Critical Discourse Analysis

(2010)

Critical Discourse Analysis
The Critical Study of Language

Second edition

NORMAN FAIRCLOUGH

Longman
is an imprint of

Harlow, England • London • New York • Boston • San Francisco • Toronto
Sydney • Tokyo • Singapore • Hong Kong • Seoul • Taipei • New Delhi
Cape Town • Madrid • Mexico City • Amsterdam • Munich • Paris • Milan

PEARSON EDUCATION LIMITED

Edinburgh Gate
Harlow CM20 2JE
United Kingdom
Tel: +44 (0)1279 623623
Fax: +44 (0)1279 431059
Website: www.pearsoned.co.uk

First edition published by Longman Group Limited 1995
Second edition published 2010

© Pearson Education Limited 1995, 2010

The right of Norman Fairclough to be identified as
author of this work has been asserted by him in
accordance with the Copyright, Designs and Patents Act 1988.

ISBN: 978-1-4058-5822-9

British Library Cataloguing in Publication Data
A CIP catalogue record for this book can be obtained from the British Library

Library of Congress Cataloging in Publication Data
A CIP catalog record for this book can be obtained from the Library of Congress

10 9 8 7 6 5 4 3 2
13 12

Set by 35 in 11/13pt Bulmer MT
Printed in Malaysia, (CTP - KHL)

Contents

Series editor's preface

Critical Discourse Analysis, in its first edition in 1995, along with its predecessor *Language in Power*, created in the world of applied linguistics and discourse analysis a way and a means of systematically approaching the relationships between language and social structure which has now not only extended across those worlds but also had its impact across social science more generally. It would be no exaggeration to say that those two books, along with Norman Fairclough's other key texts, notably *Discourse and Social Change*, and his numerous papers and edited collections, changed the face of the social analysis of language.

Critical Discourse Analysis in its first edition offered a range of students of linguistics, applied linguistics and language study, as well as communication research in professions and organisations more generally, a framework and a means of exploring the imbrications between language and social-institutional practices, and beyond these, the intimate links between language as discourse and broader social and political structures. A key innovation at that time was to critique some of the premises and the constructs underpinning mainstream studies in sociolinguistics, conversation analysis and pragmatics to demonstrate the need of these disciplines to engage with issues of power and hegemony in a dynamic and historically informed manner, while at the same time insisting on the dynamic and polysystemic description of language variation. Indeed, the focus on the dynamics of discourse has proved especially productive for students of professional discourses such as those of law, politics, social work, healthcare, language and literacy education. This is very much a consequence of his viewing critical discourse analysis as *relational* research. Indeed, making interrelations matter (whether among, and within, institutions of the social order and between them, or the social formation more generally) links

serendipitously with applied linguistic calls in recent years for just such connections. Indeed, Norman Fairclough has offered those practitioners whose
work is most obviously discoursed and languaged a means whereby they, now
often in collaboration with critical discourse analysts, can describe, interpret
and proffer explanations how their practices are discursively accomplished,
suggesting a way of clarifying the ideologically informed bases of the purposes
and methods of the professions themselves. At the same time, his focus on the
dialectics of discourse does not just provide a motivation for intellectual debate,
but also directly engages the understanding of *interdiscursivity* and its relation
to those semiotic modalities within and through which interdiscursivity is
realised, highlighting what he calls the two-way 'flow' of discourse to and from
sociological/political constructs such as hegemony and power. Here again, his
formulations speak directly to applied linguists engaged in understanding the
focal themes of contemporary social institutions. His discussion in this new
edition of how participants, in his terms, construe their worlds, and how they
reflexively seek to change aspects of such worlds, to reconstruct them, offers
considerable backing to those researchers and participants intent on pursuing
a reflexive and critical agenda. Workers in the fields of communication in
healthcare, social work, language and literacy education, restorative justice,
political agency, have come to rely on his formulations and theorising almost
as a manifesto for action. I use the word 'manifesto' in its true sense; as a statement of commitment to principle but also as a blueprint for practical action.
This is important if we are not to regard critical discourse analysis, as Norman
Fairclough manifestly does *not*, as merely a politically inspired approach to
analysing language, as it were, reading and seeking to change society 'off
the page'. Nothing could be further from the truth as this new edition, greatly
expanded with more recent papers and new sections, makes abundantly clear.

The papers in this collection represent a formidable treatise on critical discourse analysis from perhaps its leading exponent. To strike a personal note,
they go back to the early days of the formulation of such ideas when we were
colleagues at Lancaster; but now greatly enhanced both in terms of their scope,
their theoretical base, and also their influence. They provide the basis for
understanding the theoretical underpinnings of critical discourse analysis but
also the substance and warrant of its immense influence on research practice.

What are the key elements of this new edition for applied linguists engaged
with the critical exploration of discourse? Readers will discover many. For
me, firstly, it is the insistence throughout on what Norman refers to as *transdisciplinary* research. This is not merely to be seen, however, as forging links
between discourse study and sociology, politics, anthropology, *inter alia*,
central though that is to his theme, it is also *trans-professional* in enabling
discourse workers to collaborate with workers in other fields and disciplines

in a programme of exploring praxis. There are now rather many examples of just such transdisciplinary work. Secondly, it is the engagement of structure with strategy – again not necessarily at all focused on the macro contexts of the social formation, though clearly Norman's work speaks to that directly, but also in the exploration of the micro interactional order, addressing how strategic actions always are imbued with the influences of the institutional structural order, however naturalised. Here Norman Fairclough comes closest to the work of Bourdieu and of Cicourel, though with a distinctive engagement: one might venture to say this is the key trio underpinning current work in applied linguistics. Readers of the first edition of *Critical Discourse Analysis* will have found expression there, as they will do now even more substantially in this much expanded new edition, of his abiding concern for the relevance of critical discourse analytical research as an contributive agent for social change; in education, in the media, in the political order, and in respect of the economic drivers of contemporary society. It is this which has both raised hopes and stimulated action; it is also, we must acknowledge, a central focus of contention within the linguistic and applied linguistic community. Here we can emphasise a shift over time, from negative to positively motivated critique. That also derives from a broader understanding of 'critical' than has often been advanced in discussions of his work. Critical after all is not just even primarily, *criticism*, neither is it only a matter of focusing on *critical* moments in interaction (although that for many is a mainspring of engaging with discourse analysis at all); it is primarily, for me at least, a seeking of the means of explaining data in the context of social and political and institutional analysis, and in terms of *critiquing* ideologically invested modes of explaining and interpreting, but always with the sights set on positively motivated change. In this way, text analysis (however multimodal), interaction analysis (however framed), ethnographic study (however voiced) have always to be seen as each interpenetrating the other in the context of a historically and politically engaged understanding of the social order.

Such a picturing of critical discourse analysis is not as it were *sui generis*; it has its intellectual antecedents as Norman Fairclough amply displays in this new edition. More than that, however, it provides a foundation for, and a practically motivated reasoning for, the aspirations of a socially committed applied linguistics across a range of domains, sites and focal themes.

Christopher N. Candlin
Program in Communication in Professions and Organisations
Department of Linguistics
Macquarie University, Sydney
Australia

Acknowledgements

We are grateful to the following for permission to reproduce copyright material:

Tables

Table 11.1 from *Our Competitive Future: Building a Knowledge Based Economy*, HMSO (Department of Trade and Industry 1998), Crown Copyright material is reproduced with permission under the terms of the Click-Use License.

Text

Example 4, Sample 2 from 'Advertisement for Lectureship in Department of English', University of Newcastle upon Tyne, reprinted by permission of Newcastle University; Appendix 7.1 from the DWP press release; Appendix 7.2 from *New Ambitions for Our Country: A New Contract for Welfare* (Green Paper on Welfare Reform), The Stationery Office (Department of Social Security 1998), Crown Copyright material is reproduced with permission under the terms of the Click-Use License; Chapter 8, p. 217, extract from *Our Competitive Future: Building the Knowledge Driven Economy*, HMSO (Department of Trade and Industry 1998), Crown Copyright material is reproduced with permission under the terms of the Click-Use License; Appendix 9.1 from *Our Competitive Future: Building the Knowledge Driven Economy*, HMSO (Department of Trade and Industry 1998) Foreword, Crown Copyright material is reproduced with permission under the terms of the Click-Use License; Chapter 14, p. 387, paragraph from *New Ambitions for Our Country: A New Contract for Welfare* (Green Paper on Welfare Reform); Chapter 18, pp. 469–70, extract from article 'Police prepare to make thousands of arrests at G8', *Daily Telegraph*, 12 June 2005; Chapter 18, p. 472 and Chapter 22, pp. 546–7, extracts from MacDonald, R. (1994) 'Fiddly jobs, undeclared working and something for nothing society', *Work, Employment and Society*, 8(4); Appendix 20.1 from *A Strategic Goal for the Next Decade, Lisbon Declaration* (*European Councils*), reproduced with permission from the European Communities.

In some instances we have been unable to trace the owners of copyright material, and we would appreciate any information that would enable us to do so.

Norman Fairclough would also like to warmly thank the co-authors of papers included in this book (Eve Chiapello, Phil Graham, Bob Jessop, Simon Pardoe, Andrew Sayer, Bron Szerszynski) for the contribution which these various collaborations have made to the development of his thinking about critical discourse analysis.

General introduction

This book is a collection of twenty-three papers in critical discourse analysis (CDA) which I have written, or in the case of four of them co-authored, over a period of 25 years, between 1983 and 2008. It is a substantial revision of the much shorter first edition of *Critical Discourse Analysis* which was published in 1995 and contained just ten papers. I have retained six of these, and added seventeen new ones. I have grouped the papers in seven sections of which three (*Language, Ideology and Power; Discourse and Social Change; Language and Education*) correspond to sections in the first edition, while the other four (*Dialectics of Discourse: Theoretical Developments; Methodology; Political Discourse; Globalisation and 'Transition'*) reflect ways in which my work has developed since 1995. Although these sections do I think give a reasonable sense of main elements and emphases, there are inevitably some thematic overlaps between them.

My original formulation of the broad objective of my work in CDA still holds: to develop ways of analysing language which address its involvement in the workings of contemporary capitalist societies. The focus on capitalist societies is not only because capitalism is the dominant economic system internationally as well in Britain (where I have spent most of life), but also because the character of the economic system affects all aspects of social life. I am not suggesting a mechanical 'economic determinism', but the main areas of social life are interdependent and have effects on each other, and because of the dominance of the economy in contemporary societies its effects are particularly strong and pervasive. For instance, the 'neo-liberal' version of capitalism which has been dominant for the past thirty years is widely recognised to have entailed major changes in politics, in the nature of work, education and healthcare, in social and moral values, in lifestyles, and so forth.

I am working within a tradition of critical social research which is focused on better understanding of how and why contemporary capitalism prevents or limits, as well as in certain respects facilitating, human well-being and flourishing. Such understanding may, in favourable circumstances, contribute to overcoming or at least mitigating these obstacles and limits. This possibility follows from a property of the social world which differentiates it from the natural world: the meanings and concepts through which people interpret it and the knowledge they have of it are part of the social world and can contribute to transforming the rest of it (Bhaskar 1979).

My objective in publishing this book also remains the same as for the first edition: to bring together in a single place papers which have appeared in diverse and sometimes rather inaccessible locations in order to show continuities, developments and changes in one line of work within CDA. Other books I have published are also part of this picture, and I shall indicate some of the relationships between them and the papers in this volume in separate introductions to each of the sections, which summarise the papers and identify salient themes. I have kept the title *Critical Discourse Analysis* despite being conscious that it might seem misleading (and even more so in 2009 than in 1995) to use the name of what has become a substantial and diverse international field of teaching and research as the title for a collection of papers representing one line of work and tendency within this greater whole – though I think it is true to say that it has been an influential one. So let me stress that this is no more than my own particular view, changing over the years, of the field of CDA. But of course, in choosing to take this view rather than others I am suggesting that it is preferable in certain respects to others, so it is also *no less* than my own view of what CDA should be!

Colleagues in and beyond the field of CDA have contributed a great deal to the development of my views. Some of them are present in the book as co-authors (Eve Chiapello, Phil Graham, Bob Jessop, Simon Pardoe, Andrew Sayer, Bron Szerszynski), the many others include, within the field of CDA, Lilie Chouliaraki, Romy Clark, Isabela Ieţcu-Fairclough, Roz Ivanič, Jay Lemke, Gunther Kress, Ron Scollon, Teun van Dijk, Theo van Leeuwen and Ruth Wodak, as well as my former research students and members of the Lancaster 'Language, Ideology and Power' research group over a period of some twenty years, and more recently the Bucharest 'Re-scaling Romania' research group. My considerable debts to past and present researchers in CDA and other areas of study that I have not worked with so directly are partially indicated in the references at the end of the book.

I shall begin by giving my views on *discourse* and on what critical discourse analysis should be analysis *of*, on what should count as *analysis*, and what *critical* analysis should be. In doing so I shall be taking a position not only *on* CDA but also *in* CDA: in suggesting what discourse, analysis and critique are I will also be suggesting what they are not, and differentiating my position from that of others. I also suggest certain general measures to determine what research and analysis counts as CDA or does not count as CDA. I then discuss how CDA including my own work has contributed to critical social research on the 'neo-liberal' form of capitalism which has been internationally dominant over the past thirty years or so. This will lead to a 'manifesto' for CDA in the changing circumstances at the time of writing: a financial and economic crisis which promises to be severe in its effects and serious in its consequences. I shall discuss what role CDA can have, what it should be trying to achieve, and in particular how it might contribute to responses to the crisis which seek to tackle the difficulties and dangers that face us and enhance human well-being.

1 Discourse, analysis, critique

In my view CDA has these three basic properties: it is relational, it is dialectical, and it is transdisciplinary. It is a *relational* form of research in the sense that its primary focus in not on entities or individuals (in which I include both things and persons) but on social relations (see further Paper 12, pages 301–40). Social relations are very complex, and they are also 'layered' in the sense that they include 'relations between relations'. For example, 'discourse' might be seen as some sort of entity or 'object', but it is itself a complex set of relations including relations of communication between people who talk, write and in other ways communicate with each other, but also, for example, describe relations between concrete communicative events (conversations, newspaper articles etc.) and more abstract and enduring complex discursive 'objects' (with their own complex relations) like languages, discourses and genres. But there are also relations between discourse and other such complex 'objects' including objects in the physical world, persons, power relations and institutions, which are interconnected elements in social activity or praxis. The main point for present purposes is that we cannot answer the question 'what is discourse' except in terms of both its 'internal' relations and its 'external' relations with such other 'objects'. Discourse is not simply an entity we can define independently: we can only arrive at an understanding of it by analysing sets of relations. Having said that, we can say what it is in particular that discourse brings into the complex relations which constitute social life: meaning, and making meaning.

These relations are in my view *dialectical*, and it is the dialectical character of these relations that really makes it clear why simply defining 'discourse' as a separate 'object' is not possible. Dialectical relations are relations between objects which are different from one another but not what I shall call 'discrete', not fully separate in the sense that one excludes the other. This sounds paradoxical, and indeed in a certain sense it is. Let us consider 'external' relations between discourse and other 'objects'. Think of power and discourse. The power of, for instance, the people who control a modern state (the relation of power between them and the rest of the people) is partly discursive in character. For example, it depends on sustaining the 'legitimacy' of the state and its representatives, which is largely achieved in discourse. Yet state power also includes the capacity to use physical force and violence. So power is not simply discourse, it is not reducible to discourse; 'power' and 'discourse' are different elements in the social process (or in a dialectical terminology, different 'moments'). Yet power is partly discourse, and discourse is partly power – they are different but not discrete, they 'flow into' each other; discourse can be 'internalised' in power and vice-versa; the complex realities of power relations are 'condensed' and simplified in discourses (Harvey 1996). Social activity or praxis consists in complex articulations of these and other objects as its elements or moments; its analysis is analysis of dialectical relations between them, and no one object or element (such as discourse) can be analysed other than in terms of its dialectical relations with others.

What then is CDA analysis *of*? It is *not* analysis of discourse 'in itself' as one might take it to be, but analysis of dialectical *relations between* discourse and other objects, elements or moments, as well as analysis of the 'internal relations' of discourse. And since analysis of such relations cuts across conventional boundaries between disciplines (linguistics, politics, sociology and so forth), CDA is an interdisciplinary form of analysis, or as I shall prefer to call it a *transdisciplinary* form. What this term entails is that the 'dialogues' between disciplines, theories and frameworks which take place in doing analysis and research are a source of theoretical and methodological developments within the particular disciplines, theories and frameworks in dialogue – including CDA itself (see Section D, Methodology in CDA research).

Note that this is a *realist* approach which claims that there is a real world, including the social world, which exists irrespective of whether or how well we know and understand it. More specifically it is a 'critical realist' approach (see Papers 8 and 13), which means among other things a recognition that the natural and social worlds differ in that the latter but not the former depends upon human action for its existence and is 'socially constructed'. The socially constructive effects of discourse are thus a central concern, but a distinction is drawn between *construal* and *construction*: the world is discursively construed (or represented) in many and various ways, but which construals come to have socially constructive effects depends upon a range of conditions which include for instance power relations but also properties of whatever parts or aspects of the world are being construed. We cannot transform the world in any old way we happen to construe it; the world is such that some transformations are possible and others are not. So CDA is a 'moderate' or 'contingent' form of social constructivism.

So much for 'discourse' and what CDA is analysis of. Let me come to 'analysis'. Given that CDA should be transdisciplinary analysis, it should have a transdisciplinary methodology (see Section D and especially Paper 9). I use 'methodology' rather than 'method', because I see analysis as not just the selection and application of pre-established methods (including methods of textual analysis), but a theory-driven process of constructing *objects of research* (Bourdieu and Wacquant 1992) for research topics, i.e., for research themes as they initially present themselves to us (for instance, the current financial and economic crisis). Constructing an object of research for a research topic is converting it into a 'researchable object': cogent, coherent and researchable research questions. For instance, faced with the topic of the current financial and economic crisis which I discuss further below, we have to ask: what are the best, or the right, or the primary research questions to try to answer? Objects of research are constructed in a transdisciplinary way on the basis of theorising research topics in terms of the categories and relations of not only a theory of discourse (such as that of the version of CDA I work with) but also other relevant theories. These may be, depending on the topic, political, sociological, political–economic, educational, media and/or other theories.

Objects of research constructed in this transdisciplinary way allow for various 'points of entry' for the discourse analyst, the sociologist, the political economist and so forth, which focus upon different elements or aspects of the object of research. For instance the discourse analyst will focus on discourse, but never in isolation, always in its relations with other elements, and always in ways which accord with the formulation of the common object of research. For example, one object of research for the topic of 'the crisis' could be the emergence of different and competing strategies for overcoming the crisis, and the processes through which and the conditions under which certain strategies can be implemented and can transform existing systems and structures. This formulation is based upon a theory of crisis which among other things sees crises as events which arise from the character of structures, and sees strategies and structures as in a relationship such that the effects of structures give rise to strategies oriented to changing structures. If it also sees strategies as having a partly discursive character, one 'point of entry' for research could be focused on discursive features of strategies and how they may contribute to their success or failure. This might include for instance analysis of explanations of the crisis and attributions of blame, justifications for and legitimations of particular lines of action and policy, and value claims and assumptions in explanations, justifications and legitimations.

Bringing diverse theories or frameworks together to co-construct trans-disciplinary objects of research gives rise to issues of 'translation' between the concepts, categories and relations of CDA and of other theories or frameworks. Let's take the case of theories of and frameworks for analysing relations of power. Since research will be concerned with dialectical relations between discourse and power, the challenge is to find ways of coherently connecting categories and relations such as 'discourse', 'genre', 'recontextualisation' and 'argumentation' (from discourse theory) with categories and relations such as 'power', 'hegemony', 'ideology' and 'legitimacy' (from political theory). Given a particular theory of power, how can we coherently articulate its categories and relations with those of a theory of discourse so as to analyse ways in which discourse is internalised in power and power is internalised in discourse, that is, so as to be able to analyse dialectical relations between discourse and power for the particular topic and object of research? It is not a matter of substituting discourse-analytical categories and relations for political ones, or vice-versa. It is a matter of recognising the need for them to be separate (power is not *just* discourse, discourse is not *just* power) yet avoiding incoherent eclecticism. It is a matter of the translatability or *commensurability* (Jessop and Sum 2006) of concepts, categories and relations: a concern in transdisciplinary research is to both assess how good the match is between concepts, categories and relations from different theories and frameworks, and move towards increasing it. (An example is the category of 'recontextualisation' which was developed in sociology (Bernstein 1990) but interpreted in terms of CDA categories (including 'genre') in a way that increased the commensurability between the two (Chouliaraki and Fairclough 1999. See further below.) In doing so we are achieving an aim of transdisciplinary research which I mentioned above – using the dialogue between different disciplines or theories as the source of the theoretical or methodological development of each.

For CDA, analysis of course includes analysis of texts. Many methods of textual analysis have been developed in linguistics (phonetics, phonology, grammar, semantics, lexicology), pragmatics, stylistics, sociolinguistics, argumentation analysis, literary criticism, anthropology, conversation analysis and so forth. In principle any such methods might be recontextualised within CDA, though note that this implies that they may need to be adapted to fit in with CDA's principles and purposes. The particular selection of methods for a particular research project depends upon the object of research which is constructed for the research topic. But the version of CDA I work with has a general method: textual analysis has a dual character. It is firstly *interdiscursive* analysis, analysis of which discourses, genres and styles are drawn upon in a text and how they are articulated together. This mode of analysis is based on the view that texts can and generally do draw upon and articulate together multiple discourses, multiple genres, and multiple styles. And it is secondly *linguistic* analysis or, for many texts, *multimodal* analysis of the different semiotic 'modes' (including language, visual images, body language, music and sound effects) and their articulation. The level of interdiscursive analysis is a mediating 'interlevel': on the one hand, discourses, genres and styles are realised in the more concrete form of linguistic and multimodal features of texts; on the other hand, discourses, genres and styles are categories not only of textual analysis but also of analysis of orders of discourse, which are the discoursal element or moment of social practices, social organisations and social institutions. Analysis in terms of these categories therefore helps to link 'micro-analysis' of texts to various forms of social (sociological, political and so forth) analysis of practices, organisations and institutions.

Let me turn to the third question, what is critique, what is *critical* discourse analysis? Critique brings a normative element into analysis (on normative social research, see Sayer 2005). It focuses on what is wrong with a society (an institution, an organisation etc.), and how 'wrongs' might be 'righted' or mitigated, from a particular normative standpoint. Critique is grounded in values, in particular views of the 'good society' and of human well-being and flourishing, on the basis of which it evaluates existing societies and possible ways of changing them. For instance, many people (though not all) would agree that societies ought to be just or fair, ought to ensure certain freedoms, and ought to provide for certain basic needs of their members (for food, shelter, healthcare etc.). The devil of course is in the detail: people have very different ideas of justice, freedom and need, and critical social research is necessarily involved in debates over the meaning of these and other value-related concepts. The crucial point, however, is that critique assesses what exists, what might exist and what should exist on the basis of a coherent set of values. At least to some extent this is a matter of highlighting gaps between what particular societies claim to be ('fair', 'democratic', 'caring' etc.) and what they are. We can distinguish between *negative critique*, which is analysis of how societies produce and perpetuate social wrongs, and *positive critique*, which is analysis of how people seek to remedy or mitigate them, and identification of further possibilities for righting or mitigating them.

A primary focus of CDA is on the effect of power relations and inequalities in producing social wrongs, and in particular on discursive aspects of power relations and inequalities: on dialectical relations between discourse and power, and their effects on other relations within the social process and their elements. This includes questions of *ideology*, understanding ideologies to be 'meaning in the service of power' (Thompson 1984): ways of representing aspects of the world, which may be operationalised in ways of acting and inter- acting and in 'ways of being' or identities, that contribute to establishing or sustaining unequal relations of power (see Section A). This focuses on the function of ideologies (in serving power), but ideologies are also open to critique on the grounds that they represent or explain aspects of the world inadequately. This leads to another way of answering the question 'what is critique?' with radical implications for CDA: it identifies critique of discourse as an inherent part of *any* application of critical method in social research.

Critical analysis aims to produce interpretations and explanations of areas of social life which both identify the causes of social wrongs and produce knowledge which could (in the right conditions) contribute to righting or mitigating them. But interpretations and explanations already exist – inevitably, because a necessary part of living and acting in particular social circumstances is interpreting and explaining them. So along with and as part of the areas of social life which critical researchers research, they find interpretations and explanations of them. These interpretations and explanations moreover include not only those of the people who live and act in particular circum- stances, but also of those who seek to govern or regulate the ways in which they do so, including politicians and managers. And critical researchers will almost certainly find not only these interpretations and explanations but also prior interpretations and explanations of social researchers, historians, philo- sophers etc. Furthermore, it is a feature of the social world that interpretations and explanations of it can have effects upon it, can transform it in various ways. A critique of some area of social life must therefore be in part a critique of interpretations and explanations of social life. And since interpretations and explanations are discourse, it must be in part a critique of discourse.

But the critical analyst, in producing different interpretations and explana- tions of that area of social life, is also producing discourse. On what grounds can we say that this critical discourse is superior to the discourse which its critique is partly a critique of? The only basis for claiming superiority is provid- ing explanations which have greater explanatory power. The explanatory power of a discourse (or a theory, which is a special sort of discourse) is its ability to provide justified explanations of as many features of the area of social life in focus as possible. So we can say that it is a matter of both quantity (the number or range of features) and quality (justification). One aspect of the matter of quantity is the extent to which existing lay and non-lay interpretations and explanations are themselves explained, as well as their effects on social life, in terms of what it is or was about this area of social life that lead to these interpretations and explanations emerging, becoming dominant and being implemented. This is where ideology comes into the picture: interpretations and explanations can be said to be ideological if they can be shown to be not just inadequate but also necessary – necessary to establish and keep in place particular relations of power. On the matter of quality (justification), explanations are better than others if they are more consistent with whatever evidence exists, including what events take place or have taken place, how people act or have acted, what the effects of their actions are, and so forth. The relative explanatory power of different explanations, discourses and theories is of course an issue which is constantly in contention. A final point is that the explanatory power of a theory and an analysis informed by it contributes to its capacity to transform aspects of social life, which brings us back to dialectical relations between discourse and other social elements with respect to the aims of critique to not merely interpret the world but contribute to changing it.

This is a complex argument, but I think it is a strong one for CDA. Let me sum up its strengths. First, it repeats from a somewhat different vantage point my emphasis earlier on dialectical relations between discourse and other elements as a necessary part of social life. Second, it claims that critical analysis of discourse is a necessary part of any critical social analysis. Third, it provides a basis for determining which discourses (interpretations, explanations) are ideological. Fourth, it presents critical analysis as itself discourse which is dialectically related to other elements of social life. On this view of critique see Paper 12, and also Bhaskar (1979) and Marsden (1999).

The approach I have summarised in this section is based on a *transformational model* of social activity which is essentially Aristotelian in nature, 'in which the paradigm is that of the sculptor at work, fashioning a product out of the material and with the tools available' (Bhaskar 1979). Social activity is a form of production or work which both depends upon and transforms the material and tools available. Or to put it in different terms: in which society is both a condition for and an outcome of social activity, and social activity is both the production (which is transformative, effects changes) and the reproduction of the conditions of production (i.e., society). Moreover as I have suggested above social activity understood in this way consists in dialectical relations between different elements or moments including discourse. The view of discourse above conforms with the transformational model in that it fashions products (texts) out of available material and tools (languages, orders of discourse, discourses, genres, styles etc.) which are its condition of possibility and which it both transforms and reproduces. What we might call *texturing*, producing text out of available material and tools, is one moment of social activity as work or production. But what must be emphasised is its dialectical interconnection with other moments in a process of production whose character we might sum up as material-semiotic. Analysis must seek to elucidate the complex interpenetration of material and semiotic (discoursal) moments, and resist treating text and texturing as having an existence independently of these dialectical relations.

2   What is CDA, and what is not CDA

Interest in CDA has increased quite remarkably since the publication of the first edition of *Critical Discourse Analysis*. It has spread to new areas of the world, and to a great many disciplines and areas of study (Fairclough, Graham, Lemke and Wodak 2001). The proliferation of researchers who are using CDA is very pleasing and very welcome. CDA has also become more institutionalised, in the sense that there are many more academic posts and programmes of study and research, and it has become more mainstream, and certainly more 'respectable' than it was in the early days.

I have the impression that, perhaps as a consequence of these developments, work is sometimes identified as 'CDA' which is arguably not CDA. If CDA becomes too ill-defined, or the answer to the question 'what is CDA?' becomes too vague, its value in social research and its appeal to researchers may be weakened. So I think it is important to discuss the question of what counts as CDA and what doesn't. My purpose in doing so is emphatically not to advocate conformity. On the contrary, the vitality of the field depends upon people taking CDA in different and new directions, and indeed the view of transdisciplinary research as a source of theoretical and methodological development amounts to advocating a continuing process of change. But I think it is possible to draw from the discussion above of discourse, analysis and critique a few general characteristics which can differentiate CDA from other forms of research and analysis. I suggest that research and analysis counts as CDA in so far as it has all of the following characteristics.

1. It is not just analysis of discourse (or more concretely texts), it is part of some form of systematic transdisciplinary analysis of relations between discourse and other elements of the social process.
2. It is not just general commentary on discourse, it includes some form of systematic analysis of texts.

3. It is not just descriptive, it is also normative. It addresses social wrongs in their discursive aspects and possible ways of righting or mitigating them.

I have tried to make these measures for determining what is and what is not CDA tight enough to work as measures, but loose enough to encompass and allow for many different existing and new versions of CDA. They are, and are designed to be, open to various interpretations. They are not 'rules': they should not be seen or used as regulative devices; they are designed to be helpful in drawing important distinctions. I hope others will take them up as suggestions which are, of course, open to modification. They do not exclude the possibility of making use of certain CDA categories and relations (e.g., interdiscursive analysis) in work which does not itself count as CDA – on the contrary, the transdisciplinary approach to research which I have suggested entails a way of developing theory and methodology through recontextualising categories and relations from other theories and frameworks. For example, *recontextualisation* itself is a relation which originates in Bernstein's 'social of pedagogy' (Bernstein 1990) but has been 'translated' into a relation within CDA by incorporating it into the system of categories and relations of the theory of CDA (see Chouliaraki and Fairclough (1999) for details).

3 CDA and neo-liberal capitalism

I have presented CDA above as a form of critical research which seeks to understand how contemporary capitalism in some respects enables but in other respects prevents or limits human well-being and flourishing, with a view to overcoming or mitigating these obstacles and limits. Much recent research has centred upon the 'new capitalism' (now not so new – indeed some commentators are beginning to call it 'old') which has been internationally dominant for the past thirty years or so, a restructuring of capitalism which emerged in response to the crisis in 'Fordist' economies and 'welfare states' in the 1970s. The capitalism of what we can call the 'neo-liberal' era has been characterised by, among other things, 'free markets' (the freeing of markets from state intervention and regulation), and attempts at reducing the state's responsibility for providing social welfare. It has involved a *restructuring* of relations between the economic, political, and social domains, including the extension of markets into social domains such as education, and focusing the role of the state and government on strengthening markets and competitiveness. It has also involved the *re-scaling* of relations between different scales of social life – the global, the regional (e.g., European Union), the national, and the local – which has facilitated the emergence of global markets.

Governments formed by mainstream parties of both left and right have embraced 'neo-liberalism', a political project (and ideology) for facilitating the restructuring and re-scaling of social relations in accord with the demands of an unrestrained global capitalism (Bourdieu 1998a). It has led to radical attacks on social welfare provision and the reduction of the protections that 'welfare states' provided for people against the effects of markets. It has also led to an increasing gap in income and wealth between rich and poor, increasing economic insecurity and stress, and an intensification of the exploitation of labour. The unrestrained emphasis on 'growth' also poses major threats to the environment. It has also produced a new imperialism in which international agencies under the tutelage of the US and its rich allies have imposed restructuring ('the Washington Consensus'), and which has more recently taken an increasingly military form (notably the invasion of Iraq). But there have been positive achievements in this period: for instance, there is truth in the claim of apologists for neo-liberalism that millions of people have been pulled out of absolute poverty during the neo-liberal era, though to what extent that is due to the specifically neo-liberal features of the era is open to question.

The lifespan of CDA (though not of critical analysis of discourse *per se*, which has a much longer history – see, for instance, Paper 12) matches quite closely the lifespan of this new form of capitalism, and it has made quite a substantial contribution to critical research on neo-liberal capitalism. A number of the papers in this book are part of this contribution, as are publications by many other CDA researchers (e.g., Graham 2000, 2001, 2002, forthcoming, Lemke 1995, Language in New Capitalism website, http://www.cddc.vt.edu/host/inc/). What has been the role of and the justification for a significant focus on discourse and language in this research? I have answered the question of justification in general terms above: because the relations which constitute the social process of neo-liberal capitalism include dialectical relations between its discursive and 'extra-discursive' elements – no account of it (or any of its elements and relations) which neglects discourse can be adequate. This is self-evidently so given the argument above, but it would also be self-evidently so for any social analysis, and it is the most general case for a discourse-analytical dimension of (or a 'discourse turn' in) social research. But there are certain more particular features of the neo-liberal era which make the case for a focus on discourse especially clear.

One irony of neo-liberalism is that at the time when most of the 'doctrinaire' socialist societies were imploding and the 'end of ideology' was being confidently predicted, a restructuring of capitalism clearly driven by explicit pre-constructed doctrine – which means driven by discourse – was taking place. There was manifestly an 'imaginary' for neo-liberalism, a discourse of neo-liberalism, before strategies to operationalise and implement this imaginary and discourse in practice started to be effective. A liberal 'counter-revolution' against broadly social-democratic and 'statist' forms of capitalism had long been imagined and prepared by Friedrich Hayek, Milton Friedman and their followers. Moreover, this imaginary, discourse and ideology of neo-liberalism has continued to be crucial in justifying and legitimising neo-liberalism in its moments of crisis (such as the East Asian crisis of the late 1990s and its spread to other regions) and in its mission to internationalise and 'globalise' this form of capitalism (to extend and in principle universalise the 'Washington Consensus' – which it has not succeeded in doing). And, to anticipate the discussion of the current crisis, now that neo-liberal capitalism has come into what may be a terminal crisis, the crisis is clearly in part a crisis of its discourse. Furthermore, the imaginary for and partial reality of a 'knowledge-based economy' which came to be closely interwoven with the imaginary and partial reality of the 'global economy' in the neo-liberal era implies a more generally heightened significance for discourse in the dialectical relations of that form of capitalism. Much is 'discourse-driven'. For instance, the proliferation of ever new theories, models, imaginaries and discourses in the management of not only private organisations but also public organisations, not only in the economy but in many other spheres of social life (government, education, healthcare, social welfare, the arts), which are selectively and more or less effectively operationalised and implemented in new practices, identities and material forms (e.g., the design of built space).

Various aspects of the dialectical relations between discursive and non-discursive elements of neo-liberal capitalism and of its 'discourse-driven' character are addressed in papers in this book. A number of papers deal with New Labour in Britain, treating the politics of New Labour as a form of neo-liberalism and its discourse as a form of neo-liberal discourse (Papers 7, 9, 11 and 14). The focus is not only on the political discourse and ideology of the 'Third Way' but also political identities and styles, and on new forms of governance which accord with shifts in the role of the state in the neo-liberal era and whose discursive moment involves changes in the genres and 'genre chains' of governing. Papers 18 and 19 deal with what has become the internationally most powerful strategy for steering globalisation and the 'global economy', which I call 'globalism', and specifically its discourse. At the core of globalism is the strategic objective of spreading neo-liberal capitalism and neo-liberal discourse to all areas of the world, including, for instance, the formerly socialist 'transitional' countries of central and eastern Europe (the focus of Paper 20), a project which is widely identified with the 'Washington

Consensus' and the activities of the International Monetary Fund and the World Bank. Paper 19 focuses on the increasingly military character of the strategy of globalism and its connection to the 'war on terror'. Paper 4 deals with the imposition of markets in Higher Education in Britain, focusing again on its discourse moment and the marketisation of discourses, genres and styles, which is an illustration of the wider tendency for neo-liberal capitalism to incorporate more and more areas of social life into the market economy. Paper 10 is a transdisciplinary study of the new management ideology associated with neo-liberal capitalism, bringing together CDA and the 'New Sociology of Capitalism' developed in France. Paper 12 is also oriented towards CDA research on the new form of capitalism. It suggests that Marx's analytical method includes an element of critical discourse analysis *avant la lettre*, and considers what CDA research on neo-liberal capitalism might learn from it. Finally, Paper 22 discusses the development of 'critical language awareness' in education in relation to the 'global economy'.

4 Manifesto for CDA in a time of crisis

I come now to a 'manifesto' for CDA in the time of crisis which it appears (in December 2008) that we shall be living in for some time to come. I shall give an assessment of the role, purpose and possible contribution of CDA in the financial and economic crisis and ask: what should CDA be trying to achieve; what contribution can it make? A manifesto is generally understood to be a public declaration of purposes, principles and objectives and the means for achieving them, and it is usually political in character. So: why a 'manifesto' for CDA? My argument below will be that in this time of crisis the priority for critical research including CDA should shift from critique of structures to critique of *strategies* – of attempts, in the context of the failure of existing structures, to transform them in particular directions. But the business of critical research is not just descriptive analysis of these emerging and competing strategies but also normative evaluation of them, and another relative shift of priority in the present context is from negative critique of existing structures to *positive* critique which seeks possibilities for transformations which can overcome or mitigate limits on human well-being. So I use 'manifesto' to highlight the contribution that CDA might make to the political struggle for a way out of the crisis which can transform social forms and social life in ways which advance human well-being. But this will bring us back again to the question 'what is critique?' and particularly to this issue: if critical research is 'knowledge-for-action', how does the purpose of advancing knowledge connect with the purpose of supporting action for a better world?

I am writing a few months into an acute phase of a crisis which became apparent to many in the summer of 2007, and to a few earlier than that, but took a dramatic turn in the autumn of 2008 with a series of calamities (e.g., the bankruptcy of the US investment bank Lehman Brothers) which brought the banking and credit system close to collapse. Nobody can say with certainty how the crisis will develop, how long it will go on, or where it will take us. But many economists and other commentators are predicting that it is going to be severe, and far-reaching in its effects, and the crisis may well be the primary determinant of 'the state we are in', and the primary factor shaping the agenda for CDA for some time to come. Of course, that agenda is now very diverse, and includes adopting a discourse perspective on issues as different as racism, war, European identity and organisational change, but I suspect that there are few areas of it which will not be affected or coloured by the crisis.

What does it mean to say that this is a 'crisis'? It means that the institutional structures and mechanisms which allowed the financial and economic systems to continue doing what they were designed and claimed to do – to provide credit for businesses and households, to produce 'growth', dividends and profits, to keep people in employment, to maintain certain levels of prosperity and consumption, to provide certain levels of social support and welfare, and so forth – are manifestly no longer capable of doing so. There is general recognition that the these structures and mechanisms need to be either repaired or replaced, that it will take enormous efforts and resources to do so, and that the chances of success are at present uncertain. It is also generally expected that meanwhile people in many positions and circumstances all over the world will suffer in various ways – losing their jobs, losing their savings and having to face smaller pensions than they expected, having a lower standard of living, in some cases suffering more severe effects of poverty and other forms of social deprivation, and so forth. There is general agreement that three features together differentiate this from other crises since the 1970s: it is a crisis centred in the richest and most powerful capitalist countries, especially the USA, rather than in the periphery; it is a global crisis which affects virtually all countries; and it is more severe. It began as a crisis of a financial system built upon public and private debt on a stupendous scale running into many trillions of dollars; nobody is sure at this stage how many trillions, or where much of the debt is hidden (who owes what to whom); there is a general and proliferating indeterminacy of asset values, aversion to extending credit, and contraction of expenditure and demand. The crisis in finance has extended into a general economic crisis which is accentuated by pre-existing structural weaknesses in economies which the crisis exposes (including a growing problem of overproduction e.g., in the car industry, and major international imbalances in balance of payments, lending and borrowing etc.).

What is in crisis? Optimists tend to view it as a crisis in the particular form of the neo-liberal form of capitalism discussed above, suggesting or implying that we can get 'back to normal' after an indeterminate period of pain. At the other extreme is the view that it is a crisis of capitalism itself. The view I take, like many others, is that it seems to be a crisis not in neo-liberal capitalism but *of* neo-liberal capitalism – 'seems to be' because much is uncertain, and we are condemned to act and react (as we usually are) under conditions of uncertainty. But if this interpretation is right, as many analysts and commentators think, it means that we cannot expect to 'get back to normal', that some new form of capitalism must be sought for, some restructuring of capitalism, with the proviso that although capitalism has historically shown a remarkable capacity to remake itself out of the most extreme circumstances, there is nothing that guarantees that it will be able to this time. So alternatives to capitalism may come back onto the agenda, but at present it is not clear what these might be.

There is a great deal of public anger in the heartland of this form of capitalism, the USA, and in Britain and other countries, which is variously directed at speculators, bankers, politicians or others, and amounts to a sense of having been badly misled, mismanaged and let down. People were promised the earth – increasing prosperity without limits, an ever-expanding wealth of choice, possibility and opportunity, security and comfort in old age, and so forth – but the promises have proved to be largely hollow. Some people say we are all to blame, that we should not have believed the promises. Many realise now what was rarely publicly acknowledged: that the whole edifice was built upon bubbles (the dot.com bubble, the housing bubble etc.) that now appear finally to have burst, i.e., the possibility of simply moving on to the next bubble is now in serious doubt, as is the credibility of that 'solution' even if it were possible. There is nothing new about this sort of disillusion and outrage. Histories of the Great Depression and earlier crises (see, for instance, Galbraith 1955) show that the cycle of false hopes and promises followed by catastrophic failure and recriminations is part of the rhythm of capitalism, despite the hubristic claims of politicians and others in the neo-liberal age to have ended the cycle of 'boom and bust'.

We should be cautious about predicting the future consequences of the present crisis, but we can say with some confidence that it entails a range of risks which could extend far beyond the economy as such. There are political risks: a feature of the neo-liberal age has been consensus between the main political parties and governments of different hues in many countries over the main directions of economic policy, which means that mainstream politicians with few exceptions are complicit in the false promises and failures, and may in the absence of a coherent progressive alternative in many countries offer openings to a resurgent extreme right. There are self-evidently social risks associated with and arising from people losing their homes, their jobs, their pensions, and for young people their prospects, but also risks that the already fragile relations between different cultural and religious groups in many countries may deteriorate further and lead to conflicts. There are risks too that the actions essential to avoid ecological disasters which have been to a large extent evaded in times of relative plenty will be further delayed in the face of supposedly more urgent problems.

I want to suggest a change in priorities for critical research generally including CDA: a partial shift in focus from structures to strategies (on structures and strategies, see Jessop 2002). While neo-liberal capitalism was relatively securely in place, the priority was a critique of established, institutionalised and partly naturalised and normalised systems, structures, logics and discourses. This is not to say that strategies were irrelevant: it was a dynamic system seeking to extend itself, and it had to face a number of lesser but still serious crises, both of which entailed the proliferation of strategies to achieve particular changes and trajectories. Nevertheless, for a time the priority for critical research and CDA was to gain greater knowledge and understanding of it as a system. To an extent that agenda is being overtaken by events. Aspects of the character, flaws, fallacies, contradictions etc. of neo-liberalism which had largely been ignored except by its critics have come to be widely recognised, and even conceded by former apologists for 'free markets', and this applies too to its discourse. For instance, the British Prime Minister Gordon Brown said in a New Year speech that 2008 would be remembered as the year in which 'the old era of unbridled free market dogma was finally ushered out' (*Guardian*, 1 January 2009), just over a year after a speech at the Mansion House in the City of London (June 2007) which was unstinting in its praise for 'free markets' and for 'the talents, innovations and achievements' of the City of London. Those 'innovations' are now acknowledged to have been at the origin of the financial crisis. The turn-about among such formerly ardent free-marketeers in the last months of 2008 has been remarkably rapid. But shifting the priority to strategies does not mean we can ignore the structures of neo-liberal capitalism: they will not disappear overnight, and they may prove to be more resilient than seems likely at present.

Two main sorts of strategy are emerging at present: strategies to deal with and try to mitigate the more immediate effects and consequences of the crisis, and strategies for the longer term repair and modification of neo-liberal capitalism or its replacement with a different form of capitalism. Strategies for achieving changes of a particular sort are pursued in a more or less systematic and organised ways by groups of social agents in different positions, with different interests, or with different objectives. Crises lead to a proliferation of strategies which may be in competitive as well as in complementary relationships, leading to processes of strategic struggle. One set of questions is: what strategies are emerging, what are their origins, and what groups of social agents are promoting them? A second is: which strategies are emerging as 'winners' from strategic struggles; which strategies are coming to be 'selected' at the expense of others, becoming dominant, or hegemonic? A third is: which strategies get to be implemented and actually shape social transformations and, potentially, changes in structures and systems? But there is also a fourth question of a normative character: which strategies are, or are not, likely to lead to a progressive way out of the crisis which can bring real improvements in human well-being, and tackle major obstacles to human well-being in neo-liberal capitalism, including huge and growing inequalities of wealth and income, reduction of stability and security for many millions of people, ecologically unsustainable levels and forms of growth, and so forth?

CDA has an important role in critical research focused on strategies because strategies have a strongly discursive character: they include imaginaries for change and for new practices and systems, and they include discourses, narratives and arguments which interpret, explain and justify the area of social life they are focused upon – its past, its present, and its possible future. These discursive features of strategies are crucial in assessing and establishing both their practical adequacy to the state we are in and the world as it is and their feasibility, and their desirability with respect of particular ideas of human well-being.

In thinking about a role and agenda for CDA, we can draw upon the critical method I described at the end of the section *Discourse, analysis, critique*, pages 9–10 above, though we need to reformulate it to some extent because my initial formulation was oriented to critique of systems rather than critique of strategies. Critical analysis seeks to provide explanations of the causes and development of the crisis, identify possible ways of mitigating its effects and to transform capitalism in less crisis-prone, more sustainable and more socially just directions. The analysis is partly analysis of discourse, of dialectical relations between discourse and other elements: of lay and non-lay interpretations and explanations of the causes and character of the crisis and possible remedies and their association with diverse strategies, of how they construe and potentially contribute to constructing political-economic realities. It also seeks to develop theories and analytical frameworks which allow it to explain why it is that a particular range of strategies and discourses are emerging, why particular ones tend to become dominant, what effects they are having on the way the crisis develops, and how they may further contribute to social transformations. Its concerns here are partly normative: how adequate are particular strategies as responses to the crisis given its nature as established through analysis? can particular discourses be seen as not only inadequate in this sense but also 'necessary' to establish and sustain power relations, and therefore ideological? and, above all, which strategies and discourses are, or are not, likely to lead to a path out of crisis which advances human well-being?

CDA can contribute a specifically discursive or semiotic 'point of entry' to such critical analysis, maintaining a relational focus on dialectical relations between discourse and other social elements, but highlighting properties and features of discourse. It can particularly bring such a specifically semiotic focus to analysis of the proliferation of strategies, strategic struggle, the dominance of certain strategies, and their implementation in social transformations. We might formulate an agenda in broad terms as follows:

- *Emergence of discourses.* Identify the range of discourses that emerge and their link to emerging strategies. Show how the range of discourses changes over time as the crisis develops. Identify differences and commonalities between discourses in terms of a range of features such as: how they represent events and actions and the social agents, objects, institutions etc. that they involve; how they narrate past and present events and action and link these narratives to imaginaries for future practices, institutions and systems; how they explain events and actions; how they justify actions and policy proposals and legitimise imagined changed practices and systems. Show the origins of discourses: for instance, how they are formed through articulating together (features of) existing discourses. Such analysis needs to be coloured by and integrated into transdisciplinary critical analysis oriented to an object of research constructed in a transdisciplinary way, and particularly the explanation of why and how particular strategies and discourses emerge in particular social circumstances.
- *Relations of dialogue, contestation and dominance between discourses.* Show how different discourses are brought into dialogue and contestation within processes of strategic struggle, for instance in the manoeuvring for position that goes on between political parties. Show how particular discourses gain prominence or become marginalised over time, and how particular discourses emerge as dominant or hegemonic. CDA can provide particular insights into the struggle between different strategies for transforming society in different directions through rhetorically oriented analysis of

how strategic differences are fought out in dialogue, debate, polemic etc. But again such analysis must be informed by and integrated within transdisciplinary critique which seeks to explain the success of certain strategies and the failure of others, and is also 'positive' critique which seeks to identify strategies which are, as we might put it, both desirable (in that they may advance human well-being) and feasible.

- *Recontextualisation of discourses.* Show, as part of the analysis of how particular discourses become dominant or hegemonic, their dissemination across structural boundaries (between different social fields, such as education and politics) and across scalar boundaries (e.g., between local and national scales), and their recontextualisation within different fields and at different scales.

- *Operationalisation of discourses.* Show how and subject to what conditions discourses are operationalised as strategies and implemented: enacted in changed ways (practices) of acting and interacting; inculcated in changed ways of being (identities); materialised in changes in material reality. Operationalisation is partly a process *within* discourse or semiosis: discourses are enacted as changed genres, and inculcated as changed styles. But again while there is clearly a discourse-analytical dimension to analysing these ways in which discourse contributes to social transformation, the concern is largely with relations between discourse and other social elements (as well as partly relations within discourse/semiosis) and therefore a matter for transdisciplinary critical analysis. Moreover, the operationalisation of discourses is always subject to conditions which are partly extra-discursive. So we are always pushed back towards articulating together different forms of critical social analysis (of which CDA is one) to analyse relations between discourse and other elements.

Critique as I have presented it is committed to producing and deepening certain forms of knowledge and understanding: to producing theories and analyses with the explanatory power to cogently interpret and explain, in this case, the crisis in, and as I have suggested more likely of, the neo-liberal form of capitalism, as well as the process of restructuring capitalism that it seems likely to give rise to. This includes explanation of lay and non-lay interpretations and explanations of the crisis, strategies for social transformation, and the discourses associated with them. This form of knowledge production is value-driven: it is based upon certain conceptions of human well-being, and aims to explain why and how particular social forms like those of neo-liberal capitalism on the one hand enhance well-being but on the other hand place systemic limits on it, and to identify possible and feasible changes in social forms which can overcome or mitigate those limits. While it is not in itself a political praxis and strategy for achieving such social changes, it can be a part of and contribute to such a praxis and strategy in that praxis requires theory, knowledge and understanding to achieve its strategic goals. What is currently underdeveloped but needs to be developed in this time of crisis is a political strategy and movement to ensure that the social transformations which will result from it address the fundamental problems and dangers facing us which neo-liberal capitalism has either failed adequately to address or contributed to exacerbating: poverty, gross inequality, injustice, insecurity, ecological hazard. CDA can contribute.

Section A

Language, ideology and power

Introduction

The first two papers in this section, written 1983–87 and published in 1985 and 1989, come from my earliest work in CDA when I was developing a framework for studying connections between language and power. This work culminated in the publication of my first book *Language and Power* (Longman 1989, second edition 2001).

Ideology was a central concept and category in this early work on CDA, and although its salience in my later work has varied as new themes and categories have been brought in, it has been and continues to be a major concern throughout. Yet during these past twenty-five years, ideology has become much less of an issue in social research, and the number of social researchers who work with the category or indeed treat it as a necessary category has declined. This is clearly associated with the simultaneous decline in salience of *social class* as a theme and a category, for ideology as a theoretical category has developed within theories of capitalist societies as class societies, dominated by a ruling class and characterised by struggle between classes. And these changes in academic theory and analysis are just as clearly linked to radical social and political changes affecting social classes and social class relations: changes in economic production, the relative decline of traditional manufacturing industries and the industrial working class as part of the workforce, the decrease in trade union membership and the weakening of trade unions, the weakening link between political parties and social classes, and so forth. Largely in response to these changes, many social researchers now question whether either social class or ideology are significant or useful categories (Sayer 2005).

My view is that capitalist societies like Britain are still class societies, although their class structure and class relations have changed substantially since the 1970s, and that analysis of power and class relations requires the category of ideology because ideologies are a significant element of processes through which relations of power are established, maintained, enacted and transformed. Of course, power relations in societies like Britain are not *just* class relations, they are also relations between ethnically and culturally different groups, between women and men, between adults and young people, people of working age and retired people, managers and other workers, and so forth. Power differences and inequalities arise from all of these relations and others, and from complex combinations of these relations, and ideologies are significant for these various power relations, not just for social class relations. Given that analysis of ideology requires analysis of discourse, as I argue in the papers of this section, ideology therefore continues to be a significant theme and category for CDA. For instance, in the General Introduction I discussed what CDA can contribute to critical analysis of the financial and economic crisis which is unfolding as I write, and I suggested approaching this through a form of critique which includes a way of assessing whether discourses circulating in this time of crisis have an ideological character.

Paper 1, 'Critical and descriptive goals in discourse analysis' distinguishes critical discourse analysis from the dominant non-critical, descriptive trend within discourse analysis which was establishing itself within Linguistics departments at the time. The latter is criticised for its lack of concern with explanation – with how discursive practices are socially shaped, or their social effects. I also criticise the concept of 'background knowledge' as an obfuscation of ideological processes in discourse, the preoccupation with 'goals' as based upon an untenable theory of the subject, and the neglect of relations of power manifested for instance in the elevation of conversation between equals to the status of an idealised archetype for linguistic interaction in general.

The critical alternative claims that naturalised implicit propositions of an ideological character are pervasive in discourse, contributing to the positioning of people as social subjects. These include not only aspects of ideational meaning (e.g., implicit propositions needed to infer coherent links between sentences) but also for instance assumptions about social relations underlying interactional practices (e.g., turn-taking systems, or pragmatic politeness conventions). Such assumptions are quite generally naturalised, and people are generally unaware of them and of how they are subjected by/to them. The emphasis in this paper is upon discourse within the social reproduction of relations of domination. The paper suggests a view of critique as embedded within oppositional practice. Opposition and struggle are built into the view of the 'orders of discourse' of social institutions as 'pluralistic', each involving a configuration of potentially antagonistic 'ideological-discursive formations'

(handwritten margin notes: "1 Ideological discursive formations ↗" "Dominance + Resistance")

(IDFs), which are ordered in dominance. The dominance of one IDF over others within an order of discourse results in the naturalisation of its (ideological) meanings and practices. Resistance is most likely to come from subjects whose positioning within *other* institutions and orders of discourse provides them with the resources to resist.

The paper does take a dialectical view of the relationship between structure and action. But the emphasis, under the influence of Althusser and French discourse analysis (Althusser 1971, Pêcheux 1982), is upon the determination of action by structures, social reproduction, and the ideological positioning of subjects. Later papers have increasingly emphasised agency and change. The concept of IDF did not survive this paper; it gave an overly monolithic view of ideological diversity and struggle – well-defined forces in clear relations of opposition. Another characteristic of this early work is the centrality of social class in its view of power.

I would highlight three themes of the paper as particularly significant for later work. First, the claim that ideologies are primarily located in the 'unsaid' (implicit propositions). I later draw upon French discourse analysis for an intertextual account of presuppositions as the 'already-said' or 'preconstructed' (Pêcheux 1982, Fairclough 1989a). The second theme is that norms of interaction involving aspects of the interpersonal meaning and forms (e.g., turn-taking systems) may be ideological, in addition to the more widely discussed case of ideational meanings and forms – the 'content' of texts. The third theme is the theorisation of power as in part 'ideological/discoursal', the power to shape orders of discourse, to order discursive practices in dominance. Even casual conversation has its conditions of possibility within relations of ideological/discoursal power.

Paper 2 'Language and ideology' suggests that the language–ideology relation should be conceptualised within the framework of research on discoursal and sociocultural change. Following Gramsci (Forgacs 1988), the conception of ideology here focuses upon the effects of ideologies rather than questions of truth, and features of texts are seen as ideological in so far as they affect (sustain, undermine) power relations. Ideology is seen as 'located' in both structures (discourse conventions) and events. On the one hand, the conventions drawn upon in actual discursive events, which are structured together within 'orders of discourse' associated with institutions, are ideologically invested in particular ways. On the other hand, ideologies are generated and transformed in actual discursive events – the example I refer to is of ideological creativity in a Margaret Thatcher radio interview. An order of discourse may incorporate in Gramscian terms an 'ideological complex', a configuration of ideologies, and both the ideological complex and the order of discourse may be reconstructed in the course of discursive events. These possible discursive restructurings arise from contradictions in social practice which generate dilemmas for people, which they try to resolve through mixing available discourse conventions in new ways the mixtures being realised in heterogeneities of form and meaning in texts. Orders of discourse are viewed as domains of hegemony and hegemonic (ideological) struggle, within institutions such as education as well as within the wider social formation. In this process the ideological investments of particular discursive practices may change – for instance, the genre of counselling may operate, now counter-hegemonically within resistance to impersonal institutions, now hegemonically as a personalising stratagem within such institutions. The paper concludes by identifying a role for ideological analysis and critique of discourse within social struggles.

Certain features of the discussion of ideology are worth noting: the idea that discourse may be ideologically creative and productive, the concept of ideological complex, the question of whether discursive practices may be reinvested ideologically, and the broad sweep of features of texts that are seen as potentially ideological.

Paper 3 ('Semiosis, ideology and mediation. A dialectical view'), published in 2006, is a more recent return to the question of ideology which focuses upon CDA as a resource in researching the imbrications of media and mediation in ideological processes. Ideologies are initially defined as representations which contribute to constituting, reproducing and transforming social relations of power and domination, a view of ideology which is identified as *critical* in contrast with *descriptive* views of ideology, and is associated with power as *hegemony* rather than as force or violence. *Mediation* is understood in Silverstone's (1999) sense as the movement and transformation of meaning, and is associated with the CDA category of *recontextualisation*. Processes of recontextualisation and mediation may be ideological, and the paper follows Bernstein (1990) in emphasising the importance of recontextualisation in ideological representation. It also interprets ideology in terms of the *dialectics of discourse* (see Papers 7, 8 and 9). That is to say, ideologies are first representations and discourses within relations of power, but dialectical processes of *enacting* such discourses as ways of (inter)acting, *inculcating* them as ways of being (or identities), and *materialising* them in the physical world entail that actions and their social relations including genres, persons (or *subjects*) including styles, and aspects of the material world can also have an ideological character. Moreover, ideology is first a relation between texts and power, but also a relation between orders of discourse and power and between languages and power, because meanings of texts can achieve relative stability and durability in social practices and social structures. What therefore distinguishes this paper from my earlier treatments of ideology is that it incorporates ideology into the dialectical view of relations between discourse and non-discursive elements of social processes (and of relations between discourses, genres and styles within discourse in its most general sense) which I have developed in my more recent work. This view of ideology and its relation to mediation as a form of recontextualisation is used in the paper to analyse processes of re-scaling, changing relations between the national scale and international scales, in the '*transition*' of formerly socialist countries in Central and Eastern Europe towards being market economies and western-style democracies. The particular examples analysed are Romanian.

1. Critical and descriptive goals in discourse analysis

Abstract

I view social institutions as containing diverse 'ideological-discursive forma-tions' (IDFs) associated with different groups within the institution. There is usually one IDF which is clearly dominant. Each IDF is a sort of 'speech community' with its own discourse norms but also, embedded within and symbolised by the latter, its own 'ideological norms'. Institutional subjects are constructed, in accordance with the norms of an IDF, in subject positions whose ideological underpinnings they may be unaware of. A characteristic of a dominant IDF is the capacity to 'naturalise' ideologies, i.e., to win accept-ance for them as non-ideological 'common sense'.

It is argued that the orderliness of interactions depends in part upon such naturalised ideologies. To 'denaturalise' them is the objective of a dis-course analysis which adopts 'critical' goals. I suggest that denaturalisation involves showing how social structures determine properties of discourse, and how discourse in turn determines social structures. This requires a 'global' (macro/micro) explanatory framework which contrasts with the non-explanatory or only 'locally' explanatory frameworks of 'descriptive' work in discourse analysis. I include a critique of features of such work which follow from its limited explanatory goals (its concept of 'background knowledge', 'speaker-goal' explanatory models, and its neglect of power), and discuss the social conditions under which critical discourse analysis might be an effec-tive practice of intervention, and a significant element in mother-tongue education.

Background knowledge > BGK (handwritten)

1 Introduction: orderliness and naturalisation

In this section of the paper I shall distinguish in a preliminary way between 'critical' and 'descriptive' goals in discourse analysis. Data extracts are used to show (i) how the orderliness of interactions depends upon taken-for-granted 'background knowledge' (BGK for short), and (ii) how BGK subsumes 'naturalised' ideological representations, i.e., ideological representations which come to be seen as non-ideological 'common sense'. Adopting critical goals means aiming to elucidate such naturalisations, and more generally to make clear social determinations and effects of discourse which are characteristically opaque to participants. These concerns are absent in currently predominant 'descriptive' work on discourse. The critical approach has its theoretical underpinnings in views of the relationship between 'micro' events (including verbal events) and 'macro' structures which see the latter as both the conditions for and the products of the former, and which therefore reject rigid barriers between the study of the 'micro' (of which the study of discourse is a part) and the study of the 'macro'. I shall discuss these theoretical issues at the end of this section of the paper.

When I refer to the 'orderliness' of an interaction, I mean the feeling of participants in it (which may be more or less successfully elicited, or inferred from their interactive behaviour) that things are as they should be, i.e., as one would normally expect them to be. This may be a matter of coherence of an interaction, in the sense that individual speaker turns fit meaningfully together, or a matter of the taking of turns at talking in the expected or appropriate way, or the use of the expected markers of deference or politeness, or of the appropriate lexicon. (I am of course using the terms 'appropriate' and 'expected' here from the perspective of the participant, not analytically.)

Text 1 gives an example of 'orderliness' in the particular sense of coherence within and between turns, and its dependence on naturalised ideologies. It is an extract from an interview between two male police officers (*B* and *C*), and a woman (*A*) who has come to the police station to make a complaint of rape.[1]

Text 1   *Ex of orderliness* (handwritten)

1. *C*: you do realise that when we have you medically examined . . . and
2. *B*: they'll come up with nothing
3. *C*: the swabs are taken . . . it'll show . . . if you've had sexual intercourse with three men this afternoon . . .
    it'll ⌈ show
4. *A*:   ⌊ it'll show each one

5. *C*: it'll ⌈ show each one . . .
   B: ⌊ hmm

6. *A*: yeah I ⌈ know
7. *C*: ⌊ alright . . . so . . .

8. *A*: so it would show ⌈ (indist.)
9. *C*: ⌊ it'll confirm that you've had

   ⌈ sex . . . or
   B: ⌊ hm

   C: not with three men alright . . . so we can confirm it's happened . . .
   that you've had sex with three men . . . if it does confirm it . . . then
   I would go so far as to say . . . that you went to that house willingly
   . . . there's no struggle . . . you could have run away quite easily . . .
   when you got out of the car . . . to go to the house . . . you could have
   got away quite easily . . . you're well known . . . in Reading . . . to
   the uniformed . . . lads for being a nuisance in the streets shouting
   and bawling . . . couple of times you've been arrested . . . for under
   the Mental Health Act . . . for shouting and screaming in the street . . .
   haven't you . . .

10. *A*: when I was ill yeah

11. *C*: yeah . . . right . . . so . . . what's to stop you . . . shouting and
    screaming in the street . . . when you think you're going to get raped
    . . . you're not frightened at all . . . you walk in there . . . quite blasé
    you're not frightened at all . . .

12. *A*: I was frightened

13. *C*: you weren't . . . you're showing no signs of emotion every now and
    again you have a little tear . . .

14. *B*: (indist.) if you were frightened . . . and you came at me I think I
    would dive . . . I wouldn't take you on
    ⌈ you frighten me
15. *C*: ⌊ (indist.)

16. *A*: why would I frighten ⌈ you (indist.) only a little (indist.)
    ⌊ you you just   it doesn't

17. *B*: matter . . . you're female and you've probably got a hell of a temper
    . . . if you were to ⌈ go
    ⌊ I haven't got a temper

18. *A*: (indist.) a hell of ⌈ a temper
    ⌊ oh I don't know . . .

19. *C*:

20. *B*: I think if things if if things were up against a a wall . . . I think you'd
    fight and fight very hard . . .

I imagine that for most readers the most striking instance of ideologically-based coherence in this text is in 17 (*you're female and you've probably got a hell of a temper*), with the implicit proposition 'women tend to have bad tempers' which, with a further implicit proposition ('people in bad tempers are frightening to others') and certain principles of inference, allows 16 and 17 to be heard as a coherent question–answer and complaint–rejection pair. There are other, perhaps rather less obvious instances, including the following (I have taken the example in 17 as 'case' (1)).

(2)   It is taken as given (as mutually assumed background knowledge) that fear or its absence, and perhaps affective states in general, can be 'read off' from behavioural 'symptoms' or their absence. The orderliness of *C*'s talk in 9 (from *there's no struggle*) and 11, i.e., its coherence as the drawing of a conclusion (*you're not frightened at all*) from pieces of evidence (*there's no struggle*, *A* could have got away but didn't, *A* has a proven capacity for creating public scenes but did not do so in this case), depends upon this implicit proposition. Similar comments apply to 13.

(3)   It is taken as given that persons have, or do not have, capacities for particular types of behaviour irrespective of changes in time, place, or conditions. This is a version of the doctrine of the 'unified and consistent subject' (Coward and Ellis 1977: 7). Thus, again in 9 and 11, evidence of *A*'s capacity for creating a public scene in the past, and when she was suffering from some form of mental illness, is taken, despite 10, as evidence for her capacity to do so in this instance. As in the case of (2), the coherence of *C*'s line of argument depends upon the taken-as-given proposition.

(4)   It is taken as given that if a woman willingly places herself in a situation where sexual intercourse 'might be expected to occur' (whatever that means), that is tantamount to being a willing partner, and rules out rape. *C*'s apparent objective in this extract is to establish that *A* went willingly to the house where the rape is alleged to have occurred. But this extract is coherently connected with the rest of the interview only on the assumption that what is really at issue is *A*'s willingness to have sexual intercourse. To make this connection, we need the above implicit proposition.

The four implicit propositions which I have identified represent BGK of a rather particular sort, which is distinct from, say, the assumed BGK that there is some identifiable door which is closed when some speaker asks some addressee to 'open the door'. I argue below (Section 3.1) that the tendency in the literature to conflate all of the 'taken-for-granted' under the rubric of 'knowledge' is an unacceptable reduction. For present purposes, I propose to refer to these four propositions as 'ideological', by which I mean that each is a particular representation of some aspect of the world (natural or social; what is, what can be, what ought to be) which might be (and may be) alternatively represented, and where any given representation can be associated with some particular 'social base' (I am aware that this is a rather crude gloss on a complex and controversial concept. On ideology, see Althusser (1971) and Therborn (1980)).

These propositions differ in terms of the degree to which they are 'naturalised' (Hall 1982: 75). I shall assume a scale of naturalisation, whose 'most naturalised' (theoretical) terminal point would be represented by a proposition which was taken as commonsensically given by all members of some community, and seen as vouched for by some generally accepted rationalisation (which referred it, for instance, to 'human nature').

Cases (1) and (4) involve only limited naturalisation. The proposition 'women tend to have bad tempers' could, one imagines, be taken as given only within increasingly narrow and embattled social circles – one achievement of the women's movement has been precisely the denaturalisation of many formerly highly naturalised sexist ideologies. Case (4) corresponds to traditional judicial views (in English law) of rape as well as having something of a base outside the law, but it is also under pressure from feminists.

The degree of naturalisation in cases (2) and (3) is by contrast rather high, and they are correspondingly more difficult to recognise as ideological representations rather than 'just common sense'. Such ideological propositions are both open to lay rationalisation in terms of 'what everyone knows' about human behaviour and 'human nature', and traceable in social scientific theories of human behaviour and the human subject.

Texts 2–4 illustrate other ways in which orderliness may depend upon ideological BGK. My aim here is merely to indicate some of the range of phenomena involved, so my comments on these texts will be brief and schematic.

Text 2

1. *T*: Now, let's just have a look at these things here. Can you tell me, first of all, what's this?
2. *P*: Paper.
3. *T*: Piece of paper, yes. And, hands up, what cutter will cut this?
4. *P*: The pair of scissors.
5. *T*: The pair of scissors, yes. Here we are, the pair of scissors. And, as you can see, it's going to cut the paper. Tell me what's this?
6. *P*: Cigarette box.
7. *T*: Yes. What's it made from?

(Sinclair and Coulthard 1975: 96)

The orderliness in this instance is a matter of conformity on the part of both teacher and pupils to a framework of discoursal and pragmatic rights and obligations, involving the taking of turns, the control of topic, rights to question and obligations to answer, rights over metacommunicative acts and so forth (see Sinclair and Coulthard (1975) and Stubbs (1983: 40–46) for a detailed discussion of these properties of classroom discourse). The implicit ideological propositions identified in text 1 appertain to language in its 'ideational' function, whereas the discoursal and pragmatic norms of text 2 appertain to the 'interpersonal' function of language (Halliday 1978: 45–46). Moreover, while in text 1 ideologies are formulated in (implicit) propositions, in text 2 ideological representations of social relationships are symbolised in norms of interaction. Michael Halliday's claim that the linguistic system functions as a 'metaphor' for social processes as well as an 'expression' of them, which he formulated in the context of a discussion of the symbolisation of social relationships in dialectal and registerial variants (Halliday 1978: 3) also applies here. In these respects, text 3 is similar to text 2:

Text 3

1. *X*: oh hel*lǒ* Mrs Norton
2. *Y*: oh hel*lǒ* Súsan
3. *X*: yès erm wèll I'm afraid I've got ^ afraid I've got a bit of a *prò*blem
4. *Y*: you mean about tomorrow *nìght*
5. *X*: yès ^ erm you [knów I
6. *Y*: oh dèar]
7. *X*: *knòw* that that you said
8. *Y*: yéah
9. *X*: er you *wàn*ted me tomorrow night
10. *Y*: uhúh yéah
11. *X*: well I just thought erm (clears throat) I've got something else on which I just didn't think about when I arranged it with you you know and er
12. *Y*: (sighs) yés
13. *X*: I'm just wondering if I could possibly back dòwn on tomorrow
(Edmondson 1981: 119–120)[2]

Again, this is a matter of orderliness arising from conformity with interactive norms, though in this case pragmatic norms of politeness and mitigation: *X* uses a range of politeness markers, including a title + surname mode of address (in 1), 'hedges' (e.g., *a bit of a* in 3), and indirect speech acts (as in 13). These markers are 'appropriate' given the status asymmetry between *X* and

Y (*Y* is *X*'s employer, and no doubt older than *X*), and given the 'face-threatening' act which *X* is engaged in (Brown and Levinson 1978: 81).

The interactive norms exemplified in texts 2 and 3 can be seen in terms of degrees of naturalisation like the implicit propositions of text 1, though in this case it is a matter of the naturalisation of practices which symbolise particular ideological representations of social relationships, i.e., relationships between teachers and pupils, and between babysitters and their employers. The more dominant some particular representation of a social relationship, the greater the degree of naturalisation of its associated practices. I will use the expression 'ideological practices' to refer to such practices.

Texts 1–3 are partial exemplifications of the substantial range of BGK which participants may draw upon in interactions. We can very roughly differentiate four dimensions of participants' 'knowledge base', elaborating Winograd (1982: 14) who distinguishes only the first, third and fourth:

knowledge of language codes,
knowledge of principles and norms of language use,
knowledge of situation, and
knowledge of the world.

I wish to suggest that all four dimensions of the 'knowledge base' include ideological elements. I will assume without further discussion that the examples I have given so far illustrate this for all except the first of these dimensions, 'knowledge of language code'. Text 4 shows that this dimension is no exception. It is a summary by Benson and Hughes (1983: 10–11) of one of the case studies of Aaron Cicourel from his work on the constitution and interpretation of written records which are generated in the juvenile judicial process (Cicourel 1976).

Text 4

The probation officer was aware of a number of incidents at school in which Robert was considered to be 'incorrigible'. The probation file contained mention of 15 incidents at school prior to his court appearance, ranging from 'smoking' to 'continued defiance'. The probation officer's assessment and recommendation for Robert contained a fairly detailed citation of a number of factors explaining Robert's 'complete lack of responsibility toward society' with the recommendation that he be placed in a school or state hospital. Among the factors mentioned were his mother's 'severe depression', divorced parents, unstable marriage, and his inability to comprehend his environment:

the kind of factors, we should note, assembled in conventional sociological reasoning explaining the causes of delinquency.

Cicourel is concerned to show 'how "delinquents get that way" as a process managed and negotiated through the socially organised activities that constitute "dealing with crime" ' (Benson and Hughes 1983: 11). What I want to highlight is the role which the lexicon itself plays in this process. Let us focus on just four items among the many of interest in the text: *incorrigible, defiance, lack of responsibility, deliquency*. These belong to a particular lexicalisation of 'youth', or more specifically of young people who do not 'fit' in their families, their schools, or their neighbourhoods. The 'conditions of use' of this lexicon as we may call them, are focused upon by Cicourel – the unwritten and unspoken conventions for the use of a particular word or expression in connection with particular events or behaviours, which are operative and taken for granted in the production and interpretation of written records. But the lexicon itself, as code, is only one among indefinitely many possible lexicalisations; one can easily create an 'anti-language' (Halliday 1978: 164–182) equivalent of this part of the lexicon – *irrepressible* for *incorrigible, debunking* for *defiance, refusal to be sucked in by society* for *lack of responsibility toward society*, and perhaps *spirit* for *delinquency*. Alternative lexicalisations are generated from divergent ideological positions. And lexicalisations, like the implicit propositions and pragmatic discoursal practices of the earlier texts, may be more or less naturalised: a lexicalisation becomes naturalised to the extent that 'its' IDF achieves dominance, and hence the capacity to win acceptance for it as 'the lexicon', the neutral code.

It may be helpful for me to sum up what I have said so far before moving to a first formulation of 'critical' goals in discourse analysis. I am suggesting (a) that ideologies and ideological practices may become dissociated to a greater or lesser extent from the particular social base, and the particular interests, which generated them – that is, they may become to a greater or lesser extent 'naturalised', and hence be seen to be commonsensical and based in the nature of things or people, rather than in the interests of classes or other groupings; (b) that such naturalised ideologies and practices thereby become part of the 'knowledge base' which is activated in interaction, and hence the 'orderliness' of interaction may depend upon them, and (c) that in this way the orderliness of interactions as 'local', 'micro' events comes to be dependent upon a higher 'orderliness', i.e., an achieved consensus in respect of ideological positions and practices.

This brings me to certain theoretical assumptions which underpin the proposed adoption of critical goals in discourse analysis. Firstly, that verbal

verbal = social action

interaction is a mode of social action, and that like other modes of social action it presupposes a range of what I shall loosely call 'structures' – which are reflected in the 'knowledge base' – including social structures, situational types, language codes, norms of language use. Secondly, and crucially, that these structures are not only presupposed by, and necessary conditions for, action, but are also the *products* of action; or, in a different terminology, actions *reproduce* structures. Giddens (1981) develops this view from a sociological perspective in terms of the notion of 'duality of structure'.

The significance of the second assumption is that 'micro' actions or events, including verbal interaction, can in no sense be regarded as of merely 'local' significance to the situations in which they occur, for any and every action contributes to the reproduction of 'macro' structures. Notice that one dimension of what I am suggesting is that language codes are reproduced in speech, a view which is in accordance with one formulation in Saussure's *Cours*: 'Language and speaking are thus interdependent; the former is both the instrument and the product of the latter' (1966: 19). My concern here, however, is with the reproduction of social structures in discourse, a concern which is evident in Halliday's more recent work:

> By their everyday acts of meaning, people act out the social structure, affirming their own statuses and roles, and establishing and transmitting the shared systems of value and of knowledge. (Halliday 1978: 2)

But if this is the case, then it makes little sense to study verbal interactions *as if* they were unconnected with social structures: 'there can be no theoretical defence for supposing that the personal encounters of day-to-day life can be conceptually separated from the long-term institutional development of society' (Giddens 1981: 173). Yet that seems to be precisely how verbal interactions have in fact been studied for the most part in the currently predominant 'descriptive' work on discourse. Thus the adoption of critical goals means, first and foremost, investigating verbal interactions with an eye to their determination by, and their effects on, social structures. However, as I have suggested in discussing the texts, neither determinations nor effects are necessarily apparent to participants; opacity is the other side of the coin of naturalisation. The goals of critical discourse analysis are also therefore 'denaturalising'. I shall elaborate on this preliminary formulation in the following sections.

My use of the term 'critical' (and the associated term 'critique') is linked on the one hand to a commitment to a dialectical theory and method 'which grasps things . . . essentially in their interconnection, in their concatenation, their motion, their coming into and passing out of existence' (Engels 1976:

27), and on the other hand to the view that, in human matters, interconnections and chains of cause and effect may be distorted out of vision. Hence 'critique' is essentially making visible the interconnectedness of things; for a review of senses of 'critique', see Connerton (1976: 11–39). In using the term 'critical', I am also signalling a connection (though by no means an identity of views) between my objectives in this paper and the 'critical linguistics' of a group of linguists and sociologists associated with Roger Fowler (Fowler *et al.* 1979, Kress and Hodge 1979).

2 Social institutions and critical analysis

The above sketch of what I mean by 'critical goals' in discourse analysis gives rise to many questions. For instance: how can it be that people are standardly unaware of how their ways of speaking are socially determined, and of what social effects they may cumulatively lead to? What conception of the social subject does such a lack of awareness imply? How does the naturalisation of ideologies come about? How is it sustained? What determines the degree of naturalisation in a particular instance? How may this change?

I cannot claim to provide answers to these questions in this paper. What I suggest, however, is that we can begin to formulate answers to these and other questions, and to develop a theoretical framework which will facilitate researching them, by focusing attention upon the 'social institution' and upon discourses which are clearly associable with particular institutions, rather than on casual conversation, as has been the fashion (see further Section 3.3 below). My reasoning is in essence simply that (a) such questions can only be broached within a framework which integrates 'micro' and 'macro' research, and (b) we are most likely to be able to arrive at such an integration if we focus upon the institution as a 'pivot' between the highest level of social structuring, that of the 'social formation',[3] and the most concrete level, that of the particular social event or action. The argument is rather similar to Fishman's case for the 'domain' (Fishman 1972): the social institution is an intermediate level of social structuring, which faces Janus-like 'upwards' to the social formation, and 'downwards' to social actions.

Social actions tend very much to cluster in terms of institutions; when we witness a social event (e.g., a verbal interaction), we normally have no difficulty identifying it in institutional terms, i.e., as appertaining to the family, the school, the workplace, church, the courts, some department of government, or some other institution. And from a developmental point of view, institutions are no less salient: the socialisation of the child (in which process discourse is both medium and target) can be described in terms of the child's progressive exposure to institutions of primary socialisation (family, peer group, school, etc.). Given that institutions play such a prominent role, it is not surprising that, despite the concentration on casual conversation in recent discourse analysis referred to above, a significant amount of work is on types of discourse which are institutionally identified, such as classroom discourse (e.g., Sinclair and Coulthard 1975); courtroom discourse (e.g., Atkinson and Drew 1979, O'Barr 1982), or psychotherapeutic discourse (e.g., Labov and Fanshel 1977). However, most of this work suffers from the inadequacies characteristic of descriptive discourse analysis, which I detail in Section 3 of this paper.

One can envisage the relationship between the three levels of social phenomena I have indicated – the social formation, the social institution, and social action – as one of determination from 'top' to 'bottom': social institutions are determined by the social formation, and social action is determined by social institutions. While I would accept that this direction of determination is the fundamental one, this formulation is inadequate in that it is mechanistic (or undialectical): that is, it does not allow that determination may also be 'upwards'. Let us take education as an example. I would want to argue that features of the school as an institution (e.g., the ways in which schools define relationship between teachers and pupils) are ultimately determined at the level of the social formation (e.g., by such factors as the relationship between the schools and the economic system and between the schools and the state), and that the actions and events that take place in the schools are in turn determined by institutional factors. However, I would also wish to insist that the mode of determination is not mechanical determination, and that changes may occur at the level of concrete action which may reshape the institution itself, and changes may occur in the institution which may contribute to the transformation of the social formation. Thus the process of determination works dialectically.

A social institution is (among other things) an apparatus of verbal interaction, or an 'order of discourse'. (I suggest later in this section that this property only *appears* to belong to the institution itself.) In this perspective, we may regard an institution as a sort of 'speech community', with its own particular repertoire of speech events, describable in terms of the sorts of 'components' which ethnograhic work on speaking has differentiated – settings, participants (their identities and relationships), goals, topics, and so forth (Hymes 1972). Each institution has its own set of speech events, its own differentiated settings and scenes, its cast of participants, and its own norms for their combination – for which members of the cast may participate in which speech events, playing which parts, in which settings, in the pursuit of which topics or goals, for which institutionally recognised purposes. It is, I suggest, necessary to see the institution as simultaneously facilitating and constraining the social action (here, specifically, verbal interaction) of its members: it provides them with a frame for action, without which they could not act, but it thereby constrains them to act within that frame.[4] Moreover, every such institutional frame includes formulations and symbolisations of a particular set of ideological representations: particular ways of talking are based upon particular 'ways of seeing' (see further below in this section).

I shall use the terms 'subject', 'client', and '(member of) public' for the parties to verbal interaction, rather than the more familiar term 'participant'. I use 'subject' for 'members' of an institution – those who have institutional roles and identities acquired in a defined acquisition period and maintained as long-term attributes. The 'client' is an outsider rather than a member, who nevertheless takes part in certain institutional interactions in accordance with norms laid down by the institution, but without a defined acquisition period or long-term maintenance of attributes (though attribute-maintenance is no doubt a matter of degree). Examples would be a patient in a medical examination, or a lay witness in a court hearing. Finally, some institutions have a 'public' to whom messages are addressed, whose members are sometimes assumed to interpret these messages according to norms laid down by the institution, but who do not interact with institutional subjects directly. The primary concept is 'subject': 'client' and 'public' might be defined as special and relatively peripheral types of subject.

The term 'subject' is used in preference to 'participant' (or 'member') because it has the double sense of agent ('the subjects of history') and affected ('the Queen's subjects'); this captures the concept of the subject as qualified to act through being constrained – 'subjected' – to an institutional frame (see above). I shall refer to 'social subjects' as well as 'institutional subjects': the social subject is the whole social person, and social subjects occupy subject positions in a variety of institutions. The choice of terms here is not a trivial matter: I suspect the term 'participant' tends to imply an essential, integral 'individual' who 'participates' in various institutionally defined types of interaction without that individuality being in any way shaped or modified thereby. In preferring 'subject', I am emphasising that discourse makes people, as well as people make discourse.

We may usefully distinguish various facets of the subject (either 'institutional' or 'social'), and talk of 'economic', 'political', 'ideological' and 'discoursal' subjects. What I have been suggesting above can be summed up by saying that institutions construct their ideological and discoursal subjects; they construct them in the sense that they impose ideological and discoursal

Teacher Ex.

constraints upon them as a condition for qualifying them to act as subjects. For instance, to become a teacher, one must master the discursive and ideological norms which the school attaches to that subject position – one must learn to talk like a teacher and 'see things' (i.e., things such as learning and teaching) like a teacher. (Though, as I shall show in Section 1.4, these are not mechanically deterministic processes.) And, as I have suggested above, these ways of talking and ways of seeing are inseparably intertwined in that the latter constitute a part of the taken-for-granted 'knowledge base' upon which the orderliness of the former depends. This means that in the process of acquiring the ways of talking which are normatively associated with a subject position, one necessarily acquires also its ways of seeing, or ideological norms. And just as one is typically unaware of one's ways of talking unless for some reason they are subjected to conscious scrutiny, so also is one typically unaware of what ways of seeing, what ideological representations, underlie one's talk. This is a crucial assumption which I return to below.

monolithic vs. pluralistic

However, social institutions are not as monolithic as the account so far will have suggested: as ideological and discursive orders, they are pluralistic rather than monistic, i.e., they provide alternative sets of discoursal and ideological norms. More accurately, they are pluralistic to an extent which varies in time and place, and from one institution to another in a given social formation, in accordance with factors including the balance of power between social classes at the level of the social formation, and the degree to which institutions in the social formation are integrated or, conversely, autonomous.[5] The significance of the first of these factors is that pluralism is likely to flourish when non-dominant classes are relatively powerful; the significance of the second is that a relatively autonomous institution may be relatively pluralistic even when non-dominant classes are relatively powerless.

I shall say that, as regards the ideological facet of pluralism, a given institution may house two or more distinguishable 'ideological formations' (Althusser 1971), i.e., distinct ideological positions which will tend to be associated with different forces within the institution. This diversity of ideological formations is a consequence of, and a condition for, struggles between different forces within the institution: that is, conflict between forces results in ideological barriers between them, and ideological struggle is part of that conflict. These institutional struggles are connected to class struggle, though the relationship is not necessarily a direct or transparent one; and ideological and discoursal control of institutions is itself a stake in the struggle between classes (see below on 'ideological and discoursal power').

I propose to use for talking about institutional pluralism Pêcheux's term 'discursive formation' as well as Althusser's 'ideological formation'. Pêcheux

defines a discursive formation as 'that which in a given ideological formation, i.e., from a particular position in a given conjuncture determined by
the state of the class struggle, determines *"what can and should be said"*'
(Pêcheux 1982: 111). I shall refer to 'ideologicaldiscursive formations' (IDFs
for short), in accordance with what I have said above about the inseparability of 'ways of talking' and 'ways of seeing'. In so doing, I shall make the
simplifying assumption, which further work may well challenge, that there is
a one-to-one relationship between ideological formations and discursive
formations.

I have referred above to the social institution itself as a sort of speech
community and (to extend the image) ideological community; and I have
claimed that institutions construct subjects ideologically and discoursally.
Institutions do indeed give the appearance of having these properties – but
only in cases where one IDF is unambiguously dominant (see below). I suggest that these properties are properly attributed to the IDF, not the social
institution: it is the IDF that positions subjects in relation to its own sets of
speech events, participants, settings, topics, goals and, simultaneously, ideological representations.

As I have just indicated, IDFs are ordered in dominance: it is generally
possible to identify a 'dominant' IDF and one or more 'dominated' IDFs in a
social institution. The struggle between forces within the institution which I
have referred to above can be seen as centring upon maintaining a dominant
IDF in dominance (from the perspective of those in power) or undermining a
dominant IDF in order to replace it. It is when the dominance of an IDF is
unchallenged to all intents and purposes (i.e., when whatever challenges there
are do not constitute any threat), that the norms of the IDF will become most
naturalised, and most opaque (see Section 1), and may come to be seen as the
norms of the institution itself. The interests of the dominant class at the level
of the social formation require the maintenance in dominance in each social
institution of an IDF compatible with their continued power. But this is never
given – it must be constantly fought for, and is constantly at risk through a shift
in relations of power between forces at the level of the social formation and in
the institutions. I shall refer to the capacity to maintain an IDF in dominance
(or, at the level of the social formation, a network of IDFs) as 'ideological/
discoursal power', which exists alongside economic and political power, and
can normally be expected to be held in conjunction with them. I shall use
'power' in this sense in contrast with 'status': the latter relates to the relationship between subjects in interactions, and their status is registered in terms of
(symmetrical or asymmetrical) interactional rights and obligations, which are
manifested in a range of linguistic, pragmatic and discoursal features. The

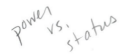

group which has ideological and discoursal power in an institution may or may not be clearly status-marked.

We are now in a position to develop what has been said so far about the naturalisation of ideologies, and what I described at the end of Section 1 as 'the other side of the coin of naturalisation', their opacity to participants in interactions; since the case for a discourse analysis with critical goals (which it is the primary objection of this paper to argue) rests upon the assumption that the naturalisation and opacity of ideologies is a significant property of discourse, it is important to be as clear as possible about these effects and their origins.

Naturalisation gives to particular ideological representations the status of common sense, and thereby makes them opaque, i.e., no longer visible as ideologies. These effects can be explained given (a) the process of subject-construction referred to above, and (b) the notion of a dominant IDF. I have argued that in the construction of the subject, the acquisition of normative 'ways of talking' associated with a given subject position must simultaneously be the acquisition of the associated 'ways of seeing' (ideological norms); that is, since any set of discursive norms entails a certain knowledge base, and since any knowledge base includes an ideological component, in acquiring the discursive norms one simultaneously acquires the associated ideological norms.

If, moreover, the process of acquisition takes place under conditions of the clear dominance of a given IDF in an institution, such that other IDFs are unlikely to be evident (at least to the outsider or novice), there is no basis internal to the institution for the relativisation of the norms of the given IDF. In such cases, these norms will tend to be perceived first as norms of the institution itself, and second as merely skills or techniques which must be mastered in order for the status of competent institutional subjects to be achieved. These are the origins of naturalisation and opacity.

If it is also the case (as it typically is) that those who undergo the process of subjection are unaware of the functioning of the institution concerned in the social formation as a whole, then the institution will tend to be seen in isolation and there will be no basis external to the institution, either, for the relativisation and rationalisation of the norms of the given IDF.

Subjects, then, are typically unaware of the ideological dimensions of the subject positions they occupy. This means of course that they are in no reasonable sense 'committed' to them, and it underlines the point that ideologies are not to be equated with views or beliefs. It is quite possible for a social subject to occupy institutional subject positions which are ideologically incompatible, or to occupy a subject position incompatible with his or her overt political or social beliefs and affiliations, without being aware of any contradiction.[6]

3   Critical and descriptive goals

I am using the term 'descriptive' primarily to characterise approaches to discourse analysis whose goals are either non-explanatory, or explanatory within 'local' limits, in contrast to the 'global' explanatory goals of critical discourse analysis outlined above. Where goals are non-explanatory, the objective is to describe without explaining: if for instance a speaker in some interaction uses consistently indirect forms of request, one points this out without looking for causes. Where goals are explanatory but 'local', causes are looked for in the immediate situation (e.g., in the 'goals' of the speaker – see below), but not beyond it: that is, not at the higher levels of the social institution and the social formation, which would figure in critical explanation. Moreover, although 'locally' explanatory descriptive work may seek to identify at least local determinants of features of particular discourses, descriptive work generally has been little concerned with the *effects* of discourse. And it has certainly not concerned itself with effects which go beyond the immediate situation. For critical discourse analysis, on the other hand, the question of how discourse cumulatively contributes to the reproduction of macro structures is at the heart of the explanatory endeavour.

Descriptive work in discourse analysis tends to share other characteristics which can be seen as following from its at best limited explanatory goals. These include a reliance upon the concept of 'background knowledge', adoption of a 'goal-driven' local explanatory model, and neglect of power in discourse and, to an extent, status; all of these are discussed below. I shall refer for convenience to 'a descriptive approach' which has these characteristics in addition to descriptive goals in the above sense, but this is to be understood as a generalised characterisation of a tendency within discourse analysis and not as a characterisation of the work of any particular discourse analyst. Thus I would regard all of the following as basically descriptive in approach, diverse though they are in other respects: Sinclair and Coulthard (1975), Labov and Fanshel (1977), Atkinson and Drew (1979), Brown and Yule (1983), Stubbs (1983). But this does not mean that I am attributing to each of them all the descriptive (or, indeed, none of the critical) characteristics.

3.1   Background knowledge[7]

My primary contention in this sub-section is that the undifferentiated concept of BGK which has such wide currency in descriptive discourse analysis places discourse analysis in the position of ('uncritically') reproducing certain ideological effects.

The concept of BGK reduces diverse aspects of the 'backgrounded material' which is drawn upon in interaction – beliefs, values, ideologies, as well as knowledge properly so called – to 'knowledge'. 'Knowledge' implies facts to be known, facts coded in propositions which are straightforwardly and transparently related to them. But 'ideology', as I have argued above, involves the representation of 'the world' from the perspective of a particular interest, so that the relationship between proposition and fact is not transparent, but mediated by representational activity. So ideology cannot be reduced to 'knowledge' without distortion.[8]

I suggested in Section 2 that where an IDF has undisputed dominance in an institution, its norms tend to be seen as highly naturalised, and as norms of the institution itself. In such instances, a particular ideological representation of some reality may come to appear as merely a transparent reflection of some 'reality' which is given in the same way to all. In this way, ideology creates 'reality' as an effect (see Hall 1982: 75). The undifferentiated concept of BGK mirrors, complements and reproduces this ideological effect: it treats such 'realities' as objects of knowledge, like any other reality.

It also contributes to the reproduction of another ideological effect, the 'autonomous subject' effect. The autonomous subject effect is a particular manifestation of the general tendency towards opacity which I have taken to be inherent to ideology: ideology produces subjects which appear not to have been 'subjected' or produced, but to be 'free, homogeneous and responsible for (their) actions' (Coward and Ellis 1977: 77). That is, metaphorically speaking, ideology endeavours to cover its own traces. The autonomous subject effect is at the bottom of theories of the 'individual' of the sort I referred to in Section 2.

Seeing all background material as 'knowledge' is tantamount to attributing it to each participating person in each interaction as a set of attributes of that person ('what that person knows'). Interactions can then be seen as the coming-together of so many constituted, autonomous persons, 'of their own free will', whose 'knowledge bases' are mobilised in managing and making sense of discourse. This conception is cognitive and psychological at the expense of being asociological; the sociological is reduced to the cognitive through the 'competence' metaphor, so that social factors do not themselves figure, only the 'social competence' of persons. The 'competent' subject of cognitive conceptions of interaction is the autonomous subject of ideology.

I am not of course suggesting that descriptive discourse analysts are consciously conspiring to give social scientific credence to ideological effects. The point is rather that unless the analyst differentiates ideology from knowledge, i.e., unless s/he is aware of the ideological dimensions of discourse, the chances are that s/he will be unconsciously implicated in the reproduction of ideologies, much as the lay subject is. To put the point more positively and more contentiously, the concept of ideology is essential for a scientific understanding of discourse, as opposed to a mode of understanding which emulates that of the partially unsighted discourse subject. But the concept of ideology is incompatible with the limited explanatory goals of the descriptive approach, for it necessarily requires reference outside the immediate situation to the social institution and the social formation in that ideologies are by definition representations generated by social forces at these levels.

3.2 Goals[9]

'Goal-driven' explanatory models of interaction tend, I suggest, to exaggerate the extent to which actions are under the conscious control of subjects. In referring to goal-driven models, I mainly have in mind 'speaker goal' models which set out to explain the strategies adopted by speakers, and the particular linguistic, pragmatic and discoursal choices made, in terms of speakers' goals (e.g., Winograd 1982: 13–20, Leech 1983: 35–44). But I shall also comment on what one might call an 'activity-goal' model, which claims that features of the 'activity type' are explicable by reference to its 'goal', i.e., 'the function or functions that members of the society see the activity as having' (Levinson 1979: 369). I include activity-goals because Levinson also suggests that there might be a connection between them and speaker-goals: in essence, the former determine the latter. Atkinson and Drew (1979) attribute analogous explanatory value to activity-goals.

My objection to the 'activity-goal' model is that it regards properties of a particular type of interaction as determined by the *perceived* social functions of that type of interaction (its 'goal'), thus representing the relationship between discourse and its determinants as transparent to those taking part. The properties which Levinson sees as so determined broadly correspond to what I have called 'ideological practices' (see Section 1), i.e., discoursal practices which vary between IDFs, and which are explicable immediately in terms of the ideological facets of IDFs and indirectly in terms of the social determinants of these ideologies. An example of ideological practices is the unequal distribution of discoursal and pragmatic rights and obligations in classroom discourse, illustrated in text 2. A distinction needs to be made between the ideologies which underlie such practices, and *rationalisations* of such practices which institutional subjects may generate; rationalisations may radically distort the ideological bases of such practices. Yet the activity type model portrays such rationalisations – the function(s) which these practices are *seen* (Levinson's term) as having – as *determinants* of these practices.

The objection to 'speaker-goal' models is similar: they imply that what speakers do in interaction is under their conscious control, and are at odds with the claim that naturalisation and opacity of determinants and effects are basic features of discourse. I have no doubt that this will be a contentious view of speaker-goal models; it will be objected that I am using 'goal' in its ordinary language sense of 'conscious objectives' ('goal 1') rather than in the technical sense ('goal 2') of 'a state which regulates the behaviour of an individual' (Leech 1983: 40), which misrepresents speaker-goal models. However, I would argue that such an objection underestimates the power of a metaphor: goal 2 includes goal 1; there is no obvious reason why one should accept this conflation of conscious goals and unconscious 'goals'; but given this conflation, it is inevitable that the sense of goal 1 will predominate, and hence that interactions will be essentially seen as the pursuit of conscious goals. Such a view is in harmony with the local explanatory goals of the descriptive approach, for it seems to offer an explanation without needing to refer to institutions or the social formation.

3.3 Power and status

Either the descriptive approach offers pseudo-explanations of norms of interaction such as that of the activity-goal model, or it regards norms of interaction as requiring descriptions but not explanation. I shall be suggesting here that in either case, given that the capacity to maintain an IDF in dominance is the most salient effect of power in discourse, the absence of a serious concern with explaining norms results in a neglect of power; that, furthermore, there has been such an emphasis on cooperative conversation between equals that even matters of status have been relatively neglected (see Section 2 for 'power' and 'status').

The descriptive approach has virtually elevated cooperative conversation between equals into an archetype of verbal interaction in general. As a result, even where attention has been given to 'unequal encounters' (the term is used in the Lancaster work referred to in note 1 for interactions with status asymmetries), the asymmetrical distribution of discoursal and pragmatic rights and obligations according to status (see below) has not been the focal concern. The archetype has developed under influences which prominently include two which I shall comment upon: the 'Cooperative Principle' of Grice (1975), and ethnomethodological work on turn-taking.

I think it is clear that Grice primarily had in mind, when formulating the 'Cooperative Principle' and the maxims in the 1975 paper, interaction between persons capable of contributing (more or less) equally; this is the implication of his focus on 'the *exchange* of information' (my emphasis, see below). But for persons to be able to contribute equally, they must have equal status. Having equal status will presumably mean having equal discoursal and pragmatic rights and obligations – for instance, the same turn-taking rights and the same obligations to avoid silences and interruptions, the same rights to utter 'obligating' illocutionary acts (such as requests and questions), and the same obligations to respond to them. I take it that having equal status also means having equal control over the determination of the concepts pre-supposed by Grice's maxims: over what for interactional purposes counts as 'truth', 'relevance', adequate information, etc. (see Pratt 1981: 13).

Of course, there do occur interactions which at least approximate to these conditions, but they are by no means typical of interactions in general. Grice himself pointed out that the maxims were stated as if the purpose which 'talk is adapted to serve and primarily employed to serve' were 'a maximally effec-tive exchange of information', and noted that 'the scheme needs to be general-ized to allow for such general purposes as influencing or directing the actions of others' (1975: 47). This proviso seems to have been often overlooked.

The impact of ethnomethodological work on turn-taking on the archetype must surely involve an influential paper by Sacks, Schegloff and Jefferson (1978), which proposes a simple but powerful set of rules to account for properties of conversational turn-taking, where 'conversation' is again very much cooperative interaction between equals. These rules tend to be taken as generally relevant for turn-taking, even though they are explicitly formulated for conversation. The paper itself argues that the 'exchange system' for conversation which it characterises 'should be considered the basic form of speech-exchange system, with other systems . . . representing a variety of transformations on conversation's turn-taking system' (Sacks *et al.* (1978: 47)). Levinson has suggested an analogous primacy for Grice's maxims, which we might view as 'specifications of some basic *unmarked* communica-tive context, deviations from which however common are seen as special or *marked*' (1979: 376). Any such assignment of primacy or 'unmarked' status to conversation strengthens the archetype I have referred to.

The neglect of 'unequal encounters' and questions of status which has resulted from the appeal of the archetype is not unconnected with the neglect of power I referred to above. For if one focuses upon 'unequal encounters', or the comparison of 'equal' and 'unequal' interactions, the variability and relativity of norms of interaction is likely to be highlighted, giving rise to ques-tions about their origins and rationales which may in turn lead to questions about ideological and discursive power; whereas if one concentrates heavily upon data where the distribution of rights and obligations is more or less symmetrical, there seems to be nothing to explain. Though from a critical perspective, of course, there is: the possibility of, and constraints upon, co-operative conversation between equals, which are themselves effects of power.

Such conversation does not occur freely irrespective of institution, sub-jects, settings, and so forth. A reasonable hypothesis perhaps is that the most favourable conditions for its occurrence would be in an institution whose dominant IDF represented (certain) subjects as diversely contributing to a cooperative venture of equals; and that those with power would be most likely to endeavour to maintain such an IDF in dominance where the conditions existed for them (or required of them) to maintain their power through actively involving the 'powerless' in the organisation and control of the institution. In contemporary Britain, academic communities approximate rather closely to these conditions.

From the critical perspective, a statement of the conditions under which interactions of a particular type may occur is a necessary element of an account of such interactions, and I have suggested that such a statement cannot be made without reference to the distribution and exercise of power in the institution and, ultimately, in the social formation. Given the limited explanatory goals of the descriptive approach, however, the concept of power lies outside its scope.

3.4 Conclusion: research objectives

I have suggested that from the at best 'locally' explanatory goals of the descriptive approach there follow certain other characteristics – its conception of BGK and its 'complicity' in certain ideological effects, its interest in goal-driven models and its image of subjects in conscious control of interactions, the absence of serious explanatory work on norms and the neglect of power and status.

I referred in Section 3.1 to the 'cognitive' conception of interaction which is implicit in the concept of BGK. Interest in cognitive theories of language and discourse is on the increase, at least in part because of their 'computer-friendliness'; Winograd (1982) presents a 'computational paradigm' as a new synthesis of the work of linguists, psychologists, students of artificial intelligence and others, around a computer-friendly cognitive theory of language. Winograd's proposals have much in common with what I have called the 'descriptive approach', including a speaker-goal model, and local goals. I suspect that the current computational explosion might make this an increasingly attractive direction for discourse analysis, which will no doubt produce significant advances in certain directions, much as tranformational-generative grammar did, and at much the same cost in terms of the desocialisation of language and discourse.

Any such development must, however, come to terms with what I would see as a major problem for non-critical discourse analysis, that of what I shall call the *rationality* of its research programme. I take a 'rational' research programme to be one which makes possible a systematic development in knowledge and understanding of the relevant domain, in this case discourse. Given the in principle infinite amount of possible data, a principled basis for sampling is necessary for such a programme. No such principled basis is possible so long as discourse analysts treat their samples as *objets trouvés* (Haberland and Mey 1977: 8), i.e., so long as bits of discourse are analysed with little or no attention to their places in their institutional matrices.

A principled basis for sampling requires minimally (a) a sociological account of the institution under study, its relationship to other institutions in the social formation, and relationship between forces within it; (b) an account of the 'order of discourse' of the institution, of its IDFs and the dominance relationships among them, with links between (a) and (b); (c) an ethnographic account of each IDF. Given this information, one could identify for collection and analysis interactions which are representative of the range of IDFs and speech events, interactional 'cruxes' which are particularly significant in terms of tensions between IDFs or between subjects, and so forth. In this way a systematic understanding of the functioning of discourse in institutions and institutional change could become a feasible target.

The same is true for 'comparative' research on discourse across institutions. The descriptive approach to such research may show interesting similarities or differences in discourse structure and organisation, as does work in the Birmingham discourse analysis model (Sinclair and Coulthard 1975: 115–18, Coulthard and Montgomery 1981). But such comparison requires a principled basis for selecting cases, given which it can contribute to the investigation of substantive social issues such as: the degree to which social institutions are integrated or autonomous in a given social formation, and centralising or decentralising tendencies; or the positions of social institutions on a hierarchy of relative importance to the function of the social formation, and how this relates to influences from one institution to another on various levels, including the ideological and discoursal. The work of Foucault (1979) is a suggestive starting point for such research.

4 Concluding remarks: resistance

The following piece of data is, like text 1, an extract from a police interview, though in this case the interviewee is a youth suspected of involvement in an incident during which a bus window was broken. *A* is the youth, *B* is the police interviewer, and the conventions are the same as for text 1.

Text 5

1. *B*: so why did ⌈ you get the other fellows to come up with
2. *A*:   ⌊ some went up first
3. *B*: you as well
4. *A*: I'm not getting on a bus with a bus load of coons me sitting there jack the lad d'you know what I mean . . .
5. *B*: why's ⌈ that
6. *A*:   ⌊ get laid into what do you mean why's that . . .
7. *B*: well they weren't attacking any other white people on the bus were they
8. *A*: no . . . that's coz there was no other skinhead on the bus that's why . . . if there was a skinhead on the bus that was it they would lay into him
9. *B*: so there's a feud is there
10. *A*: yeah . . .
11. *B*: between skinheads and blacks
12. *A*: yeah . . .
13. *B*: so when you went on the upstairs on the bus because let's face it if there was none of them downstairs was there
14. *A*: no
15. *B*: so why did you go upstairs
16. *A*: like I say there was no room downstairs anyway I don't sit on the bottom of the bus that's where all the grannies sit . . . I can't sit down there[10]

In contrast to the orderliness of the texts discussed in Section 1.1 of this paper, text 5 manifests a certain 'disorderliness', in the sense that the interviewee is in a number of respects not constraining his contributions to the interaction in accordance with institutional norms for the subject position he is in. This is a case where we have a 'client' rather than an institutional subject; as I indicated earlier, clients can normally be expected to comply with institutional norms. The client here is non-compliant in the following ways:

(a) *A* interrupts *B* (2,5)
(b) *A* challenges *B*'s questions rather than answering them (3,5)
(c) *A* questions *B* (5)
(d) *A* questions *B*'s sincerity. In 9 and 11, *A* signals prosodically as well as non-vocally that *B* is already in possession of information he purports to be asking for (and therefore not to have).

(e) *A* maintains a different 'orientation' (Sinclair and Coulthard 1975: 130–32) from *B*'s. This is marked by his use of the lexis of his peer group rather than that of police interviews (*coon, jack the lad, grannies*).

One might add that there are indications that *A* gets *B* to adapt to his orientation, whereas one would expect the reverse, i.e., one would expect the client to adapt to the orientation of the subject (and of the institution). For instance, in 6 *B* anaphorically refers to (*a bus load of*) *coons*, rather than using a different lexicalisation as one might expect him to if he were 'asserting' his orientation (and as he does in 10, with *blacks*).

Text 5 will no doubt correct any impression that may have been given in this paper that norms are necessarily faithfully mirrored in practices (see note 4). One factor determining how likely it is that a client will comply with the norms which an institution attaches to a subject position is the particular configuration of processes of subjection in other institutions which have contributed to the social formation of that client. In this instance one might wish to look into the subject positions associated with the client's peer-group, i.e., the relevant 'youth culture'. One dimension of institutional subject construction which I have not referred to in the paper so far is that the institution also constructs the subject's stance towards 'outsiders', including subjects in other institutions. In this case, it could be that the client is constructed into an oppositional stance towards the police and perhaps other public authorities.

The critique of institutional discourse, as part of the critique of social institutions and the social formation, does not take place in glorious academic isolation from the practices of institutional subjects, clients and publics. On the contrary, it is continuous with such practices, and it is only in so far as such practices include significant elements of resistance to dominant IDFs – be it through clients rejecting subject positions as in text 5, or, analogously, readers rejecting the 'preferred reader' positions which writers 'write into' their texts – or through challenges to the dominance of an IDF from other IDFs, that the critique of institutional discourse can develop into a 'material force' with the capacity to contribute to the transformation of institutions and social formations.

Given the existence of such conditions across social institutions, which may occur in a period when the struggle between social forces at the level of the social formation is sharp, it may be possible to introduce forms of critical discourse analysis in the schools, as part of the development of 'language awareness', in the teaching of the mother tongue. The desirability in principle of such a development follows from what I have claimed above: if speakers are standardly operating in discourse under unknown determinants and with unknown effects, it is a proper objective for schools to increase discoursal consciousness. However, I have stressed the conditions for such a development, because it would be naïve to think that its desirability in principle would be sufficient for it to be achieved. On the contrary, it is likely to be fiercely resisted.

Notes

1. The transcription conventions are: turns are numbered, excluding 'back channels'; beginnings of overlaps are marked with square brackets; pauses are marked with dots for a 'short' pause and a dash for a 'long' pause; material in round brackets was indistinct. For texts 2 and 3 I retain the conventions used in their sources, which are indicated. Text 1 was part of the data used in a presentation to the Language Study Group of the British Sociological Association (Lancaster Conference, June 1982) by myself and colleagues Christopher Candlin, Michael Makosch, Susan Spencer, Jennifer Thomas. It is taken from the television series *Police* as is text 5.

2. Italicised syllables carry primary stress; intonation is selectively marked; utterance segments which overlap are enclosed within one pair of square brackets; short pauses are marked '^'.

3. I use the term 'social formation' to designate a particular society at a particular time and stage of development (e.g., Britain in 1984).   The term 'society' is used too loosely and variously to serve the purpose.

4. The relationship between norms and action is not as simple as this suggests. Sometimes, which norms are the appropriate ones is itself a matter for negotiation; then there may be alternative sets of norms available (see below); and, as I show in section 4, norms may be rejected.

5. I have in mind throughout class societies, and more specifically capitalist social formations such as the one I am most familiar with: that of modern Britain.

6. Nor are ideologies to be equated with 'propaganda' or 'bias'; the latter are associated with particular communicative intentions (such as 'persuading'), the former are not.

7. The concept of BGK has a wide currency across a number of disciplines. The following, for instance, are representative of pragmatics, discourse analysis and sociology: Giddens (1976), Levinson (1983), Brown and Yule (1983).

8. I assume for present purposes that 'knowledge' and 'ideology' are clearly separable, which presupposes a much more categorical distinction between science and ideology than may be sustainable.

9. I use the term 'goal' here with respect to parties in discourse, whereas my use of the term earlier has been with respect to analytical goals. I don't believe there should be any confusion.

10. This text and some of my comments on it derive from a part of the presentation referred to in note 1 which was jointly produced by Michael Makosch, Susan Spencer and myself. I am grateful to all the colleagues referred to in note 1 for providing the stimuli which led to the writing of this paper. I am grateful to my wife Vonny for showing me how to be more coherent; remaining incoherence is my own responsibility.

2. Language and ideology

1 Introduction

This paper explores the theoretical question of what sort of relationships there are between language and ideology, and the methodological question of how such relationships are shown in analysis (which together I refer to as 'language/ideology'). It is an attempt to build from the achievements and limitations of explorations of these questions within Marxism, especially Althusser's contribution to the theory of ideology and its development by Pêcheux into a theory of discourse and a method for discourse analysis (see Althusser 1971; Haroche, Henry, Pêcheux 1971; Pêcheux 1982; Larrain 1979). I have found the self-criticism of Pêcheux and his associates in their most recent work a valuable resource for going beyond structuralist accounts of language/ideology (Conein *et al.* 1981; Maldidier 1984; Pêcheux 1988).

I discuss the merits of 'locating' ideology in language structures or language events and conclude it is present in both. I outline a conception of discourse and discourse analysis which is compatible with this conclusion, and suggest that a more diverse range of linguistic features and levels may be ideologically invested than is usually assumed, including aspects of linguistic form and style as well as 'content'. I then argue that language/ideology issues ought to figure in the wider framework of theories and analyses of power, for which the Gramscian concept of hegemony is fruitful. This implies a focus in studies of language/ideology upon change in discoursal practice and structures, seen as a dimension of change in the balance of social forces. I conclude with a discussion of the limits of ideology and the possibilities for combating ideological discourse.

2 Location of ideology

I want to argue that ideology invests language in various ways at various levels, and that we don't have to choose between different possible 'locations' of ideology, all of which seem partly justified and none of which seems entirely satisfactory. The key issue is whether ideology is a property of structures or a property of events, and the answer is 'both'. And the key problem is to find a satisfactory account of the dialectic of structures and events.

A number of accounts place ideology in some form of system of potential underlying language practice – be it a 'code', 'structure', 'system' or 'formation' (e.g., a set of expressions in specified semantic relations). These structures are defined for various varieties of a language, not for a language *per se*. The 'structure' option, as I shall call it, has the virtue of showing events, actual discoursal practice, to be constrained by social conventions, norms, histories. It has the disadvantage of tending to defocus the event on the assumption that events are mere instantiations of structures, whereas the relationship of events to structures would appear to be less neat and less compliant. This privileges the perspective of reproduction rather than that of transformation, and the ideological conventionality and repetitiveness of events. Pêcheux is a case in point, though he represents an advance on Althusser in opening up the possibility of resistance through 'counteridentification' and 'disidentification'. It also tends to postulate entities (codes, formations, etc.) which appear to be more clearly bounded than real entities are, thus privileging the synchronic moment of fixity over historical processes of fixation and dissolution.

An alternative location for ideology would be the discursive event itself. This has the virtue of representing ideology as a process which goes on in events, and it permits transformation and fluidity to be highlighted. But it can lead to an illusory view of discourse as free processes of formation unless there is a simultaneous emphasis on structures. There is a textual variant of this location: ideologies reside in texts. While it is true that the forms and content of texts do bear the imprint of ideological processes and structures, it is not possible to 'read off' ideologies from texts. This is because meanings are produced through interpretations of texts and texts are open to diverse interpretations, and because ideological processes appertain to discourses as whole social events – they are processes between people – not to the texts which are produced, distributed and interpreted as moments of such events. Claims to discover ideological processes solely through text analysis run into the problem now familiar in media sociology that text 'consumers' (readers, viewers) appear sometimes to be quite immune to the effects of such ideologies (Morley 1983).

Both the structure and discourse options (as well as the text option) have the limitation of being localised and particular. Ideologies cut across the boundaries of situation types and institutions, and we need to be able to discuss how they transcend particular codes or types of discourse (a simple example would be metaphors of the nation as a family), how ideology relates to the structuring and restructuring of relations between such entities. The concept of 'interdiscourse' is helpful here; so too is Foucault's concept of 'order of discourse' (Foucault 1971) which I shall use. Once again, the structural focus on orders of discourse needs a complementary focus on events, where these restructurings concretely take place.

An issue is what sort of entities are involved in the (re)structuring of orders of discourse. Without attempting a detailed account of the structuring of orders of discourse, I would like to suggest the entities which make them up are (a) more or less clearly defined, (b) variable in scale, and (c) in various relationships to each other, including the relationships of complementarity, inclusion and contradiction. I remarked above that structures are sometimes conceived of as more clearly bounded than they are; some entities seem to be sharply differentiated, others fuzzy. The entities which are articulated and rearticulated in discourse are not all fully fledged codes or registers; they may be smaller scale entities such as turn-taking systems, lexicons which incorporate particular classifications, generic scripts for narratives (for instance), sets of politeness conventions, and so forth. Finally, orders of discourse should, I suggest, be seen as heterogeneous in the sense that they articulate both compatible and complementary entities and contradictory entities – such as contrasting lexicalisations, or turn-taking systems. These suggested properties of orders of discourse accord with thinking in 'second-generation' French discourse analysts. They also, as I shall show, harmonise with the concept of hegemony.

Ideology is located, then, both in structures which constitute the outcome of past events and the conditions for current events, and in events themselves as they reproduce and transform their conditioning structures. In the following two sections I shall present a way of conceptualising (use of) language and a matrix for conceptualising ideology in its relation to economic and political relations which harmonise with this position.

3 Discourse and text

The Saussurean conception of language use or parole sees it in individualistic and asocial terms. In using the term 'discourse' I am claiming language use to be imbricated in social relations and processes which systematically determine variations in its properties, including the linguistic forms which appear in texts. One aspect of this imbrication in the social which is inherent to the notion of discourse is that language is a material form of ideology, and language is invested by ideology.

Also inherent to discourse is the dialectical relation of structure/event discussed above: discourse is shaped by structures, but also contributes to shaping and reshaping them, to reproducing and transforming them. These structures are most immediately of a discoursal/ideological nature – orders of discourse, codes and their elements such as vocabularies or turn-taking conventions – but they also include in a mediated form political and economic structures, relationships in the market, gender relations, relations within the state and within the institutions of civil society such as education.

The relationship of discourse to such extra-discoursal structures and relations is not just representational but also constitutive: ideology has material effects discourse contributes to the creation and constant recreation of the relations, subjects (as recognised in the Althusserian concept of interpellation) and objects which populate the social world. The parent–child relationships of the family, the determination of what positions of 'mother', 'father' and 'child' are socially available as well as the subjection of real individuals to these positions, the nature of the family, or of the home, are all shaped in the ideological processes of discourse. This could easily lead to the idealist inversion referred to earlier whereby the realities of the social world are seen as emanating from ideas. However, there are two provisos which together block this. First, people are always confronted with the family as a real institution (in a limited number of variants) with concrete practices: existing family structures are also partly constituted in ideology and discourse, but reified into institutions and practices. Second, the constitutive work of discourse necessarily takes place within the constraints of the complex of economic, political and discoursal/ideological structures referred to above – and I shall argue later in relation to particular hegemonic projects and struggle. The result is that the ideological and discoursal shaping of the real is always caught up in the networks of the real.

I see discourse as a complex of three elements: social practice, discoursal practice (text production, distribution and consumption), and text, and the analysis of a specific discourse calls for analysis in each of these three dimensions and their interrelations. The hypothesis is that significant connections exist between features of texts, ways in which texts are put together and interpreted, and the nature of the social practice (see Paper 5 for details of this framework).

Ideology enters this picture first in the ideological investment of elements which are drawn upon in producing or interpreting a text, and the ways they are articulated together in orders of discourse; and second in the ways in which these elements are articulated together and orders of discourse rearticulated in discoursal events (detailed below). In the former connection, it should be noted that the richness of the ideological elements which go into producing and interpreting a text may be sparsely represented in the text. An example might be the way in which scare quotes are used to signal a point of confrontation between ideologies (and discourses) which are not further represented in the text – around the word 'personal' in the expression 'the "personal" problems of young people' in a left-wing newspaper (for which many 'personal' problems will be social).

A further substantive question about ideology is what features or levels of language and discourse may be ideologically invested. A common claim is that it is 'meanings' (sometimes specified as 'content' as opposed to 'form') that are ideological (e.g., Thompson 1984), and this often means just or mainly lexical meanings. Lexical meanings are of course important, but so too are presuppositions, implicatures, metaphors and coherence, all aspects of meaning. For instance, coherent interpretations of texts are arrived at by interpreters on the basis of cues in the text, and resources (including internalised ideological and discoursal structures) which they bring to text interpretation. Coherence is a key factor in the ideological constitution and reconstitution of subjects in discourse: a text 'postulates' a subject 'capable' of automatically linking together its potentially highly diverse and not explicitly linked elements to make sense of it. In postulating such a subject, a text contributes to constituting such a subject.

The 'form'–'content' opposition is itself misleading, however. If content is to enter the realm of practice, it must do so in formal clothing, in texts or other material forms, though it is possible to study forms as if they were unrelated to content, as linguists sometimes do. In fact, formal features of texts at various levels may be ideologically invested. For example, the representation of slumps and unemployment as akin to natural disasters may involve a preference for intransitive and attributive rather than transitive sentence structures ('the currency has lost its value', 'millions are out of work', as opposed to 'investors are buying gold', 'firms have sacked millions' – see Fowler *et al.* (1979)). At a different level, crime stories in newspapers are written according to relatively predictable scripts which embody ideological representations of crime (Jordanidou 1990). Again, the turn-taking system in a classroom or politeness conventions operating between a manager and a secretary imply particular ideologial representations of teacher–pupil and manager–secretary relations. Nevertheless, it may be useful to think of ideologies in terms of content-like entities which are manifested in various formal features, and perhaps frame, schema, script and related concepts are of value in this respect (Schank and Abelson 1977).

Even aspects of the 'style' of a text may be ideologically significant. When for instance public bodies such as government ministries produce public information on their schemes and activities, they select a style of writing (or indeed televising) partly on the basis of the image they thereby construct for themselves. This can be regarded as a special sort of ideological process of subject constitution. A topical case in point is the Department of Trade and Industry's publicity for its 'enterprise' initiatives. The Department seems to be trying to create for itself the image of the entrepreneur of 'enterprise culture', in its efforts to persuade others to adopt the same image and identity. It does this in part stylistically. Its publicity for instance is full of categorical, authoritative and unmitigated statements about business practice aimed at businessmen (e.g., 'It's no good expecting to make the right decisions for your business if you don't start with decent information') which have I think more to do with establishing a categorical and authoritative and decisive image than with giving 'information' (or rather opinions) which addressees must already have.

4 Hegemony

The concept of hegemony originates in Lenin but is the centrepiece in an elaborated form of Gramsci's analysis of Western capitalism and revolutionary strategy in Western Europe. I shall make use of it both because it harmonises with the dialectical conception of structure/event advocated above, and because it provides a framework for theorising and analysing ideology/discourse which avoids both economism and idealism. Hegemony cuts across and integrates economy, politics and ideology, yet ascribes an authentic place to each of them within an overall focus upon politics and power, and upon the dialectical relations between classes and class fragments.

Hegemony is leadership as well as domination across the economic, political, cultural and ideological domains of a society. Hegemony is the power over society as a whole of one of the fundamental economically defined classes in alliance (as a bloc) with other social forces, but it is never achieved more than partially and temporarily, as an 'unstable equilibrium'. Hegemony is about constructing alliances, and integrating rather than simply dominating subordinate classes, through concessions or through ideological means, to win their consent. Hegemony is a focus of constant struggle around points of greatest instability between classes and blocs, to construct or sustain or fracture alliances and relations of domination/subordination, which takes economic, political and ideological forms. Hegemonic struggle takes place on a broad front which includes the institutions of civil society (education, trade unions, family), with possible unevenness between different levels and domains.

Ideology is understood within this framework in terms which bear the seeds of all Althusser's advances (Buci-Glucksmann 1980: 66) in, for instance, its focusing of the implicit and unconscious materialisation of ideologies in practices (which contain them as implicit theoretical 'premisses'), ideology being 'a conception of the world that is implicitly manifest in art, in law, in economic activity and in the manifestations of individual and collective life' (Gramsci 1971: 328). While the interpellation of subjects is an Althusserian elaboration, there is in Gramsci a conception of subjects as structured by diverse ideologies implicit in their practice which gives them a 'strangely composite' character (1971: 324), and a view of 'common sense' as both a depositary of the diverse effects of past ideological struggles, and a constant target for restructuring, in ongoing struggles. In common sense, ideologies become naturalised, or automatised. For Gramsci, ideology is tied to action, and ideologies are judged in terms of their social effects rather than their truth values. Moreover, Gramsci conceived of 'the field of ideologies in terms of conflicting, overlapping, or intersecting currents or formations' (Hall 1988: 55–6), which highlights the question of how the elements of what he calls 'an ideological complex' (Gramsci 1971: 195) come to be structured and restructured, articulated and rearticulated, in processes of ideological struggle. This is a perspective developed by Laclau and Mouffe (1985), though in terms which reject basic Gramscian positions such as the rootedness of hegemony in class (see also Laclau (1979)).

The ideological dimensions of hegemonic struggle can be conceptualised and analysed in terms of the view of discourse I have introduced above. An order of discourse constitutes the discoursal/ideological facet of a contradictory and unstable equilibrium (hegemony); notice that the view outlined above of an order of discourse as complex, heterogeneous and contradictory harmonises with the concept of ideological complex. And discoursal practice is a facet of struggle which contributes in varying degrees to the reproduction or transformation of the existing order of discourse, and through that of existing social and power relations. Let us take the political discourse of Thatcherism as an example. Thatcherite discourse can be interpreted as a rearticulation of the existing order of political discourse which has brought traditional conservative, neo-liberal and populist discourse elements into a new mix that has also constituted an unprecedented discourse of political power for a woman leader. This discoursal rearticulation materialises an ideological project for the constitution of a new political base, new political subjects, and a new agenda, itself a facet of the political project of restructuring the hegemony of the bloc centred upon the bourgeoisie in new economic and political conditions. Thatcherite discourse has been described along these lines by Hall (1988), and Fairclough (1989a) shows how such an analysis can be carried out in terms of the conception of discourse introduced above, in a way which accounts for (as Hall does not) the specific features of the language of Thatcher's political texts. I should add that the rearticulated order of discourse is a contradictory one: authoritarian elements coexist with democratic and egalitarian ones (textually, for instance, inclusive *we* coexists with indefinite *you*), patriarchal elements with feminist elements, but always with the latter member of each pair being contained and constrained by the former. The rearticulation of orders of discourse, however, is achieved not only in productive discoursal practice, but also in interpretation: because of the heterogeneous elements which go into their production, texts are open to many ambivalences which are reduced if not eliminated by particular interpretative practices which draw upon particular configurations of discoursal elements as parts of their interpretative procedures.

However, most discourse does not bear upon hegemonic struggle in such a direct way as Thatcherite discourse. In most discourse, the protagonists (as it were) are not classes or political forces linked in such relatively direct ways to classes or blocs but, for instance, teachers and pupils, counsellors and clients, police and public, women and men. Hegemony is a process at the societal level, whereas most discourse has a more local character, being located in or on the edges of particular institutions – the family, schools, neighbourhoods, workplaces, courts of law, etc. We have to honour the specificity of such institutional domains. However, hegemony still provides both a model and a matrix. It provides a model: in, let us say, education, the dominant groups also appear to exercise power through constituting alliances, integrating rather than merely dominating subordinate groups, winning their consent, achieving a precarious equilibrium which may be undermined by other groups, and doing so in part through discourse and ideology, through the constitution of and struggle around local orders of discourse, no less heterogeneous and contradictory than their societal counterpart. It provides a matrix: the achievement of hegemony at a societal level requires a degree of integration of local and semi-autonomous institutions and power relations, so that the latter are partially shaped by hegemonic relations. This directs attention to links across institutions, and links and movement between institutional orders of discourse. What is necessary but difficult to accomplish is giving proper weight to integration without thereby playing down the relative autonomy and integrity of non-class struggles: between the sexes, ethnic groups, and the various categories of institutional agent.

From the perspective of hegemony, it is processes which are in focus: local processes of constituting and reconstituting social relations through discourse, global processes of integration and disintegration transcending particular institutions and local orders of discourse. Discoursal change, and its relationship to ideological change and to social struggle and change in a broader sense, is where the emphasis must be placed, and where the language/ideology problem should be confronted. And in accordance with the dialectical view of structure/event above, a study of discoursal change needs a double focus on the discoursal event and on the societal and institutional orders of discourse.

By change in discoursal events I mean innovation or creativity which in some way goes against conventions and expectations. Change involves forms of transgression, crossing boundaries, such as putting together existing codes or elements in new combinations, or drawing upon orders of discourse or their elements in situations which conventionally preclude them in a way which gives a sense of a struggle between different ways of signifying a particular domain of experience. Change leaves traces in texts in the form of the co-occurrence of contradictory or inconsistent elements – mixtures of formal and informal styles, technical and non-technical vocabularies, markers of authority and familiarity, more typically written and more typically spoken syntactic forms, and so forth. The immediate origins and motivations of change lie in contradictions which may problematise conventions in a variety of ways. For example, contradictions which occur in the positioning of subjects, such as those involving gender relations, where gender-linked discoursal and other practices have been problematised and changed under the impact of contradictions between traditional gendered subject positions which many of us were socialised into, and new gender relations. People are faced with what Billig *et al.* (1988) call 'ideological dilemmas', which they attempt to resolve or contain through discoursal forms of struggle. On a rather different plane, Thatcher's political discourse can be seen to arise out of the problematisation of traditional right-wing discoursal practices in circumstances where contradictions become apparent between the social relations, subject positions and political practices they are based in and a changing world. Such subjective apprehensions of problems in concrete situations have their social conditions in stuctural contradictions at the institutional and societal levels, upon which discoursal events have cumulative effects. In terms of the framework for discourse analysis introduced in the previous section, social conditions and effects are analysed in the dimension of social practice, 'ideological dilemmas' and attempts to resolve them in the dimension of discourse practice, and textual traces in the dimension of text.

In respect of structural change, changes which appear to move across boundaries between institutional orders of discourse are of particular interest in their possible links to wider hegemonic projects. Let me refer to two changes of this sort. One is an apparent democratisation of discourse which involves the reduction of overt markers of power asymmetry between people of unequal institutional power – teachers and pupils, academics and students, employers/managers and workers, parents and children, doctors and patients. This tendency is manifested in a great many different institutional domains. Although there are variations between them, it appears to be generally interpretable not as the elimination of power asymmetry but its transformation into covert forms. For example, teachers may exercise control in discourse with pupils less through direct orders and overt constraints on their rights to speak than through indirect requests and suggestions and the way they react and respond (facially and physically as well as verbally) to pupils' contributions. Such discourse can be seen in terms of contradictory mixtures of discourses of equality and power. The second example is what I have called 'synthetic personalisation' (Fairclough 1989a). This is the simulation of private, face-to-face, person-to-person discourse in public mass-audience discourse – print, radio, television. Both examples are I think interpretable in hegemonic terms, though to do so properly would require more space than I have here. Discoursal democratisation is of course linked to political democratisation, and to the broad shift from coercion to consent, incorporation and pluralism in the exercise of power. Synthetic personalisation is I think a facet of a concomitant process of the breaking down of divisions between public and private, political society and civil society, as the state and its mechanisms (especially ideological) of generating consent expand into private domains. Although both cases can perhaps be seen in pessimistic terms as illusions of democracy, informality and so forth being projected for ulterior motives, the fact that orders of discourse do incorporate these elements if only in ways limited and constrained by others renders them open, if we adopt a hegemonic model, to discoursal struggle directed at promoting these elements, as it were. In this sense democratisation and personalisation as strategies are high risk.

Are discoursal changes of this order necessarily ideologically invested, and what are their implications for the language/ideology problem? It is quite conceivable that changes in discoursal practices and restructuring of orders of discourse could come about for purely rational reasons. For example, it could well be that doctors are more likely to arrive at sound medical judgements if they talk with their patients conversationally on a roughly (at least apparently) equal footing than if they merely subject them to batteries of preconstructed verbal and physical examinations. But the rational motivations for such a change are virtually bound to attract an ideological overlay by the fact that the change takes places within existing power relations inside and outside medicine. Let me spell this out: in so far as changes in practices and restructurings can be said to embody representations, propositions or assumptions which affect (sustain, undermine) relations of power, they can be said to be ideological. This is broadly similar to Thompson's view of ideology as meaning in the service of relations of domination (though I would add resistance to domination), or Frow's view of ideology as a 'political functionalisation of speech' (Thompson 1984: 4, Frow 1985: 204). For discourse, being ideological does not therefore preclude being other things as well.

This does not mean, however, that the specific ideological import of a particular element is fixed. Consider for example the apparently non-directive, non-judgemental, empathising way of talking to people one-to-one about themselves and their problems which we call 'counselling'. Counselling has its origins in therapy, but it now circulates as a technique across many institutional domains. It is highly ambivalent ideologically. Most counsellors see themselves as giving space to people as individuals in a world which increasingly treats them as ciphers, which makes counselling look like a counter-hegemonic practice. However, counselling is now used in preference to practices of an overtly disciplinary nature in various institutions, which makes it look like a hegemonic technique for subtly drawing aspects of people's private lives into the domain of power. Hegemonic struggle of an ideological order is partly through counselling and partly over counselling.

The picture of language/ideology which emerges from this discussion is moving towards Frow's view of ideology as 'a state of discourse . . . in relation to the class struggle' (1985: 204). That is, rather than attributing specific and fixed ideological 'contents' to elements, ideology is seen more dynamically as the shifting relationship of discoursal practices to hegemonic (and more local-institutional) struggle. Clearly some elements are more ideologically fixed than others – think for instance of vocabularies it would be difficult not to regard as sexist or racist. The point is, however, that many discoursal elements at least which may manifest a degree of ideological fixity may nevertheless be turned around. Foucault makes the same point in referring to the 'tactical polyvalence of discourses':

> Discourses are tactical elements or blocks operating in the field of force relations; there can exist different and even contradictory discourses within the same strategy; they can, on the contrary, circulate without changing their form from one strategy to another, opposing strategy. (Foucault 1981: 101)

This suggests a homology between discoursal 'strategies' and hegemonic political strategies for constructing alliances and incorporating subordinate groups, which underscores the value of the hegemony concept for exploring discoursal change and language/ideology. It also suggests that perhaps the relationship between discourse and hegemony is a matter of the latter limiting the potential of the former: there is no specifically discoursal reason why there should not be an unlimited articulation and rearticulation of elements. It is hegemony – history – that curtails this discoursal potential and constrains which articulations actually come about, their durability, and so forth. I should add that the view I have set out of changes in the structure of orders of discourse as facets of an evolving hegemonic struggle will hopefully evoke Foucault's explorations of discourse and the technologies of power (Foucault 1972, Dreyfus and Rabinow 1982).

5 Limits of ideology

I have suggested that discoursal practices are ideologically invested in so far as they contribute to sustaining or undermining power relations. Relations of power may in principle be affected by discoursal practices in any type of discourse, even in scientific and theoretical discourse. This precludes a categorical opposition between ideology on the one hand and science or theory on the other which some writers on language/ideology have suggested (Zima 1981, Pêcheux 1982). This does not, however, imply that all discourse is irredeemably ideological. Ideologies arise in class societies characterised by relations of domination, and in so far as human beings are capable of transcending such societies they are capable of transcending ideology. I do not therefore accept the view of 'ideology in general' as a form of social cement which is inseparable from society itself.

On a less Utopian level, it is also quite possible to combat ideology now. The fact that all types of discourse are open in principle and no doubt to some extent in fact in our society to ideological investment does not mean that all types of discourse are ideologically invested to the same degree. It should not be too difficult to show that advertising is in broad terms more heavily invested than the physical sciences, though the thrust of Foucault's work (even if he resists the concept of ideology) is to show that the social sciences have a heavy ideological investment. There are structural determinants of degrees of ideological investment, but that does not mean that ideology cannot be effectively combated in any circumstances. Ideology works, as Althusser reminds us, by disguising its ideological nature. It becomes naturalised, automatised – 'common sense' in Gramsci's terms. Subjects are ideologically positioned as independent of ideological determination. Yet subjects are also contradictorily positioned, and when contradictory positions overlap they provide a basis for awareness and reflexivity, just as they lead to problematisation and change. A critically orientated discourse analysis can systematise awareness and critique of ideology (which does not, of course, mean it is itself automatically immune from it). From awareness and critique arise possibilities of empowerment and change (Fairclough 1989a, Chapter 9). Since all such movements take place within the matrix of hegemonic struggle, however, they are liable not only to be resisted but also to be incorporated. A critical discourse analysis must aim for constant vigilance about who is using its results for what, and about whether its critique of certain practices is not helping to naturalise other equally but differently ideological practices.

Acknowledgements

I am grateful to Raman Selden for comments on a draft of this paper.

3. Semiosis, ideology and mediation. A dialectical view

My objective in this paper is to indicate how particular conceptualisations of mediation and ideology can be accommodated within a version of CDA (see Chouliaraki and Fairclough 1999; Fairclough 2000a, 2001c, 2003; Chiapello and Fairclough 2002; Fairclough, Jessop and Sayer 2004). The version of CDA which I shall work with here is somewhat different from my previous publications on media (especially Fairclough 1995b). I shall argue that this version of CDA can constitute a theoretical and methodological resource in researching media and mediation, including the imbrication of media in ideological processes, a resource which can most fruitfully be drawn upon in combination with more established resources in media studies. The term *semiosis* in the title is used in preference to *discourse* to refer to language and other semiotic modes (e.g., visual images) in a general way, so as to avoid the common confusion between 'discourse' (abstract noun) and 'discourses' (count noun). The latter will be introduced later.

1 Two examples

In the course of my discussion of ideology, I shall refer to two short mediated texts in Romanian. The first is a leaflet (a piece of A5 paper folded into two) picked up at a large furniture store (called 'Mobexpert Gallery', from 'mobilă' meaning 'furniture') in Bucharest in August 2003. The front of the leaflet reads: 'intră in Golden Club şi eşti privilegiat' ('Join the Golden Club and you are privileged'), with the first four words at the top of the page, the last three at the bottom, and the image of a carefully manicured woman's hand holding a Golden Club membership card in the middle. The top of the centre page is taken up with the same woman's hand holding a gift voucher, and the lower half by a text which reads 'bucură-te de avantajele Golden Club' ('Enjoy the advantages of the Golden Club'), followed by a list of 'advantages' (gift vouchers, special offers, price reductions etc.), and the back of the leaflet lists a number of 'condiţii' ('conditions') for membership. The furniture store's logo appears twice, with 'eşti privilegiat' ('you are privileged') incorporated into it. The second text was encountered on a visit to a bank in Bucharest also in August 2003. A metre or so in front of the cashier's desk there was a notice on a stand reading 'Pastraţi limita de discreţie. Vă mulţumim.' A close translation into English is 'Observe the limit of discretion. We thank you'. A similar notice in the UK might read something like 'Please respect the privacy of others. Thank you', though my impression is that such notices are not usual in the UK, that the semiotic cues are more minimal and covert, for example, a line painted on the ground or some other sort of boundary marker.

The practices of stores issuing 'loyalty cards', and maintenance of space between a person being served in a bank, post office etc. and others queuing, are familiar and routine in 'western' countries like the UK. One can see such practices as having been recontextualised in Romania and other formerly socialist countries of Central and Eastern Europe in the course of a decade of 'transition' towards capitalism. For each of the two cases, I shall comment on aspects of the Romanian context which are relevant to the nature and process of recontextualisation.

Romania post-1989 is a profoundly unequal society, with huge differences in wealth, income and resources between a small elite living mainly in Bucharest and the vast majority of the population, and substantial poverty and social deprivation. One might say, no doubt somewhat reductively, that there are two Romanias, two radically different lifestyles and associated expectations and values (with the proviso that the new 'western' values and practices have permeated both, if in different ways). Only members of the elite use stores such as Mobexpert Gallery, or for that matter the banks. The qualification for membership of the Golden Club is spending at least €750 on furniture, while the mean monthly wage for state employees is around €150. Most people could not afford the furniture sold at Mobexpert. The people who are offered the possibility of being 'privileged' as members of the Golden Club are already the most privileged group in Romanian society. The Mobexpert Gallery from this perspective is part of a network of spaces which the economic elite moves within, including for instance the Bucharest mall, expensive restaurants, health clubs etc., from which the rest of Romanian society is excluded by price. The Romanian economic elite are not only objectively privileged within Romanian society, they also seem to be preoccupied with their privileged position, with their distinction from others in Romanian society, with their status as an elite.

The Golden Club card is a 'loyalty card' which gives certain 'advantages' to those who hold it in terms of savings on future purchases, delivery and assembly, and so forth. The term 'privilege card' is sometimes used in the UK and the USA – such cards are represented as 'rewarding' customers for their 'loyalty'. Other terms like 'reward card' are also used. Some of these schemes seem to construe the relationship between customer and company as rather like that between courtier and monarch – the latter 'rewards' the former's 'loyalty', maybe grants 'privileges' in reward for loyalty. In many cases such contentious if not bizarre representations of the commercial relationship between company and customer are kept covert through nominal compounds like 'privilege card' which leave the verbal process and its participant relations ('who is privileging who?') opaque and vague. In the Romanian case, there isn't a nominal compound but a clause with a copular verb ('eşti', 'are') and an attributive adjective derived from the past participle of a verb ('privilegiat', 'privileged'). What the customer gains through membership of 'Golden Card' are represented not as 'privileges' but as 'avantajele', 'advantages', a term which is very widely used in Romanian advertising and media for price reductions, special offers, good deals etc. What is striking about the Romanian case, and different from similar material in the UK for instance, is not the presence of the concept of 'privilege', but its presence as an attribute ('privileged') of those who join the 'club'. The tense of the verb is significant: it is a present tense verb, not a future tense verb – the latter would be more easily amenable to being interpreted as an indirect way of saying that the customer will gain certain 'privileges' (i.e., 'advantages') as a member. The clause with the present tense verb, occurring three times in this short leaflet, construes membership of the 'club' as conveying a 'privileged' status. There seems to be an appeal to the economic elite's preoccupation with privilege, both linguistically (construing membership as 'being privileged', and as joining a 'club', which also implies exclusivity and privilege) and in terms of visual semiotics (the carefully manicured woman's hand holding the card, and the colour gold). Membership of the 'club' is offered not just as a way to get a good deal, but also as a status symbol and marker of distinction for people who are preoccupied with such symbols and markers.

The second case calls for some historical context, especially with respect to queuing. Queuing in Romania before 1989, and in many contexts still now, has been a somewhat anarchic happening. People do not stand in line, no respect is shown for another's 'place' in the queue, or for the privacy of an individual's business with an official or consultant, yet at the same time queuing is a communal affair in which information about official requirements and procedures which organisations often do not provide is freely shared and exchanged, and in which people also share their life stories, their problems and their anxieties. But queuing is now radically different in certain contexts. For instance, people queuing at cash machines in the street preserve as a matter of course a space between the person using the machine and the rest of the queue (to the point where it is often unclear whether people are waiting to use the machine or just casually standing around). One might take the notice in the Romanian bank to be socialising the public into 'western' queuing behaviour. Yet given that people observe such queuing practices without such prompts in cases like cash machines, it seems likely that customers at the cashier's desk in the bank (who would also be among the much larger group of people who use cash machines) would be aware of what is expected. Perhaps therefore the notice is as much to do with distinction as with socialisation: if it is informationally and pedagogically redundant, perhaps it works to reaffirm the common commitment of the bank and its customers to practices and values of 'discretion', and thus serves both as publicity for the bank and as a marker of distinction for the customers, an affirmation of part of what makes them different from the rest of Romanian society.

What was striking to me as a cultural outsider was that the focus is on 'observing the limit of discretion' in the queue rather than the privacy of the person at the counter. If one compares 'respect the privacy of others' with 'observe the limit of discretion', the former gives salience to what is to be respected (individual 'privacy'), the latter to how to show respect (be 'discrete') – the former perhaps takes for granted what the latter draws attention to. Although the customers at the bank may not need to be socialised into 'western' queuing practices, one can see a socialising force in the notice – the implication is that people have to be taught how to respect the privacy of others. 'Limita' in Romanian can be interpreted as both (physical) 'boundary' and in terms of social and ethical (self)-restraint or acceptability, and both senses can be seen as actualised in this case.

2 Mediation and ideology

I shall work from the view of mediation proposed by Silverstone (1999: 13), mediation as 'the movement of meaning':

> Mediation involves the movement of meaning from one text to another, from one discourse to another, from one event to another. It involves the constant transformation of meanings, both large scale and small, significant

and insignificant, as media texts and texts about media circulate in writing, in speech and audiovisual forms, and as we, individually and collectively, directly and indirectly, contribute to their production . . . Mediated meanings circulate in primary and secondary texts, through endless intertextualities, in parody and pastiche, in constant replay, and in the interminable discourses, both off-screen and on-screen, in which we as producers and consumers act and interact, urgently seeking to make sense of the world . . .

There are a number of issues here. First, as meanings move from text to text, they are open to transformation. Meanings do not simply 'circulate' unchanged between texts; movement of meanings involves both continuity and change and, I would add, how much continuity and how much change is contingent upon the nature of the events and texts that mediated meanings move into. Second, the possibility of transformation suggests that mediated meanings enter processes of meaning-making as part of the resources for meaning-making. I prefer to see movement in these terms – 'movement of meaning' is misleading given that meanings may be transformed in moving; 'movement of resources for meaning-making' is better. Third, these resources for meaning-making are both specific and general, concrete and abstract – they include for instance both concrete representations of specific events of the US/UK invasion of Iraq in particular news reports, and regular and durable ways of representing such events ('discourses' in the sense in which I shall introduce that term below). Fourth, a relationship is implied between media texts and other sorts of texts (though the movement of resources for meaning-making may be between media texts too). What differentiates media texts from other sorts of texts? I see media texts as a class of texts which are specialised for moving resources for meaning-making between texts, and more abstractly between different social practices, fields, domains and scales of social life.

Ideologies, in a first formulation (elaborated below), are representations which contribute to the constitution, reproduction, and transformation of social relations of power and domination ('ways in which meaning serves to sustain relations of domination', Thompson 1984). There are many different views of ideology (Thompson 1984; Larrain 1989; Eagleton 1991; van Dijk 1998), but a major divide is between critical versus descriptive concepts of ideology, and what essentially characterises critical concepts is that ideologies are seen as one modality of power, a modality which constitutes and sustains relations of power through producing consent or at least acquiescence, power through hegemony rather than power through violence and force. My view is that critical social science including CDA requires a critical concept of ideology, and that descriptive concepts of ideology empty the category of its distinctive import and value in social research and analysis.

I shall now briefly present the version of CDA referred to above, and then discuss how the view of mediation and ideology I have just sketched out can be accommodated within it.

3   Critical discourse analysis

CDA is based upon a realist social ontology (Sayer 2000), which sees both concrete social events and abstract social structures as part of social reality. Social structures can be conceived of as potentialities which are selectively actualised in social events – what is possible, in contrast with what is actual. The relationship between social structures and social events is mediated by social practices, which control the selective actualisation of potentials. Diagramatically, these are:

- Social structures
- Social practices
- Social events.

There is a semiotic dimension to each level of abstraction:

- Social structures: semiotic systems (languages)
- Social practices: orders of discourse
- Social events: texts (including talk, 'utterances').

The concepts of semiotic system (language) and text are familiar in language studies; the concept of order of discourse is relatively novel. Orders of discourse constitute the social structuring of semiotic variation or difference. At the concrete level of texts one finds, of course, considerable semiotic variation, which is not random but socially structured in accordance with relatively durable and stable semiotic dimensions of social practices, i.e., orders of discourse. An order of discourse is a specific configuration of discourses, genres, and styles (for these categories, see below), which define a distinctive meaning potential, or, to put it somewhat differently, which constitute distinctive resources for meaning-making in texts. The relationship between what is semiotically possible (as defined by semiotic systems) and the actual semiotic features of texts is mediated by orders of discourse as filtering mechanisms which select certain possibilities but not others.

Social events, and texts as the semiotic elements of social events, are shaped by two sorts of causal powers, understanding causality in the critical realist (non-Humean) sense as not entailing regularity – i.e., x can be said to cause y without that entailing a regular correlation between x and y, because effects have multiple causes which affect one another's operation (Sayer 2000; Fairclough, Jessop and Sayer 2004). Social events (and texts) are shaped on the one hand by social practices and social structures, and on the other hand by social agents. One may say that events (and texts) are locally and inter-actionally produced by situated agents, but in ways which depend on the continuity of structures and practices (as well as the continuity – the habitus – of persons). At the same time, texts have causal effects on non-semiotic as well as semiotic elements of social life – which is how they can do ideological work. In terms of the classical sociological distinction, both the perspective of 'verstehen' and the perspective of 'erklären' are relevant to the study of texts: texts are caught up in processes of meaning-making, but they are also (thereby) a part of the causal (including ideological) effects of events.

Texts figure in three main ways as part of events: in acting, representing and identifying. They are part of the action (talking or writing constitute ways of acting, often in conjunction with non-semiotic action); they simultaneously represent aspects of the world, and they simultaneously identify social actors, contribute to the constitution of social and personal identities. One might compare this with Halliday's concept of 'metafunctions', though the particular functions (or rather aspects of meaning) I have distinguished are different (Halliday 1994). When people act, represent, identify in (texts as parts of) events, they orient to more or less established and stabilised ways of acting, representing and identifying, which are parts of social practices, constituted at the level of social practices, and therefore of orders of discourse, but also habituses (Bourdieu and Wacquant 1992). Semiotically, the distinctions are:

- Genres: ways of acting
- Discourses: ways of representing
- Styles: ways of being.

Analysis of texts includes (a) interdiscursive analysis of which genres, discourses and styles are drawn upon and oriented to in a particular text, and how they are articulated together in the text; (b) linguistic (semiotic, pragmatic, conversational) analysis of actional, representational and identify-ing meanings, and of their realisation in the linguistic forms of the text, and of how these meanings and forms realise the interdiscursive 'mix' of genres, discourses and styles.

Events do not come singly, but in interconnected chains or, more loosely, networks which are in part chains or networks of texts. Texts also connect events, including events that are removed from each other in time and space. Media texts clearly have a particular importance in this regard. Participants in chains or networks of events orient to ways of chaining or networking which are parts of networks of social practices, including, semiotically, what I have called 'genre chains' (Fairclough 2003), genres which are regularly and predictably chained together such that meanings are moved and transformed along the chain, and recontextualised and transformed in regular ways in accordance with recontextualising principles. An example of (part of) a genre chain would be the chain that routinely links significant government statements of publications, press conferences and/or press statements, and news reports. Genre chains are among the semiotic conditions of possibility of 'globalisation' as 'action at a distance', and intensifications and shifts in globalisation are conditional upon changes in this semiotic resource.

CDA has taken the category of 'recontextualisation' from Bernstein's sociology of pedagogy (Bernstein 1990, 1996), and sought to operationalise it in discourse analysis, in fact, precisely recontextualise it, for instance by specifying processes of recontextualisation in terms of genre and genre chains. Relations of recontextualisation involve principles of selectivity and filtering devices which selectively control which meanings (which can now be specified and differentiated as which discourses, genres and styles) are moved from one field to another. But there are also internal relations within the recontextualising field which control how recontextualised meanings are articulated with, recontextualised in relation to, existing meanings – i.e., in the terms above what forms of interdiscursivity occur between recontextualised and existing discourses, genres and styles. Taking these points together, recontextualisation of meanings is also transformation of meanings, through decontextualisation (taking meanings out of their contexts) and recontextualising (putting meanings in new contexts). Moreover, recontextualisation should be seen as an appropriation/colonisation dialectic (Habermas 1984; Chouliaraki and Fairclough 1999): a matter of an opening to a potentially colonising external presence which is however potentially appropriated and 'domesticated'.

More generally, social change (e.g., the transformations of capitalism, including its globalisation, currently underway) includes change in social practices and, crucially, the networking of social practices (social fields, social domains). Following Jessop (2000), we can specify these transformations on two dimensions: 'Restructuring' (a transformation of relations between social fields and domains, such as the economic field and fields such as education or the arts) and 're-scaling' (the transformation of relations between the local, national, (macro-)regional, and global scales of social life). 'Globalisation' understood as 'a process (or set of processes) which embodies a transformation in the spatial organisation of social relations and transactions generating transcontinental and interregional flows and networks of activity, interaction, and the exercise of power' (Held *et al.* 1999), is a form of re-scaling. Changes in genres, discourses and styles, in orders of discourse, in genre chains, are a irreducible part of restructuring and re-scaling, and constitute semiotic conditions of possibility for these transformations overall. The relationship between semiotic and non-semiotic elements of social events, and at a more abstract level of social practices, is a dialectical relationship. The elements (including semiosis, social relations and organisations and institutions, material objects and means and technologies, people with their beliefs and feelings and values) are different, and the difference between them cannot be reductively collapsed, but they are not discrete: they are dialectically interconnected, semiotic elements 'internalise' non-semiotic elements, and vice-versa (Harvey 1996).

Social transformations in contemporary social life are extensively 'discourse-led', in the sense that it is discourses which change first. As new discourses enter and achieve salience or dominance in particular social fields or domains and at different social scales, or more concretely in particular organisations, or are recontextualised within them, dialectical processes may ensue in which discourses are enacted in ways of acting (e.g., new ways of managing, new procedures, routines etc.), inculcated in ways of being, in social identities (e.g., new management identities, such as new types of 'leader'), and materialised for instance in new spatial, including architectural, forms. Enactment and inculcation may be non-semiotic, i.e., involve a dialectical movement between the semiotic and the non-semiotic, or 'intra-semiotic': discourses may be enacted semiotically as genres (as well as manufacturing processes), and inculcated as styles (as well as new forms of bodylines – which are, of course, semioticised, but not reducible to semiosis).

These dialectical processes do not, however, proceed in abstraction from social relations of power. In taking recontextualisation to be a dialectic of colonisation and appropriation, I am suggesting not only the potential for struggle within the recontextualised context to inflect or deflect the colonising effect through forms of appropriation, but also the potential for struggle over forms of appropriation between social groups pursuing different strategies within the recontextualised context, which might include for instance struggles over identity which are germane to whether and how a discourse is inculcated in new ways of being.

4 Mediation and ideology

Let us come back to the questions of mediation and ideology, which I discussed in a preliminary way above, in the light of this brief theoretical sketch of a version of CDA. In terms of this version of CDA, Silverstone's discussion of mediation can be seen as suggesting a focus on recontextualisation. The processes and relations of mediation are processes and relations of recontextualisation, which specifically involve relations between the field of media and other social fields, though this 'structural' relation between fields can simultaneously be a 'scalar' relation, for instance when we consider mediation within processes of globalisation (see the discussion of the Romanian cases below). Chouliaraki (1999) has proposed that we can see media discourse ('discourse' used in a third sense, meaning the type of language used specifically in media) as 'a recontextualising principle for appropriating other discourses and bringing them into a special relation with each other for the purposes of their dissemination and mass consumption'. We can also see media texts in turn being recontextualised according to specific recontextualising principles, e.g., in government, in everyday conversation, and so forth. These relations are seen as obtaining between, in Bourdieu's terms (Bourdieu and Wacquant 1992), social fields, or relatively stable and durable networks of social practices (see below), rather than just 'discourses'. Chouliaraki (1999: 41) suggests that each genre has its own recontextualising principle, which appropriates and reconstitutes discourses (Chouliaraki 1999: 41). I shall assume rather that recontextualising principles attach to social fields (conceived as networks of social practices) such as media, whose semiotic/discoursal moment is orders of discourse, though the diversity of media – print media, broadcast media, electronic media – entails a set of connected recontextualising principles rather than a unitary one. Recontextualising principles are actualised in genres, conceived as regulative devices (Chouliaraki 1999), 'systematically distributed forms of control' (Threadgold 1989).

As I indicated above, recontextualisation and therefore also mediation may involve flows of discourses, genres and styles between fields. In the case of the mediation/recontextualisation of representational meanings – discourses – my discussion above of dialectical relations implies that discourses are open to dialectical processes of enactment, inculcation and materialisation, including 'intra-semiotic' enactment and inculcation as genres and styles. Processes of recontextualisation, including processes of mediation, may be ideological processes. Bernstein puts this in terms of the movement of discourses in recontextualisation: 'Every time a discourse moves, there is a space for ideology to play' (Bernstein 1996: 26). Bernstein is I think right to focus on the primary importance of the movement of discourses across contexts, fields, social practices, scales in the work of ideological representation. A discourse de-contextualised from its dialectical relationship with other elements of a field or network of social practices becomes an imaginary, very often working in a metaphorical way in the re-imagining of aspects of the field or practices it is recontextualised within (e.g., re-imagining student–academic relations in higher education as consumer–producer relations), and, of course, open to enactment, inculcation and materialisation. Media institutions and processes of mediation are clearly crucial in these ideological processes.

Ideology is, first, a relation between meaning (and therefore texts) and social relations of power and domination. It is one modality of power (another is physical force). And ideology is, first, a matter of representation. We may call discourses 'ideological' where social analysis plausibly shows a relation between their meanings (ways of representing) and social relations of power. In so far as discourses are ideological, their dialectical semiotic and non-semiotic internalisation in ways of acting and ways of being (enactment, inculcation), as well as their materialisation in the physical word, is also an internalisation of ideology. So if ideology is, first, representations (discourses), it is, second, (a) action and its social relations (and genres); (b) persons/subjects (and styles), as well as (c) the material world. Moreover, if ideology is, first, a relation between texts (in meaning-making) and power, it is, second, a relation between orders of discourse and power, and even languages and power, because meanings achieve relative stability and durability in social practices and social structures. The 'recontextualisation' of discourses (e.g., in processes of mediation) may constitute meaning as a modality of power relations across networks of social practices (structural relations between fields, scalar relations between local, national, regional, 'global'), i.e., it may be ideological. The specific contribution of discourse analysis to ideological analysis is (a) identifying discourses, and their linguistic realisations, (b) tracing the texturing of relations between discourses, (c) tracing the 'internal' (to semiosis) dialectic between discourses, genres and styles, (d) tracing the recontextualisation of discourses (genres, styles) across structural and scalar boundaries. That in itself does not tell us whether we are dealing with ideology. To do so requires other forms of social analysis which explore (a) the causal effects of semiosis (changing organisations, persons etc.), and (b) the relationship of all this to relations of power, domination, struggle, resistance – the 'external' dialectics of discourse.

5   The Romanian cases

The two Romanian cases introduced earlier are cases of mediation, through the medium of print, and the media genres of the advertising leaflet and public notice. Resources for meaning-making can be seen as moved from the domain of commercial organisations into the domain of consumption and thereby potentially into the world of mundane experience and living, the life world. But what is also clearly at issue if we consider such cases cumulatively over the period since 1989 is a movement across scales, a 're-scaling', recontextualising resources for meaning-making which are already established and to a degree harmonised on an international scale onto another national scale, incorporating a part of Romanian social life into the international scale, contributing to the contemporary scalar complexity of Romanian society (where international, national and local elements coexist in complex and contradictory articulation with each other). These processes can be subsumed under 'globalisation'.

But recontextualisation has been understood above as dialectic of colonisation and appropriation. Cases of this sort can easily be seen and often are seen as simply cases of colonisation, of meanings, practices, discourses etc. being imposed from the centres of capitalism onto the transitional peripheries. But in my initial notes on the two cases I began to indicate how these resources for meaning-making come to be appropriated within the specific social and power relationships and social dynamics of Romanian society, and in particular how they are appropriated as resources within the strategies of distinction of the economic elite. This is not to suggest that only the economic elite are affected by such 'western' practices – they have at least an aspirational resonance for perhaps most of the population, and are no doubt appropriated into different strategies, including strategies of distinction (for an intense preoccupation with distinction seems to be a general trait of Romanian society) elsewhere. There may also be resistance to them, though if there is resistance in Romania it would seem to be a relatively covert resistance, for it does not appear to reach the public space. Be that as it may, any account of recontextualisation in such cases has to refer, in the terms introduced above, to the 'causal powers' of social agents, their appropriating actions and strategies (specification of which with respect to particular fields contributes also to specifying the recontextualising principles according to which recontextualisation takes place), as well as to the changes in structure implied in the concept of re-scaling, and also at the level of social practices to emergent change in orders of discourse in Romania.

The moment of appropriation in processes of recontextualisation can be explored analytically through interdiscursive analysis of how recontextualised meanings are articulated in texts with existing meanings. When I came across the two Romanian cases, I found them both familiar and transparent in the light of practices in the UK and elsewhere, and yet in some respects opaque and puzzling, specifically the representation of membership of the Golden Club as making people 'privileged', and the observation of 'the limit of discretion'. This experience of opacity on the part of a cultural outsider is a pointer to interdiscursive hybridity: familiar recontextualised elements are articulated together with unfamiliar elements in these cases.

A prominent theme in public debate on change and 'transition' in Romania has been 'changing mentalities'. It is often argued by intellectuals and politicians that changes in Romanian 'mentality' are necessary for substantive social change, and for successful integration of Romania into 'western' capitalism. This focus on 'mentality' appears to have been introduced into the public sphere and social life by intellectuals influenced by the French tradition of research on 'mentality' (the cultural anthropologist Levy-Bruhl and the historian Braudel are important figures in that tradition). Similar debates in the UK for instance represent 'subjective' aspects of change more as changes in 'culture' or 'attitudes' (for instance in the Thatcher government's promotion of an 'enterprise culture' in the 1980s, Fairclough 1990). Problematic aspects of Romanian 'mentalities' are often attributed to the legacy of communism. Change in 'mentalities' is called for in various areas of social life: work, business, education and teaching, gender relations and parent–child relations in the family, the human rights of homosexuals and minorities, especially gypsies. This way of representing 'subjective' aspects of change has become an element of dominant discourses of change and transition in intellectual and political debate, but has also extended into various social fields and into the 'lifeworld' of ordinary living and experience. An indication of the latter discussions of change in Romania on computer games forums on the internet rather frequently refer to need to change, or the difficulty of changing, 'mentalities'. Both of the cases can be seen in terms of these debates on 'changing mentalities', as covertly projecting 'western' mentalities. And one aspect of recontextualisation which shows itself as interdiscursive hybridity is the articulation of recontextualised 'western' discourses and practices with this distinctively Romanian way of representing 'subjective' aspects of change in discourses of change and 'transition'.

I earlier referred to what is recontextualised as 'practices', practices of the 'loyalty card' and of discretionary spatial distance in certain sorts of queuing. The theoretical framework sketched out above points us to the question: what are these practices, these rituals, these ways of acting and interacting, an enactment of? Is there a discourse, or discourses, here which, while not being enunciated as such in these cases, nevertheless lies behind them, informs them, becomes enacted in them? When my Romanian friend and I encountered the two cases, we saw them as presences of 'western individualism'. We might say that 'behind' the practices, enacted as the practices, there are discourses of the individual, of society as made up of acquisitive and competitive individuals in pursuit of their own material and symbolic advantage, of individuals as endowed with certain rights to privacy and autonomy. In the first case, the discourse of 'competitive individualism' is enacted in the practice of the 'loyalty card', and inculcated in the identities of members of the economic elite seeking competitive advantage with respect to both material and symbolic goods through membership of the 'club'. One might add that it is materialised in the personalised, technologically sophisticated card itself (as one card holder ironically told me, 'It makes me feel important'). In the second case, the discourse of individual autonomy is enacted in the practice of preserving the 'limit of discretion', inculcated in individuals who have taken in the values and behaviours of privacy and 'discretion', and materialised in the organisation of space in the bank, including the placing of a stand with the notice on it at a distance from the counter. Thus the dialectical processes I have referred to above are in evidence in both cases.

With respect to ideology and ideological processes, the centrality of individualist ideologies to the nature and workings of contemporary capitalism is widely acknowledged. Ideas and values and practices of (autonomous, self-regulating, competitive etc.) individualism (and as pointed out above not only the discourses but also the ways of acting including genres, ways of being including styles, and material forms it is dialectically internalised in) can be adjudged ideological in the sense that these ways of being and of seeing the self and others are conditions of possibility for the operation of capitalist system (in terms of motivations to acquire and consume, innovative working practices based upon the self-regulation of employees, and so forth) and for sustaining the social and power relations of capitalism, and in the sense that they con- stitute misrecognition of the antagonisms and contradictions of the system (misrecognition of relations between social groups and forces as relations between individuals). In this respect, the recontextualisation of these interna- tional beliefs, values and practices in Romania constitutes a not insignificant part of the incorporation of Romania into the structures and power relations of international capitalism, and is in that sense an ideological process of re-scaling. This is against the background not only of the official commitment to collectivism and egalitarianism before 1989, but the practical collapse of that commitment into a form of individualism which is at odds with the individualist virtues promoted by contemporary capitalist society – a 'dependent' individualism where people were totally dependent on the state yet selfishly pursuing their own individual interests with no sense of communal responsibility (Barbu 1999; Poznanski 2000).

But there is a more complex orchestration of scale: a binding together of power relations on international and national levels (as well as the local level, in particular localities, organisations, institutions, though I have not discussed this) in which the same representations, values, practices and identities may simultaneously work ideologically in spreading the new capitalism (and its 'neo-liberal' politics) as 'the only show in town', and yet do ideological work of a different character with respect to social dynamics and power relations at national and local scales. In the Romanian case, practices and values which work ideologically to inculcate subjects into the 'global' capitalist economy and thus contribute to an emergent and expansive global hegemony also work in the pursuit of strategies of distinction, which can be adjudged ideological in the sense that they misrecognise raw relations of economic and financial power in the 'wild capitalism' of contemporary Romania as relations of distinction (e.g., 'we know how to behave in queues, they don't'), allow the rationalisation of gross differences of wealth and power which have often emerged through aggressive and even corrupt business practices and exploitation in terms of what are widely regarded as inherent (or even genetic) differences between people in intelligence and civilisation, and so misrecognise the antagonisms and contradictions of the anarchic emergence of capitalism in Romania. At the same time, the ideological import of recontextualised elements is inflected by the distinctively Romanian focus on 'changing mentalities' with respect to 'subjective' aspects of change. In so far as the failure of Romania's turn to capitalism to produce substantial improvements in the condition of the majority of Romanians is attributed to problems of 'mentality', their failure to 'change mentalities', this way of representing the 'subjective' aspect of change can be seen as a potent ideological element.

Discourse and sociocultural change

Introduction

The papers in this section were written between 1989 and 1992, and are representative of the change of emphasis in that period from developing CDA as a form of ideology critique to using CDA for bringing a focus on discourse to research on social change. This new emphasis culminated in the publication of my book *Discourse and Social Change* in 1992. The shift in direction should not be overstated: there was a concern with social change in *Language and Power* (1989), and ideology remained a major concern in *Discourse and Social Change*. Nevertheless the change in emphasis was significant in presaging the increasing interest in developing forms of *trans-disciplinary* research on social change which could effectively address relations between discursive and non-discursive elements or dimensions of social changes (see Section C).

The first paper in this section ('Critical discourse analysis and the mark-etisation of public discourse: the universities') was published in 1993. It has a certain historical value in analysing a relatively early stage of a profound transformation (which is still going on) in not only universities but also virtu-ally all public services and institutions in Britain and many other countries. They have been restructured on the model of commodity markets. This is arguably not just a simulation of markets based perhaps on their renewed pres-tige since the 1970s, but part of a change in how 'the economy' was conceived, imagined and eventually institutionalised which has shifted these public institutions either into or at least closer to 'the economy'. Universities for instance are now increasingly seen as and operating as a sector of the economy. Retrospectively, this paper seems to me to be a good early example of what CDA can contribute to social research on change.

The paper opens with a sketch of a social theory of discourse and a framework for its critical analysis, which is centred around a combination of a Gramscian theory of power as hegemony and a Bakhtinian theory of intertextuality: the creative potentialities implicit in the latter are limited by the state of hegemonic relations and hegemonic struggle. I suggest that the place and role of discourse in society and culture is a historical variable, and discuss the role of discourse within modern and especially contemporary ('late modern' according to Giddens (1991)) society. Specifically, I consider the role of discourse in a range of major contemporary cultural changes which have been thematised in recent sociological analysis: shifts towards 'post-traditional' forms of social life, more reflexive forms of social life, and a 'promotional culture'. The bulk of the paper is taken up with an analysis of discourse samples which illustrate the marketisation of higher education in contemporary Britain, as an instance of contemporaneity in discursive practices tied in with these three cultural tendencies. My examples are (extracts from) advertisements for academic posts, materials for a conference, a curriculum vitae, and undergraduate prospectuses. The focus is upon shifts in the identities of groups within higher education, especially academics, and upon authority relations between groups, for example, between institutional managements and academic staff or students. The paper concludes with a discussion of CDA as a resource for people who are trying to cope with the alienating and disabling effects of changes imposed upon them.

'Discourse, change and hegemony' links the 'macro' domain of state, government and policy with the 'micro' domain of discursive practice, by way of the concept of 'technologisation of discourse'. The technologisation of discourse is a specifically contemporary form of top-down intervention to change discursive practices and restructure hegemonies within orders of discourse (in places of work, for instance), as one element within wider struggles to reconstruct hegemonies in institutional practices and culture. It is a technology of government in a Foucaultian sense, and linked to what Gramsci calls the 'ethical state' – the state as involved in engineering its subjects to fit in with the demands of the economy (Forgacs 1988). It involves redesign of discursive practices on the basis of research into their institutional effectivity, and retraining of personnel. I discuss the emergence of various aspects of discourse technologisation, expert discourse technologists, a shift in the policing of discursive practices associated with technologisation of discourse, the role within it of context-free 'skills', and strategically motivated simulation of conversation.

The paper sketches out a version of the 'three-dimensional' CDA framework which I have used extensively elsewhere – CDA looks to establish connections between properties of texts, features of discourse practice (text production, consumption and distribution), and wider sociocultural practice. An extract from a medical interview is analysed in these terms, and I argue that the link between sociocultural practice and the other two dimensions involves the integration of 'macro' and 'micro' analysis of discursive events, where the former includes analysis of discourse technologisation processes. On the one hand, no instance of discursive practice can be interpreted without reference to its context; in this example, for instance, one cannot determine whether the 'conversationalisation' of medical discourse is democratising or manipulative without reference to the 'macro' context and to discourse technologisation processes. But on the other hand, 'macro' phenomena such as technologisation of discourse cannot be properly analysed without the evidence of their actual effects on practice, which comes from analysis of discursive events. I demonstrate this with an extract from a university prospectus, which illustrates the dilemmas that people are placed in by discourse technologisation, and strategies for resolving them through accommodation, compromise or resistance.

Paper 6, 'Ideology and identity change in political television' is an application of the framework of Paper 4 to analysis of media discourse – specifically, one section of a late-night political discussion and analysis programme which was broadcast during the 1992 General Election in Britain. The paper argues that the discourse practice of the programme effects a restructuring between the orders of discourse of politics, private life (the 'lifeworld'), and entertainment, through a mixing of some of their constituent genres and discourses. One notable presence is the emergent television genre of 'chat', which is an institutionalised simulation of ordinary conversation as a form of entertainment and humour. I suggest that humour is a design feature of the mixed genre of the programme; participants are shown to be orientating to a ground rule that requires any serious political talk to be lightened with humour. This complex discourse practice is seen as part of an unstable and shifting social practice, the scenario Habermas refers to as a 'structural transformation of the public sphere' of politics (Habermas 1989), in which the domain of politics is being restructured through a redrawing of its boundaries with leisure and the media and with the lifeworld. The complex discourse practice is realised in heterogeneities of meaning and form in the text. I focus in particular on the effect upon the textual construction of identities for the presenter of the programme and the politicians he is interviewing, suggesting that the restructuring of boundaries between forms of life and orders of discourse is condensed into their complex personalities. The complexity of the discourse practice gives rise to a high level of ambivalence, in that the mixture of genres entails uncertainty over which interpretative principles apply. The complex format also appears to place heavy demands upon participants and cause difficulties for them which are manifest in disfluencies and in failures to observe the ground rule identified above, which are treated as sanctionable behaviour by other participants. The paper concludes with a discussion of the ideological effects of these changes in political discourse.

4. Critical discourse analysis and the marketisation of public discourse: the universities

The objective of this paper is, first, to set out my own view of critical discourse analysis, and, second, to illustrate the practice of critical discourse analysis through a discussion of marketisation of public discourse in contemporary Britain. The first section of the paper, 'Towards a social theory of discourse', is a condensed theoretical account of critical discourse analysis. The second section, 'Analytical framework', sets out a three-dimensional framework for analysing discursive events. Readers will find the view of the field sketched out in these sections more fully elaborated in Fairclough (1989a, 1992a). The third section makes a transition between the rather abstract account of the first two sections and the illustrative example: it is a reflection on language and discursive practices in contemporary ('late capitalist') society, which it is claimed make a critical, social and historical orientation to language and discourse socially and morally imperative. The fourth section is a text-based examination of the marketisation of discursive practices as a process which is pervasively transforming public discourse in contemporary Britain, with particular reference to higher education. The paper concludes with a discussion of the value of critical discourse analysis, as a method to be used alongside others in social scientific research on social and cultural change, and as a resource in struggles against exploitation and domination.

1 Towards a social theory of discourse

Recent social theory has produced important insights into the social nature of language and its functioning in contemporary societies which have not so far been extensively taken on board in language studies (and certainly not in mainstream linguistics). Social theorists themselves have generally articulated such insights abstractly, without analysis of specific language texts.[1] What is needed is a synthesis between these insights and text-analytical traditions within language studies. The approach developed in this section of the paper is aiming in that direction.

'Discourse' is a category used by both social theorists and analysts (e.g. Foucault 1972, Fraser 1989) and linguists (e.g., Stubbs 1983, van Dijk 1987). Like many linguists, I shall use discourse to refer primarily to spoken or written language use, though I would also wish to extend it to include semiotic practice in other semiotic modalities such as photography and non-verbal (e.g., gestural) communication. But in referring to language use as discourse, I am signalling a wish to investigate it in a social-theoretically informed way, as a form of social practice.

Viewing language use as social practice implies, first, that it is a mode of action (Austin 1962, Levinson 1983) and, secondly, that it is always a socially and historically situated mode of action, in a dialectical relationship with other facets of 'the social' (its 'social context') – it is socially shaped, but it is also socially shaping, or *constitutive*. It is vital that critical discourse analysis explore the tension between these two sides of language use, the socially shaped and socially constitutive, rather than opting one-sidedly for a structuralist (as, for example, Pêcheux (1982) did) or 'actionalist' (as, for example, pragmatics tends to do) position. Language use is always simultaneously constitutive of (i) social identities, (ii) social relations and (iii) systems of knowledge and belief – though with different degrees of salience in different cases. We therefore need a theory of language, such as Halliday's (1978, 1994b), which stresses its multifunctionality, which sees any text (in the sense of note 1) as simultaneously enacting what Halliday calls the 'ideational', 'interpersonal' and 'textual' functions of language. Language use is, moreover, constitutive in both conventional, socially reproductive ways, and creative, socially transformative ways, with the emphasis upon the one or the other in particular cases depending upon their social circumstances (e.g., whether they are generated within, broadly, stable and rigid, or flexible and open, power relations).

If language use is socially shaped, it is not shaped in monolithic or mechanical ways. On the one hand, societies and particular institutions and domains within them sustain a variety of coexisting, contrasting and often competing discursive practices ('discourses', in the terminology of many social analysts). On the other hand, there is a complex relationship between particular discursive events (particular 'instances' of language use) and underlying conventions or norms of language use. Language may on occasion be used 'appropriately', with a straightforward application of and adherence to conventions, but it is not always or even generally so used as theories of appropriateness would suggest (see Fairclough (1992d) for a critique of such theories).

It is important to conceptualise conventions which underlie discursive events in terms of *orders of discourse* (Fairclough 1989a, 1992a), what French discourse analysts call 'interdiscourse' (Pêcheux 1982, Maingueneau 1987). One reason for this is precisely the complexity of the relationship between discursive event and convention, where discursive events commonly combine two or more conventional types of discourse (for instance, 'chat' on television is part conversation and part performance: Tolson 1991), and where texts are routinely heterogeneous in their forms and meanings. The order of discourse of some social domain is the totality of its discursive practices, and the relationships (of complementarity, inclusion/exclusion, opposition) between them – for instance in schools, the discursive practices of the classroom, of assessed written work, of the playground, and of the staff-room. And the order of discourse of a society is the set of these more 'local' orders of discourse, and relationships between them (e.g., the relationship between the order of discourse of the school and those of the home or neighbourhood). The boundaries and insulations between and within orders of discourse may be points of conflict and contestation (Bernstein 1990), open to being weakened or strengthened, as a part of wider social conflicts and struggles (the boundary between the classroom and the home or neighbourhood would be an example). The categorisation of types of discursive practice – the elements of orders of discourse – is difficult and controversial: for present purposes I shall simply distinguish between *discourses* (*discourse* as a count noun), ways of signifying areas of experience from a particular perspective (e.g., patriarchal versus feminist discourses of sexuality), and *genres*, uses of language associated with particular socially ratified activity types such as job interview or scientific papers (see, further, Kress 1988, on the distinction between discourses and genres).

By 'critical' discourse analysis I mean discourse analysis which aims to systematically explore often opaque relationships of causality and determination between (a) discursive practices, events and texts, and (b) wider social and cultural structures, relations and processes; to investigate how such practices, events and texts arise out of and are ideologically shaped by relations of power and struggles over power; and to explore how the opacity of these relationships between discourse and society is itself a factor securing power and hegemony (see below). In referring to opacity, I am suggesting that such linkages between discourse, ideology and power may well be unclear to those involved, and more generally that our social practice is bound up with causes and effects which may not be at all apparent (Bourdieu 1977).[2]

2 Analytical framework

I use a three-dimensional framework of analysis for exploring such linkages, in particular discursive events. Each discursive event has three dimensions or facets: it is a spoken or written language *text*, it is an instance of *discourse practice* involving the production and interpretation of text, and it is a piece of *social practice*. These are three perspectives one can take upon, three complementary ways of reading, a complex social event. In analysis within the social practice dimension, my focus is political, upon the discursive event within relations of power and domination. A feature of my framework of analysis is that it tries to combine a theory of power based upon Gramsci's concept of *hegemony* with a theory of discourse practice based upon the concept of intertextuality (more exactly, *interdiscursivity* – see further below). The connection between text and social practice is seen as being mediated by discourse practice: on the one hand, processes of text production and interpretation are shaped by (and help shape) the nature of the social practice, and on the other hand the production process shapes (and leaves 'traces' in) the text, and the interpretative process operates upon 'cues' in the text.

The analysis of text is form-and-meaning analysis – I formulate it in this way to stress their necessary interdependency. As I indicated above, any text can be regarded as interweaving 'ideational', 'interpersonal' and 'textual' meanings. Their domains are respectively the representation and signification of the world and experience, the constitution (establishment, reproduction, negotiation) of identities of participants and social and personal relationships between them, and the distribution of given versus new and foregrounded versus backgrounded information (in the widest sense). I find it helpful to distinguish two sub-functions of the interpersonal function: the 'identity' function – text in the constitution of personal and social identities – and the 'relational' function – text in the constitution of relationships. The analysis of these interwoven meanings in texts necessarily comes down to the analysis of the forms of texts, including their generic forms (the overall structure of, for instance, a narrative), their dialogic organisation (in terms, for instance, of turn-taking), cohesive relations between sentences and relations between clauses in complex sentences, the grammar of the clause (including questions of transitivity, mood and modality), and vocabulary. Much of what goes under the name of pragmatic analysis (e.g., analysis of the force of utterances) lies on the borderline between text and discourse practice. (See Fairclough (1992a) for a more detailed analytical framework, and see below for examples.)

The analysis of discourse practice is concerned with sociocognitive (Fairclough 1989a and Paper 1) aspects of text production and interpretation, as opposed to social-institutional aspects (discussed below). Analysis involves both the detailed moment-by-moment explication of how participants produce and interpret texts, which conversation analysis and pragmatics excel at, and analysis which focuses upon the relationship of the discursive event to the order of discourse, and upon the question of which discursive practices are being drawn upon and in what combinations. My main interest, and main concern in this paper, is the latter.[3] The concept of *interdiscursivity* highlights the normal heterogeneity of texts in being constituted by combinations of diverse genres and discourses. The concept of interdiscursivity is modelled upon and closely related to *intertextuality* (Kristeva 1980), and like intertextuality it highlights a historical view of texts as transforming the past – existing conventions, or prior texts – into the present.

The analysis of the discursive event as social practice may refer to different levels of social organisation – the context of situation, the institutional context, and the wider societal context or 'context of culture' (Malinowski 1923, Halliday and Hasan 1985). Questions of power and ideology (on ideology, see Thompson 1990) may arise at each of the three levels. I find it useful to think about discourse and power in terms of hegemony (Gramsci 1971, Fairclough 1992a). The seemingly limitless possibilities of creativity in discursive practice suggested by the concept of interdiscursivity – an endless combination and recombination of genres and discourses – are in practice limited and constrained by the state of hegemonic relations and hegemonic struggle. Where, for instance, there is a relatively stable hegemony, the possibilities for creativity are likely to be tightly constrained. For example, one might draw a rather gross contrast between dominance of cross-gender interaction by normative practices in the 1950s, and the creative explosion of discursive practices associated with the feminist contestation of male hegemony in the 1970s and 1980s.

This combination of hegemony and interdiscursivity in my framework for critical discourse analysis is concomitant with a strong orientation to historical change (Fairclough 1990a).

It may be helpful to readers to have available a summary of some of the main terms introduced in the last two sections:

discourse (abstract noun)	Language use conceived as social practice.
discursive event	Instance of language use, analysed as text, discursive practice, social practice.
text	The written or spoken language produced in a discursive event.
discourse practice	The production, distribution and consumption of a text.

interdiscursivity	The constitution of a text from diverse discourses and genres.
discourse (count noun)	Way of signifying experience from a particular perspective.
genre	Use of language associated with a particular social activity.
order of discourse	Totality of discursive practices of an institution, and relations between them.

3 Language and discourse in late capitalist society

Critical discourse analysis tends to be seen, certainly in many linguistics departments, as a marginal (and, for many, suspect) area of language study. Yet it ought, in my view, to be at the centre of a reconstructed discipline of linguistics, the properly social theory of language. My first objective in this section is to suggest that strong support for this position comes from an analysis of the 'state' of language and discourse (i.e., of 'orders of discourse') in contemporary societies: if language studies are to connect with the actualities of contemporary language use, there must be a social, critical and historical turn. A second objective is to fill in the wider context of the processes of marketisation of public discourse discussed in the next section.

My premise in this section is that the relationship between discourse and other facets of the social is not a transhistorical constant but a historical variable, so that there are qualitative differences between different historical epochs in the social functioning of discourse. There are also inevitably continuities: I am suggesting not radical disjuncture between, let us say, pre-modern, modern and 'postmodern' society, but qualitative shifts in the 'cultural dominant' (Williams 1981)[4] in respect of discursive practices, i.e., in the nature of the discursive practices which have most salience and impact in a particular epoch. I shall refer below particularly to Britain, but a *global* order of discourse is emerging, and many characteristics and changes have a quasi-international character.

Foucault's (1979) investigations into the qualitative shift in the nature and functioning of power between pre-modern and modern societies are suggestive of some of the distinctive features of discourse and language in modern societies. Foucault has shown how modern 'biopower' rests upon technologies and techniques of power which are embedded within the mundane practices of social institutions (e.g., schools or prisons), and are productive of social subjects. The technique of 'examination', for example, is not exclusively linguistic but it is substantially defined by discursive practices – genres – such as those of medical consultation/examination and various other varieties of interview (Fairclough 1992a). Certain key institutional genres, such as interview, but also more recently counselling, are among the most salient characteristics of modern societal orders of discourse. Discourse in modern as opposed to pre-modern societies is characterised by having the distinctive and more important role in the constitution and reproduction of power relations and social identities which this entails.

This Foucaultian account of power in modernity also makes sense of the emphasis in twentieth-century social theory upon ideology as the key means through which social relations of power and domination are sustained (Gramsci 1971, Althusser 1971, Hall 1982), the common-sense normalcy of mundane practices as the basis for the continuity and reproduction of relations of power. And Habermas (1984) gives a dynamic and historical twist to the analysis of the discourse of modernity through his postulation of a progressive colonisation of the 'lifeworld' by the economy and the state, entailing a displacement of 'communicative' practices by 'strategic' practices, which embody a purely instrumental (modern) rationality. The process is well illustrated, for example, in the ways in which advertising and promotional discourse have colonised many new domains of life in contemporary societies (see further below and the next section).

I ought not to omit from this brief review of language and discourse in modernity phenomena of language standardisation, which are closely tied in with modernisation; one feature of the modern is the unification of the order of discourse, of the 'linguistic market' (Bourdieu 1991), through the imposition of standard languages at the level of the nation state.

Many of these characteristics of modern society are still evident in contemporary 'late capitalist' (Mandel 1978) societies, but there are also certain significant changes affecting contemporary orders of discourse; they thus manifest a mixture of modernist and what some commentators (Jameson 1984, Lash 1990) characterise as 'postmodernist' features. The identification of 'postmodernist' features of culture is difficult and necessarily controversial in the sphere of discourse as in others. In what follows, I shall draw, very selectively, upon two recent accounts of contemporary culture, as late modernity' (see Giddens (1991) and the related discussion of the 'risk society' in Beck (1992)) and as 'promotional culture' (see Wernick (1991) and Featherstone (1991) on 'consumer culture'), to tentatively identify three sets of interconnected developments in contemporary discursive practices.

1. _Contemporary society is 'post-traditional'_ (Giddens 1991). This means that traditions have to be justified against alternative possibilities rather than being taken for granted; that relationships in public based automatically upon

Relationships

authority are in decline, as are personal relationships based upon the rights and duties of, for example, kinship; and that people's self-identity, rather than being a feature of given positions and roles, is reflexively built up through a process of negotiation (see also (3) below). Relationships and identities therefore increasingly need to be negotiated through dialogue, an openness which entails greater possibilities than the fixed relationships and identities of traditional society, but also greater risks.

emotional labour

A consequence of the increasingly negotiated nature of relationships is that contemporary social life demands highly developed dialogical capacities. This is so in work, where there has been a great increase in the demand for 'emotional labour' (Hochschild 1983), and consequently communicative labour, as part of the expansion and transformation of the service sector. It is also true in contacts between professionals and publics ('clients'), and in relationships with partners, kin and friends. These demands can be a major source of difficulty, for not everyone can easily meet them; there is a notable new focus on training in the 'communicative skills' of face-to-face and group interaction in language education.

This provides a frame within which we can make sense of the process of 'informalisation' (Wouters 1986, Featherstone 1991) which has taken place since the 1960s in its specifically discursive aspect, which I have called the 'conversationalisation' of public discourse (Fairclough 1990a, 1992a, 1994).[5] Conversationalisation is a striking and pervasive feature of contemporary orders of discourse. On the one hand, it can be seen as a colonisation of the public domain by the practices of the private domain, an opening up of public orders of discourse to discursive practices which we can all attain rather than the elite and exclusive traditional practices of the public domain, and thus a matter of more open access. On the other hand, it can be seen as an *appropriation* of private domain practices by the public domain: the infusion of practices which are needed in post-traditional public settings for the complex processes of negotiating relationships and identities alluded to above. The ambivalence of conversationalisation goes further: it is often a 'synthetic personalisation' associated with promotional objectives in discourse (see (3) below) and linked to a 'technologisation' of discourse (see (2) below).

Reflexivity

expert systems

2. *Reflexivity, in the sense of the systematic use of knowledge about social life for organising and transforming it, is a fundamental feature of contemporary society* (Giddens). In its distinctive contemporary form, reflexivity is tied to what Giddens calls *expert systems*: systems constituted by experts (such as doctors, therapists, lawyers, scientists and technicians) with highly specialised technical knowledge which we are all increasingly dependent upon. Reflexivity and expert systems even 'extend into the core of the self' (Giddens 1991: 32):

with the demise of the given roles and positions laid down within traditional practices, the construction of self-identity is a reflexive project, involving recourse to expert systems (e.g., therapy or counselling). Discursive practices themselves are a domain of expertise and reflexivity: the technologisation of discourse described in Fairclough 1990a can be understood in Giddens' terms as the constitution of expert systems whose domain is the discursive practices of, particularly, public institutions.

3. *Contemporary culture has been characterised as 'promotional' or 'consumer' culture* (Wernick 1991, Featherstone 1991).[6] These designations point to the cultural consequences of marketisation and commodification – the incorporation of new domains into the commodity market (e.g., the 'culture industries') and the general reconstruction of social life on a market basis – and of a relative shift in emphasis within the economy from production to consumption. The concept of promotional culture can be understood in discursive terms as the generalisation of promotion as a communicative function (Wernick 1991: 181) – discourse as a vehicle for 'selling' goods, services, organisations, ideas or people – across orders of discourse.

The consequences of the generalisation of promotion for contemporary orders of discourse are quite radical. First, there is an extensive restructuring of boundaries between orders of discourse and between discursive practices; for example, the genre of consumer advertising has been colonising professional and public service orders of discourse on a massive scale, generating many new hybrid partly promotional genres (such as the genre of contemporary university prospectuses discussed in the next section). Second, there is a widespread instrumentalisation of discursive practices, involving the subordination of meaning to, and the manipulation of meaning for, instrumental effect. In Fairclough (1989a), for instance, I discussed 'synthetic personalisation, the simulation in institutional settings of the person-to-person communication of ordinary conversation (recall the discussion of conversationalisation in (1) above). This is a case of the manipulation of interpersonal meaning for strategic, instrumental effect.

Thirdly, and most profoundly, and also most contentiously, there is a change in what Lash (1990) calls the 'mode of signification', the relationship between signifier, signified and referent. One aspect of this is a shift in the relative salience of different semiotic modalities: advertising, for example, had undergone a well-documented shift towards greater dependence upon visual images at the relative expense of verbal semiosis. But there is also, I suggest, a significant shift from what one might call signification-with-reference to signification-without-reference: in the former, there is a three-way relation between the two 'sides' of the sign (signifier, signified) and a real object (event, property etc.) in the world; in the latter there is no real object, only the constitution of an 'object' (signified) in discourse. Of course, the possibility of both forms of signification is inherent in language, but one can nevertheless trace their comparative relative salience in different times and places.

The colonisation of discourse by promotion may also have major pathological effects upon subjects, and major ethical implications. We are, of course, all constantly subjected to promotional discourse, to the point that there is a serious problem of trust: given that much of our discursive environment is characterised by more or less overt promotional intent, how can we be sure what's authentic? How, for example, do we know when friendly conversational talk is not just simulated for instrumental effect?[7] This problem of trust is compounded by the significance for reflexive building of self-identity of choices made among the 'lifestyles' projected in association with the promotion of goods. But the pathological consequences go deeper; it is increasingly difficult not to be involved oneself in promoting, because many people have to as part of their jobs, but also because self-promotion is becoming part and parcel of self-identity (see (1) above) in contemporary societies. The colonising spread of promotional discourse thus throws up major problems for what we might reasonably call the ethics of language and discourse.

This is, let me repeat, a tentative identification of changes in discursive practices and their relationship to wider social and cultural changes. Nevertheless, this sketch does, I hope, give some sense of aspects of 'the language question' as it is experienced in contemporary society. If this account carries conviction, then it would seem to be vital that people should become more aware and more self-aware about language and discourse. Yet levels of awareness are actually very low. Few people have even an elementary metalanguage for talking about and thinking about such issues. A critical awareness of language and discursive practices is, I suggest, becoming a prerequisite for democratic citizenship, and an urgent priority for language education in that the majority of the population (certainly of Britain) are so far from having achieved it (see Clark *et al.* 1990, 1991). There is a major role and opportunity here for applied language studies, yet it will not be capable of undertaking it unless there is the critical, social and historical turn I am calling for.

4 Marketisation of public discourse: the universities

In this section I refer to a particular case and specific texts in order to illustrate the theoretical position and analytical framework set out in the first two sections, at the same time making more concrete the rather abstract account of contemporary discursive practices in the previous section. The case I shall focus upon is the marketisation of discursive practices in contemporary British universities,[8] by which I mean the restructuring of the order of discourse on the model of more central market organisations. It may on the face of it appear to be unduly introspective for an academic to analyse universities as an example of marketisation, but I do not believe it is; recent changes affecting higher education are a typical case and rather a good example of processes of marketisation and commodification in the public sector more generally.

The marketisation of the discursive practices of universities is one dimension of the marketisation of higher education in a more general sense. Institutions of higher education come increasingly to operate (under government pressure) as if they were ordinary businesses competing to sell their products to consumers.[9] This is not just a simulation. For example, universities are required to raise an increasing proportion of their funds from private sources, and increasingly to put in competitive tenders for funding (e.g., for taking on additional groups of students in particular subject areas). But there are many ways in which universities are unlike real business – much of their income, for instance, is still derived from government grants. Nevertheless, institutions are making major organisational changes which accord with a market mode of operation, such as introducing an 'internal' market by making departments more financially autonomous, using 'managerial' approaches in, for example, staff appraisal and training, introducing institutional planning, and giving much more attention to marketing. There has also been pressure for academics to see students as 'customers' and to devote more of their energies to teaching and to developing learner-centred methods of teaching. These changes have been seen as requiring new qualities and skills from academics and indeed a transformation in their sense of professional identity. They are instantiated in and constituted through changed practices and behaviour at various levels, including changed discursive practices, though these have very much been 'top-down' changes imposed upon academic staff and students and the extent to which they have actually taken effect is open to question (see further below).

In what follows I wish to take up the discussion of 'promotional' culture in (3) in the last section. I suggest that the discursive practices (order of discourse) of higher education are in the process of being transformed through the increasing salience within higher education of promotion as a communicative function. This development is closely intertwined with the emergence of post-traditional features (see (1) in the last section), and I investigate in particular, focusing upon discursive practices, the following two interconnected questions: (a) What is happening to the authority of academic institutions and academics and to authority relations between academics and students, academic institutions and the public etc.? (b) What is happening to the professional identities of academics and to the collective identities of institutions?[10] This entails an emphasis on interpretational dimensions of textual form/meaning (recall the discussion of the multifuntionality of language and discourse in the first section), and I refer in particular to four examples that are partially and of course highly selectively representative of the order of discourse of the contemporary university: press advertisements for academic posts (*Example 1*), programme materials for an academic conference (*Example 2*), an academic curriculum vitae (*Example 3*), and entries in undergraduate prospectuses (*Example 4*). I shall draw upon the analytical framework sketched out earlier.

Example 1: Advertisements

My first example consists of three advertisements for academic posts which appeared in the *Times Higher Education Supplement* on 22 May 1992. Advertisements by the newer universities (until the summer of 1992, poly-technics) and the older universities in general follow sharply different patterns at the time of writing. Sample 1 is a typical newer-university advertisement; Sample 2 a typical older-university advertisement, though, as Sample 3 shows, there are intermediate types and incursions of the newer-university model into the more traditional one. (It will be interesting to see how practices evolve during the first few years of the post-binary system.) The analysis focuses upon Sample 1 and to a lesser extent Sample 2. I present my analysis here in accordance with the three-dimensional framework introduced earlier, but (for reasons of space) I am less systematic in discussing my other examples.

Discourse practice

Sample 1 is interdiscursively complex, articulating together a variety of genres and discourses, including elements of advertising and other promotional genres. It is an illustration of one of the features of promotionalised discursive practices I identified in the previous section – the generation of new hybrid, partly promotional genres. An obvious promotional element is the presence of features of commodity advertising genre, realised textually for instance in the 'catchy' headline (*Make an Impact on the Next Generation*) and in personalisa-tion of the reader (*you*) and the institution (*we*). In the latter respect, advertising simulates conversational genre, which is also therefore a part of the inter-discursive 'mix'. In addition to general commodity advertising elements, there are elements from the genre of prestige or corporate advertising, including the self-promotional claims at the beginning (*With our reputation . . .*) and the logo. Some of the self-promotional material draws upon narrative genre;

SCHOOL OF ENGINEERING

With our reputation as one of the UK's leading centres of teaching excellence and research innovation, we're making a lasting impact on the next generation of innovators and business leaders in the field of Engineering – and you can help.

With your ambition, energy and expertise, you will be committed to teaching at both undergraduate and post-graduate level, while enjoying the advantage of our close links with Industry and applied research initiatives to add to both your own reputation and ours.

SENIOR ACADEMIC POST
VEHICLE EMISSION TECHNOLOGY

Up to £31,500 p.a. plus substantial enhancement available by negotiation.

The School of Engineering is renowned for its innovative work in the area of Vehicle Emission Technology and is a leader in the field of Automotive Research. A team leader is now required to join this active team to help build on our success.

This leading post requires an outstanding Engineer who can bring expertise in at least one of the following:- Vehicle Pollution, Hybrid Vehicles, Air Quality Systems. You'll also need to be dedicated to progressing research and consultancy whilst lecturing to undergraduate and postgraduate students.

Along with appropriate qualifications, technological expertise and industrial experience, you will need to have energy, enthusiasm and communication skills to motivate your team.

We offer an excellent salary and benefits package, but more importantly the ideal environment and opportunity to really make a contribution to the future of automotive engineering.

You may be awarded the title of Professor if the relevant criteria are met.

For an informal discussion about the post please ring Professor David Tidmarsh, Director of School of Engineering on (0742) 533389.

Application forms and further details are available from the address below. Ref. 40/92.

LECTURERS /SENIOR LECTURERS
PRINCIPAL LECTURERS

£10,949 – £28,851 p.a.

COMPUTER AIDED ENGINEERING

With expertise in one or more of the following: CAD, CAM, FEA, Expert Systems, AMT. Ref. 41/92.

QUALITY SYSTEMS

Applications to both Design and Manufacturing Engineering, offering expertise in one or more of the following areas: TQM, SPC, BS5750, BS7000, Taguchi Methods. A capability to contribute to the teaching of operations management will be an advantage. Ref. 42/92.

MANUFACTURING TECHNOLOGY

MAKE AN With expertise in one or more of the following: Metal and Polymer Forming, Non-conventional Manufacturing, AMT, Environmental Impact of Manufacturing. Ref. 43/92.

IMPACT ON ### OPERATIONS MANAGEMENT

With expertise in one or more of the following: Expert Systems, Database Systems, Simulation, Manufacturing Planning and Control, CIM, CAPP, MRP. Ref. 44/92.

THE NEXT ### ENVIRONMENTAL ENGINEERING

(Two Posts)

GENERATION Post 1: With expertise in one or more of the following: The chemistry of air/water pollution, the impact of geology, hydrology and ecology on environmental issues, impact of transport on the environment. Ref. 45/92.

Post 2: With expertise in Electro-hydraulic Control Systems, Automation, PLCs, Environmental Noise, Noise Control, Acoustics, Vibrations. Ref. 46/92.

MATERIALS ENGINEERING : MATERIALS RESEARCH INSTITUTE

An experienced graduate Materials Scientist or Metallurgist, ideally with an appropriate higher degree, to undertake research and development work in the Metals and Ceramics Research Group. The research work will involve the use of extensive SEM/STEM/XRD and surface analysis techniques applied to a range of metallurgical problems with a particular emphasis on surface engineering. Ref. 47/92.

For all the above posts you will ideally have industry-related experience to add to your degree and a record of achievement in research and/or consultancy activities. You will be committed to teaching excellence at both undergraduate and postgraduate levels and also have the enthusiasm and ability to be part of an active group and to initiate and supervise research, consultancy and short course programmes.

If you feel you have the ideas and expertise to make an impact in a dynamic, forward-looking environment, then please send for an application form and further details to the Personnel Department, Floor 3, 5 Storey Block, Pond Street, Sheffield S1 1WB. Telephone (0742) 533950. Closing date 8th June 1992.

We are actively implementing equality of opportunity policies and seek people who share our commitment. Job share applicants welcome. Women are under represented in this area and applications from this group are particularly welcomed.

The University working in partnership with industry and the professions.

Sheffield City Polytechnic   **Promising Futures**

Example 1 Sample 1

**University of
Newcastle upon
Tyne**

Department of English
Literature

LECTURER

Applications are invited for a Lectureship
in the Department of English Literature
from candidates who have expertise in any
Post-Medieval field. The post is available
to be filled from 1st October, 1992, or as
soon as possible thereafter.

Salary will be at an appropriate point on
the Lecturer Grade A scale: £12,860 –
£17,827 p.a. according to qualifications
and experience.

Further particulars may be obtained from
the Director of Personnel, Registrar's
Office, University of Newcastle upon
Tyne, 6 Kensington Terrace, Newcastle
upon Tyne NE1 7RU, with whom
applications (3 copies), together with the
names and addresses of three referees,
should be lodged not later than 29th May,
1992.

Please quote ref: 0726/THES.
(18704)   B9905

**University of
Nottingham**

The Department of Law is a thriving
department committed to excellence in
teaching and research across a broad range
of legal disciplines. The successful
applicant will share this commitment.
Applications are invited from candidates
with an interest in any field of Law, but the
Department has a particular need in the
area of Property Law.

The appointment will be made at the
appropriate point on the Lecturer A and B
scales according to age, qualifications and
experience. Professor M.G. Bridge, is
Head of the Law Department is happy to
answer any enquiries (Ext. 3376).

Further details and application forms,
returnable not later than 26th May, from
the Personnel Office, University of
Nottingham, University Park, Nottingham
NG7 2RD (Tel: 0602 484848, Ext. 2696).
Ref. No. 1529. (18699)   B9905

Example 1 Sample 2   **Example 1** Sample 3

the section under the heading *School of Engineering*, for example, can be construed as a (simple) story about the institution's impact on the next generation.
A discourse of personal qualities is also an element of the interdiscursive mix
(e.g., *with your ambition, energy*), as is a discourse of (educational) management, realised textually most notably in nominalisations such as *teaching
excellence, expertise, a dynamic, forward-looking environment*. There are also,
of course, elements of the more traditional genre and discourse of university
job advertisements (e.g., *Application forms and further details are available
from the address below. Ref. 40/92*).

Text

I begin with more general comments on contrasting interpersonal meanings in
Samples 1 and 2, then move on to a more detailed discussion of their textual
realisations.

The institutional identity projected in Sample 2 is impersonal, distant, settled (in a sense I explain below) and conservative. The institutional voice is that of a traditional university. The institution claims authority only with respect to the post and its conditions and procedures of application. There is no attempt to project a specific professional identity for the potential applicant. Very similar interpersonal meanings are present in those parts of Sample 1 which draw upon the traditional genre and discourse of academic advertisements (e.g., *Application forms and further details are available from the address below*), but the sample is characterised by contradictory interpersonal meanings in accordance with its complex interdiscursive mix, and its most salient interpersonal meanings are drawn from the dominant, promotional and self-promotional elements in that mix. The predominant institutional identity projected is personalised and assertive (self-promotional). While the identity of the institution in Sample 2 is taken as settled and given, there is an obvious sense in which Sample 1 is actively constructing an institutional identity. Again, not only is a professional identity for the potential applicant set up in the text in contrast with Sample 2, but also it is actively constructed in parts of the text which are about the qualities of a successful applicant (e.g., *With your ambition, energy and expertise, you will be committed to teaching . . .*). In these sections, the institution is claiming authority over the identity of applicants (including in terms of what are traditionally seen as personal qualities), as well as elsewhere (like Sample 2) over the post, its conditions and application procedures. The personalisation of both institution (*we*) and addressees (*you*), and the individualised address of potential applicants (it is a singular not a plural *you*), simulate a conversational and therefore relatively personal, informal, solidary and equal relationship between institution and potential applicant, and other features (see below) reinforce this.

Realisation of these interpersonal meanings involves analysis of the text in several dimensions. The *generic structure* of Sample 2 follows traditional advertising for academic posts: a heading identifying the institution, then the main heading giving the title of the post, then details of the post and salary, then procedure for applying. Sample 1 is hybrid, showing evidence of three elements in its interdiscursive mix: commodity advertising, and prestige advertising, as well as traditional advertising for academic posts. The traditional headings are missing, and there is a catchy advertising-style headline (though not actually at the head of the advertisement) and a signature line which identifies the institution with a logo and slogan as well as its title. The body of the advertisement begins with a promotional characterisation of the institution, and a characterisation of the suitable applicant for the posts advertised. These advertising and promotional elements foreground the predominant interpersonal meanings identified above.

Parts of Sample 1 are generically structured as narratives – the section beneath the heading *School of Engineering* is an example. The rather simple story is of the reader as a possible future employee working within the institution. Such narrative is not a feature of traditional university job advertisements (nor of Sample 2), and its presence here is linked to the shift identified above towards a more active discursive construction of professional identity. Notice in this connection an otherwise rather odd feature of modality and tense, exemplified here in *you will be committed to teaching*, which occurs several times in the sample; this is a potentially face-threatening prediction about the professional ethics as well as behaviour of the potential employee, with the modal verb (*will*) marking a high level of commitment to the proposition, which, however, loses its face-threatening character in the imaginary scenario portrayed in the narrative. Although the story is, as I have said, a rather simple one, it is more elaborate than its meagre two sentences would suggest. These narrative sentences have a form of complexity which one does not find in traditional academic advertisements. Both sentences contain a number of subordinate clauses and both have prepositional phrases introduced by *with* which contain presupposed propositions. In all, there are seven propositions in this narrative (in abbreviated form: we have a reputation, we are making an impact, you can help, you have ambition, etc., you will be committed to teaching, you will enjoy the advantage of our links, you will add to your reputation and ours). Notice that the paratactic clause linked with a dash to sentence 1 (– *and you can help*) evokes a conversational style which gives a touch of informality to the personalised relationship between institution and potential applicant.

Turning to the *grammar* of the *clause*, I want to comment in turn on features of *modality, mood* and *transitivity* (Halliday 1985). The authority of the institution with respect to the post, its conditions and the procedure of application in Sample 2 is partly realised in mood and modality features. Clauses are, of course, declarative, with high-affinity epistemic (or 'probability') modalities such as *the post is available* or *salary will be . . .* There is also one instance of deontic ('obligational') modality (*applications . . . should be lodged*), and one case (*further particulars may be obtained*) with an ambivalence between epistemic and deontic modality (mixing 'possibility' with 'permission') which is characteristic for this discourse. Sample 1 has several instances of imperative mood (*make an impact on the next generation, please send for an application form*) which accord with the personalised institution–audience relationship noted above. As in Sample 2, the authority of the institution is

modality+

transitivity

marked through high-affinity epistemic modalities. However, explicit obligational modalities are absent. I noted above the frequency of clauses with modal auxiliary *will* marking futurity plus high-affinity epistemic modality. These are, in some cases, set within developed if simple narratives, as I have indicated, but this is not always so: the advertisement seems generally to cast the potential applicant in the imaginary role of future employee. But notice that these clauses (e.g., *for all the above posts you will ideally have industry-related experience*) provide *alternatives* to obligational clauses (such as *you should have industry-related experience*), in which obligational meanings can be backgrounded. This accords with the personalised, solidary and equal relationship claimed between institution and potential applicant which I described above. So also does the foregrounding of the activity of the potential applicant in these clauses (and also, for instance, in *you can help*, with a modal verb ambivalent between 'possibility' and 'ability'). Although it takes us beyond mood to pragmatics and speech acts, let me also note here the frequency of clauses which make claims about the institution (e.g., *The School of Engineering is renowned for its innovative work . . .*), which realise the self-constructive and self-promotional institutional identity I have referred to.

In terms of transitivity, there are two features of Sample 2 which contribute to its qualities of impersonality: passives and nominalisations. Both are illustrated in its opening sentence: *Applications are invited for a Lectureship*. The passive verb is agentless, so that the institution is not present in the surface grammar, and the nominalisation (*applications*) also lacks an agent, so that the potential applicant is also absent. There are elements of this impersonal style in Sample 1 (e.g., *applications from this group are particularly welcomed*) but they are not salient.

There are a number of points which might be made about the vocabulary of these samples, but I shall make just two. First, the formal-sounding and slightly archaic vocabulary of Sample 2 (such as *thereafter, particulars, lodged*) accords with the impersonality and distance of the institutional identity set up. Vocabulary of this sort is not present in Sample 1. By contrast (and this is the second point), Sample 1 uses a vocabulary and collocations of educational management (*teaching excellence, expertise, a dynamic, forward-looking environment, progressing research, research and consultancy*), as well as a vocabulary of personal qualities and skills. From the perspective of discursive practice, these vocabularies belong to separate discourses which I identified earlier as belonging to the interdiscursive mix. The appropriation of these discourses is, I think, part of the process of constructing a new corporate identity for the higher education institution.

Social practice

The observations on marketisation of universities at the beginning of this section are part of the wider social practice within which these discourse samples are located. It is also relevant that these samples appeared in a period of transition between announcement of the abolition of the binary divide between polytechnics (referred to as the 'newer' universities above) and (older) universities, and its full implementation. There are many relevant historical factors here. For example, there have been particularly strong links between the newer universities and business, and polytechnics were in conception more vocationally oriented than universities, though they have also evolved many courses which are like traditional university courses. Sample 1 illustrates a type of job advertisement found widely for posts in business. For instance, a rapid survey of *The Guardian* at the time of writing shows that the great majority of advertisements for posts in marketing resemble Sample 1 rather than Sample 2 in terms of the sorts of features discussed above. One development that is at issue here, therefore, seems to be the fracturing of the boundary between the orders of discourse of higher education and business as regards advertising, and a colonisation of the former by the latter. This can be construed as one rather particular discursive manifestation of the processes of marketisation of higher education referred to above. As Sample 3 shows, this colonisation of academic discourse affects older universities as well, though there is generally at the time of writing a rather clear correlation between the two types of advertisement and the older and newer universities. This case is, I think, an interesting one in terms of struggles to restructure hegemony within the order of discourse of higher education. At present, there are in this specific area of discursive practice two orders of discourse which have not been unified. I would predict that, with the breakdown of divisions between institutional types, that situation is highly unlikely to persist. It will be interesting to see whether and how the two orders of discourse begin to unify, and whether and how a struggle develops around the traditional advertising practice illustrated by Sample 2 and the new, interdiscursively complex practice illustrated by Sample 1. A significant issue in monitoring developments will be to monitor changes in processes and routines of drafting and production of advertisements, and it will also be interesting to monitor the responses of potential applicants to different advertising styles.

Example 2: Programme materials; Example 3: Curriculum vitae

I want to refer rather more briefly, and without systematically using the three-dimensional framework of analysis, to two of my other examples, as further instances of the incursion of promotion and self-promotion into the order of discourse of higher education, and of the reconstruction of, respectively, corporate and individual professional identities.

Example 2

The first is the 'pack' given to participants in a one-day academic conference held recently at Lancaster University.[11] The conference was a highly prestigious event with two of the foremost sociologists in Europe as its main speakers. The 'pack' consisted of

(a) a brief account of the topic of, participation in and organisation of the conference;
(b) a programme;
(c) a page of notes on 'platform participants', their academic positions, publications and other distinctions;
(d) a page on the research centre which co-organised the conference, its history, personnel, research activities, relationships with other organisations;
(e) a rather spaciously laid-out seven-page list of participants with their institutions, divided into external participants and Lancaster participants;
(f) an evaluation form for the conference.

Conferences of this sort are increasingly used as a means of promoting academic organisations, as well as being motivated for more conventional academic reasons, and this example is, I think, fairly typical of the tendency. While (a) and (d) are the most obviously promotional elements, one could argue that even (e) has a promotional function in using a rather spacious layout to underline the distinguished array of participants in the conference. Here is (a):

This one-day conference links the growing body of sociological thought on Risk in Society (as in recent studies by social theorists such as Giddens, Beck, Baumann and others), with the phenomenon of world-wide environmental concern and cultural change. It is timed to relate to the imminent first publication in English of Ulrich Beck's celebrated book *Risikogesellschaft* (*The Risk Society*), one of the most influential and best-selling works of post-war European sociology.

The conference will bring together sociologists from the UK and continental Europe on these questions for the first time. It is organised jointly by Lancaster's Centre for the Study of Environmental Change (CSEC) and Sociology Department, with the support of the Economic and Social Research Council (ESRC).

It is quite a good example of a widespread contemporary ambivalence; is this information, or is it promotion? The promotional function seems to have become more salient in ('colonised') a whole range of types of informative discourse. Does meaning (here, the giving of background information relevant to the conference) have primacy, or is it subordinated to effect (constructing the conference as a highly significant event in the minds of its participants)? For example, the information in sentence 2 is on one level certainly accurate (Beck's book has had a rapturous reception and has just been published in English). Yet why *imminent* (with its portentous associative meaning) rather than *forthcoming*? Why *first* publication (implying, but only on the basis of a guess, that there will be more)? Why *Ulrich* Beck (it was simply *Beck* in sentence 1)? Why not stop at *celebrated book* (which gives the information about the book's reception), why add the reduced relative clause (*one of the . . . European sociology*), especially since the addressees are those who have elected to attend the conference, who are mostly 'in the know'? Is this sentence on balance *referring* to the book and its imminent publication, or rather *constructing* the book and the event? In short, is this sentence mainly informative or mainly to do with promoting the book (notice the vague – one might even say euphemistic – verb *relate to*) and thereby implicitly the conference (if the book is that significant, so by implication is a conference where the author is talking about the topic of the book)? As so often in contemporary society, the giving of information is taking place in a context where there is a premium on winning people to see things in a particular way. Notice the closed nature of this promotional work; the conference is being promoted among its own participants, who constitute a significant section of the constituency empowered to give the institution the recognition it is seeking. I should perhaps add that I suspect that these promotional objectives would be no mystery to most of those who participated; people who attend such conferences seem generally prepared to live with promotional objectives, limiting themselves to ironic, distancing comments in private which suggest that for some academics at least such apparently necessary work on institutional identity does not sit easily with their sense of their own professional self-identity.

Example 3

The next example I want to look at specifically in terms of promotion – and more exactly self-promotion – is an extract from a curriculum vitae (CV). Such data are sensitive for obvious reasons, and I have therefore used an extract from a CV I prepared myself in 1991 for an academic promotions committee. The form of submissions to this committee is controlled by procedural rules which specify the maximum length of a CV and the categories of information it should contain, and require a 'supporting statement' of no more than 'two sides of A4 paper'. The extract I have chosen is a paragraph from the supporting statement. Unlike the CV proper, the content of the supporting statement is not specified in the procedural rules. I had to make informal enquiries to find out what was expected. I was able to look at previous submissions by colleagues, and I received advice from a colleague with experience of the committee. From these sources, I gathered that the supporting statement had to be a compelling account of one's contribution to, if possible, all the categories of activity in two overlapping schemes of categorisation: to research, teaching and administration; and to the department, the university, and the wider community (these categorisation schemes are actually spelt out in the procedural rules, though not specifically with reference to the supporting statement). The advice I received was that one had to 'sell' oneself to stand any chance of success. The following extract from an internal memorandum, produced shortly after I had prepared the submission, gives a sense of the prevailing wisdom at the time:

> To succeed, departments have to 'sell' their candidates. One cannot expect merit to gleam with its own halo; the halo has been assiduously polished up! Put differently, this means that one has to hone one's application to give an impression of all-round excellence, preferably over a period of time, with feedback from others.

This easily extends to an emphasis on the need for extended preparation for the well-honed application – for instance, it is helpful to have favourable student feedback on one's courses, ideally over several years. One's future promotability may become a significant factor in the planning of one's current activities. Here is the extract:

Contributions to the Department
I have I believe played a significant role in the academic and administrative leadership of the Department over the past eight years or so. I was Head of Department from 1984 to 1987 and again for one term in 1990, and I have carried a range of other responsibilities including MA and undergraduate programme coordination and admissions. I helped to set up and now help to run the Centre for Language in Social Life. Through my coordination of the Language, Ideology and Power research group and in other activities, I have stimulated research (e.g., on critical language awareness) among colleagues and postgraduate students, and helped form what is now being recognised nationally and internationally as a distinctive Lancaster position

on and contribution to study of language and language problems in contemporary British society. I am currently helping to edit a collection of Centre for Language in Social Life papers for publication.

Some of the self-promotional properties of the extract are obvious enough. There is a series of claims realised as clauses with past tense, present perfective and present continuous verbs and *I* as subject and theme. These are mainly claims which are categorical in their modality, positive assertions without explicit modalising elements, though there is a subjective modality marker in the first clause (*I believe*) which (a) foregrounds the subjective basis of judgement in the whole paragraph in that the first clause is a summary/formulation of the paragraph, but also (b) foregrounds (one might say rather brazenly) the self-promotional nature of the activity. (For the analytical terminology used here see Halliday (1994b) and Fairclough (1992a).) Except for one relational process (*I was Head of Department*), all clauses in the extract contain action processes. It would seem that material actional process verbs are consistently being selected even where other process types would be just as congruent with or more congruent with the happenings and relationships reported – for instance, although I am indeed one of the five co-directors of the Centre for Language in Social Life, it receives practically no 'running' from anyone, and I might well (indeed better) have worded this *am now an active member of.* Similarly *played a significant role in* might have been *been a significant part of, carried a range of other responsibilities* might have been *had a range of other responsibilities, helped to set up* might have been *was a founding member of,* and so forth. These changes would, I think, reduce the sense of dynamic activity conveyed in the extract. A noteworthy lexical choice is *leadership* in the first sentence. The wording of academic relationships in terms of *leadership* belongs, in my view, to a managerial discourse which has come to colonise the academic order of discourse recently, and which I actually find deeply antipathetic. In terms of the characteristics of promotional discourse discussed earlier, the extract is very much a signification/construction of its subject/object rather than just referentially based description, and meaning would seem to be subordinated to effect.

I suppose I saw the preparation of the submission as a rhetorical exercise. By which I mean that I was consciously using language in a way I dislike, playing with and parodying an alien discourse, in order to 'play the game' and convince the committee of my merits. That is rather a comforting account of events, and a common enough one; the self stands outside or behind at least some forms of discursive practice, simply assuming them for strategic effects. I felt embarrassed about the submission, but that is, I think, compatible with the rhetorical account. There are, however, problems with this account. In the first place, it assumes a greater consciousness of and control over one's practice than is actually likely to be the case. For instance, while I was quite conscious of what was at stake in using *leadership*, I was not aware at the time of how systematically I was 'converting' all processes to actions, although I *could* have been (and perhaps I ought to have been) – unlike most people I have the analytical apparatus. More seriously, the rhetorical account underestimates the incorporative capacity of institutional logics and procedures. Whereas the average academic rarely has contact with promotions committees, contact with other organisational forms whose procedures are based upon the same logics are necessary and constant. Doing one's job entails 'playing the game' (or various connected games), and what may feel like a mere rhetoric to get things done quickly and easily becomes a part of one's professional identity. Self-promotion is perhaps becoming a routine, naturalised strand of various academic activities, and of academic identities.

Example 4: Prospectuses

My final example consists of extracts from Lancaster University's undergraduate prospectuses for the years 1967–8 (Example 4.1), 1986–7 (Example 4.2), and 1993 (Example 4.3) see pages 119–124. (See also the prospectus sample in Paper 5.) I have used part of the English entry from the first, and part of the Linguistics entries from the second and third (Linguistics was taught within English in 1967–8). I focus upon differences between the 1993 and 1967–8 samples, the 1986–7 sample being included to show an intermediate stage in the development of the prospectus genre. A first observation is that the earliest and most recent entries are sharply different in their content. The 1967–8 entry (Example 4.1) consists of: (a) approximately half a page on the English BA degree, specifically on the view of the study of English it embodies; (b) an itemised list of the 'special interests' of the department; (c) approximately one page on the detailed content of the English BA degree. The 1993 entry (Example 4.3) consists of (a) a box detailing entry policy and requirements; (b) three paragraphs on the department – its staff, courses, academic links, academic achievements, and ethos; (c) a headed section on assessment; (d) a headed section on graduate careers; (e) a one-page diagrammatic summary of the undergraduate Linguistics degree. I shall focus my comments again on aspects of authority and identity.

I shall begin with textual analysis, considering specifically meanings of requirement and obligation and their formal realisations. Sections (a), (c) and (e) of the 1993 entry (entry requirements, assessment, and the undergraduate degree structure) involve requirements placed by the institution upon students or applicants. Most of the 1967–8 entry deals with degree structure, with entry requirements and assessment being dealt with elsewhere in the prospectus. Meanings of obligation and permission are extensively and overtly present in the 1967–8 entry. There are quite a few obligational and permissive modal auxiliary verbs (e.g., *subjects may be offered, each undergraduate will choose, third-year undergraduates must choose, any one course . . . may be offered*) and other modal expressions (*second-year undergraduates . . . are required to take*; compare *must take*). Obligation is expressed lexically as well as modally (in *no specialisation . . . is permitted, a very limited concentration . . . is allowed*). By contrast, although meanings of requirement and obligation are implicit in the 1993 entry, they are not explicitly worded. This is facilitated by the use of tabular and diagrammatic layout for the entry requirements and the degree structure, which allow requirements to be left implicit. For instance, while **A/AS-level grades:** *BCC or equivalent* implies that applicants are required to achieve these grades, explicit obligational meanings are conspicuously absent. The degree structure section consists mainly of phrases (or 'minor clauses' – see Halliday 1985), but where a full clause is used the wording again backgrounds requirement (e.g., *You take at least three*, rather than, for example, *You must take at least three*). The assessment section again uses minor clauses and lacks overt obligational meanings.

A related contrast is between the impersonal style of the 1967–8 entry and the personalised style of the 1993 entry. Notice, for example, that the three passive verbs in the 1967–8 entry referred to above as instances of obligational meaning (*are required to take, is permitted, is allowed*) are 'agentless', that is, they lack an explicit agent, though in each case the institution is the implicit agent (it is the department, or the university, that requires, permits and allows). There are also other agentless passives in the entry where the institution is implicit (e.g., *the Language course is so constructed as to be*). The opening sentence uses a different syntactic–semantic means to maintain impersonality; selecting *the undergraduate courses* as subject and agent of *treat*. This is, in Halliday's terms, a 'grammatical metaphor' for a 'congruent' (non-metaphorical) grammaticisation with, for example, *we* as subject/agent of *treat* and *undergraduate courses* within an adjunct (*we treat English as a whole subject in our undergraduate courses*). Another impersonalising device is nominalisation; *the special interests of the Department include the following*, with the nominalisation (*the special interests of the Department*) as clause subject, avoids more personalised alternatives like *members of the Department* (or *we*) *are particularly interested in*. . . . It is also worth noting that what appear to be merely descriptive statements about the course could be reworded and regrammaticised in personalised ways: compare (the actual) *the course consists of three parts* with *the department/we organise(s) the course in three parts*.

Actually, there are two issues involved here. First, there is the issue of to what extent participants (here the institution and the potential applicant/ student) in the processes referred to are made explicit or left implicit. Secondly, there is the issue of the grammatical person of these participants when they *are* explicit: third person, or first (*we*) and second person (*you*). (A further question is whether first and second person are singular or plural – in fact, where they are used, the institutional first person is plural (*we*) whereas the second person is singular – addressees are addressed individually.) With regard to the institution as participant, the 1967–8 entry is impersonal in both senses – not only is the institution referred to in the third person where it is explicit, it is often not explicit at all – whereas the 1993 entry is personalised in both senses as far as the institution is concerned – it is frequently explicit in the text, and it is first person.

But the picture is somewhat more complex for the addressees. There is some second-person direct address in the 1993 entry (*Linguistics does not commit you to any one career, you take at least three of*). But applicants are referred to in the third person in the opening entry requirements section (e.g., *all accepted candidates are invited to open days* – notice also the passive verb and missing institutional agent), and applicants/students are not referred to in the next section until its third paragraph (beginning *We are a friendly . . .*), and then in the third person (e.g., *the people we teach, students*). On the other hand, the 1967–8 entry is again impersonal in both senses with respect to adressees. For example:

> *. . . no specialisation in either language or literature separately is permitted until the third year of study when a very limited concentration on either is allowed.*

While the agentless passives avoid personalisation of the institution as noted above, the nominalisations acting as their subjects (*no specialisation, a very limited concentration*) avoid personalisation of addressees (compare *you cannot specialise until the third year of study*). An agentless passive is used to the same effect: *in Part II, various periods are studied*. Where the student participants are explicitly textualised, in the third person, it is generally particular groups of students who need to be explicitly identified (e.g., second-year undergraduates), though notice cases of individualised third person reference with *each* (*each undergraduate will choose*) and generic reference with the indefinite article (*may be offered by an undergraduate*).

Turning to some broader issues of social practice, these contrasting textual features mark a major historical shift in the nature and objectives of university prospectuses, in line with the wider changes in higher education I discussed earlier. The 1967–8 entry gives information about what is provided on a take-it-or-leave-it basis. In the 1993 prospectus, by contrast, the promotional function is primary; it is designed to 'sell' the university and its courses to potential applicants, in the context of a competitive market where the capacity of a university to attract good applicants is seen as one indicator of its success, and a factor which can affect how well it is funded. A revision of the prospectus can lead to a dramatic increase in applications; for instance, when Lancaster University revised its prospectus in the late 1980s, the number of applicants went up by 15 per cent for two successive years. The content and form of the contemporary prospectuses are informed by market research – evidence of what applicants most want to know (hence the prominence of careers information in the 1993 entry), an understanding of the literacy culture of young people (e.g., the salience within it of 'glossy' printed material of various sorts), an understanding of the conditions of reading documents of this sort (they are likely to be flicked through rather than carefully read), and so forth.

These changes entail a shift in discourse practice, and specifically in the processes of prospectus production, of which the textual features noted above are realisations. The primacy of the promotional function in contemporary prospectuses entails drawing upon genres associated with advertising and other forms of promotional activity as well as the more traditional informationally oriented genre of university prospectuses, so that the 1993 entry, for example, is an interdiscursively hybrid quasi-advertising genre. The two entries are strikingly different in physical appearance: the earlier entry is based upon the conventional printed page, whereas the 1993 entry uses a brochure-style page size and layout with three print-columns per page, colour (the first page of the entry uses five colours), tabular layout and a photograph. The document is drawing upon visual and design features widely used in advertising and promotional material. As to the features noted earlier, promotional considerations are certainly behind the marked change in content between 1967–8 and 1993, especially the introduction of the three paragraphs about the department, which bring in a genre of prestige or corporate promotion. The personalisation of the institution (as *we*), which occurs heavily in this part of the entry, is a part of this. Like individualised direct address with *you*, it is widely used in advertising. The avoidance of explicit obligational meanings is also in line with the elevation of the promotional function. The avoidance of explicit obligational meanings marks a significant shift in authority relations. Promotional material addresses readerships as consumers or clients, and when someone is selling to a client, the client is positioned as having authority. This is generally true in advertising. It is in contradiction with the traditional authority of the university over applicants/students, and it places the institution in something of a dilemma, for it will obviously still wish to impose requirements and conditions upon entry, course structure and assessment. This dilemma over authority is given a textual resolution (though not necessarily a very satisfactory one): these requirements *are* included in the text, but *not* in overtly obligational forms. The text effects a compromise between the demands of two different situations and the conventions of two different genres. The text also effects a compromise as regards self-identity. The series of claims about the department which make up the first three paragraphs point to a promotional genre, but the claims are quite restrained (in comparison with, for example, Sample 1 of the job advertisements). A final note is that the interdiscursive mix I have suggested here appears to be achieving a hegemonic status in higher education publicity, as part of a more general dominance of a marketing ethos in this area of higher educational activity.

Summary

The four examples I have used above can hardly be said to be properly representative of the complex order of discourse of a modern university, but they do provide four contrasting 'takes' on the discursive practices of such institutions. They have, I hope, suggested how analysis of the discourse of organisations such as universities (in the terms of analytical framework introduced earlier) in their 'text' and 'discourse practice' dimensions can illuminate such matters as shifting authority relations and shifts in self-identity within organisations. The particular shifts I have identified can be summed up as (i) the decline of stable institutional identities which could be taken for granted, and a much greater investment of effort into the construction of more entrepreneurial institutional identities, (ii) a corresponding decline in the implicit (unspoken) authority of the institution over its applicants, potential students and potential staff, (iii) a reconstruction of professional identities of academics on a more entrepreneurial (self-promotional) basis, with the foregrounding of personal qualities.

The discursive instantiation of these shifts illustrates, I think, all three of the sets of developments in contemporary discursive practices identified in the previous section. I have already sufficiently highlighted the third of these, the elevation and generalisation of the promotional function in discursive practices, and its consequences in terms of the hybridisation of discourse practice, the subordination of meaning to effect, and the mode of signification. But the shifts I have identified can also be read (with respect to the first of my sets of developments) in terms of Giddens' account of the post-traditional nature of contemporary society, and the corresponding informalisation of society which is partly constituted through a conversationalisation of discursive practices, which is also evident in my examples. The second set of developments, associated with the increased reflexivity of contemporary life and my concept of technologisation of discourse, is also relevant here: one dimension of the much increased emphasis on staff development and training in higher education is the training of staff in the discursive practices of, for instance, marketing or preparation of research proposals for research councils (itself a heavily promotional form of discourse these days).

It would be premature to draw sweeping conclusions with respect to the 'social practice' dimension of my analytical framework on the basis of such a limited range of illustrative examples. But as I indicated in Note 9, this paper is linked to a longer-term study of change in higher education. One of the questions which that study will address is whether developments in higher education amount to the emergence of a new, reconstituted hegemony, and whether one can talk of a restructured hegemony in the domain of the order of discourse in particular. It would be unwise to leap too quickly to such a conclusion before there has been some investigation of the reception of and response to the sort of changes I have illustrated among various categories of members of higher educational institutions. It may well be, for example, that largely 'top down' changes in discursive practices are widely marginalised, ignored or resisted by certain categories of staff and/or students in a significant range of their activities.

5 Conclusion

I conclude this paper with some brief reflections upon the social use and utility of a critical discourse analysis. I have tried to indicate how critical discourse analysis might contribute to more broadly conceived social research into processes of social and cultural change affecting contemporary organisations. Discourse analysis is, I believe, an important though hitherto relatively neglected resource for such research. It has the capacity to put other sorts of social analysis into connection with the fine detail of particular instances of institutional practice in a way which is simultaneously oriented to textual detail, the production, distribution and interpretation/consumption of texts, and wider social and cultural contexts.

However, discourse analysis also has the capacity to be a resource for those engaged in struggle within institutions. For many members of higher educational

English

The undergraduate courses treat English as a whole subject and not as two divergent specializations. Accordingly, when English is taken as a major subject for the degree of B.A., no specialization in either language or literature separately is permitted until the third year of study when a very limited concentration on either is allowed. For higher degrees, specialization in either language or literature may be complete or subjects may be offered which connect these two branches of study.

In the study of *language* for the B.A. degree, modern English is central and is combined with some general linguistics and phonetics, and in Part II with history of the language. Language specializations in the third year include optional courses on older forms of English, and also on various aspects of the modern language and of linguistics. The study of English language throughout the first degree course will include fieldwork, special studies of varieties of modern English and the use of language laboratory techniques. The Language course is so constructed as to be of value to those who wish to specialize in English as a second or as a foreign language. As much as possible of the material used for literary study is also used for the study of language.

In the study of *literature* the syllabus is divided into periods, each taught with emphasis on a different aspect of literary study. The first-year course, based mainly on modern literature, deals with problems of reading and with the forms and functions of literature in contemporary society. In Part II, various periods are studied, two in two-year courses and the remainder in one-year courses.

The special interests of the Department include the following:

1. Project work in the drama courses using the facilities which will be available in the Theatre Workshop, at present being designed.
2. Special studies of the relationship between language and literature, including work on literary structures from a linguistic point of view.
3. Poetry as a performed art and its links with song.
4. Relations between the study of literature and of philosophy.
5. Relations between literature and scientific thought.
6. Relations between literary and historical study.

Undergraduate studies
PART I (FIRST YEAR) COURSE

The course consists of three parts:

(a) Language: a general introduction, including some elementary phonetics and linguistics.

(b) Literature: a course on problems of reading, and the forms and functions of literature, based on modern English poetry and prose fiction and on texts from three different types of drama (Classical, Renaissance, Modern).

(c) Special courses: each undergraduate will choose one of the special courses referred to below, the choice being determined by his other first-year subjects.

Example 4.1

(i) For those taking groups involving History or Economics or Politics or French Studies or Classical Background, a study of certain historical aspects of literature in the seventeenth century.

(ii) For those taking groups involving Economics or Politics or Philosophy, a study of some of the relationships of literature and philosophy, centred on the works of William Blake.

(iii) For those taking groups involving Environmental Studies, Mathematics or Philosophy, a study of certain scientific texts from a literary and linguistic point of view.

The Part I course, or selected parts of it, will also (timetable permitting) be available as a one-year minor course for certain second-year undergraduates majoring in Boards of Studies A, B and C who did not take English in their first year.

PART II (SECOND AND THIRD YEAR) COURSES

Major course

Second-year undergraduates majoring in English are required to take four lecture courses – two in literature and two in language, from the following:

(a) Literature 1780–1860
   Literature 1660–1780
   Elizabethan Drama, including some project work in the theatre

(b) Varieties of Modern English I (study of the varieties of modern English outside the United Kingdom)
   History of the English Language I
   Principles and Techniques of General Linguistics, with special reference to English

Third-year undergraduates must choose four courses: *either* three language and one literature, *or* three literature and one language, *or* two of each. Any one course in language or literature may be offered by an undergraduate as a special option to be examined as such in the Final Examination. Third-year courses listed for 1966–67 (subject to the availability of staff) are as follows:

(a) Literature 1860–1966, Literature 1550–1660, Mediaeval Literature, Jacobean Drama.

(b) Old English, Middle English, Old Norse, Writing Systems, Linguistic Study of Style, Varieties of Modern English II, History of the Language II, Principles and Techniques of General Linguistics II.

Combined major course in English and French Studies – see page 118

Combined major course in English and Philosophy – see page 118

Combined major course in Latin and English – see page 118

Example 4.1 continued

LINGUISTICS

Linguistics (BA) Q100 Ling
Human Communication (BA) P300 Hum
  Comm
Classical Studies and Linguistics (BA) QQ98
  Class/Ling
Computer Science and Linguistics (BA) GQ51
  Comp/Ling
English and Linguistics (BA) QQ13 Eng/Ling
French Studies and Linguistics (BA) QR11
  Fr/Ling
German Studies and Linguistics (BA) RR32
  Germ/Ling
Italian Studies and Linguistics (BA) QR13
  Ital/Ling
Language and Education (BA) Y656 Lang/Educ
Linguistics and Philosophy (BA) QV17
  Ling/Phil
Linguistics and Psychology (BA) LQ71 Ling/Psy
Modern English Language (BA) Q312 MEL

Lancaster is a major centre in the United Kingdom for study in Linguistics, the science of human language. There are about five thousand languages, and their enormous diversity and complexity supply the raw data for Linguistics. Language is Man's most remarkable achievement, and its systematic study provides insights into Man's psychological and social nature. The study of language tells us something about the nature of the human mind, since languages are abstract systems of peculiar and labyrinthine structure and yet men are capable of communication in them very easily and speedily. Language is of interest sociologically, since it is the stuff that binds complex societies together: without language no sophisticated social organisation is possible. The Department of Linguistics and Modern English Language, which has a staff of 12, is unique among departments of Linguistics in the country in the way its degree schemes offer students *three* alternative but complementary perspectives: on the structure and functions of human language; on the use of symbols by humans as a means of under-

standing themselves and their place in society; on English, as one of the world's most important means of communication and the language of one of its most significant literatures. Degree schemes in Linguistics, Human Communication, English and Linguistics and Modern English Language, as well as combined schemes with other departments, provide the perspectives.

The department makes use of a variety of modes of teaching in its undergraduate programme. Typically, teaching is by lecture and small group seminars of up to 12 students, where the seminars are used to discuss readings related to the lecture topic. Many courses, especially those concerned with the collection of language data, concentrate on seminars and workshops and often involve more than one member of staff.

Linguistics and Human Communication offer useful training and expertise that are of special professional relevance to many working in education, public services and administration, industry and management, the mass media and creative arts, for example as language teachers, speech therapists, as social workers, as counsellors and as translators. Indeed an understanding of how language works and the structure and purposes of human communication is available in a whole range of careers in which there is a need for clear communication, sensitive to people's interests and needs.

A detailed departmental prospectus can be obtained from the Departmental Secretary.

Admission requirements and policy
Linguistics is not a subject taught at school, and prospective applicants should try to get some idea of the subject before committing themselves to it. (They may read, for example, one or more of the following introductory books: *The Articulate Mammal* and *Language Change: Progress and Decay* by Jean Aitchison, *Linguistics* by D Crystal,

Example 4.2

Phonetics by D J O'Connor, *Grammar* and *Semantics* by F R Palmer.) The Department usually makes conditional offers on the basis of the UCCA form. We look for evidence of a keen interest in the structure of language *per se* and a willingness to analyse it objectively. When such evidence cannot be found in the UCCA form, we interview candidates. GCE attainments in Languages and Mathematics are taken as indications of likely talent in Linguistics, but there are no specific formal prerequisites. (For the general requirements see page 178.) *We welcome applications from mature candidates.*

About 25 candidates gain admission each year to the degree scheme in Human Communication and to single and combined major degree schemes in Linguistics.

Part 1 course in Linguistics
The purpose of this course is to provide a foundation for the Part II studies of students who intend to major in Linguistics or in Human Communication and to provide a balanced and self-contained introduction for those undergraduates who go on to major in another subject.

Part I Linguistics comprises Introduction to General Linguistics (151) which is compulsory and which introduces students to core areas of the subject (Phonetics, Phonology, Syntax, Semantics, Pragmatics and Sociolinguistics), together with a set of options (152) in which students choose two of a range of more specialised topics each studied for half the year. The available options vary from year to year: they currently include Structure of a non-Indo-European Language (e.g. Chinese, Arabic or Hebrew), Writing systems, History of Modern Linguistic Thought, Field Methods, the Linguistics of Literacy.

Linguistics (3-year scheme)
Part I
Students are free to choose any two courses from the list on page 175 in addition to Linguistics at Part I, subject to timetable restrictions and departmental advice; but it is wise to select courses that will permit at least one alternative choice of Part II degree scheme (since you might wish to change your mind). Subjects that combine well with Linguistics include English and the other language subjects, Computer Studies, Educational Studies, Philosophy, Psychology, and Sociology, and the Department of Linguistics has close links with those departments.

Part II
(Six units in Linguistics, two units in a minor and a free ninth unit course: see page 18.)

Students take six units in Linguistics from a wide range of courses on various aspects of the subject. A unit can comprise either two half-unit courses or one full course. They cover the core areas studied in Part I and specialisms that include Sociolinguistics, Psycholinguistics, Stylistics, and Anthropological, Computational, Philosophical and Applied Linguistics. Some of the courses are designed specifically for the needs of the students combining Linguistics with a particular subject, while others are appropriate for all students of Linguistics. For detailed information on the courses available see the departmental prospectus.

Students also take two courses in a minor, chosen freely (subject to departmental advice and prerequisites: see page 175), and a free ninth unit course.

Human Communication (3-year scheme)
The degree scheme in Human Communication, jointly offered by the departments of Linguistics, Psychology and Sociology, places language in a broader context; it investigates human communication as a unified field of academic enquiry through the interrelated perspectives of the three subjects. Its aim is to bring the student to an awareness of the centrality of communication in human behaviour and consciousness. The only specific entry requirement is that undergraduates who take Psychology in Part I must have a pass in Mathematics at Ordinary level.

Example 4.2 continued

LINGUISTICS AND HUMAN COMMUNICATION   SOCIAL SCIENCES

Ph... ...li...
Administrative Units Human
Languages ... Unit Most
Human Communication

A/AS-level grades: BCC or equivalent; AS-levels accepted GCSE: Maths and normally a language for Linguistics courses
Scottish Highers: BBBBB
International Baccalaureate: 30pts
BTEC: at least merits in BTEC National
Mature students: we are keen to recruit mature students.

All accepted candidates are invited to open days; interviews in special cases.

The Department of Linguistics and Modern English Language is one of the largest in the UK with a teaching staff of fourteen. We offer a series of flexible degrees with a wide range of courses in 'core' areas like phonetics, grammar and discourse analysis; areas which connect strongly with other disciplines, like sociolinguistics and psycholinguistics; and more 'applied' areas like adult literacy, language teaching and the linguistic study of literature. We have strong links through collaborative degrees with English, Computer Science, the social sciences (especially Psychology and Sociology) and Modern Languages.

We received a grade 4 (national excellence in most areas of Linguistics and international excellence in some) in the 1989 research ratings carried out by the Universities Funding Council. We are especially well known for our research work in Linguistics in relation to language teaching, for the study of language in social settings (e.g. school classrooms and interaction between cancer patients and their carers), for the automatic analysis of texts by computer, and for the linguistic study of literature.

We are a friendly and flexible group of teachers who like to have social contact with the people we teach. Every year, students are invited to join staff for a walking weekend in the nearby Lake District. There are also opportunities for students to spend part of their second year in Copenhagen as part of an ERASMUS student exchange arrangement. We are currently exploring similar links with universities in other European countries.

Assessment

For Linguistic and Human Communication courses: coursework (at least 60%)

and exams. For courses run by the English Department: coursework (50% in the first year, usually 40% in later years) and exams.

What our graduates do

Linguistics and Human Communication offer useful training and expertise that are of special professional relevance to many working in education, language teaching, speech therapy, translation, industry and commerce, management, the mass media, creative arts, social work and counselling.

Recent graduates have gone to work or train as teachers of English overseas, teachers of English as a mother tongue, computer programmers and consultants, bankers, chartered accountants, O & M analysts, air traffic planners, managers in the retail industry, personnel managers, journalists, social workers, nurses and so on. A sizeable proportion of our Linguistics graduates take up employment overseas.

A degree in Human Communication or Linguistics does not commit you to any one career, but can open many doors.

Example 4.3

institutions, for example, the dramatic changes of the last decade or so have been profoundly alienating, yet their capacity to resist them has been weakened by their reluctance to fall back upon traditional practices and structures which have been widely criticised from the Left and the Right and which have been the target for change. Many have experienced a sense of helplessness, which critical discourse analysis can, I believe, help to illuminate. Part of

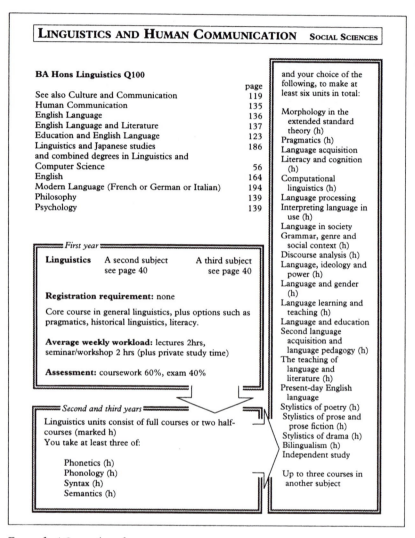

LINGUISTICS AND HUMAN COMMUNICATION   SOCIAL SCIENCES

BA Hons Linguistics Q100

	page
See also Culture and Communication	119
Human Communication	135
English Language	136
English Language and Literature	137
Education and English Language	123
Linguistics and Japanese studies	186
and combined degrees in Linguistics and	
Computer Science	56
English	164
Modern Language (French or German or Italian)	194
Philosophy	139
Psychology	139

═══ *First year* ═══

Linguistics   A second subject   A third subject
                   see page 40   see page 40

Registration requirement: none

Core course in general linguistics, plus options such as pragmatics, historical linguistics, literacy.

Average weekly workload: lectures 2hrs, seminar/workshop 2 hrs (plus private study time)

Assessment: coursework 60%, exam 40%

═══ *Second and third years* ═══

Linguistics units consist of full courses or two half-courses (marked h)
You take at least three of:

Phonetics (h)
Phonology (h)
Syntax (h)
Semantics (h)

and your choice of the following, to make at least six units in total:

Morphology in the extended standard theory (h)
Pragmatics (h)
Language acquisition
Literacy and cognition (h)
Computational linguistics (h)
Language processing
Interpreting language in use (h)
Language in society
Grammar, genre and social context (h)
Discourse analysis (h)
Language, ideology and power (h)
Language and gender (h)
Language learning and teaching (h)
Language and education
Second language acquisition and language pedagogy (h)
The teaching of language and literature (h)
Present-day English language
Stylistics of poetry (h)
Stylistics of prose and prose fiction (h)
Stylistics of drama (h)
Bilingualism (h)
Independent study

Up to three courses in another subject

Example 4.3 continued

the difficulty, which emerges from an investigation of discursive practices, is a polarisation between unacceptable traditional practices and equally distasteful, highly promotional, marketised new practices. Advertisements for academic posts are a very small but interesting case in point: they do appear to be rather starkly polarised, as I showed earlier, with no real alternative to the two main types. The situation can be conceived of in terms of an *absence* within the order of discourse: the absence of a language – of discursive practices

– through which authority relations and institutional and professional identities different from either traditional or marketised forms can be constituted. Critical discourse analysis cannot solve this problem, but it can perhaps point to the need for a struggle to develop such a new 'language' as a key element in building resistance to marketisation without simply falling back on tradition, and perhaps give a better understanding of what might be involved in doing so.

Notes

I am grateful to Teun van Dijk, Theo van Leeuwen and Ruth Wodak for their helpful comments on an earlier version of this paper.

1. I use the term 'text' for both written texts and transcripts of spoken interaction.
2. The pendulum of academic fashion seems to be swinging against such an 'ideological' view and in favour of a greater stress on self-consciousness and reflexivity (see Giddens 1991). While accepting the need for some correction in this direction (see further on reflexivity below), I believe it is wrong-headed to abandon the ideological view. See General Introduction.
3. The two are not, of course, independent. The nature of detailed production and interpretation processes in particular cases depends upon how the order of discourse is being drawn upon. See Fairclough (1992a: 18–19) for a critical discussion of conversation analysis in these terms.
4. I am using this term rather more loosely than Williams, for whom dominant, emergent and oppositional culture were tied to dominant, emergent and oppositional classes. See Wernick (1991: 183–4) for discussion.
5. Wouters (1986), however, sees informalisation and formalisation as cyclical phenomena, and suggests a new wave of formalisation since the 1970s.
6. The discussion here draws heavily upon Wernick (1991) as well as Fairclough (1989a).
7. Another question is whether practices which are widely simulated are not thereby devalued in a general way.
8. At the time of writing, the binary divide between universities and polytechnics is being dissolved. I shall refer below to the ex-polytechnics as the 'newer universities' and to the 'older universities'.
9. The account in this paragraph is drawn from collaborative work with Susan Condor, Oliver Fulton and Celia Lury.
10. The threefold focus upon changes in the market, in authority, and in self-identity broadly characterises much of the work of the Lancaster Centre for the Study of Cultural Values, of which I am a member. I draw here particularly upon a recent formulation by Russell Keat.
11. Conference on 'The Risk Society: Modernity and the Environment', 29 May 1992, Lancaster University.

5.   Discourse, change and hegemony

Abstract

In this paper I use the term 'technologisation of discourse' to identify a distinctively contemporary mode of language policy and planning, the application specifically to discourse of the sort of 'technologies' which Foucault (1979) identified as constitutive of power in modern society. Technologisation of discourse involves the combination of (i) research into the discursive practices of social institutions and organisations, (ii) redesign of those practices in accordance with particular strategies and objectives, usually those of managers or bureaucrats, and (iii) training of institutional personnel in these redesigned practices. It is being used in a widening range of types of institution, notably within the service industries and the professions, and in increasingly systematic ways.

I regard technologisation of discourse as an important resource in attempts by dominant social forces to direct and control the course of the major social and cultural changes which are affecting contemporary societies. This argument is developed below within the framework of a Gramscian theory of power in modern capitalist societies as 'hegemony', together with an assumption that hegemony and hegemonic struggle are constituted to a significant degree in the discursive practices of institutions and organisations. Discourse conventions may embody naturalised ideologies which make them a most effective mechanism for sustaining hegemonies. Moreover, control over the discursive practices of institutions is one dimension of cultural hegemony. Technologisation of discourse is part of a struggle on the part of dominant social forces to modify existing institutional discursive practices, as one dimension of the engineering of social and cultural change and the restructuring of hegemonies, on the basis of strategic calculations of the wider hegemonic and ideological effects of discursive practices. However, hegemonic projects are contested in discursive and other modes of practice, and technologisation of discourse is no exception. I argue that this mode of language policy and planning needs to be investigated not only at more 'macro' levels of policy formation and implementation, but also through a critical method of discourse analysis which can show how technologisation of discourse is received and appropriated by those who are subjected to it, through various forms of accommodation and resistance which produce hybrid combinations of existing and imposed discursive practices.

The paper is structured as follows. The first section is theoretical. It gives a necessarily skeletal account of social class, political power and the state in modern society in terms of Gramsci's concept of hegemony, and a view of how discourse and discursive change, and specifically the technologisation of discourse, fit into such a framework. The second section is methodological. It sketches out, with examples, a multidimensional 'critical' approach to discourse analysis, based upon the theoretical positions adopted in the first section, which is I suggest a suitable approach for use in research on social and cultural change and its discursive aspects. The third and final section focuses upon the policy and planning dimension of the paper and the concept of technologisation of discourse, locating it within the theoretical and methodological frameworks set out in the first two sections.

1 Discourse and hegemony

In the sphere of language as in other spheres, the nature of policy formation and implementation varies according to the political and organisational structures within which it takes place. For example, simple models of policies radiating outwards and downwards from central government do not match the complexities of modern states in developed capitalist societies such as Britain or the USA. In the case of technologisation of discourse, there are clear tendencies at national and even transnational levels which can be linked to state and dominant class (including capitalist multinational) interests without too much difficulty; yet it is not possible to trace them to one or even several particular moments of locations of central policy formation. Rather, the policies and planning which underlie processes of discourse technologisation have been determined at different levels and different times, in many different institutions and organisations, within the private domain as well as within the public domain. Of course, these instances are linked together in various ways (e.g., through a common relationship to the social scientific expertise which discourse technologisation depends upon), but the decision-making and implementational processes are autonomous.

We need therefore a theory of power, class and state in modern capitalist societies which can account for the relationship of such developments as technologisation of discourse to class and state interests, without reducing complex relationships between organisations, institutions and levels to a 'conveyor belt' view of state power. Such a theory is available in Gramsci's studies of the structures of power in Western capitalist societies after the First World War, and the sort of revolutionary strategies they implied. (See Gramsci (1971), Buci-Glucksmann (1980), Forgacs (1988). Quotations from Gramsci are taken from Forgacs (1988).) For Gramsci, the political power of the dominant class in such societies is based upon a combination of 'domination' – state power in the narrow sense, control over the forces of repression and the capacity to use coercion against other social groups – and 'intellectual and moral leadership' or 'hegemony' (Forgacs 1988: 249). Correspondingly, the state is a combination of 'political society' (the public domain, the domain of state power in the narrow sense) and 'civil society' (the private domain, the domain of hegemony) – or as Gramsci graphically puts it, 'hegemony protected by the armour of coercion' (Forgacs 1988: 235). It is the hegemonic control of the dominant class over the institutions of civil society (education, work, family, leisure etc.) within the 'outer defences' of the repressive state apparatus that makes revolutionary transformation of modern capitalist societies so difficult, and imposes upon the revolutionary party the long-term ideological and hegemonic struggles of a 'war of position', rather than direct confrontation with the state in a 'war of manoeuvre'.

Gramsci links hegemony to the functioning of the state as an 'ethical state': 'every state is ethical in as much as one of its most important functions is to raise the great mass of the population to a particular cultural and moral level, a level (or type) which corresponds to the needs of the productive forces of development, and hence to the interests of the ruling classes' (Forgacs 1988: 234). And, referring to Fordism and Taylorism in the USA, Gramsci discusses 'the need to elaborate a new type of man suited to the new type of work'. One aspect of hegemony is thus cultural and ethical engineering, the reshaping of subjectivities or 'selves' (Keat and Abercrombie 1990), and technologisation of discourse is one aspect of this process as I shall argue in more detail later. However, it is necessary first to provide an account of how discourse fits into Gramsci's theoretical framework. (See also the account of the interaction of hegemony and discourse provided in Laclau and Mouffe (1985) and

Hall (1988), working with a somewhat different concept of discourse. A fuller account is given in Fairclough (1992a).)

There is a dual relationship of discourse to hegemony. On the one hand, hegemonic practice and hegemonic struggle to a substantial extent take the form of discursive practice, in spoken and written interaction. Indeed, my use of the term 'discourse' rather than (say) 'use of language' implies the imbrication of speaking and writing in the exercise, reproduction and negotiation of power relations, and in ideological processes and ideological struggle. The concept of hegemony implies the development in various domains of civil society (e.g., work, education, leisure activities) of practices which naturalise particular relations and ideologies, practices which are largely discursive. A particular set of discourse conventions (e.g., for conducting medical consultations, or media interviews, or for writing crime reports in newspapers) implicitly embodies certain ideologies – particular knowledge and beliefs, particular 'positions' for the types of social subject that participate in that practice (e.g., doctors, patients, interviewees, newspaper readers), and particular relationships between categories of participants (e.g., between doctors and patients). In so far as conventions become naturalised and commonsensical, so too do these ideological presuppositions. Naturalised discourse conventions are a most effective mechanism for sustaining and reproducing cultural and ideological dimensions of hegemony. Correspondingly, a significant target of hegemonic struggle is the denaturalisation of existing conventions and replacement of them with others.

An example I develop in the next section is doctor–patient consultations. In contemporary British society (for example), there is a dominant traditional mode of conducting consultations, and emergent alternative modes. In the dominant mode, doctors ask questions according to pre-set agendas, patients are limited to answering questions, and trying to squeeze anything which does not fit into the doctors' agendas into elaborations of their answers. The tone is impersonal and often brusque, the patient being treated as a bundle of symptoms rather than a person. (See Mishler (1984) and Fairclough (1992a) chapter 5, for a more detailed account.) This traditional mode of consultation corresponds to conventional hegemonic relations within medicine, and it is based upon and reproduces ideological assumptions about the nature of medicine, the social identities of doctors and patients, and the nature of the doctor–patient relationship, which partly constitute those hegemonic relations. Conversely, alternative modes of consultation which have more conversational properties, often drawing upon counselling as a model, are emerging as a part of struggles to challenge and restructure existing hegemonic relations. In my view, any analysis of hegemony and hegemonic struggle within an institution such as medicine must include analysis of discursive practices and of relationships (of dominance, or of opposition and confrontation) between diverse discursive practices.

The second aspect of the dual relationship of discourse to hegemony is that discourse is itself a sphere of cultural hegemony, and the hegemony of a class or group over the whole society or over particular sections of it (or indeed, these days, hegemony on a transnational scale) is in part a matter of its capacity to shape discursive practices and orders of discourse. The importance of cultural hegemony in the sphere of discourse follows from the ideological potency of discursive practices and conventions referred to in the last paragraph. Hegemony in this sphere also includes, as Gramsci himself pointed out (Forgacs 1988: 357ff), the relationships set up between different language varieties (different languages, different dialects), and the emergence of a dominant standard variety. The hegemony of a class or group over an order of discourse is constituted by a more or less unstable equilibrium between its constitutive discursive practices, which may become unbalanced and open to being restructured in the course of hegemonic struggle. For example, in traditional forms of medical practice, doctors did act as counsellors ('lay priests') to their patients as well as body-menders, but the two sets of (discursive) practices tended to be kept distinct; in the struggle of alternative forms of medical practice against traditional forms, this boundary within the order of discourse tends to be weakened, so that the discursive practices of counselling and medicine in the narrow sense merge to produce a new discursive practice. See the next section for an illustration. I should add that hegemonic struggle includes struggle on the part of dominant forces to preserve or restructure and renew their hegemony in the sphere of discourse, as well as struggle on the part of dominated groups.

The two aspects of the relationship of discourse to hegemony distinguished above are of course closely connected, in that it is in concrete discursive practice that hegemonic structurings of orders of discourse are produced, reproduced, challenged and transformed. Any instance of discursive practice can thus be interpreted in terms of its relationship to existing orders of discourse and discursive practices (is it broadly normative, reproducing them, or creative, contributing to their transformation?), as well as its relationship to existing social structures, ideologies and power relations (e.g., in the case of consultations between male doctors and women patients, do they reproduce or challenge dominant gender relations and ideologies?).

In the paragraphs above I have already introduced a historical and dynamic dimension into the relationship between discourse and hegemony through references to hegemonic struggle: hegemonic struggle takes place to a significant extent in discourse, where the 'stakes' include the structuring of orders of discourse as well as other dimensions of hegemonies. This has important theoretical and methodological implications for the study of social and cultural change: accounts of social change need to give more serious attention to discourse than they have done in the past, and to the question of how discursive change relates to (instantiates, constitutes or reflects) social and cultural change; and discourse analysis needs to be used alongside other types of analysis (e.g., sociological, ethnographic) in research on change. The general point is that the investigation of change requires a combination of 'micro' forms of analysis (discourse analysis is one) and more 'macro' forms of analysis (see Fairclough 1992a). These conclusions have considerable current relevance, because of the radical changes which are affecting contemporary societies, and more especially because discourse is coming to be an increasingly salient and defining element in certain areas of social life such as many types of work (notably in the service industries), so that social and cultural changes *are* largely changes in discursive practices (see further below). This is the context in which technologisation of discourse is becoming increasingly prominent as a conscious and strategic intervention to reshape discursive practices on the basis of calculations of their wider hegemonic and ideological effects.

2 A critical approach to discourse analysis

My purpose in this section is to give a brief description, with illustrative examples, of an approach to discourse analysis which is based upon the theoretical positions above (see Fairclough 1989a, Fairclough 1992a). It is an approach which is, I believe, suitable for use in the sort of research into social and cultural change I referred to above. What in particular makes it suitable for such work is that it foregrounds links between social practice and language, and the systematic investigation of connections between the nature of social processes and properties of language texts. (I use 'text' for the language 'product' of discursive processes, whether it be written or spoken language; a spoken 'text' can of course be turned into a written text by being transcribed.) It also facilitates the integration of 'micro' analysis (of discourse) and 'macro' analysis (including analysis of language policy and planning). It is moreover a 'critical' approach to discourse analysis in the sense that it sets out to make visible through analysis, and to criticise, connections between properties of texts and social processes and relations (ideologies, power relations) which are generally not obvious to people who produce and interpret those texts, and whose effectiveness depends upon this opacity.

The approach I have adopted is based upon a three-dimensional conception of discourse, and correspondingly a three-dimensional method of discourse analysis. Discourse, and any specific instance of discursive practice, is seen as simultaneously (i) a language text, spoken or written, (ii) discourse practice (text production and text interpretation), (iii) sociocultural practice. Furthermore, a piece of discourse is embedded within sociocultural practice at a number of levels: in the immediate situation, in the wider institution or organisation, and at a societal level; for example, one can read an interaction between marital partners in terms of their particular relationship, relationships between partners within the family as an institution, or gender relationships in the larger society. The method of discourse analysis includes linguistic *description* of the language text, *interpretation* of the relationship between the (productive and interpretative) discursive processes and the text, and *explanation* of the relationship between the discursive processes and the social processes. A special feature of the approach is that the link between sociocultural practice and text is mediated by discourse practice; how a text is produced or interpreted, in the sense of what discursive practices and conventions are drawn from what order(s) of discourse and how they are articulated together, depends upon the nature of the sociocultural practice which the discourse is a part of (including the relationship to existing hegemonies); the nature of the discourse practice of text production shapes the text, and leaves 'traces' in surface features of the text; and the nature of the discourse practice of text interpretation determines how the surface features of a text will be interpreted. On page 133 there is a diagrammatic representation of this approach.

I want to illustrate the approach by applying it to an example which exemplifies:

1. Texts with heterogeneous and contradictory features.
2. A complex relationship between discourse practice (text production) and discourse conventions; one could show a similarly complex relationship between text interpretation and conventions, but I shall not do so here.
3. A relationship between such heterogeneous textual features and such complexity of discourse processes, and processes of sociocultural change.

The example is an extract from a consultation between a doctor (a 'general practitioner' in the British medical system) and his female patient (a dot

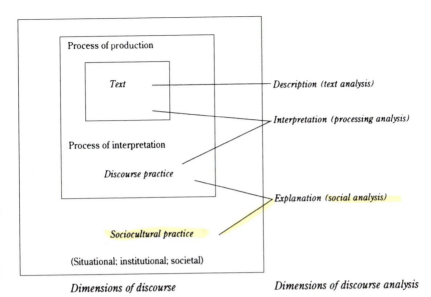

Dimensions of discourse   *Dimensions of discourse analysis*

indicates a short pause, a dash a longer pause, and overlaps are shown with square brackets).

```
 1. Patient:  but she really has been very unfair to me . got⌈ no
    Doctor:                                               ⌊ hm
    Patient:  respect for me at⌈ all and I think . that's one of the
    Doctor:                   ⌊ hm
 5. Patient:  reasons why I drank s⌈ o much you⌈ know⌈ —
    Doctor:                        ⌊ hm        ⌊ hm  ⌊ hm
    Patient:  a⌈ nd em
    Doctor:   ⌊ hm are you you back are you back on it have you started
              drinking⌈ again
10. Patient:          ⌊no
    Doctor:   oh you haven't (unclea⌈ r)
    Patient:                        ⌊ no . but em one thing that the lady on
              the Tuesday said to me was that . if my mother did turn me out
              of the⌈ house which she
15. Doctor:        ⌊ yes
    Patient:  thinks she may do⌈ . coz . she doesn't like the way
    Doctor:                    ⌊ hm
    Patient:  I've been she has turned me⌈ out be⌈ fore . and em .
    Doctor:                              ⌊ hm   ⌊ hm
```

20. *Patient*: she said that . I could she thought that it might be possible to
me for me to go to a council ⌈ flat
Doctor: ⌊ right
yes ⌈ yeah
Patient: ⌊ but she said it's a very em she wasn't
25.   ⌈ pushing it because . my mother's got to sign a
Doctor: ⌊ hm
Patient: whole ⌈ lot of ⌈ things and e: . she said it's difficult
Doctor: ⌊ hm   ⌊ hm
Patient: ⌈ and em . there's no rush over it . I I don't know
30. *Doctor*:   ⌊ hm
Patient: whether . I mean one thing they say in *AA* is that you shouldn't
change anything ⌈ . for a year
Doctor: ⌊ hm
Doctor: hm yes I think I think that's wise . I think that's
35.   wise (5 second pause) well look I'd like to keep you know
seeing you keep . you know hearing how things are going from
time to time if that's possible

The *text* is characterised by a configuration of heterogeneous and contradictory properties. I want to illustrate that in terms of a contrast between the
fact of certain occurrences and their *manner* of occurrence. On the one hand,
the fact of the occurrence of the doctor's question about whether the patient
(an alcoholic) has started drinking again (*are you back are you back on it have
you started drinking again*) in lines 8–9, which breaks topic and which is
repeated as a check (*oh you haven't (indistinct)*) in line 11; and the fact of the
occurrence of the doctor's assessment of the advice the patient has received
(*I think that's wise. I think that's wise*) in line 34; and of the doctor's directive
to the patient to see him again in lines 35–37 – *well look I'd like to keep you know
seeing you keep . you know hearing how things are going from time to time if
that's possible*. On the other hand, the manner of these contributions from the
doctor: the doctor's question in lines 8–9 both in its working (the vague initial
formulation – *are you back are you back on it* – and the reformulation – *have you
started drinking again*), and in a strikingly quiet and fast delivery (which I
have not tried to represent) which give this presumably vital medical question
the appearance of an aside; and the assessment in line 34, which includes an
explicit subjective modality marker (*I think*) which modulates its authorita-
tiveness; and the directive (lines 35–37), which is extremely tentative, hedged
(*you know* etc.) and indirect.

In terms of *discourse practice*, it appears to me that the doctor is creatively articulating two different discourse conventions, that associated with traditional medical consultations, and that associated with counselling. Of course, this is not just this doctor's personal achievement; this is a common and widespread articulation. On the one hand, the doctor as in traditional consultations pursues an agenda which controls and determines the structure of the interaction, and this is manifest in the fact of occurrence of the doctor's question, assessment and directive. On the other hand, the doctor like the counsellor in a counselling session appears to cede much of the control and leadership of the interaction to the patient. The typical apparent non-directiveness of counselling is manifest in the manner of occurrence of the question, assessment and directive. The contradictory demands of medical practice and counselling are tenuously reconciled through the choice of forms of realisation for these speech acts. A more overtly counselling feature is the degree of empathy shown by the doctor, in the textual form of his substantial back-channelling activity (*hm, right, yes*, and so on).

The nature of the discourse production process can itself be referred to the wider sociocultural practice within which it occurs. For instance, at the institutional level, the doctor belongs to a minority oppositional group within official medicine which is open to the practices of alternative medicine and counselling. Institutional members with a knowledge of relations and struggles within medicine may well interpret the doctor's articulation of diverse conventions in this instance as anti-authoritarian – against the authority of the doctor over the patient, and the authority of the medical establishment over the profession; breaking down the professional elitism of doctors by giving the patient greater control in the consultation, and sanctioning the introduction via counselling of more informal and conversational discursive practices which patients are familiar with and at the same time treating the patient as a person, an individual.

However, this particular mix of medical discourse and counselling discourse is one institutionally local instance of a global feature of the contemporary societal order of discourse; the colonisation of institutions in the public domain by types of discourse which emanate from the private domain. This tendency could be called the 'conversationalisation' of institutional discourse. Conversationalisation entails greater informality, and interactions which have a person-to-person quality in contrast with the interaction between roles or statuses which characterises more traditional institutional discourse. It also entails more democratic interaction, with a greater sharing of control and a reduction of the asymmetries which mark, say, conventional doctor–patient interaction. Conversationalisation can I think be seen as a discursive part of social and cultural changes associated at some levels at least with increased openness and democracy, in relations between professionals and clients for instance, and greater individualism.

However, while these developments cannot be simply equated with a spread of consumerism, they have come to be tied in with – one might say appropriated by – consumerism to some extent. Correspondingly, commercial organisations, including increasingly organisations like the professions, social services and even the arts which are being drawn into commercial and consumerist modes of operation, are under pressure to transform their organisational practices and 'cultures' in this direction, undertaking in many cases systematic strategies of training and other forms of intervention to achieve these ends. Technologisation of discourse is a part of this process, and in many cases a central objective of technologisation of discourse is the achievement of a shift towards more conversationalised discursive practices as a part of these broader organisational and cultural changes. Thus conversationalised discursive practices are open to contradictory investments, being linked either to democratisation or to new strategies of control, and being therefore themselves a focus of hegemonic struggle.

Returning to the example, I would suggest that it is difficult to interpret the mixing of medical discourse and counselling discourse, in the sense of arriving at a conclusion about the social value and import that it has, without placing it in the context of longer-term transformations affecting orders of discourse, tendencies of the sort referred to in the previous paragraph, and the current state of hegemonies and hegemonic struggles (including deployment of technologisation of discourse) in the discursive sphere within the institution concerned. In this case, I suspect there is at least an ambivalence about the mixing of discursive practices; it may instantiate a democratic and anti-authoritarian stance on the part of the doctor, but it may also constitute the imposition upon the patient of a new mode of control more in accordance with contemporary cultural emphases.

This discussion points to the necessary interdependence of 'micro' analyses of specific discourse samples and more 'macro' analysis of longer-term tendencies affecting orders of discourse, the construction and restructuring of hegemonies in the sphere of discursive practices, and language policy and planning. These 'macro' dimensions constitute part of the context of any discursive event, and are necessary for its interpretation. Conversely, as I shall argue in the next section, no account of discourse technologisation (or other 'macro' developments) can forgo an investigation of how planning initiatives are received and responded to (adopted, paid lip service to, accommodated, opposed), which can come only from analyses of specific discourse samples. 'Micro' and 'macro' analyses of discourse and discursive change are mutually dependent.

3 Technologisation of discourse[1]

Technologisation of discourse is a process of intervention in the sphere of discourse practices with the objective of constructing a new hegemony in the order of discourse of the institution or organisation concerned, as part of a more general struggle to impose restructured hegemonies in institutional practices and culture. In terms of the analytical method introduced in the last section, it involves an attempt to shape a new synthesis between discourse practice, sociocultural practice and texts. This is done through a process of redesigning existing discursive practices and training institutional personnel in the redesigned practices, on the basis of research into the existing discursive practices of the institution and their effectivity (be it in terms of the efficiency of organisational operations, the effectiveness of interaction with clients or 'publics', or the successful projection of 'image').

My use of the term 'technology' derives ultimately from Foucault's analyses of the alliance between social sciences and structures of power which constitutes modern 'bio-power', which has 'brought life and its mechanisms into the realm of explicit calculations and made knowledge/power an agent of transformation of human life' (Foucault 1981). Technologies of discourse are more specifically a variety of what Rose and Miller call 'technologies of government': 'the strategies, techniques and procedures by means of which different forces seek to render programmes operable, the networks and relays that connect the aspirations of authorities with the activities of individuals and groups' (Rose and Miller 1989). Referring to liberalism as a mode of government, these authors see the 'deployment' of 'political rationalities and the programmes of government' as 'action at a distance', involving the 'enrolment' of those they seek to govern through 'networks of power' incorporating diverse agents and 'the complex assemblage of diverse forces – laws, buildings, professions, routines, norms'. Discourse is, I would suggest, one such 'force' which becomes operative within specific 'assemblages' with other forces.

Technologisation of discourse has, I think been accelerating and taking on firmer contours in the past decade or so, but its lineage is longer. For example, 'social skills training' (Argyle 1978) is a well-established application of social psychological research, and technology of government, which has a partially discursive nature. Large units of practice such as interview are assumed to be composed of sequences of smaller units which are produced through the automatic application of skills which are selected on the basis of their contribution to the achievement of goals. It is assumed that these skills can be isolated and described, and that inadequacies in social (including discursive) practice can be overcome by training people to draw upon these skills. Social skills training has been widely implemented for training mental patients, social workers, health workers, counsellors, managers, salespeople and public officials. One example given by Argyle is training in the 'personnel interview' (used for instance for disciplinary interviews in workplaces), which (and this quotation points to the design element) 'can make it a pleasanter and more effective occasion' (Argyle 1978).

I shall use the following list of five characteristics of technologisation of discourse as a framework for elaborating the definition given above.

1. The emergence of expert 'discourse technologists'.
2. A shift in the 'policing' of discourse practices.
3. Design and projection of context-free discourse techniques.
4. Strategically motivated simulation in discourse.
5. Pressure towards standardisation of discourse practices.

There have long been specialists in persuasive and manipulative discourse, but what we might call contempory 'technologists of discourse' have certain distinguishing features. One is their relationship to knowledge. They are social scientists, or other sorts of expert or consultant with privileged access to scientific information, and their interventions into discursive practice therefore carry the aura of 'truth'. Another is their relationship to institutions. They are likely to hold accredited roles associated with accredited practices and routines in institutions, either as direct employees or as expert consultants brought in from outside for particular projects. For example, 'staff development' and 'staff appraisal' are two recent additions to the institutional practices of British universities. Both the training of staff and the training of appraisers are partly training in a variety of discourse practices – lecturing, organising seminars, interviewing, designing publicity materials, writing research proposals. And both directly employed staff and outside management consultants are being drawn into specialised institutional roles and practices, partly as discourse technologists. These relationships of discourse technologists to knowledge and to institutions distinguish contemporary forms of discourse technologisation from earlier forms of intervention in institutional discourse practices.

Discourse practices are, I think, normally 'policed' – subjected to checks, corrections and sanctions – though there is a great deal of variation in how overtly or how rigorously. One effect of technologisation of discourse is, I suggest, to shift the policing of discourse practices from a local institutional level to a transinstitutional level, and from categories of agent within particular institutions (be it education, law, medicine) to discourse technologists as outsiders. In addition to a shift in the location of policing agents, there is a shift in the basis of their legitimacy. It has traditionally been on the basis of their power and prestige within the profession or institution that certain categories of agent claimed the right to police its practices; now it is increasingly on the grounds of science, knowledge and truth – the discourse technologist as expert as well as outsider.

Discourse technologists design and redesign what I shall call 'discursive techniques', such as interviewing, lecturing or counselling, to maximise their effectiveness and change them affectively – recall the objective of making a disciplinary interview 'a pleasanter and more effective occasion'. Argyle recommends that an interview should end with a review of what has been agreed and 'on as friendly a note as possible', suggestions about design which involve the design of particular utterances (to be 'friendly') as well as the overall organisation of the interview. I suspect that the tendency is for techniques to be increasingly designed and projected as 'context-free', as useable in any relevant context. This tendency is evident in training, where there is a focus upon the transferability of skills – 'teaching for transfer' is a prominent theme in recent vocational education, for example. Moreover, the projection of such context-free techniques into a variety of institutional contexts contributes to a widespread effect of 'colonisation' of local institutional orders of discourse by a few culturally salient discourse types – advertising and managerial and marketing discourse, counselling, and of course interviewing (Fairclough 1989b).

The redesign of discourse techniques involves extensive *simulation*, by which I mean the conscious and systematic grafting onto a discourse technique of discourse practices originating elsewhere, on the basis of a strategic calculation of their effectivity. I have in mind particularly simulation of meanings and forms which appertain to the discursive constitution of social relationships and social identities – which have 'interpersonal' functions in systemicist terminology (Halliday 1978). The recommendation that an interview end on a friendly note is an invitation to the interviewer to simulate the meanings and forms (those of language but also other semiotic modalities) of 'friendliness', meanings and forms which imply and implicitly claim social relations and identities associated more with domains of private life than with institutional events like interviews. Opening frontiers between the private and the institutional; institutional appropriation of the resources of conversation; conversationalisation and apparent democratisation of institutional discourse (already referred to above) – these are pervasive features of the technologisation of discourse.

The final characteristic of discourse technologisation in my list is that it constitutes a powerful impetus towards standardisation and normalisation of discourse practices, across as well as within institutions and different types of work. The importance of expert outsiders as discourse technologists, the shifting of the policing of discourse to a transcendent position 'above' particular institutions, and the trend towards context-free discourse techniques – all of these are centralising and standardising pressures upon discourse practice: pressures which meet with resistance, however, as I shall suggest below.

The contemporary prominence of technologisation of discourse reflects the increasing relative importance of discursive practices in certain areas of social life, especially various types of work. It is well known that there has been an increase in service industry at the expense of manufacturing industry, and the 'skills' necessary for jobs in service industries are to a substantial extent 'communication skills'. The quality of the 'product' in service industries often depends largely upon discursive practices and capacities of workers. Even within manufacturing industry, discursive practices are becoming more important, as new technologies bring about a shift from repetitive and solitary work on a production line to more variable work in teams. In a context of rapid change in the nature of work, the engineering of change in discursive practices assumes some importance.

The engineering of change in discursive practices is part of a process of cultural engineering and restructuring cultural hegemony – as Gramsci put it, 'elaborating a new type of man suitable to the new type of work' (Forgacs 1988: 234). For example, the simulation of conversational discourse in institutional settings – the 'conversationalisation' of institutional discourse – has implications for the social identities of, and social relationships between, those who operate in them. A professional such as a doctor or lawyer cannot shift to a conversational mode of interaction with patients or clients without taking on in some degree a new social identity, and projecting a new social identity for the patient or client. These new identities draw upon models in the 'lifeworld', the private sphere. The same is true where interaction between managers and workers, and more generally those at different points on hierarchical scales, becomes more conversational. However, the engineering of social identity may have unforeseen pathological consequences; the widespread simulation of conversation and its cultural values may lead to a crisis of sincerity and a crisis of credibility and a general cynicism, where people come to be unsure about what is genuine and what is synthetic.

People in their actual discoursal practice may react in various ways to pressures for change emanating from the technologisation of discourse: they may comply, they may tactically appear to comply, they may refuse to be budged, or they may arrive at all sorts of accommodations and compromises between existing practices and new techniques. The latter is perhaps the most common and certainly the most interesting case. Study of such accommodations in the discursive practice of workplaces, for example, strikes me as a likely source of insight into the actual impact of technologies of government on practice, and into ongoing processes of change in social relations and social identities.

I want to suggest that the production of discourse under such conditions of change places producers in 'dilemmas' (Billig *et al.* (1988)) which are an effect of trying simultaneously to operate in accordance with divergent constructions of social relationships and social identities, and that these dilemmas lead to accommodations and compromises which are manifested in the ambivalence and heterogeneity of spoken or written texts.

Let me relate these suggestions to a specific example, an extract from a British university prospectus (see pages 143 and 144), using the approach to discourse analysis presented in the last section. The recent evolution of university prospectuses reflects clearly pressures on universities to operate under market conditions, and to 'sell' their courses, using discursive techniques from advertising. Some of the changes that have occurred are immediately evident in the physical appearance of prospectuses; the typical course entry has shifted in ten years from a couple of pages of quite dense writing to a mixture of written text, colour photographs, and sophisticated graphics. But prospectuses also show how academics have responded to the dilemmas that these pressures have placed them in by accommodation and compromise. These dilemmas centre upon the contradiction between a traditional professional- (or producer-) orientated relationship between university and applicant, where the university is the 'authoritor' admitting or rejecting applicants according to its criteria for entry; and a 'consumer-orientated' relationship being forced upon universities by the economic position they have been placed in, where the applicant is the authoritor choosing (as consumers do) among the range of goods on offer. On the former model, a prospectus would focally give information about courses and conditions of entry, on the latter model it would 'sell' courses. In fact, contemporary prospectuses attempt a balancing act between these two discursive practices, and in terms of professional identities, they show academics trying to reconcile being academics and being salespeople.

This dilemma shows up in the heterogeneity of the text, and in particular in how its heterogeneity in terms of semiotic modalities and genres (written text and photograph on the left, list of courses and graphic display on the right) relates to its heterogeneity in terms of meanings, or more precisely speech functions (the main ones are informing, regulating and persuading). Let me begin with regulating. It strikes me as significant that everything to do with requirements imposed by the university upon the applicant – entry requirements, course requirements – is located in the synoptic right-hand section of the entry. This allows requirements to be separated from any source or authoritor, so that the problematic meaning (problematic, that is, in the consumer-orientated model) of the university imposing requirements upon applicants does not have to be overtly expressed. This occlusion is evident in the wording of the graphic display: *you will need* rather than for instance *we require* shifts the onus onto the student, and the agentless passives (*will be accepted, candidates who are offered places will be invited*). In the written text, regulating is avoided, and aspects of the degree scheme which might normally be seen as requirements are semanticised in other terms. For example, in paragraph 3 taking courses in several disciplines comes across as an assurance (*students will gain valuable experience*) rather than a requirement; similarly in paragraph 4, taking the three specified courses in the first year comes across as a description (*students pursue . . .*) rather than a requirement.

Let me turn from regulating to the other two speech functions, informing and persuading. The most fully persuasive modality is the photograph, which positions the applicant in some unspecified but most attractive 'American' scene, co-constructing the potential student, the programme and the university within a mythical 'America'. The sentences of the written text on the other hand are in many cases ambivalent between informing and persuading – persuasion is certainly a significant speech function, but in a mainly covert form which anticipates substantial inferential work on the part of the reader (as, of course, does the photograph). The opening paragraph for instance appears on the face of it to consist of three bits of information (with *lively* as a transparently persuasive lexicalisation) – about the tradition of American Studies at the university, the introduction of a specialised degree, and content of the degree. The first two sentences are in an overtly temporal relationship marked by the contrast between present perfective and simple present verb forms, and the temporal conjunct *now*. A little inferential work on the part of the reader can construct these markers and bits of information into a persuasive narrative according to which the degree is the culmination of a cross-disciplinary tradition. Similarly in other paragraphs, persuasion is mainly covert. The academic's dilemma appears to be resolved through a compromise; the written text is designed to persuade while appearing to be merely informative.

AMERICAN STUDIES

Enquiries to: Director of Admissions
Teaching staff: members of appropriate departments

Photograph of American scene
[not reproduced here]

Lancaster students have always shown lively interest in American subjects, whether in the English, History, Politics or other departments. Now it is possible to take a specialised degree in American Studies. This degree combines different disciplinary approaches to the study of the United States and offers options covering American history, literature, and politics from the earliest colonial settlements to the present day.

In addition, American Studies majors will spend their second year at an American university, such as the University of Massachusetts at Amherst or another selected American university. Lancaster's close American connections make it possible to integrate the year abroad into the degree, so that, unusually in British universities, the American Studies degree can be completed in *three* years. Special counselling will ensure close integration between the year abroad and the two years at Lancaster.

Degree studies at Lancaster call on specialists in a number of departments,

and, as with most Lancaster degrees, students will gain valuable experience in more than one discipline. But a substantial degree of flexibility is maintained, and it is possible for students to concentrate substantially on either history or literature or politics if they so choose.

The first year is largely devoted to providing a disciplinary grounding, and students pursue the normal first year courses in the History, English and Politics departments, taking American options where they exist. Thereafter the course of study is almost exclusively devoted to American topics, and may include the writing of a dissertation of an American theme.

American Studies graduates pursue careers normally associated with a humanities or social science education: education, business, journalism, publishing, librarianship, and social service, with the wider opportunities which may come from students' transatlantic experience and perspective.

Two pages from the Lancaster University 1990 Undergraduate Prospectus (see page 144)

There are many variants of such accommodations and compromises between 'telling' and 'selling', reflecting the dilemmas of professionals in various domains faced with commodification and marketisation and pressure to use associated discourse techniques. In Fairclough 1988b, I analysed the effect of contradictory producer- and consumer-orientations and authoritor–authoritee relations on the modality of a brochure about a bank's financial services. One might also see the text analysed in the last section in similar dilemmatic terms: in terms of the compromises effected by a medical practitioner in attempting to adopt a patient-orientated counselling or therapeutic style of medical interview while maintaining control over medically important aspects of the interview. Similarly, Candlin and Lucas (1986) have shown how a family-planning counsellor tries to reconcile contradictory pressures to control clients' behaviour

B A Hons **American Studies** *Q400*

First Year
History (American options)
English
Politics

Second Year
Four or five courses in American subjects taken at a United States university, including at least one interdisciplinary course.

Third Year
Four or five courses, normally from:
History:
The History of the United States of America
Religion in America from Jamestown to
Appomatox, 1607–1865
From Puritan to Yankee: New England,
1630–1730

The Great Alliance: Britain, Russia and the
United States, 1941–1945
Cold war America: The United States from
Truman to Kennedy
English:
American Literature, 1620–1865
American Literature, 1865–1940
American Literature, 1940–1980
Politics:
The Politics of Race
United States Government: The Politics of the
Presidency
The American Policy Process
United States Foreign Policy since 1945

Assessment: see under appropriate subjects.

YOU WILL NEED

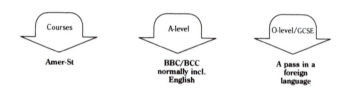

Courses	A-level	O-level/GCSE
Amer-St	BBC/BCC normally incl. English	A pass in a foreign language

or other qualifications (IB, EB, Scottish Highers) at a comparable standard.
AS-levels: will be accepted.
Interview policy: special cases only.
Open days: candidates who are offered a place will be invited.

and yet as counsellors to refrain from any form of direction, through the indirect linguistic realisation of speech acts. In all such cases, people are using discourse as one medium in which they can attempt to negotiate their identities and their relationships with others in problematical circumstances of change.

There is, however, a significant gap between such practices of accommodation and compromise, and the impetus within technologisation of discourse towards more standardised and context-free discourse practice; technologies of government generate strategies of resistance. What appear in a social psychological perspective as attempts to resolve dilemmas appear in the perspective of a politics of discourse as discursive facets of processes of hegemonic struggle in which the structuring of orders of discourse and of relationships between orders of discourse is at stake. The outcomes are restructured orders of discourse, innovative mixing of genres, and the emergence of new genres and sub-genres. One should also not exclude the possible appropriation of discourse technologisation by dominated social forces.

Let me note finally that important changes are taking place in language education and training in Britain (and I imagine elsewhere), for example, in the new national curriculum for schools and in the 'communication' elements of pre-vocational education programmes which seem to be closely linked to technologisation of discourse. There is a new emphasis on oracy and spoken language education, on face-to-face interaction and interaction in small groups, sometimes explicitly justified in terms of changing communicative requirements in work. And there is an extension to language of competence-based models of education which see knowledge operationally in terms of what people can do, and see education as training in skills. These new priorities and approaches contrast with more traditional emphases on written Standard English. Their emergence can, I think, be interpreted as the spread of a technologising orientation to discourse into the general educational system, most obviously into vocationally orientated programmes, but also to a degree into the general school curriculum. The competence- and skill-based approach harmonises with technologisation of discourse in a number of ways: it focuses upon training in context-free techniques (skills); it is a pressure for standardisation of practices; it fits with autonomous notions of the self, each individual being construed as housing a configuration of skills which can be worked upon and improved.

4 Conclusion

I have identifed technologisation of discourse as an emergent domain of language policy and planning, and have tried to locate it within a view of social and cultural change which highlights the role of discourse, insisting at the same time that discursive aspects of change, including policy and planning dimensions, should be investigated with methods which integrate 'micro' and 'macro' modes of analysis.

Note

1. This section of the paper is a modified version of part of 'Technologisation of discourse', N. Fairclough (1996) in Costas-Coulthard, C.R. and Coulthard, M. (eds) *Critical Discourse Analysis*, Routledge.

6. Ideology and identity change in political television[1]

1 Introduction

This paper is an analysis of part of a late-night political television programme entitled *Midnight Special* which was broadcast during the April 1992 British General Election campaign on Channel 4. The reporter is a well-known TV presenter and 'personality' Vincent Hanna, and this part of the programme features a panel of MPs, one from each of the three main parties (Conservative, Labour, Liberal Democrat). I shall be using the framework for CDA described in Paper 4. Let me summarise the argument of the paper. I want to suggest that the *Midnight Special* programme is complex, creative and productive interdiscursively, that is, in its discourse practice. This is manifested through a mixing of genres and discourses, including the mixing of elements of (i) conventional political interview, (ii) simulated conversation, and (iii) entertainment – performance, 'act', even including comedy routine. Following Tolson (1991), we might group together the second and third of these as constituents of 'chat', understood by Tolson as an institutionalised version of conversation which serves as a form of entertainment (see further below). The generic and discoursal mixture of the discourse practice is realised textually in heterogeneity: the text is heterogeneous in its meanings (ideational and interpersonal, and both identity and relational aspects of the latter) and in their realisations in the forms of the text. The complexity and creativity of the discourse practice accords with the complex, unstable and innovative sociocultural practice it is a part of. Putting the same points in different terms, the contradictions of the sociocultural and discourse practice are manifest in the heterogeneities of the text. The discourse practice here is representative of a more general tendency for the order of discourse of political broadcasting to be restructured, specifically through a redrawing of boundaries between the discursive practices (and orders of discourse) of the traditional political public sphere, the private sphere of the 'lifeworld', and the media as institution of entertainment. This restructuring of orders of discourse is one facet of a more general restructuring of relationships between these domains of life. One might see this in terms of the possible emergence of a new hegemonic structure in the domain of politics and political broadcasting, and associated ideological changes affecting social identities, social relations, and knowledges (see further below).

My analysis will focus upon a point in the programme immediately following a report on a Conservative Party Election Broadcast which was centred upon the origins and personality of the Prime Minister, John Major. The extract is a discussion of the report between Vincent Hanna, the presenter, and MPs Jonathan Aitken (Conservative), Robin Corbett (Labour) and Simon Hughes (Liberal Democrat).[2] I shall supplement this extract with others later. My main aims in the analysis of the first extract are to illustrate the genre mixing referred to above; show how it is realised in heterogeneous textual meanings and forms, which constitute identities, social relations, and knowledges in complex and contradictory ways; and suggest that ambivalence and disfluency are two notable and significant features of this mixed-genre discourse.

> *(talk and laughter)*
> VH: /splendid piece there by Fiona Murch# the arts   /smiling#
> correspondent . of Channel 4 news. now . . . you
> struck me during that as if you weren't sure whether
> to laugh or throw up
> 5. JA: /well I'll give him an Oscar *(laughter)* . in a loyal way.   /smiling#
> *(laughs)* it looked to me rather attractive I mean it is
> a good story you have to admit that
> VH: ⌈ yeah
> JA: ⌊ the boy from Brixton who's made it to Number 10 e:
> 10.   left school at 16 it's a ⌈ good yarn a good script. um
> VH: ⌊ (unclear)
> JA: I ⌈ should think John Schlessinger's probably (voiced
> VH: ⌊ (but unclear)
> JA: hesitation) e:m done a first class job I I'm looking for-
> 15.   ward to it. looking forward to seeing the real thing# =
> VH: = backing nervously away from this question Jonathan
> ⌈ (unclear)
> JA: ⌊ what is the question sorry *(laughter)*.
> ⌈ I said I'd give him an Oscar *(laughter)*
> 20. VH: ⌊ do you find it *(laughs)*
> /do you# find it embarrassing that the . party   /laughing#
> leaders descend to this kind of .

      JA: /no I think it's ⌈ showbusiness it's poli   /smiling#
                              ⌊ thing
25. *VH:*
      JA   ⌈   modern politics#
      VH   ⌊ right   fine OK
      JA: um . and (voiced pause) I mean I I wonder how many
               votes are in it I mean . I think in the last election we
30.   just saw a s-soupcon of it there . Neil Kinnock's
               broadcast with the Beethoven's 9th. it was an
      VH: ⌈ right
      JA: ⌊ outstanding ⌈ piece of
      VH: ⌊ Brahms Brahms 1st
35. *JA:*   /no it was Beethoven's 9th   /smiling#
      VH: no
      JA: anyway . let's not argue about the music# but it was the
               um the rather stunning um presentation of Kinnock
               /in a much better light than certainly I'd ever seen him   /smiling#
40.   before# and . it didn't make a tupenny ha'penny worth
               of votes in the end . I mean the so I think it's part of
               the razzamatazz of electioneering but . /the British   /sober#
               people are not fooled by . any . director's presenta-
               tion I think in the end . uh it is the issues an and the
45.   substantive things that count   #
      VH: well from one practising journalist to another . /Ro#   /laughing#
               Robin Corbett

I want to begin with the discourse practice and the mixing of genres. A preliminary point is that genres drawn upon within a text may be related to each other in various ways. In this extract, we have both 'sequential' and 'mixed interdiscursivity' (Fairclough 1992a: 118): to some extent there is a sequential alternation between parts of the text which seem to be primarily political interview or primarily 'chat', but many particular parts of the text (even down to individual clauses) are also interdiscursively mixed.

The most obvious presence of conventional political interview genre in the section of the programme from which the extract is taken is the control exercised by VH over turn-taking and topic. In this part of the programme, which is located between two reports, VH interacts with each of the politicians in turn. Although VH does not always ask *questions*, his talk does count as elicitations which require (and receive) an on-topic response; so while there is a direct question in lines 21–24 (*do you find it embarrassing that party leaders descend to this kind of thing*), VH's contributions in lines 2–4 (*you struck me as if you weren't sure whether to laugh or throw up*) and lines 16–17 (*backing nervously away from this question Jonathan*) are not questions, but are still elicitations requiring responses. The elicitation in lines 16–17 might also be taken as fulfilling the conventional interviewer's responsibility to sanction an interviewee who fails to answer 'the question'. But if it is a sanction it is heavily mitigated, by humour and by first-name address: the difficulty for the interpreter is to know whether the interpretative procedures associated with conventional political interview apply in this case, given a general ambivalence of genre (see further below on ambivalence).

There are also elements of political *discourse* (on the distinction between genre and discourse, see Paper 4), notably in lines 42–45, which consist of two hackneyed formulae of political speech-making ('the British people are not fooled by . . .'; 'in the end it is the issues . . . that count'). The shift into political discourse is marked by *but* in line 42, and is accompanied by a shift to a more measured delivery, and a sober facial expression which JA sustains while the camera is on him even after he has finished speaking. Although I do not have the space to pursue this dimension of the analysis here, different discourses and genres imply *bodily* as well as linguistic differences, and a text which mixes genres and discourses may entail complex and hybrid corporeal-ities (Threadgold 1989).

Turning to conversational elements in the generic mix, before VH speaks there is a snatch of talk and laughter (from RC, I think) presumably directed at the report, and VH's first word (*splendid*) is audibly said 'smilingly', and, in fact, he is smirking through the first part of this contribution. Such features would be unproblematic in conversation but would not be expected in con-ventional political interview, and the same is true of the elicitation directed by VH at JA (*you struck me during that as if you weren't sure whether to laugh or throw up*), in terms of its force (it is a comment on JA's apparent response to the report), its use of a conversational formula for reporting someone taken aback by events ('x looked as if s/he didn't know whether to y or z'), and style (note the lexical selection of *throw up*), as well as perhaps the absence of an explicit nomination of JA to respond. It is also conversational in the sense that it elicits a personal response from JA 'as an individual' rather than as occupier of an official political role (representative of the Conservative Party): a politician would not standardly feel a need to answer such a comment in a personal way even if it was made. Both VH in making the comment and JA in answering it in a personal way show an orientation to their co-involvement, conversationally, as individuals here rather than role-holders. A noteworthy feature of this exchange and the extract generally, which is indicative of this conversational orientation to person rather than position, is the density of 'mental process' clauses (Halliday 1994b). Some of the mental process verbal groups are:

struck (3), *weren't sure* (3), *looked* (6), *I should think* (12), *I'm looking forward* (14), *do (you) find* (21), *(I) think* (23), *(I) wonder* (27). A number of these operate modally as what Halliday calls 'subjective' modality markers, highlighting the subjective basis of commitment to propositions (there is an example even of the political discourse of lines 42–45 – recall my earlier suggestion that there is extensive mixed interdiscursivity). A further conversational feature of VH's talk are the responses he makes during JA's contributions, in lines 8 (*yeah*), 27 (*right, fine OK*), and 32 (*right*). Notice also how VH's elicitation in lines 16–17 'latches' onto the end of JA's contribution, giving it the force of a rejoinder. In the disagreement about the music (lines 34–37), both VH's interruption of JA to correct him and JA's assertive and mock-outraged response are again more typical of conversation than of conventional political interview.

VH's opening elicitation/comment (*you struck me as if you weren't sure whether to laugh or throw up*) is also a humorous one, delivered in a deadpan, ironic way which is part of VH's style (and 'personality'), and perhaps part of the communicative ethos of the programme. (This is perhaps an example of how 'personality' can be transformed into 'product image' in the leisure market, indicating that the preoccupation with personality in the contemporary media may not be the substantive concern for individuals that it is often represented as being). Humour is a major element of this section of the programme, and it is systematically registered by the participants through their smiles and laughter. Although there is, of course, humour in conventional political programmes such as *Question Time*, it is incidental, whereas here it is a basic and sustained feature of the talk. There is an element of 'chat' in the programme, a form of witty conversation which is at the same time entertainment, performance. In line 19, JA's humorous response to VH's (humorous) elicitation (*what is the question*) has the split-second timing of a line in a comedy double-act. Even some of the apparently serious parts of the programme have an undercurrent of humour. For instance, in JA's serious answer to VH's (serious) question in lines 24–45, there are elements of ironic humour (e.g., *we saw just a soupçon of it*, lines 29–30). The ground rules of the programme seem to require serious political talk not to be sustained for more than a few seconds without being 'lightened' by humour (see further below). There is a general correspondence in 'key' between VH's elicitations and the responses they elicit. In this case, for example, a humorous elicitation elicits a humorous response, and its humour is also marked by JA's smiling delivery. I shall have more to say about the humour of the programme shortly in discussing its high level of ambivalence.

Another aspect of the presence of elements of conversation and entertainment/performance in the generic mix is the way in which viewers are addressed and constructed in the programme. VH begins with direct address on camera to the audience, before (*now . . . you struck me*) swivelling his chair sideways to face and address JA. It is a general feature of this part of the programme that, except for VH at points of transition between report and studio discussion, the audience is not addressed, and indeed there is little surface evidence at all of orientation to audience or of contributions being designed for viewers rather than co-participants. The talk is designed ostensibly as if the studio were a private place and as if this were a private conversation. This is, of course, just an intricate pretence: like all broadcast talk, the programme is in reality carefully designed for its audience. Interestingly, the pretence is at one point explicitly alluded to by Robin Corbett when he jokingly reveals a professional secret, 'just . . . inside this studio because I know it won't go anywhere else'. Vincent Hanna joins in the joke by agreeing with him ('no'). The programme is constructed as a spectacle for, rather than interaction with, the viewer, and viewers are positioned as voyeurs surreptitiously observing the 'conversation' (including a substantial amount of close observation of participants through camera close-ups). Yet at the same time viewers are constructed in the Corbett–Hanna joke as 'knowing' with respect to the pretence and the act.

The generic mix I have sketched out above leads to a text with complex and contradictory meanings, in terms of the identities set up by/for participants and audience, the relationships between participants, and between participants and audience, and the 'knowledges' which are constituted in the text. Let me summarise some aspects of this as they show up in the extract. VH has a composite identity as part political interviewer, part entertainer, and part conversationalist, and JA's identity includes the two latter elements plus of course that of politician, and the relationship between them is correspondingly complex (interviewer–politician, double act, co-conversationalists). These complex identities and relations articulate together the three domains of public (political) life, the media as a domain of leisure and entertainment, and private life. And that articulation is anchored in, and condensed into, specific personalities. These complex identities and relations are realised in the language used, in the co-occurrence of heterogeneous meanings and styles, some details of which I have referred to above. Although I am stressing contradictoriness and heterogeneity, such language, identities and relations can come in time to be naturalised (and indeed to an extent probably is now). Audience members are as I have suggested positioned as voyeurs watching the conversation as an entertaining spectacle, but also through the elements of more conventional political discourse in the programme as political subjects, as citizens.

2 Ambivalence

One consequence of genre mixing which I have already referred to is that it produces a great deal of ambivalence. Genres are associated with particular principles of interpretation, so that the interpretation of any given linguistic text will depend upon how it is contextualised generically. Where two or more genres are operative, the question arises as to how they are hierarchised. For example, interpreters might ask whether the extract above or a part of it is still 'at bottom' political interview so that interpretative principles associated with interview should apply.

JA's response to VH's first elicitation (lines 5–15) will serve as an illustration. I am not sure whether to take it 'at bottom' as a conventional political response, a defence of his leader, mitigated in a way which accommodates it to the ground rules of this programme, or as a performance, an entertainment, where the audience is invited to share the joke of JA dutifully going through the motions of defending Major. Let me pursue first a reading according to the interpretative principles of conventional political interview. As a politician in an election campaign JA is bound to defend his leader against attack, yet in the cultivated intimacy of studio conversation he cannot solemnly defend what is commonsensically agreed to be indefensible – electoral 'razzamatazz'. Being positive about Major's performance in the indirect, metaphorical and humorous way of *well I'll give him an Oscar . . . in a loyal way* allows him to reconcile these conflicting demands. The rest of JA's contribution (from *it looked to me* to *looking forward to seeing the real thing*) seems on the face of it a more serious defence of Major. It is very defensive (notice the 'low affinity' modalities *it looked to me, I should think, probably*, the 'hedges'[3] *rather, I mean*, and *you have to admit*). There is also as VH points out a nervous quality to it, in the repetitiveness and in its rhythm of delivery. But the apparent shift to a more serious key is offset by the fact that JA continues to smile throughout, and by lexical markers of continuing humorousness (*the boys from Brixton, yarn*). The nervousness upon this reading might indicate the balancing act JA is trying to bring off, aggravated perhaps by the potentially derailing interruptions which VH seems to embark upon at two points (line 10) and the disaffiliation which VH expresses in the way he says *yeah* in line 8. Alternatively, however, one could read JA's answer according to the interpretative principles of entertainment: as a joke which depends upon our recognition of JA going through the political motions of defending his leader, where the conspicuous defensiveness and nervousness (as well as *in a loyal way*) are so many cues to help us 'see' the joke.

There is a similar ambivalence about VH's second elicitation (*backing nervously away from this question Jonathan*, lines 16–17). Like the first, it is not a question but a comment on JA's answer. On one reading, VH is 'at bottom' operating in his role as interviewer and sanctioning JA's failure to answer the 'question', but mitigating the sanction with humour, with an indirect formulation of it, and with first-name address, in accordance with the ethos of the programme. On another reading, there is no real sanctioning going on, it is just a joking way of giving the floor back to JA.

3 Disfluency

The programme is characterised by a rather high incidence of disfluency. Disfluencies seem to register the difficulties which participants are faced with in trying to negotiate the mixed genres of the programme. The following contribution by RC follows an interaction between VH and SH about a sharp rebuke administered by Paddy Ashdown to a journalist, which ends in a long and seemingly uncomfortable pause. It is not clear whether RC takes it upon himself to come to the rescue or whether VH nominates him non-verbally to do so – VH does appear to turn towards RC during the pause.

> RC: well prickly Paddy Ashdown there eh . uh I mean I have uh
>   some sneaking sympathy for him except of course that . um . we:
>   . need to feed this monster . . television . in order to try and .
>   grub around for the extra handful of votes and you're you're
> 5.   quite right . uh most of us will do : m— most things . the most
>   improbable things outside of an election period . to: snatch a
>   headline or better still get ten seconds . on film . but . um . . I
>   I agree to this extent I think that . um . . I don't think uh . Paddy
>   should have put in exactly those words but I think there is
> 10.   a line to be drawn somewhere a judgement to be made it is . .
>   is this wrong when I say this is our election and not yours .
>   ours and the electors' rather than television's.
> VH: well I— I mean you're not wrong to say anything on this pro-
>   gramme (*laughter*) you can say what you want I mean I would I
> 15.   hope it's the voters' election

The transcription only captures a part of what is going on, but nevertheless RC's disfluency is evident in the number and positioning of voiced (*uh, um*) and unvoiced pauses, the false starts, and the anacolutha (constructions which are started then abandoned, e.g., *it is* in line 10). RC's opening (*well prickly Paddy Ashdown there eh* seems to be a joke which does not come off, and there-after he is manifestly struggling to put together a coherent contribution, his discomfort even being registered at one point by a flustered and anxious look from VH. It is an indication of RC's lack of control that he effectively asks for VH's judgement on whether what appears to be his main point is legitimate (*is this wrong when I say this is our election and not yours*). This is perhaps an appeal for help, asking VH to rescue him from his discursive discomfort (which he does not do).

Apart from instances of disfluency, there are points in the programme where participants apparently fail to conform with its ground rules and ethos. I include these with disfluencies because they also are indicative of difficulties that participants have in negotiating the complex expectations of the programme. On such occasions there is sometimes evidence of sanctioning devices for keeping participants in order. The following extract includes RC's reaction to Major's 'performance' in the Conservative election broadcast:

> RC: I don't th— I shall be very surprised if that movie on
> the basis of the snatch I've seen gets a any Oscar
> nominations . the thing is a joke . . it's an absolute
> joke . . a bloke in the back of a chauffeur-driven car
> 5.   . . uh . trying to send out the message you too can do
> this sweetheart if you vote Tory . I don't believe it.
> VH: Simon Hughes
> SH: that . particular . clip of film looked pretty dire .   /laughing#
> I have to / say#

RC makes a rather sharp attack on the election broadcast which seems to be treated as 'over the top' in terms of the programme's ground rules and ethos. Perhaps the camped-up 'message' *you too can do this sweetheart if you vote Tory* is an attempt to mitigate the attack with humour, but it doesn't appear to come off; there is no audible or visible recognition of this as a joke. There is no response to RC's attack from VH – perhaps an indication that it is embarrassing or reprehensible in the context of the programme – and VH, after a pause which is perhaps just long enough to be uncomfortable, shifts squarely into the conventions of political panel interview in simply nominating SH as next speaker. SH's contribution begins with a strikingly measured (in terms of rhythm of delivery) and mitigated (through hedging – *pretty dire*, modalisation – *I have to say*, and his laughing delivery of *say*) critique of the broadcast which ostensibly does adhere to what I think are the ground rules of the programme – that political point-scoring should be mitigated. This seems to be a way for SH to dissociate himself from RC's immoderate attack and get the programme back on track. The example illustrates how participants can come unstuck in trying to negotiate the complex demands of this mixed-genre format, and also the availability of sanctioning devices for keeping participants in line with the ground rules and ethos of the programme.

A further illustration of sanctioning devices but also of ways in which a participant can try to pre-empt sanctioning is the following:

SH: but the- there's an interesting thing I mean I think that . certainly the Labour Party last time and I understand this time . and it looks like the Tory Party last time and this time . are staging most of their leaders' .
5.   appearances
VH: (unclear) what do you mean staging
JA: don't pretend Paddy Ashdown isn't
    ⌈ staging things (unclear)
SH: ⌊ well well no it in a slightly different way what I
10.   mean is the Labour Party had . ticket only rallies
    ⌈ membership only ⌈ ra⌈ llies . and and Neil Kinnock was
JA: ⌊ hm   ⌊ hm
VH: ⌊ yes
SH: only seen in front of his ⌈ own people . and it gave the
15. RC: ⌊ yes yes
SH: impression of solidarity and support . and Mrs Thatcher again generally had a prearranged careful oppor⌈ tunity
VH: ⌊ that's
    (indeed) for security ⌈ reasons
20. JA: ⌊ hm
SH: in in her case . much more than the leader of the opposition . fair to say . it looks as if John Major in the round . members again supporters . people who are not going to be hostile throw wobbly questions . I I have to say I
25.   think Paddy doesn't put himself in that position . the meetings certainly the venues that I'm aware of . anybody could turn up
    ⌈ I mean it's a risky it's risky
VH: ⌊ well it's possible but then he is the only one of the
30.   three party leaders who's trained to kill
SH: :/well yes ⌈ and maybe that#   /smiling#
JA: ⌊ he's the only one who has trouble getting a crowd

SH seems to take a great deal of trouble preparing the ground for what can be construed as the political point-scoring which occurs towards the end of this contribution. Firstly in claiming the floor for the point he wants to make he types it as 'an interesting thing', which implies he is about to make an analytical rather than a point-scoring contribution. Secondly, SH's claims are carefully and cautiously modalised: *I understand* in line 2, *it looks like* in line 3 with the meaning of appearance foregrounded through *look* being heavily stressed and carrying a falling intonation contour, *it looks as if* in line 22, and *I have to say* and *I think* (a sort of double modalisation) in lines 24–5. Thirdly, SH downtones his claims with hedges: *slightly* in line 9, *generally* in line 17. Nevertheless, his claim about 'staging' is sharply challenged in lines 6–8 by VH and JA. Thereafter, all the participants seem to be working at re-establishing a tone of reasonable discussion: the other participants' audible responses (lines 12, 13, 15) to SH's conciliatory explanation in lines 9–18 signal agreement and acceptance; VH's intervention in 18–19 is a supportive clarification rather than a challenge, and again SH is conciliatory in his response and accepts VH's point ('fair to say'). There are no audible responses from the other participants for the rest of SH's contribution until VH interrupts SH with a joke, followed by another from JA which also interrupts SH, which deflate SH's political point-scoring. All of the participants – SH in his cautious design of his contribution, the others in their response – in this exchange are demonstrating an orientation to the programme's ground rules and to the delicate balance which they require between serious (and especially partisan) politics and chat: the former is tolerated if at all only in short bursts, and preferably mitigated by humour. The implicit message is that reasonable, fair-minded non-partisan discussion is acceptable (in moderation), but partisan point-scoring is not, especially when it is not mitigated, and is a fair target for humorous attack.

4   Mediatised political discourse: a new hegemony?

Let me summarise the analysis so far in the terms of the CDA framework introduced in Paper 4. I have suggested that the *Midnight Special* programme is characterised by a complex discourse practice involving the mixing of genres and discourses of politics, conversation and entertainment; that this complexity is realised in heterogeneous and contradictory textual meanings (identities, relations and knowledges) and forms; and that it leads, on the text production side of the discourse practice, to disfluences and other difficulties in managing the complex demands of this hybrid format, and, on the text reception side, to considerable ambivalence.

I now want to comment upon how these properties relate to the sociocultural practice which the discourse practice and the text are embedded within. There are some difficulties in doing so, especially within the confines of a short article. Firstly, an account of aspects of the social context at various levels of generality which may be relevant to reaching an understanding of the discursive and textual features of the programme risks being a many-sided and highly complex account in its own right. I can do no more than identify broad themes here. Secondly, a full analysis would need to generalise over contemporary political discourse as an order of discourse and political broadcasting within that, whereas all this paper does is refer to one programme which is illustrative of one trend within that order of discourse. I think it is a particularly significant trend in the emergence of a new hegemony in political discourse, but that can obviously be no more than a hypothesis.

I want to suggest that the discourse practice illustrated in this programme is a significant part in a shift in social practice which involves, in the terms of Habermas (1989), a 'structural transformation of the public sphere' of politics. One aspect of this transformation is a restructuring of the relationship between the traditional sphere of politics, the media as a domain of entertainment, and private life. Public life, including important elements in the political process such as conferences, elections and proceedings of Parliament, has become increasingly open to media coverage. However, there is a contradiction and a gap between the public nature of media production and media sources, and the private nature of media reception, which is embedded within a home and family life. The gap has been bridged, as work by Cardiff and Scannell has recently shown (Cardiff 1980, Scannell 1992) by a progressive (if not always even) accommodation of public practices and discourses towards the private conditions of reception. One aspect of this movement has been a 'domestication' (Cardiff) or 'conversationalisation' (Fairclough 1994) of mediated public discourse – though as I suggested earlier there are also more general cultural conditions favouring conversationalisation, which is by no means confined to media (Fairclough 1994). At the same time, media consumption has evolved as an important element of leisure activity, in which audiences expect relaxation and entertainment, and in which audiences are increasingly constructed as consumers rather than citizens. 'Chat' has emerged as a genre in which an institutionalised version of private discursive practice, conversation, becomes a form of entertainment.

The mediatisation of politics has entailed a shift from the media merely transmitting political events happening elsewhere whose nature was determined autonomously, to the media generating its own political events (interviews, debates, programmes such as *Midnight Special*) and political events which happen elsewhere being reshaped to enhance their media worthiness. The revaluing of ordinary life and its practices in the media goes along with a devaluing of public, formal, impersonal, demagogic and so forth practices. Correspondingly, we can perhaps see a restructuring of hegemony in the sphere of political practice and political discourse which is placing the chatty, conversational, entertaining political discourse illustrated by *Midnight Special* in an increasingly dominant position in the order of broadcast political discourse, and the order of political discourse more generally. There is in this connection a paradoxical quality to the programme: one of its main themes is dismissing the 'razzamatazz' of electioneering and party political broadcasts, what JA in the extract calls 'showbusiness'; one thing that the participants share is a cynical view of politics in that form. And yet the programme itself is manifestly a form of 'showbusiness', an act, a performance. It is I think highly significant of the shift in dominance within the political order of discourse that more traditional forms of political performance attract general derision, whereas other emergent forms are apparently acceptable.

What is at issue in the restructuring of the order of political discourse is the nature of politics in a fundamental sense, including: political beliefs, knowledges, practices and representations; political identities; and political relations. In terms of the beliefs and knowledges, there is little space for serious debate of political issues, which is present only in a fleeting and ambivalent form; in terms of identities, politicians are reconstituted as 'real' individuals and personalities (a concept which, like 'chat', bridges the public realm of entertainment and the private realm) and the political public is reconstituted as voyeurs and consumers of spectacle, yet at the same time 'knowing' about the conventions and illusions of the new political game; in terms of political relations, politicians and public are constructed as co-members of a private domain culture whose dominant values are ordinariness, informality, authenticity and sincerity. Issues of truthfulness and authenticity have perhaps become more salient here than issues of truth.[4]

The features of the programme I noted above in the discussion of disfluencies are of interest in the latter connection: on the one hand they indicate perhaps the tolerability of disfluences and misjudgements in the new sphere of political discourse, but on the other hand they perhaps suggest the risks for politicians which go hand in hand with the opportunities offered by their new accessibility and visibility (Thompson 1990: 247). Politicians are certainly losing their traditional mystique and authority, though this is not perhaps a development which is explained only by the evolution of broadcast politics: there has been a more general shift, or apparent shift, of authority away from professional groups such as teachers, doctors and lawyers as well as politicians, which some have taken to be entailed by a shift of authority *towards* consumers in 'consumer society' (Keat, Whiteley and Abercrombie 1994).

The changes I am pointing to, and which are illustrated in *Midnight Special*, have I believe an ideological nature. Much ideological analysis of media has focused upon stability and reproduction, but analysis of change in media output and of relatively innovative types of programme such as this one provides an opportunity for investigating the emergence of ideologies. In suggesting that, for instance, the representations of traditional politics and the identities and relations set up for politicians and for the political public in this programme are ideological, I am assuming that (a) there is a difference between the actuality of political practice and its representations in the media, and (b) its representations in the media are enabling for real political practice, specifically in (c) helping to sustain relations of domination which structure real practice. I have some sympathy with the account in Pilger (1992) of apparently ever-increasing openness and visibility of the political process being underlaid by an increasingly secretive state engaged in more and more covert operations, and an increasingly disciplinary society. In this light, the restructured order of political discourse has more of a legitimising function than a democratising function, though the ambivalence of conversationalisation which I referred to earlier precludes simple black-and-white interpretations.

Notes

1. This paper is based upon a presentation at a conference on media discourse at Strathclyde University in September 1992. I am grateful for comments of other participants on the presentation.
2. Pauses are indicated as dots, one for a short pause and two for a longer pause. Overlaps are shown by square brackets. Talk which is unclear is indicated in round brackets, as are vocalisations such as laughter. Aspects of non-verbal communication simultaneous with talk (including laughter) are shown in the margin, and their onset and termination in the text are marked respectively as '/' and '#'.
3. Modalities can be differentiated in terms of the degree of speaker affinity with (commitment to) a proposition (or a person) that they express – see Hodge and Kress (1988). A hedge is a device for qualifying, toning down or mitigating an utterance – see Brown and Levinson (1978).
4. In the terms of Habermas 1984, some parts of the media are perhaps manifesting a shift in the relative salience of implicit validity claims, in favour of truthfulness and sincerity, and at the expense of truth. I am grateful for this point to Martin Montgomery and Sandra Harris, in their contributions to the conference mentioned in note 1.

Section C

Dialectics of discourse: theoretical developments

Introduction

The two papers in this section were published in 2000 and 2004, though an earlier version of the second ('Critical realism and semiosis') appeared in 2002. The theoretical framework developed in the book which I co-authored with Lilie Chouliaraki, *Discourse in Late Modernity*, informs the first one in particular, as does my book *New Language, New Labour?* The latter was aimed at a general readership, whereas this paper addresses the contribution of CDA to research on change in governance with reference to the New Labour 'reform' of social welfare in Britain for a more specialised readership. Both of these papers contribute to the goal of strengthening CDA theoretically which was part of the research programme I adopted in the late 1990s (alongside strengthening CDA methodologically, and applying it in research projects on various themes – see the General Introduction). Papers which are more focused on methodology appear in Section D, though there is some overlap between the two sections in theoretical and methodological concerns.

Several significant theoretical developments are represented in these papers.

1. Recasting CDA in terms of a differentiation of three levels of social life: the level of social structures, the level of social practices, and the level of social events and actions, with social practices being seen as mediating the relationship between (abstract) structures and (concrete) events and actions. Each level has a semiotic (linguistic–discoursal) element or dimension: languages (level of structures), orders of discourse (level of practices), texts (level of events/actions).
2. Seeing CDA as a form of relational analysis, primarily concerned with relations, specifically (a) relations between semiotic and non-semiotic

elements, (b) relations between levels, especially relations between texts and orders of discourse, (c) relations within orders of discourse and within texts. It approaches relations as articulations between semiotic and non-semiotic elements (e.g., between discourses, material practices and events, and non-semiotic elements of social relations) and between semiotic elements (e.g., between different discourses or different genres) which are variable and change over time and space.

3. Seeing relations as dialectical, i.e., as relations between elements which are different but not discrete, where one element can be 'internalised' in others.

4. Identifying action, representation (or 'construal') and identification as three primary, simultaneous and interconnected facets of social process and social interaction, and genres, discourses and styles respectively as their semiotic or discoursal elements or 'moments' at the level of social practices.

5. Working with a realist and specifically critical realist ontology which asserts that there is a real world which exists independently of our (always limited) knowledge of it and of whether or how we represent it, rejects versions of discourse theory which collapse the distinction between reality and discourse, yet also asserts that the real world is socially and discursively constructed.

The first paper in this section ('Discourse, social theory, and social research: the discourse of welfare reform') illustrates a transdisciplinary way of working in CDA research. Adopting a transdisciplinary approach affects the development of both theory and methodology in CDA; I argue in 'A dialectical–relational approach to critical discourse analysis in social research' in Section D that theory and methodology are far from being mutually exclusive, that methodology has a highly theoretical character. A commitment to transdisciplinary research is a particular way of interpreting a commitment to interdisciplinary research. It sees the theoretical and methodological development of the disciplines, theories or frameworks which come into dialogue within such research as arising from that dialogue. In this paper I discuss a transdisciplinary approach to political change, specifically change in modes of governing (or 'governance') associated with New Labour in Britain. I show how this allows categories from sociological and political theories to be recontextualised within CDA in order to enhance the capacity of CDA to contribute to deepening and strengthening transdisciplinary research on such issues. This is not an eclectic 'add-on' of such categories; it implies a process of theoretical development to 'translate' them into CDA categories and relations.

The main categories come from Bernstein's sociology of pedagogy (the categories of recontextualisation, framing and classification) and from Laclau and Mouffe's political theory (the categories of equivalence and difference). I show in the paper that CDA can make a stronger contribution to transdisciplinary analysis of the New Labour mode of governing which has been used in the process of 'welfare reform' by 'internalising' these categories within its own theory and methodology.

The second paper ('Critical realism and semiosis') was written with co-authors who institutionally belong to a sociology department and have interests in ('cultural' and 'moral') political economy and a strong association with critical realism. The paper may present difficulties for readers whose background is in discourse studies because its focus is if anything more on theoretical issues in critical realism than on issues for CDA. Nevertheless it is a significant paper for CDA, because it suggests that CDA can contribute to addressing weaknesses hitherto in critical realism in its treatment of semiosis.

The paper addresses three main issues. First, it argues that critical realism has tended to neglect issues of semiosis or discourse, and that this is a weakness which needs to be corrected. It also argues that critical realism has the capacity to go beyond the commonplace claim that semiosis can have real effects on, or produce changes in, social practices, social institutions and so forth by providing explanations of how it can have such effects. From a critical realist perspective, semiosis can be a cause as well as having meaning, so that the study of semiosis requires in classical sociological terms not only the perspective of *verstehen* (interpretative understanding) but also the perspective of *erklären* (causal explanation). However, this claim depends on a particular ('non-Humean') view of causality, adopted within critical realism, which distinguishes causal powers or potentials (of, for example, semiosis) from actual causal effects, which depend upon context. But so far these issues have been addressed in critical realism mainly in the form of the claim that 'reasons can be causes', which is implicitly a claim about the causal powers of semiosis, but fails to give an adequate semiotic account of reasons, and to recognise that the causal powers of semiosis are not limited to reasons. So if critical realism were to attend more to semiosis, it could provide better explanations of the latter's 'constructive' effects than exist elsewhere.

Second, in so recognising the importance of semiosis and its effects in social analysis, it is vital not to ignore the extra-semiotic factors and conditions 'that make semiosis possible and secure its effectivity' (including bodily and practical know-how and skills, the habitus of social actors, and the constraints and affordances of the material world). This is a rejection of the 'discourse-imperialism' that characterises much recent social theory, which collapses the distinction between semiosis and materiality, and treats semiosis as a play of differences among signs without extra-semiotic conditions and limits. The relationship between semiosis and various extra-semiotic factors (actors, social relations, practical contexts etc.) is a dialectical internal relation i.e. they are different but not discrete (see above). A distinction is drawn between construal (how things are construed or represented) and construction (the material effects of construals), where the move from the former to the latter is contingent on extra-semiotic as well as semiotic conditions.

Third, the paper gives a critical realist account of semiosis in social structuration, the dialectical interconnections between social structures and social action, which incorporates the evolutionary mechanisms of variation, selection and retention. Given that social life constantly produces variation (innovation, change) in both semiotic and extra-semiotic features of social phenomena, what factors condition which variants are selected (taken up, adopted, widely disseminated) and retained (institutionalised, materialised, have structural effects)? We propose a list of specifically semiotic conditioning factors. We also discuss the nature of semiotic structures (languages, and 'semiotic orders' or orders of discourse) and their elements (e.g., genres, discourses and styles), and analyse examples of the emergence of new semiotic features through the texturing of interdiscursive relations (between different discourses) in texts, and of how emergent semiotic features may 'flow' and 'resonate' between social fields and across social scales.

7. Discourse, social theory, and social research: the discourse of welfare reform

Recent social theory includes important insights into language which constitute a so far underdeveloped resource for socially oriented research on language and discourse. But much of this theory stops short: theoretical frameworks and categories which socially locate language are not pushed in the direction of a theorisation of language itself, which limits their operational value in research. Socially oriented research on language can draw upon social theory to produce more sophisticated theorisations and analyses of language which at the same time constitute contributions to social theory.

My aim in this paper is to explore what it means to work in a *transdisciplinary* way. I argue in particular for a transdisciplinary engagement within social theory and analysis in which the logic of one theory is put to work in the elaboration of others without the latter being simply reduced to the former. My focus is upon CDA which I here take to be a part of a broadly conceived social linguistics. I shall link this theoretical exploration to a concrete research focus by referring to a discourse analytical study of the current British ('New') Labour government, with particular reference to its 'reform' of social welfare. I shall be drawing upon the theoretical framework developed in Chouliaraki and Fairclough (1999). I have referred to some of the social theory which I find particularly fruitful to work with, but the paper is intended to suggest a way of working and in no sense offers a closed list of theorists – on the contrary, I believe that we should be open to a wide range of theory.

1 Sociolinguistic theory

The Editorial of the first issue of the *Journal of Sociolinguistics* committed it to promoting the 'building of sociolinguistic theory', arguing that on the one hand sociolinguistics has often been only 'weakly social' in failing to connect with social theory, and on the other hand language-oriented traditions in social science have 'shunned the technical resources that linguistics and semantics offer' (Bell *et al.* 1997). I agree with Coupland's more recent claim (Coupland 1998) that there is a profound interest in language in recent social theory. This constitutes a so far undeveloped potential for socially enriching sociolinguistics and socially oriented research on language more generally, including CDA. At the same time, there is a pervasive failure among social theorists to operationalise their theorisations of language in ways of showing in social research specifically how language figures in social life. This is partly a matter of theory stopping short – theoretical frameworks and concepts which centre language within social life are not pushed in the direction of theorisations of language itself. So I agree with Coupland that socially oriented research on language can advance social theory – though I see this not as a simple add-on, but as a transdisciplinary relationship wherein the logic of one theory is put to work within another (Dubiel 1985, Halliday 1993, Fairclough 1997). Coupland argues that a single integrated social theory of language is both implausible and undesirable, I would argue that integrated theorising is crucial: much recent social theory is committed to overcoming the unproductive divisions between 'macro' and 'micro' theories or 'structure' and 'action' theories by centering its theorising on the dialectic of structure and action (Bhaskar 1986, Giddens 1991, Bourdieu and Wacquant 1992, Archer 1995), and I believe that we should follow the same route.

2   The place of social linguistics in social research on modernity

The interest in language in recent social theory is substantially attributable to understandings of modernity which in one way or other centre upon language or imply an enhanced role for language in modern social life as compared with pre-modern social life. The turn to language in recent social theory resonates with a turn to language in recent social life. But different theoretical categories are used to reference similar perceptions of social change within modern society: for some theorists it's a 'turn to language' (or semiosis), a 'narrative turn', an 'argumentative turn' and so forth; for others a 'cultural turn', or an 'ideological turn', or 'a knowledge turn'. These are of course not simply different terms for the same thing, because the theoretical differences are sometimes substantive, but they do nevertheless constitute different takes on broadly the same sorts of social change. Part of the difficulty of the category of 'discourse' is that it slides between such different theorisations.

The turn to language is evident in various narratives of modernity which to some degree centre on language, e.g., the narrative of modernity as time–space compression and 'globalisation' (Giddens 1991, Harvey 1990, 1996). Social systems are contrasted in terms of their properties of temporal and spatial distantiation, the extent to which social relations are 'stretched' in time and space. Whereas social relations in pre-modern societies were centred upon people being co-present, modern society has involved a progressive 'stretching' of social relations, so that in contemporary (or 'late modern') society there is a compression of time and space to the point where relations of power can be instantaneously enacted on a global scale, e.g., massive movements of capital can destabilise economies and governments in a matter of days. Time–space compression disembeds persons and practices from particular local contexts, and undercuts traditions – it entails a process of 'detraditionalisation' and a corresponding enhancement of the reflexivity of social life, understood as living social life on the basis of knowledge about social life. People live in ways which are increasingly mediated by discourses which construct work, family, gender (femininity, masculinity), sexuality and so forth in particular ways, which emanate from experts attached to social systems and organisations, and which come to them through the mass media (print, radio, television, the internet). If the 'texts' of early modern society were printed, it is this multi-semiotic discourse (combining especially language and image) that constitutes the 'texts' of late modern society. We might say that contemporary social life is 'textually-mediated' – we live our practices and our identities increasingly through such texts. This implies a more central role for discourse, for language and other forms of semiosis, in contemporary social life in comparison with earlier social life.[1] There are other narratives of modernity which centre discourse in different ways (for instance, Habermas's version of critical theory, the post-structuralist and postmodernist theories of Foucault, Lyotard and Baudrillard, the post-Marxism of Laclau and Mouffe, and the feminist theories of Butler, Fraser and Haraway).

In addition to such 'grand narratives', the dialogue with social theory needs to include more middle-range and local social theory which opens up empirical work on specific fields, such as the theories of Bourdieu (1988, 1991) and Bernstein (1990, 1996). These two theorists at once complement the grand narratives and draw them into analysis of particular fields, and together open up a sociological theorisation of discourse. If we develop the categories of CDA in a transdisciplinary way through internalising the logic of these theories, we can operationalise this theorisation in ways of analysing discourse (Chouliaraki and Fairclough 1999).

If theories of modernity ascribe in one way or another a central place to language, they tend not to specify how it does the social work that is ascribed to it. What is missing is a theoretical specification of the social power of language which could be operationalised as ways of showing in detail within particular social research projects how language and other forms of semiosis perform the social magic which they are credited with. Smith's work is a case in point. It is immensely valuable in producing a feminist sociological account of the social effectivity of texts in contemporary social life, without specifying how texts have these effects. This is where discourse analysis (and more broadly social linguistics) can contribute to developing social theory. But this should not be conceived of as simply adding existing theorisations of language onto existing social theories. It is rather a matter of each internalising the theoretical logic of the other, and allowing it to work within its own theorising. It is a matter for instance of doing discourse analysis and developing the theoretical categories of discourse analysis in a way which tries to work with Smith's concept of textually mediated social life, and of doing sociological analysis and developing sociological categories in a way which tries to work with discourse analytical concepts such as 'interdiscursivity' (Fairclough 1992a) – in short, developing one theory in dialogue with another, being open to having one theory transformed through internalising the logic of another.

What I shall specifically do in this paper is explore how discourse and text analytical categories might be developed through internalising certain social theoretical logics. The social theoretical logics I shall discuss relate to the theorisation of: (a) social practices (Althusser and Balibar 1970, Mouzelis 1990); (b) different and competing practices (for Bernstein, 'coding modalities') within a given field (Bernstein 1990, 1996); (c) processes of classification in social practices as processes of differentiation and dedifferentiation ('equivalence' in Laclau and Mouffe's (1985) terms). Let me emphasise that my aim is not to produce a finished re-theorisation, but to explore what it means to work in a transdisciplinary way.

3 New Labour

I shall give the theoretical concerns of the paper a particular focus by referring to a discourse analytical study I am currently working on, on the political discourse of the 'New Labour' government in Britain (Fairclough 2000b). I shall refer in particular to New Labour's 'reform' of social welfare.

The Labour Party won the general election of May 1997 in the UK under the leadership of Tony Blair with a substantial majority after eighteen years of Conservative government. Under Blair's leadership, Labour came to the conclusion that its successive defeats indicated that it needed radically to reposition itself. Major changes of policy took place including the revision of 'Clause 4' of the Party's constitution, amounting to acceptance of capitalism in its new 'global', 'neo-liberal', form. Referring to the Party as 'New' Labour was also seen as important in convincing the electorate that Labour really had changed. This went along with a shift in the focus of the Party's appeal towards 'middle England', the relatively prosperous middle class and upper working class many of whom had supported the Conservatives. Although such matters of interpretation are inherently controversial, the Labour Party is widely perceived as becoming a party of the centre rather than the centre-left. The repositioning of 'New' Labour has involved significant changes in British politics and government. It represents itself as initiating a 'new politics', a politics of the 'Third Way', which transcends the division in British politics between the ('old') left and the ('new') right. There is a new political discourse which combines elements from Thatcherite Conservative discourse with elements of communitarian and social democratic discourses (a favourite way of summing this up is 'enterprise as well as fairness' – 'enterprise' is a Thatcherite word, 'fairness' is 'New' Labour's preferred alternative to the social democratic 'equality'). There is an attempt to 'reinvent' (or 'modernise') government, involving new forms of 'partnership' between the government, business, and the voluntary sector. And there is a change in political style which is most obvious in the leadership style of Tony Blair. What is open to question is whether the 'new politics' of 'New' Labour constitutes a new form of social democracy (Giddens 1998), or is a neo-liberal politics which is essentially a continuation of the Thatcherite 'new right' (*Marxism Today* 1998).

Given that political and governmental processes are substantively linguistic processes, there is a clear general rationale for using the resources of language and discourse analysis in researching politics and government. However, the case is even stronger for New Labour, not only because there has been an unprecedented focus on questions of language both within the government itself and among those who have commented on it, but also because the 'reinvention' of government (Perri 6 1997, 1998) seems to entail a relative 'turn to discourse' in the way government is conducted. In particular, a move towards a more 'networked' form of governing involving what New Labour calls 'partnerships' with for instance business and the voluntary sector (as opposed to a hierarchical-bureaucratic form of governing) means that government becomes more 'dispersed' among agencies whose activities cannot be directly overlooked from the centre (though the shift towards such networking is in tension and contradiction with New Labour's drive for strong central control). The emphasis consequently shifts to government interventions to change 'cultures' ('cultural governance'). For example, the government is intent on introducing 'customer-focused services' in welfare and public services, treating the public as customers and consumers. Changing the 'culture' of government agencies in that direction is very much a matter of changing the language, getting staff to adopt and internalise a new language (e.g., renaming claimants as 'customers'). At the same time, the government is giving unprecedented attention to how its policies and actions are represented in the media, to putting an advantageous media 'spin' on everything it does, and therefore to carefully designing its language (Fairclough 2000b).

4 Texts and social practices

My objective in this section is to work with the logic of a theory of social practice in order to specify theoretical categories for the social analysis of texts (*text, texture, genre, discourse, style, intertextuality, order of discourse*), and to show how the theoretical framework which emerges from this can be used in a textually oriented political analysis of New Labour.

4.1 Social practices

The analysis of social practices constitutes a theoretically coherent and methodologically effective focus for social scientific research (Bhaskar 1986, Bourdieu and Wacquant 1992, Archer 1995, Chouliaraki and Fairclough 1999). The great strength of the concept of practice is that it allows analysis of social structures to be brought into connection with analysis of social (inter)action – see further below.

All social practices involve forms of work, identification, that is the construction of social identities, and representations of the social world (this is a reworking of Mouzelis (1990) – see also Chouliaraki and Fairclough (1999)). All social practices are practices of production – work. In claiming that all social practices are work, the aim is not economic reductionism, but on the contrary to insist that people collaboratively produce their social lives in all domains of life, so that economic production is only one special form of social production. All social practices can be characterised in terms of the materials they work on, and the means of production available (techniques, methods, theories), and the social relations within which they produce (Althusser and Balibar 1970: 41). Furthermore, all practices involve identification, the construction of social identities – every practice is associated with particular 'positions' for people (Bhaskar (1986) refers to the 'positions-and-practices system') in terms of which their identities and social relations are specified.

However, there are different 'performances' in these positions depending on the social (class, gender, ethnicity, etc.) memberships and life histories of those who occupy them (Archer 1995), and different identities attach to different performances. Finally, people also produce representations of the social world, including representations of themselves and their productive activities – people never simply act, their representations of their actions and domains of action are an inherent part of action, action is reflexive. Different representations tend to be produced from different positions.

4.2 Texts – the dialectics of discourse

A social practice as a practice of production brings together different elements of life into a specific local relationship – types of activity, spatial and temporal locations, material resources, persons with particular experiences, knowledges and wants, semiotic resources including language. We can roughly distinguish four major categories of elements: physical elements, sociological elements, cultural and psychological elements, and text (or 'discourse' as an abstract noun). I understand 'text' in a broad sense, including spoken as well as written language, and combinations of language with other forms of semiosis including gesture and visual images. In that these diverse elements are brought together to constitute a practice, we can call them 'moments' of that practice (Harvey 1996). A focus of analysis is on processes of 'articulation' (Laclau and Mouffe 1985) – on how elements are brought together as moments within practices, which may achieve stabilisation as relative permanencies, but may also be disarticulated. In being articulated together within a practice, elements are transformed. The moments of a practice are in a dialectical relationship – each moment 'internalises' the others without being reducible to any of them (Harvey 1996). It is in this sense that text is physical activity, is power, is knowledge and desire, etc., yet at the same time something different from all of them. Each of the four categories of elements contributes its own distinctive generative powers to the production of social life, though the generative powers of each works through the mediation of the generative powers of the others. From this 'critical realist' perspective (Bhaskar 1986, Collier 1994, Archer 1995) it is relevant to ask, what is the distinctive generative power of text? The question of how texts figure in social practices, how in specific terms they are dialectically related to other moments, has to be answered empirically practice by practice, and for each of the three major aspects of practices distinguished above (work, identification, representation).

What is the distinctive generative power of text? What in Hasan's terms is the 'semologic' (Hasan 2000)? It is the power to socially produce, i.e., to work, in its textual moment; the power to produce texts. I shall refer to this as 'texturing', adapting the term 'texture' from Systemic Functional Linguistics (Halliday and Hasan 1976). So the production of social life in social practices is partly the production of texts. The creativity of texturing as a mode of social production consists in generating new meanings through generating new combinations of elements of semiotic systems (including new 'wordings'). Any difference of wording entails a difference of meaning, though the nature of that difference is a matter for social negotiation and renegotiation as wordings are repeated in shifting contexts (Derrida 1978, Hasan 2000). Is the generative power of text attributable purely to properties of language and other semiotic systems? Language and other semiotic systems are open systems with an unlimited capacity to make meaning through generating syntagmatic and paradigmatic connections. Yet there is also a social structuring of semiotic diversity – the social order of discourse (see below) – which limits the generative capacity of language and other semiotic systems by limiting the combinatorial possibilities of genres and discourses. What I am suggesting is that there is a double structuring of the semiotic, the structuring of semiotic systems and the structuring of orders of discourse, and that the specification of the generative power of text needs to be in terms of both.

4.3 Genres, styles and discourses

I shall give a specific interpretation to the categories of genre, discourse, and style in terms of the theoretical framework above.

For any particular practice, the question of genre is the question of how texts figure (in relation to other moments) within work, the production of social life, and therefore within the social interaction that constitutes work. Different genres are different means of production of a specifically textual sort, different resources for texturing. Social production, i.e., work, both produces social life and reproduces social life; it is simultaneously creative and conservative. Our theorisation of genre must capture that; Bakhtin's (1986) theory of genre is indispensable in its subtle combination of the relative fixities of genres and their openness to new articulations.

The question of styles is the question of how text figures (in relation to other moments) in the identification of people involved in the practice (the construction of identities for them, and differences between them). Different styles attach to different identities.

The question of discourses is the question of how texts figure (in relation to other moments) in how people represent the world, including themselves and their productive activities. Different discourses are different ways of representing associated with different positions. They constitute different visions of, for instance, the field of government and the wider conjuncture of social fields it is a part of, and different classification (or di-visions) of that social world.

4.4 Field, order of discourse, intertextuality

There is one further important characteristic of social practices – they are organised into networks. Networks are more or less stable, more or less fluid. Networks articulate together different forms of work (social relations), different identifications, and different representations, corresponding to the different practices they combine. Practices are networked together within particular areas of social life which have a relative internal coherence and are relatively demarcated from others (for instance, politics, or education). Following Bourdieu, I shall call these 'fields' (Bourdieu and Wacquant 1992). Both the internal organisation of fields, and the way social life is divided between fields, are open to change. The social relations of fields are relations of power and struggle, in which the external boundaries and internal structure of the field are stakes. Since social practices are always networked within fields, analysis of the textual moment is always concerned with specifying how different genres, different discourses, and different styles are articulated together in particular sorts of relationships. We can use the term 'order of discourse' (Fairclough 1992a) to talk about fields as relative permanences specifically in terms of these articulations within the moment of text. The term 'intertextuality' (or 'interdiscursivity', Fairclough 1992a) can be used on the other hand to talk about shifting articulations of genres, discourses and styles in specific texts.

4.5 Structure and action

'Men (sic) make their own history, but not of their own free will; not under circumstances they themselves have chosen but under the given and inherited circumstances with which they are directly confronted' (Marx 1973). A preoccupation in recent social theory has been how to overcome the unproductive divide between theories of structure and theories of action, though the quotation from Marx above symbolises a long tradition of dialectical thinking about structure/action. Theorisations and analyses oriented only to structure are incomplete because structure as well as being the precondition for action is the outcome of action, is transformed in action. This is what Bhaskar (after Giddens) calls the 'duality of structure' (Bhaskar 1986). Theorisations and analyses oriented only to action are incomplete, because action not only produces social life, it also reproduces structures which are its precondition. This is what Bhaskar calls the 'duality of praxis'. Social science should include theories and analyses of both structure and action, and of their interconnection. Social analysis based upon social practices and positions constitutes a theoretically coherent and methodologically effective focus for social research precisely because it allows structure and action to be brought into connection (Bhaskar 1986). On the structural side, positions within practices are pregiven 'slots' in which people have to act, and the position–practice system has a relative durability over time. But, on the action side, although positions are defined abstractly for collective actors, they are occupied by individuals who belong to diverse categories of social agent (working class, middle class; women, men; black, white; and so forth), and who have an individual sense of self (Archer 1995). The dynamics of the social and individual relations played out in practices transcend and transform the position–practice system.[2]

Analysis of the textual moment of social practices mediates between the perspective of action, that is the specificity of the particular text, its specific forms of intertextuality, and the perspective of structure, i.e., the order of discourse. The order of discourse is seen as both a precondition for and constraint on textual action, texturing as a mode of work, and an effect of textual action, both reproduced and transformed through textual action. The categories of genre, style and discourse are understood in a way which facilitates movement between the perspectives of structure and action. They are categories both of the order of discourse and of the text. Genres, styles and discourses are on the one hand relatively permanent elements of orders of discourse, and on the other hand instantaneously and shiftingly constituted in specific texts in ways which may to a greater or lesser degree reproduce or transform the permanences of orders of discourse. Those who favour neatness may regard this tension within the categories as simply confusing, but it is essential to a dialectical movement between the perspectives of structure and action in the analysis of texts and discourse.

4.6 New Labour, government and text

The field of government can be seen from the perspective of this paper as a network of social practices, which changes over time and varies from place to place. Therefore, to characterise the field of government in a particular time and place, one needs to look at how exactly practices are networked together. Part of that exercise is looking at the textual moment of the field, at how different genres, discourses and styles are articulated together within its order of discourse. Some changes in practices and orders of discourse can be identified with specific governments, others are longer term. Although the specific network of practices under New Labour is distinctive, some of its features are longer term and apparent, for instance in the Conservative governments which preceded it.

The 'reinvention of government' (Perri 6 1997, 1998) under New Labour involves shifts in the field of government. We can think of this as shifts between the field of government and other related fields which transform the field of government itself – the 'inside' of government is transformed through transformations in its relationship to the 'outside'. This involves shifts in the relationship between the fields of government, politics, media, market research, business, voluntary work, and so forth. Shifts in these relationships are internalised as a new conjuncture of practices constituting the field of government itself (the field of government selectively 'takes in', recontextualises (Bernstein 1990, 1996), practices of politics, media, market research and so forth). For instance, the state becomes 'managerial', incorporating business management practices into government (Clarke and Newman 1997). This applies also for the textual moment: government under New Labour is a new order of discourse, a new articulation of genres, discourses and styles. Althusser and Balibar (1970) characterise practices of production in terms of the sort of 'effects' they produce. The work of government produces social effects (new social practices and conjunctures of practices) through producing political effects (groupings and alliances of people around/behind desired social effects). Part of the analysis of a particular form of government is specifying the genres of government, the textual means of governing and producing the effects of government.

New Labour has meant changes in the genres of government, including changes in which genres are articulated together and how they are articulated together, for instance, 'focus group' discussion has been incorporated into the array of genres, and articulated with more mainstream genres through the mediation of research reports and press releases which 'translate' focus group discussions into forms which can then be incorporated into, say, official documents. Or again, media genres such as the press release or newspaper feature article have taken on a more prominent role among the genres of government and come in a sense to dominate mainstream governmental genres (Franklin 1998). At the same time, the adoption of more 'managerial' practices in government means that mainstream genres such as consultation documents (so-called 'Green Papers') have also changed (see below). In broad terms, New Labour has accentuated the longer-term shift towards achieving the effects of government through managerial rather than political means. This means that, in terms of the textual moment, the political discourse of New Labour is a promotional discourse, which avoids and excludes political dialogue.

Another part of the analysis is the specification of the range and distribution of political discourses and their relationship to positions within the political field. New Labour has had a radical impact on political discourse through the discourse of the 'Third Way', which has appropriated much of the Conservative discourse of Thatcherism (and is in that sense 'post-Thatcherite' (Driver and Martell 1998)) which it has combined into a new mix with elements of communitarian and social democratic discourses, leaving the Conservative Party floundering in search of a distinctive political discourse of its own.

A third part of the analysis is specifying the distribution of political styles, and how they figure in the constitution of identities and differences. These include the identities of parties, tendencies and individuals. New Labour has (especially through the person of Tony Blair) achieved a dominant political style, a textual construction of an identity which is effective in conveying its mix of values (youthfulness, compassion, toughness, etc.) and capturing the cultural mood. (I am writing in the northern hemisphere spring of 1999 – this might, of course, change.)

5   New Labour welfare 'reform': the textual moment

I focus now on analysis of the textual moment of a specific aspect of New Labour in government, the 'reform' of social welfare. I shall pursue the theme of working in a transdisciplinary way by drawing upon other theoretical logics in addition to the theorisation of social practice – specifically, Bernstein's sociological theory of the field of pedagogy (1990, 1996), and Laclau and Mouffe's theorisation of hegemonic struggle (1985).

5.1   'Reform' of social welfare

One of the major commitments of the 'New' Labour government is the 'reform' of the welfare state. I use scare quotes for 'reform' to indicate that it is a contentious representation of what the government is doing – for instance, in the words of an *Observer* editorial (14 February 1999) an 'anodyne' term which represents as 'neutral, technological and essentially benign' what can otherwise be represented as 'the salami slicing of welfare benefits' and 'the rebasing of the welfare state around means-testing rather than universalism and income redistribution'. The government argues that 'reform' is necessary because the system is increasingly expensive yet ineffective in relieving poverty and 'tackling' social exclusion, and encourages a 'dependence' on welfare among people who could work. Welfare state reform in Britain is in many ways analogous to reforms underway elsewhere – the US shift from welfare to 'workfare' for instance is widely recognised as having been a model for New Labour, and there are similar attempts at reform in other EU countries. But international 'neo-liberal' tendencies to reduce welfare provision do not preclude national specificity: Clarke and Newman (1997, 1998) argue that the post-war British welfare state was part of specific social and organisational 'settlements' which have been 'unsettled' by radical social change (e.g., in gender relations).

Welfare reform is a major process which is likely to extend over several years. I shall focus on just one point in that process, the publication of the so-called 'Green Paper' on welfare reform. A Green Paper in the British system is a consultative document in which the government sets out options and its own position and solicits public discussion. It is a preliminary to legislation. The welfare Green Paper (entitled 'New Ambitions for Our Country: A New Contract for Welfare') was published in March 1998. This particular point in the reform process itself involves a network of practices, and in its textual moment a network of genres, discourses and styles.

5.2 Generic chaining

The production of effects within the field of government depends upon the constituent practices articulated together (networked) within it being 'chained' together in particular ways. For instance, there are two practices whose positioning in these chains seems to be regarded by commentators as distinctive for government under New Labour. The first is 'experiments in democracy' (Giddens 1998) such as using focus groups and citizens' juries (e.g., the 'People's Panel'). One view of the function of such experiments is in testing reactions to government initiatives as part of a wider strategy for managing consent. The strategic location of these legitimising exercises in the chaining of practices is important. So too is the location of enhanced forms of media management which have been critically referred to as 'government by media "spin"' (Franklin 1998), which can be seen as part of the shift towards 'cultural governance' (which entails a preoccupation with representations and the control of representations). One feature of New Labour noted by commentators such as Franklin is that every move by government appears to come with a prepared media strategy, implying a chain structure punctuated by media-oriented practices.

One aspect of texturing as work (social production) in a textual mode is the arrangement of genres in what we can call 'generic chains' as part of the chaining of practices, i.e., the regular sequential ordering of different genres. We find generic chains of the following general form in the welfare reform process: . . . speech <press release> – (media reports) – document <press release> – (media reports) – speech <press release> . . . That is, a document such as the Green Paper on welfare reform is likely to be prepared for and followed up by speeches on the part of important ministers, but each of these (like the document itself) comes with its own press release (systematically incorporating a media 'spin' – see below on this term), and each subsequent move in the chain is responsive to media reactions to earlier moves. Practices such as focus groups may be inserted into such chains through research reports which also come with press releases attached. On occasion press conferences will also figure in such chains.

The press release for the Green Paper on welfare reform is reproduced in Appendix 1 (see pages 193–6). I shall begin the analysis of it here, but go into more detail in Section 5.6. This is a 'boundary' genre which links the fields of government and media, and it is apparently a combination of two genres: a media genre – a press report, with the familiar beginning of headline + lead; and a governmental (administrative) genre or rather sub-genre (i.e., occurring as part of other genres) – a set of background notes. The latter also hybridises the former: the date and reference number between the headline and lead paragraph. The 'report' is also a resource for producing reports, and the latter part of it consists of important elements of that resource – key principles of the Green Paper, key quotes from Field and Blair. It is in a sense an official summary, but a summary which selects and orders what it summarises with a partly promotional intent. In this respect too the 'report' hybridises media and governmental genres. It is a sort of 'transitional' genre. In sum, the hybridity of the press release as a genre arises from its positioning in generic chains.

The process of summarising is crucially important not only in press releases but throughout the practices of government. The Green Paper itself includes its own internal summaries – the first chapter is a summary of the whole document; there is a summary of the main points in the last chapter; the Prime Minister's Foreword incorporates his summary; the press release constitutes a summary oriented to media uptake, and the document is then summarised over and over again in speeches. It is through summarising that media 'spin' is added. By media 'spin' I mean a particular representation of an event or series of events (including a speech or a document) designed to manage the way they are perceived by the public. Differences in summaries are also significant in the negotiation and contestation of political differences within the government as well as between the government and other parties and interested groups and organisations. Summarising is a form of representation and is linked to the question of discourses – the different summaries referred to above involve differences in discourses.

5.3 Recontextualisation

Summarising can also be seen as an aspect of what Bernstein calls 'recontextualisation' (1990, 1996). Every practice (and every network of social practices – every field) recontextualises other social practices according to principles which are specific to that practice/field, which derive from the particular form of social production (work) associated with that practice/field. For instance, the press release is a practice which here recontextualises according to its own particular logic two other practices: a press conference held by Frank Field to launch the Green paper, and the documentary practice of the Green Paper itself (also Blair's Foreword as a distinct genre or perhaps sub-genre within that practice). Practices in being recontextualised are so to speak uprooted, torn from their own social circumstances, and they appear in the recontextualised form of discourses.[3]

The concept of recontextualisation draws attention to the link between production (work) and representation: the way other practices are represented depends on the work that is going on, as well as different positions occupied by people who are involved in the work. Using the concept of recontextualisation to think about the textual moment draws attention to links between genres (ways of working in the textual mode) and discourses (textual representations). It points to processual ways of analysing texts, which see representation as an ongoing process within the social dynamics and struggles of work. This entails a close link between analysis of genres and analysis of discourses (and indeed analysis of styles). But in order to move in this direction we need to look elsewhere for a perspective and categories which will allow us to operationalise a processual view of representation. I suggest we can find them in the political theory of Laclau and Mouffe (1985). But further categories of Bernstein's are needed to make that connection: the categories of 'framing' and 'classification'. Thinking with these categories is a way of socially enriching the text-analytical categories of 'genre' and 'discourse'.

5.4 Genre and framing

'Framing' in Bernstein's theory is a matter of control – in the terms I have been using, the control and regulation of work, i.e., of social production, and therefore of the action and interaction which constitute work. Framing according to Bernstein is either 'strong' (where control is one-sided) or 'weak' (where control is shared). I want to suggest, following Chouliaraki (1998), that it is productive to think of genres as devices for framing, i.e., as means for controlling work in a textual mode. Framing is a matter of both properties of individual genres and the chaining of genres. In the case of welfare reform, the chaining of genres constitutes a strong 'framing' of its process of production, i.e., one facet of the powerful one-sided control and management of the process of achieving political consent by the government. I shall focus in this section on one chapter of the Green Paper itself (Chapter 3, 'The importance of work'), returning to the press release in Section 5.6. Readers will find the first 14 paragraphs of the chapter (there are 40 in all) in Appendix 2 (see pages 196–200).

The Green Paper consists of a (signed) Preface by the Prime Minister, Tony Blair, followed by a Summary of the whole document, Chapter 1, which sets out the case for welfare reform, Chapter 2, which identifies four 'ages' of welfare, and eight 'key principles' of welfare reform which constitute the topics of Chapters 3–10. Chapter 11 is about the longer-term future of welfare, and there is an Appendix on the evolution of social security.

I have already suggested that the political effects of government in the production of consent are sought by New Labour not through political dialogue but through management and promotion, despite representations of the welfare reform process which suggest otherwise (e.g., 'It is vital that reform is informed by a full debate on the proposed framework', Summary chapter, paragraph 31). The framing of this promotional practice of governance is strong; that is, the government tightly and unilaterally controls the process. Referring specifically to the Green Paper, it is characterised by a strongly framed promotional genre.

Each of the central chapters (3–10) is structured as follows: a chapter title ('The importance of work' in the case of Chapter 3) below which there is a coloured box containing one of the eight 'principles' of the proposed welfare reform. In this case 'Principle 1': *The new welfare state should help and encourage people of working age to work where they are capable of doing so.* There is then an unheaded introductory section focusing on past and present welfare practices, and the case for reform (paragraphs 1–5); a section headed 'Policy Direction' taking up the bulk of the chapter (paragraphs 6–40) setting out proposed future welfare practices; and under the heading 'Measures for Success' a short list of criteria against which the success of the proposed reforms will be judged (end of paragraph 40). Each of the chapters tells readers what the case is for welfare reform but above all what the government has done, is doing and intends or aims to do in the way of welfare reform.

In these accounts, welfare reform is represented as a managerial process of problem-solving, finding solutions to obstacles in the way of the objectives formulated in the eight 'principles', with the problem-solver represented as virtually exclusively the government itself. Specifically in this chapter: work is the means of averting poverty and welfare dependency, but there are obstacles to people working, so the government will take certain steps to facilitate work. This argumentative structure is repeated in places within the central 'Policy Direction' part of the chapter, though its focus is heavily on the 'solutions' (the predominant type of clause has an actional process with the government as agent – what the government has done, is doing, or will do). Representing welfare reform as managerial problem-solving and structuring these central chapters of the document in terms of problem-solving is part of what makes the genre promotional: the government's policies are sold as merely technical solutions to an agreed problem.

Although in the nature of things there are many unanswered questions at this consultative stage in the reform process, no questions are asked:[4] the grammatical mood is declarative. The potential for questions is indicated by their marginal presence at the end of the Summary chapter where the reform process is constructed as debate:

> it is also vital that reform is informed by full debate on the proposed frame-work. We are consulting widely on the content of this Green Paper and we want your views. For instance, how can we best deliver on our guiding principles? Are there ways in which the policy direction can be improved? Are our tracking measurements for success right?

Statements are categorical assertions – again, although in the nature of things there are uncertainties about what has happened or what is the case and hesitations about what should be done, there are no 'maybes' here. The government is constructed as in full and solitary control. The simulation of certainty and being in control are part of the representation of welfare reform as problem-solving and part of the promotional rhetoric of the document.

Moreover, there is a slippage between the process of consultation over proposed welfare reform and the process of implementation, between consultation document, planning document, and publicity document. This is evident in the use of coloured boxes (eight in all) in the chapter. These boxes contain bullet points or in one case numbered points, with or without headings. Such boxes are widely used in planning documents. The clearest example of this sort of use is at the end of the chapter, the 'Success Measures': there is no discussion of 'success measures' as part of welfare reform, just a list of four measures, as if this were itself a planning instrument in the implementation of welfare reform. Such boxes are also widely used in publicity. The document oscillates between describing the proposed welfare reform, and publicising it, as it might publicise particular schemes to claimants in implementing the welfare reform. Welfare reform is not simply represented as problem-solving in the document (which would be a matter of what discourse is drawn upon), is enacted as problem-solving – there is an ambivalence of genre.

These boxes figure as a structuring device: they mark and signal to readers careful authorial planning of and tight control over the text and texturing. They are a resource for strong framing, strong unilateral control by the writer (the government) over the texturing. For instance, the box in paragraph 5 lists in their sequential order the main sections of the 'Policy Direction' part of the chapter which takes up 35 of its 40 paragraphs. The boxes also figure as a pedagogical device, directing the reader to the main points and the main structures of the projected new world of welfare. These are 'reader-friendly' but also thereby reader-directive features, which construct the social relations of the document as asymmetrical relations not only between the one who tells and the one who is told but also more specifically between teacher and learner, with strong classification (insulation) between the two subject positions (see Section 5.5). The many section headings work in a similar way.

There is an oscillation between informing and persuading ('telling' and 'selling') throughout the document – correspondingly between the social relations of 'telling' constructed in the pedagogical way referred to above, and the social relations of 'selling' (relations between the one who sells (persuades) and the one who potentially buys (accepts)). Take paragraphs 5–7 as an example. One aspect of this oscillation is the shift between third person ('the government', paragraph 5, the first and third sentences of paragraph 6, the second sentence of paragraph 7) and first person ('we', the second sentence of paragraph 6 – notice the explicit commitment to changing culture, 'cultural governance', the first sentence of paragraph 7). This oscillation between 'the government' and 'we' occurs throughout the document in the 'solutions' part of the problem–solution structure. Notice that 'we' is open to an ambivalence which is an aspect of the promotional character of the genre; for instance, is the 'we' of 'our ambition' in paragraph 6 the government, or the Labour Party? and more generally, is the Green Paper government report or party 'propaganda'? Another aspect of the oscillation between informing and persuading is the shift in explicitness of evaluation. The two sentences with first person are also the two most explicitly evaluative – the first including the noun 'ambition' which has a marked positive evaluation in contrast with 'aim' (which occurs here twice as a verb), and 'nothing less than'; the second including several words/expressions which are positively (first two) or negatively (second two) evaluative in this context: 'comprehensive', 'break the mould', 'old', 'passive'.

Bourdieu
Ref 7 'symbolic
violence'

5.5 *Discourse and classification*

I referred earlier to different discourses constituting different visions (representations) of the social world which are also classifiications or divisions. If genres are framing in its textual mode, i.e., forms of control, discourses are classification in its textual mode, i.e., forms of power. Discourses are forms of what Bourdieu calls 'symbolic violence' (Bourdieu 1991). Discourses classify people, things, places, events etc. – and indeed other discourses. The central question is what sort of boundaries and 'insulations' (Bernstein 1990) are set up between discourses. The recontextualisation of practices as I said earlier transforms them into discourses, and imposes upon them classifications and divisions, variably according to different positions in the recontextualing practice. Classification may be strong or weak (Bernstein 1990) – entities may be sharply or loosely divided, strongly or weakly insulated from each other.

The Green Paper selectively recontextualises social practices to constitute a discourse of social welfare, a vision of the world of welfare. The first division, classification, is between what is included and what is excluded – the analysis of discourses has to attend to absences as well as presences. For instance, the population of the world of welfare in this discourse of social welfare is a sparse one, consisting essentially of the government and welfare claimants. Welfare staff figure in a very few instances, and a claimant organisation ('lone parent organisations') only once in this chapter – claimant and campaign organisations are rare in the document as a whole. On the other hand, welfare professionals such as doctors are simply absent.

The second division is among the entities (persons, things, events, discourses etc.) which are included. This 'internal' classification is strong – in the case of persons included within the world of welfare, the government and welfare claimants are strongly divided, insulated from each other. Overwhelmingly, the agent in actional processes is the government – 'the government', 'we', or a government initiative such as one of the 'New Deals'. Overwhelmingly, claimants figure as goals or beneficiaries in actional processes. The government acts, claimants are acted upon. Welfare staff rarely act, welfare professionals never, and claimants generally only where their actions are initiated/managed by the government (e.g., in paragraph 9: it aims to help young unemployed people . . . to find jobs). The dominance of the government over the process of welfare reform enacted in the strong framing is in a sense repeated in the strong classification, the exclusive agency of the government in the represented world of welfare.

Claimants (and staff) do, however, figure if only marginally in another participant role: as agents in verbal processes and experiencers in mental processes, mainly in paragraph 14. There is also a scatter of other examples elsewhere in the chapter where claimants are subjects of mental process verbs (e.g., 'the vast majority of single parents want to work', 'some people feel forced to give up their job'). These can be seen as recontextualisations of what people say in other practices; they take the form of reports of particular things people have said or thought (i.e., they are 'reported speech' and 'reported thought'). In the reporting of speech, the practice that is being recontextualised is sometimes explicitly identified, and sometimes not. Here it is not, but it is evident that the practice is market research (opinion polls, surveys, perhaps focus groups) – that is the only practice reported in terms of what claimants (and staff) say or think. Notice in particular the way in which thought is reported, e.g., in 'the vast majority of single parents want to work': not only is the practice where these 'wants' were expressed unspecified, so also is who precisely expressed them (possible alternative: 'in a poll of single parent opinion, the vast majority of those asked said they wanted to work'). The government speaks for these people. Part of the classification which divides the government from claimants is that the latter do not act (without government management) but do react (verbally, mentally), though both the ways in which they react and how reactions are represented are controlled by government (van Leeuwen 1995). One might say that this 'reinvented' form of government includes market research as a technology for legitimising the government speaking for the public. Apart from these examples, what others (including relevant others such as welfare professionals, claimant groups) say is not reported. The Green Paper is monological, univocal, dominated by the voice of the government and excluding other voices.

The government's welfare reform policy is summed up as 'welfare to work', getting people off welfare and into work, so the practice of work is heavily but again very selectively recontextualised. A key issue is what is seen as included within the practice of work – what 'work' is. Work is overwhelmingly constructed in the document as 'jobs' in the traditional sense – relatively stable and regular work providing enough to live on. The fact that an increasing proportion of work is casual, part-time, and poorly paid, is not focused upon in the document. Nor is the question of whether, for example, women's work in households counts as 'work'. Recent debate over what should count as 'work' does not figure – whether e.g., governments should deliberately stimulate the 'third' (e.g., voluntary) sector and legitimise it as 'work' (Giddens 1998). This is an aspect of the first division, between what is included and what is excluded: these other discourses of work are not explicitly included, though they do have an implicit presence.

For the most part, the word 'work' is used without modification to mean 'jobs' in the sense above. However, there is a shift to the expression 'paid work' twice in the document, once in paragraph 1 of Chapter 3. Why this shift? It is significant that it occurs here, at the beginning of the chapter dealing centrally with work. The shift is informationally backgrounded – 'paid work' in sentence 3 is the unmarked theme and is thus constructed as simply a repetition of 'work' in sentence 1. There is no explicit contrast between paid and other sorts of work. Nevertheless, the shift does implicitly signal a contrast – the specification of 'work' as 'paid work' is an implicit acknowledgement that there are other understandings (and discourses) of work. There is also a trace of an alternative discourse of 'work' later in the chapter in Paragraph 9 which is the only such case in the document. A list of 'opportunities' for young unemployed people includes: 'work with an employer who will receive a job subsidy', 'work with a voluntary sector organisation', and 'work on the Environmental Taskforce'. Only the first is a 'job' in the usual sense. On the other hand, when the document refers to what parents do in caring for children, it does not refer to that activity as 'work'. As with reported speech so with discourses, an important variable is whether they are attributed (to voices) and located (in practices). What we have here is a covert recontextualisation of what people say about work in other practices (not of specific things they say – not reported speech as above – but more abstractly of their discourse) which neither attributes nor locates this discourse.

The Green Paper is cut off from debates over the nature and future of work, through strong classification which is manifested in the exclusion of relevant other voices, and in the dominance of one discourse of work over an alternative which is only covert. Yet one might think that these debates are crucial for a policy which depends entirely on moving people from welfare into work, given that the number of 'jobs' in the traditional sense is shrinking. Without some fundamental rethinking of the nature of work, the policy looks at best incoherent, at worst dishonest.

By contrast with the representation of work, there is a diversity of discourses in the representation of the social relations of welfare within the document, and that diversity is evident to a degree in the introductory section of this chapter, specifically in paragraph 5, which includes the following representations of the practices of the new world of welfare: 'promote work', 'help people move from welfare to work' (and in Principle 1, 'help and encourage people to work'), 'develop flexible . . . services', 'responsibilities and rights are fairly matched'. The construction of the social relations of welfare as 'helping' relations has been central to the British welfare state, but 'helping' is mainly focused in this document on getting people off welfare and into work.

'Promoting' and 'developing flexible . . . services' by contrast belong to a managerial discourse, and the former connotes cultural intervention. There is also legal/contractual discourse in 'responsibilities and rights'. But the main feature of the construction of the social relations of welfare is the mixture of bureaucratic/professional welfare discourse ('helping' etc.) and managerial/cultural ('promoting' etc.), with the latter predominant. An example of the latter is in paragraph 21 of Chapter 3: 'personalised', 'flexible' services are 'delivered', through a single 'gateway' for 'customers' by 'personal advisers' who develop 'tailor-made action plans' for individuals. There is a new discourse here which 'relexicalises' (Fowler, Hodge, Kress and Trew 1979) welfare services. Cultural effects can be achieved in so far as the government can win acceptance for such shifts in discourse and the new identities and values they entail. In so far as this document represents (as it is claimed to) a 'third way' between traditional social democracy and neo-liberalism, it would seem to lie in this discoursal diversity in the recontextualisation of (the social relations of) the new world of welfare – a point at which the classification and division between subjects is relatively open.

5.6 Equivalence and difference

If we use Bernstein's categories of framing and classification to think about genre and discourse, we can analyse the Green Paper as simultaneously regulating the work and social relations of government, and representing the world of welfare (producing a vision of that world through division). But we still need a way of showing how regulation and representation are bound together in the process of texturing; that is, we still need a way of analysing representation processually. Classifications are not simply imposed through the generic framing of interaction, they are ongoingly produced but also subverted in the course of interaction.

We can draw upon the political theory of Laclau and Mouffe (1985) to find a way of theorising and operationalising this perspective. They theorise the political process (and 'hegemony') in terms of the simultaneous working of two different 'logics', a logic of 'difference' which creates differences and divisions, and a logic of 'equivalence' which subverts existing differences and divisions. I want to suggest first that this can usefully be seen as a general characterisation of social processes of classification: people in all social practices are continuously dividing and combining – producing (also reproducing) and subverting divisions and differences. Social practice, as Laclau and Mouffe suggest, is an ongoing work of articulation and disarticulation. My second suggestion is that this can be applied specifically to the textual moment of social practices. Elements (words, phrases etc.) are constantly being combined and divided in texts; prior combinations and separations are constantly being subverted. The point that texts are constantly combining some elements and dividing others is a rather obvious one. But what I am suggesting is that we see these processes as part of the textual moment of the social process of classification, and that by doing so we can see the integration of that textual process with the textual work of controlling and regulating social relations and interactions. That is, we can see the integration of discourses with genres.

It is easier within the limits of an article to show this process in a short text than in a long one, so I shall refer again to the Green Paper press release (Appendix 1). The press release is a recontextualisation of a press conference given by Frank Field and of the Green Paper itself including the Prime Minister's foreword. It is a recontextualisation which is shaped by the genre of the press release, the work it is doing (the effects it is trying to produce) and the way the work is regulated and controlled.

As I said in Section 5.2, the press release is a combination of two genres, 'report' and background notes. I am only concerned here with the former. The headline and lead (which I take to include the first three paragraphs – i.e., sections separated by spaces) give a summary of the Green Paper and press conference which is elaborated in the rest of the 'report'. The logic of the report genre is an additive and elaborative one favouring repetition and expansion. The 'report' is also a promotion, and the summary in the headline and lead also incorporates a particular 'spin' which needs to be subsequently sustained and developed. The direct reproduction of the eight 'principles' which constitute the Green Paper's self-summary falls outside these reporting and promotional logics – the press release is also a sort of official summary which is expected to give the 'complete picture'.

Turning to discourse and classification, the headline and lead selectively focus certain aspects of the vision of the 'reformed' world of welfare in the Green Paper: the reform as a 'contract', 'promoting opportunity instead of dependence', 'work for those who can, security for those who can't'. This selective focus constitutes the 'spin'. There is actually internal evidence of differences of position and focus between Field and Blair (Field takes a more ethical stance towards welfare reform, Blair sees it more in terms of a contract – see further below). There is also internal evidence in the press release of the selectivity of the focus – compare the eight principles with the rest of the report. For instance the construction of welfare as a 'contract' is not included in the principles, and is not prominent in the Green Paper until Chapter 11, which deals with the long-term future rather than the immediate reform. The section selected from Blair's foreword is the last four paragraphs which are the only ones in which he refers to the new welfare 'contract'. This focus is therefore a significant one, and it had an effect on media coverage of the Green Paper – several national newspapers, for instance, reproduced a table from Chapter 11 summarising the vision of a 'new welfare contract' for 2020 as if it were a summary of the proposed more immediate reform.

Let me come to division and combination – the logics of difference and equivalence. The second paragraph of the lead incorporates two divisions taken from the Green Paper – 'opportunity instead of dependence', and 'work for those who can, and security for those who can't'. The latter is a double division: the division between those who work and those who can't is mapped onto the division between 'work' and 'security', restricting by implication the social security offered by the welfare system to those who are unable to work. These divisions condense important features of the New Labour welfare 'reform': an acceptance of the New Right construction of welfare as morally objectionable in promoting 'welfare dependency', the commitment to 'equality of opportunity' as an alternative to 'welfare dependency', shifting the focus of welfare towards getting people off welfare and into work (which gives the division between those who can work and those who can't primacy over the division between those who have work and those who haven't).

These divisions are repeated and elaborated in the quotations from Field. The first paragraph of those quotations contains in addition to a repetition of 'work for those who can; security for those who cannot' a division between 'a cycle of dependency and insecurity' and 'an ethic of work and savings'. Although the various elements put together here can be found in the Green Paper, this particular division is Field's; it is 'spin' as creative elaboration, a process of representational work. It is combination as well as division: 'dependency' combined with 'insecurity', 'work' with 'savings'. The division is again a double one – 'dependency and insecurity' as against 'work and savings', but also 'cycle' as against 'ethic'. The latter seems somewhat incoherent. Field's specific position and difference from others within New Labour is evident both in the foregrounding of the ethical aspect of welfare 'reform' – which is present in the Green Paper, but marginal – and more subtly in the rewording of 'dependence' as 'dependency', which is a more direct evocation of the New Right theories of 'welfare dependency' referred to above and again foregrounds the moral dimension. The two instances of 'genuine' in the third and fourth paragraphs of the Field quotation also accentuate the moral dimension, and also show that division can be covert – 'those in genuine need' are covertly set off from those not in genuine need (those whose claimed needs are not genuine). The moral division between the deserving and undeserving poor is echoed here.

At the same time, the division between those who can and those who cannot work is elaborated and developed in the third and fourth paragraphs, into a division (among the disabled) between 'people who want to work' and 'those who cannot work', and 'those of working age' and 'those in genuine need who can't work'. The former hybridises two divisions, 'can/cannot' and 'want to/don't want to', formulating the shift in New Labour thinking from seeing work as an option for the disabled to expecting those who are able to work to do so. The latter generalises the category of those who can work to those of working age – the message is that if you are of working age you work unless you are too severely disabled to do so, a message which is underscored by the combination of 'work' and 'welfare' which subverts the division between them – 'work is the best form of welfare'.

Summing up the quotation from Field, the vision of welfare which is summarised in the divisions of paragraph two of the lead is further worked up through the divisions and combinations of the quoted material. This is a localised instance of how the politics of New Labour, the 'Third Way', is constantly in process as its elements are worked (textured) together in texts – in this case for instance in a way which foregrounds ethical and moral aspects of welfare 'reform'. The process of working up the discourse takes place according to the logic of the genre, involving in this case a movement from summarising gist in the headlines and lead, to repetition and elaboration in the rest of the 'report'. The genre is, of course, a relatively simple one, and the interplay between discourse/classification/division and genre/interaction/regulation is much more complex, for instance, in the Green Paper itself.

Differences of position and perspective between Field and other New Labour leaders which are well known and can be extensively documented elsewhere are also evident here. The ethical focus is Field's rather than Blair's – which does not mean that it is absent from Blair's political discourse, just that it is not worked into the same salience. Conversely, it is the Blair quotations which elaborate the construction of welfare as a 'contract' – though again it is also part of Field's political discourse. In the first paragraph of the Blair quotation there is a three-way division which sets the 'third way' against 'dismantling welfare' and 'keeping it unreformed', and constructs the former as a 'new contract between citizen and state', and in terms of a marked form of combination which is pervasive in New Labour discourse – the 'but also' relation.

I use this term for combinations which can be paraphrased with 'x but also y' (or 'not only x, y'). The example here is: 'we keep a welfare state from which we all benefit, but on terms which are fair and clear' (or: 'but we also make the terms fair and clear'). Other instances of the 'but also' relation are: '. . . the vast majority of us benefit . . . But we all contribute . . .', 'We benefit but we pay', 'fair not just for the existing generation, but fair between generations'. The pervasiveness of the 'but also' relation in New Labour is a part of the politics of the 'Third Way' – the 'Third Way' is all about transcending divisions, reconciling what had been seen as unreconcilable, combining themes from the 'old' left and 'new right'. There is a very prominent New Labour 'but also' relation which is alluded to here and most directly formulated in the lead as 'reciprocal duties between government and the individual' but interestingly not formulated in its usual form – 'rights and responsibilities'. By developing the focus on 'contract' through the 'but also' relation, Blair is linking it to the core logic of the politics of the 'Third Way'. Also, by combining universality ('we all benefit') with the everyday concept of 'fairness', and constructing the contract as a 'fair deal', Blair connects the 'reform' with everyday values and criticisms of the existing system (in terms of 'unfair' abuses of it). This everyday and one might say populist construction stands in contrast with the austere, theoretical, and moral construction of the lead: 'reciprocal duties between government and the individual' – one might see this as part of a difference in style between Field and Blair.

6 Conclusion

In addressing the question of sociolinguistic and social linguistic theory which I raised in the opening section, I have drawn upon several social theories in a transdisciplinary way, using them to think theoretically about language within the operational context of research on the political discourse of New Labour, trying to enhance the capacity of the particular area of social linguistics I have been concerned with (discourse analysis) to advance social theory in the direction of language. There are gains, I am suggesting, both for the social linguist and for the social theorist. The gains for the social linguist from thinking with theories of social practice are more explicit and coherent specifications of how the semiotic (language, discourse in the abstract sense, text) figures as an element of the social. What I have specifically argued is that there is a textual moment in any social practice, and that the textual moment has three facets for which we can use the categories of genre, discourse (as a count noun), and style. The category of intertextuality can be specified as the textual aspect of the articulatory character of social practice. Other categories such as dialect and register could also be grounded and differentiated in theorisations of social practice. I argued that theories of practice can be enhanced with theories of fields as networks of practices whose textual aspect is orders of discourse. I also argued that a socially grounded theorisation of texts as processes involving the interplay of genre and discourse (as a count noun) could be developed through thinking with the categories of recontextualisation, classification and framing, and the logics of difference and equivalence. What this gives is a way of specifying the process of texturing as work – the production of social life in its textual moment. My concern has been to discuss a particular way of working, in a transdisciplinary mode, and again this could be pushed in different directions, for instance towards the concern of many sociolinguists with linguistic constructions of identity.

The gains for the social theorist are in pushing social theory in the direction of language so that social research flows into language research rather than stopping (as so often) on the threshold of language.[5] These gains come from the incorporation of social theories into theorisations and eventually analyses of language so that the latter become more fruitful for social theorists to think, theorise and analyse with. The key issue is textual analysis, and the place of textual analysis in social research. The concept of 'texturing' claims that there is always a textual moment to the work, the production of social life, in any social practice, and this entails that textual analysis is an inescapable part of social analysis. The challenge for social linguists is to develop forms of textual analysis (including, of course, interactional analysis) which are socially compelling, and I am suggesting that the way to do this is by drawing social thought into our theorisation and analysis of texts.

APPENDIX 1   Frank Field launches new contract for welfare

Date: 26 March 1988
Ref: 98/077

Frank Field, Minister for Welfare Reform, today unveiled the Government's Green Paper on Welfare Reform 'New Ambitions for Our Country – A New Contract for Welfare'.

Mr Field said the Government's programme for welfare reform would promote opportunity instead of dependence, and would be based on work for those who can, and security for those who can't.

The Green Paper, for the first time, sets out a series of success measures to be achieved over the next 10–20 years. It presents a new welfare contract, based on reciprocal duties between government and the individual.

The Green Paper sets out eight key principles guiding welfare reform:

- The new welfare state should help and encourage people of working age to work where they are capable of doing so.
- The public and private sectors should work in partnership to ensure that wherever possible, people are insured against foreseeable risks, and make provision for their retirement.
- The new welfare state should provide public services of high quality to the whole community, as well as cash benefits.
- Those who are disabled should get the support they need to lead a fulfilling life with dignity.
- The system should support families and children as well as tackling the scourge of child poverty.
- There should be specific action to tackle social exclusion and help those in poverty.
- The system should encourage openness and honesty and the gateways to benefit should be clear and enforceable.
- The system of delivering modern welfare should be flexible, efficient and easy for people to use.

Mr Field said:

> This Green Paper has a central aim: work for those who can; security for those who cannot. We want to replace a cycle of dependency and insecurity with an ethic for work and savings.
>
> The document builds on the £3.5 billion New Deal for the young and long term unemployed and the Budget that made work pay, raised Child Benefit and put quality childcare within reach of all families. At the same time we are modernising and putting money into schools and hospitals and will soon have the first ever national minimum wage to help the low paid.
>
> The arguments for reform are clear, society has changed and the state has not kept pace with it. As such, spending on Social Security has doubled yet more people live in poverty and insecurity.
>
> The Green Paper offers pensioners a decent income in retirement and a new beginning for disabled people. Those disabled people who want to work will get help to do so, while those who cannot work will get genuine support.
>
> Work is the best form of Welfare. To those of working age we offer greater help to get into work, and a modern system to provide help for those in genuine need who can't work.

In a foreword to the Green Paper, the Prime Minister said:

> We must return to first principles and ask what we want the welfare state to achieve. This is the question this Green paper seeks to answer. In essence, it describes a third way: not dismantling welfare, leaving it simply as a low-grade safety net for the destitute; nor keeping it unreformed and under-performing; but reforming on the basis of a new contract between citizen and state, where we keep a welfare state from which we all benefit, but on terms that are fair and clear.
>
> There is a very simple reason why we need such a contract more than ever today. The welfare state we have is one from which the vast majority of us benefit through a state pension or Child Benefit or use of the NHS. The welfare state isn't just about a few benefits paid to the most needy.
>
> But we all contribute through taxes and charges. We benefit but we pay. It is a contract between us as citizens. As such, it needs to be a fair deal, within a system that is clearer, more relevant for the modern world, efficiently run and where costs are manageable. One that is fair not just for the existing generation, but fair between the generations.
>
> That is the fundamental reason for reform. It will take time. Frank Field has started the process in this Green Paper. Now that the process is underway, we want all the nation to be part of it. There will be consultation and time for discussion at every stage. Our objective is to build a genuine national consensus behind change. The welfare state belongs to us all. It is part of our inheritance. We must now all work together to re-build it for the new century that awaits.

Notes to editors

1. The Green paper *New ambitions for our country: A NEW CONTRACT FOR WELFARE* is available from Stationery Office bookshops. It is also available in Braille, audio cassette and in Welsh (Cmd 3805, price £11.50).
2. A summary version of the Green paper has also been produced and is available free of charge from the following address:

Welfare Reform
Freepost (HA4441)
Hayes
UB3 1BR
Tel: 0181 867 3201
Fax: 0181 867 3264

The lines are open Monday to Friday from 9am–5pm

3. Consultation

Feedback on the content of the Green Paper should be addressed to:

The Welfare Reform Green Paper Consultation Team
Department of Social Security
7th Floor, The Adelphi
1–11 John Adam Street
London WC2 6HT

People are also invited to respond using the following email address:
welfarereform@ade001.dss.gov.uk

Comments should reach DSS by 31 July 1998.

Press enquiries: 0171 238 0866
(Out of hours: 0171 238 0761)
Public enquiries: 01717 712 2171
Internet Address: http://www.dss.gov.uk

APPENDIX 2   Excerpt from Green Paper on welfare reform

Chapter Three   The importance of work

Principle 1

The new welfare state should help and encourage people of working age to work where they are capable of doing so.

1. The Government's aim is to rebuild the welfare state around work. The skills and energies of the workforce are the UK's biggest economic asset. And for both individuals and families, paid work is the most secure means of averting poverty and dependence except, of course, for those who are retired or so sick or disabled, or so heavily engaged in caring activities, that they cannot realistically support themselves.
2. For many people the absence of paid work is a guarantee of a life on low income. One of the reasons children make up a higher proportion of those at the bottom of the income distribution is that a growing number of parents, especially lone parents, are out of work. Paid work also allows people to save for their retirement.

3. For too long, governments have abandoned people to a life on benefits. Far too many individuals and families are penalised, or gain too little, if they move from benefit to work.

4. Chapter One described how work has changed over the last 50 years. The rewards for skills have grown, widening the wage gap. Some people reap the rewards of fairly paid work, while others are either stuck on benefit or switching between benefit dependency and short-term, low-skilled jobs. There has also been a shift in balance from full-time manual jobs to part-time and service-sector posts. In households with two working adults, the loss of a job for one can mean that the other would be better off giving up work too.

5. The Government aims to promote work by:

- **helping people move from welfare to work through the New Deals and Employment Zones;**
- **developing flexible personalised services to help people into work;**
- **lowering the barriers to work for those who can and want to work;**
- **making work pay, by reforming the tax and benefit system, including a Working Families Tax Credit, reforming National Insurance and income tax, and introducing the national minimum wage; and**
- **ensuring that responsibilities and rights are fairly matched.**

Policy direction

Welfare to Work – The New Deals

6. The Government's biggest investment since taking office has been in a large-scale welfare to work programme. Our ambition is nothing less than a change of culture among benefit claimants, employers and public servants – with rights and responsibilities on all sides. Those making the shift from welfare into work will be provided with positive assistance, not just a benefit payment.

7. Our comprehensive welfare to work programme aims to break the mould of the old, passive benefit system. It is centred on the five aspects of the New Deal for:

- **young unemployed people;**
- **long-term unemployed people;**
- **lone parents;**
- **people with a disability or long-term illness; and**
- **partners of the unemployed.**

8. Alongside these national programmes, we are also piloting targeted help for areas of high long-term unemployment through the new Employment Zones.

Young unemployed people

9. For young people, entering the labour market is a critical rite of passage to adulthood. One of the factors causing social exclusion is an unacceptably high level of youth unemployment. The New Deal for Young People is a radical step forward because it emphasises quality, choice and above all meeting the needs of individuals. It will address all the barriers to work that young people face, including homelessness and drug dependency. It aims to help young unemployed people, aged 18 to 24, to find jobs and remain in employment. In the Budget, the Chancellor also announced that partners of young unemployed people who have no children would be included in the New Deal, and given access to the same opportunities for work.

The New Deal for young people

- **Is being piloted in 12 pathfinder areas.**
- **Will go nationwide in April 1998.**
- **Is an investment of £2.6 billion.**
- **Will offer participants, aged 18 to 24, four opportunities:**

  - **work with an employer who will receive a job subsidy of up to £60 a week;**
  - **full-time education or training;**
  - **work with a voluntary sector organisation; or**
  - **work on the Environmental Taskforce.**

  All these options involve training.
- **Support will also be given to those young people who see self-employment as the best route out of benefit dependency.**
- **Includes a special £750 grant to employers to provide their New Deal employees with training towards a recognised qualification.**
- **For those who do not wish to take up offers of help there will be no 'fifth option' of simply remaining on benefit.**

10. Every young person who receives Jobseeker's Allowance (JSA) for six months without securing work will enter the New Deal Gateway – an exercise in promoting job-readiness and providing a tailor-made package

of help. People with particular disadvantages may enter earlier. For those with adequate skills and appropriate work experience – the 'job-ready' – the immediate focus will be on securing an unsubsidised job. For those young people less equipped to enter the job market, the Gateway will provide careers advice and guidance, assessment of training needs, work trials with employers and tasters of other options. This Gateway period may last for up to four months.

Long-term unemployed people

11. For those who lack skills and become unemployed, the risks of remaining out of work for a long period are high. So prevention is better than cure. The Government's plans for lifelong learning, described in Chapter Five, are designed to raise skills in the adult population and promote employability, so that people find it easier to get and keep jobs.

12. There is already a sizeable group of long-term unemployed people who may need additional help to overcome barriers to work. Employers are often sceptical of the job-readiness of a person who has been out of the labour market for long periods. And, over time, skills, confidence and health can deteriorate. The New Deal for the Long-Term Unemployed represents the first serious attack on the waste of talents and resources represented by long-term unemployment.

The New Deal for the long-term unemployed

- **Due to start in June 1998.**
- **Initial investment of £350 million.**
- **For those aged over 25 who have been out of work for more than two years.**
- **Substantial job subsidy of £75 a week for employers for six months.**
- **Changes to benefit rules to improve access to full-time education or training. Additional pilots are due to start in November 1998:**

  - **Pilots of an intensive approach for 70,000 people, providing individualised advice, counselling and help, which may include training and work experience, at a cost of £100 million.**
  - **Special assistance tailored to the needs of those aged over 50.**

Lone parents

13. The twin challenges of raising children alone and holding down a job are considerable. The vast majority of single parents want to work, to gain a

decent wage and a foothold on the ladder out of poverty. But the old welfare system did little to help, simply handing out benefits rather than offering active support in finding and securing work, training or childcare. The New Deal for Lone Parents will provide a more active service.

The New Deal for lone parents

- **Piloted in eight areas since July 1997, offering help to 40,000 lone parent households.**
- **Available nationwide to lone parents making a new or repeat claim for Income Support from April 1998.**
- **Available to all lone parents on Income Support from October 1998.**
- **The service is aimed at lone parents whose youngest child is at school, but is also available to those with pre-school children.**

14. There will be a full, independent evaluation of the first phase of the New Deal for Lone Parents, available in autumn 1999. Early indications are encouraging. Lone parent organisations, employers and lone parents themselves have all welcomed this New Deal, and the staff responsible for delivering the service have been particularly enthusiastic. The staff have welcomed the opportunity to become involved in providing practical help and advice. The first phase of this New Deal has aroused considerable interest: lone parents in other parts of the country are asking if they can join in.

Notes

1. In policy terms, the recent emphasis on the 'learning age', the need (especially the economic need) for 'lifelong learning', can be construed as a recognition of this (Department of Education and Employment1998).
2. With respect to the social dynamics, Bourdieu (Bourdieu and Wacquant 1992) gives a different account, in terms of the dual inscription of the social in places/institutions (fields and their positions) and in bodies (and habitus), and tensions between position and habitus as a source of transformation.
3. They appear in an 'imaginary' form according to Bernstein, and it is the transformation from real to imaginary, that is the space in which the play of ideology takes place. I do not develop the point here, but this strikes me as an interesting basis for thinking about discourse and text ideologically. See Chouliaraki and Fairclough (1999), and also Paper 3 of this collection.
4. The Green Paper on Learning (Department of Education and Employment 1998) makes an interesting contrast in this respect, and shows what is

possible. Questions are directed to the reader throughout the document, and gathered together over four pages in the final chapter.

5. Let me give one example of social theory stopping on the threshold of language, where the rubicon of text analysis really needs to be crossed. According to Bernstein (1990, 1996), although the symbolic violence of classification imposes 'voices' on subjects which limit their 'messages' in social interaction, 'message' can subvert 'voice' – what is repressed in classification can re-emerge in social interaction. There is, in other words, a voice–message dialectic. Bernstein does not acknowledge the need for text analysis in formulating this important position, yet it is through close analysis of texturing, of textual processes, that this dialectic can be shown in practice (Chouliaraki and Fairclough 1999).

[Handwritten margin note: Semiosis = any form of activity/conduct, or process that involves, including the production of meaning. → sign process (?)]

8. Critical realism and semiosis

Norman Fairclough, Bob Jessop and Andrew Sayer

This paper explores the mutual implication of critical realism and semiosis. At least three major sets of questions can be posed in this regard.[1]

First, we argue that critical realism cannot afford to ignore semiosis, provisionally defined as the intersubjective production of meaning,[2] in its more general approach to social relations, their reproduction and transformation (see Section 1). In discussing this issue we interpret social relations broadly to include individual actions, the relations between these interactions, and the emergent properties of institutional orders and the domain of the lifeworld. Apart from addressing the closely related, controversial, but nonetheless analytically distinct, issue of whether reasons can also be causes, critical realists have paid little attention to the nature and significance of semiosis. Prioritising the former at the expense of the latter is quite unjustified because reasons are merely one (albeit important) aspect of the causal efficacy of semiosis. In addition, their effectiveness can only be understood in and through the operation of semiosis.

Second, and equally important for our purposes, we inquire into the social preconditions and broader social context of semiosis. This set of problems is well suited to the application of critical discourse analysis (CDA) because the latter can provide explanatory contextualisations of the production, communication, and reception of semiosis and therefore provide a means of thinking about the articulation of the semiotic and extra-semiotic in social transformation (see Chouliaraki and Fairclough 1999). But we also show that, depending on the explicandum, it may be necessary or appropriate to supplement CDA through more concrete, complex analyses of extra-discursive domains. This implies that, in so far as semiosis has been studied in isolation from its context, this is bound to lead to an incomplete account of social causation and therefore risks committing one or more kinds of reductionism (see Section 2).

Finally, we turn to a third set of questions. These concern the nature of semiotic structures, the dialectics of their constitutive role in and emergence from texts and textual practices, and their role in social structuration (see Section 3). We exemplify these issues by drawing on critical semiotic analysis (especially CDA), which is a form of text analysis that is not only compatible with critical realism but also provides major insights into the role of semiosis in social structuration (see Section 4). Overall, Sections 3 and 4 seek to show that semiosis involves mechanisms that are intelligible from a critical realist point of view. Our concluding section draws these different themes together to argue that semiotic analysis might benefit from paying attention to other aspects of critical realism and that critical realism might benefit from paying more attention to semiosis when exploring the social world.

Addressing these three sets of questions involves identifying and exploring the real mechanisms of semiosis as a first step towards making progress on the larger problem of mind–body–semiosis–sociality–materiality. This is clearly an ambitious project and we do not expect to produce a solution in this paper. Moreover, since critical realism *qua* philosophy does not entail commitments to any particular substantive social or psychological theory, alternative critical realist accounts of semiosis could also be advanced. If so, we hope our own proposals will stimulate fellow critical realists to present them.

1 Why critical realism must address semiosis

Critical realism has tended to take semiosis for granted. For example, its practitioners often defend the claim that reasons can be causes without making any substantial reference to semiosis as such. Our first objective is to oppose this neglect. We will then demonstrate how a critical realist approach might be used to illuminate semiosis.

Social theorists and discourse analysts routinely defend semiotic analysis on the grounds that semiosis has real effects on social practice, social institutions, and the social order more generally. They argue, in short, that semiosis is performative. Though it is certainly possible for us to communicate unintentionally, we normally speak or write in order to produce some kind of response. Yet answers to the question of how semiosis produces effects are generally conspicuous by their absence in much social science analysis. This could well be due to the many uncertainties and/or controversies over the nature of explanation in the social sciences. For some social theorists, explaining how semiosis produces effects would require a causal explanation that first identifies the social entities that produce observed effects and then attributes causal responsibility to these entities in terms of an underlying causal mechanism (or mechanisms). But many other theorists reject causal explanation as being wholly inappropriate to the study of semiosis. For example, hermeneutics is generally taken to reject causal explanation (*erklären*) in favour of interpretive understanding (*verstehen*). Its advocates deny that semiosis and its effects can be explained in the same way as the production of chemical reactions and their effects; all that is possible (and all that is required) is to elucidate what a specific text 'means'. This rejection of *erklären* in favour of *verstehen* is often (but not always) tied to a Humean account of causal explanation in terms of 'constant conjunctions' between causes and effects.[3] Thus advocates of *verstehen* typically argue either that such regularities do not characterise communication and are therefore totally excluded; or that causal explanation is simply redundant in so far as it adds nothing to our understanding. Given the semiotic character of reasons (see below), this argument is linked to their conclusion that reasons are not to be treated as causes of behaviour. Instead, according to advocates of *verstehen*, reasons are propositions that precede or accompany behaviour and must simply be 'understood'. If this line of reasoning were to be accepted, however, it would be meaningless and/or pointless to inquire into the causal efficacy of semiosis.

In contrast, we argue that semiosis is both meaningful and causally efficacious, and we therefore need to demonstrate, using critical realist concepts, how it produces effects. To do this we need to recall some key features of critical realist philosophy.

First, critical realists distinguish the real from the actual and the empirical. The 'real' refers to objects, their structures or natures and their causal powers and liabilities. The 'actual' refers to what happens when these powers and liabilities are activated and produce change. The 'empirical' is the subset of the real and the actual that is experienced by actors.[4] Although changes at the level of the actual (e.g., political debates) may change the nature of objects (e.g., political institutions), the latter are not reducible to the former, any more than a car can be reduced to its movement. Moreover, while empirical experiences can influence behaviour and hence what happens, much of the social and physical worlds can exist regardless of whether researchers, and in some cases other actors, are observing or experiencing them. Though languages and other semiotic structures/systems are dependent on actors for their reproduction, they always already pre-exist any given actor (or subset of actors), and have a relative autonomy from them as real objects, even when not actualised.[5]

Second, critical realism views objects as structured and as having particular causal powers or liabilities. That is, they are able to act in certain ways and/or suffer certain changes. Thus a person who has learned a language has a rich set of (causal) powers to communicate, and she has these powers even though she does not use them all the time.[6] These powers exist (often, of course, in latent form) but they can be activated in certain situations. If and when they are activated, the effects depend on the context. Thus if we ask someone the way to the Town Hall, the effects of the question will depend on whether she speaks the same language, whether she knows the area, and so on. But regardless of whether the answer is 'round the corner', 'I'm sorry I don't know', or 'why do you want to know?', it is at least co-produced by the question, and this is true irrespective of whether the relationship between the question and answer is regular or irregular. Causation is about what produces change (the activation of causal powers) not about (whether observers have registered) a regular conjunction of cause events and effect events. Hence, regularities are not necessary for explanation, whether of physical or social phenomena. Even where we do find regularities they still have to be explained in terms of what produces them. Thus critical realism rejects the Humean, constant conjunction view of causation.

Third, as the preceding example suggests, critical realists argue that reasons can operate as causes, that is, can be responsible for producing a change. Indeed, when someone tries to persuade us that we are wrong to make this argument by giving us reasons, they in turn presuppose that offering reasons can be causative in at least some circumstances. This applies irrespective of whether there are regularities for us to record, for the general absence of regularities between giving or recognising reasons and subsequent behaviour is not fatal to causal explanation. On the contrary, as we have seen, regularities are not essential for causal explanation even in the physical sciences. The effects produced by semiosis certainly depend on texts being understood[7] in some fashion but not necessarily just in one, and only one, fashion. Thus a speech made during an election campaign may offer people strong reasons for voting in a certain way. The fact that the speech might be construed differently by different individuals (even leading them to vote contrary to the reasons adduced) and hence does not form part of a constant conjunction or event regularity does not mean that it can have no influence on voting (Bhaskar 1979, Collier 1994).[8] Understanding (*verstehen*) and explanation (*erklären*) are therefore not antithetical.

Crucial though this issue of reasons as causes has been in the philosophy of social science, it fails to address the specific nature of 'reasons' and how they come to motivate action. In particular, it ignores the semiotic character of reasons and, in the most extreme cases, treats them as simple, singular triggers of action. Yet reasons are diffuse and hard to identify unambiguously. Indeed, it would be better be think of them as emergent elements in more extensive networks of concepts, beliefs, symbols and texts. As we show in Section 2, they presuppose languages, intentionality, particular concepts and prior understandings and interests, intertextuality, conventions of inference and evidence, and so on. Even a brief reflection on the implications of this semiotic and social embedding of reasons is enough to bring home the inadequacy of a simplistic treatment of reasons. What matters is the resonance of the reasons offered to the partners in a social interaction and this depends on more than their formal content. In addition, if we reflect more broadly upon what kinds of semiotic features and events can bring about changes in behaviour (if only at the level of how people think or feel), we notice that it is not only reasons that change what we do. We may be influenced more by the tone (e.g., warmth, hostility) or imagery of a speech than by any reasons for action that it might present. Consideration of these expressive qualities of communication exposes the narrowly rationalist character of the reasons-as-causes answer to the question of how texts produce effects. We therefore need to go beyond the reasons-as-causes argument, important though it is, to examine the nature of semiosis more generally and its place within the overall logic of the social.

2   The social preconditions and context of semiosis

Social scientists who have shown interest in semiosis have tended to ignore its broader social context. We aim to correct this bias in the semiotic turn by putting semiotic processes into context. This means locating them within their necessary dialectical relations with persons (hence minds, intentions, desires, bodies), social relations, and the material world – locating them within the practical engagement of embodied and socially organised persons with the material world.

Semiosis – the making of meaning – is a crucial part of social life but it does not exhaust the latter. Thus, because texts are both socially-structuring and socially-structured, we must examine not only how texts generate meaning and thereby help to generate social structure but also how the production of meaning is itself constrained by emergent, non-semiotic features of social structure. For example, an interview is a particular form of communication (a 'genre' in the terminology we introduce below) that both creates a particular kind of social encounter and is itself socially-structured, for example by conventions of propriety, privacy and disclosure, by particular distributions of resources, material and cognitive. In short, although semiosis is an aspect of any social practice (in so far as practices entail meaning), no social practice (let alone all behaviours) is reducible to semiosis alone. This means that semiosis cannot be reduced to the play of differences among networks of signs (as if semiosis were always purely an intra-semiotic matter with no external reference) and that it cannot be understood without identifying and exploring the extra-semiotic conditions that make semiosis possible and secure its effectivity.[9] We therefore reject the Foucauldian-inspired conflation of discourses and material practices as one more instance of the 'discourse-imperialism' that has infected social theory for the last two decades. This conflation also eliminates the distinction – so crucial for critical realism – between the transitive and intransitive dimensions of scientific inquiry. It thereby produces the epistemic fallacies associated with strong social constructionism (Sayer 2000).

The intersubjective production of meaning and other semiotic effects is exceptionally difficult to explain, not least because it involves more or less inaccessible mental processes. Thus, although we offer a way of explaining the power of semiosis to generate meaning, and even though semiosis involves the listener/reception as much as speaker/production, we will leave open the question of how minds make sense of *texts*. While meaning and motive are emergent phenomena of semiosis, they need minds with certain capabilities to co-construct social action and interaction (and bodies to enact them).

Accordingly, our approach to semiosis goes beyond semiotic systems (including languages) and texts. Language acquisition itself is both preceded by, and ongoingly presupposes, various bodily and practical forms of non-linguistic knowledge or know-how, skills and sense. Regarding language acquisition, we acknowledge Margaret Archer's demonstration of the importance of the embodied, practical and non-semiotic, indeed non-social (in the sense of intersubjective) dimensions of human practice, and their status as preconditions of language-learning and use (Archer 2000). Thus infants have to learn a considerable amount without the aid of semiotic systems before they are able to acquire the latter. In addition, text producers and interpreters subsequently continue to rely heavily upon non-semiotic knowledge, bodily awareness or know-how in order to carry out both simple and complex tasks. Once these linguistic and non-linguistic skills have been acquired, further issues arise. First, we are often only more or less subliminally aware of 'events' at the margins of our fields of perception. Second, we may also respond more or less subconsciously to 'events'. And, third, if we were not intentional, desiring beings with needs, semiosis would be redundant, for it would simply not matter what existed in reality or actuality (which provides part of the overall basis for the referential function of semiosis), there would be no performativity, and no affect or expressive communication. More generally, semiosis presupposes embodied, intentional, practically-skilled social actors, social relations, material objects and spatio-temporality.

Semiosis is also influenced by the habitus, i.e., by the semi-conscious dispositions that people, particularly in their early lives, acquire through social/material interaction with their habitat and through the social relations in their part of the social field (Bourdieu 2000). Habitus and the feel for particular games that it provides can include different degrees of facility with respect to language use, for example, differing capacities to deal with and learn new discourses or genres or styles (see below) (Bourdieu 1991).

The relationship between these elements – actors, language, texts, social relations, practical contexts – is one of dialectical internal relations, i.e., although distinct, they are not discrete (Laclau and Mouffe 1985, Ollman 1993, Harvey 1996). Nonetheless the relative weight of these different elements within the overall configuration of a social action is bound to vary from case to case. In this regard it is worth noting that there is a range of 'semioticity' in so far as different social actions, events, or social orders may be more or less semioticised. For example, whereas a football match is an event that is not primarily semiotic in character, though it has semiotic aspects, a lecture is a primarily semiotic event, even though it has material aspects. Indeed, one might be able to construct a continuum ranging from technological systems through to religion in terms of the relative weight of semiosis and materiality in their overall.

No account of semiosis can evade the issues of what Habermas terms truth, truthfulness and appropriateness. Thus the production and interpretation of any text rests upon generally implicit (and often counterfactual) validity claims with respect to what is the case (the 'truth'), the intentions, beliefs, integrity, etc., of agents ('truthfulness'), and the relation of the text to its social context ('appropriateness'). In addition, the interpretation of texts by social agents in the course of social events may also involve the attempt to arrive at explanatory accounts of the motives of other social agents for speaking or writing as they have, and of less immediate social causes. This does not mean that understanding implies agreement, though some disagreements (and agreements) may be based on misunderstanding. Of course, such interpretative effort is applied very selectively to texts and many receive scant attention, and the interpretability of texts (and even their comprehensibility) depends upon a measure of shared assumptions between social agents about what is the case, intentions and beliefs, and social relations. (For instance, religious or various types of expert [e.g., technical] texts may be incomprehensible to certain social agents because of radical disparities in assumptions about what is the case.)

Semiosis has a dual presence in the production and identification of social events. On the one hand, social action and social processes may be more or less semiotic in character. Thus, referentially, expressively and in terms of social relations, such action and processes will typically engage the ways of thinking, specific identities, emotional responses or commentaries, vocabularies of motives, goals, and reasons for action that are available to the various actors and frame the situation in which the actors 'find' themselves. Whether these semiotic features of social action and social processes come from public communication or inner conversations, they can be related to real semiotic causal powers and thus one of our main tasks is to try to illuminate semiotic causal powers and how they might be actualised (their mechanisms). And, on the other hand, the identification of an 'event' and its constitutive elements (persons, objects, places etc.) from the ongoing flow of social action and social processes necessarily requires some act of semiotic interpretation, even if what happens is totally non-semiotic (i.e., purely material, physical action). This holds true even though (and, perhaps, precisely because) much of social life escapes the notice of any particular observer and, perhaps, all possible observers.

Semiosis is multi-functional (Jakobson 1990, Halliday 1994). It is simultaneously referential (or propositional, or ideational), social-relational (or interpersonal) and expressive. Thus, in the Habermasian terms introduced earlier, semiosis raises validity claims of truth, truthfulness/sincerity and appropriateness. Though it should hardly need saying, we insist on the importance of all three, including, contra Saussureans, the role of reference: there are not only signifiers (e.g., 'book' as a phonic or visual form) and signifieds (concepts) but also referents.[10] The 'play of difference' among the former could not be sustained without extensive embedding of semiosis in material practice, in the constraints and affordances of the material world. Just because the relation of reference between individual words or phrases and objects to which they refer is not one-to-one or self-sufficient, it does not follow that language and ways of thinking are unconstrained by the world. Not just anything can be constructed.[11] This does not mean that the differentiations and qualities of the world dictate the content of knowledge – for the latter is a fallible construction and to assume otherwise is to commit the ontic fallacy. But nor is the world or being dependent on knowledge – if one assumes that it is, one commits the epistemic fallacy. This pair of arguments is important in helping us to disambiguate 'construction' into its two moments of construal (the fallible ideas that inform it) and construction (in the sense of the material processes, if any, that follow from it) (cf. Sayer 2000). Indeed, even in the case of social constructions such as institutions, what gets constructed is different from how it is construed; and the relative success or failure of this construal depends on how both it and the construction respond to the properties of the materials (including social phenomena such as actors and institutions) used to construct social reality. Of course, the construal need not refer to the material world: it could also refer to other semiotic phenomena, to images, smells, sounds or feelings and states of mind.

3 The role of semiosis in social structuration

A critical realist account of social structuration must be sensitive to the complex dialectic that is entailed in the emergence, reproduction and transformation of social structures from social actions and the reciprocal influence of these emergent structures on ongoing social action (see Bhaskar 1979, Archer 1982, Jessop 2001). An important aspect of this dialectic is the operation of the evolutionary mechanisms of variation, selection and retention that shape the relationships between semiosis and social structuration. These mechanisms are common to natural and social evolution[12] (a distinction that itself becomes less distinct, of course, as human action acquires an increasing role in natural evolution) but, as suggested earlier, their operation in the social world is bound to involve semiotic as well as extra-semiotic factors.

Accordingly, we now want to highlight three interrelated semiotic aspects of social structuration. First, semiotic conditions affect the differential reproduction and transformation of social groups, organisations, institutions and other social phenomena. Second, these mechanisms are reflexive in the sense that semiotic conditions affect the variation, selection and retention of the semiotic features of social phenomena. And, third, semiotic innovation and emergence is itself a source of variation that feeds into the process of social transformation. Overall, then, semiosis can generate variation, have selective effects, and contribute to the differential retention and/or institutionalisation of social phenomena.

We can elaborate these arguments by listing some semiotic conditions involved in the selection and retention of the semiotic and extra-semiotic features of any social phenomenon in the face of the continuing variation in behaviour as social actors wittingly or unwittingly innovate in the conduct of their lives and new consequences, intended or unintended, arise:

(a) The *selection* of particular discourses (the privileging of particular discourses over others available internally and/or externally) for interpreting events, legitimising actions, and (perhaps self-reflexively) representing social phenomena. Semiotic factors operate here by influencing the differential resonance of discourses. Some resonant discourses will subsequently become retained (e.g., through their inclusion into widely accepted hegemonic projects or their inclusion into an actor's habitus) (see (d) below).

(b) The enactment of these selected discourses as modes of conduct, both semiotically (in genres) and non-semiotically (e.g., in organisational procedures).

(c) The inculcation of these discourses in the ways of being/identities of social agents both semiotically (e.g., ways of talking) and somatically (bodily dispositions).

(d) The objectification of these discourses in the built environment, technology etc., in organisational practices, and in the form and function of the body/bodies (hexis).

(e) The development of filtering devices within procedures for selecting these discourses and filtering out others, including genre chains. For instance, chains of genres in policy formation that might include policy proposals, consultations in meetings of stakeholders, and reports recommending policy decisions. A variety of different and potentially conflicting discourses may figure (e.g., within stakeholder meetings) but in so far as the genre chain is legitimised these may be unproblematically filtered to favour selected discourses in a report.

(f) The selection of strategies for agents (strategies for acting and for interpreting) which privilege these discourses (genres, styles).

(g) The resonance of these discourses (genres, styles, strategies) within the broader ensemble of social phenomena to which the relevant social phenomenon belongs as well as the complementarity of these discourses (etc.) with others within the network.

(h) The capacity of the relevant social groups, organisations, institutions etc., to selectively 'recruit' and retain social agents whose predispositions fit maximally with requirements (a)–(g).

While the preceding list has been phrased to emphasise the role of semiosis in securing social reproduction, semiotic conditions may also militate against this. For example, relationships of contestation between discourses (i.e., relationships of contestation within a social practice in their semiotic aspect, and/or relations of contestation between the social practices in question and other practices in their semiotic aspect) may impede the selection/privileging of particular discourses for interpreting events, legitimising actions, and (perhaps self-reflexively) representing the phenomenon and associated phenomena. Where such contestation occurs, factors (b)–(g) in the preceding list will either be absent or, at least, limited in their overall operation.[13] This will create in turn conditions favourable to successful innovation in the semiotic and extra-semiotic dimensions of the social world in the sense that significant variations are selected and retained to produce a durable transformation in that world. Among the relevant semiotic conditions here are the internal relations between discourses and the external relations that obtain between discourses concerned with associated social practices. Both are germane to questions of intertextuality. For their relations should be such that a new selection/privileging of discourses is possible, allowing the development of factors favouring the retention of selected discourses (b)–(g). Examples of this would include the absence/weakening of competing discourses internally or the development of new relations between such phenomena of a (partially) semiotic character favouring the recontextualisation of external discourses with regard to that phenomenon. Rather than pursue such arguments in the abstract, however, we will illustrate how these mechanisms actually operate.

4 Semiotic formations and their emergent properties: from abstract to concrete

It is precisely because semiosis is the making of meaning through recourse to language and other semiotic systems that, as critical realists, we need the tools and skills of critical semiotic analysis (linguistic analysis, discourse analysis etc.) to reflect (critically) on any text. Competent language users typically get by on a day-to-day basis, of course, without knowing about the arcana of critical semiotic analysis (hereafter CSA); but, if, as critical realists, we are interested in how actual semiotic effects are generated, we must focus on the complexities of the real mechanisms that, according to semantic content and overall context, produce effects that tend to escape the attention of lay persons and non-specialist social scientists alike. This is the *semiotic* aspect of critical semiotic analysis. As regards its *critical* aspect, CSA (e.g., CDA) is concerned with the truth, truthfulness and appropriateness of texts, their production, and their interpretation. That is, it is concerned with the relationship between semiosis and the material and social world; persons and their intentions, beliefs, desires etc.; and social relations. It is concerned with the description of texts, the interpretation of how people produce and interpret texts, judgements of texts in terms of truth, truthfulness and appropriateness, and explanation of the social causes and effects of texts.

Thus a CR approach to the explanation of concrete phenomena such as semiosis analyses them as conjunctions of structures and causal powers co-producing specific effects. To do this it abstracts these structures, identifying them and considering their respective causal powers and liabilities. Having done this, it then moves back towards the concrete, combining the abstracted constituent elements, noting how they combine, with what consequences. While, for the sake of simplicity of exposition of critical realist method, it is usual to consider simple cases involving discrete structures and mechanisms, semiosis is an extreme case where concrete phenomena are the product of dialectically related elements, and hence whose interaction is non-additive. Hence the abstractions made by CDA are analytical distinctions that have to be used in a way which acknowledges their dialectical interdependence. Concrete events have a more or less semiotic ('textual') character but even primarily semiotic events are co-produced by mental, social and material as well as specifically semiotic structures.

Semiotic structures include semiotic systems – most obviously languages – which have distinctive properties (e.g., the properties formulated in grammatical rules) not found in other structures. Nevertheless, even languages show the dialectical interpenetration of otherwise operationally autonomous structures, i.e., they are overdetermined by other structures. Thus there is a differentiation of major components of grammatical systems corresponding to the referential and social relational functions of language (Halliday 1994b). But semiotic systems can only partially account for texts (semiotic facets of events). In CR terms the gap between the productive potential ('real') of semiotic systems and the 'actual' of semiotic facets of events is such that other structures need to be postulated at lower (i.e., closer to the concrete) levels of abstraction. We call these 'semiotic orders'.

Semiotic orders (or orders of discourse, Fairclough 1992a) comprise the forms of social structuring of semiotic variation. Their main elements are genres, discourses and styles. Genres are ways of acting and interacting in their specifically semiotic aspect; they are ways of regulating (inter)action. An example would be (a specific form of) interview. Discourses are positioned ways of representing – representing other social practices as well as the material world, and reflexively representing this social practice, from particular positions in social practices. An example would be a particular political discourse – let us say the political discourse of the 'third way' (New Labour). Styles are ways of being, identities in their specifically semiotic (as opposed to bodily/material) aspect. An example would be the 'new' managerial style described by Boltanski and Chiapello (1999). A semiotic order is a specific configuration of genres, discourses and styles, which constitutes the semiotic moment of a network of social practices (e.g., a field in Bourdieu's sense, for instance the political field).

The relationship between genres, discourses and styles is dialectical. Thus discourses may become enacted as genres and inculcated as styles. What enters a practice as a discourse such as the discourse of 'new public management' may become enacted as new ways of (inter)acting, which will in part be new genres (new ways of (inter)acting discursively). And such a discourse may become inculcated as new ways of being, new identities, including both new styles and new bodily dispositions. Moreover, in addition to the intra-semiotic flows between discourses, genres and styles, there are also flows between semiosis and other elements/moments of social practices. For example, discourses may become materialised in new buildings, new technologies etc. It is important to stress again 'may': there is nothing inevitable about these 'socially constructive' effects of discourse; they are conditional upon the specificity of the practice.

Elements of semiotic orders such as genres are overdetermined to a greater extent than semiotic systems through their dialectical articulation with other structures. For this reason, whereas semiotic systems can be studied in relatively abstract-simple terms, semiotic orders are best studied in relatively concrete-complex terms. The categories of semiotic systems are abstract-simple (i.e., relatively autonomous from other structures, e.g., 'noun', 'sentence') whereas those of semiotic orders are more concrete and complex (i.e., over-determined by the categories of other structures, e.g., 'discourse', 'genre', 'dialect').

Thus, while critical semiotic analysis attributes causal effectivity to semiotic/linguistic forms, it does so without falling into a semiotic/linguistic formalism. The effectivity of forms depends upon their semantic content and their social context. For example, processes in the material world may be semiotically represented as events or as objects, in the linguistic form of finite clauses (e.g., 'Multinational corporations are changing the ways in which different countries trade with each other') or of nominalisations (e.g., 'The modern world is swept by *change*'). But the social effectivity of nominalisation depends upon what is nominalised (reducing processes to their effectivity and thus conceal-ing details of both process and agency) and on the specific social context in which it occurs (for more extended examples, see below). Attending to nomin-alisation as a linguistic form is germane to the critical analysis of the social effectivity of semiosis but this attention must be combined with an account of meaning and how meaning is mediated in and through textual interpreta-tion. It would make a difference, for example, whether or not there were widespread critical awareness of such features of texts. This lack of one-to-one relations between formal features of texts, interpretations, and social effects implies that generalisations about semiosis are difficult. However, there is nothing exceptional about this. Social systems – and, indeed, most physical systems – are open and hence unpredictable. As critical realists have emphasised, the contingent emergence of new phenomena in and through the complex interactions between systems and their environments makes con-stant conjunctions rare.

Semiosis is an instance of emergence par excellence and in moving back towards the concrete we attempt to register how meanings emerge in texts. When post-structuralists emphasise the endless possibilities for meanings to emerge from the play of difference, they are referring in CR terms to emergence. Intertextuality is a crucial property of semiosis in terms of emergence. It has more concrete and more abstract aspects. Concretely, particular texts report, echo etc., particular other texts for both speaker and listener. More abstractly, texts may stand in complex relationships to semiotic orders – they may articulate the discourses, genres and styles of different semiotic orders together in complex ways.

The objection to post-structuralist accounts of emergence is that they idealise semiosis – they ignore reference and truth conditions and attribute properties to semiosis as such in a way that ignores the dialectical inter-penetration of semiotic and non-semiotic facets of social events. The 'play' of difference is materially, socially and psychologically constrained. This is clear if we think about intertextuality. Texts may and do articulate different discourses, genres and styles together in innovative ways, but these semiotic articulations are at the same time articulations of social fields, social groups, social activities, space–times, desires etc.

Semiotic emergence is tied not only to shifting articulations of discourses, genres and styles as such, but also to texts as processes, the 'texturing' of texts, the working together of diverse elements in texts over time and in space. Texturing manifests the causal powers of agents in texts. The following texts illustrate the processes at work here. The first text is an extract from a meeting of (mainly) supervisors in an Australian subsidiary of an American multi-national company, discussing the introduction of team management (the data was collected by Lesley Farrell):

Ben   we thought you know maybe maybe I should be the facilitator for Grace's group or something where I'm away from the people a bit and um
Sally   yeah
Ben   just have a background in what's going on but just sort of keep them on the right track and let them they've got to really then rely on each other instead of relying on the supervisor to do the work
Grace   well I think kind of in the groups that are gonna come along that's what's gonna have to happen. I mean I know the the first ones that start off I think we have to go down this path to try to direct people onto the path and therefore we kind of will be in charge of the meeting but then we have to get people to start their own teams and us sort of just being a facilitator rather than
James   the team leader

[. .]   yeah
Grace   I mean it's hard to get started I think that's where people are having trouble and that's why they're kind of looking to you Ben and you know things like that
Peter   I'm not the only one I'm having trouble maintaining the thing
[. .]   yeah
Peter   I just can't maintain it at the moment you know a couple of days you know a couple of days crook there and you know just the amount of work that builds up it just goes to the back of the queue sort of thing it's shocking
James   so what you really want is the um you've got a a group you start a group and you want one of those people to sort of come out and [. .] facilitate the group
Peter   just to maintain the group you know like just to keep it just keep the work flowing
Ben   what I'm trying to get across
Peter   cause
Ben   is I'm too close to those people because I
[. .]   yeah
Ben   already go outside of the group and then I'm their supervisor outside on the on the floor where maybe if I was facilitating another group where I'm not I'm not above them you know I'm not their supervisor or whatever um I can go back to my job they can go back to theirs and they still um you know it's this their more their team than
Sally   yours

This extract shows an element of the (new) 'global' discourse of team management ('facilitating') being locally appropriated by being worked in the course of the interaction into a relationship of equivalence with elements of existing discourses (e.g., 'keep them on the right track', 'they've got to really rely on each other', 'people . . . start their own teams'), and into a relationship of difference from other elements of existing discourses (e.g., '(being) the team leader', 'direct people onto the path', 'be in charge of the meeting'). The 'work' of texturing these relations of equivalence and difference is evidenced in the high incidence and the distribution of 'hedging' expressions such as 'or something', 'just', 'kind of', 'sort of', and 'modalising' expressions such as 'maybe', 'we thought', 'I think', which mitigate in various ways degrees of commitment to propositions and proposals. The texturing of such relations of equivalence and difference can cumulatively produce new configurations of discourses and, in so far as they are enacted and inculcated, of genres and styles (in this case, the meeting itself can be seen as a generic enactment of the new discourse which it is locally appropriating). If we assume a social theory of learning as active participation in the innovative meaning-making practices of a community (Lave 1998, Wenger 1998), such examples can be seen as instances in cumulative processes of organisational learning that can produce changes in knowledge, social relations and social identities (semiotically: in discourses, genres and styles).

To show how instances of semiotic emergence figure in processes of social transformation we must also consider the resonance of emergent semiotic properties within orders of discourse. The second example is a foreword by Tony Blair to a White Paper on competition produced by the Department of Trade and Industry (1998).

> The modern world is swept by change. New technologies emerge constantly, new markets are opening up. There are new competitors but also great new opportunities.
>
> Our success depends on how well we exploit our most valuable assets: our knowledge, skills and creativity. These are the key to designing high-value goods and services and advanced business practices. They are at the heart of a modern, knowledge-driven economy.
>
> This new world challenges business to be innovative and creative, to improve performance continuously, to build new alliances and ventures. But it also challenges Government: to create and execute a new approach to industrial policy.
>
> That is the purpose of this White Paper. Old-fashioned state intervention did not and cannot work. But neither does naïve reliance on markets.
>
> The Government must promote competition, stimulating enterprise, flexibility and innovation by opening markets. But we must also invest in British capabilities when companies alone cannot: in education, in science and in the creation of a culture of enterprise. And we must promote creative partnerships which help companies: to collaborate for competitive advantage; to promote a long-term vision in a world of short-term pressures; to benchmark their performance against the best in the world; and to forge alliances with other businesses and employees. All this is the DTI's role.
>
> We will not meet our objectives overnight. The White Paper creates a policy framework for the next ten years. We must compete more effectively in today's tough markets if we are to prosper in the markets of tomorrow.
>
> In Government, in business, in our universities and throughout society we must do much more to foster a new entrepreneurial spirit: equipping ourselves for the long term, prepared to seize opportunities, committed to constant innovation and enhanced performance. That is the route to commercial success and prosperity for all. We must put the future on Britain's side.
>
> *The Rt Hon Tony Blair MP, Prime Minister*

This example shows the texturing together of the space-time of 'global' economic change and the space–time of national policy formation. The text is organised on a problem–solution model: the problem is defined in 'global' space–time in terms of irresistible processes without social agents (e.g., 'new markets are opening up', not for instance 'business corporations are opening up new markets') in a timeless present and an undifferentiated 'universal' space; the solution is defined in a national space–time in terms of what national agencies ('we', '[the] government', 'business') 'must' do. We can relate this to the general problems that face any social formation (indeed, any social inter-action short of fleeting contacts) in articulating different space–times (Harvey 1996, Jessop 2000). At one level this articulation tends to become a banal accomplishment of everyday life events, and a banal accomplishment in texturing but there is also a problem around securing relative compatibility among different spatio-temporal horizons in different contexts, different institutional orders, and on different scales. One aspect of contemporary social transformation associated with neo-liberalism is the sort of articulation of global and more local space–times illustrated here, and now a pervasive feature of neo-liberal discourse in business, government, education etc., and at international (e.g., agencies like the OECD), national, regional and local levels. Unlike the first example, the Blair text does not show semiotic emergence in process, but is rather one of many possible illustrations of the extraordinary resonance and 'flow' between fields and across scales of a recently emergent semiotic re-articulation of space-times.

5 Conclusions

We wish to draw three main conclusions from this first cut at promoting a debate between critical realists and critical discourse analysts. First, we have argued that the study of semiosis would benefit from articulation with critical realism. This has already occurred in critical discourse analysis, of course, with its even-handed concern with context as well as text. But we suggest that it should be extended to other forms of semiotic analysis. This does not mean that we reject the hermeneutic approach; rather, we argue that hermeneutics by itself cannot provide an adequate explanation of social phenomena even at the level of face-to-face communication and interaction. There is always an extra-semiotic context to the operation of hermeneutics (especially if this is extended to the notion of the 'double hermeneutic' practised by social scientists) and any serious explanation of social phenomena must be adequate both at the level of meaning and at the level of social (extra-semiotic) causation. Once we reject a Humean account of causation in terms of constant conjunction, *verstehen* and *erklären* are not so much antithetic as complementary. Given the prolific nature of semiosis with its infinity of possible meaningful communications, understandings and misunderstandings, it is important to explore the various extra-semiotic mechanisms that contribute to the variation, selection and retention of semiosis as well as the contribution of semiosis to the reproduction and transformation of social structures.

Second, we have argued that critical realism would benefit from sustained engagement with semiotic analysis. For critical realism has tended to operate with an insufficiently concrete and complex analysis of semiosis. It has tended to take symbol systems, language, orders of discourse, and so on for granted, thereby excluding central features of the social world from its analysis. One consequence of this is that critical realism cannot give an adequate account of the complex semiotic, social and material overdetermination of that world. Semiosis has its own distinctive elements, necessary properties and emergent effects and, even though (and precisely because) these qualities and their associated causal powers and liabilities interpenetrate, interfere with, and overdetermine other types of social relations and institutional orders, they must be integrated into a more comprehensive critical realist analysis of the social world. In this way we can move to provide explanations that are 'socially (or semiotically) adequate' as well as 'objectively probable' in the sense that they establish the discursive as well as extra-discursive conditions of existence of the explicandum at an appropriate level of concretisation and complexification.

And, third, in exploring the distinctive features of semiosis, we began by emphasising how semiosis frames social interaction and contributes to the construction of social relations. Within this context we then discussed the construction of identities, modes of calculation, vocabularies of motives etc., and their role in providing the motivational force behind actions. At the same time we took pains to argue that semiosis works in conjunction with extra-semiotic (or extra-discursive) elements. By mapping some key aspects of semiosis, especially its extra-discursive conditions of existence and effectivity, we attempted to block off a purely rationalist or ideologist view of social relations. In developing this argument, we oppose theorists such as Laclau and Mouffe (1985), who, in a manner reminiscent of the analysis of the production of commodities by means of commodities offered by Sraffa (1960), one-sidedly emphasise the discursive production of discourse from discourse. This leads them to neglect the extra-discursive as well as the discursive factors that shape the resonance of semiosis and the willingness and capacity of actors (and other social forces) to respond to interpellations, appeals to their identities and interests, hegemonic projects etc. Against this, we argue for at least equal weight to be given to the consumption of semiosis as well as its production. In particular, we have stressed that both the production and the consumption of symbolic systems (orders of discourse etc.) are overdetermined by a range of factors that are more or less extra-semiotic.

Notes

1. A fourth question that some may want to raise is that of naturalism and, more specifically, whether semiotic analysis can be assimilated to the methodology of the natural sciences. We regard this question as misguided. What is important is not whether their methods of analysis match those of the natural sciences but whether they are appropriate for their subject matter. Answering the former question incidentally supplies a response to the latter, of course; our paper answers yes and no to the latter question, for the study of semiosis requires both similar and different methods from those of natural science.

2. We use the term 'semiosis' throughout this paper. Although we initially gloss it as the inter-subjective making of meaning, our understanding of semiosis as an element/moment of 'the social' is necessarily relational and will therefore emerge more fully during the paper. We prefer 'semiosis' to 'language' and 'discourse' (used as abstract nouns) for two reasons. First, semiosis involves more than (verbal) language – it also involves, for example, 'visual language' (photographs, pictures, diagrams etc.). And, second, 'discourse' as an abstract noun is a notoriously problematic and confusing term. In any case, we later use 'discourse' as a count noun for particular positioned ways of representing aspects of the world. Likewise, we shall later use 'languages' (count noun) for particular language systems (e.g., English). When referring to concrete social events from a semiotic perspective, we use the term 'texts' (count noun) in an extended sense to include not only written texts but also spoken conversations, 'multi-semiotic' texts such as TV ads (which mix words, images, sound effects etc.), and so on. This extended use of 'texts' is common in certain areas of linguistics, though we recognise that it is not a very satisfactory term.

3. For example, in her critique of Bourdieu, Judith Butler (2000) assumes a Humean concept of causation. Unsurprisingly, then, she fails to note that to acknowledge performativity is to concede the causal efficacy of discourses.

4. Empirical is not an ontological category counterposed to the 'real' or the 'actual' but an epistemological one. Parts of the real as well as the actual may be observable.

5. Critical realists have debated whether social structures, such as those of language, exist independently of their enactment (Bhaskar 1979, 1989, Benton 1981, Collier 1994).

6. This is an example of a set of powers that needs a certain amount of use if they are to be sustained but, at least in the short run, we have these powers even though they are only activated intermittently.

7. 'Felt' or 'sensed' might better describe some of the less articulated responses.

8. Interestingly, according to Ringer (2000), this view was shared by Max Weber, one of the founders of interpretive sociology. While Weber is widely associated with an allegedly unsuccessful attempt to unite explanatory (causal) and interpretive (hermeneutic) analysis, this negative judgement arises because most interpreters have assumed that Weber followed a Humean model of causation based on constant conjunctions. However, Ringer shows that Weber rejected this model as well as related arguments that anticipated Hempel's neo-positivist, deductive nomological 'covering law' model of causal analysis. Weber came to appreciate that 'reasons' could be causes. He concluded that an adequate explanation of a specific historical, cultural or social phenomenon must be adequate both in terms of motivational intelligibility (i.e., its social meaning for the relevant actors) and its production through the contingent interaction of causal processes in specific circumstances. Bhaskar's first critical realist defence of the possibility of naturalism incorrectly cites Weber as seeing constant conjunctions as necessary for an adequate explanation (1989: 2, 137–8). He presents Weber as combining a neo-Kantian methodology with methodological individualism and contrasts this approach with Marx's realist methodology and relational ontology (1989: 31). He also argues that there are two key differences between Weberian sociology and transcendental realism: (a) whereas Weber accepts, realism rejects constant conjunctions; (b) whereas Weber denies, realism accepts that correction of agents' perceptions may be a necessary part of a social scientific investigation (1989: 135–8). Bhaskar is wrong on both counts since Weber also discussed 'wrong thinking' and other forms of irrationality. Another problem that is directly relevant to our own analysis below is that Weber does not adequately distinguish between the actual and the real. In using terms such as 'pressing toward', 'developmental tendencies', 'moving forces', and 'impeding' factors, Weber supported a dynamic conception of causal analysis. But he also argued that such notions do not constitute 'real causal interconnections' at an 'elementary' level but involve no more than tactically useful constructs in the practice of historical reasoning (Ringer 2000: 76).

9. For an interesting discussion of semiosis and its conditions in relation to realism and pragmatism, see Nellhaus (1998).

10. The signifier/signified relationship is often mistakenly interpreted as one of text to referent. It is part of a threefold relation among signifier/signified/referent. See Thibalt.

11. See Archer (2000) for an interesting argument on the pre-linguistic and material bases of logic.

12. On the role of variation, selection, and retention in evolution, see Campbell (1969).

13. Long-term critical engagement with a contested discourse can, of course, serve to reproduce the terms of a given debate at the expense of moving beyond it (e.g., the relationship between base and superstructure in Marxism or the primacy of structure or agency in sociology).

Methodology in CDA research

Introduction

Methodology vs. Methods

I use *methodology* in preference to *method*. Settling on a methodology for a particular research project is not just a matter of selecting from an existing repertoire of methods. It is a theoretical process which constructs an *object of research* (a researchable object, a set of researchable questions) for the research topic by bringing to bear on it relevant theoretical perspectives and frameworks. Methods (e.g., of data collection and analysis) are selected according to how the research object is constructed. So one cannot neatly separate and oppose theory and method in the conventional way. This is more fully explained and illustrated in the first paper ('A dialectical–relational approach to critical discourse analysis in social research').

The five papers in this section were published between 2002 and 2009. They are all concerned with issues of methodology in CDA research, but they differ in how they approach these issues. The first is a systematic presentation and illustration of a methodology for the version of CDA I am working with at the time of writing (2008). The second ('Understanding the new management ideology. A transdisciplinary contribution from critical discourse analysis and the new sociology of capitalism') is an exploration of how a transdisciplinary research methodology might be developed between CDA and an approach to analysing changes in capitalism developed by French sociologists, 'New Sociology of Capitalism'. It was written with Eve Chiapello, the co-author of a major study using that approach. The third ('Critical discourse analysis in researching language in the new capitalism: overdetermination, transdisciplinarity and textual analysis') focuses on the implications of a transdisciplinary research methodology for methods of analysing texts, and discusses common ground and differences between CDA and systemic functional linguistics. The fourth ('Marx as a critical discourse analyst: the genesis of a critical method and its relevance to the critique of global capital') is a study with Phil Graham of Marx's analytical method, focusing on the ways in which it foreshadowed and might inform CDA. The fifth ('Critical discourse analysis, organisational discourse and organisational change') is an invited contribution to the journal *Organization Studies* on developments in research on organisational discourse, which advocates a CDA methodology based upon critical realism in preference to the postmodernist and extreme social constructivist approaches often adopted.

The first paper ('A dialectical–relational approach to critical discourse analysis in social research') presents a methodology which is a form of what Bhaskar (1986) calls 'explanatory critique'. The same methodology in essence was proposed in the book I co-authored with Lilie Chouliaraki, *Discourse in Late Modernity* (1999), though I have modified it here. The methodology can be formulated in four 'stages' (which can be further elaborated into a number of 'steps'):

Stage 1: Focus upon a social wrong, in its semiotic aspect.
Stage 2: Identify obstacles to addressing the social wrong.
Stage 3: Consider whether the social order 'needs' the social wrong.
Stage 4: Identify possible ways past the obstacles.

The methodology follows the practice in critical research of focusing research on *wrongs*, a term I use here in preference to *problems*, which Chouliaraki and I used, for reasons explained in the paper. Wrongs include injustices and inequalities which people experience, but which are not necessary wrongs in the sense that, given certain social conditions, they could be righted or at least mitigated. These might be, for instance, matters of inequalities in access to material resources, lack of political rights, inequalities before the law or on the basis of differences in ethnic or cultural identity. Stage 1 also indicates a focus on wrongs which can be productively researched in terms of relations between semiotic and extra-semiotic elements, and one 'step' within Stage 1 is constructing a research object for researching the wrong in a transdisciplinary way. Stage 2 asks: what is it about the nature of the social order in which this wrong exists that makes it difficult to right it? Since the 'point of entry' in CDA research is semiotic, we need to consider particularly semiotic aspects of the obstacles, and to answer this question we need to analyse dialectical relations between semiotic and extra-semiotic elements in relevant practices, institutions and events, which entails collecting and analysing relevant texts. Stage 3 asks: is this social wrong inherent to the social order so that it can't be righted without changing the social order (though perhaps it can be mitigated), or something that can be righted without such radical change? Stage 4 asks how the obstacles identified in Stage 2 might be overcome, and since these obstacles are partly semiotic in character, it focuses on how people actually deal or might deal with the obstacles in part by contesting and changing discourse. The social wrong I take as an example to illustrate this methodology is a political one: suppression of political differences over how to respond nationally to major international economic changes ('the global economy', as many construe it) in favour of creating a consensus, which is a social wrong in that it undermines democracy but also poses the danger that dissent which cannot be politically articulated may emerge in nationalist or xenophobic forms. The problem is one of *depoliticisation*, keeping issues and people out of political debate and dialogue, and the research object is: semiotic aspects of depoliticisation and politicisation (the latter because we are also concerned – Stage 4 – in how they may be brought back in).

This paper appeared in a collection of papers which presented a variety of 'methods' in CDA (Wodak and Meyer 2001). Labelling different approaches to CDA (as 'dialectical–relational', 'discourse–historical' etc.) has the advantage of showing that there are in indeed differences in approach, but also the substantial disadvantage of potentially ossifying different tendencies and emphases into mutually exclusive territories. I think it is misleading to overemphasise, and especially to institutionalise, these differences – which amounts to advising readers not to make too much of the title of this paper. For instance, my approach to CDA is, like the approach labelled 'discourse-historical' in the collection of papers, discourse–historical, and dialectical relations are a focus for all the approaches in the book, though my treatment of both these facets of CDA is different and sometimes markedly different from others.

The second paper ('Understanding the new management ideology. A transdisciplinary contribution from critical discourse analysis and the new sociology of capitalism') begins from the concept of and analysis of the 'spirit of capitalism' in the book of that title by Luc Boltanski and my co-author, Eve Chiapello (Boltanski and Chiapello 1999). The book offers an account of changes in capitalism since 1960, focusing upon one aspect of the new 'spirit of capitalism' associated with the new form of capitalism which began to emerge in the 1980s, an ideology which justifies people's commitment to this form of capitalism: new management ideology. The book includes analysis of two bodies of texts, management literature from the 1960s and from the 1990s. Given this textual dimension of the book's analytical method, our paper seeks to develop a transdisciplinary methodology which brings together the new sociology of capitalism and my version of CDA, and to assess what it can add to research on transformations in capitalism. To make this methodological endeavour more concrete we include an analysis of part of a book by an influential management 'guru' Rosabeth Moss Kanter who was one of the authors included in Boltanski and Chiapello's corpus of texts from the 1990s.

The third paper ('Critical discourse analysis in researching language in the new capitalism: overdetermination, transdisciplinarity and textual analysis') focuses upon textual analysis, and how discourse analysts and linguists can make a strong case to social scientists for textual analysis as a significant element in social research, specifically research on current transformations of capitalism. This is a theme I addressed in an earlier paper in the journal *Discourse & Society* (Fairclough 1992e) and more extensively in my book *Analyzing Discourse: Textual Analysis for Social Research* (2003). A central claim both of that book and of this paper is that although there is much in existing forms of textual analysis which can be drawn upon in this regard (and I emphasise particularly the contribution of systemic functional linguistics (SFL)), working in the transdisciplinary way I am proposing for CDA also entails developing a transdisciplinary way of approaching textual analysis. This means seeking to operationalise categories and perspectives in other theories in ways of analysing texts, as I also sought to do for categories from Bernstein's sociological theory and Laclau and Mouffe's political theory in the paper 'Discourse, social theory and social research: the discourse of welfare reform' in Section C (pages 167–201). The paper also takes up what I see to be the main difference between my version of CDA and SFL with respect to textual analysis: for CDA, textual analysis includes interdiscursive analysis of how genres, discourses and styles are articulated in texts, for SFL it does not.

The fourth paper ('Marx as a critical discourse analyst: the genesis of a critical method and its relevance to the critique of global capital'), co-authored with Phil Graham, is a study of the development of Marx's method in a range of his economic, political and historical texts. We show that it was based upon a view of language as an element of material social processes which is dialectically related to other elements, that critique of language was therefore part of Marx's critical method, that one can see the latter as in part a form of CDA *avant la lettre*, and that applications of CDA in transdisciplinary critical research on contemporary capitalism may gain from a study of Marx's method. The paper argues that his method drew not only from the philosophy of his day and especially from Hegel but also from the classical tradition, Aristotle in particular. We trace these influences and the ways in which he transformed them with respect to the theory of abstraction, the dialectical method, and ideology. We then analyse extracts from six texts (*Critique of Hegel's Doctrine of the State, Economic and Philosophic Manuscripts,*

Capital, Critique of the Gotha Programme, The Eighteenth Brumaire of Louis Napoleon, and the *Grundrisse*). We suggest that critique of texts (the texts of the political economists, of Hegel, and of others) was a crucial element and stage in Marx's method, and that the central focus of this critique, and the basis for the development of his own analyses, was, as he put it in the *Economic and Philosophic Manuscripts*, failure 'to grasp the interconnections within the movement' of social history and social reality. It is a critique of relations, or of what we call 'connectivity', in texts. We suggest that what it points to for CDA is 'a critical analysis of the whole formal and conceptual architecture of texts' (e.g., the texts of political economy – or the texts produced around and in relation to what is emerging at the time of writing (winter 2008) as a major economic crisis) 'focusing on texts as relational work . . . as producing certain relations and not producing others . . . as well as . . . being produced from within certain relations and not from within others'.

The fifth paper ('Critical discourse analysis, organisational discourse and organisational change') is a polemical comment piece on the analysis of organisational discourse within the field of organisation studies, which takes issue with postmodernist and extreme social constructivist positions. I argue against the reductions that characterise the latter: the reduction of organisations to organisational discourse, and the reduction of organisational analysis to the 'organising' that goes on in organisational processes. I suggest by contrast that discourse analysis is consistent with a realist approach to organisational research which distinguishes organisational process and agency from organisational structures, and focuses research on the relations and tensions between them. Incorporating discourse analysis into a realist approach both ensures that questions of discourse are properly attended to in organisational studies, and avoids these forms of reduction. Within such a realist approach, discourse analysis can make a significant contribution to researching organisational change, and addressing such general concerns as the following: When organisations change, what is it that changes? What makes organisations resilient in the face of change, resistant to change, or open to change? How are external pressures for organisational change internalised in organisations, how may organisational members respond to them, and what outcomes are possible? Such questions cannot, of course, be addressed by discourse analysts alone, but my argument is that effectively researching them does depend on a substantive element of discourse analysis in transdisciplinary research on organisational change.

9. A dialectical–relational approach to critical discourse analysis in social research[1]

In this paper, I introduce and illustrate a methodology for using a dialectical–relational version of CDA in transdisciplinary social research (Chouliaraki and Fairclough 1999, Fairclough 2003, 2006). I begin with a theoretical section explaining the dialectical–relational approach, including my view of discourse, of critical analysis, and of transdisciplinary research. In the second section, I explain the methodology, presenting it as a series of stages and steps, and identify a number of core analytical categories. In the third section, I present an example, showing the application of this methodology in researching a political topic, and I illustrate the approach to political analysis in the fourth section with respect to particular texts. The sixth section summarises what can be achieved with this methodology and discusses possible limitations.

1 Theory and concepts

First, a terminological point. Discourse is commonly used in various senses including (a) meaning-making as an element of the social process, (b) the language associated with a particular social field or practice (e.g., 'political discourse'), and (c) a way of construing aspects of the world associated with a particular social perspective (e.g., a 'neo-liberal discourse of globalisation'). It is easy to confuse them, so to at least partially reduce the scope for confusion, I prefer to use semiosis for the first, most abstract and general sense (following Fairclough, Jessop and Sayer 2004), which has the further advantage of suggesting that discourse analysis is concerned with various 'semiotic modalities' of which language is only one (others are visual images and 'body language'). Semiosis is viewed here as an element of the social process which is dialectically related to others – hence a 'dialectical–relational' approach. Relations between elements are dialectical in the sense of being different but not 'discrete', i.e., not fully separate. We might say that each 'internalises' the others without being reducible to them (Harvey 1996) – e.g., social relations, power, institutions, beliefs and cultural values are in part semiotic; they 'internalise' semiosis without being reducible to it. For example, although we should analyse political institutions or business organisations as partly semiotic objects, it would be a mistake to treat them as purely semiotic, because then we couldn't ask the key question: what is the relationship between semiotic and other elements? CDA focuses not just upon semiosis as such, but on the relations between semiotic and other social elements. The nature of this relationship varies between institutions and organisations, and according to time and place, and it needs to be established through analysis.

This requires CDA to be integrated within frameworks for transdisciplinary research, such as the framework I have used in recent publications, *cultural political economy*, which combines elements from three disciplines: a form of economic analysis (the 'Regulation Approach'), a neo-Gramscian theory of the state, and a form of CDA (Jessop 2004, Fairclough 2006). Transdisciplinary research is a particular form of interdisciplinary research (Fairclough 2005b). What distinguishes it is that in bringing disciplines and theories together to address research issues, it sees 'dialogue' between them as a source for the theoretical and methodological development of each of them. For example, recontextualisation was introduced as a concept and category within CDA through a dialogue with Basil Bernstein's sociology of pedagogy, where it originated (Chouliaraki and Fairclough 1999).

In what sense is CDA critical? Critical social research aims to contribute to addressing the social '*wrongs*' of the day (in a broad sense – injustice, inequality, lack of freedom etc.) by analysing their sources and causes, resistance to them and possibilities of overcoming them. We can say that it has both a 'negative' and a 'positive' character. On the one hand, it analyses and seeks to explain dialectical relations between semiosis and other social elements to clarify how semiosis figures in the establishment, reproduction and change of unequal power relations (domination, marginalisation, exclusion of some people by others) and in ideological processes, and how in more general terms it bears upon human 'well-being'. These relations require analysis because there are no societies whose logic and dynamic, including how semiosis figures within them, are fully transparent to all: the forms in which they appear to people are often partial and in part misleading. On the other hand, critique is oriented to analysing and explaining, with a focus on these dialectical relations, the many ways in which the dominant logic and dynamic are tested, challenged and disrupted by people, and to identifying possibilities which these suggest for overcoming obstacles to addressing 'wrongs' and improving well-being.

The social process can be seen as the interplay between three levels of social reality: *social structures, practices* and *events* (Chouliaraki and Fairclough 1999). Social practices 'mediate' the relationship between social structures at the most general and abstract level and particular, concrete social events; social fields, institutions and organisations are constituted as networks of social practices (see Bourdieu on social practices and fields – Bourdieu and Wacquant 1992). In this approach to CDA, analysis is focused on two dialectical relations: between structure (especially social practices as an intermediate level of structuring) and events (or between structure and action, structure and strategy) and, within each, between semiotic and other elements. There are three major ways in which semiosis relates to other elements of social practices and of social events – as a facet of action; in the construal (representation) of aspects of the world; and in the constitution of identities. And there are three semiotic (or discourse–analytical) categories corresponding to these: *genre, discourse* and *style*.

Genres are semiotic ways of acting and interacting, such as news or job interviews, reports or editorials in newspapers, or advertisements on TV or the internet. Part of doing a job, or running a country, is interacting semiotically or communicatively in certain ways, and such activities have distinctive sets of genres associated with them. *Discourses* are semiotic ways of construing aspects of the world (physical, social or mental) which can generally be identified with different positions or perspectives of different groups of social actors. For instance, the lives of poor people are not only construed through different discourses associated with different social practices (in politics, medicine, social welfare, academic sociology) but through different discourses within each practice which correspond to differences of position and perspective. I use 'construe' in preference to 'represent' to emphasise an active and often difficult process of 'grasping' the world from a particular perspective (Fairclough 2009). *Styles* are identities, or 'ways of being', in their semiotic aspect – for instance, being a 'manager' in the currently fashionable way in business or in universities is partly a matter of developing the right semiotic style.

The semiotic dimension of (networks of) social practices which constitute social fields, institutions, organisations etc. is *orders of discourse* (Fairclough 1992a); the semiotic dimension of events is *texts*. Orders of discourse are particular configurations of different genres, different discourses and different styles. An order of discourse is a social structuring of semiotic difference, a particular social ordering of relationships between different ways of meaning-making – different genres, discourses and styles. So, for example, the network of social practices which constitutes the field of education, or a particular educational organisation such as a university, is constituted semiotically as an order of discourse. Texts are to be understood in an inclusive sense, not only written texts but also conversations and interviews, as well as the 'multi-modal' texts (mixing language and visual images) of television and the internet. Some events consist almost entirely of texts (e.g., a lecture or an interview), while in others, texts have a relatively small part (e.g., a game of chess).

Discourses which originate in some particular social field or institution (e.g., to anticipate the example, neo-liberal economic discourse, which originated within academic economics and business) may be *recontextualised* in others (e.g., in the political field or the educational field). Recontextualisation has an ambivalent character (Chouliaraki and Fairclough 1999): it can be seen as the 'colonisation' of one field or institution by another, but also as the 'appropriation' of 'external' discourses, often the incorporation of discourses into strategies pursued by particular groups of social agents within the recontextualising field. For example, the 'transition' to a market economy and western-style democratic government in the formerly socialist countries of Europe (e.g., Poland, Romania) has involved a 'colonising' recontextualisation of discourses (e.g., discourses of 'privatisation') which were, however, incorporated differently into the strategies of new entrepreneurs, government officials, managers of state industries, etc. (Fairclough 2006).

Discourses may under certain conditions be *operationalised* or 'put into practice', which is a dialectical process with three aspects: they may be *enacted* as new ways of (inter)acting, they may be *inculcated* as new ways of being (identities), and they may be physically *materialised*, e.g., as new ways of organising space, for example in architecture. Enactment and inculcation may themselves take semiotic forms: a new management discourse (e.g., the discourse of marketised 'new public management' which has invaded public sector fields like education and health) may be enacted as management procedures which include new genres of interaction between managers and workers, or it may be inculcated as identities which semiotically include the styles of the new type of managers.

CDA oscillates, as I have indicated, between a focus on *structures* (especially the intermediate level of the structuring of social practices) and a focus on the *strategies* of social agents, i.e., the ways in which they try to achieve outcomes or objectives within existing structures and practices, or to change them in particular ways. This includes a focus on shifts in the structuring of semiotic difference (i.e., shifts in orders of discourse) which constitute a part of social change, and on how social agents pursue their strategies semiotically in texts. In both perspectives, a central concern is shifting relations between genres, discourses and styles, and between different genres, between different discourses and between different styles: change in the social structuring of relations between them which achieves relative permanence and stability in orders of discourse, and the ongoing working and reworking of relations between them which is regarded in this approach to CDA as a normal feature of texts.

The term *interdiscursivity* is reserved for the latter: the interdiscursivity of a text is an aspect of its intertextuality (Fairclough 1992a), a question of which genres, discourses and styles it draws upon, and how it works them into particular *articulations*. Textual analysis also includes linguistic analysis, and analysis where appropriate of visual images and 'body language', and these features of texts can be seen as realising its interdiscursive features.

2 Methodology

I have referred to a 'methodology' for using a dialectical–relational version of CDA in transdisciplinary social research rather than a 'method', because I also see the process as a theoretical one in which methods are selected according to how the *object of research* (Bourdieu and Wacquant 1992) is theoretically constructed. So it is not just a matter of 'applying methods' in the usual sense – we cannot so sharply separate theory and method. This version of CDA is associated with a general method, which I discuss below, but the specific methods used for a particular piece of research arise from the theoretical process of constructing its object.

We can identify 'stages' or 'steps' in the methodology only on condition that these are not interpreted in a mechanical way: these are essential parts of the methodology (a matter of its 'theoretical order'), and while it does make partial sense to proceed from one to the next (a matter of the 'procedural order'), the relationship between them in doing research is not simply that of sequential order. For instance, the 'step' I refer to below of constructing the object of research does need to precede subsequent steps, but it also makes sense to 'loop' back to it in the light of subsequent steps, seeing the formulation of the object of research as a preoccupation throughout. It is also helpful to distinguish the 'theoretical' and 'procedural' from the 'presentational' order one chooses to follow in, for instance, writing a paper – other generally rhetorical factors will affect the order in which one presents one's analysis.

The methodology can be seen as a variant of Bhaskar's 'explanatory critique' (Bhaskar 1986, Chouliaraki and Fairclough 1999) and can be formulated initially as four 'stages':

Stage 1: Focus upon a social wrong, in its semiotic aspect.
Stage 2: Identify obstacles to addressing the social wrong.
Stage 3: Consider whether the social order 'needs' the social wrong.
Stage 4: Identify possible ways past the obstacles.

4 stages (again.)

Research helpful

Stage 1: Focus upon a social wrong, in its semiotic aspect

CDA is a form of critical social science geared to a better understanding of the nature and sources of social wrongs, the obstacles to addressing them and possible ways of overcoming those obstacles. 'Social wrongs' can be understood in broad terms as aspects of social systems, forms or orders which are detrimental to human well-being, and which could in principle be ameliorated if not eliminated, though perhaps only through major changes in these systems, forms or orders. Examples might be poverty, forms of inequality, lack of freedom or racism. Of course, what constitutes a 'social wrong' is a controversial matter, and CDA is inevitably involved in debates and arguments about this which go on all the time.[2] We can elaborate Stage 1 in two steps:

> Step 1: Select a research topic which relates to or points up a social wrong and which can productively be approached in a transdisciplinary way with a particular focus on dialectical relations between semiotic and other 'moments'

We might, for instance, conclude that such an approach is potentially 'productive' because there are significant semiotic features of the topic which have not been sufficiently attended to in existing social research. A topic might attract our interest because it has been prominent in the relevant academic literature, or is a focus of practical attention in the domain or field at issue (in political debate or debates over questions of management or 'leadership', in media commentary and so forth). Topics are often 'given', and they sometimes virtually select themselves – who could doubt for instance that 'immigration', 'terrorism', 'globalisation' or 'security' are important contemporary topics, with significant implications for human well-being, which researchers should attend to? Selecting such topics has the advantage of ensuring that research is relevant to the issues, problems and wrongs of the day, but also the danger that their very obviousness can lead us to take them too much at face value. We cannot assume that such topics are coherent research objects; to 'translate' topics into objects, we need to theorise them.

Step 2: Construct objects of research for initially identified research topics by theorising them in a transdisciplinary way

Anticipating the example I shall discuss below, let us assume that the selected research topic is the relationship between national strategies and policies and the 'global economy': strategies and policies which are developed for the global economy, or the adaptation of national strategies and policies for the global economy. We might pin this down by focusing, for instance, on strategies and policies to enhance 'competitiveness' in particular countries (the example I discuss relates to competitiveness policies in the UK). As a topic for critical research, this seems plausible enough: a preoccupation of contemporary governments is indeed adapting to the 'global economy', and this process does indeed have implications for human well-being (it is widely presented as a way towards greater prosperity and opportunity, but as entailing suffering and insecurity for some people). One – controversial – formulation of the social wrong in this case might be that the well-being (material prosperity, security, political freedom etc.) of some people – arguably the majority – is being unfairly or unjustly sacrificed for the interests of others. I shall focus below on one particular political aspect of the social wrong: the suppression of political differences in favour of a national consensus on strategies and policies.

Constructing an object of research for this topic involves drawing upon relevant bodies of theory in various disciplines to go beyond and beneath the obviousness of the topic, and since the focus is on a specifically semiotic 'point of entry' into researching it, these should include theories of semiosis and discourse. There are no 'right answers' to the question of which theoretical perspectives to draw upon: it is a matter of researchers' judgements about which perspectives can provide a rich theorisation as a basis for defining coherent objects for critical research which can deepen understanding of the processes at issue, their implications for human well-being and the possibilities for improving well-being. One must work in a transdisciplinary way, either in research teams which bring together specialists in relevant disciplines, or by engaging with literature in such disciplines.

What theoretical perspectives might be drawn upon in this case? These might include (political) economic theories which theorise and analyse the 'global economy' and take positions on whether and how it constitutes a 'realm of necessity', a fact of life; state and political theories which probe the character and functioning of the state and of national and international politics in the era of 'globalisation'; theories of 'global ethnography' which address how local groups and individuals seek to adapt to but also sometimes test and challenge the 'global economy' as a claimed realm of necessity. The importance of discourse theory is indicated by this implicit questioning of the 'global economy': a central issue in both the academic literature and practical responses to the 'global economy' in politics, workplaces and everyday life is the relationship between reality and discourse – the reality and the discourses of the 'global economy' and of its impact, implications and ramifications. We can initially identify analysis of the complex relationship between reality and discourse as a general formulation of the object of research for a semiotic 'point of entry' into this topic, but I shall suggest a more specific formulation, linked to the example I shall discuss, in the section below on political discourse analysis.

Stage 2: Identify obstacles to addressing the social wrong

Stage 2 approaches the social wrong in a rather indirect way by asking what it is about the way in which social life is structured and organised that prevents it from being addressed. This requires bringing in analyses of the social order, and one 'point of entry' into this analysis can be semiotic, which entails selecting and analysing relevant 'texts' and addressing the dialectical relations between semiosis and other social elements. Steps 1–3 can be formulated as follows:

1. Analyse dialectical relations between semiosis and other social elements: between orders of discourse and other elements of social practices, between texts and other elements of events.
2. Select texts, and focuses and categories for their analysis, in the light of and appropriate to the constitution of the object of research.
3. Carry out analyses of texts, both interdiscursive analysis and linguistic/semiotic analysis.

Taken together, these three steps indicate an important feature of this version of CDA: textual analysis is only a part of semiotic analysis (discourse analysis), and the former must be adequately framed within the latter. The aim is to develop a specifically semiotic 'point of entry' into objects of research which are constituted in a transdisciplinary way, through dialogue between different theories and disciplines. The analysis of texts can effectively contribute to this only in so far as it is located within a wider analysis of the object of research in terms of dialectical relations between semiotic and other elements which comprehend relations between the level of social practices and the level of events (and between orders of discourse and texts).

I shall not elaborate much on the three steps at this stage, because I think they will be clearer when I work through them using the example below. There is one point about Step 3, however. I said above that although the particular methods of textual analysis used in a specific case depend upon the object of research, this version of CDA does have a general method of analysis. I alluded to this in the first section: textual analysis includes both linguistic analysis (and, if relevant, analysis of other semiotic forms, such as visual images) and inter-discursive analysis (analysis of which genres, discourses and styles are drawn upon, and how they are articulated together). Moreover, interdiscursive analysis has the crucial effect of constituting a mediating 'interlevel' which connects both linguistic analysis with relevant forms of social analysis, and the analysis of the text as part of an event with the analysis of social practices – in more general terms, the analysis of event (action, strategy) with the analysis of structure. Why so? Because interdiscursive analysis compares how genres, discourses and styles are articulated together in a text as part of a specific event, and in more stable and durable orders of discourses as part of networks of practices, which (qua social practices) are objects of various forms of social analysis.

Stage 3: Consider whether the social order 'needs' the social wrong

It is not awfully obvious what this means, and I shall try to clarify it by again anticipating the example. I indicated above that the social wrong I shall focus on when I get to the example is the suppression of political differences over the global economy and national responses to it in favour of seeking to create a national consensus, which is substantively realised in discourse. In what sense might the social order 'need' this? Perhaps in the sense – again anticipating the discussion below – that the internationally dominant strategy for globalising an economic order based upon neo-liberal principles requires that states be able to operate in support of this strategy without being encumbered by the 'old' adversarial politics. Stage 3 leads us to consider whether the social wrong in focus is inherent to the social order, whether it can be addressed within it, or only by changing it. It is a way of linking 'is' to 'ought': if a social order can be shown to inherently give rise to major social wrongs, then that is a reason for thinking that perhaps it should be changed. (Which leads to the question of whether it can be changed – whether the contradictions of the social order are such, and the forces and resources which might be deployed against it are such, that change is feasible as well as desirable.) It also connects with questions of ideology: discourse is ideological in so far as it contributes to sustaining particular relations of power and domination.

Stage 4: Identify possible ways past the obstacles

Stage 4 moves the analysis from negative to positive critique: identifying, with a focus on dialectical relations between semiosis and other elements, possibilities within the existing social process for overcoming obstacles to addressing the social wrong in question. This includes developing a semiotic 'point of entry' into research on the ways in which these obstacles are actually tested, challenged and resisted, be it within organised political or social groups or movements, or more informally by people in the course of their ordinary working, social and domestic lives. A specifically semiotic focus would include ways in which dominant discourse is reacted to, contested, criticised and opposed (in its argumentation, its construal of the world, its construal of social identities and so forth).

3 An example: political discourse analysis

The texts I shall discuss below are political texts: the foreword to a government document written by former British Prime Minister Tony Blair, and a critique of Blair's 'New Labour' government by two former members of the Labour Party. As I have said, how a research topic is constituted as an object of research determines both the selection of texts for analysis and the nature of the analysis. In this section, I shall suggest a more specific formulation of the object of research for the research topic anticipated above ('adapting national strategy and policy for the global economy'), which entails some discussion of political theories of the contemporary 'political condition', and the main issues and priorities it suggests for analysis of politics and political discourse. I shall discuss theoretical perspectives on the character of contemporary politics and the State especially in advanced capitalist countries like Britain, but I should emphasise that this discussion is necessarily partial given limitations of space. The material in this section will also help with Step 1 of Stage 2 of the methodology when we get to the texts – analysing dialectical relations between semiosis and other elements, especially at the level of social practices and orders of discourse.

Let me begin with a highly condensed summary analysis of the contemporary 'political condition', in the form of four major claims:

- Globalisation in its dominant neo-liberal form has been associated with changes in the state and national (as well as international) politics (Harvey 2003, Pieterse 2004).
- There is a tendency of the state to become a 'competition state' with the primary objective of securing competitive advantage for the capital based within its borders (Jessop 2002).
- There is an associated tendency within mainstream politics for the political division and contestation (e.g., between political parties) characteristic of the previous period to weaken, and for consensus to emerge on the main strategy and policy issues (Rancière 2006).
- This tendency constitutes a fundamental political danger; not only is it a threat to democracy, it also creates a vacuum which can be filled by nationalism and xenophobia (Rancière 1995, Mouffe 2005).

The fourth point is based upon particular views of the general character of (democratic) politics and of politics in modern democracies. I shall refer specifically to Rancière's view. He argues that democracies, both ancient and modern, are mixed forms, as anticipated by Aristotle when he characterised 'a good regime' as a 'mixture of constitutions . . . there should appear to be elements of both (oligarchy and democracy) yet at the same time of neither . . . the oligarch sees oligarchy and the democrat democracy' (see Aristotle, *Politics IV*: 1294b). This follows from the fact that 'the question of politics begins in every city with the existence of the mass of the *aporoi*, those who have no means, and the small number of the *euporoi*, those who have them' (Rancière 1995: 13). The task of politics is to calm and control the irreducible conflict between rich and poor, which means curbing the excesses of democracy. What we now call 'democracies' are actually oligarchies in which government is exercised by the minority over the majority. What makes them specifically democratic is that the power of oligarchies rests upon the power of the people, most obviously because governments are elected. In democracies, oligarchy and democracy are opposing principles in tension, and any regime is an unstable compromise between them. The public sphere is the sphere of encounters and conflicts between these principles: governments tend to reduce and appropriate the public sphere, relegating non-state actors to the private sphere; democracy is the struggle against this privatisation, to enlarge the public sphere and oppose the public/private division imposed by government.

In contemporary democracies, the 'conflictual equilibrium' associated with popular sovereignty is being undermined. The oligarchic system is being combined with a 'consensual vision' on the claim that contemporary reality, the global economy and the prospect of endless 'growth' which it promises, do not leave us with a choice. Government is the business of 'managing the local effects of global necessity', which requires consensus and an end to the 'archaic' indulgence of political division. Oligarchies are tempted by the vision of governing without the people, i.e., without the division of the people, which means effectively without politics, rendering popular sovereignty problematic. But the suppressed division inevitably returns, both in the form of mobilisation outside the political system (e.g., against the negative effects of neo-liberal globalisation or the Iraq war) and in the dangerous form of extreme-right nationalism and xenophobia.

A priority for political analysis is consequently contemporary processes of *depoliticisation*, which is by no means a new strategy (according to Rancière 1995, it is 'the oldest task of politics') but is now emerging in a particularly profound and threatening form. Depoliticisation is the exclusion of issues and/or of people from processes of political deliberation and decision – placing them outside politics. But politicisation is equally a priority if we are to analyse the tension between the principles of oligarchy and democracy, the democratic response to depoliticisation, and how responses might develop a momentum capable of contesting the push towards depoliticisation. Others have also identified depoliticisation and politicisation as priorities (Palonen 1993, Sondermann 1997, Muntigl 2002, Hay 2007), but from different theoretical perspectives.

This prioritisation provides a basis for questioning the centrality which has been attributed to other problems and issues. Let me briefly mention two. First, the centrality attributed to 'sub-politics' or 'life politics' by theorists of 'reflexive modernity', which is linked to the recent prominence of 'identity politics'. This accords with the perspective above in giving prominence to 'grassroots' political action, but clashes with it in construing such politics as an alternative to adversarial politics centred around the political system. The 'grassroots' politics of politicisation is both defined and limited by the opposing logic of depoliticisation, which means that state- and government-focused adversarial politics is by no means outdated. Second, the centrality attributed by, for instance, those influenced by Habermas to 'deliberative democracy' also tends to be associated with the assumption that adversarial politics can be superseded and to construe political dialogue as a rational process of consensus-formation, rather than a process which allows divisions, differences and conflicts to be contained within a shared political community without the assumption that these are just 'problems' waiting to be 'solved'. In different theoretical terms, we could say: these are *contradictions*, and although they can be managed, they cannot be solved within the parameters of the existing system (Jessop 2002). This does not diminish or ignore cooperation in politics: conflict in political dialogue requires cooperation (only those who are cooperating at a certain level can stage a conflict), and adversarial politics necessarily includes cooperative moments (e.g., the formation of alliances).

We can fruitfully develop a specifically semiotic 'point of entry' into analysing the processes of depoliticisation and politicisation. I shall illustrate this below in my analysis of the texts. This does not exclude other issues and associated categories which have tended to receive more attention in political discourse analysis, and indeed I shall refer to some (legitimation, manipulation, ideology, cooperation and identity). But it does imply a different 'mapping' of the relations between categories which may lead to reconceptualising or changing some of them.

Politicisation and depoliticisation are high-level strategies or 'macro-strategies'; so are legitimation and delegitimation. Strategies combine goals and means, and these macro-strategies are both means for achieving oligarchic or democratic goals (e.g., governing with minimal interference from political divisions, or pushing political differences into the public sphere), and goals in their own right associated with further strategies as means. We can identify strategies for (de)politicisation and (de)legitimation – for instance, 'authorisation' and 'rationalisation' have been suggested as legitimation strategies (van Leeuwen and Wodak 1999, van Leeuwen 2007). All of these are political strategies, not semiotic (or 'discourse') strategies, though they are generally realised semiotically. I suggested above that the object of research could be broadly formulated as the complex relationship between discourse and reality in adapting national strategy and policy for the global economy. We can now reformulate it more precisely: semiotic realisations of strategies of depoliticisation and politicisation in national responses to the 'global economy', focusing on the competitiveness policy in the UK.

4 An illustration: analysing political texts

I come now to the analysis of two sample texts. The one I shall begin with is the foreword written by the former British Prime Minister Tony Blair to the Department of Trade and Industry's White Paper, *Our Competitive Future: Building the Knowledge-Driven Economy* (1998) – see Appendix 1, page 253. I shall organise my comments according to the stages and steps listed in the Methodology section, but I have just been effectively discussing aspects of Stage 1 so I shall keep my comments on it brief.

Stage 1: Focus upon a social wrong, in its semiotic aspect

The social wrong I shall focus upon is the suppression or marginalisation of political differences over important issues of strategy and policy – how to respond nationally to radical international economic changes (and the prior question of what the changes actually are) – in favour of creating a consensus, which is, as I indicated above, a social wrong in that it undermines democracy but also poses the danger that dissent which cannot be politically articulated may emerge in nationalist or xenophobic forms. A semiotic point of entry is possible and fruitful, focusing upon semiotic realisations of the macro-strategy of depoliticisation, in accordance with the construction of the object of research which I have discussed above. The second text, an extract from a book (Brown and Coates 1996) written by former members of the Labour Party criticising Blair's 'New Labour' government, exemplifies semiotic realisations of the macro-strategy of politicisation. (Note that both macro-strategies may, however, be at work in the same text.) Blair's text is representative of the dominant tendency of the times towards depoliticisation; but this tendency coexists with politicising responses such as that of the second text, even if the latter often have a relatively marginal effect on government strategy and policy. I have already discussed steps 1 and 2 above, on the construction of an object of research for the research topic, in anticipation of the illustration, so we can move on to Stage 2.

Stage 2: Identify obstacles to addressing the social wrong

I shall discuss Stage 2 by taking each of the three steps it includes in turn.

Step 1: Analyse dialectical relations between semiosis and other social elements (orders of discourse and elements of social practices, texts and elements of events)

Step 1 also implicitly includes the dialectic between structures (at the intermediate level of social practices) and events (and strategies). I have already (in the previous section) given an indication of the social practices and orders of discourse at issue here, but let me fill this out a little with respect to the *restructuring* and *re-scaling* (Jessop 2002) tendencies associated with contemporary capitalism, and a brief note on New Labour in Britain. Restructuring is changes in structural relations, notably between economic and non-economic fields, which include extensive 'colonisation' of the latter (including politics and the state) by the former; re-scaling is changing relations between global,

regional, national and local scales of social life, including changes in government and governance. Analysing these tendencies would help contextualise
the UK strategies and policies which are in focus, i.e., help determine what
they are a part of. National governments are increasingly incorporated within
larger networks which include not only other governments but also international agencies (e.g., the European Union, the World Bank, the IMF), business networks and so forth. Governments, according to Castells (1996), are
increasingly coming to function as 'nodes' within a transnational network
based upon a business–government complex, whose central 'functions' are
focused upon creating the conditions (financial, fiscal, legal, 'human capital'
etc.) for successful competition in the 'global economy'. If the government
strategies and policies in focus here are locked into this powerful network, this
in itself constitutes a substantial obstacle to addressing the social wrong.

But these processes of restructuring and re-scaling have an important
semiotic dimension: the networks of social practices which they entail are
also orders of discourse which themselves cut across structural and scalar
boundaries. For example, the dominant neo-liberal discourse of globalisation
illustrated in the first text is dominant in education as well as politics, and in
the European Union, the World Bank and many other countries apart from
Britain. There are also genres and styles which are disseminated structurally
and in scale in a similar way (Fairclough 2006). Moreover, the semiotic dimension is fundamental to restructuring and re-scaling, in the sense that these
processes are 'semiotically driven'. They begin as discourses which constitute
'imaginaries' (Jessop 2004, 2008) – imaginary projections – for new relations
of structure and scale in economies, government, education and so forth;
these may become hegemonic, or dominant, and may be widely recontextualised; in so far as they do become hegemonic, they may be 'operationalised'
in new structures, practices, relations and institutions; and the operationalisation itself has a partly semiotic aspect in the emergence and dissemination of
genres and 'genre networks' (see below), which enable the governance of these
complex new networks, as well as styles. The semiotic dimension, deeply
embedded within and constitutive of the new structural and scalar relations, is
itself a part of the obstacles to addressing the social wrong.

With respect to the dialectic between texts and other elements of social
events, the general point is that political texts are not some superficial em-
broidery upon political events but a fundamental, constitutive part of them. In
this case, for example, the strategies and policies of the Blair government for
building British 'competitiveness' in adapting to the 'global economy' have
a clearly textual character. They are formed, disseminated and legitimised
within complex chains and networks of events (committee meetings, reports,

parliamentary debates, press statements and press conferences etc.) which are largely chains and networks of texts, i.e., different types of texts which are regularly and systematically linked together. They are linked, for instance, in accordance with the 'genre networks' I referred to above – systematically linked genres (e.g., discussion, report, debate) which semiotically constitute procedures – in this case, procedures of governance (on 'chains' of events, texts and genres, see Fairclough 2003). These strategy and policy processes thus have a largely textual character, and require textual analysis. The illustrative examples are just two small samples from the complex networks of texts involved.

The analysis would need to go into some detail about politics and social change in Britain. I have no space for such detail here, but let me make a couple of points (see further Fairclough 2000b). First, 'New Labour' abandoned the traditional social democracy of the British Labour Party to embrace the neo-liberalism of preceding Conservative governments (those of Margaret Thatcher and John Major). The effect was to produce a neo-liberal consensus on major policy issues within mainstream politics and a common political discourse – the associated tendency to exclude opposition is precisely the 'social wrong' I am addressing. Second, the infamous preoccupation of New Labour with media 'spin' (close management and manipulation of the presentation of policies and events in the media) indicates the growing importance of semiotic processes (political 'communication') in government. Thus, the form of politics which has developed with New Labour poses specifically semiotic obstacles to addressing the social wrong at issue.

Step 2: Select texts and categories for analysis

With respect to Step 2, the constitution of the object of research indicates the selection of texts in which the macro-strategies of depoliticisation and politicisation are semiotically realised. My examples here are both written texts, but one would also want to include, for instance, not only discussions, debates and interviews on TV and radio, and websites, but also material from campaigns, protests and demonstrations centred upon 'the global economy' and government strategy and policy oriented towards it, and material representing how people experience and react to the drive for 'competitiveness' in a variety of situated contexts (e.g., conversations and discussions within workplaces). Appropriate focuses and categories for the analysis include semiotic strategies which realise de/politicisation, including argumentation and rhetorical strategies, as well as semiotic aspects and realisations of legitimation, manipulation, ideology, cooperation and identity. I shall be more specific about some of these in discussing the texts.

Step 3: Carry out analyses of texts

The first text is structured as an argument whose structure we can schematically reconstruct as follows:

> *Premises*: The modern world is changing. There are opportunities to succeed and prosper in the modern world. If we want to succeed and prosper, we must compete effectively.
> *Implicit premise*: (We do want to succeed and prosper.)
> *Conclusion*: Therefore, we must compete (more) effectively.

The argumentation realises semiotically the macro-strategy of legitimation, and specifically the strategy of rationalisation: it is an example of the government's attempt to legitimise its political strategy and the policies associated with it as necessary responses to the situation. The argument is formally valid, but whether it is sound or not (i.e., whether it is a reasonable argument) depends upon the truth of its premises. We can challenge the argument, argue that it is fallacious, by challenging the truth of its premises (Ieţcu 2006). I want specifically to question the premises on the grounds that they (a) predicate the possible success of a problematic identity category as subject ('we'), and (b) falsely claim that the change attributed to the modern world is simply an inevitable fact of life which 'we' must accept.

Both of these flaws in the premises can be associated with the macro-strategy of depoliticisation. With respect to the first flaw, the identity category 'we' is problematic in that it is based upon a false equation between 'we' = 'Britain' and 'we' = all the citizens of Britain: if Britain achieves 'success' or 'prosperity', it does not follow that all of its citizens do. This is the 'fallacy of division', when a general category has properties which are mistakenly attributed to each of its parts. One sentence clearly implies that this does follow: 'That is the route to commercial success and prosperity for all'. This fallacy is a banal feature of governmental discourse, but it is fundamental to the macro-strategy of depoliticisation, whose basic strategic goal is to dedifferentiate potentially antagonistic identities – the internal division of the political community into 'us' and 'them'. In this sense, identity and the semiotic construal of identities are a major focus in analysis which prioritises depoliticisation.

The issue in semiotic terms is personal deixis. There are two personal 'deictic centres', or positionings of the author (Blair) with respect to identity: he positions himself within two group identities – 'we' = the government, and 'we' = the country. It is commonplace in the literature on identity that identity entails difference – 'we' entails 'they' (Connolly 1991). We might say that 'we' = the government is implicitly construed in opposition to 'they' = previous governments which pursued strategies which are rejected because they 'did not and cannot work': 'old-fashioned state intervention' and 'naive reliance on markets'; whereas 'we' = the country is construed in opposition to 'competitors'. But notice that the construal of personal deixis excludes a 'we/they' division both within the political community ('Britain') and within the contemporary political field (political system), where no contemporaneous political 'opposition' is construed. The implication is that there is consensus within both the political community and the political field. This is depoliticisation.

Texts semiotically construe identities and simultaneously seek to make these construals persuasive. The fact that we can show fallacies in Blair's argument does not mean that it will be widely perceived as fallacious, and we must consider what might make the argument and construal of identities persuasive. This brings us to the second flaw, in the construal of world change. Dominant construals of 'the new global order' have certain predictable linguistic characteristics (on the linguistic categories I mention below, see Fairclough (2003)): processes of change are construed without responsible social agents; they are construed in a timeless, ahistorical present; statements about the new economy (which are often very familiar truisms) are construed categorically and authoritatively as unmodalised truths, and there is a movement from the 'is' of the economic to the 'ought' of the political – from what is categorically the case to what 'we' ought to do in response; the new economic reality is construed as indifferent to place; and series of evidences or appearances in the new economy are construed paratactically as lists. I have shown elsewhere (Fairclough 2000b) that these features are sustained through recontextualisation, appearing in economic texts (e.g., texts of the World Bank), political texts, educational texts and so forth, as well as on different scales. They are also evident in Blair's text, and they can be seen as aspects of the semiotic realisation of depoliticisation. In the construal of economic change in the 'modern world', there is an absence of responsible social agents. Agents of material processes are abstract or inanimate. In the first paragraph, 'change' is the agent in the first (passive) sentence, and 'new technologies' and 'new markets' are agents in the second sentence – agents, notice, of intransitive verbs ('emerge', 'open up') which construe change as happenings or processes without agents. The third sentence is existential – 'new competitors' and 'new opportunities' are merely claimed to exist, not located within processes of change. Notice also that in the third paragraph, the inanimate 'this new world' is the agent of 'challenges', construing change itself as articulating what responses to it are necessary. By contrast, when it comes to national responses to these implacable and impersonal processes of world change, social agents are fully present – business, the government, the DTI and especially 'we'.

Turning to time, tense and modality, world change is construed in the ahistorical 'timeless' present tense, as indeed are national responses, and, in terms of modality, through authoritative categorical assertions of truisms (e.g., 'The modern world is swept by change', and indeed all five statements in the first paragraph). The only historical reference is to the 'old-fashioned' strategies in paragraph 4. There is a movement from 'is' to 'ought'. 'Ought' is implicit in paragraphs 2 and 3: 'our success depends on how well we exploit our most valuable assets' implies that we should exploit them; 'this new world challenges business to be innovative' and 'government to create' imply that business and government should do these things. From paragraph 5 onwards, 'ought' is explicit and recurrent – the modal verb 'must' occurs six times. The domain of 'is' is world change; the domain of 'ought' is national responses: a divide is textually constructed between economics and politics (there is an 'industrial policy', but focused on enabling the economic process rather than radically shaping it), fact and value, which excludes the former from the latter. This differs from the social democratic tradition from which New Labour has come; earlier Labour governments used political power to change the economy, for example by nationalising private industries, taking them into state control. In contrast with economic processes, political processes do have responsible social agents: the agent in processes modalised with 'must' is in five cases 'we' and in one case 'the government'. Summing up, world change is a process without a history which 'we' must respond to. Moreover, world change is implicitly construed as indifferent to place – there are no place expressions in the first or third paragraphs.

The syntax is paratactic,[3] in relations between both sentences and phrases within sentences. The first paragraph, for instance, consists of three paratactically related sentences (the second and third contain paratactically related clauses), listing evidences of world change. The same is true of the second paragraph. Notice that the sequencing of these sentences is not significant and is changeable (with minor rewording) without any substantive meaning change. Indeed, what is included in this list of evidences is somewhat arbitrary; for instance, the second sentence of the first paragraph might have been 'Huge amounts of money move across the globe in a fraction of a second, and even our family cat, Socks, has his own homepage on the World Wide Web'. The second clause is fanciful only in that Blair does not have a cat called Socks. It was actually included in a very similar list in a book by Bill Clinton. What is significant, rhetorically, is the relentless accumulation of evidences of change – what Clarke and Newman (1998) call 'the cascade of change' – which persuasively (and manipulatively) establishes the new economy as simple fact, what we must live with and respond to.

Summing up, change is authoritatively construed as lists of known appearances (and truisms) in the present which are indifferent to place and whose social agency is effaced, and which must be responded to in certain ways. These features together construe the new economy as a simple fact to which there is no alternative. They locate the 'global economy' within the 'realm of necessity', and therefore outside the 'realm of contingency and deliberation', i.e., outside the realm of politics, semiotically realising the macro-strategy of depoliticisation (Hay 2007). We can say that in so far as this sort of discourse achieves significant public acceptance, which it has, it is part of the obstacles to addressing the social wrong.

Let me briefly comment on interdiscursive analysis. One can see Blair's text as recontextualising analyses of the 'global economy' more fully elaborated in texts produced for instance by the World Bank, and their particular discourse (construals of, narratives of and arguments about the 'global economy'). Blair's text is not primarily an analytical text but an advocative text, arguing for 'necessary' policies. But it is interdiscursively complex in grounding this advocative argument in the recontextualised analysis, combining analytical and advocative genres (as well as economic and political discourses). This type of recontextualisation and interdiscursive hybridity is common as a semiotic realisation of a favoured legitimation strategy: legitimising by appeal to expert knowledge. Notice that the expert discourse is not the same here as it might be in specialist economic texts. For instance, in the first paragraph, the construal of change in the global economy is stripped down to three short sentences which furthermore incorporate characteristic features of political rhetoric (the dramatic metaphor 'swept by change', the antithesis of 'new competitors but also great new opportunities'), and which constitute dramatic and potentially persuasive formulations of premises in the argument. Recontextualisation involves transformation to suit the new context, which affects forms of interdiscursive hybridity.

In discussing Stage 2, I have identified a number of obstacles to addressing the social wrong at issue, and shown that they are partly semiotic in nature. Let me summarise them: the national and international networks that government strategies and policies are embedded within; the consensual character of mainstream politics in Britain; and an influential political discourse, exemplified in the Blair text, which in various ways contributes to depoliticising the global economy and national responses to it.

Stage 3: Consider whether the social order 'needs' the social wrong

I anticipated this example in discussing Stage 3 in the Methodology section, where I suggested how the suppression of political differences in favour

of consensus might be interpreted as necessary for states to operate effectively within the hegemonic, neo-liberal strategy. We might add that achieving
a broad consensus within the political system depends upon semiotic
conditions – achieving semiotic hegemony, or broad acceptance of the sort
of discourse we have here. And as I noted above, this can be interpreted in
terms of ideology as the naturalisation of meanings which sustain relations
of power and domination. So it seems plausible that the social order does
'need' the social wrong in this case – addressing it might require wider
changes in the social order – and that, since the wrong has a partly semiotic
character, it also 'needs' certain characteristics of contemporary political
discourse.

Stage 4: Identify possible ways past the obstacles

At this point, I shall introduce the second text (see Appendix 2, page 254), an
extract from a book (Brown and Coates 1996) written by two long-standing
members of the Labour Party about New Labour's view of what they call
'capitalist globalisation'. This will allow some necessarily brief, partial and
sketchy comments on the other main macro-strategy – politicisation.

I mentioned one adversarial feature in the first text: a rejection of the 'old
fashioned state intervention' and the 'naive reliance on markets' of previous
governments, while implying that there were no contemporaneous divisions
on the nature of 'world change' or the national strategies needed to adjust to it.
The second text, by contrast, enters into adversarial dialogue with contemporaries, specifically Blairites. The macro-strategy of politicisation is semiotically realised in the text's dialogicality. Specifically, there are claims which
are denials of claims made 'elsewhere', by New Labour politicians among
others: 'What has changed is not that capital is more mobile' and 'it is not true
that national governments – and by extension the European Union – are totally
lacking in powers to employ against the arbitrary actions of transnational
capital'. In this respect, the strategy is to politicise by construing the nature of
'world change' and government responses as controversial matters, subject to
political difference and division.

The second text also politicises by counterposing to the New Labour
narrative of collaboration between government and business a narrative of
conflict between government and business, capital and labour. Notice that
both texts construe the global(ised) economy as a reality which countries need
to adjust to, but in radically different ways. In the second but not the first, the
construal of the global(ised) economy does include responsible social agents:
the companies, whose actions are construed in general and negative terms

('moving internationally from bases . . .', 'the arbitrary actions of transnational capital', 'divide and conquer'). The text also construes relations between the companies and national governments, contrasting the 'clientelist' relations which tend to exist and which New Labour advocates ('nation-states . . . clients of transnational companies') with adversarial relations which could and by implication should exist ('employing' their 'powers . . . against the arbitrary actions of transnational capital', 'making or withholding tax concessions', 'bargaining'). The same contrast between what is and what could/ should be is construed in relations between the EU and national governments ('reinforcing' the status of nation states as 'clients' of the companies, versus 'offering a lead and challenge to the nation-states').

In sum, whereas the first text depoliticises by construing a consensus on the global economy as an inevitable fact of life and building national competitiveness as a necessary response, the second text politicises by construing the globalised economy as a stake in struggles between governments and transnationals, and capital and labour, and by opposing that construal to the government's consensualist construal.

But the mere existence of texts which politicise in this way does not amount to 'ways past the obstacles'. This text offers an imaginary for a different, politicising strategy in response to a differently conceived global(ised) economy; it shows that different imaginaries are possible and indeed exist, but we would also need to consider how feasible it would be to operationalise this or some other imaginary in a strategy which could actually succeed and be implemented in the face of the sort of obstacles I have begun to indicate. It's not impossible, but it's difficult to see how at present: there are abundant alternative imaginaries, but there is currently no clear counter-hegemonic strategy. A fuller treatment than I have space for would include an analysis of attempts to develop oppositional strategies and their semiotic dimensions.

5 Discussion

The theoretical claim that relations between semiosis and other social elements are dialectical in character, and the methodological focus on these relations rather than on semiosis as such, mean that this approach to CDA is particularly attuned to transdisciplinary research, to working with the grain of various bodies of social theory and research, but at the same time bringing to them an enhancement of their capacity to address often neglected semiotic dimensions of their research objects, as well as taking from them perspectives and research logics which can contribute to the further development of the dialectical–relational approach itself.

As with any approach, there are things about which the dialectical–relational approach has little to say. We should distinguish, however, between issues and problems it has not got around to because others seemed more pressing or more interesting or simply because life is short, and issues and problems which fall outside its remit and are thus not issues and problems for it (though they may be for other approaches). An example of the former is a relative emphasis on the workings of power rather than the workings of reception, reaction and resistance to power – I stress relative because the latter have not been entirely neglected (see, for instance, Fairclough (2006)). Critics might reasonably say that I have 'done it again' in this chapter, spending more time on depoliticisation than politicisation. This has been a bias in my work, perhaps partly because of the sort of left-wing politics I was involved with in the 1970s, but it is not in my opinion a limitation of the approach as such. An example of the latter is a lack of attention to psychological and cognitive matters. I would agree that cognitively oriented research on discourse can complement the dialectical–relational approach, but I would not accept that an absence of attention to cognitive issues is a 'blindspot' in the approach, still less that it in some sense invalidates the approach.

Chilton, for example, has suggested that a proper understanding of the cognitive capacities of humans may lead to the conclusion that CDA is trying to teach people what they already know. 'Put bluntly, if people have a natural ability to treat verbal input critically, in what sense can CDA either reveal in discourse what people can . . . already detect for themselves or educate them to detect it for themselves?' (Chilton 2005). Yet the closing sentences of Chilton (2004) note that 'if people are indeed political animals . . . then they are also in principle capable of doing their own political critique. The important question is whether they are free to do so'. I agree. Chilton (2005) argues that although there are various conditions under which people are not free, 'it is doubtful that any of them can be elucidated by purely linguistic or discourse-analytical means. For they would seem to have to do with economic forces or socio-political institutions'. The main problem with this argument is indicated by the contrast between 'purely' linguistic or discourse-analytical factors and economic forces or socio-political institutions. From a dialectical–relational perspective, economic forces and socio-political institutions are in part semiotic, and analysis has to be in part semiotic analysis. The fact that people have cognitive capacities which make them in principle capable of seeing through manipulative intentions and even doing their own political critique (which CDA, far from discounting, presupposes) does not mean that they are generally capable in practice of seeing through the complex dialectical relations between semiotic and non-semiotic elements which constitute the social, political and economic conditions of their lives.

APPENDIX 1   Building the knowledge-driven economy
Foreword by the Prime Minister

The modern world is swept by change. New technologies emerge constantly, new markets are opening up. There are new competitors but also great new opportunities.

Our success depends on how well we exploit our most valuable assets: our knowledge, skills and creativity. These are the key to designing high-value goods and services and advanced business practices. They are at the heart of a modern, knowledge-driven economy.

This new world challenges business to be innovative and creative, to improve performance continuously, to build new alliances and ventures. But it also challenges Government: to create and execute a new approach to industrial policy.

This is the purpose of this White Paper. Old-fashioned state intervention did not and cannot work. But neither does naïve reliance on markets.

The Government must promote competition, stimulating enterprise, flexibility and innovation by opening markets. But we must also invest in British capabilities when companies alone cannot: in education, in science and in the creation of a culture of enterprise. And we must promote creative partnerships which help companies: to collaborate for competitive advantage; to promote a long-term vision in a world of short-term pressures; to benchmark their performance against the best in the world; and to forge alliances with other businesses and employees. All this is the DTI's role.

We will not meet our objectives overnight. The White Paper creates a policy framework for the next ten years. We must compete effectively in today's tough markets if we are to prosper in the markets of tomorrow.

In Government, in business, in our universities and throughout society, we must do much more to foster an entrepreneurial spirit: equipping ourselves for the long term, prepared to seize opportunities, committed to constant innovation and enhanced performance. That is the route to commercial success and prosperity for all. We must put the future on Britain's side.

The Rt Hon Tony Blair MP, Prime Minister

APPENDIX 2

Capital has always been global, moving internationally from bases in the industrialised countries. What has changed is not that capital is more mobile . . . but that the national bases are less important as markets and production centres. In other words, the big transnational companies are not only bigger but more free-standing . . . The European Union, far from offering a lead and a challenge to the nation-states of Europe, reinforces their status as clients of the transnational companies. Indeed, this clientism applies not only to companies based in Europe . . . While it is true that a national capitalism is no longer possible in a globalised economy, it is not true that national governments – and by extension the European Union – are totally lacking in powers to employ against the arbitrary actions of transnational capital. There is much that governments can do in bargaining – in making or withholding tax concessions, for example . . . But such bargaining has to have an international dimension or the transnational companies can simply continue to divide and conquer . . . New Labour appears to have abandoned what remained of Labour's internationalist traditions . . . Yet the ICTFU, the European TUC and the Geneva trade groups all offer potential allies for strengthening the response of British labour to international capital (Brown and Coates 1996: 172–4).

Notes

1. I am grateful to Isabela Ieţcu, Michael Meyer and Ruth Wodak for commenting on a draft version of the chapter.
2. In the first edition of this book and in other publications, I referred to social 'problems' rather than 'wrongs'. I have changed this because I think that construing all wrongs as 'problems' which need 'solutions' – which can in principle be provided even if they have not been so far in practice – is part of the self-justifying (and one might say ideological) discourse of contemporary social systems in countries like Britain. The objection to it is that some wrongs are produced by systems and are not resolvable within them.
3. Paratactic–syntactic relations are relations between sentences, clauses or phrases which are grammatically equal, and are coordinated; they contrast with hypotactic relations, where there is one main sentence, clause or phrase, and others are subordinated.

capitalism

10. Understanding the new management ideology. A transdisciplinary contribution from critical discourse analysis and the new sociology of capitalism

Eve Chiapello and Norman Fairclough

Language of new capitalism

trans-disap.

Our aim in this paper is to explore how one might approach the language of new capitalism working in a transdisciplinary way. We come from different disciplinary and theoretical traditions, Economic Sociology and 'new sociology of capitalism' (Eve Chiapello) and a form of CDA developed within Linguistics (Norman Fairclough). We shall focus upon 'new management ideology', and in particular on a recent book of a highly influential management 'guru', Rosabeth Moss Kanter, who is Professor of Business Administration at Harvard Business School (Kanter 2001). To fit the scope of our analysis within the confines of a single paper, we concentrate on one chapter of the book, Chapter 9, 'Leadership for change'.

CDA is analysis of the dialectical relationships between discourse (including language but also other forms of semiosis, e.g., body language or visual images) and other elements of social practices. Its particular concern (in this approach) is with the radical changes that are taking place in contemporary social life, with how discourse figures within processes of change, and with shifts in the relationship between discourse/semiosis and other social elements within networks of practices. We cannot take the role of discourse in social practices for granted, it has to be established through analysis. And discourse may be more or less important and salient in one practice or set of practices than in another, and may change in importance over time. The new sociology of capitalism offers an account of the changes in the developed capitalist societies since the 1960s, using as pivotal the concept of 'spirit of capitalism' which comes from Weberian sociology but which has been reworked to fit analysis of contemporary capitalism. An alliance of the two approaches can, we believe, be productive for the study of language of new capitalism.

We see transdisciplinary research as a particular form of interdisciplinary research. Our concern is not simply to bring together different disciplines and theoretical–analytical frameworks in the hope of thereby producing richer insights into new management ideology. We are also concerned with how a dialogue between two disciplines and frameworks may lead to a development of both through a process of each internally appropriating the logic of the other as a resource for its own development.

We begin with a discussion of new management ideology based particularly upon the work of Boltanski and Chiapello (1999), followed by a brief outline of the version of Critical Discourse Analysis we draw upon, and an analysis of Chapter 9, focusing upon a number of extracts, which brings these two perspectives together. In the conclusion we consider the implications of the analysis for transdisciplinary research.

1   The theoretical framework of the 'new spirit of capitalism'

New management ideology is part of the broader ideological system of 'the new spirit of capitalism'. It is the part addressed to managers and people occupying intermediate levels in big companies. It focuses on explaining and justifying the way the companies are organised, or should be organised.

1.1   The notion of the 'spirit of capitalism'

The 'spirit of capitalism' is the ideology that justifies people's commitment to capitalism, and which renders this commitment attractive. It is a necessary construct because in many ways capitalism is an absurd system: wage-earners have lost ownership of the fruits of their labour as well as any hope of ever working other than as someone else's subordinate. As for capitalists, they find themselves chained to a never-ending and insatiable process. For both of these protagonists, being part of the process of capitalism is remarkably lacking in justification. Capitalistic accumulation requires commitment from many people, although few have any real chances of making a substantial profit. Many will be scarcely tempted to get involved in this system, and might even develop decidedly adverse feelings. This is an especially thorny problem in modern economies that require a high level of commitment from their employees, in particular from managers. The quality of the commitment that one can expect depends not only on economic stimuli, but also on the possibility that the collective advantages that derive from capitalism can be enhanced.

The 'spirit of capitalism' is the ideology which brings together these reasons for commitment to the system. The term 'ideology' is used here in a different sense from common conceptions which define it in terms of truth and falsehood. The 'spirit of capitalism' does not just legitimise the process of accumulation, it also constrains it – indeed it can only legitimise it in so far as it constrains it, for people are endowed in this neo-Weberian sociological perspective with real critical capacities with effects on the world. If one were to take the explanations contained in the spirit of capitalism to their logical conclusion, then not all profit would be legitimate, nor all enrichment fair, nor all accumulation legal. Actors' internalisation of a particular spirit of capitalism thus serves in the real world as a constraint on the process of accumulation. A spirit of capitalism approach thus provides a justification both for capitalism and for the criticisms that denounce the gap between the actual forms of accumulation and the normative conceptions of social order.

An ideology is a system of ideas, values and beliefs oriented to explaining a given political order, legitimising existing hierarchies and power relations and preserving group identities. Ideology explains both the horizontal structure (the division of labour) of a society and its vertical structure (the separation of rulers and ruled), producing ideas which legitimise the latter, explaining in particular why one group is dominant and another dominated, one why person gives orders in a particular enterprise while another takes orders. Ideology is thus closely linked to Weber's concept of legitimacy, for according to Weber domination and compliance require the belief of the dominated in the legitimacy of the dominant. Ideology is one of the central vectors of this legitimacy, even though Weber lacked a concept of ideology (Ricoeur 1997).

As Schumpeter and Marx realised perfectly well, one of the main characteristics of capitalism as a social order is that it constantly transforms itself. Capitalism in the general sense is capable of assuming highly variable historical forms, which continue to be capitalist through the continuity of a number of central features (wage-labour, competition, private property, orientation to capital accumulation, technical progress, the rampant commodification of all social activities). The 'spirit of capitalism' is therefore an ideology which serves to sustain the capitalist process in its historical dynamism while being in phase with the historically specific and variable forms that it takes. Thus there are in a sense two levels within the configuration of ideas of the 'spirit of capitalism' of a particular epoch: those which account for the process of capitalism over the long term (most of which have been shaped by economic theory), and those which accord with its historical incarnation at a given period of time within a given region of the world.

Three dimensions play a particularly important role at this second level in providing a concrete expression for the spirit of capitalism:

1. The first dimension indicates what is *stimulating* about an involvement with capitalism – in other words, how this system can help people to blossom, and how it can generate enthusiasm. This 'stimulating' dimension is usually related to the different forms of 'liberation' that capitalism offers.
2. A second set of arguments emphasises the forms of *security* that is offered to those who are involved, both for themselves and for their children.
3. Finally, a third set of arguments (and one that is especially important for our demonstration) invokes the notion of *justice* (or *fairness*), explaining how capitalism is coherent with a sense of justice, and how it contributes to the common good.

Thus one might argue that to successfully commit people to the capitalist process, the ideology which legitimises it needs to provide answers to these three implicit questions: what is stimulating about it, how does it provide security, how does it assure justice?

When seen in this light, the spirit of capitalism can be said to have undergone a number of historical changes. From the literature on the evolution of capitalism, one can sketch at least three 'spirits' that have appeared, at least in western Europe, one after the other, since the nineteenth century.

1. The first, described among others by Sombart, corresponds to a predominantly domestic form of capitalism. Its main incarnation is the entrepreneurial *bourgeois*. The 'excitement' dimension is manifested by an entrepreneurial spirit; its security dimension by respect for *bourgeois* morality. In this instance, fairness mechanisms essentially revolve around charity and personal assistance.
2. A second 'spirit' (descriptions of which were found between the 1930s and the 1960s) which focuses on the idea of the large, integrated firm. Its main incarnation is the salaried director. Security is to be achieved through mechanisms such as career development and by the link between private capitalism and the rise of a welfare state. Fairness takes on a very meritocratic form in that it incorporates skills whose certification involves the awarding of credentials.
3. A third form of capitalism, which began to manifest itself during the 1980s.

Boltanski and Chiapello (1999) focused on the way in which the spirit of capitalism changed between the 1960s and 1990s. They devoted the first two chapters (of a book containing seven) to describing the changes on the basis of an analysis of texts (as Weber and Sombart had done previously) that provide moral education on business practices. For our era, this meant two bodies of work from the field of management studies: one from the 1960s and one from the 1990s (each representing around 500 pages and 50 texts). The text we chose to analyse in this article is a good example of the kind of texts they studied, and, in fact, Kanter was one of the authors (in French translation) in the 1990s' corpus.

From a CDA perspective, a 'spirit of capitalism' can be regarded as an 'order of discourse', a configuration of discourses articulated together in a particular way, dialectically enacted as ways of acting (and discoursally in genres)

Table 10.1 Three spirits of capitalism

	First spirit End of nineteenth century	Second spirit 1940–1970	Third spirit Since 1980s
Forms of the capital accumulation process	Small family firms Bourgeois capitalism	Managerial firms Big industrial companies Mass production State economic policy	Network firms Internet and biotech Global finance Varying and differentiated production
Excitement	Freedom from local communities Progress	Career opportunities Power positions Effectiveness possible in 'free countries'	No more authoritarian chiefs Fuzzy organisations Innovation and creativity Permanent change
Fairness	A mix of domestic and market fairness	Meritocracy valuing effectiveness Management by objectives	New form of meritocracy valuing mobility, ability to nourish a network Each project is an opportunity to develop one's employability
Security	Personal property, Personal relationships Charity Paternalism	Long-term planning Careers Welfare state	For the mobile and the adaptable, the ones who know how to manage themselves, companies will provide self-help resources

Cité = justificatory regime (handwritten)

and inculcated as ways of being or identities (and discoursally in styles). See further below.

1.2 The fairness dimension of the spirit of capitalism: the 'cité' model

To be able to identify the exact nature of the notion of fairness as depicted in the management texts they studied, Boltanski and Chiapello (1999) used a theoretical construct that Luc Boltanski had developed together with Laurent Thévenot in an earlier publication (Boltanski and Thévenot 1991): the 'justificatory regime' model ('cité' in French). This construct had initially been designed with a view to highlighting the conditions that make it possible to say whether an evaluation or distribution of goods was being done in a fair and legitimate manner. Such judgements can be accepted as legitimate and support an agreement between different people because they are supposed to be unrelated to the characteristics of those who have made them and, particularly, independent of their power. They refer to 'legitimate orders' which are endowed with a very general validity, and which are at a level above the concrete and particular situations evaluated, constituted by conventions generally accepted in a society for judging the fairness of social arrangements.

Boltanski and Thévenot (1991) called these legitimate orders '*cités*' (thus referring to classical political philosophies whose object had been to design a legitimate order based on a principle of justice) and argued that they can be used to reach *agreement* as well as to support *criticism*. However, as opposed to political philosophies that had usually attempted to anchor this social order in a single principle, they argued that, in complex modern societies, several justificatory regimes can coexist within the same social space, even though their relevance may vary in accordance with the situation (i.e., with the material or symbolic nature of the objects involved).

They identified six justificatory regimes:

1. the Inspirational *Cité*,
2. the Domestic *Cité*,
3. the *Cité* of Renown,
4. the Civic *Cité*,
5. the Market *Cité*, and
6. the Industrial *Cité*.

Each of these justificatory regimes is based upon a different principle of evaluation ('equivalency principle') which entails a form of general equivalency (a standard) without which comparative evaluations become impossible. In terms of a given standard (e.g., efficiency in the Industrial *Cité*), people's 'test results', and hence their specific (e.g., industrial) value for the rest of society, can vary. A person's worth, assessed through a legitimate process and in terms of a given standard, was called his/her 'greatness'.

In the Inspirational *Cité*, greatness is defined as being akin to a saint who has reached a state of grace (or an inspired artist). This quality appears after a period of ascetic preparation, and is expressed mostly through manifestations of inspiration (sainthood, creativity, an artistic sense, authenticity etc.). In the Domestic *Cité*, people rely on their hierarchical position in a chain of personal interdependencies in order to achieve greatness. The political ties that unite people spring from a model of subordination which is based on a domestic pattern. These ties are thought of as a generalisation of generational ties that combine tradition and proximity. The 'great one' is the elder, the ancestor, the father to whom respect and allegiance are due, and who in turn grants protection and support. In the *Cité* of Renown, greatness depends only on other people's opinions, i.e., on the number of persons who will grant credit and esteem. The 'great one' in the Civic *Cité* is the representative of the group, the one who expresses its collective will. In the Market *Cité*, the 'great' person is the one who makes a fortune for him- or herself by offering highly coveted goods in a competitive marketplace – and who knows when to seize the right opportunities. Finally, in the Industrial *Cité*, greatness is based on efficiency and determines a scale of professional abilities.

Justificatory regimes are described using a basic 'grammar' that specifies among other things:

(a) an *equivalency principle* (in reference to which an evaluation can be made of all actions, things and persons for that particular *Cité*);

(b) a *state of greatness*, a 'great one' being a person who strongly embodies the *Cité*'s values, and the *state of smallness*, defined as lack of greatness;

(c) a *format of investment*, this being a major precondition for each *Cité*'s stability since, by linking greatness to sacrifice (which takes a specific form in each *Cité*), it ensures that all rights are offset by responsibilities;

(d) a *paradigmatic test* which, for each justificatory regime, best reveals a person's greatness. In order to avoid an idealistic construction that is overly reliant on verbal argumentation, people's claims have to be confronted with the real world, hence pass a series of more or less standardised procedures called *tests* ('*épreuve*' in French). In the end, it is the outcome of these tests that lends substance to the judgements people make. This is what provides them with the strength that they need to stand up to challenges.

In terms of justificatory regimes or '*cités*', the dimension of justice of the first spirit of capitalism depends mainly upon the Domestic and Market regimes, whereas the Industrial and Civic regimes become more salient in the second.

In their study of the third spirit of capitalism, Boltanski and Chiapello (1999) showed that the six justificatory regimes identified by Boltanski and Thévenot (1991) cannot fully describe all of the types of justification that can be found in the 1990s' texts. A new and increasingly influential justificatory logic has emerged which emphasises mobility, availability, and the variety of one's personal contacts: a Projects-oriented or Connectionist *Cité*. This refers to a form of justice or fairness that is appropriate in a world which is organised by networks which are connectionist and reticular in nature.

In the Project-oriented *Cité* the general standard with respect to which greatness is evaluated is *activity*. In contrast with the Industrial *Cité* where activity means 'work' and being active means 'holding a steady and wage-earning position', in the Project-oriented *Cité* activity overcomes the oppositions between work and non-work, steady and casual, paid and unpaid, profit-sharing and volunteer work. Life is conceived as a series of projects: the more they differ from one another, the more valuable. What is relevant is to be always pursuing some sort of activity, never to be without a project, without ideas, to be always looking forward to, and preparing for, something along with other persons, who are brought together by the drive for activity. When starting on a new project, all participants know that it will be short-lived. The perspective of an unavoidable and desirable end is built in the nature of the involvement, without curtailing the enthusiasm of the participants. Projects

Table 10.2 Part of the grammar of the Project-oriented or Connectionist *Cité*

Equivalency principle (general standard): activity; project initiation; remote links between people

A state of smallness: inability to get involved, to trust in others, to communicate; closed-mindedness, intolerance, stability, over-reliance on one's roots, rigidity

A state of greatness: adaptability, flexibility, polyvalence; sincerity in face-to-face encounters; ability to spread the benefits of social connections, to generate enthusiasm and to increase team members' employability

Format of investment: ready to sacrifice all that could curtail one's availability, giving up lifelong plans

Standard (paradigmatic) test: ability to move from one project to another

are well adapted to networking for the very reason that they are transitory forms: the succession of projects, by multiplying connections and increasing the number of ties, results in an expansion of networks.

In the Project-oriented *Cité*, a 'great one' must be adaptable and flexible. But these qualities by themselves cannot suffice to define the state of 'being great' because they could also be implemented in an opportunistic way, to pursue a strictly selfish course towards success. By contrast, a 'great' person will take advantage of his/her given qualities to contribute to the common good. In the Project-oriented *Cité*, a 'great one' therefore also generates a feeling of trust. S/he does not lead in an authoritarian way, as did the hierarchical chief, but manages the team by listening to others with tolerance and by respecting their differences. S/he redistributes among them the connections s/he has secured through networks. Such a project manager hence increases all his/her team-mates' *employability*.

The corpus of 1990s texts is marked by the salience of legitimations based upon the Project-oriented *Cité*, and the decline of the Industrial and Civic *Cités* which were salient in the second spirit of capitalism, as well as the virtual disappearance of the Domestic, part of whose vocabulary is nevertheless drawn upon but completely recontextualised within the Project-oriented *Cité*. There is also an increase in the salience of the Inspirational and, to a lesser degree, the Merchant *Cités*.

Boltanski and Chiapello (1999) is oriented to the language of the new capitalism, seeing each *Cité* or justificatory regime as associated with a specific vocabulary in terms of which the categories of the 'grammar' of each *Cité* (the state of 'greatness', the state of 'smallness', the format of investment etc.) can be described. In terms of CDA, a *Cité* or justificatory regime can be regarded as a discourse. Since a *Cité* is a durable and transferable structure (transferable across fields, e.g., between the capitalist organisation, the family, the political system) at a relatively high level of abstraction, we use 'Discourse' with a capital 'D'. This convention is also useful in that each such Discourse is itself analysable as a configuration of discourses (lower case 'd') as we show below. Many of these discourses appear as metaphors or similes, e.g., the 'change-masters' of Kanter's text become 'idea scouts', they 'establish their own listening posts'; creativity is 'like looking at the world through a kaleidoscope'. In analysing a text such as the one we focus on here, CDA is concerned not only with identifying within it elements of the order of discourse and the Discourses of a particular 'spirit of capitalism' and particular *Cités*. It is also concerned with how the work of texturing, making texts as a part of making meaning, in such influential texts as Kanter's itself contributes to the dissemination of the new 'spirit of capitalism'.

2 Critical discourse analysis

Critical discourse analysis is based upon a view of semiosis as an irreducible element of all material social processes. Social life is seen as interconnected networks of social practices of diverse sorts (economic, political, cultural, family etc.). Centring the concept of social practice allows an oscillation between the perspective of social structure and the perspective of social action and agency – both necessary perspectives in social research and analysis (Chouliaraki and Fairclough 1999). By 'social practice' we mean a relatively stabilised form of social activity. Examples would be classroom teaching, television news, family meals, medical consultations, or work situations inside innovation projects (like the one represented in the Kanter text).

Every practice is an articulation of diverse social elements in a relatively stable configuration, always including discourse. Let us say that every practice includes the following elements: activities, subjects, and their social relations, instruments, objects, time and place, forms of consciousness, values, discourse (or semiosis). These elements are dialectically related (Harvey 1996). That is to say, they are different elements but not discrete, fully separate, elements. There is a sense in which each 'internalises' the others without being reducible to them. So, for instance, social relations, social identities, cultural values and consciousness are in part semiotic, but that does not mean that we theorise and research social relations for instance in the same way that we theorise and research language – they have distinct properties, and researching them gives rise to distinct disciplines.

Discourse figures in broadly three ways in social practices:

1. It figures as a part of the social activity within a practice. For instance, part of doing a job (for instance, as a shop assistant or a manager) is using language in a particular way; so too is part of governing a country. Discourse as part of social activity constitutes genres. Genres are diverse ways of acting, of producing social life, in the semiotic mode. Examples are: everyday conversation, meetings in various types of organisation, political and other forms of interview, book reviews, or guides for managing e-firms (like Kanter's book).
2. Discourse figures in representations. Social actors within any practice produce representations of other practices, as well as ('reflexive') representations of their own practice, in the course of their activity within the practice. They 'recontextualise' other practices (Bernstein 1990, Chouliaraki and Fairclough 1999), that is, they incorporate them into their own practice, and different social actors will represent them differently

according to how they are positioned within the practice. Discourse in the representation and self-representation of social practices constitutes discourses (note the difference between 'discourse' as an abstract noun, and 'discourse(s)' as a count noun). For instance, the lives of poor and disadvantaged people are represented through different discourses in the social practices of government, politics, medicine and social science, and through different discourses within each of these practices corresponding to different positions of social actors.

3. Discourse figures in ways of being, in the constitution of identities – for instance the identity of a political leader such as Tony Blair in the UK is partly a semiotically constituted way of being. Discourse as part of ways of being constitutes styles – for instance the styles of business managers, or political leaders.

Social practices networked in a particular way constitute a social order – for instance, the emergent neo-capitalist global order referred to above, or at more local level, the social order of education in a particular society at a particular time. The discourse/semiotic aspect of a social order is what we can call an *order of discourse*. It is the way in which diverse genres and discourses and styles are networked together. An order of discourse is a social structuring of semiotic difference – a particular social ordering of relationships among different ways of making meaning, i.e. different discourses and genres and styles. One aspect of this ordering is dominance: some ways of making meaning are dominant or mainstream in a particular order of discourse, others are marginal, or oppositional, or 'alternative'. For instance, there may be a dominant way to conduct a doctor–patient consultation in Britain, but there are also various other ways, which may be adopted or developed to a greater or lesser extent in opposition to the dominant way. The dominant way probably still maintains social distance between doctors and patients, and the authority of the doctor over the way interaction proceeds; but there are others ways which are more 'democratic', in which doctors play down their authority. The political concept of 'hegemony' can usefully be used in analysing orders of discourse (Laclau and Mouffe 1985, Fairclough 1992a) – a particular social structuring of semiotic difference may become hegemonic, become part of the legitimising common sense which sustains relations of domination, but hegemony will always be contested to a greater or lesser extent, in hegemonic struggle. An order of discourse is not a closed or rigid system, but rather an open system, which is put at risk by what happens in actual interactions.

The 'spirit of capitalism' as defined above can be seen as an order of discourse characterised by dominant discourses (enacted as genres, inculcated as styles) but also by oppositional or 'alternative' discourses (genres, styles). This accords with the view in Boltanski and Chiapello (1999) that any capitalist order is constantly traversed by critique. They show how the birth of the third spirit of capitalism is a response to and incorporation of what they call the 'artistic critique' of the 1960s and 1970s.

We said above that the relationship between discourse and other elements of social practices is a dialectical relationship – discourse internalises and is internalised by other elements without the different elements being reducible to each other. They are different, but not discrete. If we think of the *dialectics of discourse* in historical terms, in terms of processes of social change, the question that arises is the ways in which and the conditions under which processes of internalisation take place. Take the concept of a 'knowledge economy' and 'knowledge society'. This suggests a qualitative change in economies and societies such that economic and social processes are knowledge-driven – change comes about, at an increasingly rapid pace, through the generation, circulation, and operationalisation of knowledges in economic and social processes. The relevance of these ideas here is that 'knowledge-driven' amounts to 'discourse-driven': knowledges are generated and circulate as discourses, and the process through which discourses become operationalised in economies and societies is precisely the dialectics of discourse.

Discourses include imaginaries – representations of how things might or could or should be. The knowledges of the knowledge-economy and knowledge-society are imaginaries in this sense – projections of possible states of affairs, 'possible worlds'. These imaginaries may be enacted as actual (networks of) practices – imagined activities, subjects, social relations etc. can become real activities, subjects, social relations etc. Such enactments include materialisations of discourses, in the 'hardware' (plant, machinery etc.) and the 'software' (management systems etc.). Such enactments are also in part themselves discoursal/semiotic: discourses become enacted as genres. So new management discourses become new genres, for instance genres for team meetings. Discourses as imaginaries may also come to be inculcated as new ways of being, new identities. The dialectical process does not end with enactment and inculcation. Social life is reflexive. That is, people not only act and interact within networks of social practices, but they also interpret and represent to themselves and each other what they do, and these interpretations and representations shape and reshape what they do.

There is nothing inevitable about the dialectics of discourse. A new discourse may come into an institution or organisation without being enacted or inculcated. It may be enacted, yet never be fully inculcated. For instance, managerial discourses have been quite extensively enacted within British universities (for instance as procedures of staff appraisal, including a new genre of 'appraisal interview'), yet arguably the extent of inculcation is very limited – most academics do not 'own' these management discourses. This has a bearing on theories of 'social constructionism' (Sayer 2000). It is a commonplace in contemporary social science that social entities (institutions, organisations, social agents etc.) are or have been constituted through social processes, and a common understanding of these processes highlights the effectivity of discourses: social entities are in some sense effects of discourses. Where social constructionism becomes problematic is where it disregards the relative solidity and permanence of social entities, and their resistance to change. In using a dialectical theory of discourse in social research, one needs to take account, case by case, of the circumstances which condition whether and to what degree social entities are resistant to new discourses.

The Boltanski and Chiapello (1999) argument can be formulated in these terms. A spirit of capitalism is an order of discourse where discourses are dialectically enacted in 'action models' (e.g., 'tests') which are partially semiotic in character, i.e., it is partly a matter of discourses being enacted as genres, and dialectically inculcated in ways of being (identities) such as new manager identities, partly again a semiotic inculcation of discourses in styles, partly a matter of extra-semiotic embodiment – with the proviso that the dialectical movement continues as these enactments/inculcations of the discourse are themselves ongoingly and diversely represented in new discourses. This reformulation seems to us to clarify the position of discourse (semiosis) in the Boltanski and Chiapello (1999) model, while avoiding any reductive discourse idealism, which is a shared concern for both CDA and the new sociology of capitalism.

3 Analysis of the sample text

We have chosen a recent text of one of the best-known management 'gurus'. Boltanski and Chiapello (1999) point out that this type of literature, aimed at informing managers about the latest innovations in managing enterprises and people, is one of the main places of inscription of the spirit of capitalism. Though, as dominant ideology, it has a general capacity to penetrate the mental representations of the epoch – political and trade union discourses, journalism, research and so forth. Like the spirit of capitalism, which is oriented both to capital accumulation and to principles of legitimation, management literature contains both new methods of running enterprises and making profit, and justification for the way these are done – arguments which managers can use to respond to criticisms and to demands for them to justify themselves.

The sample text is thus a good example of the many texts which contribute to the constitution and inculcation of the new 'spirit of capitalism', in terms of the dimensions of stimulation, security and justice and in terms of the *Cités* which are drawn upon to ground legitimation in terms of justice, and those which are conversely devalued. We shall look at it in terms of the three inter-connected but analytically separable aspects of genre, style and discourses. That is, what sort of activity is this a part of; what sort of interaction charac-terised by what sort of social relations (genre); what sort of authorial identity is constituted here (style); what sort of representations do we find here of work and organisations and their members in the new economy (discourses)?

3.1 Genre

The blurb on the book cover can give us an initial sense of genre. The book 'provides a hands-on blueprint for adopting the core principles of e-culture', 'identifies and analyses the emergence of e-culture – and provides a lively roll-up-your-sleeves guide to profiting from tomorrow'. So in addition to being an 'analysis', it is a 'guide', a 'blueprint'.

The chapter we are focusing on is the ninth of ten chapters, which are divided into three Parts. Part One ('Searching, searching: The Challenge of Change') sets forth 'a variety of challenges' – centrally, the challenge of the internet. Part Two analyses 'the implications for business of the advent of the Internet and identifies best practices in implementing e-culture principles'. Part Three (which Chapter 9 is in) 'offers a practical guide to change – how to move fast to transform a whole organization, how to lead change, and how to cultivate the human skills required for an Internet-enabled world'. Chapter 9 focuses on 'how to lead change'.

Chapter 9 is made up of an introduction which identifies seven 'classic skills involved in innovation and change', a section on each 'skill', and a con-cluding section entitled 'The Rhythm of Change'. The dominant genre is a form of self-help guide, embedded in an actional sequence which potentially moves from acquiring knowledge to applying knowledge, from learning to doing. Its social relations are those of expert advice, between an expert and would-be learners and users. One might see presentation of research results as a subsidiary genre, though its relationship to the dominant genre is complex as we show below, and it is only marginally present. Shifts in genre imply shifts in social relations, for instance, there is a brief levelling of the ground between writer and readers at the beginning of the chapter as the genre shifts to dialogue ('Wait a minute. Haven't we heard this before? Of course we have.') In accordance with the genre, targeted readers are 'managers' and 'executives', as indicated by appreciative comments about the book quoted on the cover: they all come, with one exception, from Chief Executive Officers of companies, i.e., from those with whom ambitious managers identify. It is assumed that to succeed in one's professional life as they have done, one must apply Kanter's prescriptions.

Genres are realised in semantic and lexico-grammatical features of texts. Let us look at the dominant genre in these terms. Most of the sections on 'skills' begin with statements which make categorical claims. Some of these are explicitly normative statements with obligational modalities ('A raw idea that emerges from the kaleidoscope must be shaped into a theme that makes the idea come alive', 'Sensing an opportunity on the horizon is only part of the picture; an additional mental act of imagination is needed to find a creative new response to it.'). Others are apparently statements of fact (e.g., 'Innovation begins with someone being smart enough to sense a new need') but with an implicitly normative force ('To be innovative, leaders must be smart enough . . .'). There are many such ostensible descriptions which are implicit prescriptions in the chapter (e.g., 'Changemasters find many ways to monitor external reality', 'Changemasters sense problems and weaknesses before they represent full-blown threats'), and they are more frequent than explicit prescriptions. This gives the sense that 'analysis' predominates over prescription. Yet although the book is said to be based upon responses from 785 organisations, 300 original interviews in nearly 80 companies, and detailed case studies of over two dozen companies, this is not a scientific analysis, and neither the claims made nor the examples given are documented with evidence from the data. Nor is there a methodological section explaining how the collection and analysis of the data ground the claims made in the book, though there is a summary of 'selected survey findings' in an Appendix. All that is said about the relationship of the research and the book is that the results 'are reflected in the lessons of this book'.

There is an oscillation between explicit or implicit normative claims or prescriptions, and examples which are summarised anecdotally in a sentence or two, or just a quotation from a Chief Executive Officer. Here is an example of this oscillation from the section on 'Skill 3':

Extract 1
Changemasters have to focus people's eyes on the prize – to get them to see the value beyond the hardship of change to the prize waiting at the end. When honkong.com changed its business model and set a new theme,

director Rudy Chan reported: 'We needed to go through quite a lot of explaining. We had to tell them why. And what's in it for them in terms of career opportunities. And we needed to do that several times. It was a lot of communication.'

The anecdotal examples often presuppose a knowledge of the case or the company as this does – 'When honkong.com changed its business model and set a new theme' presupposes that (assumes reader knowledge that) honkong.com did change its business model and set a new theme.

In terms of taxis, or the way in which clauses and sentences are related to each other, the syntax is predominantly paratactic, one clause or sentence constituting an addition to others, so that meanings (e.g., the meaning of 'leadership') are cumulatively built up. This is most obvious in the predilection for lists. There are seven lists in the chapter which are set off in the text, either numbered or with bullet points (for instance: 'The customer avoidance trap, The competitor avoidance trap, The challenger avoidance trap'), and other lists embedded in the text (e.g., 'preselling, making deals, getting a sanity check' as the 'actions' which constitute 'coalition-building'). Such lists are easily memorised, and facilitate the transition from prescription to action (think of shopping lists, or 'to do' lists). On the other hand, a paratactic additive relationship is inimical to complexity, analysis and argumentation. But the paratactic relationship is not by any means limited to lists. It predominates in the way sentences are related to each other in paragraphs, the way paragraphs are related to each other, the way clauses and phrases are related to each other in sentences. Take for instance the extract on 'Skill 2'.

Extract 2
Skill 2. Kaleidoscopic Thinking: Stimulating Breakthrough Ideas
Sensing an opportunity on the horizon is only part of the picture; an additional mental act of imagination is needed to find a creative new response to it. Changemasters take all the input about needs and opportunities and use it to shake up reality a little, to get an exciting new idea of what's possible, to break through the old pattern and invent a new one.
    Creativity is a lot like looking at the world through a kaleidoscope. You look at a set of elements, the same ones that everyone else sees, but then reassemble those floating bits and pieces into an enticing new possibility. Innovators shake up their thinking as though their brains are kaleidoscopes, permitting an array of different patterns out of the same bits of reality. Changemasters challenge prevailing wisdom. They start from the premise that there are many solutions to a problem and that by changing the angle on the kaleidoscope, new possibilities will emerge. Where

other people would say 'That's impossible. We've always done it this way,' they see another approach. Where others see only problems, they see possibilities.

There are additive paratactic relations between the two paragraphs; between all the sentences in each paragraph; between clauses within sentences (e.g., the first and second sentences). There are also some hypotactic relations within sentences (e.g., the purpose clauses in sentence 2, 'to shake up . . . invent a new one' – notice that they themselves constitute three paratactically related clauses). In addition to additive paratactical relations, there are contrastive paratactical relations marked by 'but' and 'whereas'. A portrait of the kaleidoscopic thinking of 'changemasters' is cumulatively built up by adding one statement to others, and contrasting the 'changemaster' with 'others'.

The contrastive or adversative element is itself a significant feature of the syntax of the text, and it can be related to the Boltanski–Chiapello view of the 'grammar' of justificatory regimes (or *Cités*): they incorporate a contrast and a relation between 'the great ones' and 'the small ones', those who strongly embody the *Cité*'s values those who do not. This is a defining characteristic of this genre of 'popular management discourse' as opposed to 'academic, practical and political' management discourses (Furusten 1999). The 'great one' is an example to readers; the 'small one', always described in unfavourable terms, serves as a foil. It is obvious that a text which aims at action and implementation will represent prescribed behaviour in its best light and devalue alternatives, especially when the latter are not (in contrast to criminal behaviour, for instance) inherently negative. The 'great ones' are also systematically associated with the future, the 'small ones' with the past, on the basis of a banal ideology of progress.

3.2 Style

The issue here is the sort of identity which is projected in the text for its author. We can see this in terms of what the author is implicitly committed to by the way the text is written – being a particular sort of person, claims about what is the case, value claims about what is good and desirable. The author is clearly projected as an expert through the explicit prescriptions and implicit prescriptions (apparent descriptions) which are pervasive through the text. Overwhelmingly, their modality is 'strong' – that is, the prescriptions of what should be done and the descriptions of what is the case are categorical, unmitigated, not hedged. Take, for example, 'Changemasters sense problems and weaknesses before they represent full-blown threats' and 'Leaders must wake people out of inertia'. There are various ways in which the claim of the former and the prescription of the latter might be mitigated and made less categorical: replacing 'sense' with 'often sense' or 'tend to sense' or 'may sense' in the former, replacing 'must wake' with 'ought to wake' or 'should try to wake' in the latter. There are exceptions in the chapter, cases where modality is mitigated, for example: '. . . changemasters *are often* more effective when they are insiders bringing a revolutionary new perspective. A foundation of community and a base of strong relationships inside large organisations *can speed* the change process'. These are the (relatively rare) points in the text where we hear at least a trace of the more circumspect voice of the academic researcher reporting on the results of research, and they can be seen as contributing to a hybrid style – the author is projected primarily as an expert guide (and all-knowing 'guru') but with marginal traces of the academic researcher. There are also other relatively marginal diversities, including the brief shift to dialogue alluded to above ('Wait a minute. Haven't we heard this before? Of course we have.'), where the author is projected as a co-participant with the reader in an event such as a seminar or meeting.

Style is also linked to values – the value commitments made in the text are part of the constitution of an authorial identity. Values can be made explicit through evaluations, e.g., 'These pieces of the picture are *important* because sometimes people just don't understand what the change leader is talking about'. But for the most part values are implicit – they are value assumptions. For instance: 'an additional mental act of imagination is needed to find a *creative new response*'. 'Finding a creative new response' is assumed to be a good thing to do, though it is not explicitly said to be desirable. Such assumed values are pervasive through this text – and the assumption is that they are shared values, shared within the reading community of the text. These values emanate in Boltanski and Chiapello's terms from the 'equivalency principles' of the *cités* (the Discourses) which are present in the text, in particular the 'inspirational' (e.g., 'find a creative response') and 'connectionist' (e.g., 'coalition building') *cités*, as in the majority of popular management texts of the 1990s. The values associated with other *cités* are present in the adversative relations of the text – as rejected values.

The author, Rosabeth Kanter, is what is normally called a management 'guru'. Being a guru is partly a matter of credentials and standing (e.g., being a professor at the prestigious Harvard Business School), and partly a matter of book sales and the attractiveness and cost of the seminars one leads (Huczynski 1993, Jackson 2001). It is centrally a matter of having the authority to project, predict and interpret the future (Kanter 'predicts how the Internet will alter the way we work in the future', according to the description of her book on Amazon.com), prescribe what people need to succeed in the future, and have people act on those prescriptions. The slippage from description to prescription which we have described above is a central feature of guru style: the performative power of statements which aim to bring about what they represent as actual. Bourdieu (1991) has described this prescriptive power of descriptions in political discourse. Visionaries, gurus, traditionally belonged to the domains of religion and politics; they have now extended their domain into management. Kanter constructs herself as 'changemaster' in this text, as an incarnation of the new business hero she presents to readers. Her creativity is foregrounded in the opening words of the book: 'Evolve! – The song. Lyrics by Rosabeth Moss Kanter'. And the text itself can be seen as enacting the 'kaleidoscope thinking' it attributes to leaders: 'You look at a set of elements . . . but then reassemble those floating bits and pieces into an enticing new possibility'. There is an enticing, seductive character to Kanter's text. The sheer semantic heterogeneity of the text is striking – the diversity of the discourses, metaphors and similes which are articulated together in the construal of leadership.

3.3 Discourse

To win conviction and enhance the prospects for action, texts in this genre must address the three dimensions of legitimation distinguished by Boltanski and Chiapello (1999): stimulation, security and justice. It is the first of these dimensions (the promise of stimulation) that is most prominent, while the others (security and justice) are relatively underdeveloped in Kanter's book as in the texts studied by Boltanski and Chiapello. For instance, there is nothing about what happens to 'laggards' or to leaders ('changemasters') who fail. Boltanski and Chiapello (1999) predict this for the early stages of a new spirit of capitalism before its novelty wears off. As the element of stimulation diminishes, people begin to see the limits of the new order in terms of security and justice, and the spirit of capitalism must strengthen these dimensions to stand up to critique.

The promise of stimulation evokes a world of change, innovation, creativity ('to offer a dream, to stretch their horizons', 'to create the future'), liberty ('the free-expression atmosphere'), personal development ('a call to become something more'). The promise of security can be seen in the representation of a team as a protected cocoon (where one is 'nurtured', 'fed' by a leader who is also the 'advocate' of the team and ensures sufficient 'flexibility' for it to surmount obstacles). The promise of fairness can be seen in giving people 'recognition', 'a warm glow', 'making everyone a Hero'. One feature of the ideal new world depicted in management literature is that security is seen as emanating from people's capacity to adapt. Either they are flexible and adaptable, open to change, capable of finding new projects, and live in relative personal security, or they are not and will be put aside when the current project finishes. Security in mobility is the reward, which is why new management can be seen as introducing a new conception of justice (a new *cité*). Someone who contributes well to a project will be helped to find another – his/her reputation will be built up as a reward for his/her merits. In Kanter's words: 'Recognition is important not only for its motivational pat on the back but also for publicity value. The whole world now knows (. . .) who has done it, and what talents reside in the community gene pool'.

The main Discourses (*Cités*) are the Inspirational and Connectionist, though others are also less saliently present. In particular, there is a protagonist-antagonist relation (textured as contrastive/adversative relations, see below) between these two Discourses, and the Industrial and Domestic Discourses, which are contested ('challenging prevailing wisdom', challenging 'stifling bureaucracy').

Each Discourse can be specified in terms of what Boltanski–Thévenot call its basic 'grammar', which includes: which 'subjects' or participants are represented as involved in the processes of the capitalist organisation; which are 'great ones', which are 'small ones'; what sort of actions (material, mental, verbal) and attributions are characteristic for each type of subject; what relations there are between 'great ones' and 'small ones'; what 'objects' (e.g., technologies) are represented as involved in the processes of the organisation; what values are assumed (which we have discussed above). The text can be analysed in terms of how it textures together the subjects, actions, relations, objects and values of different Discourses.

The 'subjects' represented in the text are: the 'great one' (the leader), the 'small one' (the 'laggards', 'skeptics' etc.) and the leader's helpers (his/her 'people', 'stakeholders' etc.). The 'great ones' are represented as: 'change-masters, leaders, pacesetters, idea scouts, innovators, lead actors, producer-directors', and so forth, the two most frequent representations being 'leaders' and 'changemasters' ('change leaders' also occurs). These representations of 'great ones' articulate together different discourses, including discourses of entertainment ('ideas scouts', cf. 'talent scouts') and theatre ('lead actors', 'producer-directors'). The 'small ones' are represented primarily as 'laggards' (also 'skeptics', 'resisters'); 'laggard' is drawn from the moral discourse of everyday life.

It is the 'great ones' who are the predominant actors or agents in the text – it is their actions as well as attributes that are in focus. The range of actions and attributions includes elements from two main *Cités* – the 'Inspirational' and 'Connectionist'. With respect to the former, the 'great ones' 'sense problems and weaknesses', exhibit 'curiosity', 'create', 'imagine', 'improvise', 'dream', have 'visions', 'shake up' reality and their own thinking, and so forth. Like all artists they are a little mad – 'neurotic', 'paranoid'. They are charismatic: they 'inspire' others, and 'raise aspirations' with their visions, they 'wake people out of inertia', and so forth. With respect to the latter, the 'great ones' 'reassemble', 'combine', form 'alliances' and build and 'widen' 'coalitions', 'build' and 'nurture teams', have a 'network of contacts' etc. There are traces of other *Cités* – the 'Industrial' ('delivering on deadline') and the 'Merchant' ('making deals'), but the 'deals' have a 'connectionist' character which points to a merger of *Cités*. In these 'deals', exchange is not balanced to the point that parties are 'quits' and can therefore sever connection, as it is in the 'merchant' world when one pays the price of the object purchased. Here there always remains a debt to pay, which allows for relations to be built on a long-term basis ('this can involve some creative exchange of benefits, so that supporters get something of value right away. Some changemasters seek contributions beyond the amount they actually need because investment builds the commitment of other people to help them').

3.4 *Texturing*

The diverse Discourses which constitute *cités*, and the diverse discourses which constitute each *cité*, are articulated, 'textured', together in the text in accordance with its genre and the syntactic features which we have identified above as realising the genre (most saliently, additive and adversative paratactic relations).

On the one hand, leadership is constructed through relations of equivalence between different discourses (and Discourses) emanating from (the orders of discourse of) different areas of social life and social experience, and so between these areas. On the other hand, relations of difference are set up between the Inspirational/Connectionist and Industrial/Domestic Discourses (and constituent discourses). The text builds a protagonist (Inspirational/Connectionist) – antagonist (Industrial/Domestic) relation between them.

Let us begin with relations of difference. In Extract 3, a relationship of difference is textured between 'pacesetters' and 'laggards', in terms of, on the one hand, the Inspirational and Connectionist Discourses (with a particular appropriation of the Domestic Discourse which we come to shortly), and, on the other hand, the Industrial Discourse. This relationship is textured as a protagonist–antagonist relation (Martin 1992).

Extract 3

Companies that are successful on the web operate differently from their laggard counterparts. On my global e-culture survey, those reporting that they are much better than their competitors in the use of the Internet tend to have flexible, empowering, collaborative organizations. The 'best' are more likely than the 'worst' to indicate, at statistically significant levels, that:

- Departments collaborate (instead of sticking to themselves).
- Conflict is seen as creative (instead of disruptive).
- People can do anything not explicitly prohibited (instead of doing only what is explicitly permitted).
- Decisions are made by the people with the most knowledge (instead of the ones with the highest rank).

Pacesetters and laggards describe no differences in how hard they work (in response to a question about whether work was confined to traditional hours or spilled over into personal time), but they are very different in how collaboratively they work.

Working in e-culture mode requires organizations to be communities of purpose. Recall the elements of community sketched in chapter 1. A community makes people feel like members, not just employees – members with privileges but also responsibilities beyond the immediate job, extending to colleagues in other areas. Community means having things in common, a range of shared understandings transcending specific fields. Shared understandings permit relatively seamless processes, interchangeability among people, smooth formation of teams that know how to work together even if they have never previously met, and rapid transmission of information. In this chapter we will see how the principles of community apply inside organizations and workplaces, sometimes facilitated by technology but also independent of it. And I will examine the challenges that have to be overcome to create organizational communities.

The greater integration that is integral to e-culture is different from the centralization of earlier eras. Integration must be accompanied by flexibility and empowerment in order to achieve fast response, creativity, and innovation through improvisation. Web success involves operating more like a community than a bureaucracy. It is a subtle but important distinction. Bureaucracy implies rigid job descriptions, command-and-control hierarchies, and hoarding of information, which is doled out top-down on a need-to-know basis. Community implies a willingness to abide by standardized procedures governing the whole organization, yes, but also voluntary collaboration that is much richer and less programmed. Communities can be mapped in formal ways, but they also have an emotional meaning, a feeling of connection. Communities have both a structure and a soul.

The texturing of the relationship of difference is effected through a range of contrastive or antithetical relational structures and expressions: *x instead of y, x not just y, x but also y, x is different from y, more like x than y*. The clearest case is in the list in the centre of the extract, where protagonist practices represented before the brackets are set off against antagonist practices within the brackets.

This extract illustrates how the meanings of words drawn from the vocabulary of the Domestic Discourse is changed through their recontextualisation within a largely Connectionist–Inspirational context. The new world has nothing in common with the original Domestic *Cité* one finds for example in texts from the 1930s, where 'the great ones' are old, carriers of tradition etc. in a hierarchical world where one should respect one's elders. This world accorded with the bourgeois capitalism of the time, but does not accord with the contemporary elevation of rupture and innovation into supreme values. This particular appropriation of the Domestic Discourse is clear in the final paragraph, where 'communities' are attributed with Inspirationist attributes – notably 'a soul' – and the two Discourses are worked into a relation of equivalence. A relationship of difference is textured between this Domestic–Inspirational hybrid and the 'bureaucracy' of the Industrial *Cité*.

Turning to relations of equivalence, this extract also textures relations of equivalence between different discourses within each Discourse. Firstly, vocabulary items which are in equivalent positions in contrastive relations are thereby textured as equivalent, e.g., *integration* and *community* on the one hand, *centralization* and *bureaucracy* on the other. Secondly, such relations of equivalence are textured through additive paratactic structures, sometimes with the conjunction 'and' (e.g., 'flexible, empowering, collaborative', where the three elements belong to different discourses). There are also contrastive relations within the 'protagonist' conjunction of Discourses: 'members, *not just* employees'; 'privileges *but also* responsibilities'; 'a willingness to abide by standardized procedures governing the whole organization, yes, *but also* voluntary collaboration that is much richer and less programmed'; 'Communities can be mapped in formal ways, *but* they *also* have an emotional meaning, a feeling of connection . . . both a structure and a soul'. These contrastive relations do double duty: they both register contrastive features on the protagonist side, and the contrast between the complexity of the latter (*x but also y*) and the simplicity of the antagonistic Industrial Discourse (*x*).

There is also a combination of relations of equivalence and difference in Extract 4:

Extract 4

Skill 1: Sensing Needs and Opportunities: Tuning in to the Environment

Changemasters sense problems and weaknesses before they represent full-blown threats. They see the opportunities when external forces change – new technological capabilities, industry upheavals, regulatory shifts – and then they identify gaps between what is and what could be. Recall the divergent paths to e-business success taken by pacesetter companies compared with the laggards in Chapter 3. Whereas laggards respond to hints of new developments on the horizon with denial and anger, pacesetters exhibit curiosity.

Changemasters find many ways to monitor external reality. They become idea scouts, attentive to early signs of discontinuity, disruption, threat, or opportunity. They can establish their own listening posts, such as a satellite office in an up-and-coming location, an alliance with an innovative partner, or investments in organizations that are creating the future.

Through additive paratactic relations, equivalences are again textured between elements of Inspirational ('sensing', 'tuning in', being 'idea scouts') and Connectionist ('establishing listening posts', 'an alliance') Discourses; between discourses of intuition ('sensing') and, through a metaphorical extension of radio electronic discourse, a discourse of self-reflexivity ('tuning in'), an entertainment discourse ('idea scouts' – cf. 'talent scouts') or a discourse of military intelligence or espionage ('establish listening posts').

Through a contrastive paratactic relation, a relation of difference is textured between a psychoanalytical discourse ('denial or anger') and perhaps a discourse of child psychology which is a part of the 'Inspirational' Discourse ('exhibit curiosity'). The texturing work here is both the texturing of these equivalence relations through additive and contrastive paratactic constructions, and through collocations: the collocation of 'scouts' with 'idea' is the most obviously creative collocation; 'identify gaps' (conventional strategic management discourse) is collocated with '(between) what is and what could be' – religion/charismatic politics, even revolutionary politics. Note also collocations of 'sense' (discourse of intuition) and 'needs and opportunities'/ 'problems and weaknesses' (conventional strategic management discourse).

Extract 5 is the list of the seven 'skills':

Extract 5

Seven classic skills are involved in innovation and change: tuning in to the environment, kaleidoscopic thinking, an inspiring vision, coalition building, nurturing a working team, persisting through difficulties, and spreading credit and recognition. These are more than discrete skills; they reflect a perspective, a style, that is basic to e-culture.

The list textures together in a relation of equivalence elements of the Inspirational Discourse ('tuning in to the environment', 'an inspiring vision') and the Connectionist Discourse ('coalition building', 'nurturing a working team', 'spreading credit and recognition'). 'Persisting through difficulties' is more difficult to place, but perhaps evokes an Inspirational world and the unrecognised genius able to carry on alone in the face of opposition for the sake of recognition in posterity. 'Kaleidoscopic thinking' evokes both Inspirational and Connectionist Discourses, creativity taking a connectionist form, the form of a new relation rather than an invention *ex nihilo*. The list textures together elements of discourses of charismatic politics or perhaps religion ('inspiring vision'), self-reflexivity/counselling ('tuning in'), cognitive theory and perhaps play (and childhood) ('kaleidoscopic thinking') within the Inspirational Discourse, politics ('coalition building') and parenting ('nurturing') within the Connectionist Discourse.

4 Conclusion

We shall conclude with some thoughts on this collaboration as an exercise in transdisciplinarity, returning to the theme we raised in the Introduction. We suggested there that transdisciplinary research is a particular form of interdisciplinary research which does not simply bring together different disciplines and theoretical-analytical frameworks. It also initiates a dialogue between two disciplines and frameworks which may lead to a development of both through a process of each internally appropriating the logic of the other as a resource for its own development. We consider what we have achieved first from the perspective of CDA, second from the perspective of the new sociology of capitalism.

From the perspective of CDA, our collaborative analysis has appropriated the logic of the new sociology of capitalism in ways which point to the development of the theoretical concepts of 'order of discourse', 'discourse' and 'style'. We have suggested that a substantive change in the form of capitalism entails a change in the 'spirit of capitalism', and we have seen the latter both as an ideology and as an order of discourse – a particular configuration of discourses enacted as genres and inculcated as styles. We have also suggested that the *cités* which are configured within the constitution of the 'spirit of capitalism' are Discourses, which are in turn analysable as configurations of discourses. We have also associated styles with values, and especially implicit values, which we have suggested can be seen as emanating from the 'equivalency principles' of particular *cités*. In suggesting these connections between the categories of the two theories, we are opening up various directions of theoretical elaboration for CDA by 'putting to work' within it the logic of new sociology of capitalism: the relationship between capitalist formations, ideologies, and orders of discourse; the various levels of abstraction or generality at which discourses (and 'Discourses') need to be identified; the relationship between D/discourses, styles and legitimation.

From the perspective of New Sociology of Capitalism, collaborating with CDA allows an elaboration and deepening of a text analysis which was mainly thematic and centred upon pre-established analytical categories (the *cités*, dimensions of legitimation of a spirit of capitalism). The linguistic tools of CDA have encouraged us to look more closely at how texts are structured, how ways of writing construct, for example, equivalences and differences, how the author of a text constructs him/herself through the discourse, and so forth.

More generally, we believe that the study we have carried out is not merely of interest in terms of collaboration between disciplines. It also provides a relatively in-depth analysis of an influential management 'guru' text, allowing its codes to be exposed, which is one of a variety of ways in which social researchers can de-sacrilise the words of these new prophets. De-sacrilisation seems to us an important undertaking, for such texts have a real influence on the maintenance of dominant ideologies and on the actions of managers who read them. Yet the lack of a scientific apparatus and a relatively unsophisticated style lead social scientists to treat them with disinterest or contempt, as is more generally the case with popular literature and television. Consequently such texts are rarely subjected to critique, leaving the field free for them to do their doctrinal work. It seems to us, by contrast, that studying such texts is one of the tasks of social science as we conceive it – to subject to debate what presents itself as given and obvious, and to expose to critique all the social agencies which impose themselves on people, in order to enhance democratic debate.

11. Critical discourse analysis in researching language in the new capitalism: overdetermination, transdisciplinarity and textual analysis[1]

Capitalism has the capacity to overcome crises by radically transforming itself periodically so that economic growth and profitability can continue. Such a transformation towards 'New Capitalism' has been taking place since the 1970s in response to a crisis in the post-Second World War model ('Fordism'). This transformation involves both *restructuring* of relations between the economic, political and social domains (including the commodification and marketisation of fields such as education which become subject to the economic logic of the market), and the *re-scaling* of relations between different scales of social life – the global, the regional, e.g., the European Union, the national, and the local. Governments on different scales, social democratic as well as conservative and liberal, have embraced 'neoliberalism': a political project for facilitating restructuring and re-scaling of social relations in accord with the demands of an unrestrained global capitalism (Bourdieu 1998a). It has been imposed on formerly socialist economies as allegedly the best means of rapid system transformation, economic renewal, and integration into the global economy. It has led to radical attacks on social welfare provision and the reduction of the protections that 'welfare states' provided for people against the effects of markets. It has also led to an increasing division between rich and poor, increasing economic insecurity and stress even for the 'new middle' classes, and an intensification of the exploitation of labour. The unrestrained emphasis on growth also poses major threats to the environment. It has also produced a new imperialism in which international financial agencies under the tutelage of the US and its rich allies indiscriminately impose restructuring, sometimes with disastrous consequences, e.g., Russia and Argentina – an imperialism which has recently taken a military form in the 'war on terrorism' and the invasion of Iraq. It is not the impetus to increasing international economic integration (or 'globalisation' in that sense) that is the problem, but the particular form in which this is being imposed, and the particular consequences, e.g., in terms of unequal distribution of wealth, which are being made to follow. All this has resulted in the disorientation and disarming of economic, political and social forces committed to radical alternatives, and has contributed to a closure of public debate and a weakening of democracy.

1 Language in new capitalism

Knowledge-based (handwritten margin note)

The common idea of new capitalism as a 'knowledge-based' or 'knowledge-driven' socio-economic order implies that it is also 'discourse-driven', suggesting that language may have a more significant role in contemporary socio-economic changes than it has had in the past. If this is so, discourse analysis has an important contribution to make to research on the transformations of capitalism. The significance of language in these transformations has not gone unnoticed by social researchers. Bourdieu and Wacquant (2001: 3) for instance point to a 'new planetary vulgate', which they characterise as a vocabulary ('globalisation', 'flexibility', 'governance', 'employability', 'exclusion' and so forth), which 'is endowed with the performative power to bring into being the very realities it claims to describe'. That is, the neo-liberal political project of removing obstacles to the new economic order is discourse-driven.

But, as well as indicating the significance of language in these socio-economic transformations, Bourdieu and Wacquant's paper suggests that social research needs the contribution of discourse analysts. It is not enough to characterise the 'new planetary vulgate' as a list of words, a vocabulary; rather, texts and interactions need to be analysed to show how some of the effects that they identify are brought off, e.g., making the socio-economic transformations of new capitalism and the policies of governments to facilitate them seem inevitable; representing desires as facts; and representing the imaginaries of interested policies – the interested possible realities they project – as the way the world actually is (Fairclough 2000b). Bourdieu and Wacquant's account of the effectivity of neo-liberal discourse exceeds the capacity of their (otherwise extremely powerful) sociological research methods.

But it is not only text and interactional analysis that discourse analysts can bring to social research on the new capitalism, it is also a satisfactory theorisation of the *dialectics of discourse* (elaborated further below). If the restructuring and re-scaling (Jessop 2000) are changes in the networking of social practices, they are also a restructuring and re-scaling of discourse, of 'orders of discourse' (the term is explained below). The restructuring of orders of discourse is a matter of shifting relations, i.e., changes in networking, between the discourse elements of different (networks of) social practices. A prime example is the way in which the language of management has colonised public institutions and organisations such as universities, although I should add that this process is a colonisation/appropriation dialectic, i.e., not only a matter of the entry of discourses into new domains, but the diverse ways in which they are received, appropriated, and recontextualised in different locales, and the ultimately unpredictable outcomes of this process. The re-scaling of orders of discourse is a matter of changes in the networking of the discourse elements of social practices on different scales of social organisation – global, regional, national and local, for instance, the enhanced and accelerated permeability of local social practices (local government, small-scale industry, local media) in countries across the world to discourses which are globally disseminated through organisations like the International Monetary Fund (IMF) and the World Bank. Working the above account of the transformation of capitalism into a dialectical theory of discourse provides a theoretical framework for researching the global penetrative power of the 'new planetary vulgate' which Bourdieu and Wacquant (2001) allude to, as well as its limits.

This theoretical framework is also needed to research what Bourdieu and Wacquant (2001: 4) call the 'performative power' of the 'new planetary vulgate', i.e., its power to 'bring into being the very realities it describes'. How does this discourse come to be internalised (Harvey 1996) in social practices, and under what conditions does it construct and reconstruct (rather than merely construe) social practices including their non-discoursal elements? How does it come to be enacted in ways of acting and interacting, e.g., organisational routines and procedures including genres and inculcated in the ways of being, i.e., the identities of social agents? How does it come to be materialised in the 'hardware' of institutions and organisations? Researching this crucial issue requires detailed investigation of organisational and institutional change on a comparative basis, such as the study by Salskov-Iversen *et al.* (2000) of the contrasting colonisation/appropriation of the new 'public management' discourse by local authorities in Britain and Mexico, but working with the sort of dialectical theory of discourse I sketch out below. (See also Iedema 1999.)

2 An example: the Blair text

Having given above a general account of the transformations of new capitalism, and a general rationale for a language focus in researching new capitalism,

Table 11.1 Text by Tony Blair

Paragraph	Text
Paragraph 1	The modern world is swept by change. New technologies emerge constantly, new markets are opening up. There are new competitors but also great new opportunities.
Paragraph 2	Our success depends on how well we exploit our most valuable assets: our knowledge, skills and creativity. These are the key to designing high-value goods and services and advanced business practices. They are at the heart of a modern, knowledge-driven economy.
Paragraph 3	This new world challenges business to be innovative and creative, to improve performance continuously, to build new alliances and ventures. But it also challenges Government: to create and execute a new approach to industrial policy.
Paragraph 4	That is the purpose of this White Paper. Old-fashioned state intervention did not and cannot work. But neither does naïve reliance on markets.
Paragraph 5	The Government must promote competition, stimulating enterprise, flexibility and innovation by opening markets. But we must also invest in British capabilities when companies alone cannot: in education, in science and in the creation of a culture of enterprise. And we must promote creative partnerships which help companies: to collaborate for competitive advantage; to promote a long-term vision in a world of short-term pressures; to benchmark their performance against the best in the world; and to forge alliances with other businesses and employees. All this is the DTI's role.
Paragraph 6	We will not meet our objectives overnight. The White Paper creates a policy framework for the next ten years. We must compete more effectively in today's tough markets if we are to prosper in the markets of tomorrow.
Paragraph 7	In Government, in business, in our universities and throughout society we must do much more to foster a new entrepreneurial spirit: equipping ourselves for the long term, prepared to seize opportunities, committed to constant innovation and enhanced performance. That is the route to commercial success and prosperity for all. We must put the future on Britain's side.
	Tony Blair (signature) *The Rt Hon Tony Blair MP, Prime Minister*

I now want to focus on specific issues which arise from a single text. Table 11.1 is the 'Foreword' to a UK Department of Trade and Industry White Paper, 'Our Competitive Future: Building the Knowledge-Driven Economy', written by (or at least signed by) the Prime Minister, Tony Blair. I have used a tabular layout in paragraphs for purposes of clarity. (Note that this is one of the texts analysed in the first paper in this section, 'A dialectical–relational approach to critical discourse analysis in social research', but the focus of the analysis is different in this paper.)

One thing I find striking about this text (and many other contemporary texts in politics and government but also other fields such as education) is the texturing of a relationship between the 'global'[2] and the national. The relevance of this feature of the text to the concerns of this paper is that this way of construing the global and the national and the relationship between them is, as I shall argue in more detail later, characteristically neo-liberal – using that term as above for the dominant political position within current transformations of capitalism. In using the term 'texturing', I am focusing on the 'work' that is done textually, i.e., the textual 'working up' of that relationship. Blair is writing about, and texturing a relationship between, 'the modern world' (more specifically the 'new global economy', an expression he uses often although not in this text) and Britain. Let us refer to these as different 'space-times': the global space–time and the national space–time. I shall come back to that term later. For instance, Paragraph 1 represents the global space–time of the 'modern world'. The first sentence of the Paragraph 2 can be seen as combining representations of global and national space–times. The relation between 'success' and exploitation of 'assets' is global (it applies anywhere in the 'new global economy'), but the relational process verb ('depends on') links a nominalisation ('our success') and an embedded clause ('how well we exploit. . . .') which represent processes in British national space–time. The second and third sentences of Paragraph 2 represent the global space–time. I shall comment first on how these space–times are constructed, and then on how they are textured together.

3 The global space–time

Global space is represented as an entity, a place, 'the modern world', 'this new world'. It is a participant in processes rather than a circumstance (as it would be in, for example, 'new markets are opening up on an international level'). It is the passive subject (and 'logical object') in the first sentence of Paragraph 1 and the active subject in the first sentence of Paragraph 3: 'this new world challenges . . .'. It is also the theme of the text's opening sentence and, one might say, of the first paragraph.

Global time is represented as present although what that means needs some clarification. The verbs are present tense, either simple present or present continuous ('are opening up'). In most cases the simple present is 'timeless present', representing an indeterminate stretch of time which includes but pre-dates and post-dates the present. The present continuous with the event verb 'open up' has both the meaning of inception and incompletion ('are beginning to open up') and an iterative meaning ('keep opening up'), as does the simple present 'emerge' combined with the adverb 'constantly'.

The modality of representations of the processes and relations of the global space–time is epistemic and categorically assertive: positive statements without modal markers which represent processes as real and actual. These statements of some of the truisms of the age are of a somewhat gnomic character. Yet, 'are opening up' and 'emerge constantly' bring covert predictions ('will carry on emerging and opening up') of an 'irrealis' future into the representation of global space–time as 'realis' present (Iedema 1998, Graham 2001). So too does the contrast in Paragraph 6 between 'today's tough markets' and 'the markets of tomorrow'; there is an implicit prediction of the competitive character of these future markets.

The processes of the global space–time are material (the three processes in the first two sentences of Paragraph 1, 'is swept', 'emerge', 'are opening up'), existential (the third sentence of Paragraph 1), relational ('depends on', 'are', Paragraph 2) and verbal ('challenges', Paragraph 3). The actors in the material processes are non-human, inanimate ('new technologies', 'new markets') or nominalised ('change'), and the actor in the verbal process is 'this new world'. The global space–time is represented as processes without human agency.

The representation of relations between processes is also worth noting, especially in Paragraph 1. Semantically, the relationship between the first sentence and the rest of the paragraph is elaboration; the relationship between the second and third sentences, and between the two clauses of the second, is addition, and the relationship between the two phrases of the third can be seen as both additive ('also') and contrastive ('but') (Halliday 1994). Grammatically, there are three sentences, the second and third containing paratactically related clauses and phrases, respectively. The global space–time is represented as a list of processes. But there is also a nominalised process ('change') and two inanimate nouns ('markets', 'opportunities') which, like the nominalisation, represent processes, i.e., people trading in new ways, and people being able to do new things, as entities, two of which ('change', 'new markets') are actors in material processes.

4   The national space–time

National space is also represented as a place, Britain, although it is implicitly evoked through some of its attributes ('we', 'the government' etc.) rather than directly represented – 'Britain' does not appear until Paragraph 7, and 'British' appears just once in Paragraph 5. It is also differentiated (see the final paragraph) in terms of fields ('Government', 'business', 'our universities') in which, as 'throughout society', 'a new entrepreneurial spirit' is to be 'fostered', bringing all domains of social life under the sign of business.

In contrast to the predominant timeless present of the global space–time, the temporality of the national space–time is predominantly future, for instance, in Paragraph 5. Notice also that the future is to be put 'on Britain's side' (Paragraph 7). The verbs of the main clauses of the first three sentences of Paragraph 5 are deontically modalised ('must'), and the meanings are 'present necessity of future action'. The implicit normative framework is not, for instance, ethical but pragmatic and circumstantial, i.e., we are forced by circumstances. On the other hand, in using 'must' rather than 'have to', Blair commits himself to these necessities rather than locating their source elsewhere. Whereas statements about the global space–time are descriptive, statements about the national space–time are predominantly prescriptive, though Paragraph 6 begins with a sentence which is epistemically modalised, i.e., a prediction ('we will not meet our objectives overnight'). The national space–time is represented mainly in terms of 'irrealis' processes: what things should be like and must be made like rather than what they are like. The processes of subordinate and embedded clauses ('stimulating', 'opening', 'collaborating', 'benchmarking') are also irrealis through a process of 'propagation' of the irrealis processes of main clauses analogous to the 'value propagation' discussed by Lemke (1998), but so too are the embedded processes of nominalisations ('competition', 'flexibility'). As well, the irrealis processes are in (irrealis) causal relation with each other, e.g., 'creative partnerships' lead to 'collaboration' which leads to 'competitive advantage'. The processes of the national space–time are predominantly material and, in contrast to the global space–time, the actors in material processes are human, either represented by the pronoun 'we' or collective nouns ('the Government', 'companies').

I shall comment on the representation of relationships between processes just in Paragraph 5. The semantic relationship between the first sentence and the second and third taken together is both additive ('also') and contrastive ('but'); the relationship between the second and third sentences is addition; and the relationship between the first three sentences and the fourth is elaboration. In terms of relations between sentences, the representation of global space–time in Paragraph 1 and national space–time in Paragraph 5 have a similar list-like quality. But there is a difference in relations within sentences.

In the first sentence of Paragraph 5, the first non-finite clause (from 'stimulating') is subordinate to the preceding finite clause while the second non-finite clause ('by opening') is subordinate to the first non-finite clause. Semantically, the relations are elaboration and means, respectively. In the second sentence, the second finite clause (from 'when') is subordinate to the first, i.e., the semantic relation is apparently temporal but perhaps rather causal ('because companies alone cannot'). There is layered embedding in the third sentence: a restrictive relative clause (beginning 'which help') embedded in a noun phrase, and a list of coordinated non-finite clauses in a semantic relation of addition (from 'to collaborate') which are embedded in the relative clause as complements of 'help'. There are many nominalised processes ('competition', 'flexibility', 'innovation' etc.) although in contrast with Paragraph 1, they do not function as actors.

The text as a whole, in the representation of both global and national space–times, is notable for the number of lists: elements in a semantically additive and grammatically paratactic relationship. Using a terminology I shall come back to, these lists texture *relations of equivalence* among elements. In some cases, equivalent elements are co-hyponyms, for instance 'our assets: knowledge, skills and creativity' in Paragraph 2 where 'knowledge', 'skills', and 'creativity' are co-hyponyms of 'assets' (the superordinate term). 'New technologies emerge constantly', 'new markets are opening up', '(there being) new competitors', and 'new opportunities' are co-hyponyms of 'change' in Paragraph 1; 'education', 'science', and '(the creation of) a culture of enterprise' are co-hyponyms of 'British capabilities' in Paragraph 5. But 'equipping ourselves for the long term', '(being) prepared to seize opportunities', '(being) committed to constant innovation and enhanced performance' are co-meronyms of 'fostering a new entrepreneurial spirit' – the former are aspects of the latter (Martin 1992). Elsewhere, elements are textured in equivalence relations without being in such hierarchies, as co-members of a class which is not labelled (what van Leeuwen (1996) calls 'associations'), for instance in Paragraph 3, 'to be innovative and creative', 'to improve performance continuously' and 'to build new alliances and ventures'. In the last sentence of Paragraph 2, the relation of equivalence between 'modern' and 'knowledge-driven' can be taken as the semantic relation of elaboration (Halliday 1994).

Let me come to how the global space–time is textured into a relationship with the national space–time in the Blair text.

(a) The overall semantic pattern or rhetorical formation of the text can be seen as the 'problem-solution' pattern (Hoey 2001). The problem is the incontrovertible and inevitable reality that people are faced with (the global economy); the solution is what they must do to succeed in this new reality. A relationship is textured between 'is' and 'must', reality and necessity, which precludes real policy options.

(b) A relationship of subordination of national space–time to global space–time (national policy to global economy) is textured through projection in Paragraph 3, in verbal processes in which 'this new world' is addresser (posing 'challenges') and (national) 'business' and 'Government' are addressees.

(c) A relationship of subordination of national space–time to global space–time is textured in Paragraph 2 as the relation between national policy action (the embedded clause in sentence 1) and an implicit global reason (sentences 2 and 3) for this action. Notice the slippage from national to global in the anaphoric reference at the beginning of sentence 2: 'these' refers anaphorically not to 'our knowledge, skills and creativity', but to 'knowledge, skills and creativity' generally.

(d) Processes on a national level are framed by circumstantial elements ('in a world of short-term pressures', 'in today's tough markets' 'the markets of tomorrow') which embed them within processes on a global level in Paragraphs 5 and 6.

(e) The national space–time is populated, one might say colonised, by the entified and spatialised processes of neo-liberal representations of the 'global economy' ('flexibility', 'enterprise', 'innovation', 'partnerships' etc.) which are positively valued, i.e., verbs such as 'stimulate' and 'promote' can be seen as textual triggers for positive valuation.

5   CDA in research on new capitalism

Let us come back to relations of equivalence, using 'knowledge, skills and creativity' as an example. There is potentially a negative aspect to texturing elements as equivalent: it can subvert prior differences. What is striking about this example is that it makes equivalent words which come from different discourses that are historically associated with different domains of social life: education and learning ('knowledge'), crafts and trades ('skills'), and art ('creativity'). This subversion of the difference between prior discourses is constitutive in the making of a new discourse. A discourse is a representation of some area of social life from a particular perspective. One might refer rather to 'registers', but 'discourses' implies that all domains of social life (and of language use) are multi-perspectival, e.g., representing economic production in terms of 'creativity' might be abhorrent from certain perspectives in the artistic field. The new discourse in this case is neo-liberal. That is a way of labelling a particular perspective within the political field, and a characteristic of this labelling is that it makes these words equivalent as co-hyponyms of 'assets'. I should add that there are issues of time-scale here: the equivalence of 'knowledge' and 'skills' is older than their co-equivalence with 'creativity'. Furthermore, some texts are original in texturing new equivalences while others (including this one) are typical of large bodies of texts which characteristic-ally texture particular equivalences. This text is typical, I would suggest, of a body of texts which draws upon the political discourse of New Labour, of the 'Third Way', which one can see as a particular variant of the political discourse of neo-liberalism (Fairclough 2000b).

So, at one level of analysis, the relations textured by texts constitute discourses in relation to (and potentially in subversive relation to) other discourses. The particular constructions of global and national space–time can be seen in the same terms. They are characteristic of neo-liberal political discourse and, at the same time subversive of prior political discourses; in this case, the neo-liberal political discourse of the 'Third Way' is subversive especially of the social democratic discourse of 'old Labour'. The relations of equivalence in particular point to what I suggest is a general property of texts: they hybridise discourses in constituting discourses. Actually, that is only one aspect of other, more general processes: they also hybridise genres in consti-tuting genres and hybridise styles (in the sense of ways of being, i.e., identities, in their language aspect) in constituting styles. This is an aspect of the multi-functional character of texts, but I am suggesting that texts not only simult-aneously have representational, actional, and identificatory functions in their linguistic features, they also have these functions 'interdiscursively' at the level of discourses, genres and styles. (The version of multifunctionality I am adopting here is, of course, different from the most familiar version of the ideational, interpersonal, and textual metafunctions in systemic functional linguistics (SFL), but the principle of multifunctionality is the same (Halliday 1994, Fairclough 2003)).

In CDA, *interdiscursive* analysis of texts is the mediating level of analysis which is crucial to integrating social and linguistic analyses (Fairclough 1992a, Chouliaraki and Fairclough 1999). I prefer to use the term *semiosis* rather than 'discourse' as an abstract noun. One advantage is that it is a reminder that what is at issue is not just (verbal) language but also other semiotic modalities (Kress and van Leuwen 2000); another is that it avoids confusion with 'discourses' as a count noun in the sense I have just discussed. Semiosis is an element of social practices which is *dialectically* interconnected with other elements – in the terminology of dialectical theory, it is a 'moment' of the social. What this means is that, while different elements of social practices – including forms of activity, social relations, and their institutional forms; persons with beliefs, values, emotions, histories; material objects (including the means or technologies of activities); and semiosis – are indeed *different* and cannot be reduced to each other and, therefore, demand different social scientific theories and methodologies, they are *not discrete*. They flow to one another; they 'internalise' one another in Harvey's terminology (Harvey 1996, also Fairclough 2001c, 2003). Discourses, genres and styles are three main ways in which semiosis figures in social practices as part of the action (genres), in representation (discourses), and in identification (styles).

Social practices are networked. One way of describing a particular social field in the sense of Bourdieu (Bourdieu and Wacquant 1992) or indeed a social order is in terms of the networking of social practices which characterises it. Social change is change in the networking of social practices; therefore, the transformations of new capitalism can be analysed in terms of changes in network relations, i.e., both structural changes (changes in relations between fields or domains), and scalar changes (changes in relations between global, regional, national and local), in the terminology I introduced earlier. The semiotic element or moment of a network of social practices is an *order of discourse* – a particular articulation or configuration of genres, discourses and styles. Orders of discourse are the social structuring of semiotic difference or variation. Interdiscursive analysis of texts is the mediating link between linguistic analysis and social analysis because, on the one hand, the 'mix' of genres, discourses and styles in a text is realised in its semantic, lexicogrammatical and phonological features and, on the other hand, that 'mix' constitutes a particular working at the level of the concrete event of the semiotic moment of social practices – orders of discourse. A particular text can simultaneously, depending on the 'mix' of genres, discourses and styles, constitute a reworking of prior, habitual or familiar constellations of linguistic features, e.g., relations of equivalence, and a reworking of the relatively durable articulations of genres, discourses and styles which constitute orders of discourse and relations between orders of discourse (and hence, given the dialectical view of semiosis as a moment of the social, relations between social practices). Thus, the equivalences noted in the text not only rework relations between orders of discourse but also between the social practices they are moments of (education, crafts/trades, art). Interdiscursive analysis, thus, enables textual analysis to be properly integrated into social analysis, and in the case of the particular focus in this paper, to be properly integrated into social analysis of the transformations of new capitalism.

I have focused upon the political discourse of Blair's text. It would also be possible to analyse its genre and its style, i.e., to analyse it as a form of political action (specifying what such 'Forewords' are doing) and as a form of constituting the identity of a political leader. But I want, rather, to comment on relations between discourses, genres and styles in terms of the historical process within which this text is positioned. I described the temporality of the national space–time as 'irrealis'. To put it differently, this sort of political discourse deals in imaginaries: it projects ways of acting and ways of being. Whether it remains merely a construal of possible ways of acting and being, or comes to construct real ways of acting and being, is a contingent matter (Sayer 2000). Discourses can be socially constructive, i.e., social life can be remodelled in their image, but there are no guarantees in that regard. There are conditions of possibility for discourses to have such constructive or performative effects (Fairclough, Jessop and Sayer 2004). If they do have such effects, then the dialectics of discourse takes effect: discourses may be enacted in ways of acting and interacting, and they may be inculcated in ways of being, i.e., identities. Take, for instance, 'creative partnerships'. For 'creative partnerships' to go beyond the realm of imaginary construal into the realm of actual existence, people would need to start acting, interacting and being 'differently'. Partly, these enactments and inculcations are themselves semiotic, entailing new genres and styles. But partly they are non-semiotic: for instance, the dialectical internalisation of discourses in new management systems and forms of embodiment; or their materialisation in new architectural forms; or new ways of organising urban space. Texts such as this one are, of course, precisely in the business of creating imaginaries as a step towards changed realities. One needs a dialectical view of semiosis to grasp that potential process in a way which gives due force to the impact of language in initiating it and in carrying it through.

Blair's text is positioned in complex chains or networks of texts with which it contracts intertextual relations, both 'retrospective' and 'prospective', i.e., both with prior texts, which in one way or other have shaped it or which it is oriented to or in dialogue with, and with subsequent texts which report, represent, echo, and so forth the text and which it may anticipate. The concept of *recontextualisation* helps to grasp the dynamics of these relations (Bernstein 1990). But these relations on the concrete level of relations between specific events and texts are shaped by the more durable relations of networks of social practices and orders of discourse as their semiotic moments. Orders of discourse are characterised by 'chain' relations as well as 'choice' relations. In particular, relations within as well as between orders of discourse are regulated by genre chains, i.e., relatively durable and institutionalised relationships between genres characterised by particular principles of recontextualisation and transformation. Thus, the genres of politics and government are chained with the genres of mass media in such a way that the recontextualisation of a political document like the Blair text within a press report, and the transformations from the one to the other, have a relatively regular and predictable character. Social change importantly includes change in these relations of recontextualisation and genre chains. For instance, the 'globalising' character of the transformations of new capitalism includes the emergence of relations of recontextualisation and genre chains which enable and regulate more fluid ways of acting across scales (at the limit, from the global to the local). Texts such as this not only represent relations between space–times, they are also positioned within such relations. And any account of the constitutive or performative effects of semiosis in the transformations of new capitalism must include these shifts in relations of recontextualisation.

At the same time, however, recontextualisation should be seen in terms of a colonising/appropriating dialectic (Chouliaraki and Fairclough 1999). In this case, for instance, one might refer to recontextualisation relations between the economic field and the political field (and their orders of discourse), and between the global scale and the national scale. Blair's representation of global space–time can be seen as a recontextualisation of representations of the 'new economic order' and economic 'globalisation' which are pervasive in texts, for instance, of the World Bank, IMF and Organisation for Economic Cooperation and Development (OECD). One can meaningfully consider how national political discourse is being colonised by global economic discourse. But, at the same time, this narrative of economic change can be seen as appropriated into doing particular sorts of ('rhetorical') work in particular sorts of text. Thus, Hay and Rosamund (2002) claim that, by legitimising national policy change in terms of inexorable and uncontrollable processes, globalisation is a rhetorical strategy used in domestic political discourse in Britain (though not British political discourse within international agencies such as the United Nations), but not in France where the legitimising narrative is one of 'European integration'. Textually, one can look at how such a recontextualised narrative is transformed – in this case, into a very minimal narrative compared with the elaborated versions one finds, for instance, in World Bank texts (Fairclough 2000b) – and worked into a relation with other elements, in this case, elements of policy formulation, in ways which are rhetorically motivated.

6 Overdetermination and transdisciplinarity

I have distinguished above different levels of concreteness and abstractness: social events and texts on the one hand, social practices and orders of discourse on the other. I assume a realist social ontology, in which social structures as well as social events are part of social reality. Social structures are abstract entities which define potentials, i.e., sets of possibilities. However, the relationship between what is structurally possible and what actually happens, i.e., between structures and events, is a very complex one. Events are not in any simple or direct way the effects of abstract social structures. Their relationship is mediated: there are intermediate entities between structures and events. I call these *social practices*. Social practices can be thought of as ways of controlling the selection of certain structural possibilities and the exclusion of others, and the retention of these selections over time, in particular areas of social life.

Language is an element of the social at all levels. Schematically, these are:

Social structures: languages
Social practices: orders of discourse
Social events: texts.

Languages can be regarded as among the abstract social structures I have just been referring to. A language defines a certain potential, certain possibilities, and excludes others. But texts as elements of social events are not simply the effects of the potentials defined by languages. There also exist intermediate organisational entities of a specifically linguistic sort: the linguistic moments of networks of social practices, i.e., orders of discourse. The elements of orders of discourse are not, for instance, nouns and sentences (elements of linguistic structures), but discourses, genres and styles. These elements select certain possibilities defined by languages and exclude others; they control linguistic variability for particular areas of social life. So orders of discourse can be seen as the social organisation and control of linguistic variation. There is an argument in Chouliaraki and Fairclough (2000) for an extension of Hasan's (2000) account of 'semologic' to include orders of discourse.

When moving from abstract structures towards concrete events, it becomes increasingly difficult to separate language from other social elements. In the terminology of Althusser, language becomes increasingly *overdetermined* by other social elements (Althusser and Balibar 1970).[3] So at the level of abstract structures, the analyst can talk more or less exclusively about language – more or less – because 'functional' theories of language view even the grammars of languages as socially shaped (Halliday 1978). The way I have defined orders of discourse makes it clear that, at this intermediate level, there is a much greater overdetermination of language by other social elements. Orders of discourse are the social organisation and control of linguistic (semiotic) variation, and their elements (discourses, genres, styles) are correspondingly not purely linguistic categories but categories which cut across the division between semiosis and non-semiosis and can act as a bridge between disciplines in transdisciplinary research. When one comes to texts as elements of social events, the 'overdetermination' of language by other social elements becomes massive: texts are not just effects of linguistic structures and orders of discourse, they are also effects of other social practices and structures as well as of the casual powers of social agents. Therefore, it becomes difficult to separate out the factors shaping texts (Fairclough, Jessop and Sayer 2004).

It follows, I suggest, that researchers should work in a *transdisciplinary* way (Dubiel 1985, Halliday 1993) in doing discourse analysis and text analysis. 'Interdisciplinarity' covers a multitude of practices, including the coming-together of researchers with different disciplinary backgrounds and training for the purposes of a particular research project, without any implication that the contributing disciplinary theories or methods are affected or changed by the experience. Working in a transdisciplinary way is one method of working in an interdisciplinary way, which is distinguished by a commitment to enter a dialogue with other disciplines and theories, and put their logic to work in the development of one's own theory, methods, research objects and research agendas. It is not simply a matter of adding concepts and categories from other disciplines and theories, but working on and elaborating one's own theoretical and methodological resources so as to be able to address insights or problems captured in other theories and disciplines from the perspective of one's particular concerns. It makes sense to do so in the light of what I said above about overdetermination: semiosis is an analytically separate element of social events whose analysis requires its own theories, categories and methods but, at the same time, one must be seeking to analyse the language element of events – text – in ways which elucidate its dialectical relations with other elements. Disciplinary specialisation is simultaneously necessary and insufficient, desirable and dangerous.

The critical realist distinction between the *real*, the *actual* and the *empirical* is also germane to this issue. I have already, in effect, distinguished between the 'real' and the 'actual': the 'real' for critical realism is structures and their associated 'mechanisms', i.e., the structural delimitation of the possible, whereas the 'actual' is the concrete, i.e., what actually happens as opposed to what could happen. (This critical realist sense of 'real' is unfortunate because both the 'real' and the 'actual' are real in any reasonable sense of the term.) The empirical is what is available as knowledge of the real and the actual. However, the real and the actual cannot be reduced to the empirical, i.e., one cannot assume that what is known exhausts what is. When applying this perspective to texts, it implies that analysts should be somewhat cautious about what they know as linguists about texts, avoid any claims for a positive science of texts, and recognise the need to work on the common social opacity of textual analyses by developing their resources for textual analysis through a trans-disciplinary way of working.

7 Space–time and equivalence/difference relations

With these considerations in mind, let me come back to the Blair text and to put into focus the incipient transdisciplinary character of the analysis I have done by positioning the text in relation to social scientific theories of space–time on the one hand, and logics of equivalence and difference on the other.

The use of the category of 'space–time' in recent geographical and social theory registers the view that there is an 'indissoluble link' between space and time (Harvey 1996). People in modern societies simultaneously inhabit different spaces: their immediate localities ('places'), sub-national regions (e.g., 'the North' in the UK), nation states, and international spaces (e.g., the European Union, the 'global'). These are also characterised by differences in temporality. Furthermore, these space–times are not externally given but are socially constructed. So too are relationships which are established (and negotiated and contested) between them. These relationships can prove to be problematic in different ways for different classes and groups of people. For instance, Harvey (1996) discusses the persisting problem in working-class politics of how to connect the 'militant particularism' (the term is Raymond Williams's) of trade union and political activists in particular places (localities, workplaces) with universalist national and international agendas for social emancipation. At the same time, there are mundane and banal ways in which relationships between different space–times are lived and experienced in people's daily lives.

The transformations of new capitalism include changes in the social construction of space–times and of relations between space–times. The emergent new social order brings new problems in relating and moving between simultaneously occupied space–times, and between new social divisions which have been discussed, for instance, by Castells (1996) in terms of the differences between those who primarily occupy global as opposed to local networks (also Bauman 1998). It also brings new problems in achieving and legitimising normalised, banal, relations between space–times. The significant points in terms of my present concerns are that (a) these processes of establishing, negotiating and legitimising space–times and relations between space–times are processes which are omnipresent in texts, and (b) an elucidation of these processes (whether for theoretical purposes of understanding them or for political purposes of contesting them) requires the resources of textual analysis. At the same time, however, those resources need to be enhanced in a transdisciplinary way by exploring methods by which one can 'operationalise', in textual analysis, perspectives on space and time which have been developed in social theory.

My earlier analysis of the Blair text, in which I attempted a transdisciplinary approach, is intended to suggest the significance of texts and texturing in the shifting constructions of global and national space–times and of the relationship between them associated with the new capitalism and neo-liberal political discourse. Global space–time is represented, and described, as a reality of the undelimited ('timeless') present although as I pointed out in a somewhat contradictory way in that the 'realis' description disguises some 'irrealis' prediction. The processes of global space–time are also represented as spatially universal (though 'great new opportunities' might seem rather difficult to see for millions of people in the poorest countries). Its processes are processes without responsible human agents. For instance, technologies simply 'emerge', i.e., they are not developed and promoted by human agents (such as corporations or governments) in connection with particular purposes and interests. Such processes are described rather than analysed or explained; a sense of their reality is built up through a cumulative list of evidences and appearances rather than through analysis of causes and effects. A relationship is textured between the global space–time and of the national space–time which frames the latter within the former: the global space–time is an incontrovertible and inevitable reality, and 'we' must respond to it in ways which allow us to live and succeed within it. This is reminiscent of accounts of 'time–space compression' and its implications in terms of enhanced connectivity between scales of social life, and the inescapability of global processes and events at other scales (Giddens 1991, Harvey 1996). National space–time is irrealis, a set of prescriptions for future action to achieve success in the global reality. Its agents are human and collective. Policies and actions which are prescribed are, in some cases, rationalised and legitimised. Ends are associated with means, e.g., 'by opening markets'; reasons are given, although generally implicitly, e.g., 'companies alone cannot (invest in British capabilities)' is a reason for 'us' doing so, and being in 'a world of short-term pressures' is a reason for promoting a long-term vision. In contrast with the description of the global in terms of appearances, there is a causal logic at work in these national policy prescriptions.

Heller (1999) characterises modernity as legitimising present actions in terms of grand visions of the future. The Blair text has something of this character but without its optimistic or visionary aspects. The national space–time is not envisioned in terms of progress in the modernist sense. The inevitable and imperative global space–time, which broods over the national space–time, enforces a particular direction of change: the grand vision (if such it be) is coloured by an implicit sense of risk and danger from 'new competitors'; 'success' is contingent; and failure to compete effectively now will mean we will not 'prosper in the markets of tomorrow'. Neo-liberalism may, as Gray (1993) suggests, share the 'canonical thinking' of socialism, but without its optimistic sense of progress for the betterment of humankind. The prescribed future is more a matter of acting to create reality in accordance with a neo-liberal blueprint so as not to fail.

Let me turn more briefly to relations of equivalence and difference. Laclau and Mouffe (1985) theorise the political process (and 'hegemony') in terms of the simultaneous working of two different 'logics': a logic of 'difference' which creates differences and divisions, and a logic of 'equivalence' which creates equivalences in 'subverting' existing differences and divisions. This can usefully be seen as a general characterisation of social processes of classification: people in all social practices are continuously dividing and combining and, thereby, producing (also reproducing) and subverting divisions and differences. Social interaction, as Laclau and Mouffe (1985) suggest, is an ongoing work of articulation and disarticulation. This is true of the textual moment of social events. Elements (words, phrases etc.) are constantly being textured into relations of equivalence and relations of difference; prior equivalences and differences are constantly being 'subverted'; and these processes are an important part of the textual moment of the social process of classification. By operationalising this theory in textual analysis, one also strengthens the claims of textual analysis to be able to contribute to social research on classification and processes of articulation and disarticulation. Laclau and Mouffe's (1985) political theory is already a discourse theory in a Foucaultian sense, but what it lacks is a text analytical capacity.

8 Conclusion

What is at issue on one level in this paper is how we (as systemic linguists or critical discourse analysts) can make a strong case to other social scientists for textual analysis as a significant element in social research on the transformations of new capitalism (or 'globalisation'). Traditions of textual analysis in linguistics already have much to offer, and I have, of course, drawn upon SFL in particular in the analysis. But I have also made a case for a transdisciplinary way of working in textual analysis in which one attempts to maintain a dialogue with social theoretical and research perspectives and to develop and enhance textual analysis by seeking to operationalise within it categories and insights from these perspectives. I have also argued that interdiscursive analysis of texts is a crucial mediating link between linguistic analysis and social analysis, a link which is needed, I would argue, if one is to succeed in incorporating textual analysis more substantively within social research. The rationale and clarification of how interdiscursive analysis can act in this mediating way depends upon theoretical categories and perspectives within CDA which I have briefly discussed.

There is much in SFL which is of value in this project, including a long-standing concern with socially oriented analysis of text and a linguistic theory which is itself socially oriented and informed. Also, the dynamic, process view of text as 'texturing' echoes thinking within SFL (Lemke 1998). The key difference regards interdiscursivity and the category of 'order of discourse' (Chouliaraki and Fairclough 1999). One can put this in terms of the levels of concreteness and abstractness I have distinguished; just as the general relationship between social structures and social events needs to seen as mediated by social practices, so also does the relationship between semiotic structures (languages) and texts need to be mediated by orders of discourse, the semiotic moment of social practices. The interdiscursivity of texts is the correlate at the concrete level of social events of orders of discourse at the more abstract level of social practices. Incorporating interdiscursive analysis into textual analysis provides, as I suggested earlier, a way to link linguistic analysis to social analysis and, thus, places us in a stronger position to make a substantive contribution to social research.

Notes

1. I am grateful to Isabela Ieţcu (formerly Preoteasa) for her helpful comments on a draft of this paper.
2. I shall sometimes put 'global' in scare quotes to indicate the contentiousness of claims about 'globalisation'. A key issue is the relationship between real processes of increased international trade, international operation of corporations, international cultural flows etc., and their representation as 'globalisation'. Some argue that 'globalisation' is more of a partial and interested and ideological way of representing actual changes than a real process (Held *et al.* 1999).

3. Althusser takes the term 'overdetermination' from Freud who uses it to describe the condensation of a number of thoughts in a single image in dreams or the transference of psychic energy from a potent thought to an apparently trivial image. Althusser uses the term to describe the effects of the contradictions of each practice within a social formation on the social formation as a whole, with respect to relations of domination/subordination between contradictions. (See Glossary, Althusser and Balibar 1970.) Althusser (Althusser and Balibar 1970: 188) notes that this was not an arbitrary borrowing from Freud but a necessary one, 'for the same theoretical problem is at stake in both cases: with what concept are we to think the determination of either an element or a structure by a structure?' Similarly, my use of the concept reflects my concern with the same theoretical problem (Fairclough, Jessop and Sayer 2002).

12. Marx as a critical discourse analyst: the genesis of a critical method and its relevance to the critique of global capital

Norman Fairclough and Phil Graham

I n this paper we identify elements in Marx's economic and political writings that are relevant to contemporary critical discourse analysis (CDA). We argue that Marx can be seen to be engaging in a form of discourse analysis. We identify the elements in Marx's historical materialist method that support such a perspective, and exemplify these in a longitudinal comparison of Marx's texts.

1 Introduction

This paper has developed as one part of a wider project: the critique of language in new capitalism. By 'new capitalism' we mean the emergent form of capitalism, variously referred to as 'globalisation', 'the global economy', 'the knowledge economy', 'the information society', and so forth. It is the form of capitalism which is currently emerging as a new and dominant form of social organisation on a global scale (Jessop 2000). Among its more salient characteristics are the importance of international and 'global' institutions, and the ways in which the actions of such institutions are integrated with national, regional and local scales and, more particularly, a systemic emphasis on commodifying the most intimate aspects of human existence, including thought, language, attitudes, and opinions (Graham 1999, 2000).

There are various ways in which language and other discursive artefacts (for instance, imagery) are of greater importance to this new socio-economic formation than to its predecessors. Let us for instance briefly pursue this argument with respect to its 'knowledge-based' nature. The very idea of a 'knowledge-based' economy, and its counterpart 'information society', entails a discourse-based economy and society, in the sense that these more or less valuable knowledges are inevitably produced, exchanged and consumed as discourses. Put more plainly, more or less valuable knowledges presuppose more and less valued ways of knowing, which are always institutionally defined as such in discourse (Graham 1999, 2000). Moreover, the cycle of knowledge production, exchange and consumption includes 'operationalisation': on the one hand the 'enactment' of knowledges (discourses) as social practices, as ways of acting and interacting; and on the other hand the 'inculcation' of knowledges (discourses) as ways of knowing one's self and the world, as ways of being, as identities (Fairclough 2000a, Graham 2000: 141).

Language is intricately involved throughout this cycle: the enactment of discourses includes the creation of new genres through 'generic chaining', or generic convergence (Fairclough 2000a); the subtle but profound effects wrought by new ways of mediating linguistic and discursive exchanges (Graham 2000); and the inculcation of discourses, including the creation of new styles, new discursive ways of being, knowing and having; and new artefacts and institutions of knowledge (Fairclough 2000, Graham 2000). At every point in this cycle, language is both implicated and exposed as a decisive element. The diffusion, operationalisation, enactment and inculcation of discourses is crucial in the integration of different scales of economic activity. If the socio-economic order is discourse- and language-based in this sense – and we must assume it is – understanding of it, resistance to it, and struggle against it must also incorporate a significant discursive element (Melucci 1996).

We shall not attempt an extended rationale for the critique of the new capitalism here – we assume that readers will be familiar with evidence of alarming disparities between, on the one hand familiar claims to enhance human progress, welfare, poverty-relief, and so forth through 'economic growth', and on the other hand an increasingly pronounced gap between rich and poor, declining economic and social standards for millions if not billions of people, major damage to both ecological systems and the social fabric, and so forth (cf. Saul 1997, Bauman 1998, Kennedy 1998, Graham 1999, Hart 1999, Jessop 2000). The important point to make for this paper is that the critique of the new capitalism is incomplete without a significant element of language critique. One might say the same about any form of capitalism, or indeed about other socio-economic systems. But if the resources of discourse, and in particular language, do indeed, as we suggest, carry more weight in the constitution and reproduction of the emergent form of global capitalism, then language critique becomes correspondingly more important.

Why then go back to Marx? It is uncontentious that Marx's critique of capitalism has been the single most substantial and influential critique, and we believe that Marx's method remains important in understanding the emergent new capitalism. What has not been sufficiently recognised, however, is the significant place of critique of language in the critical method which he applied to capitalism. Indeed, we argue that Marx's method includes elements of what is now generally known as 'critical discourse analysis'. Our aim in looking at Marx as a discourse analyst 'avant la lettre' is first of all to establish this, and secondly to ask whether there are insights we can take from Marx which are of theoretical and/or methodological value in developing a critical analysis of language as part of the contemporary critique of capitalism. We shall argue that there are. We believe that this sort of critique should start from a view of language as an element of the material social process which is dialectically interconnected with other elements (Chouliaraki and Fairclough 1999, Fairclough 2000a, Graham 1999, 2000), and that the production of social life (both economic production and production in non-economic domains) is based within the articulation together of diverse elements and aspects of sociality into relatively stable configurations which always essentially and inherently include language (or more generally, discourse). This view stands in contrast with the predominant approach to the sociality of language within linguistics, which has consisted in a double movement of first abstracting language from its material interconnectedness with the rest of social life, treating language as an 'ideal' and non-material entity, and then construing the sociality of language as relations 'between' language – so constituted as an object of linguistic theory and analysis – and society, as if these were two separately constituted realities which subsequently, or even accidentally, come into contact with each other. What emerges in particular from our reading of Marx is precisely his emphasis on the dialectical interconnectivity of language and other elements of the social, which we believe is an essential basis for a form of language critique which can do full justice to social power of language in new capitalism without reducing social life to language, removing language from material existence, or reifying language.

Of course, to speak of Marx's method as if it were a monolithic and homogenous 'thing' is to do a great violence to the perspective. His approach was profoundly transdisciplinary, many-faceted, and ever-changing, both drawing on and inspiring studies in political theory, political economy, jurisprudence, philosophy, social theory, anthropology and historiography. Further, to view the whole of Marx as a theoretical monolith is to ignore or disallow the development of thought and the path of self-clarification common to any intellectual career. Here we examine Marx's development with the assumption that it can, at least in part, be viewed as the development of a critical understanding of just how central language is to social organisation, social change, and to the reproduction of social forms, as well as to understanding relations between these phenomena.

2 Critical discourse analysis: a brief overview

The perspective from which we approach the wider research project and the reading of Marx is 'critical discourse analysis' (Fairclough 1992a, 1995, Fairclough and Wodak 1997). Critical discourse analysis (hereafter CDA) analyses language as 'discourse', which we take to mean that language is conceived as one element of the social process dialectically interconnected with others along the lines sketched out above. It is a 'critical' analysis of discourse in that it sets out precisely to explore these often opaque dialectical interconnections within the tradition of critical social science. That is, it shares the concern of critical social science to show how socio-economic systems are built upon the domination, exploitation and dehumanisation of people by people, and to show how contradictions within these systems constitute a potential for transforming them in progressive and emancipatory directions. In our understanding, CDA differs from other critical (e.g., Foucaultian, 'postmodern', 'post-structural', 'social constructivist' etc.) approaches to discourse in its view of spoken, written and multimediated texts. CDA views texts as a moment in the *material* production and reproduction of social life, and analyses the social 'work' done in texts as a significant focus of materialist social critique.

CDA builds upon 'critical linguistics' (Fowler *et al.* 1979) by centring the conceptualisation of language as 'discourse' and more explicitly locating critical language analysis within critical social science (Fairclough 1989a, 1992a). Critical linguistics and CDA have both been shaped by Marxism, especially twentieth-century 'western Marxism' (Fairclough and Wodak 1997). Although the analysis of language in relation to the power relations and ideologies of capitalism has been a concern throughout, there has more recently developed a particular concern with contemporary processes of socio-economic change and the ways in which language figures within them (Fairclough 1992a, 2000c, Graham 2000). The 'language in new capitalism' project (Fairclough *et al.* 2000) is currently giving a tighter focus to this work, and a more explicit political orientation, linking CDA more closely to contemporary analyses of the form and contradictions of new capitalism, and the forms of resistance and struggles for change which are developing in response to it.

Critical research on new capitalism is, by nature and necessity, inter-disciplinary. We envisage critical discourse analysis as working within such a conjunction in a 'transdisciplinary' way (Fairclough 2000c); that is, entering a dialogue with other disciplines, theories and methods, putting their logic to work in developing critical discourse analysis as a theory and method in relation to the particular object of research. The relationship between object of research, theory and method is conceived of as a dynamic relationship, not a matter of pre-existing theory and method being 'applied' to a new object, but of theory and method (in our case, the theory and method of critical discourse analysis) evolving in the encounter with the object of research, whose con-struction is in turn ongoingly developed through this process of evolution. Marxism and the work of Marx in particular is obviously a significant partner-in-dialogue for critical discourse analysis given the focus on capitalism. We therefore see this paper as initiating a process of putting a Marxist logic to work in developing critical discourse analysis as theory and method to enhance its capacity to address the object of research.

We proceed by outlining the origins and development of Marx's method, highlighting the explicit and implicit role of language as his method matures over the course of a life. We draw these elements together by focusing on examples from six of Marx's works. A caveat to this paper is that it is *not* a crit-ical analysis of Marx's discourse. Rather, it is an exposition of the elements in Marx that we believe can contribute theoretically and methodologically to CDA, and, more specifically, to CDA's contribution to the transdisciplinary project of critically engaging contemporary capitalism.

3 Marx, classical scholarship and language: an historical contextualisation

Critics of Marx who suggest that he lacked a systematic 'theory of language' (e.g., Cook 1982: 530, Lepschy 1985) overlook the nature of nineteenth-century scholarship. While much attention has been directed towards under-standing the historical links between Kant, Hegel and Marx (e.g., Hook 1928a, Bloom 1943, Adorno 1966/1973, 1994, Cook 1982, Warminski 1995), little attention has been given to the broader historical tapestry in which these writers appear as pivotal figures in the history of western thought (Bloom 1943). The contributions of Marx, Hegel and Kant cannot be under-stood without taking into account the enduring influence of classical scholar-ship in general (Bloom 1943). Nor can we grasp the centrality of language critique to Marx's method without taking into account nineteenth-century scholarship in general, and, in particular, his philosophical and juridical education in Germany at a time when Hegel's philosophy was considered to be a revolutionary intellectual force (cf. Hook 1928: 114, Bloom 1943, Tucker 1972: xvii–xviii, Colletti 1975: 46). An understanding of language was central to scholarship during the time Marx studied. It was, in fact, the foundation of classical scholarship (Grote 1872, Adorno 1973: 56, 1994: 18–21, 116–118, Cook 1982: 530).

In the following section, we outline three conceptual elements that are central to understanding the discursive aspects of Marx's critical method. The elements we have chosen to highlight are: the doctrine of abstraction, Aristotle's conception of dialectic, and the late-eighteenth to mid-nineteenth century conceptions of ideology, the philosophical counterpart of post-revolutionary political economy in France and Germany. When we trace these themes out in their historical significance, what we find in Marx's formulation is an intense mixture of naturalism and humanism intertwined with a funda-mentally discursive approach to analysing social phenomena.

4 The 'doctrine of abstraction' and its significance to Marx's thought

Hegel substitutes the act of abstraction revolving within itself for these fixed abstractions; in so doing he has the merit, first of all, of having revealed the source of all these inappropriate concepts which originally belonged to separate philosophers, of having combined them and of having created as the object of criticism the exhaustive range of abstraction rather than one particular abstraction. We shall later see why Hegel separates thought from the subject; but it is already clear that if man is not human, then the expression of his essential nature cannot be human, and therefore that thought itself could not be conceived as an expression of man's being, of man as a human and natural subject, with eyes, ears, etc., living in society, in the world, and in nature. (Marx 1844/1975a: 398)

While much is made of Marx's materialist critique of Hegel, rarely is it acknowledged that it merely extends a debate that has continued for thou-sands of years (Colletti 1975: 22–24). The very earliest written record we have in the western tradition of antagonism between idealism and materialism can be found in Aristotle's arguments against Plato's 'ideal forms' (Grote 1872: 29–30, Colletti 1975: 24, Lawson-Tancred 1998: xxvii).[1] It is here that we find Aristotle deploying the concept of abstraction in an attempt to reconcile 'ideal' and 'material' aspects of human existence. The notion of 'abstraction' as being essential to human cognition has its origin in Aristotle's materialist critique of Plato's idealism.[2] Central to Aristotle's rebuttal of idealism is his insistence that the 'Forms of material things are not separate realities, yet we seem to be able to consider them without considering the matter or without considering other concrete features of material things' (Weinberg 1968: 1). This, of course, was in contradiction to Plato and his followers who held that form had a separate existence from matter, and that humans were able to link these separate aspects because of knowledge gathered during a previous existence, thus rendering a theory of abstraction unnecessary (page 1). Aristotle argued against this, claiming that because 'form and matter are joined in physical objects', a theory of abstraction is 'both possible and neces-sary' (page 1).[3] Aristotle's materialist theory of cognition is the foundation upon which the scholastics developed their 'doctrine of abstraction' (page 2).

The doctrine remained the fundamental tool for reasoning about ques-tions of cognition throughout the height of the scholastic period, persisting throughout the enlightenment and beyond (McKeon 1928: 425–426). It was also an object of contention, and thus underwent all the usual twists and turns that such pivotal ideas do (Randall 1940). Descartes' ontological dualism owes its existence to the doctrine of abstraction, as does Kant's theory of the a priori.[4] Logical positivism is similarly derived. But essentially, Aristotle's formulation, as it was passed down by the scholastics, remained intact until Hegel reshaped it in a very specific way: by adding the concept of genesis – change over time. This was in contradistinction to doctrinaire abstraction, as it was most fully developed by the scholastics, which was concerned with the immutable and Universal attributes of isolated things, the Universal charac-teristics of objective matter. Hegel, on the other hand, added the dimension of social time – history – and formulated a theory of abstraction that assumed the effects of dynamic, antagonistic and antithetical social processes through-out history, thus bequeathing us the concept of the evolving 'Idea' (Marx 1844/ 1975a: 398, McTaggart 1893, Hook 1928a: 117).

The significance of Hegel's contribution cannot be overestimated. Rather than being confined to a dry logic of 'things', Hegel reshaped the static tool of abstraction into a dynamic system that describes how universal categories themselves evolve over time (McTaggart 1893: 490).[5] For Hegel, this change over time – this evolution of historical consciousness – was a matter of thought becoming conscious of itself through dynamic, contradictory and inter-dependent processes of abstraction working upon themselves, the historical culmination of which is to be 'Absolute Knowledge or Spirit knowing itself as Spirit' (Hegel 1807/1966: 808).[6] History is thus 'the process of becoming in terms of knowledge, a conscious self-mediating process – Spirit externalized and emptied into Time' (page 807). The 'goal' of History is 'the revelation of the depth of spiritual life' (page 808).

It is precisely these 'mystical' aspects in Hegel that drive Marx's pivotal critique of idealism. For Hegel, 'self-realising self-consciousness', the historical movement of abstract thought, determines the course of human history (Marx 1846/1972: 118). For Marx the opposite is true: human life – social activity – determines the form, nature and consequences that our conscious abstractions take (Marx 1846/1972: 118, Warminski 1995: 118).[7] But Marx's is no simple inversion of Hegel, 'that is what the Young Hegelians do and what he criticises them for' (Warminski 1995: 120). His approach is, rather, 'a full-scale "deconstruction" of both consciousness *and* life and the "relation" between them' (1995: 120). But for Marx, language and *social* consciousness are identical – 'language *is* practical consciousness' (1846/1972: 122); the one cannot be practically distinguished from the other:

> Language does not transform ideas, so that the peculiarity of ideas is dissolved and their social character runs alongside them as a separate entity, like prices alongside commodities. Ideas do not exist separately from language. (Marx 1857/1973: 163)

For Marx, Hegel's (1910) *Phenomenology* is 'concealed and mystifying criticism' because it hides the social character of our ideas, the social nature of shared abstractions (Marx 1844/1975a: 385). But he sees that Hegel has grasped an important feature of abstraction: *genesis*, 'the moving and producing principle', the dynamic, processual, intrinsically productive nature of human social activity which, once given a materialist orientation, is the basis of Marx's critical method (1844/1975a: 386).

5 Dialectics: outlines of a method

> Dialectics – literally: language as the organon of thought – would mean to attempt a critical rescue of the rhetorical element, a mutual approximation of thing and expression, to the point where the difference fades. Dialectics appropriates for the power of thought what historically seemed to be a flaw in thinking: its link with language, which nothing can wholly break [. . .]. Dialectics seeks to mediate between random views and unessential accuracy, to master this dilemma by way of the formal, logical dilemma. But dialectic inclines to content because content is not closed, not predetermined by a skeleton; it is a protest against mythology. (Adorno 1966/1973: 56)

The classical formulation of dialectical method is a relational, socially grounded approach to analysing assertions. Its methods and categories are derived from language in use, from 'common speech'; its objective is to challenge 'common sense' (Grote 1872: 385–390). In ancient Greece, it has been argued, dialectical method was the essence of 'free speech and free thought', and thus was considered to be the essence of democracy (Berti 1978). If Hegel's dynamic treatment of abstraction is the foundation of Marx's theoretical perspective, Aristotle's dialectic may be viewed similarly as his analytical method. As defined by Aristotle, dialectic is a critical linguistic method formulated to challenge the dogmas of received wisdom (Adorno 1966/1973, Grote 1872: 384). A crucial aspect of Aristotlean dialectic is its relational logic.[8] Various misunderstandings of relational logic have led to antithetical, 'substantialist' (Bourdieu 1998c: 4) readings of important categories in Marx's work, 'social class' for example. From a relational perspective, any property we care to identify as a significant 'distinction' in social life, including social class, 'is nothing other than *difference*, a gap, a distinctive feature, in short, a *relational* property existing only in and through its relation with other properties' (Bourdieu 1998c: 6).[9] Bourdieu's relational logic, like Marx's, is fundamentally Aristotlean.

In its classical form, dialectical argument is organised around Aristotle's Categories, the most fundamental of these being *Entia* (Grote 1872: 90). '*Entia*' are defined relationally within propositions, and while the term has a rough correspondence to 'Essences' or 'Substances', it is best viewed as a *gradation* of essences, as 'more and less essential' essences (Grote 1872: 90, Lawson-Tancred 1998: xxviii–xxvix).[10] But the most important of the Categories is *Relation*. Considered in the most comprehensive sense, all of Aristotle's categories 'are implicated and subordinated to Relation', even the fundamental category of 'essence' (Grote 1872: 115–120). Relation, 'understood in the large sense which really belongs to it, ought to be considered as a Universal, comprehending and pervading all the Categories' (page 120). Relations in Aristotle are organised around the concept of *Relata* (pages 100–104). *Relata* are '*of other things*, or are said to be in some manner *towards something else*' (page 100). They are 'so designated in virtue of their relation to another *Correlata*; the master is master *of a servant* – the servant is servant *of a master*' (Grote 1872: 101, cf. also Hegel 1807/1966: 228–240, Marx 1844/1975b). Relata and Correlata are mutually defining; they are *simul naturâ*. If you suppress one of the pair, the other vanishes' (Grote 1872: 102). It is no selective contrivance on our part that we choose to highlight the relational aspect of Aristotle's system. Aristotle describes Relation, 'not as one amongst many distinct Categories, but as implicated with all the Categories' (Grote 1872: 126).[11] And this primacy of the relational in Aristotle can also be clearly seen throughout Marx.

Dialectical arguments, then, are primarily concerned with language. They have 'for their province words and discourse; they are . . . powers or accomplishments of discourse' (page 384). The objects of dialectic are 'Endoxa', 'premises, propositions and problems' which are 'borrowed from someone among the varieties of accredited or authoritative opinions' – from 'a particular country', 'an intelligent majority' or from 'a particular school of philosophers or wise individuals' (page 383). They are found 'exclusively in the regions of . . . received opinions', and are supported to varying degrees by 'the mass of opinions and beliefs floating and carrying authority at the same time' (page 389). In any given community, endoxic propositions are often contradictory, and will have many meanings and interpretations within that community. They are an important focus for dialectical investigation for precisely this reason. Each individual, as they mature, 'imbibes these opinions and beliefs insensibly and without special or professional teaching . . . and it is from them that the reasonings of common life . . . are supplied' (1872: 385). In other words, endoxa form the basis of what we call 'common sense'.[12] Dialectical argument 'searches for a "counter syllogism" of which the conclusion is contradictory . . . to the [endoxic] thesis itself' (page 390).[13] The primary function of dialectic is that of 'dissipating the false persuasions of knowledge' based on fallacious first principles or taken-for-granted, commonsense beliefs and assumptions (page 391). The subject matter may be 'ethical', 'physical', or 'logical' (Grote 1872: 394).[14]

Abstraction again becomes significant when we encounter the human 'essence' in Marx. That is because Marx does not regard it as some vague, immutable, and constant 'abstraction inherent in each individual' (Marx 1844/1975a: 423). The reality of the human 'essence' is, rather, a dynamic set of relationships, 'the ensemble of social relations' in which each person is embedded (Marx 1844/1975a: 423). Aristotle defines 'essences' under ten categories.[15] The most noteworthy aspect of the categories is, though, *how* Aristotle develops them. He considers them 'in their *relation* to Propositions; and his ten classes discriminate the relation which they bear to each other as parts or constituent elements of a proposition' (Grote 1872: 94). Even more significantly for socially grounded linguistics, the categories are drawn from 'common speech; and from the dialectic . . . which debated about matters of common life and talk, about received and current opinions' (pages 94–95). Aristotle's Categories are derived from language-in-use within specific social contexts. They are sociolinguistically derived.

'Essences' may be either abstract or concrete, but in Aristotle, 'Abstract alone can be predicated of abstract; concrete alone can be predicated of concrete. If we describe the relation between the abstract and the concrete, we must say, The Abstract is in the Concrete – the concrete contains or embodies the Abstract' (Grote 1872: 91). But Marx, like Hegel before him, is concerned with showing the historical relationship between abstract and concrete aspects of human experience through the deployment of dialectical argument (Hook 1928: 120–123).[16] The aim of dialectic is not to discover truth, but rather to 'convict an opponent of inconsistency' and to propose counter assertions (page 385). The method is designed to investigate the common meanings – the accepted assumptions, definitions and understandings – of a given subject by way of investigating the received, authoritative statements about it. It proceeds by laying out the orthodoxies of, for instance, a particular science, into its accepted propositions; differentiating between the various uses and meanings of these; and showing the relationships of these parts to the whole subject matter.

The dialectical method that Marx deploys should not be confused with the *reductio ad absurdum* carried on by the late scholasticism of the counter-reformation (cf. McKeon 1928, Saul 1992, 1997). Rather, it is as an expression of what we know as 'scientific method' (Randall 1940). The 'free thinkers' among the scholastics, especially those in the school of Padua, developed through dialectic method, a method based on the 'careful analysis of experience' that 'left their hands with a refinement and precision . . . which the seventeenth century scientists who used it did not surpass in all their careful investigation of method' (Randall 1940: 178). In this sense, 'scientific method' and 'critical method' are identical. Both are founded, dialectically, on a healthy scepticism towards common sense, dogma, and taken-for-grantedness. At their very foundation they are relational and dynamic, social and empirical linguistic methods. Critical praxis stands opposed to what is now often called 'ideology', but which has *always* been the dominating myths propagated by vested interests (Horkheimer and Adorno 1947/1998: 20, Adorno 1966/1973: 56). This brings us to a central and overt object of Marx's critical engagement with language: ideology.

6 Ideology: language and language critique

The term 'ideology' has for some time been understood as 'false consciousness', 'ruling class ideals', 'belief systems', 'mistaken common sense', 'religious dogma', or something similar (see, e.g., Roucek 1944: 479, Burks 1949, Huxley 1950: 10, Bergmann 1951, Lipset 1966, Sartori 1969, Kennedy 1979: 353). However, ideology was conceived of in the first instance as an intellectual discipline to fill the perceived void left by the Church's moral authority and the scholastic system's associated monopoly on knowledge in post-Thermidorian France (Roucek 1944, Kennedy 1979). As such, it dominated the last few years of eighteenth-century France, and continued as a dominant influence for the first half of the nineteenth century throughout Western Europe, including Italy and Spain, even having considerable influence in the United States (Roucek 1944: 482, Kennedy 1979: 362–364).[17] As a terminology and an intellectual project, 'Ideology' was initially conceived of by Destutt de Tracy (1754–1836) with the explicit purpose of dominating the whole human intellectual environment, including the fields of morality, political economy, physics, calculus and, ultimately, politics proper (Kennedy 1979: 356–358). Tracy intended that ideology should replace theology as the 'queen' of human intellectual endeavour (Kennedy 1979: 356). Its formulation was an attempt to stabilise post-revolutionary France in the very image of the Enlightenment:

> At stake was a whole political and social philosophy, a conservative post-Thermidorean liberalism of a part of the propertied class, an Ideology which was strongly materialist in its conception of the relationship between the physical and the moral. (page 356)

Throughout the first half of the nineteenth century, Ideology was a much-contested movement, especially in the social and political sciences of France and Germany. 'Ideology' was meant literally as the 'science of ideas' (Kennedy 1979: 355). It was first announced as such by Tracy in 1796, with a full social, political, educational and economic agenda later being published by him in a four-volume work in 1805 (Roucek 1944: 482, Kennedy 1979). Late eighteenth century scholars associated with the movement searched to unite political economy, moral philosophy and the liberal arts to develop 'a sound "theory of the moral and political sciences" which embraced grammar, logic, education, morality, and "finally the greatest of arts, for whose success all the others must cooperate, that of regulating society"' (Kennedy 1979: 355, cf. also Neill 1949). And that was *Ideology*, a liberal science of human thought with the ultimate purpose of regulating social morality. Its central focus was language and its relationship to thought (Kennedy 1979: 364–366).

In the genesis of Marx's method, his critique of *The German Ideology* (1846/1972a,b) is the point at which his relational social logic, his materialist perspective on dynamic abstraction, and his conception of socio-historical transitivity as productive human activity are first fully expressed. *The German Ideology* marks a watershed in Marx's intellectual project. It synthesises and summarises his political, economic, historical, social and philosophical positions; it contains a statement of the first principles of Marx's political economy; and it is the beginnings of the 'mature' Marx. Not surprisingly, it is here that we find Marx formulating his most explicit and sustained treatment of language and consciousness as material processes of production, as aspects of the social production process which are inherently bound up in the totality and materiality of human experience.

Marx's much referred to comments about language in *The German Ideology* (1846/1972a,b) are best seen as a critical response to the idealist, alienated conceptions of language and consciousness widely propagated by the formal 'ideologists', or, in the Napoleonic perjorative, 'ideologues', of the day, particularly those associated with Tracy. The French ideologists had their German counterparts in the 'Young Hegelians', led in the early nineteenth century by Bruno Bauer (1809–1882) and Max Stirner (1806–1856). It is the Germans who are the main targets of Marx's critique. In Germany, the 'Young Hegelians' developed their own 'science of ideas' based on Hegel's philosophy and his intensely conservative conceptions of the state. Ideology, both in its French and German formulations, was essentially a legitimising discipline comprising 'Natural Order' apologists for the French and Prussian aristocracies of the day (Marx 1846/1972a,b, Neill 1949, Kennedy 1979).

Marx and formal ideology were contemporaries.[18] He saw ideology as a contrivance by vested interests to fill the moral void left by the diminished influence of the Church and 'Divine Right' monarchies, and *a fortiori* their socially sanctioned authority. The intentions of ideology's earliest proponents, 'a group of propertied intellectuals in power after Thermidor', was to 'transform and stabilize post-revolutionary France' by supplanting the eroded authority of the Church and the monarchy with the study of ideology (Kennedy 1979: 358). The express focus of ideology was language and its relationship to thought: '[w]e can never pay too much attention to the illusions which certain words produce. Nothing proves better how vague and confused their meaning is' (Tracy 1805, in Kennedy 1979). For the most enthusiastic of the French School, 'Ideology' was to be 'the torchlight of grammar' (Lemare 1812, in Kennedy 1979: 363). Marx's pejorative construal of ideology, which includes references to the French *and* German schools in *The German Ideology* (1846/1972a,b), *Grundrisse* (1857/1973), and *Capital* (1976, 1978, 1981), comes 'not from Hegel . . . but only from the cumulative usages current in the 1830s and 1840s and specifically from Destutt De Tracy' (Kennedy 1979: 366). *The German Ideology* firstly critiques ideological conceptions of the relationship between language, consciousness, social life and 'civil society'.

The ideologists had emphasised the unity of language and thought, language being for them a system of arbitrary signs, the externalised artefacts of thought 'abstracted from time and men' (Frank 1844, in Kennedy 1979: 364). For Tracy, ideas are 'the only things that exist *for us*, the only means we have to know things' (Kennedy 1979: 364).[19] Hegel is identical to the French ideologists in his conception of language and thought:

> The strictly raw material of language itself depends more upon an inward symbolism than a symbolism referring to external objects; it depends, i.e., on anthropological articulation, as it were the posture in the corporeal act of oral utterance. For each vowel and each consonant accordingly, as well as for their more abstract elements . . . and for their combinations, people have tried to find the appropriate signification. But these dull subconscious beginnings are deprived of their original importance and prominence by new influences, it may be by external agencies or by the needs of civilization. Having been originally sensuous intuitions, they are reduced to signs, and thus have only traces left of their original meaning, if it be not altogether extinguished. As to the formal element, again, it is the work of analytic intellect [*Verstand*] which informs language with its categories: it is this logical instinct which gives rise to grammar. (Hegel 1830/1998: 306)

Marx held an almost opposite perspective on the relationship between language and thought:

> The production of ideas, of conceptions, of consciousness, is at first directly interwoven with the material activity and the material intercourses of men, the language of real life. Conceiving, thinking, the mental intercourse of men, appear at this stage as the direct efflux of their material behaviour. The same applies to mental production as expressed in the language of politics, laws, morality, religion, metaphysics etc. of a people. Men are the producers of their conceptions, ideas, etc. – real active men, as they are conditioned by a definite development of their productive forces and of the intercourse corresponding to these, up to its furthest form. Consciousness can never be anything else than conscious existence, and the existence of men is their actual life-process. If in all ideology men and their circumstances appear upside-down as in a camera obscura, this phenomenon arises just as much from their historical life-process as the inversion of objects on the retina does from their physical life-process. (Marx 1846/1972a,b: 118)

For Hegel, language functions to externalise the internal and intuitive state of isolated individuals. It is 'the imagination which creates signs', and these signs are language (Hegel 1833/1998: 303). In Hegel's ideology, meaning made in language moves from abstract intuition and imagination to symbolise and particularise already universalised meanings (i.e., a system of already-thought-of abstractions), 'reason' being the universalising force, mechanism, or system into which the categorical effects of language 'fit' (page 305). Language, as a system of signs, is 'a product of intelligence', and 'gives to sensations, intuitions, conceptions, a second and higher existence than they naturally possess – invests them with the right of existence in the ideational realm' (Hegel 1833/1998: 303–305, cf. also Hegel 1807/1966: 340–341). Hegel's view is that the *written* word drives language forward to 'perfection' (1833/1998: 307). He derides the 'hieroglyphic mode of writing' for keeping the 'Chinese vocal language from reaching that objective precision which is gained in articulation by alphabetic writing' (page 307). Alphabetic writing 'is on all accounts the more intelligent: in it the word – the mode, peculiar to the intellect, of uttering its ideas most worthily – is brought to consciousness and made an object of reflection' (page 307). But for Marx, language is firstly a social and material phenomenon, not the reified object of abstract speculation. It is, rather, a dynamic social product that emerges from the material relationships between people and their social and material environments: 'language, like consciousness, only arises from the need, the necessity, of intercourse with other men' (1846/1972: 122). For Marx, meaning travels in entirely the opposite direction from Hegel.

Similarities can be seen between the German ideologists and the hard-line social-constructivist school that rose to prominence in the last quarter of the twentieth century in western social theory:

> Since the Young Hegelians consider conceptions, thoughts, ideas, in fact all the products of consciousness, to which they attribute an independent existence, as the real chains of men . . . it is evident that the Young Hegelians have to fight only against these illusions of consciousness. Since, according to their fantasy, the relationships of men, all their doings, their chains and their limitations are products of consciousness, the Young Hegelians logically put to men the moral postulate of exchanging their present consciousness for human, critical, or egoistic consciousness, and thus removing their limitations. This demand to change consciousness amounts to demands to interpret reality in another way, i.e., to recognise it by means of another interpretation. (Marx 1846/1972a,b: 113)

Like the latter-day constructivists, the Young Hegelians find themselves at war with 'phrases. They forget, however, that to these phrases they themselves are only opposing other phrases, and that they are in no way combating the real existing world when they are merely combating the phrases of this world' (page 113). Marx is clear that 'the language of real life' – a many-sided metaphor for social *praxis* – is materially implicated in a reciprocally causal relationship with the whole of social life, including language in the abstract, its categories, and the social relations in which these are produced by people.

These are the foundations, history and context of Marx's critical approach. It is a critical praxis that views productive processes, not as merely or exclusively 'economic' activities, but more precisely, as the network of social activities by which societies reproduce themselves at every level: materially, socially, relationally, consciously, economically and *linguistically* (Graham 2000: 137). The dialectic is Marx's method of analysis. A materialist approach to the problem of abstraction is his theoretical underpinning. Language, consciousness and praxis are considered to be in an inseparable relationship of 'causal reciprocity' (Hook 1928a: 124). Combined, the theoretical and methodological tools outlined here provide a critical, linguistic, *propositional* method of analysis, the main purpose of which is to challenge the taken-for-grantedness of common-sense ideas about human life, precisely by *beginning* with human life rather than deducing it *a posteriori* from eternal ideas. Dialectical materialism 'is what Aristotle becomes when modified by Hegel and Darwin. It is an emergent naturalism with a strong anti-religious flavor struggling with the problem of "time"' (Hook 1928a: 122).

Language critique is thus central to Marx's approach; an historical, materialist, critical understanding of language is the very foundation of his method. But language is not a separate or independent 'thing' for Marx, not the object of decontextualised contemplation. The transitivity of the clause and the transitivity of human social life are predicated of one and the same subject: *human social activity*, 'the language of real life'. Critical language analysis is central to Marx's method precisely because language is the only way we have of grasping the diachronics of changing social circumstances – not language as an abstract system of signs, but as a mutually determining product and substance of changing material circumstances and practices; not as the abstract representative of externalised ideas, but as both product, producer, and reproducer of social consciousness, which in turn is in a reciprocally causal relationship with the whole of the human experience. In these very important respects, Marx's method and the methods of CDA are identical.

7 Language critique in the development of Marx's method

We now discuss a number of Marx's texts – two economic texts (*Economic and Philosophic Manuscripts*, 1844/1975a, and *Capital* [vol. 1], 1867/1976), two political texts (*Critique of Hegel's Doctrine of the State*, 1843/1975, *Critique of the Gotha Programme*, 1875/1972), and an historical analysis (*Eighteenth*

Brumaire of Louis Bonaparte, 1851–2/1973). The aim here is twofold. First, to discuss the development of Marx's critical method in terms of how language critique figures within it, especially with reference to the economic texts. Second, to illustrate how Marx deploys critical linguistic analysis in different ways in different types of text – economic, political and historical.

Throughout the early Marx, through to the *Grundrisse*, we can clearly identify elements of a classical Aristotlean method, especially in the predominance of specific analytical and taxonomic terminologies: 'subjects and predicates'; 'Ens', 'genus' and 'species'; 'differentia and semblances'; 'accidents and errors in language', and so on.[20] A longitudinal shift in Marx's method can be seen in both his political and economic texts. In the earlier economic texts, up to and including the *Grundrisse* (1857–8), Marx deploys the method we have outlined above: a close reading and dialectical critique of the texts of the classical political economists. In his mature work, *Capital*, his own alternative to the theory of the political economists is presented. This does not mean that texts of the political economists do not figure in *Capital* – there are many quotations, especially in the footnotes – but they have a different role, and there is less explicit critique of the language of the texts. At this point, he uses the words of classical political economy, as well as parliamentary reports and submissions, as either 'documentary proof' of his assertions, or as 'a running commentary to the text, a commentary borrowed from the history of economic science' (Engels 1883, in Marx 1976: 108).[21] We begin our exposition with a political text, *Critique of Hegel's Doctrine of the State* (1843/1975).

8 *Critique of Hegel's Doctrine of the State*

Marx's much-refined Aristotelian method, one that is immediately recognisable as such, is especially evident in Marx's early works. The following is a passage from *Critique of Hegel's Doctrine of the State* in which Marx deploys a classic dialectical method, directly and critically engaging one of Hegel's texts (Hegel's is the first paragraph, italics are in the original):

> [§ 267] 'This *necessity* in ideality is the inner *self-development* of the Idea. As the substance of the individual *subject*, it is the **political** *sentiment* [patriotism]; in distinction therefrom, as the substance of the *objective* world, it is the *organism* of the state, i.e., it is the strictly political state and its *constitution*.'
>
>   The subject here is 'necessity in ideality', the 'inner self of the Idea', the *predicate – political sentiment* and the *political* constitution. In plain words this means: *political sentiment* is the subjective substance of the state, the political constitution its *objective substance*. The logical development from

the family and civil society to the state is, therefore, mere *appearance* as we are not shown how family and civil sentiment, and family and social institutions, as such are related to political sentiment and political institutions. [. . .]

The crux of the matter is that Hegel everywhere makes the Idea into the subject, while the genuine, real subject, such as 'political sentiment', is turned into the predicate. The development, however, always takes place on the side of the predicate. (Marx 1843/1975: 65, italics in original)

This critique appears to be almost entirely logico-grammatical in its approach. Marx critiques Hegel for what seems like a grammatical error. More precisely, though, it is a critique of Hegel's idealistic inversion of reality: 'the Idea' is forced erroneously into the position of 'subject', which is clearly understood here by Marx as an *active, transitive* entity, and an entity *definable* as such by its logical position and its 'development' in the text. Hegel is mistakenly asserting agency for 'the Idea' rather than for a 'genuine, real subject', 'political sentiment', for instance. It is worth noting here that Marx is careful to firstly engage Hegel within the realm of abstraction; he avoids asserting in the first instance that 'the political constitution' ought to be predicated of family, civil sentiment, social institutions, and the relations between these, thus avoiding predicating abstract qualities of concrete relations in a single step, according to the traditions of dialectical critique (Grote 1872: 91).[22] He chooses instead to take Hegel on his own terms, that is, entirely in the realm of abstraction. Even here, he points out that Hegel is mistaken: 'political sentiment' ought to be subject and 'the state' its predicate – abstract object predicated *of* abstract subject; the 'state' as manifest 'political sentiment'.

This brief fragment of critical analysis achieves a threefold effect. First, Marx identifies the agency that Hegel typically and erroneously attributes to 'the Idea'. Second, he proposes the correct logical abstract relations of Hegel's proposition. Third, Marx formulates the concrete, materialist alternative: that the *real* relations, which Hegel reduces to 'mere *appearance*', an illusory expression of 'the Idea' at work, are to be found in the relationships of 'family and civil sentiment' and 'family and social institutions' to 'political sentiment and political institutions'. This shows quite clearly that Marx is not merely inverting Hegel. He does that in the first move by rearranging subject and predicate, *by firstly* rearranging the relations in Hegel's proposition, and then by framing the *materialist form of the problem*. Rather than attempting to reveal relations between abstract subjects and predicates in a single step, Marx presents an emergent, materialist formulation of the problem. He presents 'family', the smallest social institution of society, in its relation to 'civil sentiment' on the one hand, and to 'social institutions' on the other, as the correct formulation of the problem.[23] We see, then, that Marx is indeed concerned with investigating 'both consciousness *and* life and the 'relation' between them' (Warminski 1995: 120). Warminski's scare quotes around *relation* denote the fact that Marx does not see consciousness and life as separate 'things', even though consciousness in particular is a clearly definable aspect of human life in general.[24] For Marx, life, language, social activity, and consciousness are essential and inseparably related aspects of human phenomena in terms of materiality and causality. By noting this, we are concerned again with stressing Marx's materialist perspective on meaning-making and its inseparability from human experience in all its aspects. Designating concrete relations in terms of 'subjects' and 'predicates' is for Marx, quite clearly, the act of asserting historically dynamic, causal, reciprocal, co-extensive relations among elements in language, and consequently among the elements of human life itself.

Aristotle directs the dialectician to investigate propositions in a particular way: they are to be put in the most general terms possible and stated as Universal if they are generally believed to be true (Grote 1872: 401). They are then to be reduced as far as possible into their particulars. But this is not to be done in a single step, 'not at once as separate individuals, but as comprised in subordinate genera and species; descending from highest to least divisible' (Grote 1872: 413).[25] Both Hegel and Marx clearly deploy such an approach in their critical analyses. Here, Marx is again testing Hegel's assertions about the constitution of the State (Hegel's words are in the quotation marks):

(1) 'This *organism* is the differentiation of the Idea into various elements and their objective reality.' It is not argued that the organism of the state is its differentiation into various elements and their objective reality. The real point here is that the organism of the state is its differentiation into various elements and their reality is *organic*. The *real differences* or the *various aspects of the political constitution* are the presupposition of the subject. The predicate is their definition as *organic*. Instead, the Idea is made into the subject, the distinct members and their reality are understood as its development, its result, whereas the reverse holds good, viz. that the Idea must be developed from the real differences. The organic is precisely the *Idea of the differences* and their ideal determination.

(2) Hegel, however, talks here of the *Idea* as of a subject that becomes differentiated into *its* members. Apart from the reversal of subject and predicate, the appearance is created that there is an idea over and above the organism. The starting point is the abstract Idea which then develops into the *political constitution* of the state. We are not concerned with a political Idea but with the abstract Idea in a political form. The mere fact

I say 'this organism (i.e., the state, the political constitution) is the differentiation of the Idea into various elements etc.' does not mean that I know anything about the *specific idea* of the political constitution; the same statement can be made about the organism of an *animal* as about the organism of the *state*. How are we to *distinguish* between *animal* and *political* organisms? Our general definitions do not advance our understanding. An explanation, however, which fails to supply the *differentia* is *no* explanation at all. (Marx 1843/1975: 67)

Here is another formal term of Aristotelian dialectic by which propositions are separated into their constituent parts: *differentia* (Grote 1872: 417). But this should be understood as dynamic differentiation, the *real* and transitive splitting of a whole into its constituent parts over time, and conversely, the emergent formation of constituents into 'wholes', in language as in life. Closely related to this is the concept of *organic* relations between constituent elements, 'predicates', of the 'subject'.[26] In short, these are the participant-elements of the state which stand in logically necessary and constitutional relationships with each other and with the state; the state *emerges* from the relations between these human elements. Thus, according to the argument Marx is putting forward against Hegel, any assertions about the nature of the state should be deduced from the differences between its constituent parts, and, as a corollary of this, from the nature of the essential relationships between these elements. The *organic* is thus the *ideal* expression of the sum total of all relations *within* the state between the different constituents *of* the state. Hegel does not go far enough. He stops at the most general of terms, failing even to differentiate between the *organic* nature (constituents) of, for instance, *animals*, and the organic nature of the state. Hegel is admonished for his *misuse* of abstraction, as well as for his failure to show the real constituent parts of these.

By absolutising the Idea, Hegel *objectifies* human consciousness; he attributes abstract ideas with historical agency, a phenomenon most clearly expressed in the dogmas of religion (1844/1975a,b: 382–385). Hegel's idealism, like contemporary neo-liberal economics, reduces real human history, real human activity, to a purely theoretical abstraction, a universalised *idea* which can have no meaningful relation to particular people because it is a closed system of abstractions which can only refer to its own insubstantial and circular elements. In such a system

Real man and real nature become mere predicates, symbols of this hidden, unreal man and this unreal nature. Subject and predicate therefore stand in a relation of absolute inversion to one another; a *mystical subject–object* or *subjectivity encroaching upon the object*, the *absolute subject* as a *process*, as a subject which alienates itself and returns to itself from alienation, while at the same time re-absorbing this alienation, and the subject as this process; pure, ceaseless revolving within itself. (page 396)

Here, we see further allusions to language in what seems like quite a metaphorical form: humanity and nature become 'predicates' of the 'subject', which is 'God, absolute spirit, the self-knowing and self-manifesting idea' (page 396). Marx then reconstrues 'subject' to expose the tension between passive and active elements in the relationships implicit in Hegel. Hegel's subject [self-realising self-consciousness] stands in a conflated relationship with its object [humanity in the abstract, i.e., as already-thought-of, theoretical humans]. In asserting a relationship between the universal idea and the abstract idea of thinkers, Hegel, in fact, separates real thought from real thinkers, leaving a pure abstraction, the idea, as the motivating force of history. Hegel's conflated 'subject–object' is thus devoid of meaningful content: because it is

nothing more than the abstract, empty form of that real living act, its content can only be a formal [i.e., abstract] content, created by abstraction from all content. Consequently there are general, abstract forms of abstraction which fit every content and are therefore indifferent to all content; forms of thought and logical categories torn away from real mind and real nature. (pages 396–397)

His subject, the absolute idea, with its historical universe of dependent predicates – namely abstract humanity and abstract nature – is thus separated from its source, humans actively thinking (and, presumably, speaking, acting, and so on). Hegel's subject therefore has no meaningful content because it can only refer to a constituency of abstract aspects of itself, all of which stand in a predefined relationship with the abstract subject, the Idea. Here again we find oblique allusions to language: abstractions that are indifferent to all content, logical categories and forms of thought torn from their realities. Marx is both critiquing Hegel's theoretical discourse, and indicating an alternative way of constituting a theoretical discourse, i.e., through identifying the relationships, the interconnected and mutually defining activities, of real life.

In engaging Hegel's assertions about the state, Marx develops in incipient form the foundational elements of his critical method. And, in identifying the historical significance of Hegel's dynamic understanding of abstraction, he formulates the rationale for his materialist method:[27]

Hegel's positive achievement in his speculative logic is to present deter-minate concepts, the universal fixed thought-forms in their independence of nature and mind, as a necessary result of the universal estrangement of human existence, and thus also of human thought, and to comprehend them as moments of abstraction (page 397). [. . .]

But nature too, taken abstractly, for itself, and fixed in its separation from man, is nothing for man. It goes without saying that the abstract thinker who decides on intuition, intuits nature abstractly.[28] Just as nature lay enclosed in the thinker in a shape which even to him was shrouded and mysterious, as an absolute idea, a thing of thought, so what he allowed to come forth from himself was simply this abstract nature, nature as a thing of thought. . . . Or, to put it in human terms, the abstract thinker discovers from intuiting nature that the entities he imagined he was creating out of nothing, out of pure abstraction, in a divine dialectic, as the pure products of the labour of thought living and moving within itself and never looking out into reality, are nothing more than abstractions from natural forms. (pages 398–399)

By investigating the way in which Marx engages Hegel's idealism regarding the State, we can see that many of the foundational concepts that Marx deploys in his critique of political economy later on are developed using the elements of language critique that we have outlined above (abstraction, dialectic and ideology): alienation; conceptual fetishism; objectification and reification; the labour process; labour as an all-embracing conception of productive human activity; and the primacy of material reality, including social reality, in deter-mining consciousness – all of these aspects can be identified in incipient form in Marx's critical engagement with Hegel's idealist discourse on the politics of the state.

9 *Economic and Philosophic Manuscripts*

We now move to the First Manuscript of the *Economic and Philosophical Manuscripts* (1844/1975a,b). This marks an important turning point in Marx's work, and not merely in terms of his new focus upon political eco-nomy. He brings the conceptual elements incipient in the critique of Hegel (objectification, alienation, conceptual fetishism, the labour process) to bear upon the problems of political economy. Marx gives his own account of what he is doing in much of the *Manuscripts*, especially in the first part. We can see that he proceeds from the 'endoxa', the received wisdom, of classical political economy, explicitly confining his empirical investigation 'to the propositions of political economy' in order to challenge its foundational assertions and formulate a contradictory thesis, or, in the formal terminology of dialectic, 'counter syllogisms', of his own (Marx 1844/1975a,b: 315). We receive further explicit evidence that Marx is engaged in language critique from the Preface of the *Manuscripts*:

> It is hardly necessary to assure the reader who is familiar with political economy that I arrived at my conclusions through an entirely empirical analysis based on an exhaustive critical study of political economy. (1844/1977: 13–14)

By 'political economy', Marx means the texts of the political economists. There is an oscillation of voices in the *Manuscripts* which is sometimes difficult to keep track of (Carver 1998): there are many quotations from the political economists, and there is Marx's own voice, which is sometimes echoing the political economists, sometimes critiquing them. What sort of critique is this? We argue that it is a critical analysis of what would nowadays be called the discourse of the political economists, which sometimes refers to their language, sometimes to their 'propositions', 'arguments', 'presuppositions'. At all levels of analysis, though, Marx keeps the socially positioned and conditioned representations of capitalism made by political economy in view.

The *Manuscripts* begins with a section on 'The Wages of Labour' which at first is purely in Marx's own voice and which hardly refers to the political economists, other than paraphrasing Smith (1776/1997) briefly. This introductory section is a summary of the conclusions he draws about wage labour in *Excerpts from James Mill's 'Elements of Political Economy'* (1844), the original version of which contains a total of 97 quotations from Mill.[29] Then Marx writes: 'Let us put ourselves now wholly at the standpoint of the political economist, and follow him in comparing the theoretical and practical claims of the worker'. Much of the pages which follow consists of Marx's own representations of 'what the political economist tells us', or extracts from the political economists, sometimes with minimal connecting linkages from Marx. For the most part, according to dialectical method, we are hearing the political economists 'in their own words'. But there are also some critical recontextualisations from Marx. For example, he writes at one point: 'Let us now rise above the level of political economy and try to answer two questions . . .' (1844/1977: 44).

The section numbered VII, 1–3 consists of a summary of claims of 'the political economist' about labour, set out in a pattern of concessional + main clauses which highlight contradictions in the political economists' discourse:

> Whilst according to the political economists it is solely through labour that man enhances the value of the products of nature . . . according to this

same political economy the landowner and the capitalist . . . are everywhere superior to the worker and lay down the law to him. (1844/1977:
22–3)

Here, we see Marx highlighting conflicting views of the relationships that
define capital as a form of social organisation. Marx concludes this set of
contradictory claims as follows:

> But it follows from the analysis made by the political economists, even
> though they themselves are unaware of the fact, that labour itself – not
> merely under present conditions, but in general, insofar as its goal is
> restricted to the increase of wealth – is harmful and destructive. (1844/
> 1977: 23)

Marx is drawing a conclusion from the arguments and the words of the political economists which is implicit in them, a conclusion which the political
economists were not aware of, and which 'rises above the level of political
economy' ('transcends' it in Hegelian terms). It is a conclusion which is highly
contradictory with the arguments of Smith, Mill, Ricardo, and so on.

Marx uses the same technique in subsection (4) of the section headed
'The Profit of Capital'. He critiques the political economists by showing the
contradictions in their own words with respect to their claim that:

> the sole defence against the capitalists [and against monopoly] is com-
> petition, which according to the evidence of political economy acts
> beneficently by both raising wages and lowering the prices of commodities
> to the advantage of the consuming public. (1844/1975a: 300)

This is dialectical argument, on the basis of quotations from the political
economists, aimed at producing a counter-syllogism to that of the political
economists, namely that competition leads to its opposite, monopoly; that
'competition among capitalists increases the accumulation of capital . . . the
concentration of capital in the hands of the few'; and that 'if labour is a commodity, it is a commodity with the most unfortunate characteristics' because it
is doomed to reduce its own worth along with those of other commodities as
productivity increases (1844/1977: 37). Marx notes later that although 'the
doctrine of competition' in political economy is 'opposed' to 'the doctrine of
monopoly', competition is conceived as an 'accidental, deliberate, violent
consequence' of monopoly, and not its 'necessary, inevitable, and natural'
consequence (1844/1977: 62).[30] Today's monopolistic global megaliths,
institutional and corporate, which preside over the most systematic, overt,

and pronounced social inequalities in history, continue to propound the doctrine of monopoly in precisely the manner Marx is criticising here. Marx's critique of classical political economy discourse also holds true for its contemporary counterpart. Marx's earliest critique remains relevant.

The section headed 'Rent of Land' includes a discussion of feudal landed property (XVII–XVIII). Here, Marx's relational logic is foregrounded. The 'essence' of feudal landed property is the 'domination of the land as an alien power over men. The serf is the adjunct of the land. Likewise, the lord of an entailed estate, the first-born son, belongs to the land' (1844/1975a: 318). In terms of the Aristotelian method of dialectic discussed earlier, the serf and the lord are 'predicates' of the essence, its co-defining 'relata' and 'correlata', without which feudal relations could not exist. But the illusory 'appearance' expressed in these relations is 'a more intimate connection between the proprietor and the land', and between the lord and the serf. It does not 'appear directly as the rule of mere capital' (1844/1977: 56–7). The 'appearance' of this form of social organisation is 'expressed' in the language, '*nulle terre sans mâitre*' (page 318).[31] The foundation of the lord–serf relationship is the blending of land and master, the personification of feudal land as the lord who carries the name of the land, and as such belongs to *it*. As objects of the land, lord and serf are feudalism's socio-historical enactment. However, for capital, 'it is inevitable that this appearance be abolished – that landed property . . . be drawn completely into the orbit of private property and become a commodity; that the rule of the property owner should appear as the naked rule of private property' (page 319).

'Appearance' here is shifting 'forms' which the 'essence' of feudal organisation (the domination of the land as an alien power over men) takes, at first 'disguised' then 'naked'. It is also how the feudal property relationship 'appears' to the people whose relationships define it as such, as their consciousness of these historical relationships. The dynamic process of landed property in the movement from feudalism to capitalism – from land as 'common weal' to land as private property, as the foundations of capital – leads to 'the abolition of the distinction between capitalist and landowner', the relationship between its 'essence' and its 'forms' of 'appearance', how they 'appear' to people, and the language in which these 'appearances' is 'expressed'. Marx's account grasps the interconnection between land and capital as forms of property relations in their historical movement, rather than just registering 'appearances' (temporary forms, forms given to consciousness in the social practice of historically entrenched relations, including the language in which these are expressed and defined). He shows, in reality, that the qualitative transformation from feudalism to capitalism is a relational and institutional transformation which in effect removes the illusion of personal domination to reveal capital's rule of 'the thing over the person' which lies latent in feudal relations:

> the rule of person over person now becomes the universal rule of the *thing* over the *person*, the product of the producer. Just as the *equivalent*, value, contained the determination of the alienation of private property, so now we see that *money* is the sensuous, corporeal existence of that *alienation*. (Marx 1844/1975b: 270)[32]

The final section of the First Manuscript is headed 'Estranged Labour'. It is a critique of commodification and alienation. Marx begins:

> We have started out from the premises of political economy. We have accepted its language and its laws. We presupposed private property; the separation of labour, capital and land, and likewise of wages, profit and capital; the division of labour; competition; the concept of exchange value, etc. From political economy itself, using its own words, we have shown that the worker sinks to the level of a commodity, and moreover the most wretched commodity of all; that the misery of the worker is in inverse proportion to the power and volume of his production; that the necessary consequence of competition is the accumulation of capital in a few hands and hence the restoration of monopoly in a more terrible form; and that finally the distinction between capitalist and landlord, between agricultur-alist worker and industrial worker, disappears and the whole of society must split into the two classes of *property owners* and propertyless *workers*. (Marx 1844/1975a: 322)[33]

This passage from the *Manuscripts* again highlights the dialectical and rela-tional foundations of Marx's method of language critique. Starting with the *premises, language and laws* of political economy, which construe the move to a capitalist economy as inherently triumphalist (a familiar theme in today's global order), Marx presents an alternative view of the historical move from feudal relations to capitalist ones, and the critical implications thereof. He also presents three foundational and essential aspect of his later critical formulation in *Capital*: class antagonism based on ownership rights; the commodification of productive human activity; and, as a corollary to these, the alienation of labour itself, its belonging to someone, or more importantly some *thing*, else.

Listed later in the section: 'the more the worker produces, the less he has to consume; the more values he creates, the more valueless, unworthy, he becomes', etc. These are the realities – the laws of political economy are mere euphemistic explanations, mistakes of *comprehension*:

It [political economy] does not *Comprehend* these laws – *i.e.*, it does not show how they arise from the nature of private property. . . . Precisely because political economy fails to grasp the interconnections within the movement, it was possible to oppose, for example, the doctrine of competition to the doctrine of monopoly, the doctrine of craft freedom to the doctrine of the guild, and the doctrine of the division of landed property to the doctrine of the great estate; for competition, craft freedom, and division of landed property were developed and conceived only as accidental, deliberate, violent consequences of monopoly, of the guilds, and of feudal property, and not as their necessary, inevitable, and natural consequences. (1844/1975: 322–323)

And later in the section: *'Political economy conceals the estrangement in the nature of labour by ignoring the **direct** relationship between the worker (labour) **and production** (page 325).'*
Marx's repeated criticism of political economy here is that it 'fails to grasp the interconnections within the movement' – it fails to give a dynamic account of relationships that give rise to its analytical abstractions, which are merely 'appearances' and 'expressions' of deeper relationships. It is a failure in the discourse of political economy – a problem of socially positioned representation, a problem of its recontextualisation but also misappropriation of the world in political economic discourse. Therefore,

We now have to grasp the essential connection between private property, greed, the separation of labour, capital and landed property, exchange and competition, value and the devaluation [*Entwertung*] of man, monopoly, and competition, etc. – the connection between this entire system of estrangement [Entfremdung] and the *money* system. (1844/1977: 62)

Marx goes on to give an extended account of how the worker is alienated in capitalist production – alienated from the product of labour, from him/herself ('self-estrangement'), from common humanity ('species-being'), and from other workers by the intermediation of money and property relations. The alienated relationship of workers to what they produce, their consciousness of themselves and each other, the relationship between work and capitalist, private property, wages etc. are all shown to be interconnected facets and effects of the social relations and processes entailed by capitalist production.
What can CDA take from this? The critique of political economy is fundamentally a critique of its failure to grasp 'the interconnections within the movement' of social history, social *reality*. It is a critique of the discourse of

political economy focused upon its lack of understanding, and consequently its mistaken construal, of social relations. From a discourse analytical perspective, Marx's critique of political economy is a critique of the connectivity in its texts: semantic relationships between words, argumentative relationships between propositions, temporal relationships between processes, syntactic relationships between and within sentences, relationships between what is asserted and what is presupposed, etc. What it points to is a critical analysis of the whole formal and conceptual architecture and texture of political economy texts, focusing on texts as relational work (Fairclough 2000a), texts as producing certain relations and not producing others, as foregrounding selected elements of those relations, as well as their being produced from *within* certain relations and not from within others.

10 *Capital*

Marx's critique of the political economists is a critique of their failure to go beyond appearances in their representation of capitalism and to challenge their own presuppositions. The same line of critique is evident in what is generally seen as Marx's most mature and complete work, *Capital* (1976, 1978, 1981). We comment in particular on the famous analysis in Chapter 1 of the first volume of the 'fetishism of commodities'.[34]

Marx points to the 'enigmatical character of the product of labour' when it 'assumes the form of commodities':

> The equality of all sorts of human labour is expressed objectively by their products being all equally values; the measure of the expenditure of labour power by the duration of that expenditure, takes the form of the quantity of value of the products of labour; and finally, the mutual relations of the producers, within which the social character of their labour affirms itself, takes the form of a social relation between the products. (1867/1976: 76–7)

In the commodity, 'the social character of men's labour appears to them as an objective character stamped upon the product of that labour . . . a definite social relation between men . . . assumes, in their eyes, the fantastic form of a relation between things'. Things and their values appear in the place of real social relations; they become the appearance of social relations. This is 'the fetishism of commodities', which has its origins in 'the peculiar social character of the labour that produces them', i.e., as alienated labour; as labour alienated from its own products. To producers, 'the relations connecting the labour of one individual with that of the rest appear, not as direct social relations . . . but as what they really are, material relations between persons and social relations between things' (page 78).

> The determination of the magnitude of value by labour-time is therefore a secret, hidden under the apparent fluctuations in the relative values of commodities. . . . It requires a fully developed production of commodities before, from accumulated experience alone, the scientific conviction springs up, that all the different kinds of private labour . . . are continually being reduced to the quantitative proportions in which society requires them.

That is, the incommensurable qualities of individuals' lives are rendered commensurable by money, which is also commensurable with all other things.

> The categories of bourgeois economy . . . are forms of thought expressing with social validity the conditions and relations of a definite, historically determined mode of production viz the production of commodities. . . . Political economy has analysed, however incompletely, value and its magnitude, and has discovered what lies beneath these forms. But it has never once asked the question why labour is represented by the value of its product and labour-time by the magnitude of that value. These formulae, which bear it stamped upon them in unmistakable letters that they belong to a state of society, in which the process of production has the mastery over man . . . appear to the bourgeois intellect to be as much a self-evident necessity imposed by Nature as productive labour itself.

Marx does not explicitly refer to language here, but he notes elsewhere the similarity between language and values. Value is not objective, nor is it inherent in things; rather, it is an abstract concept that 'transforms every product of labour into a social hieroglyph' (Marx 1976: 167). Value and language share a generative source, productive human activity: 'the characteristic which objects of utility have of being values is as much men's social product as is their language' (1976: 167). We can treat this extract as a critique of discourse, both the discourse of everyday life and the discourse of the political economists. With respect to the former, the fetishism of commodities is a matter of a particular form of consciousness, how 'the social character of men's labour appears to them', which arises from 'the peculiar social character' of their labour. But as the *German Ideology* puts it, consciousness is always 'burdened' with 'matter' – with language. What is at issue here is in contemporary terms the discourse of producers and production.

   With respect to the political economists, Marx's critique echoes the critique in the *Economic and Philosophic Manuscripts*: the 'formulae' (a word he also used in the earlier text) of political economists appear to them as 'self-evident', they do not ask 'why', they do not delve into the underlying relations to reveal the 'secret' of the determination of the magnitude of value by labour-time – nor could they, for that requires a 'fully developed production of commodities'; the 'formulae' of the political economists belong to the 'state of society' in which they lived (1970: 85). Both the fetishistic discourse of producers and the 'formulae' of the political economists are flawed in failing to grasp underlying relations – and again therefore open to critique of what we referred to above as the 'connectivity' of texts (and in texts). Thus the critique of discourse remains an important part of Marx's method in *Capital*, even though explicit engagement with and critique of the texts of the political economists is more muted.

11 *Critique of the Gotha Programme*

A similar conclusion for CDA can be drawn from another of Marx's mature works, the *Critique of the Gotha Programme* of 1875, the last of Marx's major political critiques, which is a critique of a draft programme of the German Socialist Party. We shall focus on the following extract, in which Marx discusses a section of the programme which claims that 'the proceeds of labour' belong 'with equal right' to all members of society. He is discussing 'with equal right', which he refers to as 'ideological nonsense', with respect to a future socialist society:

> What we have to deal with here is a communist society, not as it has *developed* on its own foundations, but, on the contrary, just as it *emerges* from capitalist society; which is thus in every respect, economically, morally, and intellectually, still stamped with the birthmarks of the old society from whose womb it emerges. Accordingly, the individual producer receives back from society – after the deductions have been made – exactly what he gives to it. What he has given to it is his individual quantum of labour . . . the same principle prevails as in the exchange of commodity equivalents: a given amount of labour in one form is exchanged for an equal amount of labour in another form.
>
> Hence, *equal right* here is still in principle – *bourgeois right* . . . while the exchange of equivalents in commodity exchange exists only on the average and not in the individual case . . . this equal right is still constantly stigmatized by a bourgeois limitation. The right of the producers is *proportional* to the labour they supply; the equality consists in the fact that measurement is made with an *equal standard*, labour.
>
> But one man is superior to another physically, or mentally, and supplies more labour in the same time, or can labour for a longer time; and labour, to

serve as a measure, must be defined by its duration or intensity, otherwise it ceases to be a standard of measurement. This *equal* right is an unequal right for unequal labour . . . it tacitly recognizes unequal individual endowment, and thus productive capacity, as a natural privilege. It is, therefore, a right of inequality, in its content, like every right. Right, by its very nature, can consist only in the application of an equal standard; but unequal individuals (and they would not be different individuals if they were not unequal) are measurable only by an equal standard insofar as they are brought under an equal point of view, are taken from one definite side only – for instance, in the present case, are regarded *only as workers* and nothing more is seen in them, everything else being ignored. . . . To avoid all these defects, right, instead of being equal, would have to be unequal. (1875/1972: 387–388)

Marx is arguing that 'equal rights' is the application of an 'equal standard' of measurement, no different from money, which reduces people to mere 'workers', to abstract labour, ignoring other characteristics of people which affect the work they are capable of doing (hence, 'from each according to their ability; to each according to their needs'). The result must be to produce inequality under the 'bourgeois', 'ideological', guise of 'equality' of 'rights'. The mistake is falsely rendering the incommensurable commensurable by standardised measurements. The (intertextual) critique of the appearance of this bourgeois discourse in a socialist programme, and of the exclusion from it of 'the realist outlook' which had already 'taken root' in the Party, again centres upon a failure to grasp underlying relationships – between 'rights', 'standards', and a reductive equalisation of people to nothing but abstract labour. Again, from the perspective of CDA, it is a critique of the conceptual architecture and textual connectivity of the discourse. Here we have Marx in a mature text engaging in the sort of close textual critique which we saw in the early *Economic and Philosophic Manuscripts*, with fundamentally the same target.

12   *The Eighteenth Brumaire of Louis Bonaparte*

The Eighteenth Brumaire of Louis Bonaparte (Marx 1851–2/1973) is in contrast to the other texts we have discussed an analysis of actual historical events – the process leading to Louis Bonaparte's *coup d'etat* in France in 1851 – which includes Marx's analysis of how language figured in this socio-political process. We shall begin with the celebrated opening passage:

Hegel remarks somewhere that all facts and personages of great importance in world history occur, as it were, twice. He forgot to add: the first time as tragedy, the second as farce . . .

Men make their own history, but they do not make it just as they please; they do not make it under circumstances chosen by themselves, but under circumstances directly encountered, given and transmitted from the past. The tradition of all dead generations weighs like a nightmare on the brain of the living. And just when they seem engaged in revolutionising themselves and things, in creating something that has never existed. . . . they anxiously conjure up the spirits of the past to their service and borrow from them names, battle cries and costumes in order to present the new scene of world history in this time-honoured disguise and this borrowed language. Thus Luther donned the mask of the Apostle Paul, the revolution of 1789 to 1814 draped itself alternately as the Roman republic and the Roman empire, and the Revolution of 1848 knew nothing better than to parody, now 1789, now the revolutionary tradition of 1793 to 1795. (1851–2/1973: 95–96)

And later in the text:

One sees: all 'idees napoleoniennes' are ideas of the undeveloped small holding in the freshness of its youth; for the small holding that has outlived its day they are an absurdity. They are only the hallucinations of its death struggle, words that are transformed into phrases, spirits transformed into ghosts . . . the parody of the empire. (page 131)

Revolutions are made in 'borrowed language' – 'language' in a metaphorical sense, but including language in a literal sense. Marx is talking, in Bakhtinian terms, about heteroglossia, the heteroglossic or intertextual resources that are drawn from the past in the enactment of the present (cf. Fairclough 1992a: Chapter 4, Lemke 1995: Chapter 3). But once the 'sober reality' and real 'content' of the revolution emerge, the borrowed 'phrases' disappear, and new discourses emerge. Thus the French Revolutionaries of 1789 'performed the task of their time in Roman costume and with Roman phrases, the task of unchaining and setting up a modern bourgeois society', a 'self-deception' in order to 'conceal from themselves the bourgeois limitations of the content of their struggles'. But 'the new social formation once established, the ante-diluvian Colossi disappeared and with them the resurrected Romanity. . . . Wholly absorbed in the production of wealth and peaceful competitive struggle, it no longer comprehended that ghosts from the days of Rome had watched over its cradle'.[35]

Marx contrasts these 'earlier revolutions' – where the 'phrase' (an empty shibboleth) conceals the 'content' (the meaning, the world historical conse-quences) – with the 'social revolution' struggled for by the communists, which must 'arrive at' its 'content' without 'superstition with regard to the past'. This is summed up in the powerful *chiasmus* at the end of this extract:

The social revolution of the nineteenth century cannot draw its poetry from the past, but only from the future. It cannot begin with itself before it has stripped off all superstition with regard to the past. Earlier revolutions required recollections of past world history in order to drug themselves concerning their own content. In order to arrive at its own content, the revolution of the nineteenth century must let the dead bury their dead. *There the phrase went beyond the content; here the content goes beyond the phrase.* (Our italics, page 99)

The contrast between 'phrase' and 'content', 'phrase' and 'reality', recurs throughout the text. The German word 'Phrase' is most often used by Marx in a pejorative way, as we can see later in the text:

And as in private life one differentiates between what a man thinks and says of himself and what he really is and does, so in historical struggles one must distinguish still more the phrases and fancies of parties from their real organism and their real interests, their conception of themselves, from their reality. (page 119)

But the relationship between 'phrase' and 'content' can be more complex. In the revolution of 1848, 'the social republic appeared as a phrase, a prophecy'. It 'indicated the general content of the modern revolution' (i.e., the socialist revolution), but it was a content which could not be realised then, because it 'was in most singular contradiction to everything that, with the material available, with the degree of education attained by the masses, under the given circumstances and relations, could be immediately realised in practice. . . . In no period do we find a more confused mixture of high-flown phrases and actual uncertainty and clumsiness . . .'. Nevertheless the content of 'social republic'

haunts the subsequent acts of the drama like a ghost. The *democratic republic* announces its arrival. On June 13 1849, it is dissipated together with its *petty bourgeois*. . . . The *parliamentary republic*, together with the bourgeoisie, takes possession of the entire stage; it enjoys its existence to the full, but December 2 1851 buries it to the accompaniment of the anguished cry of the royalists in coalition: 'Long live the Republic!'. . . . The overthrow of the parliamentary republic . . . was '*the victory of Bonaparte over parliament, of the executive power over the legislative power, of force without phrases over the force of phrases*'.

The phrase 'social republic' was 'prophetic' in 'indicating' (pointing towards) real social revolution. It 'haunts the subsequent acts of the drama', however, like 'a ghost', an insubstantial phrase at odds with the content, being (in contemporary CDA terms) successively recontextualised (appropriated but simultaneously transformed) in 'democratic republic' and 'parliamentary republic', but its 'force' as a phrase at odds with content was no match for the 'force without phrases' of Bonaparte.

'This Bonaparte, who constitutes himself chief of the lumpenproletariat . . . is the real Bonaparte, the Bonaparte sans phrase' (page 138). Here we find Marx describing the politics of cynical, corporatist populism, the precursor to twentieth century fascism (Saul 1992: Chapter 10, 1997: Chapter 4). He saw through the 'borrowed language': 'An old crafty roué, he conceives the historical life of the nations and their performances of state as comedy in the most vulgar sense, as a masquerade where the grand costumes, words and postures merely serve to make the pettiest knavery' (page 138). Yet after his 'victory', he himself falls victim to his own phrases, the elements of his own 'ideology':

> he become(s) the victim of his own conception of the world, the serious buffoon who no longer takes world history for a comedy but his comedy for world history. . . . with official phrases about order, religion, family and property in public, before the citizens, and with . . . the society of disorder, prostitution and theft, behind him . . .

The real content of a phrase may be 'revealed' through experience:

> The defeat of the June insurgents . . . had shown that in Europe the questions at issue are other than that of 'republic or monarchy'. It had revealed that here *bourgeois republic* signifies the unlimited despotism of one class over other classes. It had proved that . . . *the republic signifies in general only the political form of revolution of bourgeois society* and not *its conservative form of life*. (page 104)

Forms of consciousness and 'phrases' are positioned and positioning – the force of their utterance depends upon positions in social relations, in the social hierarchy, both for their social validity, and for their (often constitutive) perspective on the constitution of society:

> But the democrat, because he represents the petty bourgeoisie, that is, *a transition class*, in which the interests of two classes are simultaneously mutually blunted, imagines himself situated above class antagonism generally . . . they, along with all the rest of the nation, form *the people*. What they

represent is *the people's rights*; what interests them is *the people's interests*. Accordingly, when a struggle is impending . . . they merely have to give the signal and *the people* . . . will fall upon *the oppressors*. (page 123)

This is one of a number of instances of free indirect speech in the text – Marx is parodying 'the democrat' – the italicised phrases (apart from 'a transition class') are 'the democrat's' phrases, phrases which constitute an 'imaginary' consciousness arising from a 'transitional' historical position in class relations.

The relationship between 'phrase' and 'content' can be more nuanced than we have suggested so far. Marx contrasts the 'awakening of the dead' in the 1789 and 1848 revolutions: 'Thus the awakening of the dead in those revolutions' – he means the 1789 revolution, as well as the English revolution – 'served the purpose of glorifying the new struggles, not of parodying the old; of magnifying the given task in imagination, not fleeing from its solution in reality; of finding once more the spirit of revolution, not making its ghost walk about again'. Each of these antithetical clauses sets 1789 against 1848, and the contrast is made explicit: 'From 1848 to 1851 only the ghost of the old revolution walked about'. So 'borrowed phrases' can serve constructive and essential purposes in revolutionary struggles even while 'concealing the bourgeois limitations of their content' – or they can merely summon up 'ghosts'.

What is of value here for CDA, especially in the context of a critique of the language of the new capitalism? Marx shows how revolutions (and counter-revolutions) 'borrow' their 'language' from the past – in the terms of CDA, it is a recognition of social heteroglossia, of intertextuality, of how change involves the selective recontextualisation and interdiscursive appropriation of existing (past) discourses, and of this as a process which is socially positioned, relative to different social positionings. There is an ambivalence about this process: while it conceals the 'content' beneath the 'phrase', Marx suggests that it may either be a positive and necessary recourse for 'finding once more the spirit of revolution', or conversely a mere 'parody', a 'ghost'. Derrida (1994) questions Marx's confident claim that social revolutions are/will be different: Marx points to the way in which the phrases of the past continue to 'haunt' the present, as the phrases of Marxism 'haunt' us today – can we really expect an end to this?

The economic transformations of today – which appear to have the character of a counter-revolution against welfare state capitalism – certainly do not borrow the heroic language of 'Romanity', but they do nevertheless conceal their 'content' in 'phrases' from 'borrowed languages', especially that of the 'golden age' of capitalism, which in turn is borrowed from scholastic dogma

(Graham 2001).[36] For instance, the language of 'individual freedom' which is applied not only to the 'freedom' of people as 'consumers' 'to choose' from the unprecedented range of 'choice', the provision of which capital not infrequently represents as its *raison d'être*, but also for instance with more obvious cynicism to the 'freedom' which people gain from a market which is increasingly demanding part-time and short-term workers. Of course critiques of such ideological language are common in CDA, but what Marx valuably emphasises is that the ideological 'force' of such 'phrases' comes from their potency in historical consciousness in memory – it was the power of the memory of the first French revolution and the first Napoleon which gave the 'phrases' of the second their force.

13 Marx and CDA

What can CDA learn from Marx's critique of discourse? Some aspects of Marx's critique are already familiar within CDA – for instance, his 'transformational criticism' of texts of Hegel in which the focus is Hegel's idealist attribution of agency to 'the idea':

> The idea is made the subject and the actual relation of family and civil society to the state is conceived as its internal imaginary activity. Family and civil society are the premises of the state; they are the genuinely active elements, but in speculative philosophy things are inverted. (Marx 1843/1975: 62)

The critique of texts in terms of their representations of agency is a central concern of 'critical linguistics' and CDA. Also, Marx's view of language as just one element in the productive activity of social life, always dialectically interconnected with others as an ever-present moment and aspect of the production (meant here in the broadest possible sense to include all human activity) and reproduction of social forms (consciousness, physical activity, institutionalised forms) has certainly received some (if so far insufficient) development within CDA (e.g., Chouliaraki and Fairclough 1999, Graham 1999). So too the recognition that different discourses are tied to different positions within given systems of social relations – though Marx's stress on the development of discourses as conditional upon stages of development of systems of social relations and production adds a crucial historical dimension to the positionality of discourses.

In the commentary on selected texts above, however, we have focused on what we have referred to as the 'connectivity' in texts: relations, contradictions, and tensions between elements. We see the critique of texts in these terms as firstly tied to materialist view of texts as a modality of social production, but secondly dependent upon methods of analysing texts which are so far underdeveloped (Fairclough 2000a). Hitherto, text analysis in CDA as elsewhere has been limited by theories of language which focus on the sentence, and tend to see texts in terms of extensions of the grammar of the sentence. We need ways of seeing and analysing texts as processes, as work, as 'working up' specific relations between elements to the exclusion of other possible relations – semantic, conceptual and classificatory relationships between words, logical relationships between propositions, temporal relationships between processes, syntactic relationships between and within sentences, relationships between what is asserted and what is presupposed, and so forth. This 'work' of texts is closely integrated within the productive activities of social life (Halliday 1993: 8); it dialectally internalises other facets of these productive activities and is dialectically internalised within them, while nevertheless remaining a distinctively discoursal process which needs to be grasped in terms of its own logic, as well as its connection with others. Marx does not, of course, say any of this (perhaps because he doesn't see discourse/text/language as separate from the rest of human existence), but his critical method includes a sophisticated, developmental critique of discourse that *calls* for it.

Developing CDA in this direction is not a purely 'academic' challenge. A widely noted feature of contemporary social life is its 'fragmentation', and a widely noted obstacle to formulating alternatives to the new capitalism is its opacity as system which goes with and is sustained by that fragmentation. This opacity is not lessened merely by awareness of its existence. There is surely truth still in Marx's insight that it takes a certain level of development of the new system of social, a certain accumulation of experience, to be able to see the relations which underlie its appearances and to go beyond these. From this point of view, if CDA is to engage in the critique of language in the new capitalism, we need to be in tune with the most developed work in contemporary political economy and other political and social sciences. Nevertheless, unlike in Marx's time, the visibility of the system to those who live within it, suffer from it, and would wish to change it, is conditioned by elaborate networks of mediation.

The task is not only a critique of our own 'bourgeois economists', but also a critique of our government agencies, our armies of 'experts' (including academics), our 'news', our 'entertainment', our corporations, and so forth. But connectivity and the relational logic thereof is a focal concern throughout. Just to take one banal example: the defence of the spokesperson for a company accused on one of the many 'consumer affairs' slots within the media of producing foods for children which damage their health: 'Our concern is to ensure that parents have a wide choice'. 'Choice' appears pervasively as what Marx might have called an 'empty phrase' whose emptiness comes from its confinement to 'appearances', its abstract and equivocal nature, the historical baggage it carries, and crucially the failure of indeed many contemporary discourses to register underlying relationships which connect 'choice' to relations of production, extortion, and monopoly, rather than just fragmented (and frenzied) consumption.

14 Marx as discourse analyst

On one level it is simply anachronistic to suggest that Marx was a discourse analyst. Discourse analysis did not exist in his time. On another level, however, it is a claim that has some substance: Marx's view of language and mode of language critique are similar to those of some contemporary critical discourse analysts.

Let us finally try to justify this claim about his view of language by referring to a section of the *Grundrisse*, from the chapter on money:

> Every moment, in calculating, accounting etc., that we transform commodities into value symbols, we fix them as mere exchange values, making abstraction from the matter they are composed of and all their natural qualities. On paper, in the head, this metamorphosis proceeds by mere abstraction; but in the real exchange process a real mediation is required, a means to accomplish this abstraction. . . . In the crudest barter, when two commodities are exchanged for one another, each is first equated with a symbol which expresses their exchange value, e.g., among certain Negroes on the West African coast, $= x$ bars. One commodity is $= 1$ bar; the other $= 2$ bars. They are exchanged in this relation. The commodities are first transformed into bars in the head and in speech before they are exchanged for one another. They are appraised before being exchanged, and in order to appraise them they must be brought into a given numerical relation to one another. . . . In order to determine what amount of bread I need in order to exchange it for a yard of linen, I first equate the yard of linen with its exchange value, i.e., $= 1/x$ hours of labour time. Similarly, I equate the pound of bread with its exchange value, $= 1/x$ or $2/x$ hours of labour time. I equate each of the commodities with a third; i.e., not with themselves. This third, which differs from them both, exists initially only in the head, as a conception, since it expresses a relation; just as, in general, relations can be established as existing only by being *thought,* as distinct from the subjects which are in these relations with each other. . . . For the purpose of merely

making a comparison – an appraisal of products – of determining their value ideally, it suffices to make this transformation in the head (a transformation in which the product exists merely as the expression of quantitative relations of production). This abstraction will do for comparing commodities; but in actual exchange this abstraction in turn must be objectified, must be symbolized, realized in a symbol. . . . (Such a symbol presupposes general recognition; it can only be a social symbol; it expresses, indeed, nothing more than a social relation.) . . . The process, then, is simply this: the product becomes a commodity, *i.e., a mere moment of exchange.* The commodity is transformed into exchange value. In order to equate it with itself as an exchange value, it is exchanged for a symbol which represents it as exchange value as such. As such a symbolized exchange value, it can then in turn be exchanged in definite relations for every other commodity. Because the product becomes a commodity, and the commodity becomes an exchange value, it obtains, at first only in the head, a double existence. This doubling in the idea proceeds (and must proceed) to the point where the commodity appears double in real exchange: as a natural product on one side, as exchange value on the other (i.e., the commodity's exchange value obtains a material existence separate from the commodity).

(The material in which this symbol is expressed is by no means a matter of indifference, even though it manifests itself in many different historical forms. In the development of society, not only the symbol but likewise the material corresponding to the symbol are worked out – a material from which society later tries to disentangle itself; if a symbol is not to be arbitrary, certain conditions are demanded of the material in which it is represented. The symbols for words, for example the alphabet etc., have an analogous history). (1857/1973: 142–145).

There is a dialectical view of discourse as one element of social life in this extract. Money 'expresses a relation'; relations 'can be established as existing only by being thought', but the relation of value is only 'established' by thought when people begin to engage in exchange (e.g., barter). While the value relation continues to work as an 'abstraction', a relation established 'in the head and in speech' and 'on paper', in the appraisal of products, for the actual exchange of commodities the 'abstraction' must be 'objectified', 'symbolized, realized in a symbol' – 'exchange value obtains a material existence separate from the commodity'. This is a constitutive view of discourse: discourse shapes the development of 'real exchange' as the value relation, a relation in thought/speech – a discourse – becomes 'objectified'. It is not, however, an idealist view of discourse, but a dialectical one: 'real exchange' shapes the development of discourse – it is only at a certain stage in the development of 'real exchange' that the value relation is 'established in thought' – which shapes the development of 'real exchange'. The constitutive work of discourse is not viewed idealistically as ideas being realised in material reality: the value relation as an 'abstraction' is already material – language is the 'matter' which the mind is 'burdened with', as the German Ideology put it – and the 'abstraction' is 'objectified' as a 'symbol', itself a synthesis of idea and matter. Moreover, there is a non-arbitrary relationship between money as a symbol and 'the material in which this symbol is expressed' – it has to be 'divisible at will', for instance.

15 Conclusion

We claim that Marx was a discourse theorist *avant la lettre* because he had a discourse view of language as one element of social life which is dialectically interconnected with others, and an element which is thoroughly present in the dialectical movement between consciousness, 'real exchange', and material (in the sense of physical) existence overall. Marx was also a discourse analyst *avant la lettre* because he put this dialectical view of discourse to work in his economic, political and historical analyses. Perhaps in one sense he was a better discourse analyst than many of us are now: although his work does not obviously stand up well to contemporary expectations (in linguistics journal articles, for instance) of a sustained and systematic focus on language, nor does it suffer from the reifying and idealising consequences of abstracting language from the social process, if only to connect it back to the social process in analysis.

But perhaps the clearest message that Marx has left us as discourse analysts is that we must analyse the relationships that characterise this period as unique, the relationships that *define* it as such: are we even living in capitalist societies; or have the relationships changed so drastically as to make this new global system definable as something else, as a 'new' economy or a 'post' capitalist society? What are the implications of global organisations, both of the entrepreneurial (i.e., transnational corporations) and governmental (WTO, IMF, ILO, OECD, EU, etc.) kind? What are *their* relationships? What are the consequences of global 'shareholder' capitalism, 'social capital' in Marx's words? What does the waning of national power mean for people from different walks of life? What does it mean for democracy? How do new media change the kinds of relationships and representations that we can have? *How* do we interact to do what we do (productive activity), and how does this define our social roles and institutions? *What do we value and how?* These are the questions left to us by Marx. These are the challenges for CDA.

Notes

1. While much is made of Feurbach's materialist influence on Marx, we concur with Colletti (1975: 24) that to overstate the case is 'naïve'. Marx was an avowed Aristotlean, and as such thoroughly familiar with Aristotle's thought, as well as that of the ancient Greeks in general (Fenves 1986: 433). Feurbach's move, while clearly approved of by Marx, was merely another variation on 'one of the most profound and ancient themes in philosophical history, and recurs constantly in the debate between Idealism and Materialism' (Colletti 1975: 24). We can assume that Marx was quite aware of all this, well before Feurbach formulated his abstract materialist theses against neo-Hegelianism (cf. Fenves 1986).

2. Aristotle used the terms '*aphairesis*' and '*korismos*' which he used in different ways to describe the process of concept formation by abstracting form from matter (Weinberg 1968: 1). The term 'abstaction' is again a contribution of the scholastics.

3. The primary concern of both Plato and Aristotle was to explain how it was that people were able to consider, in universal terms, the properties of an object – a brass ring for instance – and consider 'circularity' as a universal property without taking into account any other sensuous aspects of the matter. For Aristotle, abstraction is the method by which people come to know Universal characteristics of categories, such as the mathematical characteristics of 'circle' or 'triangle' (Weinberg 1968: 2). Abstraction rests on the assumption that the abstracted forms (formal) elements of matter, *as such*, exist only in the mind, and that these are the 'fundamental elements of thought which are the referents of the verbal elements of spoken discourse' (page 2).

4. Even though Kant's debt to the scholastic doctrine is negative in this respect.

5. Those more familiar with Aristotle might well argue that his concept of abstraction was not static in the first place, and that the scholastic influence has more to do with this. While the point is clearly arguable, here is not the place to take that argument up. We can note, though, that as well as treating 'substance' or 'essence' in terms of abstraction, Aristotle also treats *causes* in the same way (1998: 440–452), although this remains an undeveloped aspect of *The Metaphysics*. 'OK. OK. Enough examples of what happens on this theory. Many more could be marshalled, but enough. The endless, endless difficulties about production, the total non-obtaining of any mode of schematizing, which afflict Form numbers are surely plausibly construed as a sign. They are a sign that [abstractions] DO NOT EXIST IN SEPARATION FROM PERCEPTIBLE OBJECTS (as widely advertised) and that PRINCIPLES OF THIS KIND GIBT ES NICHT' (Aristotle 1998: 452).

6. We note with a sense of irony that such a view is now widely adopted by techno-fetishists throughout the developed world. Its expression can be seen

in such terms as 'knowledge economy' and 'perfect information' (cf. Graham 2000).

7. We note here that abstraction is not necessarily a perjorative term, either in Marx or anywhere else. For Marx, it is how we predispose ourselves to our own abstractions (e.g., our attitudes to religion) that make them more or less damaging.

8. Readers familiar with Bourdieu (e.g., 1990, 1991, 1998c) will be familiar with the concept, if not its foundation.

9. There is absolutely no foundation whatsoever for suggesting that Marx held a conception of class as a static immutable 'substance' that properly belongs to a particular group of people. According to Marx, even at its most well-developed, 'class articulation does not emerge in pure form . . . From this point of view . . . doctors and government officials would also form two classes, as they belong to two distinct social groups . . . The same would hold true for the *infinite fragmentation of interests and positions* into which the division of social labour splits' (Marx 1981: 1025–1026, emphasis added). Class, like capital, is not a 'thing'; it is the dynamic result of things people *do*.

10. Entia have four aspects – as Accident, as Truth of Falsehood, as Potential or Actual, or as Categorically defined subject matters – but are 'not species under a common genus'; neither are they in 'co-ordinate' (paratactic/ co-meronymous) or 'subordinate' (hypotactic/co-hyponymous) relationships (Grote 1872: 86). They merely have 'a relationship with a common term' (the *fundamentum* or 'First Essence' or Subject) but 'no other necessary relation with each other' (page 86). For the dialectic, however, it is the last of these aspects of Entia that concern us, that which is defined under the ten Categories outlined by Aristotle, to be outlined presently, and in which Aristotle 'appears to blend Logic and Ontology into one' (page 88).

11. Aristotle's ten categories were reduced, via a multitude of historical interpretations, to 'four principle Categories – Substance, Quantity, Quality, and Relation', yet '[e]ven these four cannot be kept clearly apart: the predicates which declare Quantity or Quality at the same time declare Relation; while the predicates of Relation must also imply the fundamentum either of Quantity or of Quality' (Grote 1872: 129).

12. Those familiar with critical theory will recognise contemporary notions and definitions of 'ideology' and 'hegemony' in the definitions of Endoxa.

13. Dialectic does not proceed from first principles. Rather, its purpose is to 'open a new road to the first *principia* of each separate science' (page 391). In any case, the first *principia* of a science 'can never be scrutinized through the truths of the science itself, which *presuppose them and are deduced from them*' (page 391, our emphasis).

14. Propositions and problems fall under four Heads, or categories, which are types of predicates that belong to the subject matter (*Ens* or *Entia*): *Genus*

and *Differentia*; and *Proprium* or *Accident* (Grote 1872: 398). Aristotle defines 'four sorts of matters (Entia)' which are distinguished 'in reference to their functions as constituent members of propositions' (page 83): that which is part of the subject matter (essential predicate); that which is 'affirmable of a Subject' but is not actually part of the subject matter (non-essential predicate); that which is 'both in a Subject and affirmable of a Subject' (essence); and that which is neither part of a subject nor affirmable of it (accident) (page 83). *Ens* 'is not a synonymous or univocal word' (page 84), it is, rather, '*multivocal* . . . having many meanings held together by multifarious and graduated relationship to one common *fundamentum*' (pages 84–85).

15. The specific type of essence or *Ens* with which Aristotle's dialectic is concerned is the form in which *Ens* is defined most completely: '*Ens*, in its complete state – concrete, individual, determinate – includes an embodiment of all these ten Categories; the First *Ens* being the Subject of which the rest are Predicates' (Grote 1872: 93). Anything which may be said about a subject, according to Aristotle, must fall 'under one or more of these ten general heads; while the full outfit of the individual will comprise some predicate under each of them' (page 93). These categories – which Aristotle suggests are exhaustive – are (1) Essence or Substance; (2) How Much; (3) What Manner or Quality; (4) *Ad Aliquid* – in relation to something (*Relatum* and *Correlatum*); (5) Where; (6) When; (7) In what posture (How); (8) To have (attributes); (9) Activity (what is the subject doing); (10) Passivity (what is being done to the subject) (page 93). Each of these categories has 'more or fewer species contained under it, but not being itself contained under any larger genus (*Ens* not being a genus)' (page 94).

16. The difference between what is *in*, or part of a subject, and what is *predicated of* (i.e., logically follows from, or naturally associated with) the subject depends entirely on the actual relationships between a 'subject' and its 'predicates', and, in a formal sense, this turns on the *grammatical status of the predicate* (Grote 1872: 91). Such sensitivity to linguistic, grammatical, and discursive subtlety ought not be overlooked in Marx's most favoured classical scholar (Fenves 1986: 433), especially when Marx makes much of how humanity tends to objectify its linguistic abstractions and place particular of them 'in charge' of society (e.g., God, the Church, Money, The Market, 'Globalisation', Technolgy, etc.). The linguistic tendency towards 'thinginess' is, as Adorno (1966/1973: 56) and Halliday (1993: 11) quite rightly point out, a function and tendency of language-in-use. As such, it goes directly to the foundations of dialectic method.

17. Thomas Jefferson translated De Tracy's *Elemens de Ideologie* into English in 1816.

18. Kennedy points out that Marx considered Tracy, because of his 'labour theory of value' and his theory of the 'concours de forces', 'to a certain point

a light among the vulgar economists' (in Kennedy 1979: 376). However, Kennedy ignores Marx's scathing comments directed towards Tracy in Vol. 2 of *Capital* (1978: 556–564).

19. Kennedy is concerned to emphasise that Tracy was a materialist. Even though his *Ideology* contained 'a strain of idealism', this was 'virtually nullified' by Tracy's fundamental conception of ideology as part of 'zoology'. It is also nullified for Kennedy by the fact that Tracy set himself in opposition to the idealisms of Malebranche and Berkeley (1979: 364).

20. These are Latin terms developed by the scholastics, although their pedigree is clearly Aristotlean (Lawson-Tancred 1998: xxx–xxxi).

21. Today, the use of authoritative quotations as the basis of arguments is conventional. In Marx's day, argument from authority was considered to be the weakest form of argumentation. His manner of using quotes in *Capital*, we think, indicates that by the time Marx wrote *Capital*, he felt he had argued out a sufficiently developed and entirely new apprroach to political economy by means of his earlier dialectical 'counter syllogising'. It is such an unusual method of using quotes that in the preface to the third edition of *Capital*, Engels feels the need to explain 'Marx's manner of quoting, which is so little understood' (in Marx 1976: 108).

22. Aristotle details four 'helps' for proceeding with dialectical engagement. The dialectician *must*: (i) 'have a large collection of propositions' on the subject; (ii) 'study and discriminate the different senses in which the Terms of these proposition are used'; (iii) 'detect and note Differences'; and (iv) 'investigate Resemblances' (Grote 1872: 401). On the first point, propositions may be collected 'out of written treatises as well as from personal enquiry'. If the proposition is 'currently admitted as true in general or in most cases, it must be tendered . . . as a universal principle' (page 401). In fact, '[a]ll propositions must be registered in the most general terms possible, and must then be resolved into their subordinate constitute particulars, as far as the process of subdivision can be carried' (page 402). On the second protocol, terms must be investigated for 'Equivocation' because, often, they have different, double, or multiple meanings in common usage; their usage and therefore their predicates may differ vastly (page 402). On the third and fourth protocols, terms must be studied for Differences and Resemblances because terms that seem closely allied may, because of their usage or equivocation, have vastly different meanings. Conversely, 'subjects of great apparent difference' may bear resemblance for precisely the same reason: context of usage; if the different meanings of terms are not known, then dialecticians 'cannot know clearly' what they are saying (page 406). The third and fourth 'helps', the investigation of Differences (*Differentia*) and Resemblances among predicates, are useful for ascertaining, in the case of Differences, 'the essence or definition of any thing; for we ascertain this by exclusion of what is foreign thereunto, founded on the appropriate differences in each case' (page 407).

From Resemblances, we can inductively derive counter-syllogisms: from the 'repetition of similar particulars a universal is obtained', and we are 'entitled to assume as an Endoxon or doctrine conformable to common opinion, that what happens to any one' element in a string of similar cases 'will also happen to the rest'. On these bases, we can develop the major proposition of a counter-syllogism, an assertion that contradicts the endoxic thesis.

23. It might well be argued that 'family' etc. are abstractions, and rightly so. But Marx explicates his materialist formulation shortly thereafter: '. . . men [sic], who daily remake their own life, begin to make other men, to propagate their kind: the relationship between man and woman, parents and children. The family, which to begin with is the only social relationship, becomes later, when increased needs create new social relations and the increased population new needs, a subordinate one . . . , and must then be treated and analysed according to the existing empirical data, not according to "the concept of the family," as is the custom in Germany' (Marx 1846/1972a,b: 120–121).

24. This point is made most clearly in *The German Ideology* (1846/1972a,b), wherein Marx identifies 'the language of real life' as 'the material activity and the material intercourse of men' (1846/1972a,b: 118).

25. Grote calls this method a form of 'Sokratic brachiology' because of the branching, relational complexity that such an aproach entails.

26. 'Organic', we propose, is best understood here as 'instrumental and essential constituents', in this case, of 'the state, the political consitution'. That is why Marx says that, in Hegel, the 'organic is the *Idea of the differences* and their ideal determination', but that 'their reality is organic': the relationships that constitute the state – family, civil sentiment, social institutions, political sentiment, political institutions, etc. – are the state's essential elements; they are functionally, antagonistically, and instrumentally related to the state and are inseparable from it; they both define and create the state, and are thus its organic constituents.

27. Throughout the whole of his work, Marx's method is marked by a 'working out' process in his texts. For instance, 'when Marx wrote the *Critique of Hegel's Doctrine of the State* he had not yet arrived at theoretical communism. He arrived at this goal *in the course of writing it*' (Colletti 1975: 45).

28. Note here the sensitivity to nominalisation and its implications which 'goes without saying': the person who accepts 'intuition', a nominalised thing, has already presupposed an abstraction from real activity, intuiting.

29. In introducing *Excerpts*, Colletti (1975: 259) notes that 84 quotes have been edited from the original manuscript. Thirteen remain in the text.

30. 'Accidental' here is meant in the formal Aristotlean sense; i.e., it could belong to other forms of social organisation, but it is construed by Adam Smith *et al.* as deliberately deployed by capitalists to break up the monopolies of mercantilist states (see Smith 1776/1997: 251).

31. 'No land without a master'.

32. This passage is from *Excerpts from James Mill's 'Elements of Political Economy'* (1844/1975b) which Marx wrote at the same time as the EP Manuscripts.

33. It is worth noting what Marx means by 'property': he means the property rights that stem from legal rights in land. 'Property ownership' should not be confused with simple possession, a mistake of communists, socialists, conservatives, and liberals of all stripes.

34. Marx's use of the fetish concept is central in his critique of alienation and can be traced to his earliest work, in particular his critique of religion. In his critique of political economy, the concept is worked up throughout, from *Economic and Philosophical Manuscripts* onwards: 'It is the same in religion. The more man puts into God, the less he retains within himself. The worker places his life in the object; but now the object no longer belongs to him, but to the object. The greater his activity, therefore, the fewer objects the worker possesses. What the product of his labour is, he is not' (1844/1975a: 324).

35. On 'ghost', 'spirit', etc. metaphors in Marx, see Derrida (1994).

36. This is especially so where the discourse of 'choice' is concerned. It has its historical content in the State's urge to dispense with church doctrine against usury. Interestingly, it was Aristotle's concept of 'free will' – today evolved into 'rational choice' theory – that was firstly decisive in bringing church prohibitions against usury to the status of a lesser sin (Langholm 1998: 74). The scholastics first shifted the burden of sin, by a dubious twist of one of Aristotle's comments ('Forced will is will'), from the person who lent money to the person who *borrowed* it: 'One who pays usury does so voluntarily in the same sense in which one jettisons cargo when in peril at sea can be said to act voluntarily, namely, in the sense that he prefers to lose his property rather than his life' (page 74). Thus, a newly distorted conception of 'free will', and thus of 'free' choice, became currency for mainstream economic thought and has remained so ever since. Marx quite rightly savages this particularly perverse discourse of false freedom (e.g., Marx 1976: 280, Chapter 28).

13. Critical discourse analysis, organisational discourse and organisational change

I am grateful to the editors of *Organization Studies* for this opportunity to comment as a relative outsider on developments in the study of organisational discourse. Not perhaps entirely an outsider, in that I have written on organisational discourse (e.g., Fairclough 1993, Fairclough and Thomas 2004), and contributed to conferences, but the discourse of organisations as such has not been a major focus of my work. Yet there are certainly overlaps. My central interest in discourse as an element in processes of social change, for instance in my current work on 'transition' in Central and Eastern Europe, necessarily raises issues to do with organisations and organisational change; and CDA, including my own work, has been influential within research on organisational discourse.

Let me sum up my argument in this paper. First, studies of organisation need to include analysis of discourse. Second, however, its commitment to postmodernism and extreme versions of social constructivism limits the value of one prominent tendency within current research on organisational discourse for organisational studies. Third, a version of CDA based on a critical realist social ontology is potentially of particular value to organisation studies. I refer especially to its value in researching organisational change. I agree with those whose specific concern is research into organisational discourse that analysis of organisational discourse should be seen as an important part of organisation studies. This follows from certain ontological assumptions about the nature of social (and therefore also organisational) life, namely, that social phenomena are socially constructed, i.e., people's concepts of the world they live and act within contribute to its reproduction and transformation; and that social phenomena are socially constructed in discourse. As I have implied above, however, certain extreme forms of social constructivism should be rejected (I return to this issue below).

Like others, I use the term 'discourse' for linguistic and other semiotic elements (such as visual images and 'body language') of the social, but I use it in a relational way, with a focus on relations between linguistic/semiotic elements of the social and other (including material) elements. 'Discourse analysis' is generally taken to be the analysis of 'texts' in a broad sense – written texts, spoken interaction, the multimedia texts of television and the internet, etc. As I shall explain in more detail later, I take 'texts' to be the linguistic/semiotic elements of social events, analytically isolable parts of the social process.[1] But some versions of discourse analysis (which are typically Foucaultian in inspiration) limit themselves to identifying the presence and forms of combination of recurrent and relatively stable and durable 'discourses' in texts, whereas others carry our various forms of detailed linguistic analysis (e.g., analysis of grammar, semantics, vocabulary, metaphor, forms of argumentation or narrative, and so forth) and/or detailed analysis of other semiotic features of texts such as their visual aspects. Some versions of discourse analysis do both, and that is the position I adopt. More specifically, I adopt a position of 'analytical dualism' (see note 1, and Sayer 2000) which applies to discourse as well as to other elements of the social, which regards 'discourse' as subsuming both linguistic/semiotic elements of social events and linguistic/semiotic facets of social structures, as well as of the 'social practices' which, as I explain below, I see as mediating the relationship between events and structures. 'Discourses' in a Foucaultian sense are for me elements of social practices. 'Discourse analysis' correspondingly has a doubly relational character: it analyses relations between discourse and other elements of the social, and it analyses relations between linguistic/semiotic elements of social events and linguistic/semiotic facets of social structures and social practices, including 'discourses'.

I shall take a critical stance towards one prominent tendency within the work which has been carried out in the study of organisational discourse, on the grounds that it equates a shift in focus towards discourse in organisation studies with the adoption of postmodernist and extreme social constructivist positions. My position is that commitment to such positions does not in any way follow from a commitment to giving discourse analysis its proper place within organisation studies. I shall argue instead for a critical realist position which is moderately socially constructivist but rejects the tendency for the study of organisation to be reduced to the study of discourse, locating the analysis of discourse instead within an analytically dualist epistemology which gives primacy to researching relations between agency (process, and events – see note 1) and structure on the basis of a realist social ontology. I shall argue that this form of critical discourse analysis has more to offer organisation studies than broadly postmodernist work on organisational discourse. In the final section of the paper, I shall justify this argument through a discussion of organisational change. So, in sum, this paper is simultaneously an argument that the analysis of discourse is an essential and unavoidable part of organisation studies, and an argument against certain prominent forms of discourse analysis which are currently carried out within organisation studies.

1 Organising, organisation and organisational discourse

Research on organisational discourse encompasses various theoretical and methodological positions. Putnam and Fairhurst (2001) distinguish eight approaches, and Kieser and Müller (2003) note that a number of distinct research networks have emerged. I shall not attempt to address or characterise this substantial and complex body of work as a whole. I want to focus on a particular tendency within this research, which has been highly influential without being universal, to distance itself from more conventional work in organisation studies by rejecting conceptions of organisation as organisational structures in favour of conceptions of organisation as an interactive accomplishment in organisational discourse, as 'organising' (e.g., Weick 1979, Mumby and Clair 1997, Tsoukas and Chia 2002, Grant *et al.* forthcoming). The theoretical bases for this tendency have come from ethnomethodology (Boden 1994), actor-network theory (Law 1994) and Foucaultian poststructuralism (Reed 2000). Ackroyd and Fleetwood (2000) suggest that it is associated with a reductive opposition which researchers have set up between positivist and postmodern research – since positivism is unacceptable for well-known reasons, postmodernism is seen as the only viable possibility. As these authors argue, it is not: there is a strong tradition of realism in organisation studies which is equally adamant in rejecting positivism without embracing postmodernism.

Mumby and Stohl, for instance, argue that researchers in organisational communication most centrally differ from those in other areas of organisation studies in that the former problematise 'organisation' whereas the latter do not.

> For us, organization – or organizing, to use Weick's (1979) term – is a precarious, ambiguous, uncertain process that is continually being made and remade. In Weick's sense, organizations are only seen as stable, rational structures when viewed retrospectively. Communication, then, is the substance of organizing in the sense that through discursive practices organization members engage in the construction of a complex and diverse system of meanings. (Mumby and Stohl 1996: 58)

Another formulation of this shift in emphasis from organisations as structures to 'organising' (or 'organisational becoming' (Tsoukas and Chia 2002)) as a process is that of Mumby and Clair (1997: 181):

> . . . we suggest that organizations exist only in so far as their members create them through discourse. This is not to claim that organizations are 'nothing but' discourse, but rather that discourse is the principal means by which organization members create a coherent social reality that frames their sense of who they are. (1997: 181)

Reed (2004) argues that, despite the disclaimer at the beginning of the second sentence, this formulation can be seen as collapsing ontology into epistemology, and undermining the ontological reality of organisational structures as constraints on organisational action and communication.

From the perspective of critical realism and the realist view of discourse which I outline below, it makes little sense to see organising and organisation, or more generally process/agency and structure, as alternatives one has to choose between. With respect to organisational change, both organisational structures and the agency of members of organisations in organisational action and communication have causal effects on how organisations change. Organisational communication does indeed organise, produce organisational effects and may contribute to the transformation of organisations, but organising is subject to conditions of possibility which include organisational structures.

Organisational discourse studies have been associated with postmodernist positions (Chia 1995, Grant *et al.* 2001, Grant *et al.* forthcoming), though the field as a whole is too diverse to be seen as simply postmodernist. Chia identifies a postmodern 'style of thinking' in organisational studies which 'accentuates the significance, ontological priority and analysis of the micrologics of social organizing practices over and above their stabilized "effects" such as "individuals"' (1995: 581). As this indicates, the focus on organising rather than organisation is strongly associated with this 'style of thinking'. Like the dialectical–relational ontology I advocate below, this 'style of thinking' sees objects and entities as emergent products of processes. The key difference is that this 'style of thinking' tends towards a one-sided emphasis on process, whereas the realist view of discourse analysis I advocate centres on the tension between process and pre-structured (discoursal as well as non-discoursal – see below) objects.

Both Mumby and Stohl (1991) and Mumby and Clair (1997) set up the contrast between 'organising' and 'organisation' as a contrast between discourse (or 'communication') and organisational structures. I would argue that the relationship (or, for some, the choice) is not between organisational discourse and organisational structures, because organisational structures themselves have a partly linguistic/semiotic character. So too do the 'social practices' which I shall argue mediate the relationship between structures and processes (and events). It is productive to see organisations at one level of analysis as networks of social practices. In the version of CDA I sketch out below, a network of social practices includes an 'order of discourse', a relatively stabilised and durable configuration of discourses (as well as other elements, 'genres' and 'styles', which I explain below) which is a facet of a relatively stabilised and durable network of social practices. CDA is concerned with the relationship and tensions between the relative 'permanences' of organisational orders of discourse as moments of networks of social practices (and, more indirectly, the languages and other semiotic systems of whose potentials they are a selective social ordering), and organisational texts conceived as processes of texturing and organising and as the semiotic elements of social events. Thus the relations between discourse and non-discursive elements of the social should not be confused with the relationship between social process (and isolable social events), and social (practices and) structures.

Viewing discourse as a facet of practices and structures as well as of processes/events is in my view important for achieving coherent theories which can extend our knowledge of organisations and organisational change. Grant and Hardy (2004: 6) in the Introduction to a recent special issue of *Organization Studies* on organisational discourse state that:

> The term 'discourse' has been defined as sets of statements that bring social objects into being (Parker 1992). In using the term *'organizational discourse'*, we refer to the structured collections of texts embodied in the practices of talking and writing . . . that bring organizationally related objects into being as those texts are produced, disseminated, and consumed . . . Consequently, texts can be considered to be a manifestation of discourse and the distinctive unit . . . on which the researcher focuses. Accordingly, *discourse analysis* is the systematic study of texts.
>
> The papers in the special issue 'identify and analyse specific, micro-level instances of discursive action and then locate them in the context of other macro-level, "meta" or "grand" discourses'.

One problem I have with this formulation is that contingent effects of texts ('bringing organizationally related objects into being') are collapsed into the theoretical categories of 'discourse' and 'text', leaving us no way of analysing the contingency of these effects: I would argue that texts *may* have such effects, depending on certain conditions. Another problem is with the categories of 'discourse' and 'text'. I assume that 'discursive action' is equivalent to 'texts', though this is not made clear. I also assume that 'other' in the last sentence implies that 'discursive action' (and 'texts') are *themselves* 'discourses'; this would also resolve the unclarity of what *a particular* 'structured collection of texts' is – *a* discourse? – and the apparent redundancy of (organisational) 'texts' both being (organisational) 'discourse' and being 'a manifestation of' (organisational?) 'discourse'. If this is the case, it would appear that 'texts' are (micro-level?) discourses and are located 'in the context of' ('macro-level') 'discourses'. I am not sure that the authors would go along with this attempt to spell out relations between the categories; my point is rather to suggest that the relations are opaque in a way which undermines theoretical coherence, and that this opacity is at least in part due to a failure to explicitly and clearly differentiate levels (processes/events, practices and structures).

The other editors of the special issue refer in a concluding paper (Keenoy and Oswick 2004) to some papers focusing on 'big "D" discourse (that is a Grand Discourse or Mega-Discourse approach)' whereas others focus on 'small "d" discourse (that is, a micro- or meso-discourse approach)'. This is inconsistent with the claim of Grant and Hardy that all of the articles 'identify and analyse specific, micro-level instances of discursive action and then locate them in the context of other macro-level, "meta" or "grand" discourses'. In fact neither seems to be accurate: there are articles which include detailed textual analysis which also identify 'big "D" discourses' (e.g., Iedema *et al.* (2004) show how the 'doctor-manager' their analysis is focused on weaves three 'big "D" discourses' together); there are also articles (e.g., Maguire 2004) which discuss 'big "D" discourses' without any detailed textual analysis. In terms of the version of CDA I shall describe below, one cannot choose between 'big "D"' and 'small "d"' approaches in discourse analysis: discourse analysis is concerned with the relationship between processes/events and practices (as well as structures), texts and discourses (as well as genres and styles), and therefore, in the terms of the distinction used by Keenoy and Oswick, the relationship between 'big "D"' and 'small "d"' discourses. This entails the claim which I shall elaborate below, that analysis of organisational discourse should include detailed analysis of texts, both analysis of linguistic and other semiotic features of texts, and the 'interdiscursive' analysis of texts which I discuss next.

Grant *et al.* (forthcoming) emphasise the increasing importance of the category of 'intertextuality' in research on organisational discourse, and this is the particular focus of Keenoy and Oswick (2004). They propose the notion of 'textscape' to 'refer to the multiplex intertextualities which inform and underpin the meaning(s) of any given piece of discourse'. They see intertextuality as supporting their 'preference to approach the social phe-nomenon of "organization" as a (discursive) process – "organizing"', again privileging of processes over structures. Does it? I think not. The general con-cept of 'intertextuality' includes relations between actual texts (and events), one obvious example of which is 'reported speech', which are indeed complex and 'multiplex'. But it also includes what I call 'interdiscursivity': one important way in which (types of) texts are different from one another and distinctive is in how they draw on and combine together relatively stable and durable discourses (as well as 'genres' and 'styles', as I explain later), and this feature of texts can only be investigated in terms of relations between processes (and events) and the networks of practices and associated orders of discourse which mediate the relation between process and structure (as I argued in, for instance, Fairclough 1992a, 1995, 2003). This entails an 'inter-discursive' as well as linguistic/semiotic analysis texts, i.e., an analysis of how they articulate different discourses (as well as genres and styles) together. Intertextuality is indeed an important aspect of any research on discourse, but this does not provide support for an overemphasis on process at the expense of structure.

Let me close this section by referring to one particularly good and the-oretically sophisticated paper in the special issue of *Organizational Studies* (Iedema *et al.* 2004) to elaborate what I have been saying about the relation-ship between organisation and 'organising'. It is an analysis of how a 'doctor-manager' in a teaching hospital in Australia manages 'the incommensurable dimensions' of his 'boundary position between profession and organization' by positioning himself across different discourses, sometimes in a single utter-ance (Iedema *et al.* 2004: 15). The authors identify a heteroglossia 'that is too context-regarding to be reducible to personal idiosyncracy, and too complex and dynamic to be the calculated outcome of conscious manipulation'. They see the doctor-manager's talk as a 'feat' of 'bricolage', not as a display of 'behaviours that are pre-programmed'. Nor is it an instantiation of a 'strategy', for 'strategies' are, they assume, 'conscious'. Although the authors recognise that organisations can 'set limits' on what workers can say and do, impose 'closure', they see the doctor-manager as successfully 'deferring closure on his own identity and on the discourses that realize it' (2004: 29).

One can take this as an interesting and nuanced study of organisation as the 'organising' that is achieved in interaction (nuanced in that it does not exclude organisational structures, though it does suggest that they are more 'fluid' and less 'categorical' than they have been taken to be, and in that it does recognise their capacity to impose 'closure'). I would like to make a number of con-nected observations on this paper.

First, one might see the doctor-manager's 'feat' in this case as a particular form of a more general organisational process, the management of contradictions. Second, discourse figures differently in different types of organisation (Borzeix 2003, referring to Girin 2001). The type of organisation in this case seems to be in Girin's terms a 'cognitive' (or 'learning', or 'intelligent') organisation, in which the normative force of (written) texts (rules, procedures) is limited, and there is an emphasis on learning in spoken interaction. There seems to be, in other terms, a relatively 'network' type of structure rather than a simple hierarchy, where management involves a strong element of participatory and consultative interaction with stakeholders. Third, connecting the first two points, spoken interaction in this type of organisation accomplishes an ongoing management of contradictions which contrasts with the management of contradictions through suppressing them by imposing rules and procedures, which one finds in certain sorts of organisation, and one might perhaps find in this sort of organisation in certain situations. Fourth, the doctor-manager's 'feat' can be seen as a performance of a strategy as long as we abandon the (somewhat implausible) claim that all aspects and levels of strategic action are conscious – the doctor-manager would, one imagines, be conscious of the need to sustain a balancing act between professional and managerial perspectives and priorities, and of certain specific means to do so, but that does not entail him being conscious of *all* the complex interactive means he uses to do it.

Fifth, while particular performances of this strategy (or, indeed, any strategy) are not 'pre-programmed', the strategy is institutionalised, disseminated, learnt, and constitutes one might say a facet of the networks of social practices which characterise this type of organisation, i.e., a facet of organisational structure. Sixth, it strikes me that bringing off a sense of creative bricolage is perhaps itself a part of the managerial style of this type of organisation, i.e., part of the strategy, the network of social practices, the order of discourse. My conclusion is that, even given the nuanced position taken on the relationship between organising and organisation in this paper, there may be undue emphasis on organising rather organisation, performance rather than practice, 'feat' rather than strategy.[2]

2 A critical realist approach to discourse analysis

I shall begin this section with a brief sketch of certain central features of critical realism, and then move on to outline, still briefly but more fully, a critical realist approach to discourse analysis.

2.1 Critical realism

Realism is minimally the claim that there is a real world, including a real social world, which exists independently of our knowledge about it. Critical realism is a particular version of realism which is particularly associated with the work of Bhaskar (Bhaskar 1986, Archer 1995, Sayer 2000). Critical realists argue that the natural and social worlds differ in that the latter but not the former is dependent on human action for its existence – it is socially constructed. The social world is pre-constructed for any human being, and its socially constructed nature does not preclude there being aspects of it which human beings have no or limited or mistaken knowledge of. So for critical realists ontology must be distinguished from epistemology, and we must avoid the 'epistemic fallacy' of confusing the nature of reality with our knowledge of reality. This does not at all imply that reliable knowledge about reality is easy to come by, but it does mean a rejection of 'judgemental relativism' – of the view that all representations of the world are equally good – and a search for grounds for determining whether some representations constitute better knowledge of the world than others.

Critical realists assume a 'stratified ontology', which sees processes/events and structures as different strata of social reality with different properties. A distinction is drawn between the 'real', the 'actual', and the 'empirical': the 'real' is the domain of structures with their associated 'causal powers'; the 'actual' is the domain of events and processes; the 'empirical' is the part of the real and the actual that is experienced by social actors. The 'actual' does not in any simple or straightforward way reflect the 'real': the extent to which and ways in which the particular causal powers are activated to affect actual events is contingent on the complex interaction of different structures and causal powers in the causing of events. Causal powers, moreover, are not exclusively the properties of structures: social agents also have causal powers which affect the actual. The view of causality therefore is not a (Humean) 'constant conjunction' view according to which a causal relation between x and y entails a regular (and in principle predictable) relation such that where x appears, y will appear. On the contrary, the production of such 'constant conjunctions' require human intervention, notably in the form of experiments (which are generally more possible in natural than in social sciences).

As I have already indicated, critical realism claims that mediating entities are necessary to account for the relationship between structures and processes/ events. These mediating entities are 'social practices', more or less durable and stable articulations of diverse social elements, including discourse, which constitute social selections and orderings of the allowances of social structures as actualisable allowances in particular areas of social life in a certain time and place. Social practices are networked together in distinctive and shifting ways. Social fields, institutions and organisations can be regarded as networks of social practices.[3] Critical realist ontology is also 'transformational': human agency produces effects through drawing on existing structures and practices which are reproduced and/or transformed in action. Critical realism aims at explanation: at explaining social processes and events in terms of the causal powers of both structures and human agency and the contingency of their effects.

Social research proceeds through abstraction from the concrete events of social life aimed at understanding the pre-structured nature of social life, and returns to analysis of concrete events, actions and processes in the light of this knowledge. Thus, for instance, it is through investigation of sets of concrete events and texts in contemporary 'marketised' universities that one arrives at a knowledge of the pre-structured networks of social practices which constitute them as 'marketised' organisations, which have discoursal facets which I shall refer to as 'orders of discourse' (see below). Analysis of concrete events and texts then centres on the relationship between them as occasioned and situ-ated events and texts and pre-structured networks of social practices and orders of discourse, which both constitute preconditions for them and are open to transformation by them (Fairclough 1995a). This form of realism is not subject to the tendency within modernist social research which is criti-cised by Woolgar (1988) to take the objects it arrives at through abstraction (which would include in the case of CDA orders of discourse, as well as languages and other semiotic systems) to be exhaustive of the social reality it researches. The key difference in this case is whereas this form of modernist research moves from the concrete to the abstract and then 'forgets' the con-crete, the dialectical–relational form of realism I advocate crucially makes the move back to analysis of the concrete. Thus a critical realistic discourse ana-lysis is not merely concerned with languages and orders of discourse; it is equally concerned with texts as (elements of) processes, and with the relations of tension between the two.

Realist discourse analysis on this view is based in a dialectic-relational social ontology which sees objects, entities, persons, discourses, organisa-tions and so on as socially produced 'permanences' which arise out of processes and relations (Harvey 1996) and which constitute a pre-structured reality with which we are confronted, and sets of affordances and limitations on processes. The concern in research is with the relationship and tension between pre-constructed social structures, practices, identities, orders of discourse, organisations on the one hand, and processes, actions, events on the other. People with their capacities for agency are seen as socially produced, contingent and subject to change, yet real, and possessing real causal powers which, in their tension with the causal powers of social structures and practices, are a focus for analysis. Discourse analysis focuses on this tension specifically in textual elements of social events.

2.2 Critical discourse analysis[4]

This version of discourse analysis has been developed in connection with transdisciplinary research on social change. Transdisciplinary research is more than a short-term collaboration of disciplines around particular research projects; it is a long-term dialogue between disciplines and theories with each drawing on the concepts, categories and 'logics' of the others in pursuing its own theoretical and methodological development (Fairclough 2003, 2005d). Critical discourse analysis specifically contributes to such research a focus on how discourse figures in relation to other social elements in processes of social change. This includes the integration of detailed analysis of texts into research on social change.[5]

This version of CDA views discourse as an element of social processes and social events, and also an element of relatively durable social practices, though neither are reducible to discourse: they are articulations of discourse with non-discoursal elements. 'Discourse' subsumes language as well as other forms of semiosis such as visual images and 'body language', and texts (the discoursal elements of social events) often combine different semiotic forms (e.g., the texts of television characteristically combine language and visual images, and in many cases music or various 'sound effects'). But the use of the 'term' 'discourse'[6] rather than 'language' is not purely or even primarily motivated by the diversity of forms of semiosis; it primarily registers a relational way of seeing linguistic/semiotic elements of social events and practices as interconnected with other elements. The objective of discourse analysis, on this view, is not simply analysis of discourse *per se*, but analysis of the relations between discourse and non-discoursal elements of the social, in order to reach a better understanding of these complex relations (including how changes in discourse can cause changes in other elements). But if we are to analyse relations *between* discourse and non-discoursal elements, we must obviously see them as different elements of social reality – as ontologically (and not just epistemologically, analytically) different. They are different, but we might say that they are not discrete, in the sense that other elements of the social (e.g., the social relations and material division and structuring of space in organisations), in being socially constructed through discourse, come to incorporate or 'internalise' particular discursive elements (including particular discourses) without being reducible to them. The relations between them are dialectical, in Harvey's sense (Harvey 1996, see also Chouliaraki and Fairclough 1999, Fairclough 2003, Fairclough, Jessop and Sayer 2004).

As I have indicated, I adopt the 'stratified' view of ontology characteristic of critical realism, along with the claim that the relationship between structures and events is mediated by social practices. This means that discourse analysis has a doubly relational character: it is concerned with relations between discourse and other social elements, *and* relations between texts as discoursal elements of events and 'orders of discourse' as discoursal elements of networks of social practices (and, ultimately, languages and other semiotic systems as social structures). Networks of social practices include specifically discoursal selections and orderings from languages and other semiotic systems which I call 'orders of discourse', appropriating but redefining Foucault's term (Foucault 1984, Fairclough 1992a).

Orders of discourse are social structurings of linguistic/semiotic variation or difference. That is to say, linguistic and semiotic systems make possible (can 'generate') texts which differ without limit, but the actual range of variation is socially delimited and structured, i.e., through the ways in which linguistic and semiotic systems interact with other social structures and systems. An order of discourse can more specifically be seen as a particular combination of different discourses, different genres and different styles, which are articulated together in a distinctive way.

A *discourse* is a particular way of representing certain parts or aspects of the (physical, social, psychological) world; for instance, there are different political discourses (liberal, conservative, social-democratic, etc.) which represent social groups and relations between social groups in a society in different ways. A *genre* is a particular way of acting socially, which means acting together, i.e., interacting; for instance, there are different genres for consulting, discussing or interviewing. A *style* is a particular way of being, i.e., a particular identity; for instance, there are distinguishable ways of managing or 'leading' in organisations which can be characterised as different styles. Whereas one can see ways of representing as having a purely discoursal or semiotic character, ways of acting and ways of being have only a partially discursive character, and entail relations between discoursal and non-discoursal social elements. In some forms of social action (e.g., certain commodity production processes) discourse is secondary to material action, in others (e.g., meetings) action consists almost entirely of discourse; and particular ways of managing include bodily habits and dispositions as well as ways of communicating.

An order of discourse is not adequately specified simply in terms of the sets of discourses, genres and styles it comprises; the relations between them – how they are articulated together – are crucial. So the order of discourse of a particular organisation will include discourses, genres and styles whose distribution is complementary, corresponding to different parts and facets of the organisation, but also discourses, genres and styles which are potentially conflicting alternatives, whose relations are defined in terms of dominance, resistance, marginalisation, innovation, and so forth. If an order of discourse constitutes a system, it is a system which may be more or less stable and durable, or stable in some parts and unstable in others, more or less resistant to change or open to change.[7]

I shall use the term 'text',[8] in a generalised sense (not just written text but also spoken interaction, multi-semiotic televisual text, etc.) for the discoursal element of social events. Texts are doubly contextualised, first in their relation to other elements of social events, second in their relation to social practices, which is 'internal' to texts in the sense that they necessarily draw on orders of discourse, i.e., social practices in their discoursal aspect, and the discourses, genres and styles associated with them. However, events (and therefore texts) are points of articulation and tension between two causal forces: social practices and, through their mediation, social structures; and the agency of the social actors who speak, write, compose, read, listen to, interpret them. The social 'resource' of discourses, genres and styles is subject to the transformative potential of social agency, so that texts do not simply instantiate discourses, genres and styles; they actively rework them, articulate them together in distinctive and potentially novel ways, hybridise them, transform them. The 'interdiscursive' analysis of texts (Fairclough 1992a; Chouliaraki and Fairclough 1999) in this version of CDA shows how texts articulate different discourses, genres and styles together, potentially drawing from diverse orders of discourse, and potentially showing the capacity of social agents to use existing social resources in innovative ways which, subject to certain conditions, may contribute to changing the character of and relations between social practices.

The causal powers of social agents in social events are thus conditional on pre-structured properties of social life, knowledge of which can only be produced by abstraction, and knowledge of which is necessary for analyses of concrete events which can show the socially transformative and constructive powers of social agents. Interdiscursive analysis allows the analyst to assess the relationship and tension between the causal effects of agency in the concrete event and the causal effects of practices and structures, and to detect shifts in the relationship between orders of discourse and networks of social practices as these are registered in the interdiscursivity (mixing of genres, discourses, styles) of texts. The interdiscursive properties of texts can be seen as 'realised' in their linguistic and semiotic features.[9] Analysis of texts comprises both interdiscursive analysis and linguistic/semiotic analysis.

Texts can be seen as product and as process. Texts as products can be stored, retrieved, bought and sold, cited and summarised and so forth. Texts as processes can be grasped through regarding what we might call 'texturing' (Fairclough 2003), the making of texts, as a specific modality of social action, of social production or 'making' (of meanings, understandings, knowledge, beliefs, attitudes, feelings, social relations, social and personal identities). Halliday (1994) has used the term 'logogenesis', seeing the text itself as a time-frame within which entities (objects, persons, spaces) can be constructed or 'textured'. For instance, an important logogenetic process in the texts of organisations is 'nominalisation', which is linguistically a shift from verbs (and the subjects, objects, tense and modal operators and so forth which are co-constructed with verbs in sentences) to a particular class of nouns in the representation of actions and processes (for instance, from 'I *commenced* work' to 'job *commencement*').

Nominalisation is associated with a shift from the representation of actions and processes situated in the 'here and now', involving specific persons in specific places at specific times, a disembedding, dedifferentiation and time–space distantiation of actions and processes from concrete and particular situations to an abstract representation of them as applicable 'wherever, whenever and involving whoever' (Iedema 2003: 73). Iedema argues that 'organisation is contingent upon people being able to produce and reproduce these kinds of "distanced meanings"' (2003: 79). Nominalisation transforms processes and actions into a type of pseudo-entities, but at the same time has potentially (re)constructive effects on organisational identities and social relations. Analysis of nominalisation in organisational texts constitutes one case where a specific and focused form of linguistic analysis can be connected to questions about social construction in organisations.

From the perspective of this version of CDA, the general case for incorporating discourse analysis into social and organisational research includes the claim that such research should include detailed analysis of texts. The argument is a rather obvious one: one cannot research relations between discourse and other social elements, including the constructive effects of discourse, in the absence of methods for analysing linguistic, semiotic and interdiscursive features of texts in some detail. This, of course, is widely recognised as a problem for many social researchers who wish to undertake discourse analysis without a background in linguistics or language studies, and it is one good reason for developing transdisciplinary collaboration in social and organisational research.

The approach to research methodology associated with this version of discourse analysis sees methodology as the process through which one constructs 'objects of research' (Bourdieu and Wacquant 1992) from research topics. One should not assume that the research topic is transparent in yielding up coherent objects of research. The process of constructing them involves selecting theoretical frameworks, perspectives and categories to bring to bear on the research topic. It is only on the basis of such theorisation of the research topic and the delineation of 'objects of research' that one can settle on appropriate methods of data selection, collection and analysis. In certain cases, this would be the work of an interdisciplinary research team; in others it may be a matter of a discourse analyst drawing on literature from other disciplines and theories. This means that discourse analysis on this view involves working in dialogue with particular bodies of social theory and approaches to social research, identifying specific research questions for discourse analysis within the object of research, and seeking to ensure that relations between discourse and other social elements are properly addressed.

For example, Fairclough (2000b) addressed the political phenomenon of 'New Labour' from a discourse analytical perspective, formulating research questions in dialogue with objects of research constructed by political researchers. Critical realism is a philosophy of (social) science, not a (social) theory, and a critical realist approach is consistent with diverse social scientific theories which CDA might productively enter dialogue with (see for instance the dialogue with Jessop (2002) in Fairclough 2005d).

3 Discourse analysis in a critical realist approach to organisational studies and organisational change

I shall begin this section with a brief discussion of critical realist approaches to organisational studies, and then focus on how the version of discourse analysis I have set out above can contribute to research on organisational change which is consistent with a critical realist position.

3.1 Critical realist approaches to organisational studies

Ackroyd and Fleetwood (2000) address the tendency within organisation and management studies towards a polarisation between positivist and post-modernist research. The objection of the authors in this collection is that this polarisation of positions has ignored both the claims of realism (and particularly critical realism) to be an alternative to both positivism and post-modernism in organisation and management studies, and the substantive body of existing research which is based on realist principles. The critical realist critique of postmodernist research in organisational studies focuses on two interconnected issues which have already featured in my discussion above: the view of organisations as consisting of only discourse, and a 'flat ontology' which makes no ontological distinction between process (and agency) and structure. These features of postmodernist positions are held to cause various problems for organisation and management studies which critical realist positions can overcome.

Without a dualist ontology, methodological examination of conditions for organisational stability or organisational change becomes impossible. Collapsing the distinction between agency and structure, far from leaving researchers free to account for neglected aspects of agency, makes the causal powers of agents and their actualisation impossible to analyse: the capacity of social agents to radically transform organisational structures, and the conditions under which that capacity can be actualised; differences between agents, according to their positions within the social relations of organisations, to effect changes; and so forth. Furthermore, texts may have *dis*organising as well as organising effects on organisations (Ackroyd 2000), but one cannot assess the effects of texts on organisations, or indeed whether changes in texts have any wider effects at all, unless one can look at relations between discourse and other social elements and between process (and agency) and structure. One limitation of critical realism with respect to the incorporation of discourse analysis into organisational studies is that it has tended to give little systematic attention to language and discourse. However, a recent paper by Fairclough, Jessop and Sayer (2004) has tried to go some way towards redressing this neglect, and has argued that certain work in CDA (particularly the sort of approach I have described above) is consistent with critical realism.

3.2 CDA and organisational change

The tendency within research on organisational discourse which I have criticised above, privileging 'organising' over organisation, is also evident in a recent paper on organisational change by Tsoukas and Chia. The authors argue that:

> Change must not be thought of as a property of organization. Rather, organization must be understood as an emergent property of change. Change is ontologically prior to organization – it is the condition of possibility for

organization . . . we argue that change is the reweaving of actors' webs of beliefs and habits of action as a result of new experiences obtained through interactions. . . . Organization is an attempt to order the intrinsic flux of human action, to channel it towards certain ends, to give it a particular shape, through generalizing and institutionalizing particular meanings and rules. At the same time, organization is a pattern that is constituted, shaped, emerging from change. (Tsoukas and Chia 2002: 567)

The view that organisations, like all objects or 'permanences', are emergent effects of social process, and that change is inherent in social process, is consistent with the dialectical–relational version of critical realist ontology I have been advocating. But once constituted, such objects as organisations become durable entities with their own causal powers to shape processes and events, though always in contingent ways which are conditional among other things on the causal powers of social agents and the unpredictable character of events. Tsoukas and Chia recognise this. Part of their argument, however, is that the categories and practices which are institutionalised in organisations are inevitably subject to adaptation and change as organisational agents engage in a range of processes and events which is inherently too complex and fluid to be anticipated or pre-programmed. This is clearly the case.

My first problem with their account of organisational change, however, is that it does not address the relationship between 'organisational becoming' (change as ongoing in organisational interaction) and change in organisational structures. They do acknowledge that much of the change in organisational interaction does not become 'institutionalised', but this is in the context of a discussion of organisational resistance and inertia. But it is not just a matter of organisations sometimes failing to change when there are good reasons for arguing that they need to. One can argue rather that it is a property of organisational structures – and not merely a fault – that they can remain relatively stable despite the change and variation which organisational processes routinely produce, even despite radically *dis*organising processes (Ackroyd 2000). From the perspective of analytical dualism, structures and processes (and agency) have different properties, including different properties of continuity and change, and a theory of organisational change needs to clarify these differences, and in so doing clarify the relationship between change as an inherent feature of organisational processes and change in organisational structures. The authors' view that 'organisation scientists need to give theoretical priority to microscopic change' (Tsoukas and Chia 2002: 572) strikes me as an obstacle in this respect: neither 'microscopic' change nor structural change should be given theoretical priority; what theory needs to address is the relationship between them.

I would argue that research on organisational change benefits not only from adopting analytical dualism, but also from a clear and coherent account of the difference and relations between discourse and other elements of the social. This brings me to my second problem with Tsoukas and Chia's paper. It strikes me that they merge together (for instance in the quotation above) aspects of change which need to be analytically teased apart: change in discourse (which they do not explicitly distinguish or address as such), 'new' experiences, change in beliefs, change in habits of action, and change in organisation. The metaphor of 'reweaving' is a congenial one for the version of discourse analysis I have set out above. But I was suggesting there specifically that change in discourse is a matter of novel interdiscursive relations, the 'reweaving' of relations between different discourses, genres and styles. One can certainly relate this to new experiences. But it is necessary to distinguish such change in discourse from change in beliefs, change in habits of action and (as I have already indicated) change in organisation. Whether or not change in discourse leads to change in beliefs or habits of action, as well as change in organisations, is a contingent matter. Change in discourse may for instance be rhetorically motivated, to do with persuading others without necessarily implying change in one's own beliefs. Or even if it is not rhetorically motivated it can be ephemeral, without durable effects on beliefs or habits of action. Whether it does or does not have such effects is contingent on other factors, including long-term ('habitus') and short-term characteristics of social actors, and the latitude available within the 'pattern' of organisation for variation in habits of action. Changes in discourse certainly can and do contribute to change in beliefs, habits of action, and indeed organisations, but it is only by consistently regarding the difference between such social elements that one can investigate the relations between them.

The issues can be formulated in terms of evolutionary theory, which Jessop (2002) has integrated into a theoretical framework for researching changes in governance and the state which is consistent with critical realism and a dialectical–relational ontology. Social interaction inherently produces changes in discourse which add to social variation. But to account for the relationship between such change and change in pre-constructed objects such as persons (with their beliefs and habits of action) and organisations, one needs to address the factors and conditions which determine how particular variants are selected and retained, whereas others are not.

I have argued above that the version of discourse analysis I am advocating is best deployed within transdisciplinary research on social change, providing a specifically discourse analytical perspective in researching 'objects of research' which are constituted on a transdisciplinary basis. This entails working as a discourse analyst in dialogue with the particular theoretical resources and frameworks drawn on in constituting objects of research for research topics. Let me refer to three examples in my own work. I have already mentioned the study of 'New Labour', in which the particular research questions formulated for a discourse analytical approach to New Labour were established through dialogue with social and political theories of which related change in the political field to economic globalisation and the associated political project of neo-liberalism. Chiapello and Fairclough (2002) was an attempt to set up a dialogue between the 'new sociology of capitalism' (Boltanski and Chiapello 1999) and CDA, interpreting what Boltanski and Chiapello identify as the 'new spirit of capitalism' in discourse analytical terms as being in part a change in orders of discourse within business organisations, including for instance changes in the styles of managers and 'leaders'. Fairclough (2005c) is a study of 'transition' in post-communist countries focusing on Romanian strategies for building an 'information society' and 'knowledge economy', which formulated specific objects of research and specific research questions for discourse analysis on the basis of a theorisation of 'transition' in terms of 'new' or 'cultural' political economy. None of these studies has addressed change in particular organisations, but they do I think begin to set out an approach to incorporating discourse analysis into transdisciplinary research on change which can be productively extended to organisational change.

From what I have said so far, two central principles for such research have emerged: (1) that while change in discourse is a part of organisational change, and organisational change can often be understood partly in terms of the constructive effects of discourse on organisations, organisational change is not simply change in discourse, and relations between change in discourse and change in other elements of organisations are matters for investigation, which entails a clear and consistent analytical distinction between discourse and other social elements; (2) that while ongoing change in social process, in social interaction, can contribute to organisational change, the relationship between change in social interaction and change in organisational structures is complex and subject to conditions of possibility which need to be investigated, which entails a clear and consistent distinction between social process (including texts), social practices (including orders of discourse) and social structures.

One cannot proceed without theoretical assumptions about organisational change. Proposing a general theory of organisational change is clearly beyond the scope of this paper (not to mention my own capabilities), but I do need to make a number of assumptions about organisational structures and organisational change in order to consider them from a discourse analytical perspective.

These assumptions draw from the version of cultural political economy I used in Fairclough (2005c), and especially from Jessop (2002).[10]

1. Organisational structures are hegemonic structures, structures which are based in and reproduce particular power relations between groups of social agents, which constitute 'fixes' with enduring capacity to manage the contradictions of organisations in ways which allow them to get on with their main business more or less successfully.
2. Organisational structures may come into crisis, generally as a result of a combination of both external and internal changes and pressures, when the 'fix' is perceived as no longer viable.
3. In situations of crisis, groups of social agents develop their own particular (and opposing) strategies for achieving a new 'fix', and through a process of hegemonic struggle a new hegemonic 'fix' may emerge.
4. Strategies have a partly discoursal character, including particular discourses and narratives[11] which represent in particular ways what has happened and is happening, and construct imaginaries for what could happen. Discourses and narratives may be 'recontextualised' from other organisations.
5. Change in the social process, including change in texts, may have transformative effects on organisational structures in so far as it becomes incorporated within successful strategies.
6. The implementation of a successful strategy is a matter of the operationalisation of new representations and imaginaries (new discourses and narratives) in new ways of acting and being and new material arrangements.

An important part of these assumptions is that the category of 'strategies' is seen as mediating the relationship between the change which is inherent in social interaction and texts, and change in organisational structures. With respect to my reference to evolutionary theory above, the selection and retention of variants is a matter of their being incorporated into successful strategies. Strategies constitute imaginaries for changes in the networks of social practices of organisations, changes in organisational structure, including changes in the orders of discourse of organisations; and in so far as strategies are successful, such imaginaries may be realised in actual changes.

In connection with these assumptions, I would suggest that there are four broad sets of research issues which can productively be addressed specifically by discourse analysts in transdisciplinary research on organisational change: the problems of emergence, hegemony, recontextualisation and operationalisation:

Emergence: the processes of emergence of new discourses, their constitution as new articulations of elements of existing discourses.

Hegemony: the processes of particular emergent discourses (and not others) and associated narratives becoming hegemonic in particular organisations.

Recontextualisation: the dissemination of emergently hegemonic discourses across structural boundaries (e.g., between organisations) and scalar boundaries (e.g., from local to national or international scale, or vice versa).

Operationalisation: the operationalisation of such discourses, their enactment in new ways of (inter)acting, including genres, their inculcation in new ways of being or identities, including styles, their materialisation as objects and properties of the physical world.

Emergence

The problem of emergence is approached on the principle that nothing comes out of nothing – new discourses emerge through 'reweaving' relations between existing discourses. These may include 'external' discourses existing elsewhere which become recontextualised in an organisation – recontextualisation (see further below) involves questions of reception and appropriation, working 'external' discourses into relations with internal discourses. These processes of 'reweaving' can be identified in analysis of texts as processes (as 'texturing'). There is an analysis of a specific example in Fairclough, Jessop and Sayer (2004: 35–36). And Iedema *et al.* (2004) show how the doctor-manager 'reweaves' relations between different discourses (a process of 'bricolage', as they describe it). An emergent new discourse may be 'institutionalised' within a changed order of discourse, a process which is conditional on it being incorporated into a successful strategy (see the discussion of 'hegemony' below). What 'reweaving' goes on, which new discourses emerge, are not dependent on internal properties of social process and text alone – they are not socially arbitrary, not merely an effect of the normal flux or 'play' of interaction. As Iedema *et al.* point out, the doctor-manager's 'feat' (as they see it) is conditional on the particular contradictions thrown up by organisational restructuring in public services such as medicine, and the marketisation and managerialisation of organisations such as hospitals. In other words, new discourses which may contribute to changes in organisational structures have their own conditions of possibility in the structures of organisations, the strategies of social agents, the habitus of social agents, and so forth.[12] Therefore, while problems of emergence can be researched through analysing change in social processes, social interaction and text, including chains and series of interconnected texts over time and across organisational space, they also require reference to these structural, strategic and other factors.

Hegemony

The effect (or lack of effect) of emergent phenomena in social process and text depends on whether they are selected for incorporation into the strategies of social groups, and the success or failure of competing strategies in processes of hegemonic struggle. Researching the hegemony problem entails carrying out discourse analytical research in dialogue with social scientists who investigate relations between social groups in organisations and the strategies of social groups. This is a matter both of textual analysis, and of seeking to identify what distinctive discourses and narratives are associated with particular strategies (which shifts the focus towards emerging social practices and associated orders of discourse), as well as analysing texts with a focus on contradictions and struggles between competing discourses and strategies. This entails what one might call strategic critique (as opposed to the ideological and rhetorical critique which are also familiar within CDA), focusing on how discourse figures within the strategies pursued by groups of social agents to change organisations in particular directions. Strategies effect distinctive articulations of discourses, often organised around a dominant 'nodal discourse' (the discourse of 'new public management', or 'total quality management' might be examples) which organises relations between other constituent discourses (Jessop 2002, Fairclough 2005c).

The success or failure of strategies depends on various conditions, some of which have a discoursal character: for instance, some discourses are more 'resonant' than others (Fairclough *et al.* 2004b), better able to capture and encapsulate the experiences of social agents, better able to complement or organise existing discourses. The success or failure of strategies also depends on the resilience, resistance or inertia of existing organisational structures, including how well embedded existing discourses are.

Recontextualisation

The concept of recontextualisation is taken from Bernstein's sociology of pedagogy and has been operationalised as a category in CDA (Bernstein 1990, Chouliaraki and Fairclough 1999), a case of internal theoretical development through transdisciplinary dialogue. Recontextualisation identifies the ('recontextualising') principles according to which 'external' discourses (and practices) are internalised within particular organisations – particular organisations (schools, businesses, media organisations) constituted in particular ways have their own distinctive ways of internalising 'external' discourses. Chouliaraki and Fairclough see recontextualisation as a colonisation-appropriation dialectic: organisations may be seen as colonised by external discourses, but they actively appropriate them (setting the new in relation with the old) in ways which may lead to unpredictable transformations and outcomes. Given that contemporary organisations are characteristically embedded within complex networks of organisations which render them subject to powerful external pressures which affect trajectories of internal change, and given that these inter-organisational processes are often 'discourse-led', researching the recontextualisation of discourses is an important part of discourse analytical research on organisational change. For instance, research on 'transition' in the post-communist countries involves questions about how the neo-liberal discourses which were so salient in the interventions of external agencies in the early years of 'transition' have been recontextualised within post-communist countries and within particular organisations and institutions. Linking the problem of recontextualisation with the problem of hegemony, one might argue that such external discourses have substantive internal effects only on condition that they are incorporated within successful strategies, i.e., that the effectivity of the 'flow' of discourses across structural boundaries between organisations and across scalar boundaries between 'global', 'macro-regional' (e.g., EU), national and local boundaries (specific organisations would be 'local' in this sense) is conditional on how they enter into internal social relations and social struggles.

Operationalisation

I have referred so far only to discourses, without mentioning the other categories which constitute orders of discourse (genres, styles), or how discourses are dialectically transformed into other social elements. These are interconnected. Successful strategies may be operationalised, i.e., cease to be merely imaginaries for change, and effect real change. Operationalisation includes enactment: discourses may be dialectically transformed into new ways of acting and interacting. For instance, the discourse of 'appraisal' entered higher educational organisations in Britain as a discourse, an imaginary for change, which was then enacted as universities negotiated and adopted procedures for appraising staff. And, as this example indicates, enactment includes the dialectical transformation of discourses into genres: these procedures included new genres, including the 'appraisal interview', which was designed to regulate interaction between appraiser and appraisee in particular ways (see Fairclough (2003) for analysis of a particular organisation). Operationalisation also includes inculcation – the dialectical transformation of discourses into new ways of being, new identities, which includes new styles. For instance, the emergent hegemony of the discourse of 'new public management' in such organisations as local government authorities includes changes in the identities of public service managers and workers, including changes in their communicative styles. Finally, operationalisation includes materialisation: a new management system in an organisation may include changes in the structuring of organisational space, e.g., in the design of office space. Through these forms of operationalisation, networks of social practices and the orders of discourse which are parts of them may be transformed.

I have formulated these four problems in general terms to give a general view of the sort of contribution CDA can make to research on organisational change. They are, of course, not alternatives. For any particular research project, discourse analysts can contribute in dialogue with other researchers to the constitution of objects of research for research topics, and the likelihood is that the particular research questions it contributes will involve a combination of versions of some or all of the problems. For instance, my research on New Labour (Fairclough 2000b) addressed the emergence of the discourse of the 'third way', its incorporation within a hegemonic strategy for change, its recontextualisation (e.g., from UK domestic politics to international politics), and to some extent its operationalisation through the formulation and implementation of policies.

4 Conclusion

I have argued that a commitment to discourse analysis in organisational studies entails neither a reduction of organisations to organisational discourse, nor a reduction of organisational analysis to the 'organising' that goes on in organisational processes. Discourse analysis is consistent with a realist approach to organisational research which distinguishes organisational process and agency from organisational structures, and focuses research on the relations and tensions between them. Incorporating discourse analysis into a realist approach both ensures that questions of discourse are properly attended to in organisational studies, and avoids these forms of reductionism. Within such a realist approach, discourse analysis can make a significant contribution to researching organisational change, and addressing such general concerns as the following: When organisations change, what is it that changes? What makes organisations resilient in the face of change, resistant to change, or open to change? How are external pressures for organisational change internalised in organisations; how may organisational members respond to them, and what outcomes are possible? Such questions cannot of course be addressed by discourse analysts alone, but my argument is that effectively researching them does depend on a substantive element of discourse analysis in transdisciplinary research on organisational change.

Notes

1. I take an analytically dualist position, as I explain later in the paper, which distinguishes 'social process' and 'social structure' as ontologically distinct though interconnected facets of the social, and focuses research on the relationship between them. Analysis of social process includes analysis of agency, so another way of formulating the fundamental ontological distinction is 'agency v structure'. As Fairclough, Jessop and Sayer (2004) argue, the analytical isolation of distinct events and chains of events in the social process is itself an interpretative accomplishment which involves and depends on discourse, even where the events concerned do not have a mainly discursive character (e.g., a football match, as opposed to a lecture, which does have a mainly discursive character).

2. The authors state that 'the portrait painted' in the paper 'celebrates this one person's talk as a performativity'. As conversation analysts have shown, there is a sense in which any talk is a performativity or feat to be celebrated, and that surely applies to the more-or-less skilled performances of managers in any form of organisation. I suspect the authors are confusing novelty with performativity – yet there are no doubt already managers for whom performances of this sort are rather routine.

3. Or perhaps more adequately, social fields can be regarded as configurations of institutions, and organisations can be regarded as institutions of a distinctive type, where organisations and other types of institution are configurations of social practices (Ackroyd 2000).

4. Together with a broad consensus which is sufficient to identify CDA as a distinct research tradition, there are substantial differences on certain issues within the field (Fairclough and Wodak 1997), as well as shifts over time in the positions of individual researchers, including my own. If we bring into the picture the rapidly expanding applications of CDA in a great many disciplines and fields in social science (see Fairclough, Graham, Lemke and Wodak 2004), then the positions and approaches which count as, or claim to be, CDA expand considerably. Since I believe that research in CDA is most fruitfully carried out in transdisciplinary dialogue with other disciplines, theories and forms of research, this proliferation of CDA *within* various areas of social scientific research is a welcome advance on the earlier situation of

CDA often camping precariously on their borders. But it does pose some problems in making what counts as CDA. See note 5.

5. Critical discourse analysis has been one of a number of methodological influences within research on organisational discourse (others include conversation analysis, linguistic pragmatics, sociolinguistics, and systemic functional linguistics). What counts as 'critical discourse' analysis is subject to the same diversity in this area of research as in others. It should be clear from what I have said that my position does not constitute a blanket endorsement of all the research on organisational discourse which has identified itself as critical discourse analysis.

6. There are arguments for using the term 'semiosis' rather than 'discourse' in the abstract sense as an element of the social in relation to other non-discoursal elements of the social, given the widespread confusion between 'discourse' in this sense and (particular) 'discourses', and the widespread reduction of 'discourse' to 'discourses' which I discuss later (Fairclough, Jessop and Sayer 2004). However, I shall use the more familiar term 'discourse'.

7. Languages and other semiotic systems as social structures, and orders of discourse as facets of networks of social practices, are in critical realist terms both objects with particular generative mechanisms or causal powers. Languages have the causal power to contribute to the production of a limitless set of semiotic (elements of) events, far beyond the actual. Orders of discourse can in part be seen as constructs which account for the gap between the causal powers of languages (and other semiotic systems) and the semiotic actual. But a distinction must still be drawn between the causal powers of an order of discourse and the semiotic actual – the latter is in a sense both less than and more than the former, for the extent to which the former are actualised is conditional on contingencies, and the fact that texts are effects of the causal powers of objects other than orders of discourse (or languages) means that may exceed the possibilities defined by orders of discourse.

8. The term 'text' is not really felicitous for the general sense of the discoursal element of events, because it is so strongly associated with written language. However, I have not found a more satisfactory alternative.

9. I subsume a variety of particular forms of analysis under 'linguistic' analysis, including grammatical analysis, semantic analysis, analysis of vocabulary and metaphor, analysis of argumentation and other forms of rhetorical analysis, narrative analysis, pragmatic analysis, conversational analysis and other forms of interactional analysis. See Fairclough 2003.

10. Jessop's concern is with change in political economies (interconnected changes in economic systems and systems of governance), not with change in organisations. There are clearly difficulties in simply extrapolating from the one to the other, but I think that nevertheless this set of (tentative) assumptions will allow me to indicate schematically how I envisage the contribution of discourse analysis to research on organisational change.

11. Narratives are distinctive both with respect to discourses and with respect to genres – they involve particular ways of representing the social and organisational world (discourses) and particular ways of telling stories about them (genres). For my present purposes, the focus is on the discourses associated with particular narratives rather than questions of genre.

12. In Fairclough and Thomas (2004) we argue for instance that structural factors as well as the strategies of groups of social agents are germane to explaining the emergence of the discourse of 'globalisation' in the past few decades, especially given that globalisation is widely regarded as a process which is centuries old. 'Why here, why now?' are pertinent questions to ask.

Political discourse

Introduction

The papers in this section, published between 1998 and 2006, address diverse aspects of and issues in analysis of political discourse. The first paper is a previously unpublished English version of a paper published in the Romanian journal *Secolo 21*. It gives a condensed account of the analysis of the political discourse of New Labour in Britain which is more fully developed in my book *New Labour, New Language?* (2000b). The second and third papers are concerned with the political public sphere, understood as a sphere of politics outside government and the political system, in which the privileged actors are citizens. And the fourth paper is a discussion of the controversy around 'political correctness', which I treat as a recent political controversy of some significance. Political discourse has been a focus throughout my work within CDA, and readers should note that a number of papers in other sections of the book also address questions of political discourse analysis, including Papers 6, 7, 8, 11, 12 and 19.

The first paper ('New Labour: a language perspective') can be seen as a partial account of the political field in its semiotic dimension (the political 'order of discourse') in Britain around the turn of the twenty-first century, partial in that the focus is one major position within the political field – New Labour. To a degree it builds upon the analysis of the political discourse of Thatcherism in *Language and Power* (1989a). The language of New Labour is presented as having three main dimensions or facets: political discourses (representations and imaginaries of diverse fields and domains of social life which are subjected to government, as well as government itself), govern-mental genres (ways of acting and interacting in the processes of government, or ways of regulating these processes in their discourse aspect), and political styles (ways of being, identities, of New Labour politicians and ministers, including the Prime Minister Tony Blair).

The second paper is entitled 'Democracy and the public sphere in critical research on discourse'. There is a widespread contemporary perception that democracy is in decline if not in crisis, and that the travails of democracy can be productively understood in terms of the weakness of the political public sphere. Major theorists of the public sphere, including Jürgen Habermas and Hannah Arendt, have indicated that the strength of public spheres depends upon their discursive features, and this suggests that CDA may have a significant contribution to make to this area of political research. For reasons explained in the paper, I develop a framework for a CDA approach to researching public spheres on the basis of Arendt's position in particular. I suggest that any discursive practice is simultaneously a *regulative* practice, a space of *emergence*, a principle of *recontextualisation*, and a constituent of *action*, and that taken together these can constitute both a framework for description and a normative template for evaluation of public dialogue in terms of its quality or success in instantiating or creating a public sphere.

The third paper ('Critical discourse analysis and citizenship'), co-authored with Simon Pardoe and Bron Szerszynski, arose out of an EU-funded research project (the PARADYS project) on field trials of genetically modified crops in several European countries. The focus of the project was citizenship, but more precisely citizenship *as a communicative achievement* within the process of authorising and regulating farm trials. In this paper we present a CDA approach to citizenship as a communicative achievement and illustrate it from the material we collected and analysed as part of the section of the PARADYS project devoted to the UK. A central argument of the paper is that a simple shift from concerns with what citizenship *is* to concerns with how citizenship is communicatively achieved or *done* is not feasible, because the ways in which people enact citizenship are always oriented to, reflective of and often in tension with diverse coexisting preconceptions about and pre-constructions of citizenship. In the light of this argument, we address the question of how people position themselves as subjects (and specifically as citizens) by focusing on struggles over genre, switches in and struggles over voice and style, and discourses around public participation in public meetings concerned with the field trials.

The fourth paper ('Political correctness') takes the controversy around 'political correctness' (PC) as a political controversy in which both sides are engaged in a politics that is focused upon representations, values and identities – in short, a 'cultural politics'. The objective on both sides is cultural change as a trigger for broader social change. And because changing culture is conceived on both sides as partly a matter of changing language, the 'PC' controversy is partly, but only partly, a controversy over language. I focus here on the language aspect in addressing three questions. First, what explains the apparently increasing focus in politics on achieving social and political change through changing culture and changing language (a 'cultural turn' in politics)? Second, how are we to understand the relationship between culture, language and other elements of social life, and the relationship between change in culture and language, and social change? Third, for those who are politically committed to substantive change, what place can a politics centred around culture and language have in a political strategy?

14. New Labour: a language perspective[1]

The UK Labour Government which was elected under the leadership of Tony Blair in 1997 differentiated itself from its predecessors by identifying itself as 'New Labour'. Being 'New Labour' was associated with making a break from the history and traditions of the Labour Party, most notably by renouncing the commitment to 'the common ownership of the means of production, distribution and exchange' in Clause 4 of the Labour Party Constitution. It can be seen as an accommodation with the 'New Right', neo-liberal agenda of Thatcherism, an inflection of the Thatcherite agenda rather than a rejection of it. New Labour also had a new 'modern' political style, including a sophisticated use of mass media which came to be widely disparaged as the cultivation of 'media spin'.[2]

It is remarkable how much political and journalistic commentaries on and analyses of New Labour have focused upon questions of language. The political discourse of the 'Third Way', New Labour's political discourse, has been criticised for instance for the 'vagueness' of its language, New Labour's 'media spin' has been satirically associated with endless collocations with 'new' ('New Deal', 'New Britain', 'new Europe', 'new partnerships' and so forth – giving rise to scurrilous additions such as 'new underpants'), and Blair's political leadership style has been identified and criticised for its cultivation of a merely apparent sincerity and artlessness.

I wish to argue that analysis of language (or 'discourse analysis' see below) can substantially enhance political analysis. The focus of people who are not language specialists on the language of New Labour perhaps provides a *prima facie* justification for approaching the politics of New Labour from a language perspective. But there are also more substantive reasons, which one can perhaps see commentators, critics and satirists as implicitly responding to. First, the political philosophy, strategy and values of New Labour are not pre-given; they have been and continue to be, so to speak, talked and re-talked into being in speeches by Blair and in other New Labour texts. This has led some commentators to question whether they can properly be said to exist as coherent objects at all. But what this means is that attending to the shifts in the language of New Labour is analytically important in arriving at an analysis of the politics of New Labour. Second, the 'modernisation' or 'reinvention' of government which New Labour has associated itself with, including some devolution of government to unelected advisery groups which entails new forms of control by the centre, places an enhanced emphasis on public rep-resentations and construals of government and politics (and 'media spin') which again calls for close linguistic analysis. Third, contemporary politics centres upon the personality of political leaders such as Blair, whose com-municative style is professionally designed, and demands linguistic and semiotic analysis.

1 Critical discourse analysis

The theory and method used in my study of New Labour are drawn from CDA.[3] 'Discourse' is used, as an abstract noun, for language and other semiotic modes (such as 'body language' and visual images) seen as an element of social events and, more abstractly, social practices, which is dialectically[4] related to other elements (forms of activity, social relations and institutional forms, persons with knowledge, beliefs, attitudes and values, and elements of the material world). These diverse elements are seen as different without being discrete – elements 'internalise' other elements[5] (the 'external' dialectics of discourse). At the level of social practices, discourse in this abstract sense figures in three main ways: as ways of (inter)acting (or 'genres'), as ways of representing (or 'discourses' used as a concrete noun), and as ways of being or identities ('styles'). The relationship between genres, discourses and styles is also dialectical (the 'internal' dialectics of discourse): discourses may be enacted as genres (as well as non-discoursal facets of activity), and inculcated as styles (as well embodied). I see CDA's research agenda as focusing on how discourse figures in (and often, in the 'knowledge' or 'information' society, 'drives') more general processes of social change, especially contemporary changes associated with 'new capitalism', 'neo-liberalism' and 'globalisation', with respect to social relations of power and domination. Methodologically, it analyses text and talk 'interdiscursively', i.e., in terms of how different genres, discourses and styles are drawn upon and 'textured' together, and in terms of how these articulations are realised in the meanings and forms (generic, grammatical, lexical, phonological, as well as those of non-linguistic semiotic modes) of texts. It makes connections between texts in their linguistic detail and social processes and change via the mediation of shifting articulations of genres, discourses and styles. This form of CDA is designed as a resource for social scientists and social research.[6]

2   CDA of the language of New Labour

The focus of analysis is New Labour in government, and the concern is therefore both with the language of a political party, and the language of the style of government practised under the auspices of that political party. The aim is to delineate a social practice in its discourse aspect – or an 'order of discourse'. An 'order of discourse' is a particular relatively durable articulation of discourses, genres and styles. Orders of discourses constitute the social regulation of linguistic and semiotic difference or variation. The 'order of discourse' in this case is properly the politico-governmental order of discourse, including the discourse of diverse political positions within the Labour Party and of other parties, but my focus here is exclusively on New Labour.

The language of New Labour includes political discourses (representations and imaginaries of diverse fields and domains of social life which are subjected to government, as well as government itself), governmental genres (ways of acting and interacting in the processes of government, or ways of regulating these processes in their discourse aspect), and political styles (ways of being, identities, of New Labour politicians and ministers). The 'external' dialectics of discourse is a matter for instance of how imaginaries of a new order of social welfare, or 'partnerships' between government, business and non-governmental organisations,[7] are enacted in new institutions and procedures, and inculcated (more or less) in new subjects, as well as materialised, for instance architecturally. The 'internal' dialectics of discourse is a matter, for instance, of how such imaginaries are enacted as genres and inculcated as styles. An interesting insight into the dialectics of discourse within the politics of New labour is given, from a practical perspective, by Philip Gould, a political consultant who was one of Blair's leading advisers, in a memorandum written in 1994 called 'Consolidating the Blair identity': Blair 'must build on his strengths, and build an identity as a politician that is of a piece with the political positions he adopts'. We might gloss this as follows in the terms I am using: the construction of Blair's political identity is a matter of the inculcation of aspects of the political discourses of New Labour (particularly their associated 'values') in a communicative style, and a form of embodiment. I shall not explore these dialectical relations much further in this short paper, but briefly discuss in turn: the political discourse of the 'Third Way'; New Labour's genres of government; and the political style of Tony Blair.

3 The political discourse of the 'Third Way'

Discourses (and the same is true of genres and styles) can be differentiated on different levels of generality or abstraction. The political position of New Labour has been identified by Blair and others as the 'Third Way'. On a relatively high level of generality, we might approach the 'Third Way' as the political discourse of New Labour, though with certain provisos. First, its unity and coherence as a discourse are a matter of dispute. Second, we have to grasp it as an emergent discourse, a discourse in process of formation, as I indicated earlier. Third, at a lesser level of generality one can identify many different discourses within the political discourse of the Third Way, both in terms of the diverse areas of social life which are represented and imagined (e.g., social welfare, governance through partnerships, crime), and in terms of the diverse perspectives on these areas of social life. With respect to the latter, I want to highlight one recurrent feature of representations of the 'Third Way' which is illustrated in the following extract from a speech by Blair:

Third Way – our values
There is a clear theme running through the annual report. It is the third way.
There is something genuinely new about the politics of this government.
When you look at the record of the past year ask yourself:
What other government this century would have cut corporation tax to help business yet introduced a minimum wage to help the poorest paid?
What other government would have given financial independence to the Bank of England as well as setting up a unit to deal with homelessness?
What other government would work so hard to offer jobs, and new skills to young people as well as cracking down on youth crime?
What other government would reform the workings of government to make the centre of government stronger and more strategic, yet devolve power dramatically to local people throughout Britain?
What other government would put huge extra resources into health and education yet still keep to tough overall spending ceilings?
This is the third way. A belief in social justice and economic dynamism, ambition and compassion, fairness and enterprise going together.
The third way is a new politics that helps people cope with a more insecure world because it rejects the destructive excesses of the market and the intrusive hand of state intervention. It is about an enabling government that gives people the chance of a better future in which all people can play their part.[8]

One aspect of such representations is marking out the relationship and difference between the 'Third Way' and the political positions it is represented as displacing and transcending – in one formulation, the 'old-style intervention of the old left and the *laissez-faire* of the new right',[9] or in the example above, 'the intrusive hand of state intervention' and 'the destructive excesses of the market'. The pamphlets, speeches and newspaper articles of New Labour politicians are full of descriptions of how the 'Third Way' differs from the 'old left' and 'new right', often in the form of extended lists, as in this case, in which what had hitherto been seen as incompatible opposites are represented as reconciled. The meaning 'not only . . . but also' pervades the political discourse of New Labour, realised in a variety of expressions ('yet' and 'as well as' in this case, but also others: 'enterprise *yet also* fairness', 'enterprise *as well as* fairness', 'enterprise *with* fairness', 'enterprise *and* fairness', with *and* stressed), which both draw attention to assumed incompatabilities, and deny them: what has been seen as mutually exclusive, belonging to either left (e.g., 'social justice') or right (e.g., 'economic dynamism'), is not. A new political discourse is in part constituted as a hybridisation of elements of existing political discourses, those of the social democratic left and the Thatcherite right.

Political and journalistic commentaries on the discourse of the 'Third Way' often question the relationship between what New Labour says and what it does, the 'rhetoric' in one sense of that term, whether it is 'mere words' at odds with action. Indeed the central controversy about New Labour is whether its 'Third Way' is indeed a new form of centre-left politics as it claims, or a somewhat disguised continuation of the neo-liberal politics of the New Right. For instance, is the claim to 'reject the destructive excesses of the market and the intrusive hand of state intervention' mere words, or are actions being taken which prevent the destructive excesses of the market without recourse to state intervention? What are these actions – indeed, what could they possibly be? Is there any way except the power of the state for preventing these excesses? Of course, we cannot answer the question about 'rhetoric' simply by reference to language, for it asks about the relationship of language to other elements. But language is a significant focus in such a political analysis – for instance, one aspect of the pervasive meaning 'not only . . . but also' is that the two previously-incompatible terms that are made compatible (e.g., 'social justice and economic dynamism') are construed as having equal weight. In actuality, there may be policies oriented to 'social justice', but they may be secondary or marginal in comparison with policies oriented to 'economic dynamism'. Moreover, the paratactic, listing syntax which is pervasive in constructions of the 'Third Way' constructs equivalences which are contentious as contestable (e.g., in what way are 'giving financial independence to the Bank of England' and 'cracking down on youth crime' equivalent?). It is easy to be carried along by the 'rhetoric', the persuasive patterning of the language (in this case, the repeated questions beginning 'What other government would . . . ?'), which some commentators have seen as papering over the incoherence and contradictions of New Labour.[10]

I have only touched on one aspect of the discourse of the third way among many which are of interest – for instance its representation of 'work', or 'rights and responsibilities', of 'values', or 'social exclusion' and social inclusion. Quantitative corpus studies of collocative patterns can enhance the more qualitative text analysis of CDA in these cases.[11] For instance, a comparison between corpora of New Labour and earlier Labour Party texts showed that 'into' and 'back to work' are frequent collocations in the former, whereas 'out of work' is a frequent collocation in the latter. The former also include as frequent collocative patterns such as: '(from) welfare to work', 'seeking' work, 'encouraging' work, 'opportunities' to work, 'desire' to work. The latter include: 'right to work', 'democracy at work', 'health and safety at work', 'equality of opportunity' at work. These collocative patterns are indicative of the significance of textual 'work' in embedding questions of employment and unemployment is radically different policy frames.

4 Genres of government

Democratic government depends upon achieving a sufficient measure of consent for particular intended changes in social life. There are various ways in which consent can be achieved. It can be achieved politically, through dialogue in which disagreement and dissent can be expressed. One of the criticisms of New Labour has been that it is intolerant of dissent, and that it takes active measures to silence dissent within the Government and the Labour Party as well as more widely.[12] Although New Labour constantly initiates 'great debates' and calls for debate and discussion around its policy initiatives (e.g., welfare reform), it seems in broad terms that it sets out to achieve consent not through political dialogue but through managerial methods of promotion and forms of consultation of public opinion (e.g., in focus groups) which it can control. The Government tends to act like a corporation treating (and 'testing') the public as its consumers, rather than as citizens.

The New Labour way of governing is in part a way of using language. One issue is ways in which New Labour's language of government is promotional rather than dialogical. Let me take the process of reforming the welfare system as an example, and note three ways in which language works promotionally within that process, and therefore in a way which discourages dialogue and debate (see also Paper 7, pages 167–201). Firstly, the overall process was carefully stage-managed. For instance, the Green Paper (the Government's consultation document) on welfare reform was published in March 1998;[13] its publication was preceded by a series of meetings around the country addressed by the Prime Minister and a series of papers published by the Department of Social Security making the case for welfare reform. These were widely seen as preparing the ground. Each initiative was accompanied by a press release. The management of the process was partly the management of language – there was a constant process of summarising the proposed welfare reform, selecting particular representations of it, particular wordings, which would be most effective in achieving consent – what has been called media 'spin'. The process is promotional, not dialogical, although it was referred to as a 'debate'.

Secondly, the Green Paper itself is univocal, monological. In the real world of welfare, there are many voices, many opinions on what the problems are and how they should be resolved. Yet a striking feature of the language of the Green Paper is that there is very little reported speech – very few reports about what various relevant people or groups have said or written on the issue of welfare reform. Certain central 'players' in the real world of welfare are virtually and in some cases totally absent from the document – the staff who 'deliver' welfare, the professional experts who work within the welfare system or write about it, various claimant or campaigning organisations.

Thirdly, the Green Paper does not engage its readers in dialogue. Of course, there are few direct readers of such official documents, but millions of indirect readers (so to speak), people who hear or read reports about it in the media. The document is organised with such indirect readers in mind – its first chapter is a Summary of the whole document which many journalists would draw upon, and there is also a press release about the document, as well as a foreword by the Prime Minister – more summaries. The focus throughout is upon promoting the Government's proposed solutions to what it takes to be the problems of the welfare system. This is evident in certain features of the language. Although there are in the nature of things a great many unanswered questions in undertaking such a huge policy change, there are virtually no questions in the Green Paper – readers are hardly ever asked, they are told. And although in the nature of things there is a great deal of uncertainty, readers are told things as if they were certain – statements are predominantly categorical assertions or denials; there are few which are modalised as possibilities or probabilities (with modal markers such as modal verbs or adjuncts like 'perhaps'). The following brief paragraph gives some idea of the promotional flavour of the document:

3.7 Our comprehensive welfare to work programme aims to break the mould of the old, passive benefit system. It is centred on the five aspects of the New Deal for:

> young unemployed people;
> long-term unemployed people;
> lone parents;
> people with a disability or long-term illness; and
> partners of the unemployed.

The Government speaks in the first person plural ('our') rather than being referred to in the third person; its programme is positively evaluated (it is 'comprehensive', it aims to 'break the mould') and the existing system negatively ('old', 'passive', and a 'benefit' rather than 'welfare' system), and the common promotional device of bullet points is used – a device which may be 'reader-friendly', but is by the same token reader-directive, and does not encourage dialogue.

5 Blair's political style

Tony Blair's style has been immensely successful, though critiques have intensified recently. Perhaps the clearest example before the NATO war against Yugoslavia, and more recently the 'War on Terrorism', was his widely acclaimed success in 'capturing the popular mood' after Princess Diana's death in the autumn of 1997. Here is the beginning of the short statement he made on that occasion:

> I feel like everyone else in the country today – utterly devastated. Our thoughts and prayers are with Princess Diana's family – in particular her two sons, two boys – our hearts go out to them. We are today a nation, in Britain, in a state of shock, in mourning, in grief that is so deeply painful for us.

Why were these words so effective in 'striking a chord' with many people?[14] One important point is that it was not just his words but his overall bodily performance, the way he looked and acted as well as what he said. But the language was an important factor. Notice in particular that it is a mixed language. There are two threads running through it. Let me 'extract' one of them:

> Our thoughts and prayers are with Princess Diana's family, in particular her two sons, our hearts go out to them. We are today a nation in mourning.

This is the conventional sort of language which leaders use to speak on behalf of the nation on such occasions. Blair uses the first person plural ('we'), and predictable pre-constructed expressions (clichés) – 'thoughts and prayers', 'our hearts go out to them', 'a nation in mourning'. But threaded into this conventional public language there is a more personal language (Blair begins speaking for himself, in the first person singular, and about his own feelings) and a more vernacular language. It is as if Blair (and his advisers) had started with the official form of words, then personalised and informalised it. He uses a vernacular language of affect as well as a public one – 'utterly devastated', 'in a state of shock'. Notice also the way he rewords 'her two sons' as 'two boys', which again is a shift between a more formal way of referring to them in terms of their relationship to Diana and a more intimate, family way. Blair says he feels 'like everyone else' – he is not only speaking formally for 'the nation', he is also speaking informally for ordinary people; and part of the power of his style is his ability to combine formality and informality, ceremony and feeling, publicness and privateness.

A crucial part of the success of Blair's style is his capacity to, as it were, 'anchor' the public politician in the 'normal person' – the necessary posturing and evasions of politics are it seems at least partially redeemed by Blair's capacity to constantly reassert his normal, decent, likeable, personality. In his speeches and interviews, there is always a mix between the vernacular language of the normal person, and the public language of politics. The sort of 'normal person' that comes across is very much 'middle class' and 'middle England' in values, outlook and style – Blair's communicative style might be said to have inculcated the discourse of the 'Third Way' in this respect, as also in the way he has learnt how to be (i.e., talk as well as act) 'tough' (well evidenced in the course of the 'War on Terrorism'), which he was initially not very good at, and how to assert moral authority in the way he speaks.

Blair's leadership personality and style are not pre-given, they are carefully constructed. For instance, according to Gould,[15] New Labour learnt the political advantage it could gain from being and talking 'tough', and talking about being 'tough', from his research on focus groups – Blair's 'toughness' has been self-consciously built into his communicative style as a matter of policy and strategy. Blair's apparent and claimed preference for acting on the basis of his political 'instincts' is at odds with the careful calculation of effects on 'public opinion' which goes into every move that he and New Labour make.[16] Blair is according to his biographer Rentoul an accomplished showman, an actor. Of course, the circumstances of contemporary politics are not of his making – all politicians have to act, to pretend, or to put it more harshly (though not perhaps unfairly) to 'live a lie'. Though one might argue that individual leaders can nevertheless respond to those circumstances in various ways – by trying to be more accomplished at pretending than others, or by doing what they can to change the circumstances.

I alluded above to the Kosovo war and the post-September 11 'war on terrorism'. Blair has become an international statesman, and wartime leader, of some considerable stature, largely on the basis of his actions during these international crises. His political style changed to a degree, though these changes were already established at the time of the Kosovo war. The changes are partly a matter of 'body language' – for instance I first saw a new style of photographic image of Blair in the German newspaper *Die Zeit* in early 1999 which makes him look much harder, more formidable and more forbidding than hitherto. But it is also partly a matter of language. Here is a short extract from a very influential speech on 'the doctrine of the international community' which Blair made in Chicago in April 1999:

> This is a just war, based not on any territorial ambitions but on values. We cannot let the evil of ethnic cleansing stand. We must not rest until it is reversed. We have learned twice before in this century that appeasement does not work. If we let an evil dictator range unchallenged, we will have to spill infinitely more blood and treasure to stop him later . . . Success is the only exit strategy I am prepared to see.

The force of this language is based upon a combination of Blair's claims to moral authority (e.g., judgements of 'evil') and his toughness (notably in the last sentence, where he implicitly claims a personal veto over what he ironic- ally calls the 'exit strategy'). He claims to speak for the whole alliance and indeed the international community as a whole (the import of the first per- sonal plural pronoun), making categorical assertions (e.g., 'this is a just war'), using morally powerful strong deontic modalities (e.g., 'we *cannot* let the evil of ethnic cleansing stand') and making explicit claims for the moral high ground (the war is 'just', based on 'values'), and drawing upon an archaic political language in a Churchillian tradition ('spill . . . blood and treasure', and indeed the moral–religious term 'evil').

Tony Blair may stand for New Labour in the popular imagination, but New Labour is, in fact, a rather disparate alliance of different political posi- tions associated with different communicative styles (that of his deputy, John Prescott, for example). Another important issue is how distinctive New Labour is, both from its predecessors in Britain and from similar political positions in other countries. What similarities for instance are there between Margaret Thatcher and Tony Blair, or Bill Clinton and Tony Blair? Is the Blair rhetorical style a purely local and individual achievement, or is it part of a wider cultural change? Is the new political style of Blair perhaps comparable with the new management style represented for instance in Britain by the man who was reputedly Margaret Thatcher's favourite businessman, Richard Branson? Such issues can be approached in terms of what Alistair MacIntyre has called the distinctive 'characters' of the new capitalism.[17]

6 Conclusion

The significance of language, or discourse, in social life and social change has been extensively documented in recent social research. For instance, Bourdieu and Wacquant have written in recent years of the significance of neo-liberal discourse in what they see as the neo-liberal political project for removing obstacles to economic 'globalisation'.[18] Yet social researchers have lacked both the theoretical elaboration of discourse as an element of the social, dialectically interconnected with others, and the methodological resources to produce analyses of discourse which go much beyond mere lists of vocabulary items. Critical discourse analysis aims to fill these gaps, and create a bridge and a dialogue between language studies and social science.

Notes

1. See Fairclough (2000b) for a more extended treatment.
2. On New Labour, see Brown (1994), Barratt and Coates (1996), Rentoul (1997), Blair (1998a), Driver and Martell (1998), Giddens (1998), Gould (1998), Hall (1998), Levitas (1998), Marquand (1998), Jones (1999), Fairclough (2001a).
3. Fairclough (1992a, 1995, 2000a, 2001c), Chouliaraki and Fairclough (1999), Fairclough and Wodak (1997), Chiapello and Fairclough (2002).
4. Dialectical thinking has a long tradition which goes back to the Greeks and includes major figures such as Leibniz and Hegel, as well as Marx. In focusing upon dialectics, I am making the ontological assumption the processes, relations and flows have primacy over entities and things (see further, Harvey (1996)). I certainly do not have in mind the sterile, rigid and mechanical version of 'dialectical materialism' which became the official credo in, for instance, Romania during the Ceausescu regime.
5. Harvey (1996), Fairclough (2001c).
6. See, for instance, Chiapello and Fairclough (2002), Preoteasa (2002), Fairclough, Jessop and Sayer (2004).
7. Fairclough (2000b), Platt (1998).
8. Blair (1998c).
9. Blair (1998c).
10. Hall (1998), Marquand (1998).
11. Fairclough (2000b).
12. Barnett (1998), Hall (1998).

13. Department of Social Security (1998).
14. See Montgomery (1999) for a fuller analysis of this speech. Montgomery discusses how Blair's hesitancy and pausing in delivery may contribute to the impression that he is sincere.
15. Gould (1998).
16. Rentoul (1997).
17. MacIntyre (1985), Boltanski and Chiapello (1999), Chiapello and Fairclough (2002).
18. Bourdieu and Wacquant (2001).

15. Democracy and the public sphere in critical research on discourse[1]

In a recent study of the discourse of focus groups, Myers (1998) notes that they can be seen as experiments in constituting a public forum, which have the characteristic of constituting people as individuals bearing opinions. It is the objective of focus groups to elicit the fullest possible range of these opinions. An opinion is construed as an attribute of a person, like age, gender or region origin. The practical interest in using focus groups may be social research, but increasingly it is economic (as in market research) or political (as in the use of focus groups by parties to test their policies against public opinion – by New Labour in Britain for instance).

Myers suggests that if you analyse what actually goes on in focus groups it is difficult to sustain the idea of opinions as pre-existing attributes of individuals ready to be elicited by social scientific methods. For despite the fact that the people involved are usually strangers to each other, and despite the control exercised over the interaction by the 'moderator', things emerge in the course of and through the dialogical interaction of the participants, and these things arguably include opinions (as well as topics, identities, and so forth). It seems generally more plausible to see opinions as 'things' that are communicatively and collectively developed in interaction, rather than pre-existing attributes of individuals which are simply expressed in interaction.

How are we to interpret these experiments in public forums for the elicitation of pre-given opinions? I want to focus on their use within politics, and ask how it is related to the question – and the crisis – of the public sphere. That question can be summed up as follows: is it possible to overcome the formidable structural obstacles (such as the structural relations between mass media and other fields) in contemporary societies to people deliberating together as citizens on matters of common concern, in ways which shape the formation of policy and the directions societies take? Is it possible, that is, to reconstruct the public sphere under contemporary social conditions? For it cannot be a matter of reviving past forms of the public sphere (Athenian or early capitalist) whose structural conditions of possibility have gone.

I'll come back to the example of focus groups shortly in a circuitous way via two further questions about the public sphere: why should it be (as I believe it should) at the centre of critical social research on politics? And what specific contribution has CDA to make to that research?

I take it that critical social research has, as Habermas put it in his earlier work, a 'knowledge interest' in emancipation which is in contrast with the instrumental and technical knowledge interest of much social research – though that critical knowledge interest needs to be construed in a broad way to include the new politics of recognition as well as the old politics of emancipation (Fraser 1995). The objective is to deepen understanding of the obstacles to emancipation as well as discerning possibilities in the unrealised potential of the present. The agenda for critical research has to be ongoingly redefined as social life changes and presents people with new possibilities and constraints. I take it that critical social research at present needs to focus on the new global form of capitalism and its ideology of neo-liberalism. One formulation comes recently from Bourdieu in a series of politically engaged writings (1998a, 1998b) in which he argues that although the new economic regime projected in neo-liberal discourse is pervasively construed as immovable fact-of-life, it is rather a rational utopia for finance capital which the latter is trying to impose upon reality and make real. Obstacles to realisation – especially collective institutions with the capacity to resist, notably nation states but also, for instance, trade unions – are relentlessly dismantled or disabled. In the process the existing structures and forms of democracy are being destroyed and not being effectively replaced – for instance, national parliaments and parties are losing power and legitimacy without effective supranational replacements, e.g., within the EU. Touraine puts the problem in terms of a pincer movement on the political space: 'squeezed between a globalised economy and aggressively introverted cultures that proclaim an absolute multiculturalism implying a rejection of the other, the political space is fragmenting and democracy is being debased' (Touraine 1997: 2).

There are two provisos here. First, one can be alive to the deep flaws of contemporary democracy yet still regard the current dangers it faces with dismay – it is not a question of idealising it. Second, nation states still have considerable power if they can be persuaded to use it in concert – it has been after all reversible decisions by nation states on deregulating currency markets,

GATT, and most recently the Multilateral Agreement on Investment, that have largely shaped global capitalism.

Recent literature on the troubles of democracy (e.g., Benhabib 1996, Touraine 1997) has linked the debasement of democracy to the debasement of the public sphere, and seen the reconstruction of democracy as hinging upon the reconstruction of the public sphere. This link is not simply contemporary: it has been widely aired in the wake of Habermas's analysis of the rise and fall of the bourgeois public sphere (Habermas 1989/1962). So there are good reasons for locating the question of democracy and within that the question of the public sphere at the centre for critical social research on politics. What then is the specific contribution CDA can make to this research? The foundational work of Arendt and Habermas has made it clear that the question of the public sphere is centrally – though as I shall argue shortly, not exclusively – the question of what discursive practices, what forms of dialogue, are available for civic deliberation. What CDA can contribute is a linguistically and semiotically sophisticated but still socially framed understanding of the properties of practices of public dialogue. This can help in evaluating existing practices and discerning potential alternatives from the perspective of the public sphere. There are three broad contributions CDA can make: (a) describing the dynamic structuring of social orders of discourse in ways which locate diverse discursive practices of the public sphere in relation to other discursive practices and to each other, and the tendencies of insulation and flow affecting those locations; (b) analysing particular discursive practices (actions) conjuncturally in terms of their selective interdiscursive articulation of practices (permanencies) from across social orders of discourse; (c) providing a framework for 'internal' analysis of any particular discursive practice which highlights properties germane to their functioning within the public sphere. I should add that just as democracy and the public sphere are at the centre of critical social research on politics, so also they should in my view be at the centre of critical analysis of political discourse.

CDA is always by implication a critique of certain discursive practices in favour of alternative practices – though the alternatives are usually left implicit. In this case, an explicit identification of properties which make for effective public sphere dialogue is called for. Where do we get these from? For present purposes, I am going to short-circuit the process and draw upon Hannah Arendt's account of the public sphere – I will explain that choice shortly. But I also want to suggest a more satisfactory process which goes to the heart of what CDA is about. I see CDA as a theoretical practice which produces theoretically based accounts of a range of other social practices with a focus on discourse, in a way that is informed by emancipatory struggles within those practices, and oriented to generating resources for those struggles whose uptake depends upon the practical politics of those practices. CDA neither invents problems nor produces solutions. In the particular case of the public sphere, both a critique of what is and a sense of what is needed are produced within the practical political struggles of the social practices CDA theorises; that is where we should ultimately look for a sense of what properties dialogue needs in order to work within the public sphere.

Let me return briefly to focus groups before discussing Arendt. I just want to make two comments. First, political uses of focus groups might be seen as attempts to stimulate and simulate public sphere dialogue which are apparently in some cases at least also attempts to legitimise parts of the political system at a point where its legitimacy is seriously compromised. Is this a move to systemically colonise the public sphere? Secondly, however, Myers's analysis suggests as we have seen that despite this participants in focus groups are dialogically productive of topics, knowledges and opinions, evoking Arendt's observation that public spheres can be constituted in the most unpromising of circumstances, 'wherever men (sic) are together in the manner of speech and action' (Arendt 1958), even in this case perhaps where the action they are jointly embarked upon is cooperatively producing 'opinions' for mediators.

My reason for drawing more on Arendt than Habermas is that although Arendt's political theory has major weaknesses which Habermas himself among others has pointed to (Habermas 1977, d'Entreves 1994), it is also suggestive of ways of overcoming some of the problems which have been identified in Habermas's work on the public sphere by feminists and others (Benhabib 1992, 1996, Calhoun 1992, Meehan 1995). The following is a summary in point form of questions which have come out of recent debates on the public sphere which are by implication critical of Habermas's foundational work on the bourgeois public sphere.

1. Are there not many public spheres rather than one? But if so, how is dialogue achieved between them?
2. Isn't the line between public and private (as witnessed by the emergence within public spheres of 'private' issues such as sexuality) inherently problematic?
3. Are public spheres just for reaching consensus? Are they not in culturally diverse contemporary societies also about constituting and negotiating identities, winning recognition, etc.?
4. Is not democratic dialogue a pervasive need in contemporary societies, for instance in work and personal relationships as well as politics (Giddens 1994)?

5. Don't we need pubic spheres at various levels of social organisation, including now international and even global public spheres? How could they work?
6. Is the public sphere just a matter of talk or also a matter of action, people acting together to change the world?

I shall proceed as follows. First, I summarise Arendt's account of the public sphere drawing on d'Entreves (1994). Second, drawing on Arendt, Habermas, past work in CDA, and Bernstein's work on pedagogic discourse (1990, 1996), I shall sketch out a framework for critical discourse analysis of public sphere discourse. Third, I shall briefly illustrate it with an example. Fourth, I shall argue equally briefly that discourse analytical research on European identity should focus upon the emergence of a European public sphere, and obstacles to that process.

1 Arendt on the public sphere

Arendt contrasts action with labour and work: 'Labour is judged by its ability to sustain human life, work is judged by its ability to build and maintain a world fit for human use and for human enjoyment, and action is judged by its ability to disclose the identity of the agent, to affirm the reality of the world, to actualize our capacity for freedom and to endow our existence with meaning.' (D'Entreves 1994: 65–66). D'Entreves's summary of how these different activities are evaluated suggests the primacy given to action by Arendt. Action has two essential features: it instantiates freedom, in the sense of the capacity to do the unexpected, to create; and it presupposes plurality – it inherently involves other people, and, moreover, instantiates a dialectic between what they have in common and what makes each individual unique. Action inherently goes with speech – it involves in another terminology a reflexive loop through which discursive constructions of action are part of action. Action is based upon consent between participants, and speech figures within it as persuasion. Action is the locus of power, which Arendt understands as the capacity of people to act in concert for public–political purposes, and which depends upon the synthesis of action with speech already alluded to. This 'living power of the people' is the source of legitimacy for public institutions – without it they petrify and decay. In action/speech, people 'disclose' themselves, 'reveal actively their unique personal identities and thus make their appearance in the human world', not in the sense of showing what is already there but in the sense of only becoming who one is through action with others. The stories that people tell about action retrospectively determines meanings and identities, as well ensuring the remembrance of action and so its capacity to be a resource for the future. Action is unpredictable in its outcomes, and this applies with respect to the individual and collective identities that are disclosed in action. It is only through action that people develop the judgement, the capacity to see things 'not from one's own point of view but in the perspective of all those who happen to be present', which converts mere opinions into public discourses.

The public sphere is defined by on the one hand being based in a shared world, 'a world in common', and on the other hand by the emergence of 'spaces of appearance' understood as both shared spaces and shared practices 'wherever men are together in the manner of speech and action'. Modernity has undermined the 'world in common' through its one-sided emphasis on labour and economic production, so we are now faced with the task of trying to reconstruct the public sphere. Spaces of appearance are contingent, often short-lived, and can emerge in the most unlikely places and circumstances. Political action in the public sphere is based in a logic of identity – it crucially involves not negotiation between pre-given identities but the ongoing construction of a 'we', a collective identity.

Let me very briefly identify some virtues of this account of the public sphere in the light of recent debates. First, it firmly links speech to action and to power. Second, it focuses on the emergence of collective and individual identities. Third, in its view of plurality it suggests a dialectic of universal and particular, collective and individual identities. There are also as I have indicated a number of problems. There is, as D'Entreves puts it, an unresolved duality between two theories of action in Arendt's political theory, an expressive theory in which the emphasis is on the disclosure of individual identities, and a communicative theory where the emphasis is upon the collective nature of action; and this duality carries over into Arendt's view of the public sphere (as a dramatic setting for outstanding individuals, or as a discursive space) and citizenship (as heroic, or participatory). The expressive tendency in the theory has led to charges of elitism. And Habermas (1977) has argued that Arendt's Aristotelian separation of action from labour and work leads to the political being exclusively seen as praxis, action in the public sphere, losing sight of the strategic, structural dimensions of politics and its links to the economic and the social.

2 Framework for CDA of the public sphere

Drawing on Arendt and other sources I mentioned earlier, I propose in summary form five analytical focuses, the first four of which constitute the basis for evaluating particular discursive practices as public sphere dialogue. The fifth locates public sphere discursive practices within social orders of discourse.

1. A discursive practice as a regulative practice.
2. A discursive practice as a space of emergence.
3. A discursive practice as a principle of recontextualisation.
4. A discursive practice as a constituent of action.
5. Public sphere discursive practices within social orders of discourse.

2.1 A discursive practice as a regulative practice

The first focus links to the concern in Habermas's work on the public sphere with the procedural properties of public sphere communication. The concern is to specify the regulative properties of a discursive practice in the sense of how contributions are controlled. I use here Bernstein's concepts of classification and framing (1990, 1996). Classification is a matter of which categories (which discourses, subjects, voices) are included in a practice, and of whether they are strongly or weakly insulated from each other – whether the classification is strong or weak. Framing is a matter of how interaction is managed – if it is jointly managed then framing is weak, if it is asymmetrically managed then framing is strong. Effective public space dialogue entails a regulative practice which is maximally open to diverse discourses and subjects, where insulations between these categories are weak, and where there is jointly managed control of interaction, i.e., weak framing. The sociological categories of classification and framing translate into the discourse analytical categories of genre, discourse and voice (or style) – what I mean by that is that working in a transdisciplinary way (Halliday 1993, Fairclough 1997) as opposed to a merely interdisciplinary way means that the logic of one theory can be put to work within (the logic of) another without the one being reduced to the other. It means for instance that discourse analytical conceptions of genre are enriched by thinking genre in terms of Bernstein's categories, as Chouliaraki has shown (1998).

2.2 A discursive practice as a space of emergence

Looking at discursive practices as regulative practices is a familiar exercise in CDA, looking at them as spaces of emergence is perhaps less so. Working from Arendt's concept of disclosure, the point is to assess to what degree individual and collective identities, social relations, and knowledges are collectively constituted in dialogue. Public space dialogue has this property of joint production, emergence. Referring specifically to identities, Touraine (1997) like Arendt suggests a dialectic of individual and collective identities, but with a further differentiation of universal and particular moments of collective identity. The suggestion is that in effective public sphere dialogue there is a process of becoming in which people's individual identities, their collective identities as members of particular and diverse groups, and their universal identities-in-common as citizens and human beings are collectively constituted simultaneously through a complex weaving together of different facets of the self.

2.3 A discursive practice as a principle of recontextualisation

The concepts of recontextualisation and recontextualising principle are also taken from Bernstein (1990, 1996). Particular discursive practices assimilate other discursive practices in ways which are specific to them – they have their own distinctive principles of recontextualisation. Recontextualised practices are always transformed, but the particular ways they are transformed depend upon the specific logic, the recontextualising principle, of the recontextualising practice. Bernstein suggests that in being recontextualised, discursive practices are cut off from their embeddedness in action and transformed into discourses which are articulated together in new ways according to the logic of the recontextualising practice; and transformed from real to imaginary, and brought into the space of ideology.

I am introducing the concept of recontextualisation here as a way of addressing the question I briefly raised earlier about the implications of accepting that there are many public spaces: how then are diverse public spheres brought in relation with each other? I want to suggest that certain public sphere discursive practices recontextualise others. The point is of particular relevance in relation to what Habermas has referred to as the 'abstract', mediated public spheres of especially television, which extensively recontextualise others. The issue here is one of the 'terms of exchange' when different public spheres are brought together: the concept of recontextualisation draws attention to the transformations, reductions, and ideological appropriations public spaces may undergo – for instance, to the price social movements may have to pay for the privileges of accessing the virtual public spheres of television. Actually there is a complementarity between the concept of recontextualisation and the concept of 'colonisation', associated with Habermas (1984): the former focuses on the bringing of external practices into the space of the recontextualising practice, the latter on the incursion into a particular practice of external practices. As against both, the focus on effective public sphere discourse seeks to specify how different discursive practices might be dialogically hybridised to form a new practice which is reductive of neither.

2.4 A discursive practice as a constituent of action

Arendt says that 'power is actualised only where word and deed have not parted company, where words are not empty and deeds not brutal'. The danger of empty words is a real one in respect of the public sphere. Effective public sphere discourse is a constituent of action and tied into power in Arendt's sense, but much dialogue-in-public seems more like 'mere words'. We need a theoretical and analytical apparatus here such as the one proposed by Harvey in his discussion of the 'dialectics of discourse' (1996 – see also Hennessy 1993): discourse is one moment in the social process, others are material practices, power, social relations, institutions/rituals, and beliefs/desires/ values; these moments are in a dialectic; discourse internalises all the other moments, so it is possible and fruitful to analyse discourse as power, as insti- tution, as material practice etc.; and all other moments internalise discourse; but no moment is reducible to any other. This framework can be combined with the concept of articulation (Laclau and Mouffe 1985). Analysis of any social practice involves showing the practice of articulation which structures it: how discourse is articulated with non-discursive moments; how each of these moments is articulated from relative permanencies which constitute resources for action (in the case of discourse: genres, discourses, voice or style); how different social agents with different resources are conjuncturally articulated together within a particular social activity. A public sphere is not just discourse, it is an articulation of diverse moments within which discourse constitutes an effective constituent of action.

2.5 Public sphere discursive practices within social orders of discourse

Current thinking stresses the diversity of public spheres along various dimen- sions. Habermas, for instance, in a recent book (Habermas 1996) differentiates between episodic (e.g., transitory conversations in bars), occasional (e.g., public meetings) and abstract (i.e., mediated, virtual, where people are not physically co-present) public spheres; and as I suggested earlier we need to conceive of global or international as well as national and more local public spheres. A contribution CDA can make is not only in tracing the diversity of forms of public sphere but also in specifying how these practices are located within orders of discourse in relation to other discursive practices – for instance, how public sphere discursive practices are dispersed within the complex network of diverse discursive practices in television, not only in terms of for instance questions of sequencing and scheduling, but also in terms of embedding relations (e.g., the incidence of public sphere discursive practices within soaps), and in terms of the representations of diverse public spheres both within and outside television in different television genres (e.g., news programmes, comedy programmes). CDA can also specify intertextual chain relations which connect public sphere discursive practices with for instance discursive practices within the political system – what systematic relations of transformation 'carry' public space discourse into other discursive practices. This is one factor in the embedding of discourse within action, and it also connects to the concept of recontextualisation. CDA is not concerned with producing static representations of structural relations – there is an orientation towards the dynamism of orders of discourse, to flows between different public sphere discursive practices, but also to shifting relations between public sphere discourse and other discursive practices (bearing in mind for instance Giddens contention (1994) that 'dialogical democracy' now transcends divisions between political, economic and intimate spheres). Finally, there is a concern throughout with reflexivity – with how representations of the discursive practices of the public sphere are reflexively assimilated into and transform these practices.

3 Example: *monarchy – the nation decides*

A number of changes in the mode of operation of the British monarchy were announced in March 1998. According to a *Times* report:

> The Palace has long accepted the need for a change of style; but there are three main factors behind the present flurry of activity. The first is a Blair Government intent on creating a 'people's monarchy'; the second is the wave of public dissatisfaction at the present monarchical style after the death of Diana, Princess of Wales; and the third is a series of 'focus group' discussions held with members of the public by MORI, which showed that the monarchy was widely held to be too distant and to have too many unnecessary trappings. (*The Times*, 9 March 98)

We might gloss the three factors referred to here as: government policy, action in the public sphere, and opinions elicited in a simulated public sphere (focus groups). The death of Diana appears to have been marked by the conjunctural emergence of an abstract public sphere in Habermas's sense (as well as episodic and occasional public spheres). Its scale and dispersion make it difficult to discern in detail, but there was an articulation of speech and action which has had material effects.

My example (an extract from which is transcribed in the Appendix, pages 407–11) stands somewhat outside that, but it does make the point that the remarkable reaction to the death of Diana did not come out of nowhere. It is a much-publicised two-hour long TV 'debate' on the future of the monarchy which was simultaneously a 'referendum' by telephone on the question 'Do you want a monarchy?' ('debate' and 'referendum' are the producers' self-descriptions). It was unprecedented in publicly raising this question, but also experimental in format ('the biggest live debate ever staged on television', according to the journalist who anchored the programme), and there are suggestions that it was seen as a straw-in-the-wind for some form of 'electronic democracy' which would raise again the question of simulation of the public sphere. There were sharp criticisms of the format from participants during the course of it ('this is not debate, it is licensed cock-fighting') and subsequently in the media.

The format is based upon rapid and carefully scheduled and timed shifts between the following elements:

Openings and closings from the 'anchor' in the studio
Filmed reports by 'columnists'
Studio panel of 'experts' etc. 'crossing swords'
Studio reporter: results of a public opinion poll about the monarchy
Polls of opinions of studio audience (presented by 'anchor')
Reporter soliciting studio audience members' opinions
Commercial breaks.

The introduction to the programme (Extract 1 in the Appendix, page 407) depicts it in terms of the audience casting their votes after rationally weighing up the evidence and opinions and arguments provided in the programme – in fact, the rational sequence of deliberation then action was practically impossible given that all votes had to be cast before the programme ended, and the lines were jammed from the moment it started. There is also an implication ('we'll be assessing the outcome and asking what the royals should do next') that the referendum is a part of a process of constitutional change, and may thus have material effects. Thus the programme seems to claim to be constituting a public sphere drawing citizens into speech and action. How do its claims stand up to scrutiny – and how, in particular, does it rate as public sphere discourse in terms of the framework I have suggested? I shall just briefly comment on the first four analytical focuses within the framework.

3.1 Regulative practice

The programme is broadly characterised by weak classification and strong framing – notably in the panel of experts (Extract 2) and the soliciting of audience opinions (Extract 3). The classification is weak in the sense that a wide range of discourses, subjects and voices are assembled, and insulations between them are generally weak – so, for instance, the audience includes many celebrities who might equally have been on the panel, and the panel includes columnists who produce filmed reports; on another level, Roger Cook who chairs the panel shifts between chairing a debate, conducting interviews, cross-questioning a witness, and aggressively challenging an antagonist in argument – and this articulation of diverse positions entails an interdiscursively hybrid discourse. Carpignano *et al.* (1990) seem to have weak classification in mind in their upbeat assessment of the democratic potential of the television chat show:

> More than any other television genres the new talk shows exemplify the transformation of these relationships (i.e., between performance and audience) which radically shifts the framework within which the apparatuses of mass communication and popular culture operate. They call into question the very structure of the separation between production and consumption of cultural products, they problematize the distinction between expert and audience, professional authority and layperson. Ultimately they constitute a 'contested space' in which new discursive practices are developed in contrast to the traditional modes of political and ideological representation.

But what their analysis overlooks is that weak classification in such shows is generally accompanied by strong framing (though there are cases where framing is weakened), which means that the dynamics of the interaction are not under the joint control of its participants. Where this is the case, claims about democratisation have to be treated with caution. In this case, the strong framing is linked to the elaborate format and the time pressure this generates, which is in turn linked to the pressure to make the programme work aesthetically as an entertainment in the context of a competitive market – journalists often refer to the pressure on time and are constantly trying to curtail contributions and move on.[2] But another aspect of framing is control of topic: in neither the panel nor the elicitation of audience views are contributors allowed to decide for themselves what aspects of the topic of debate to address; they are asked by the journalists to address specific topics.[3] In the elicitation of audience views, this means that contributions are disconnected – there is virtually no dialogical connection between them. We are back to eliciting pre-given opinions – the programme indeed celebrates the rich variety of opinions assembled, and actually construes this disconnected airing of opinions as 'debate'. But debate only takes place – in the panel – in so far as participants ignore the control of contributions built into its exchange system.[4] This illustrates again that people do manage to come into dialogue even in the most unfavourable of circumstances. But Roger Cook does let this happen to an extent – the breaking of the rules of exchange makes for a good televisual spectacle.

3.2 Space of emergence

Emergence requires dialogue, and since the strong framing of this programme inhibits dialogue there is little by way of emergence. Take the emergence of collective identities. There is no space for the emergence of a 'we' in the disconnecting elicitation of audience opinions. There is, one might say, the emergence of a 'we' in the studio audience through their collective reactions to contributions (applause, shouting, jeering etc.), sometimes a matter of taking collective reactive action through the limited options available to show their frustration with the programme. But this is tenuous and marginal. This is not otherwise a space in which people acting and talking together can collectively constitute identities, relations or knowledges. In that sense it is not a public space.

Principle of recontextualisation

I want to focus here on one contribution in the elicitation of audience views in Extract 3, including the journalist's elicitation and response.

> *John Stapleton*: OK . gentleman over here gentleman over here in our Manchester camp you said e: no these scandals haven't damaged the country's reputation why do you take that view
> *Audience 2*: for the simple reason (unclear) for centuries the ordinary working class out there couldn't care less what royalty do they've got more to think about trying to make ends meet find a job than worry about what the royal family's doing
> *John Stapleton*: OK let me let me introduce you all to someone who I suspect we could describe as Britain's most ardent royal family

The audience member here ('Audience 2') is a working-class man from Manchester. I want to focus on his contribution because of its apparent incoherence – it's not obvious how it coherently connects with the discourse it is embedded within, or how it coherently answers the question the journalist puts to him. The point is that to see it as a coherent contribution requires some understanding of a practice which this fragment is recontextualised out of and uprooted from – a local working-class practice of public sphere discourse whose spaces are localities of face-to-face, small group interaction (pubs, trade union meetings etc.) which is not easily, or comfortably, recontextualised within an abstract televisual public sphere. Expressions which can appear to be merely empty clichés if we see this only as an individual audience member's contribution to this programme (*couldn't care less, more to think about, trying to make ends meet*) appear rather as condensations of a particular life experience from the perspective of the public sphere they originate from. I would suggest that one aspect of the recontextualising principle of television is that it generally selects for recontextualisation those practices which are relatively easy to assimilate into its own, which, of course, is also a principle of exclusion.

One rarely comes across recontextualisation of this sort of public sphere discourse in serious political television. It is also evident from this example how recontextualisation works ideologically: this fragment slides easily onto an old media stereotype of the northern working man – quaint, colourful, but not making much sense. A general observation on this programme – and this is an aspect of its strong framing – is that it ruthlessly converts practices into discourses which it assembles according to its own logic and purpose (including the eliciting of opinions). There is no space for the coming together of different public spaces and practices of public space discourse in a mutually exploratory, dialogical way.

Discourse as a constituent of action

We might wonder in what sense there is action at issue here, in that this is not a matter of people coming together 'in the manner of speech and action', but being brought together within an ostensibly political event which is, of course, also an entertainment and in a broad sense an aesthetic event. But as I have indicated, people can produce action in the most unpromising of circumstances, though this happens here only in marginal ways I have referred to above.

This programme does not rate very highly as public sphere discourse. But it does raise the question of what the object of research should be here – where one should look to find the abstract public sphere Habermas refers to. In so far as there are public spheres associated with the broadcast media, should we not be looking for them not just within television or radio programmes but also within the practices those programmes enter into? How do people use television programmes like this? What do they do with them? Modern societies are increasingly mediated societies, and if we think of that in discoursal terms it means that people live their lives in what Dorothy Smith has called 'textually-mediated' ways (Smith 1990). This would imply that in constituting public spheres people bring to the conjunctural assembly of persons and resources a range of mediated including televised practices which they in turn recontextualise as discourses. This points to a complex dialectic of colonisation and appropriation which ties together abstract public spheres and more local (episodic, occasional) public spheres: the latter are resources for mediation, but they also appropriate mediated practices as resources for their own.

4 Conclusion

I shall conclude by linking the question of public space and the public sphere to the question of European identity, with reference to some observations of Bourdieu (1998a) which contrast the project of a neo-liberal Europe, a banker's Europe, with a 'really European' Europe in terms which connect with the question of public space:

> Resistance to the banker's Europe . . . can only be European. And it can only be really European, in the sense of freed from interests, assumptions, prejudices and habits of thought that are national and still vaguely nationalistic, if it is the deed of all Europeans, in other words a concerted combination of intellectuals from all the European countries, of trade unions from all the European countries, and of the most diverse associations from all the European countries. That is why the most urgent task at the moment is not the composition of common European programmes, but the creation of institutions – parliaments, international federations, European associations of this or that: truckers, publishers, teachers, and so forth, but also defenders of trees, fish, mushrooms, pure air, children and all the rest – within which some common European programmes can be discussed and elaborated.

Although he does not use the term, the task Bourdieu is prioritising here is the creation of European public spheres. From this point of view, the European identities essential to a 'really European Europe' can only emerge from the large-scale involvement of people from the European countries in public spheres on a European scale, perhaps ultimately at a higher level a unitary European public sphere (as an articulation of particular public spheres). It is upon this process and the obstacles to it that a critical discursively oriented analysis European identity should perhaps centre.

APPENDIX

The following sample from the TV programme *Monarchy – the Nation Decides* includes the opening of the programme by the 'anchor' Trevor McDonald (Extract 1), extracts from the studio panel of 'experts' chaired by Roger Cook (Extract 2), and a reporter, John Stapleton, soliciting audience opinions (Extract 3).

Extract 1

Trevor McDonald: welcome to *Monarchy – the Nation Decides* – good evening . there's only one thing the country's been talking about and that's this programme and your role . in the future of the monarchy . it's been headline news for the past week . and that shows the importance of your vote . at home . tonight we're inviting you to take part in a unique royal referendum . these two telephone numbers will stay on screen throughout the programme . as we ask . do you want a monarchy . we'll be examining the costs, the benefits, the scandals and analysing the most comprehesive opinion poll ever undertaken . on the royal family – gathered here tonight hand-picked is the biggest studio audience ever assembled . they too will be canvassed for their views in a series of instant polls . and to help you decide we have exclusive reports from some of the country's top columnists . like the *Mirror*'s royal-watcher James Whittaker Andrew Neale former editor of the *Sunday Times* and the king of gossip columnists Nigel Dempster of the *Daily Mail* . . .
that then is the challenge for the next ninety minutes and after *News at Ten* which I won't be doing tonight we'll be assessing the outcome and asking what the royals should do next now though we ask how deep is the crisis facing the House of Windsor our first report comes from a royal correspondent for three decades the *Mirror*'s James Whittaker

Extract 2

Roger Cook: Stephen Haseler as chairman of the Republican Movement e do you as James Whittaker suggests e: are you about to lead the storming the ramparts
Stephen Haseler: no we're not going to storm anything but we – we're increasingly em attracting more and more people to our cause and republicanism is now on the agenda of British politics really for the first time since the nineteenth century this <audience: 'rubbish'> show is an is an example of that and

republicanism can only grow but contrary to James Whittaker who has spent most of his life prying into the royals poking around them and now wants to defend them contrary to him I don't think that the issue is simply the scandals of the royal family e: there have been enough of those we have an insensitive Prince and so on that's not the real issue the real issue I think is that the British public are increasingly wanting to choose their next head of state (unclear)

Roger Cook: that they may well do and that they may get a chance to indicate this evening – Frederick Forsyth is the monarchy . in terminal decline

Frederick Forsyth: no I don't think it is e:m it's going through an extremely troubled period that actually has happened oh twenty thirty forty fifty times . in the course of em the the monarchic history of this country which goes back nearly a thousand years e: it's been troubled e:m these past few years but I think that one has to get one thing quite certain if we are talking about . the royal family OK I don't know what we are talking about on this programme by the way but I'd like you to adjudicate are we talking about the royal family because if we are OK . there are thirty five members of them all descended from three dukes

Roger Cook: we're talking about the monarchy

Frederick Forsyth: right or are we talking about the monarchy if we're talking about the monarchy and the monarch then let's do that let's talk about a magnificent Queen who has been forty four years a monarch and put no foot wrong . you sir are not British . you are not (unclear) Mr Haseler . (*SH*: this country) because every family every family with thirty five members in it in this country has got a couple . (*SH*: th-) that they really would prefer not to have

Stephen Haseler: this country is not no no

Roger Cook: the Queen the Queen can't reign for ever we have to look forward . and that's where that's where the problems lie surely

Frederick Forsyth: no no no let's be let's be realistic the Queen

SH: we   we're facing Frederick we're facing Charles the Third the real reason

RC: hold on hold on

FF: you're not facing (unclear)   you're not facing anything

SH: the real reason why this programme's on and why republicanism is growing is because we're facing the prospect of Charles the Third now I admit when the Queen

FF: when when

SH: I'll tell you I'll tell you when the Queen when the Queen when the Queen

FF: you haven't the faintest idea

SH: came to the throne she came with a united country when Charles the Third takes over he is going to divide this country and that is why people are now thinking about this issue and they want to choose their next head of state they don't want

FF: no

SH: him imposed on them

Peter Hitchens: a fat a fat lot Stephen a fat lot Stephen Haseler cares about dividing this country if his movement is successful the country will be divided exposed to all kinds of dangers and left unprotected the the monarchy the monarchy is one of our human rights in this country it it defends it defends this country against people who want to tear away tradition property the family (someone on the panel laughs) loyalty honour all the things that are fundamental as far as human nature is

RC: is that right Claire is that right Claire Rayner

PH: concerned

Claire Rayner: it is it is precisely the reverse it is because the people of this country want want to have the freedom to be citizens rather than subjects of a particular individual

PH: but we are

CR: we want

PH: we are citizens in this country

CR: no listen please

PH: Claire we're among we're among the freest people we're among the freest people in the world

CR: forgive me we are not we are not the freest

PH: we've been so free for so long that we don't realise (unclear)

CR: we have so much secrecy so much deference so much bowing and scraping

RC: Roz Miles what does history tell you about this . Claire

CR: that's what we must get rid of

RC: Roz Miles what does history tell you about this

PH: what the republicans what the republicans want to do is to use (Roz Miles: British history) the popularity of Princess Diana (*RC*: hold on hold on) as a battering ram against the institution they hate

RC: right Roz Miles please

Extract 3

John Stapleton: OK let's find out some views behind those votes from our audience here and on the day when the Queen has been to Sandringham

where better to start than th- with our friends from East Anglia you said yes
you did think that these scandals have e damaged the country's reputation why
do you take that view

Audience 1: well I think like any scandal presidents of the United States these
scandals have damaged and reflected badly on our country what we're doing
here and what Mr S- people like Mr Starkie are doing is turning it our monarchy into some kind of royal soap opera trivialising it we've got the Duchess
of York being referred to as Fergie and we're not really addressing the issues
the royal family is not a soap opera and I think we ought to raise the level of
debate and that's the real problem here we've lowered it to real guttersnipe
gutter street level

John Stapleton: OK . gentleman over here gentleman over here in our
Manchester camp you said e: no> these scandals haven't damaged the country's reputation why do you take that view

Audience 2: for the simple reason (unclear) for centuries the ordinary working
class out there couldn't care less what royalty do they've got more to think
about trying to make ends meet find a job than worry about what the royal
family's doing

John Stapleton: OK let me let me introduce you all to someone who I suspect
we could describe as Britain's most ardent royal family you'll know what I
mean when you look around Margaret Tyler's rather remarkable house

FILM INSERT *Margaret Tyler voice-over*: well I have actually got the Queen and
the Duke on my balcony waving to the neighbours of course and sometimes
you can find me sitting on the throne I have to say I suppose you could call me
Queen Margaret of North Wembley I just collect everything about the royal
family and I really love them Charles and Diana are my very favourite couple
and I absolutely loved their wedding day and I do think that one day they
might just get back together again

JS: well . well Queen of North Wembley there was a mixture of cheers and
jeers there do you really mean that

MT: I would like it to happen very much

JS: I think you might be the only person in the
audience who would Alan Aherst down here former Conservative MP is your
place a shrine to the royal family

AA: no it isn't the Qu- the Queen is the head of the Church of England she's
the richest woman in the world she's the head of a rotten class-ridden corrupt political and social establishment which is directly responsible for this
nation's dreadful decline I have no problem with that lady's royal nick-nacks
but I am just saddened that she should want to glorify people who are basically
parasites and hypocrites

JS: isn't it a rather . if you don't mind me saying so isn't it a rather odd posture for a former Tory MP
AA: no I've seen the light this is the truth she is a symbol of everything that is rotten about this country and the sooner we get rid of her the better
JS: OK just . just a . cheers jeers and boos just a taste of our audience's views lots more later on

Notes

1. This is a revised version of Fairclough 1999 which also draws upon Fairclough 1998.
2. The journalists sometimes refer directly to these time pressures (Roger Cook: *you've got ten seconds Andrew, I'm afraid I'm going to have to stop you there*) or to the number of people waiting to contribute. Notice that time constraints are sometimes worded with modalities which convey externally imposed obligations (Roger Cook: *I'm going to have to stop you there*, and referring to a shift to the MORI poll *we have to pause for a moment*). Moreover, Roger Cook and John Stapleton are constantly working to control pacing, especially to limit the time taken by contributors – Cook for instance repeatedly tries (not always successfully) to move to the next contributor before the current one has finished (for instance, he makes several attempts to close down the argument between Peter Hitchens and Claire Rayner and bring in Roz Miles on 'what history tells you' – see Extract 2 in the Appendix).
3. Trevor McDonald orchestrates major topical shifts through the programme in terms of framing questions (e.g., *How deep in the crisis facing the House of Windsor? Money and the monarchy: are they worth it?*), but both Roger Cook and John Stapleton exercise lower-level topic control in inviting particular people not to just contribute to the debate but to address particular topics.
4. As in a formal debate, Cook distributes and controls access to the floor, but this repeatedly breaks down as the panel members argue, interrupt, shout each other down, etc. (for instance the sequences in Extract 2 involving Frederick Forsyth and Stephen Haseler, Claire Rayner and Peter Hitchins).

16. Critical discourse analysis and citizenship

Norman Fairclough, Simon Pardoe and Bronislaw Szerszynski

1 Researching citizenship

How does one empirically research the phenomenon of 'citizenship'? And how does one do so when notions of 'citizen' and 'citizenship' are highly contested in both theory and practice? The many recent contributions from political theory, sociology and other disciplines to the reconceptualisation of citizenship tend to draw only indirectly on empirical research, and are predominantly normative in character. Against this background, it is useful to attend more closely to the practices of citizenship 'on the ground'. The PARADYS project was therefore concerned with empirically researching and theorising 'the ways in which participants themselves act and are treated by others as citizens' (Bora and Hausendorf 2001: 4). In particular, the project focused on 'citizenship . . . as an ongoing communicative achievement' (Bora *et al.* 2001: 3), and particularly how concepts of citizenship are deployed in 'the dynamics of social positioning' (Bora and Hausendorf 2000: 1).

One way of reading this emphasis on citizenship as a communicative achievement is that it is an attempt to get us away from preconceptions about what citizenship *is*, and to force us to look at how it's *done* – at the range of ways in which people position themselves and others as citizens in participatory events. However, the contrast between preconception and practice, between the theoretical and the empirical, is not so simple. To illustrate this, let us take, as an example, the first participatory event that the present authors recorded as part of the PARADYS research – a local public meeting called by a parish council, held in a village hall near a GM crop site, with three speakers from key organisations involved in the procedures and the wider public debate.

In many ways this was clearly a public sphere event – an occasion where individuals formally gather together to debate and/or hear about issues of public concern. Yet during the meeting there was no evidence that participants were themselves working explicitly with the categories of 'citizen' or 'citizenship'. The participants certainly did not use these terms, though they did use other terms one might think of as related, such as 'consultation'. Even without using these terms, the participants were nevertheless interacting in ways which analysts might see as the ongoing communicative achievement of citizenship. So where is this analytical category of 'citizenship' coming from? Whose category is it?

In the next section we explore this question, and draw out some implications for the way that participatory events should be studied in order to understand the ways in which citizenship is enacted within them. We begin with the problem, as addressed by Bourdieu, of constructing the 'object of research' (in this case, 'citizenship' within and around the procedures for the Field Scale Trials of GM crops). We argue that constructing citizenship as an object of research entails (i) recognising ontologically the dialectic between preconstructions of citizenship and the performance of citizenship within everyday practice, and (ii) recognising epistemologically the dialectic between theoretical insights on citizenship and empirical research practice, or 'method'.

Building on a version of critical discourse analysis (CDA),[1] we then present an analytical framework for this empirical research of citizenship as a communicative achievement. The intention behind our developing this framework was to suggest a methodological and theoretical approach which would involve a dialectical relationship between theory and method, able to bridge the linguistic and sociological dimensions of the project, but would still be able to accommodate different repertoires of linguistic-analytic tools for micro-analysis.

2   Constructing the object of research

In a discussion of the construction of the 'objects of research', Pierre Bourdieu notes that:

> most of the time, researchers take as objects of research the problems of social order and domestication posed by more or less arbitrarily defined populations, produced through the successive partitioning of an initial category that is itself pre-constructed: the 'elderly,' the 'young' 'immigrants', . . . The first and most pressing scientific priority, in all such cases, would be *to take as one's object the social work of construction of the pre-constructed object.*
>
> (Bourdieu and Wacquant 1992: 229, italics in the original)

Here Bourdieu is saying that, rather than researchers simply operationalising a term such as 'immigrants' in their research (by, for example,
locating immigrants and interviewing and characterising them), part of the
research process should involve identifying and characterising the processes
whereby the term 'immigrants' has been given determinate and/or functional meaning. This shift away from simply using socially pre-constructed
categories or objects, towards exploring the practices involved in their construction and maintenance, is commonplace in disciplines and approaches
germane to the PARADYS research, such as science studies and discourse
analysis.

As Bourdieu puts it, the 'construction of the object' is 'no doubt the most
crucial research operation and yet the most completely ignored'. The conventional sociological division between theory and methodology should be
'completely rejected':

> the most 'empirical' technical choices cannot be disentangled from the
> most 'theoretical' choices in the construction of the object. It is only as
> a function of a definite construction of the object that such a sampling
> method, such a technique of data collection and analysis, etc., becomes
> imperative. More precisely, it is only as a function of a body of hypotheses
> derived from a set of theoretical presuppositions that any empirical datum
> can function as a proof or, as Anglo-American scholars put it, as *evidence*.
> (Bourdieu and Wacquant 1992: 225, italics in the original)

Since 'citizenship' would seem to be such a pre-constructed object, what
would it mean to follow Bourdieu's advice? If we were to explore the processes
whereby 'citizenship' has been given some determinate and/or functional
meaning (however implicit), this would take us into the fields of government
and law, as well as into academic theory and research. Yet it would be a mistake
to see the conceptions of citizenship emanating from those fields either as
'finished products', or as simply being taken up and acted out by individuals
in those situations where they are called upon to act as citizens. If we were to
trace historically the social work of construction of this pre-constructed
object, we would find an iterative relationship between these fields and wider
social practices (such as public participation) where citizenship is enacted.
These iterative relationships might be thought of in general terms in two ways
– as governance relationships (between governing and governed fields), and
as theory/practice relationships (between theoretical and practical fields).
And, of course, governing and theoretical fields are themselves intricately
interconnected.

It is perhaps useful here to illustrate this iterative relationship between governing and governed, and to show the ways in which conceptions/ pre-constructions of citizenship may be very implicit and highly embedded within social practices. The discourses,[2] practices and materialities of governance inevitably make available to people a range of resources out of which specific instances of 'citizenship' can be assembled. Administrative and legal discourses, as well as popular culture, provide a range of ways of thinking and talking about oneself as a citizen. Diverse practices such as voting and referenda, letters to newspapers or MPs, jury duty, civil and criminal procedures, public inquiries and other participatory events, marches and demonstrations, provide practice-specific meanings and experiences that can evoke the label of 'citizenship'. A range of material objects and spaces such as public buildings and parks, passports and driving licences, tax returns, and even private property can be seen as a material correlate or condensation of citizenship. All of these resources add up to a 'banal citizenship' that parallels what Michael Billig (1995) calls 'banal nationalism' – a pervasive but unremarked set of Discourses, practices and materialities that in different ways serve as 'signifiers' of citizenship – as indexes of citizenship identity, status or values. But as well as being signifiers they also carry with them determinate, pre-constructed meanings, meanings which fill the 'empty signifier' of citizenship (Laclau 1996), however temporarily, with specific content.

When identifying the cultural resources in this way, it is of course important to emphasise that individual citizens generate their performances of citizenship in relation to these rather than simply acting out pre-constructed scripts. As ever, these are the product of a tension and negotiation between the power of the pre-constructed, and the power of situated agency.

It is also important to emphasise that social conceptions and practices of citizenship are developed and enacted partly within the public sphere and within the media, and therefore beyond the formal processes of public participation in the operations of the state. Inevitably, there is also an interactive relationship between these. This has important implications for theorising citizenship: to limit the domain of research to, for example, formal public participation would have the effect of limiting the theoretical conceptions of citizenship that can be developed. Furthermore, performances of citizenship outside formal institutions and practices are not simply undertaken without reference to official conceptions and framings. Indeed, within our data it is notable that conceptions and practices of citizenship are often developed and enacted in response to the *exclusion* of the public from governmental decision-making processes, as well as to its mode of *inclusion*.

This recognition both of the implicit social and governmental conceptions/pre-constructions of citizenship, and of the conflicts and shifts over time and across the social, governmental and theoretical fields, makes it clear that the empirical study of citizenship as a communicative achievement has to attend both to the performance of citizenship and to its various pre-constructions. The research must entail seeing the object of research – citizenship – as a continuing focus of thought and debate. The progressive development and refinement of the empirical insight into citizenship involves (inevitably and necessarily) a conjoint build-up of social categories, theoretical perspectives and analytical methods.

In terms of the *research process*, an exploration of social categories and theoretical perspectives is clearly necessary to inform what the analyst looks for, what s/he is potentially capable of noticing within the data, and the analytic methods s/he selects. The insights from this empirical research process will in turn respond to and even challenge these categories and theoretical perspectives, and thereby demand both further empirical analysis and some potential reworking and refining of these. In other words, in terms of the research *process*, researching citizenship empirically requires an explicitly reflexive research process; it involves recognising (as both inevitable and necessary) the dialectic between theoretical insights on citizenship and empirical research practice.

In terms of the *research object* – citizenship – Bourdieu's advice suggests something more. It suggests that the empirical analysis must explore the dynamic relationship between normative, social, institutional and theoretical pre-constructions of citizenship and what is communicatively achieved in participatory events. In other words, the research must involve recognising and researching the dialectic between pre-constructions of citizenship and the performance of citizenship within everyday practice.

In summary, research into participatory events must therefore not put aside the social, governmental and theoretical preconceptions about citizenship. Instead it must be oriented to the tension between those preconceptions (plural) and what is achieved in communication. The only alternative is the problematic one of working as if one knows what citizenship 'is' – either by uncritically adopting one of the many pre-existing conceptions of citizenship, or by bracketing off all such pre-constructions in the name of a naïve empiricism. For to attempt to research citizenship without any preconception of what citizenship might be – to 'let the facts speak for themselves', as it were – can only be unwittingly to implicitly reproduce an unexamined conception of citizenship, in order to choose which facts are to be allowed to speak in the first place. Even to identify citizenship as whatever happens in a particular kind of participatory procedure is already to have performed an act of pre-construction.

While one focus of research has to be the tension between those preconceptions of citizenship and what is achieved in communication, another has to be the tension between the various contested pre-constructions within and across social, governing and theoretical fields. The research object is inevitably formed in the changing interactions between these fields – between theory, empirical research, government and the governed.

3 A practical and theoretical framework for the analysis of participatory events

The fundamental challenge presented by the PARADYS project was to develop a micro linguistic analysis of subject positioning which was capable of offering wider sociological and theoretical insight into citizenship 'as an ongoing communicative achievement' (Bora *et al.* 2001: 3). The project thus sought to analyse empirically the many ways in which 'citizenship [is] constituted, reproduced and modified within the very process of communication' *in such a way* as to enable that analysis to provide a basis for building and/or contributing to wider sociological 'theory of communicated citizenship' (Bora and Hausendorf 2000: 1). It was therefore intended to produce an analysis that was (i) empirically accountable and (ii) capable of engaging with theoretical perspectives on citizenship within sociology and philosophy, as well as current social and political debate.

In this section we describe the practical framework that we developed to take up this challenge. To do so, we drew on our chosen version of critical discourse analysis, which itself offers a practical and theoretical framework designed to address the question of how micro-linguistic analysis can be used to develop wider sociological and theoretical insight.[3]

3.1 The value of CDA in researching citizenship as a communicative achievement

Critical discourse analysis (CDA) developed as a response to the traditional disciplinary divide between linguistics, with its expertise in the micro analysis of texts and interactions, and other areas of social science such as sociology, with expertise in exploring macro issues of social practice and social change. The challenge CDA has raised and addressed for linguists is what the empirical linguistic analysis of patterns in talk and writing can potentially contribute to, for instance, sociological questions and claims about social and institutional discourses and social change. The challenge it has raised and addressed for sociologists is how their claims about social discourses and social change can be grounded in the actual empirical analysis of language in use.

In contrast with many branches of linguistics which define their research questions within their own discipline, CDA typically takes up social scientific questions and claims about social or institutional change, and explores how these changes may be taking place at the micro level of texts and interactive events. Or, to put the point in more general terms: CDA explores how discourse figures in relation to other social elements in processes of social or institutional change. This is our challenge in empirically researching citizenship.

CDA can be briefly characterised as follows (see Fairclough and Wodak 1997, Chouliaraki and Fairclough 1999, Fairclough 1992a, 2001a, 2001c):[4]

> It starts from social scientific questions, seeking to rework them as ques-
> tions partly about discourse (for example, questions about 'public space'
> are in part questions about forms of dialogue). It is used in conjunction with
> other methods, such as ethnography and political economy, to address
> such social research themes. It aims to show specifically how discourse
> (language, semiosis – 'texts' of all kinds) figures in social processes, social
> change, in dialectical relations with other elements of the social. It is *critical*
> in the sense that it aims to show non-obvious ways in which language
> is involved in social life, including power/domination, and in ideology;
> and point to possibilities for change. It works in a 'transdisciplinary' not
> just 'interdisciplinary' (or even 'postdisciplinary') way: it aims to develop
> theoretically and methodologically in dialogue with other areas of social
> theory and research.

As a heuristic, our version of CDA offers a way of conceptualising social and institutional practices in terms of three dimensions. These are designed deliberately to conceptualise the more sociological concepts of discourse, action and identity in terms which can be explored empirically through reper-toires of linguistic (in conjunction with non-linguistic) analysis.

- **Discourses:**[5] ways of *representing* the world from particular perspectives – in the context of this research, this includes the ways of representing the issues, the potential benefits, the risks and dangers, the relevant institutions, the relationships, the concerned and indifferent publics, the protesters, the farmers, the processes of public participation, the natural and agricultural environment, the crops, and the herbicides.
- **Genres:** ways of *acting* and *interacting* with other people, in speech or writing – in this case socially recognisable ways of doing meetings,

interviews, letters, reports, press releases, and so on which effectively enact, produce, reproduce or counter particular kinds of *social relations*.

* **Styles/voices**: ways of *identifying*, constructing or enunciating the self, including both social and institutional identities – in this case, styles of citizenship (ways of being a citizen), for instance.

Fundamental to the concepts of discourse, genre and style (and indeed to any research which is oriented both to the macro-sociological and the micro-linguistic analysis) is the dialectical relationship between concrete individual events and more abstract (relatively durable and stable) social practices. Within this dialectic, individual texts and events instantiate, juxtapose and creatively negotiate practices, while these practices are cumulatively developed, maintained, modified and challenged by individual texts and events.

This dialectic is the reason why individual texts and events cannot be regarded as simply representing social practices; discourses, genres and styles cannot simply be 'read off' from linguistic features of individual texts and events. The significance of individual texts and events, and their relations with others, and with social practices, is itself a necessary focus of research. Yet with that focus in mind, this dialectic is what makes the individual texts and events, and the patterns of similarity and difference within and across these, interesting in sociological terms. It is what makes it possible to explore social and institutional change through the analysis of individual texts and events.

CDA is not a toolkit for analysing text and talk (e.g., participatory events) which can be evaluated against competing toolkits. CDA does not offer special forms of 'micro' analysis; it is a way of framing any choice of modes of 'micro' analysis. It is a resource for tracing relations between the processes and relations and patterns one can discern in text and talk, and wider social (economic, political, legal etc.) relations and processes and practices and structures. It is a resource for setting up dialogue between analysts of text and talk (conversation, interaction) and sociological, political etc. theorists and analysts. It attempts to work in a transdisciplinary rather than a purely interdisciplinary way, working with categories and concepts in various areas of social theory and research to develop ways of analysing text and talk which are informed by these categories and concepts, and formulating questions and perspectives from social theory and research in ways which elucidate their specifically linguistic/semiotic aspects.

For example, the relationships between practical, theoretical and governmental fields referred to above can be seen as discoursal relationships (explained further below). Critical discourse analysis has developed categories for analysing events (such as public participation events) in their text/talk aspect as parts of chains or networks of events on a concrete level, and mapping such concrete chains or networks of events onto more abstract (durable, long term, institutionalised etc.) networks of social practices (see Fairclough 2003). CDA attends to these different levels of abstraction by oscillating in focus between analysing text/talk in concrete events, and building an emergent account of Orders of Discourse understood as the linguistic/semiotic facet of networks of practices, or the social structuring of linguistic/semiotic difference.[6]

3.2 Researching the chains of events and texts: intertextuality, interdiscursivity and recontextualisation

To explain the issues of intertextuality, interdiscursivity and recontextualisation, it is useful to illustrate these in terms of the events and texts we have been analysing in the project. The spoken interactions include interviews, public–public interactions and public–institutional interactions around the permitting procedures for the planting of GM crops. In line with the remit of this particular project, we have focused on interactions and texts about particular sites.

While each GM crop site may be geographically remote in a rural village, the various interactions about the GM crops are clearly not isolated events. The participants in an event inevitably draw on their own networks of communication and on a range of information sources. Thus, an interview may not be the first time people have talked about the issues, or heard others talking about them; similarly, a public meeting is usually called as a consequence of requests from local people. So both events may follow other events. People may have written letters, and asked for information and expressed concern in other ways. They may have read various sources of information on the GM crop trials, and may equate this issue and debate with similar issues and debates before. They may have attended previous meetings and/or heard from people attending similar meetings elsewhere. In terms of the issues at hand, and the ways they are discussed, they have already developed confidence, anxieties, expectations, priorities, doubts, irritations, assumptions and so on. These may be based on their own previous experience, interactions and correspondence, on the experience of others, and on socially available representations in society and the media.

In this way a particular text or interview or participatory event is oriented to by its participants not as an isolate but as a part of an *intertextual* chain or network of texts and events. Different groups of participants may see the event as located in different chains or networks. What is said and done and written in a particular event or text is intertextually related to other events and texts: people inevitably draw on, anticipate and respond to other events and other texts. So we cannot understand particular events or particular texts, or the significance of these for the participants, without exploring (and asking about) these wider intertextual chains.

In our data collection we tried to follow the intertextual chains of events and texts related to each case. We attended public meetings (where these took place within the research period), instigated group discussions, and conducted deliberative semi-structured interviews. We sought copies of letters, e-mails, press-releases, leaflets, magazine and newspaper articles, and so on, which are related to the particular sites and meetings. We also assembled a small corpus of media reports, Government statements, website information, e-mails and so on, which people in particular sites may draw on and respond to. Together, these intertextual chains provided a basis for exploring the ways in which particular social practices recur, develop, change, get taken up and so on, within, between and beyond particular sites.

The exploration of the links within and between these intertextual chains leads directly to a more fundamental point in sociological and linguistic terms. This is that in any communication people inevitably draw on, anticipate and respond to particular social and institutional practices (ways of doing things), both explicitly and implicitly. They are involved in an *interdiscursive* process of creatively drawing on the potential range of established discourses, genres and styles. For example, the organisers of a meeting do not have to invent the nature of a meeting, but can selectively draw on and adapt familiar ways of organising meetings and of interacting within them. Similarly, the participants in a meeting or interview do not have to invent ways of acting and interacting, or ways of talking about the issues, from scratch, but can selectively draw on and adapt familiar and effective ways of doing these. These social practices may be highly institutionalised, or from the public sphere, or as we have argued, developed from an interaction between these. The processes of drawing on them, juxtaposing them, negotiating them and/or challenging them may be implicit or partly observed by the participants.

Within these intertextual and interdiscursive chains, the anticipation of future texts and events is also important. For example, some participants may anticipate organisational or official reports or media reports of the interview or public event in which they are participating, and their contributions to the event itself may well be differentially shaped by these anticipations.

It is through an analysis of intertextuality and interdiscursivity that the particular event becomes potentially interesting in macro-sociological terms. The analysis involves identifying the available social practices which people may repeatedly draw on, anticipate and respond to in particular kinds of events and interactions. It also involves exploring the ways in which these social practices can be included, excluded, juxtaposed, negotiated and played out within the interactive events. This offers insight into the social practices as well as the particular chains of events.

It is, of course, fundamental to this kind of analysis that the resources which people and institutions draw on do not simply get reproduced 'intact'. (These resources may include individual words, utterances, scientific claims, useful concepts, ways of doing things, and so on, all of which may be embedded within social and institutional discourses, genres and styles). When these resources are set in different contexts, and used by different people and institutions, they are potentially transformed (both deliberately and unwittingly, but often systematically) by this process of *recontextualisation*. Discourses may be recontextualised in particular ways within particular genres and vice versa.

The sociological concept of 'recontextualisation' (Bernstein 1990) has therefore been operationalised in CDA in order to explore the potentially distinctive recontextualising principles associated with different fields or networks of practices (governmental, academic, public sphere etc.) which affect, at the concrete level, how one type of text or event is transformed into others in flows along chains and through networks. These flows are not simply unidirectional – there are flows into 'practical' events from governmental and theoretical fields, as well as flows in the other direction.

In this brief account we are beginning to indicate how we can research practically, in a discourse-analytical way, the relationships between the governing and governed, and theoretical and practical fields, which we have taken above to be an inherent aspect of citizenship.

4 Three interrelated strands for the analysis

From our experience of attending the participatory events, our experience of talking to people in the interviews, and our initial analysis of the texts and transcripts from these, we identified three practical and fundamental strands for our empirical analysis of citizenship as a communicative achievement. They are represented in Figure 16.1. As the arrows indicate, these three analytic strands are clearly interrelated and complementary. Moreover, 'subject positioning' is located in the centre of the diagram in order to keep in mind the intended focus of this empirical analysis of citizenship, and therefore the common focus of these strands. Within the chains of texts and events in our data, we were interested in the particular identities and social relations which

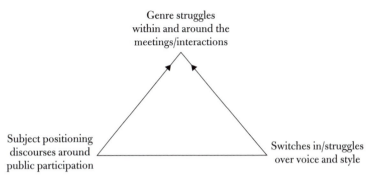

Figure 16.1 Three interrelated strands which provide a framework for a linguistic and sociolinguistic analysis of the ways in which social relations and identities of citizenship are constituted, reproduced and modified through subject positioning within and around public interactions.

participants establish and negotiate – for themselves as participants, for other participants, for the relevant institutions, and for the wider public beyond. In particular, we wanted to identify and explore those identities and relations that may be relevant to citizenship. In the next section we explain each strand and its contribution to this primary focus.

This framework is intended to provide the kind of rationale and theoretical understanding necessary to guide and underpin the micro-level linguistic analysis. By this we mean that the three strands below are intended to give direction and focus to the empirical analysis, to inform the processes of selecting from the range of potential data, from the range of potential avenues for analysis, and from the vast array of possible linguistic-analytic tools.

4.1 Strand 1: The genre struggles within and around the public interactions

A focus on the nature of the participatory event is very much central to researching citizenship as a communicative achievement within the processes of public participation and public debate. Moreover, the term *participatory event* is preferable to the term *administrative procedure* since it recognises the inevitably contingent nature of interactive events. Interactive events do not simply follow or instantiate procedures, and their significance for the participants and institutions is not simply what the organising institution intended. Similarly, the concept of *genre* also has important advantages over the notion of 'procedure'. It is a concept with which we can address the heterogeneity of the event, and the ways in which the participants draw on familiar genres in negotiating the nature of this event. Our interest in genres is an interest in the socially available resources which institutions and publics draw on in developing and negotiating the participatory events.

In analysing the transcripts of the local public meetings around GM crops it is evident that there are some interesting battles taking place over the nature of the event and, specifically, over the various genres of interaction that participants appear to be drawing on within it. Key points of struggle include what kind of event it is, what it is possible to say and do, what the various identities, social relations and forms of authority are, and the possibility and legitimacy of drawing conclusions or making decisions within it.

These struggles are, of course, partly prompted by the wider institutional context of current UK Government practice. The local village meetings we have researched are described by DEFRA (the UK Department for Environment, Food and Rural Affairs) as providing public information, rather than as the opportunity for public participation and consultation which many of the organisations and local people attending the meetings believed they should be. At the same time, the 'factual' information about the GM crop trials provided by DEFRA is itself regarded as controversial rather than neutral by many of those attending the meetings. Therefore the very nature and function of the meeting – as public information or public participation (or public relations) – is precisely one of the points of contention.

With different views of what the event should be, the participants draw explicitly and implicitly on potentially competing genres. For example, the events frequently shift between being a lecture with a subsequent question and answer session, as envisaged by DEFRA, and a more participatory public discussion. Specifically, there are frequent struggles over whether the public are allowed to provide information and to comment or only to ask questions, and over whether they can respond to the answers given by the panel. The chairperson may articulate rules for the event and demand conformity to these, yet people may insert comments or information as 'givens' (or 'presuppositions') within a question. Equally, the audience may demand that members of the panel answer a question.

Here is one example taken from a public meeting which we recorded in one site where farm trials took place. The meeting was chaired by a well-known local figure; there were several speakers in the first part of the meeting, and in the second part of the meeting members of the audience were invited to put questions to the speakers. The speakers were experts of different types – a government official with expert knowledge of the farm trials, a representative of a company which produces GM seed for farmers who is a scientist, and a representative of an organisation which promotes organic farming who has expert knowledge of the implications of GM agriculture for organic farming. The example is an exchange in the second part of the meeting involving two male members (*M1*, *M2*) of the audience and the government official.

M1: There are two or three problems or concerns really. One really is the lack of time the parish has been given with respect of when we know. We don't know when the site is to be. We only know when the site is to be drilled. The county council has put a motion through that we would ask DEFRA to let us know when the site is agreed, and then we could have a meeting like this if you like before it all gets out of hand. The other thing is there's a massive increase in nose problems through spores that are in the air now. Years ago we used to have hay fever problems at hay time, now we seem to get them – Is there any difference between the spores of genetically modified crops and the conventional crop? I think those are two major concerns that locally are causing problems. I don't know whether there's an answer to both but there certainly is an answer in time delay and there may be an answer to the other.

M2: Could I just make a point as well? I mean the first part of that, this year the first we knew about these crops was in the newspaper.

M1: Exactly.

M2: And when we did draw some information off the Internet, it was the day they'd stated for sowing. So that's when the parish council knew –

M1: The county council has asked the government to – if we can know – when the site is decided upon then we need the information. And I think that will give us a reasonable length of time to evaluate whether it is or isn't going to be a problem.

Government official: Can I [unclear word]. Well, I think that I said that our practice is to write to all parish councils when a trial site is proposed and we did that –

M1: No, that isn't what happened –

Government official: Could I just say what we do? [Extended account of the notification procedure omitted.] So we do our very best to make sure that the people know.

M1: At what point do you know which site you are going to use?

M1 begins by making statements – not asking questions – about the two 'problems or concerns', and then asking a question about the second of them. Another shift away from the 'rules' of such meetings is that *M1* and *M2* are working collaboratively to elaborate the first problem, against the normative expectation of 'one speaker at a time'. Furthermore, *M1* interrupts the government official's response, challenging what he is saying, and then continues in direct dialogue with him by asking a further question, rather than only addressing questions 'through the chair' as the 'rules' would require. More-over, *M1* would seem to be asking for more than answers to questions; that is, more than information, he would seem to be asking for solutions to problems – the 'answer in time delay' he is asking for is a *change in the official procedure*. One tension in such meetings is thus that while the 'rules' limit interaction to giving and asking for *information*, contributions from audience members are often advocating or calling for *action*. Such exchanges are frequent in this and similar meetings: audience members, usually unostentatiously but persistently, breach the 'rules' about 'questions' to get across the points and criticisms and challenges they want to get across.

Within this process, the institutions and the public are not inventing from scratch what the meeting is and might be, the roles and responsibilities of the participants, or the forms of interaction within it. Rather, they are implicitly and explicitly drawing on known, respected and functional forms of inter-action from other contexts. At the same time, they are not simply taking these genres 'off the shelf': they are actively and creatively juxtaposing, interweaving and negotiating them within this particular event. In the example, for instance, one can see *M1* and *M2* as drawing upon a genre of open debate or discussion (between colleagues, for instance), but not simply as a replacement for the genre of expert–public interaction which is specified in the 'rules' – the two are interwoven, in that the 'question–answer' format of the latter is still drawn upon.

This process of actively drawing on other genres is reflected in the micro-linguistic features of what people do when they speak, the social relations they construct and counter, the rules of the meeting they break and follow, and the identities they construct within the meeting. These are interesting in macro-sociological terms, both in identifying the apparently available genres which people draw on, and in exploring how these are played out in practice. We are, of course, particularly interested in the *subject positioning of the participants* as the genres are juxtaposed, interweaved, developed and changed. Particular genres make particular subject positions more possible or less possible. That is partly why there is a struggle over genres. Conversely, the invoking, shifting and constraining of subject positions is a significant part of negotiating and creatively (re)defining the generic nature of the event. In this way, exploring an event in terms of the genres being invoked becomes a helpful way of guiding, prompting, understanding and organising our detailed linguistic analysis of subject positioning.

This kind of investigation of genre needs to be very alert to the subtle differences in the social relations within and between events: we know from experience of analysing other public consultations that subtle differences in the framing and the identities and relations within an event can produce very fundamental differences in the nature of the interactions. This contingency of the interactions is, after all, partly why we are talking in terms of genres rather than procedures.

The contingency of the event also underlines our second focus of interest within our investigation of genre. This is an interest in the *subject positioning of the event* – by which we mean the processes of construing significance to the event itself. Consistent with micro-sociological research in science studies, applied linguistics and elsewhere, it is important to recognise that there can be considerable contingency within a participatory event in terms of what the participation is seen as counting for. One cannot assume that this is determined by the intended procedure. The significance attributed to the event (and the interactions within it) by the different participants is to be researched rather than assumed. This significance and positioning will be constituted in the interactions and intertextual chains within and around the event. For the different participants, the event may be part of different intertextual chains.

4.2   Strand 2: Switches in/struggles over voice and style

Within CDA, *styles* are what we might informally call 'ways of being' – or identities – in language (as opposed to bodily, somatic aspects). Styles, like discourses and genres, are identified and differentiated at the (relatively abstract, durable) level of social practices. In particular events (such as participatory events) people may have a range of styles available to draw upon, combine, switch or struggle over.

An analysis of styles provides one important frame for the analysis of subject positioning. Shifts in styles are one key part of the process of enacting, challenging and negotiating genres and discourses – through challenging the subject positioning available within these. But making an analytical separation between styles (or voices) and the other two categories (genres, discourses) also allows us to bring in aspects of identity which are not covered otherwise, especially the relationship between particular persons and the repertoire of available social identities or roles.

There are two concerns here. The first is how people represent themselves and are represented by others. (Van Leeuwen (1996) offers a useful framework for a detailed analysis of this.) The second is how they enact particular identities and social relations in the way they talk. For instance, people may talk ironically or aggressively, as strategies or resources for dealing with officialdom. In addition, different kinds of statements – descriptive, evaluative, implicitly evaluative, normative etc. – may be used with very different frequencies by the various participants in an event.

From research of people enacting and negotiating their identities in writing, Ivanič (1997) offers three aspects which seem useful to explore within our research. First, people bring to any event an 'autobiographical self'. This is their personal autobiography up to that moment; it is the life experiences, the socialisations and the familiar social practices they are able to draw on, explicitly as well as implicitly. Second, people create a 'discoursal self' in their talk or writing, from the ways in which they draw on socially available discourses and subject positions. When people use a particular discourse, 'they identify themselves with the interests, values, beliefs and power relations that are associated with it' (1997: 138). Third, in different situations people will, to varying degrees, establish an 'authorial self' – establish themselves as the authors of what they are saying or writing, and establish their own authority. For instance, in our research people may use unmodalised present tense assertions for scientific information, or for reporting local concerns. They may explicitly identify themselves (individually or collectively) as the source of value judgements. Or they may avoid these. Inevitably, both experts and non-experts have to negotiate a fine line between sounding appropriately authoritative and overstepping the limits of their authority.

Ivanič thereby shows the ways in which identities are negotiated even within apparently factual and impersonal texts and utterances. The constructions of identity within a text or dialogue link both to the social and personal histories, and to the socially available discourses, genres and styles.

Styles can be seen as a facet of people's habitus (Bourdieu 1977, 1984), which brings variables of life history and life experience into account. Thinking of styles within the analysis can mean thinking also of the relationship between social role and personality. Styles can be seen to involve a tension between social identity and personal identity – social identities, or at least those key social identities which MacIntyre identified as 'characters' (MacIntyre 1985, see also Archer 2000), come to be personally invested. Analysis is oriented to the relationship and tension between personal and social facets of identities.

When researching citizenship as a communicative achievement, we can explore this relationship and tension between personal and social facets of identities. We may explore the ways in which the citizen (in addition to MacIntyre's therapist and manager) may be a character in MacIntyre's sense. It may be that a 'good citizen' successfully invests the social role with his or her personality, and does it in a distinct way. Seen as a 'character' of the contemporary social order, such personal investment of the social role of citizen may be a *sine qua non* of people coming to be citizens in a real sense, or as we might put it, coming to be 'good citizens'.

It is important to note that this implies a mode of analysis which is not merely descriptive – we can describe what people do and how they are in participatory events, but interpreting this in terms of 'doing citizenship' involves a normative perspective. Further, these points on the personal investment of social roles apply also to the experts involved in participatory events. For instance, the speaker from the GM crop industry in the data we have referred to has a distinctive expert style whose analysis demands attention to how social identities and roles are personally inflected and invested. It is a performance of personality as well as social identity:

> *Industry representative*: Why would the farmer be interested in this technology? Okay, well I've already talked about yield and I'll come back to that yet again in a second. But what's great about this is you can use a particular sort of herbicide called Liberty. Now normally with oilseed rape what you do as a farmer is you go in and you put a thin layer of herbicide onto the soil, okay. This is what they call a pre-emergence herbicide. And what happens is that as the weeds come through they come into contact with the herbicide and they die. Okay? . . .
>
> Liberty is different, no point spraying it on the soil, it's just about inactivated on contact. What that means is you have to spray it onto the weeds. There is no point spraying it onto the soil and letting the weeds come through it. The weeds just carry on growing. Okay? If that's the case what we're looking at now is rather than a 'just in case' it's an 'if we actually need it'. So the farmer will come along, look and see those weeds in that crop and say 'ok, do I need to spray?' and 'if so how much do I need to spray?' So there are weeds in that field and he'll make that decision. So we're moving away from the idea of 'oh well I'll spray it just in case anything comes through' to 'if we need to we'll use it'. And that's a very exciting thing for a farmer.

While the government official represents himself as 'explaining' things in his presentation, the GM industry speaker says that he aims to give people 'a feeling for what it's all about'. These are two different styles of being an expert. The company scientist shows a more interactive orientation to the audience, for instance in this extract by checking (with 'okay?') that the statements he has made have been understood, and asking a question in a simulated question–answer exchange rather than just making statements. And unlike the government official, he also uses explicit evaluative statements alongside statements of fact (e.g., 'what's great about this', 'that's a very exciting thing for a farmer').

He also dramatises his presentation by 'doing' the voice of the farmer. In drawing more than the government official upon the resources of colloquial conversation to achieve greater dialogicality, the speaker is also opening up spaces for personally investing his enactment of the role of expert – for instance, 'doing' the voice of the farmer gives him the space for his own particular dramatic performance.

4.3 Strand 3: The discourses around public participation

The issue of public participation was an explicit focus of much of the discussion at the public meetings. Some of the interaction concerned why the government department DEFRA was not explicitly consulting the public on the sowing of GM crops, why it was not responding to public opinion, and why it was seemingly ignoring a local survey or referendum. Yet in many ways this focus was simply an extension of a theme within government discourses around the Farm Scale Trials, which seem subtly and effectively to give the listener or reader the sense that they have little or no part to play in the permitting procedures.

For example, one section of the publicity material about the Field Scale Trials that was made available by DEFRA on its website and in a printed leaflet opened as follows:

Q: What is being done to involve people with sites in their locality in the Farm Scale Evaluation programme?
The Government involves local people in the Farm Scale Evaluation (FSE) process by providing both information about the release and an opportunity for the public to comment on the safety assessments that have been made.

There are various ways in which the choice of words here means that, at the same time that the text describes a process of public participation, it also serves to constrain it. For example, the ambivalent word 'involve' is used in a way which renders the public as passive: it is used in the transactive sense of something which an organisation or person does to people, and therefore, which people have done to them. The use of the nominalisation 'sites in their locality' represents the GM crop sites as given physical entities, rather than the product of a decision-making process, representing the choice of sites as prior to the process of any public involvement. And 'local people' casts the population as a collection of individuals rather than a political collectivity or *citizenry*, effectively backgrounding the democratic power of those involved, and the democratic significance of the process. The collective effect of these discoursal choices is to close the space for participation, and to justify and maintain the existing absence of public participation.

However, the debate about public participation was also played out in a more implicit and subtle way within the public meetings. In particular, the institutional discourse(s) of DEFRA at the meetings seemed to construct a political, administrative, environmental and commercial world of experts, committees and procedures in which there was no intrinsic need for, and little place for, public participation.

With this in mind, we are using the phrase '*discourses around public participation*' to refer not only to ways of talking about public participation or citizenship, but also to discourses that are ostensibly not concerned with participation or citizenship at all, but which routinely get drawn into the processes of public participation, or which are influential in any debate about the need and possibilities for public participation. These include discourses of science, administration, governance, commerce and so on; through the implicit views of knowledge, expertise, procedures and so on, these bring with them assumptions about the potential role, nature and limits of participation as citizens, and about the possible subject positions (identities and relations) within any public–institution interaction. For the participants, the act of invoking such established institutionalised discourses within an event can be immensely powerful. Discourses effectively bring with them the authority relations, the subject positions, and the views of knowledge from the contexts in which they have been used.

For example, discourses of science and administration could be used by government and industrial actors in ways which served to depoliticise the trials, reducing them to a simple technical procedure and thus not an appropriate topic for political debate. However, during the public meetings there were also moments when both discourses were drawn upon by members of the public in order to assert their citizenly rights to be meaningfully consulted. In the following extract, scientific principles of openness and peer review are drawn on in order to call both the government and the biotechnology industry to account:

F1: My name is [name] and I am a voluntary campaigner based in [name of town] for [name of NGO] and I have devoted much of the last year to campaigning and finding out all about GM crops.
I have a simple question . . . I would like umm the two speakers from DEFRA and GM crop and herbicide company tonight, *to supply me*, by speaking to you all, *the names and reference numbers of any independent*

research to deal with safety, as regards these two crops, maize and oil seed rape.

This is for example: umm, if I was to breathe in the pollen, could they tell me please what tests have been done by independent scientists to say whether that will leave me totally healthy or whether there may be some risk; if a cow was to eat some grass, upon which the pollen had dropped in its short life, coming from these crops. *Can we say that these things have BEEN tested*, to see the result of that? That sort of thing. Thanks very much.

Audience: [applause]

Industry representative: Umm, yes. I CAN answer that question. The answer, when it comes down to INDEPENDENT research, umm I can't give you an answer to that.

To my knowledge *I'm not aware of INDEPENDENT research*. I AM aware of a lot of research that has been done both by OUR company and by OTHER companies, which has been *looked at INDEPENDENTLY*. ALL the results have been looked at INDEPENDENTLY, on a NUMBER of occasions, they umm, both in this country and in other countries around the world. And that is the only reason WHY we are allowed to grow these things in this country. So I may not be able to answer your question in terms of INDEPENDENT RESEARCH, but certainly this information that has been presented has been looked at INDEPENDENTLY, yes.

F1: Have you got *the research papers* please, so I can read them too? . . . Can I go on the internet, and actually READ this information. This is what I want to be able to do.

Industry representative: Okay, if you're talking about maize you can certainly look on OUR Internet or on, come to that DEFRA's Internet, and look at what *safety information* there. Yes. And there is *safety information* in there.

Chair: All right, next question please.

[While the chair asks for the next question, members of the audience point out that the question has not been answered by the government representative. They ask for him to answer it. It becomes evident that the Government representative is not going to answer. The chair still asks for the next question. *F1* returns to the microphone.]

F1: I have been *writing to the government*, at least once a month for seven months, and before that quite frequently. The Department of the Environment, Margaret Beckett, Michael Meacher. Written to in parliament, at one or two addresses that I've had for them. I have NEVER had a reply other than the STANDARD reply, which are just like [the industry representative] kindly said. Years, dossiers full of it. *NEVER have they answered my question with ONE research paper number or title. I DO not believe this exists.*

[*Loud 6* second applause. The chair invites another question.]

In the extract, the industry spokesman is using a discourse of science as *prod-uct*, as objective fact, one which elides the backstage processes of scientific knowledge making by which facts are fabricated, stabilised and made ready to circulate in society. By contrast, *F1* is framing science as a *process* – one of conjecture and refutation, in which scientific claims are open to scrutiny and testing, thus seeking to open up the process of scientific claims-making to citizenly intervention (see Latour 2004). The discourse of science is thus a resource which is drawn on in various ways in our participatory events, ways which can both close down and open up possibilities of citizenly intervention.

5 Conclusion

As we argued at the beginning of this chapter, one key challenge in researching citizenship as a communicative achievement is to identify when the identities and relations produced in communication are potentially relevant to the issue of citizenship. More fundamentally, this challenge raises the question of how we understand citizenship within this research.

We suggested that an emphasis on citizenship as a communicative achieve-ment could be seen as an attempt to get away from preconceptions about what citizenship *is*, and look at how it is *done* – at the range of ways in which people position themselves and others as citizens in participatory events. In response to this, we argued that the empirical study of citizenship as a communicative achievement cannot proceed in isolation from these preconceptions. An empirical analysis of citizenship as a communicative achievement entails seeing the object of the research – citizenship – as a continuing focus of thought and debate within the research. The progressive development and refinement of the empirical insight into citizenship involves a focus on social categories, theoretical perspectives and analytical methods (see above).

Within this process, theoretical perspectives have practical as well as the-oretical importance. Researchers cannot rely on their informants or data to tell them what citizenship is, or to indicate which elements of their discourse are relevant to citizenship; this is, after all, an analysis of things which are implicit (even ideological) within discourse, and which are communicated implicitly through subject positioning. Similarly, researchers cannot rely on their own existing intuitive notions of citizenship as the starting point; the danger is that these will be limited, highly cultural, and embedded within those current discourses of citizenship which should be the focus of analysis. Theoretical perspectives on citizenship provide at least a starting point for that continuing process of thought and debate about citizenship as the object of research. This is a process through which the researcher becomes better able to notice and observe popular and institutional notions of citizenship that are implicit within the data. It also provides the mechanism by which this empirical research may in turn contribute to those theoretical perspectives.

However, as we have argued, merely exploring and drawing on theoretical notions of citizenship is not enough. This would be to ignore the fact that some notions of citizenship are more salient and currently more powerful than others. It would be to ignore the powerful social categories around citizenship, and the notions of citizenship pervasive within the fields of governance. To understand citizenship as a communicative achievement, we therefore need to be able to understand the ways in which the participants may orientate to, draw on, respond to and counter these powerful and implicit articulations of citizenship. This is vital in a context where implicit, complex and contradictory notions of citizenship may be used by government institutions, the GM crop industry and environmental organisations to enrol the public into their institutional perspectives.

This is the point we argued at the start of this chapter: the empirical research of citizenship must involve recognising and researching the dialectic between pre-constructions of citizenship and performances of citizenship within everyday practice. It must involve an exploration of the dynamic relationship between the normative, social, institutional and theoretical pre-constructions of citizenship, and what is communicatively achieved in participatory events.

However, as we argued in our discussion of the final analytical strand, discourses of citizenship are also embedded within a wider range of discourses. They intersect with, and are identifiable across, current discourses of science, governance, administration, commerce, media and so on. Within the particular events and texts which we research, people may be using, negotiating and juxtaposing competing discourses of citizenship. For the researcher, to identify the apparent discourses of citizenship can be an interesting research process in itself, but it is particularly interesting when it enables us to explore their potential functioning and significance, within the wider discourse formations currently associated with science, governance, commerce, media, environmental concern and public participation.

It would be wrong, though, to interpret this emplacement of the participatory event within an overlapping set of institutional discourses as denying the possibility of agency and change. Linguistic analysis can reveal the participatory event as a moment in which discourses are actively brought together in potentially innovative ways. Similarly, the discourses around public participation are important resources for negotiating the genre(s) of the particular event. They are resources upon which institutions and members of the public draw in the process of guiding, defining, understanding, negotiating and contesting (i) the nature of public interactions about GM crops, (ii) the significance of these interactions, and (iii) the subject positions the participants may occupy within them. In turn, the generic nature of the event is critical in terms of what discourses are prompted, encouraged and/or excluded. For example, heterogeneity in the nature of the event, its unfamiliarity to the participants, or conversely, the familiarity and confidence of the participants in the event, can all enable a wider range of public and non-institutional discourses to be aired.

This interrelation of genres and discourses inevitably offers possibilities for a circular impasse, and, conversely, for learning, innovation and change. It is often the narrow conception of the potential genres of public participation that is a key factor in maintaining the established discourses which devalue and sideline public participation. The sometimes dominant assumption that public participation can mean only (a) oppositional public meetings, (b) letter-writing and website responses, or (c) a simplistic referendum, is very powerful. This rests on, and then maintains, the assumption that public participation in decision-making is about adding up individual opinions, as opposed to engaging in a debate about the complex issues in order to identify the important questions and reach informed judgements (Rawles 1998, O'Neill 2001, Skogstad 2003). It maintains the sometimes dominant institutionalised discourses around public participation, in which public participation is construed as being of limited value, potentially dangerous, and contrary to the desired goal of basing decisions on 'sound science'. Social and institutional change therefore involves changes in the discourses, genres and styles around public participation.

In terms of social learning, innovation and change, it is clear that direct experience of taking part in public consultation events can radically impact on the ways in which both institutions and publics come to talk about public participation. Moreover, the direct experience of public exclusion from particular decision-making processes can have a similarly radical impact. Such experiences can prompt reflection and learning about the current practices and the potential role and value of public participation. And as we have found in the context of GM crops, the experience of public exclusion can sometimes also prompt an explicit reflection about the wider nature and functioning of democracy.

In this way, experiences of public participation, or of the absence of it, can become moments of discoursal realignment and innovation. In particular, they can prompt social and institutional shifts in the subject positioning of experts, authorities, self and the public. The contribution of this research into citizenship as a communicative achievement is that it can potentially offer detailed empirical and theoretical insight into these important aspects of current social change.

Notes

1. There are a number of different approaches within critical discourse analysis (for overviews see Fairclough and Wodak 1997, Wodak and Meyer 2001). The version we adopt is that developed by Fairclough and his collaborators in recent publications including Chouliaraki and Fairclough (1999), Fairclough (2003), Fairclough, Jessop and Sayer (2004). In the event we did not fully apply this framework in our contribution to the project in the interests of harmonisation with other contributions to PARADYS.

2. Here we are using the terms Discourse or Discourses to mean particular ways of representing or constructing particular areas of knowledge and experience (see below, and Fairclough 1992a: 127–8). For clarity, in this document we follow the convention of using (big 'D') Discourse(s) in this way, while using (small 'd') discourse as a very general term to refer to spoken, written and non-verbal interaction.

3. We use the word 'framework' deliberately here, to indicate that this is not a recipe for the analysis, or even a toolbox of methods, but a framework within which particular forms of linguistic analysis, relevant to the particular data and context, can be used to develop a wider theoretical insight. It is intended to be used innovatively in particular research contexts. It is important to keep the more detailed level of the particular linguistic analyses fairly open: as analysts we need to draw on and develop our repertoires of linguistic-analytic tools in the course of the analysis.

4. This characterisation of CDA reflects the particular version we are using, but would be broadly accepted by other critical discourse analysts in terms of the general positions it includes, if not these specific formulations of them.

5. As stated in footnote 2, we follow the convention of using (big 'D') Discourse(s) in the way explained here, whilst using (small 'd') discourse as a very general term to refer to spoken, written and non-verbal interaction.

6. Orders of Discourse can be conceived as configurations of Genres and Discourses and Styles that achieve a relative permanence.

17. 'Political correctness': the politics of culture and language

We might see the controversy around 'political correctness' (PC) as a political controversy in which both those who are labelled 'PC' and those who label them 'PC' are engaged in a politics that is focused upon representations, values and identities – in short, a 'cultural politics'. An immediate caveat is that the homogeneity of 'PCers' (those who are labelled 'PC') is no more than a constructed homogeneity produced through the labelling, but I shall leave that until later. The objective on both sides is cultural change (in a sense of 'culture' I shall explain shortly) as a trigger for broader social change. This makes sense of the observation, which a number of commentators have made, that there is a sort of performative contradiction in critiques of 'PC' because they would seem themselves to be instances of the sort of cultural politics which is the object of critique (see e.g., Cameron 1995). Because changing culture is conceived on 'both sides' as partly a matter of changing language, the 'PC' controversy is partly, but only partly, a controversy over language. I shall focus here on the language aspect. It seems to me that in order to increase our understanding of what has been going on in the 'PC' controversy, as well as for those who see themselves as broadly committed to political change for the enhancement of social justice to learn tactically and strategically from it, there are several questions which need to be addressed.

1. A question about social history and social change in the socio-historical context of the 'PC' controversy: why this apparently increasing focus in politics on achieving social and political change through changing culture and changing language? What has happened socially that can explain the 'cultural turn' and the 'language turn' in politics, in social and political theory, and in other domains of social practice? (Section 1)

2. A question about theory: how are we to understand the relationship between culture, language and other elements of social life and social practices (including institutions and organisations, urban or industrial infrastructure, social relations)? How are we to understand the relationship between change in culture and language, and social change? (Section 2)
3. A question about political strategy and tactics: for those who are politically committed to substantive social and political change (whether on the right or on the left), what place can a politics centred around culture and language have in a political strategy which is to have some chance of success? (Section 3)

1 Socio-historical context: society, culture and language

The question of the relationships and changing relationships among society, culture and language is a highly complex question to which I can give only rather summary attention in this article. I want to follow Williams (1981) in theorising a culture as a 'signifying system' constituted as an articulation of representations, values and identities. Social analysis is concerned with the dialectical interrelations between signifying systems and other analytically separable systems (economic systems, political systems, kinship and family systems etc.). I call these analytically separate because, although there are reasons for seeing them as different, they are not discrete, i.e., the relationship between them and signifying systems *is* dialectical in that for instance the economic system internalises, enacts and inculcates (see Section 2 on theory) signifying systems. Necessarily so, because human beings are reflexive, there is always a dialectical interconnection between what they do and how they represent, value and identify themselves and what they do. Seeing cultures as signifying systems also helps clarify the relationship between culture and language: cultures exist as languages, or what I shall rather call discourses (and in their enactment as 'cultural forms' and inculcation as identities, as genres and styles – see Section 2). But cultures are not only discourses, they are also systems and forms of consciousness, and they may be ideologies – again, neither excludes discourses, neither is discrete, but they are analytically different. Let us say that a particular form of social life is a particular networking of social practices (the 'systems' referred to in Williams's terminology above) including particular articulations among culture, language (discourse) and other elements of social practices; and let us say that social change is a change in the networking of social practices and the articulation of elements.

This will have to suffice as a theoretical basis for approaching the question about social history and change. In broad terms, an increasing salience of culture and discourse in (an increasingly reflexive) social life is a feature of modernity, and perhaps especially of changes in social life over recent decades. The 'cultural turn' and the 'language turn' are first of all 'turns' in social life itself, and only secondarily turns in philosophy and social theory. Let me quickly review some more recent aspects and indications of this change. First, the 'culture industries', including broadcasting, have become increasingly important domains of social practice, and their networking with other domains of social practice (the economy, politics, family life etc.) has become an increasingly significant feature of social life. Culture industries such as television are (as the term suggests) entities on an economic level as well as others, but they are specialised for 'signifying systems' in Williams's terminology – and the representations, values and identities constructed in and projected and circulated through them are uncontroversially of increasing social significance. Other domains of social practice (e.g., politics, family life, community life) work more and more through the mediation of the culture industries, and cultural representations and values (and therefore the discourses which circulate through television and other media) play an increasingly salient role in the way in which politics, family life and so on, work. Second, culture and discourse are increasingly significant in economic production and consumption. It is a truism that commodities are now consumed for their cultural or 'sign' value rather than just their 'use' value, and are accordingly produced as embodiments of cultural values and discourses, targeted with ever greater precision at culturally differentiated 'niche markets' (defined in terms of generation, gender, lifestyle etc.). Another truism is that economies are increasingly 'informational' or 'knowledge-based' and 'knowledge-driven', which amounts to discourse-driven – driven for instance by shifting managerial discourses that come to be enacted as managerial systems in business and industry. By the same token, the knowledge, skills, aptitudes and attitudes of employees, their values and their identities, and therefore their ('lifelong') education and training, become a major concern for business.

There are other respects in which identities come to be an increasingly salient concern. Economic transformations have radically changed the social relations of work. The system of social classes defined primarily by social relations within economic production has lost its potency as the principle shaper of social identities and differences. The attachment of political parties and governments to particular social class interests has virtually disappeared. Governments are instead in increasingly close 'partnerships' with business, and see a large part of their role as creating the financial, infrastructural and 'human resources' conditions for success in the highly competitive 'global economy'. Education becomes a primary concern, but also forms of 'cultural governance', the formation and transformation of identities and values. Meanwhile, left politics, unable to respond to these social transformations and the ideological assault of the New Right and neo-liberalism with an effective counter-hegemonic strategy (Hall 1994), has become fragmented. They are no longer centred upon the political parties and social classes but oriented to 'single issues' and to a politics of recognition, identity and difference as much as to a politics of redistributive social justice.

This brief sketch has brought us to the point of entry of the controversy over 'political correctness', because as I indicated above this controversy is located within the shift to 'cultural' politics, the politics of recognition, identity and difference. The point of arriving at this politics by the rather circuitous route I have taken above, however, is that 'PC' needs, I believe, to be framed rather more broadly than it has generally been within the social transformations of recent decades. Cultural interventions directed at changing representations, values and identities, and (given the particular focus of this article) doing so in part through changing language (discourse), are actually pervasive in contemporary social life. They are pervasive in economic practices, through the inculcation of employees into new ways of working and new identities corresponding to them, partly through attempts to get them to not only use but also 'own' new discourses (some of the buzz-words are: 'teams', 'networks', 'partnerships', 'flexibility'). They are pervasive in politics and in the mediation of politics through the press and broadcasting – as, for instance, Hall (1994) points out, the hegemonic projects of Reagan and Thatcher were orchestrated at different levels, and were partly projects for changing culture and discourse.

From this perspective, one striking feature of the 'PC' controversy is its narrow focus on one relatively small part of this pervasive process of cultural and discursive intervention. For one thing, as Hall (1994) points out, the left cultural politics which was labelled 'PC' by the right really took off during the Reagan–Thatcher era, which was characterised by substantial cultural and discursive interventions on the part of government. These were linked to the development and diffusion of a neo-liberal political agenda and political discourse especially on the part of New Right 'think tanks' (such as the Adam Smith Institute in the UK), which were closely linked to the Reagan and Thatcher governments. The 'terrorism' of feminists and anti-racists in, for instance, their attempts to gain institutional acceptance for guidelines for anti-racist and anti-sexist language use (see Section 3 of this article) seem small beer in comparison with the systematic diffusion and imposition of neo-liberal discourse through international organisations such as the World Bank and the OECD, and through the very media which were loudest in condemning 'PC'.

Of course there are significant differences in forms of cultural and discursive intervention, which can make it difficult to see the generality of the process. A primary target of critiques of 'PC' has been attempts by feminists, anti-racists and others to persuade organisations such as workplaces or universities to adopt guidelines which ask people to think about how they act and speak, to avoid certain behaviour and language (e.g., sexist language), and to adopt alternatives. There are also considerable variations in what one might call the illocutionary stance of such activists (asking, urging, demanding), but what is going in such cases is an *overt* attempt to challenge and change individual behaviour and language. By contrast, the neo-liberal project to change identities, values and representations (e.g., to inculcate 'flexibility' and 'individual responsibility', or extend market identities such as 'customer' or 'consumer' to public services such as education) has mainly relied upon the *covert* power of systems (international agencies, national governments, media, business or public service organisations).

Let us come back to the question of the apparent performative contradiction in critiques of 'PC'. Critics of 'PC' assemble together a diverse range of actions and interventions on the part of diverse groups of people (teachers, academics, feminist activists, etc.) within the category of 'PC', and sometimes refer to them collectively as if they constituted some sort of homogeneous social movement. It is easy enough to show that they do not; moreover, few of those identified as 'PCers' accept themselves to be such. 'Political correctness' and being 'politically correct' are, in the main, identifications imposed upon people by their political opponents. But this in itself is also a form of cultural politics, an intervention to change representations, values and identities as a way of achieving social change (Cameron 1995). And it has relied primarily on the complicity of sections of the media. The isolation of 'PC' from the more general process of cultural and discursive intervention has proved to be a remarkably effective way of disorienting sections of the left (see Section 3). At the same time, it has perhaps helped to divert attention from the more general, more pervasive, more profound and effective processes of cultural and discursive intervention referred to above. It is worth considering why critics of 'PC' readily say that it is 'PC' to suggest that adult females should be referred to as 'women' and not 'girls', but do not see it as 'PC' when 'bank accounts' are relabelled as 'financial products'. This relabelling is certainly prescriptive for bank employees, and imposed on customers, and in that sense has to do with what is 'correct'. But I imagine it is not generally seen as 'political'. The critique of 'PC' assumes a liberal separation between the 'political' and the 'economic', whereas from the perspective of political economy the 'economic' is 'political' (Sayer 1995) – the generalisation of markets and the commodity form to finance, to public services, and indeed to most of contemporary social life which such relabelling is a part of is an eminently 'political' change.

2 Theory: language, social practices and social change

Let me turn to the theoretical question, which I have already begun to address in Section 1. How are we to understand the relationships among culture, language and other elements of social life and social practices (including institutions and organisations, urban or industrial infrastructure, social relations)? How are we to understand the relationship between change in culture and language, and social change?

I suggested above that a particular form of social life is a particular networking of social practices including particular articulations among culture, language and other elements of social practices; and that social change is a change in the networking of social practices and the articulation of elements. A social practice (e.g., commodity advertising, secondary education) is an articulation of analytically different elements which are not, however, discrete but dialectically interconnected such that each internalises the others (Harvey 1996, Chouliaraki and Fairclough 1999, Fairclough 2000a). Let us say that the analytically different elements are:

- activities;
- subjects (endowed with representations, knowledge, beliefs, values, purposes, attitudes);
- social relations;
- instruments;
- objects;
- time and place;
- discourse.

Social practices are inherently reflexive – people interact, and at the same time they represent to themselves and each other what they do (sometimes drawing upon representations of what they do which come from other practices, including governmental and 'expert' practices). What they do is then shaped and reshaped by their representations of what they do. We can understand the dialectical internalisation of discourse within other elements in these terms: activities for instance are enactments of discourses (e.g., the way a teacher teaches is an enactment of particular representations, particular discourses, of teaching – maybe even developed 'theories' of teaching).

This perspective is the basis of theories of social constructionism – theories of social life as socially (discursively) constructed as an effect of discourses. Such 'discourse theory' has helped shape the forms of cultural politics that have been labelled as 'PC'. Processes of cultural and discursive intervention, including what is referred to as 'PC', can be seen in these terms as attempts to change discourses on the assumption that changing discourses will, or may, lead to changes in other elements of social practices through processes of dialectical internalisation. For instance, if people can be persuaded to talk of 'partner' rather than 'the person I'm living with' or 'lover' (or even 'mistress'), or if people being 'sacked' is partly displaced in public discourse by organisations 'downsizing', there will (or may) be consequential changes in how non-marital relationships and economic restructuring are perceived, and how people act and react towards them. Changes of discourse are not merely relabellings but shifts to different spheres of values. In the case of 'partner', this involves a shift for some people to the values of business relationships, which has made the term uncomfortable even for many who use it; in the case of 'downsizing' there is a shift to the values of a particular form of economics. Part of the controversy over 'PC' is attributable to often implicit differences between those who assume some form of 'discourse theory', which implies that representations are always positioned, value-laden and chosen against alternative representations. This compares with those who assume a transparent and direct relationship between what is said/written and 'the language', without the mediating level of discourse (Cameron 1995).

However, one has to be cautious about how one understands social (discursive) constructionism. First, the dialectical internalisation also works 'the other way round', which amounts to saying that discourses do not come out of nowhere. Second, the internalisation of discourses in other elements of social practices (including their physical–material elements, e.g., the plant and machinery of an industry) is a conditioned and contingent process. To see why this is so, we need to look more closely at the dialectics of discourse.

Let me distinguish among three principle ways in which discourse figures in social practices. It figures firstly as *discourses* (note the distinction between 'discourse' as an abstract noun and as a count noun – the latter is just one aspect of the former). Discourses are positioned representations (including reflexive self-representations of social practices) – positioned in the sense that different positions in the social relations of a social practice tend to give rise to different representations. Secondly, it figures as *genres* – ways of acting and interacting in their discourse (more broadly: semiotic) aspect. For instance, interviewing, lecturing and conversing are genres. Thirdly, it figures as *styles* – ways of being, identities, in their discourse (semiotic) aspect. For instance, there are various ways of being a political leader or a manager, which are partly bodily and partly discursive.

With these distinctions in mind, let us turn to the dialectics of discourse. Discourses include not only representations of how things are, they can also be representations of how things could be, or 'imaginaries'. They can represent or imagine interconnected webs of activities, instruments, objects, subjects in social relations, times and places, values etc. As imaginaries, they may come to be *enacted* as actual webs of activities, subjects, times and places, values etc. – they can become actual ways of acting and interacting. Such enactments include genres – the dialectical enactment of discourses is partly a movement within the discursive/semiotic moment/element of social practices, and partly a movement between this moment/element and others. They may also come to be *inculcated* as new ways of being, new identities – including new styles (but also new bodily behaviours).

'May' is crucially important: what I am suggesting is a moderate form of 'social constructivism' (Sayer 2000) which recognises that discourses may construct and reconstruct social practices, social structures and social life, but which also recognises that there are no guarantees of such constructive effects – the sedimentation of institutions and the habituses of people may make them resistant. The general point here is that a dialectical view of social practices should also include a recognition of the formation of (relative) permanences, which may limit the dialectical flow between elements (Harvey 1996). These relative permanences are of two main types. First, the relative permanence of institutions, organisations, networks of practices, structures. The point is a rather obvious one: structures and institutions develop internal rigidities that can make them resistant to any form of change and resistant, in particular, to cultural and discursive change. Second, the relative permanence of habituses. The habitus of a person (Bourdieu and Wacquant 1992) is a set of dispositions, stances, knowhows and so forth (discursive and non-discursive), which develops over time and can also be resistant to change. The conclusion, which I elaborate in political terms in Section 3, is that the socially constructive effects of discourses are contingent upon the resistances of structures and habituses.

3 Political strategy and tactics: the politics of culture and language

Let me turn now to the third question, about political strategy and tactics. For those who are politically committed to substantive social and political change (whether on the right or on the left), what place can a politics centred around culture and language have in a political strategy which is to have some chance of success?

Let me approach this issue via another question: why is it that the critique of 'PC' has been so successful? Why is it that it has divided the left, and confused and disoriented some sections of it? Why is it that labelling one's opponents as 'PC' has proved to be such a durable tactic, still widely resorted to (e.g., by the current and previous leaders of the British Conservative Party, Iain Duncan-Smith and William Hague) presumably because it is seen as still effective? Was it perhaps because the critiques of 'PC' have a real target to shoot at, that there is something really problematic about the forms of cultural politics which were the primary target?

That is the view of Hall (1994), whose critique I broadly subscribe to, although I think he is wrong to himself refer to the cultural politics he is critiquing as 'PC'. Hall locates the 'PC' controversy in Britain within the aftermath of the Thatcher government's abolition of the Greater London Council (GLC), whose leader was Ken Livingstone, now Mayor of London. Hall sees the GLC as having been an incipient left counter-hegemonic project to the hegemonic project of Thatcherism, successfully bringing together the cultural politics of the new social movements (anti-racism, feminism etc.) with more traditional left politics based on the trade unions and the labour movement. The political and especially media offensive against the 'loony left' GLC was, as Hall points out, a critique of 'PC' *avant la lettre*. With the demise of the GLC, the constituents of the alliance around it became fragmented, and some engaged in what Hall sees as a voluntarist form of 'vanguardist' cultural politics centring upon 'PC' – it lost any sense of the need for a strategic, counter-hegemonic, dimension. Hall is careful to distinguish between the validity of a cultural politics focused upon a critique of language in the construction of social identities and differences, and the vanguardist way in which this politics was pursued – its attempt to police language and behaviour, an ultra-left politics of 'demands'. Having said that, the danger of people on the left, such as Hall, using the label 'PC' (see also Eagleton 2000: 89) is that it fails to recognize that the differentiation he is seeking to make within left politics' tactics and strategies are fudged over in the critique of 'PC' – his own more cautious cultural and discursive interventions are just as likely to be critiqued as 'PC'.

Critics of 'PC' had a plausible target because some (but only some) of the forms of cultural and discursive intervention labelled as 'PC' smacked of the arrogance, self-righteousness and puritanism of an ultra-left politics, and have caused widespread resentment even among people basically committed to anti-racism, anti-sexism etc. I recall, for instance, a discussion with a respected

political activist some years ago after a political meeting in which the debate
was interrupted by what he saw as self-righteous, holier-than-thou, hectoring,
which fetishised a rather minor matter of wording (someone referred to the
chair as 'Mr Chairman') that was irrelevant to the point at issue, and was damaging to the meeting as a political event. My impression is that such reactions
were common. It is true, as critics of the critique of 'PC' have often pointed
out, that some of the favourite chestnuts were apocryphal (e.g., 'coffee without
milk' instead of 'black coffee'), but nevertheless the resonance which these
critiques have had indicates that they did connect with people's experiences.
The critiques are certainly reactionary, they certainly depend upon a spurious
construct called 'PC', they isolate one form of cultural and discoursal intervention from other forms, but like most successful ideologies they contain a
partial truth.

What follows from all this is that if the politics of culture and language are to
work as part of a political strategy with some prospect of success, they have
to be integrated within a politics of structures and habituses – a hegemonic
politics, in Hall's terms, which brings together interventions at various levels
of the social. For example, not focusing on sexist or racist language use in an
organisation through non-sexist/non-racist guidelines *in isolation from* other
potentially discriminatory aspects of the social relations of the organisation,
such as salary differentials or procedures for promotion. The right has understood this better than the left, though some on the left (still branded within the
catch-all ideological category of 'PC') have understood it too. Neo-liberal and
New Right politics have targeted structures and institutions, educational
systems (and thereby the formation of habituses), as well as cultural representations, values and identities. That in itself is no guarantee of success, and there
are manifestly resistances both to enactment and inculcation of neo-liberal
discourses. Moreover, relatively successful enactment does not guarantee
relatively successful inculcation: there is a stage short of inculcation at which
people may acquiesce to new discourses without accepting them – they may
mouth them rhetorically, for strategic and instrumental purposes, as happens,
for instance, with market discourse in public services such as education.

4 Conclusion

The editorial in the British daily newspaper the *Daily Mail* on 11 April 2000
was headlined 'Deplorable bid to stifle debate', and attacked the 'liberal
fascism' of the Liberal Democrats for their complaint to the Commission for
Racial Equality about the language of both Labour and Conservatives in
public statements about people seeking political asylum in Britain. A focus of

debate was asylum seekers being described as 'bogus'. The *Sun* editorial on the same day, under the heading 'Bogus issue', said: 'What a sad commentary on this PC-obsessed country that, instead of confronting the problem head on, we are talking about the "right language" to use!' It also says: 'There IS a flood of illegal immigrants . . . The majority ARE bogus' and 'The issue has nothing to do with race.'

The controversy over political asylum in Britain during the past couple of years is an example of the apparent continuing effectiveness of the strategy of wheeling out charges of 'PC' against political opponents. But how might those who are committed to more socially just policies towards refugees as well as 'economic migrants' respond to this strategy, both tactically in particular instances like this, and strategically in aiming in the long run to make the strategy ineffective? And how might discourse analysts and sociolinguists contribute? These are big issues which I can only touch upon here.

Strategically, critics of globalisation, neo-liberalism and more specific aspects of them such as policies on migration lack, as Hall (1994) points out, a hegemonic strategy. There is a widespread understanding that the emerging socio-economic order is deeply problematic, that, for instance, large business corporations have too much power and elected governments have too little power, that the advocacy of 'liberalisation' in the free movement of money and goods stands in stark contrast to the harsh restrictions on the movement of people. Yet, so far, there is no coherent alternative vision of a social order which can attract the support and conviction that might lead to a hegemonic strategy. Whether and when such a strategy will emerge we cannot know. But one of its preconditions is better theory and analysis.

There is clearly a need for a better theoretical understanding of the 'PC' controversy on, broadly, the left. Discourse analysts and sociolinguists can contribute through researching and theorising the 'PC' controversy, and seeking ways to bring their perspectives into the political debates. What is missing on the left is a general understanding of the significance and nature of cultural and linguistic interventions in the transformations of contemporary social life. We need a balanced view of the importance of language in social change and politics, which avoids a linguistic vanguardism as well as dismissing questions about language as trivial, and an incorporation of a politics of language within political strategies and tactics.

What does this imply tactically for responding to the critique of 'PC' in contexts such as the controversy over political asylum? First, that this particular issue be contextualised within contemporary patterns of migration, analysis of the causes of migration, including analysis of how pressures towards migration are produced through the damaging effects of the contemporary neo-liberal 'global' restructuring on the economic, political and social fabric of the poorer countries and regions of the world. Second, that the role of governments, politics and the media in legitimising the restructuring, in (as Bourdieu (1998a) puts it) clearing away obstacles to the restructuring be placed upon the political agenda, and be related to specific issues such as political asylum and immigration policy. Third, that the importance of language, of discourse, in both the restructuring and its legitimation with respect to particular issues like this one, become a matter for political debate. And fourth, that the strategic use of the critique of 'PC' in reducing and mystifying the linguistic and discoursal aspects of restructuring and legitimation, and as an instrument of political struggle, also become a matter for political debate within this wider frame. Of course, none of this is easy. But 'PC' needs to be addressed seriously by the left, because the critique of 'PC' remains an effective and damaging strategy.

Acknowledgements

I am grateful to Phil Graham (University of Queensland) and Sally Johnson (Lancaster University) for helpful comments on a draft of this article.

Globalisation and 'transition'

Introduction

The three papers in this section were written and published between 2005 and 2009 and deal with various aspects of globalisation, 'Europeanisation' and the 'transition' in the formerly socialist countries of Central and Eastern Europe from single-party state socialism towards the 'market economy' and western-style democracy. The three papers are primarily linked by a shared concern with what has become the internationally dominant strategy for shaping and 'steering' globalisation and especially the global economy, 'globalism', which was the focus of my book *Language and Globalization* (2006). Globalism is as it were the global wing of neo-liberal capitalism, its central strategic goal being to extend the dominance of this form of capitalism internationally.

Paper 18 ('Language and globalisation') is a presentation of my CDA approach to globalisation and globalism. I argue that 'globalisation' is both a discourse, or rather a set of discourses associated with diverse strategies, and transformations in material reality, and that the discoursal or semiotic facet of globalisation and its material facet are dialectically interconnected. Discourse is an irreducible part of globalisation, though globalisation cannot be reduced to 'just discourse', and critical analysis of globalisation needs to address these dialectical relations. I discuss different strategies for steering globalisation in particular directions and the discourses associated with them, including the dominant strategy of 'globalism'; how processes of globalisation impact at different 'scales' (local, national, international) and especially the national scale; the implication of the mass media in processes of and struggles over globalisation, and people's 'lay' experience of and responses to globalisation. I also include a discussion of the 'war on terror' on the grounds that it is part of a militaristic and imperialistic turn in 'globalist' strategy.

Paper 19 ('Global capitalism, terrorism and war: a discourse-analytical perspective') is built around an analysis of the American *National Security Strategy* (2002), which has played a major part in defining the shift in American strategy especially since 2001 in a more militaristic direction. My concern in the analysis is with the 'texturing' (textual production) of a discourse in this document (among others), which can be seen as the discoursal dimension or 'moment' of the development of a new American strategy. The general research concern is with a transdisciplinary approach to changes in international relations, and this paper is exploring a specifically discoursal or semiotic 'point of entry' into transdisciplinary analysis of strategies for change. I focus on the question of the causal powers of discourse – the conditions under which particular ways of *construing* reality in a document of this sort may have *constructive*, transformative effects upon reality. I suggest that these conditions include both having a measure of *practical adequacy* (construing reality as it actually is to a sufficient degree) and having the capacity to win people's *conviction*. I distinguish two sorts of constructive effects, material and mental (effects on attitudes and beliefs), and suggest that ideology combines the two; and I further distinguish *consent* and *legitimacy* as mental effects on the grounds that while the former may be achieved by persuasive means of any sort (i.e., just rhetorically), the latter requires argumentation which is dialectically sound. I also discuss *displacement*, in the sense of a rhetorically motivated gap between construals of the strategy for public consumption and other construals where the intentions and objectives of power are more transparent, and limits on degrees of displacement in public discourse.

Paper 20 ('Discourse and "transition" in Central and Eastern Europe') deals with the role of discourse in 'transition' from centralised state socialism to market capitalism and Western forms of democratic government in Central and Eastern Europe (CEE). I focus on attempts specifically in Romania to construct a 'knowledge-based economy' (KBE) and 'information society' (IS). The importance of discourse in processes of 'transition' is quite widely recognised in social research but it has so far produced only a limited understanding of how discourse actually figures in these processes, partly because the theories of discourse which are drawn upon do not constitute an adequate basis for full and nuanced accounts of how discourse interacts with other non-discursive facets of 'transition', partly because abstract statements about discourse have not generally been translated into detailed analysis texts or talk. I view KBE and IS as strategies for achieving and stabilising a new 'fix' between a regime of capital accumulation and a regime of political regulation (in the terms of the 'regulation approach') in the aftermath of the demise of the 'fix' commonly referred to as 'Fordism' (Jessop 2004). These strategies are being pursued in 'the West' including the western area of the EU, and recontextualised in CEE as part of the processes of 'transition'. These strategies have a partially material and partially discursive character – they include discourses which represent and 'imagine', simplify and condense, complex economic, political, social and cultural realities. To analyse them we need to use a framework such as the one Jessop proposes, a 'cultural political economy' which incorporates CDA and allows analysis of the relationships between discourse and materiality in processes of change, including the potentially 'constructive' or transformative effects of discourse on non-discursive realities. I discuss the recontextualisation of these strategies and discourses in Romania with particular reference to a government policy text, the *National Strategy for the promotion of the New Economy and the implementation of the Information Society* (2002).

18. Language and globalisation

L et me begin from two very general and abstract formulations of the highly complex sets of changes which have been recently referred to as 'globalisation': 'a process (or set of processes) which embodies a transformation in the spatial organisation of social relations and transactions . . . generating transcontinental or interregional flows and networks of activity, interaction, and the exercise of power' (Held *et al.* 1999); 'complex connectivity . . . the rapidly developing and ever-densening network of interconnections and interdependencies that characterise modern social life' (Tomlinson 1999: 2). These 'flows', 'networks' and 'interconnections' are generally seen as very diverse in character, and including flows of goods and money and international financial and trading networks in the economic field; intergovernmental networks and interdependencies and interactions and interconnections between international agencies such as the United Nations (UN), the International Monetary Fund (IMF), and the World Trade Organisation (WTO) and government agencies at national and regional levels; the mobility of people as migrants, tourists, or members of commercial or governmental organisations; flows of images and representations and interactions through contemporary media and forms of technology; and so forth.

We can make three initial observations about discourse in processes of globalisation in this sense. First, that the networks, connectivities and interactions crucially include, and one might say depend upon, particular forms (or 'genres') of communication which are specialised for transnational and interregional interaction, such as the genres of global news networks; and that the 'flows' include flows of representations, narratives and discourses, such as neo-liberal economic discourse. In that sense, it is partly discourse that is globalising and globalised. Second, that it is important to make a distinction between actual processes and tendencies of globalisation, and representations or discourses of globalisation. We cannot get away from the fact that globalisation is both a set of changes which are actually happening in the world (though what the set includes is highly controversial), and a word – 'globalisation' – which has quite recently become prominent in the ways in which such changes are represented. But this is a simplification, because the word 'globalisation' is used in various senses within more complex discourses, which are partly characterised by distinctive vocabularies in which 'globalisation' is related in particular ways to other 'keywords' such as 'modernisation', 'democracy', 'markets', 'free trade', 'flexibility', 'liberalisation', 'security', 'terrorism', 'cosmopolitanism' and so forth; and these discourses are more than vocabularies – they have certain lexico-grammatical features (e.g., does 'globalisation' figure as a causal agent in material processes, as in 'globalisation opens up new markets'?), certain narratives, certain forms of argumentation, and so forth.[1] Third, having made this distinction, it is equally important to consider what the relationship is between actual processes of globalisation and representations of globalisation. In broad terms, we can say that representations and discourses of globalisation do not merely construe processes and tendencies of globalisation which are happening independently (though they do so construe them, for instance in political rhetoric), they also contribute to creating and shaping actual processes of globalisation, though in complex and contingent ways.

A vast amount has been said and written about globalisation, and this in itself makes it a difficult and confusing issue to write about. It is made more confusing if we do not distinguish what has been said by whom, and differentiate the main 'voices' within all this talk and writing. I shall distinguish five: academic research and analysis; government agencies in a broad sense – national governments, political leaders, agencies which are a part of national governments, agencies of international governance such as the UN or the WTO, and so forth; non-governmental agencies, again in a very inclusive sense including for instance business corporations, charities such as Oxfam, campaigning or monitoring organisations such as Greenpeace or CorpWatch; the media (television, radio, press etc.); and people as citizens or members of various sorts of community – people acting out their 'ordinary' lives. These voices are not fully discrete: there are flows between them – for instance, academic analysis directly or indirectly contributes to the language of governmental and non-governmental agencies, and academic analysis itself draws from management literature. And, of course, differentiating just five major sources inevitably simplifies the plethora of actual voices.

The six sections of the paper partly correspond to these diverse 'voices'. In Section 1, I summarise views on discourse as a facet of globalisation in the academic literature, and then summarise my own approach, which is based upon a version of 'critical discourse analysis' (CDA) which is envisaged as a component of a 'cultural' political economy. In Section 2, I discuss different strategies of globalisation (and regionalisation) emanating from governmental and non-governmental agencies, and the different discourses which constitute elements of these strategies. In Section 3, I discuss how processes of globalisation impact upon specific spatial 'entities' (nation states, cities, regions etc.) in terms of the idea of 're-scaling', i.e., changing relations in processes, relationships, practices and so forth between local, national, and international (including 'global') scales. I focus here upon the national scale in its relation to the global scale and the scale of international regions (in particular, the process of 'European integration'). In Section 4, I deal with the media and mediation. In Section 5, I discuss people's ordinary experience of globalisation, and its implications for and effects upon their lives.

Section 6 deals with war and terrorism. A discussion of this issue may seem surprising in a paper on the theme of language and globalisation, so let me briefly explain it, and in so doing clarify the particular stance I am taking on globalisation and its discourse facet. I shall focus in Section 2 on what Steger (2005) has called 'globalism' (see also Saul 2005), which is the strategy and discourse (and 'story') of globalisation which has become most influential, has had most effect on actual processes of change. The key feature of 'globalism' as a discourse is that it construes (and aims to construct, or more contentiously hijack) the actual processes of globalisation in a neo-liberal way – as centrally the liberalisation and global integration of markets. Latterly the 'war on terror' has been construed as a necessary element in defending and advancing 'globalisation' in this reductive sense (and, the claim is, human progress). I focus on 'globalism' not because it exhausts globalisation – it does not, globalisation is a much bigger phenomenon – nor because 'globalism' is the only current discourse of globalisation (it is not) but because it is the discourse which has become hegemonic.

1 Views on discourse as a facet of globalisation

There are various attempts to classify the vast and diverse academic literature on globalisation, including the well-known differentiation between 'hyperglobalist', 'sceptical', and 'transformationalist' positions in Held *et al.* (1999) (see also Hay and Marsh 2000, Cameron and Palan 2004). But I want to suggest a classification more suited to the purpose of this paper, based upon different views of discourse as a facet of globalisation. Four main positions can be distinguished: objectivism, rhetoricism, ideologism and social constructivism. Objectivism treats globalisation as simply objective fact, which discourse may either illuminate or obscure, represent or misrepresent (the position basically adopted for instance in Held *et al.* 1999). Rhetoricism focuses on how various discourses of globalisation are used for instance by politicians to persuade publics to accept certain (sometimes unpalatable) policies (see, for example, Hay and Rosamond (2002)). Ideologism focuses upon how particular discourses of globalisation systematically contribute to the legitimation of a particular global order which incorporates asymmetrical relations of power such as those between and within countries (e.g., Steger 2005). Social constructivism[2] recognises the socially constructed character of social life in general and forms of globalisation in particular, and sees discourse as potentially having significant causal effects in processes of social construction (e.g., Cameron and Palan 2004). Let me stress that these are recognisable general positions, which particular authors often use in combination – for instance, although Steger's emphasis is on ideology, he also discusses the socially constructive force of discourses.

From this classification of positions we can identify five general claims about discourse as a facet of globalisation:

1. Discourse can represent globalisation, giving people information about it and contributing to their understanding of it.
2. Discourse can misrepresent and mystify globalisation, giving a confusing and misleading impression of it.
3. Discourse can be used rhetorically to project a particular view of globalisation which can justify or legitimise the actions, policies or strategies of particular (usually powerful) social agencies and agents.
4. Discourse can contribute to the constitution, dissemination and reproduction of ideologies, which can also be seen as forms of mystification, but have a crucial systemic function in sustaining a particular form of globalisation and the (unequal and unjust) power relations which are built into it.
5. Discourse can generate imaginary representations of how the world will be or should be within strategies for change which, if they achieve hegemony, can be operationalised to transform these imaginaries into realities, i.e., particular actual forms of globalisation.

The fifth claim is the strongest one, and it is the claim I have committed myself to above. But this does not mean that we should reject the others – on the contrary, there is truth in all of them. What is generally lacking in the existing literature, however, is a systematic approach to theorising and analysing discourse as a facet of globalisation which can show these various effects of discourse and the relationship between them, and help explain them.

My approach to discourse is a particular version of CDA (Chouliaraki and Fairclough 1999, Fairclough 2000a, 2000b, Fairclough 2003, Fairclough, Jessop and Sayer 2004, Fairclough 2005a, 2005b), but I think it is fruitful in researching discourse as a facet of globalisation to work with a 'cultural' political economy (Jessop and Sum 2001, Jessop 2004) which incorporates the former. Political economy differs from classical economics in asserting that economic systems and economic changes are politically conditioned and embedded (Polanyi 1944). Cultural political economy asserts that economic and political 'objects' in the widest sense (including economic systems, economic organisations, the division of labour, the state, forms of management and governance) are socially constructed, are co-constructions of subjects and objects (and hence also culturally conditioned and embedded), and are in part effects of discourse. What I have called actual processes and tendencies of globalisation are highly complex, diverse, uneven, multidimensional (economic, political, social, cultural, ecological and so forth) and incapable of being fully controlled by any human intervention. Nevertheless, as in any actual scenario, strategies are developed to regulate, direct and control elements of these real processes, which may if successful inflect and partly redirect their overall trajectory, and such strategies centrally include discourses which represent and narrate past and present processes and imagine possible futures, possible economic (social, political, cultural) orders. Even if, as in the case of globalism, the primary objectives of the strategy are economic, the non-economic conditioning and embedding of economic systems, objects and processes which I have alluded to means that a strategy is only likely to succeed if it aims for general social and cultural change.

In situations of disorientation and crisis such as that associated with the difficulties of post-war Fordist economic systems and the Keynsian welfare state (Jessop 2002) which preceded the emergence of globalism, one finds a proliferation of discourses imagining alternative forms of organisation for economy, state and society. One central question for cultural political economy is the mechanisms and processes which connect variation, selection and retention, i.e., how certain of the discourses which are circulating are selected, and how they come to be retained (or institutionalised) and thereby come to be capable of having constitutive effects on real economic, political and social processes. This is a question one can ask about the discourse of globalism – how did it come to be selected from a range of alternatives and retained (institutionalised)? How did it come to shape actual processes and tendencies of globalisation or, in other words, come to be operationalised and implemented? Operationalisation points to the dialectical character of relations within discourse and between discourse and other elements or moments of the social. A discourse is operationalised through being enacted in ways of acting and interacting which themselves have a partially discursive character in that they include genres (ways of interacting communicatively), for instance in ways of working, managing, governing, or conducting politics; through being inculcated in ways of being, social and personal identities, which also have a partly discursive character in that they include styles (ways of being in their specifically communicative or discursive aspect, as opposed to their bodily or somatic aspects), for instance the identities of workers, entrepreneurs, managers, politicians, teachers; and through being materialised physically in technologies, infrastructures, architectures and so forth. From a discourse-analytical perspective a successfully operationalised strategy constitutes a new order of discourse (Fairclough 1992a), i.e., a new structured (though flexibly structured) configuration of discourses, genres and styles. Globalism, neo-liberal globalisation, is in part an order of discourse in this sense. It is important to add, however, that the hegemony of such a strategy, discourse, and operationalised social order can never be complete – because actual processes always exceed even successfully constructed construals of them; because there are always alternative and even counter strategies and discourses, and because any successfully reconstituted reality is a contradictory and crisis-prone reality (Jessop 2004).

2 Discourses of globalisation

'Globalism' is a discourse of globalisation which represents it in reductive neo-liberal economic terms within a strategy to inflect actual processes of globalisation in that direction. Steger (2005) identifies six core claims of 'globalism' (as well as providing arguments against all of them):

1. Globalisation is about the liberalisation and global integration of markets.
2. Globalisation is inevitable and irreversible.
3. Nobody is in charge of globalisation.
4. Globalisation benefits everyone.
5. Globalisation furthers the spread of democracy in the world.
6. Globalisation requires a war on terror.

The first claim is the most crucial one, and most central to the question of how this particular discourse came to be selected and retained from the range of alternatives, especially in what it assumes as a general and therefore globally applicable truth, that the most effective form of capitalist economy is one based upon 'liberalised' markets. The plausibility and resonance of this assumption rest upon what have been pretty successfully established as facts about the post second-world-war socio-economic order, and especially the 'fact' that markets are self-regulating and interference by states (as this history is claimed to have shown) are economically counter-productive and damaging. There is, of course, the contrary 'fact' that unregulated markets have been shown to produce chaotic and disastrous effects (Polanyi 1944), but in the aftermath of the economic troubles of the 1970s powerful agents and agencies were unreceptive to it. For in addition to a perceived objective plausibility in real experience, market liberalisation gained the support of the most powerful states (the USA and Britain were forerunners) and influential politicians, international agencies which these states effectively control (the World Bank, IMF, WTO, OECD etc.), private corporations, and many other agents and agencies. Steger describes globalism as a 'story' (or narrative), a discourse, and an ideology. The term 'ideology' is not inappropriate: globalism can be seen as having created a space for unconstrained and highly profitable action on the part of the corporations of the most powerful countries on earth, especially the USA, on the basis of a claim that markets work benignly without external regulation which the crises of the late 1990s (in East Asia, Latin America, and Russia) have shown to be false. Yet the strategy and discourse have proved relatively resilient and capable of accommodating certain concessions to regulation without major change. It has also gained influence within the European Union despite continuing commitment to some form (if a 'modernised' and arguably weakened one) of the European Social Model.

Epistemologically, discourses are abstract entities which established on the basis of repetition and recurrence over time and in diverse social sites, but ontologically they appear in the concrete form of particular texts. One contribution that CDA can make to (cultural) political economic analysis is methods for analysing texts which illuminate their contribution to strategies, discourses, and their operationalisation and implementation, as well as their recontextualisation in different places (e.g., countries, regions) and different fields of social life, and their adaptation to changing events and circumstances. CDA in itself cannot, however, tell us which texts are significant within the constitutive effects of discourse on social life – that requires institutional and historical forms of analysis.

I shall illustrate the contribution of textual analysis in the case of a speech (Eizenstat 1999) whose significance arises from the standing of the speaker (US undersecretary of State, Stuart Eizenstat) and the context of crisis for globalism within which it was delivered and which it addresses (it was delivered in the wake of the Asian economic collapse in the late 1990s), constituting a response by the US government to crises which threatened the strategy they supported. In essence, Eizenstat acknowledges the threat while arguing that 'globalisation' must not be abandoned, that the crisis was largely due to flaws in the countries affected, and that international help must be given to remedying them, and thus restoring confidence in the capacity of the system to deliver on its promises. The speech is clearly globalist, and it illustrates some of the central globalist claims identified by Steger: that 'globalisation' benefits everyone ('By any measure, globalisation is a net benefit to the United States and the world. In an increasingly globalised and interdependent economy, the quest for prosperity is the opposite of a zero sum game'), that it is inevitable and irreversible ('Globalisation is an inevitable element of our lives. We cannot stop it anymore than we can stop the waves from crashing on the shore'), and that it strengthens democracy. Yet there is evidence in apparent incoherencies within the speech that its attempt, to justify continuing adherence to a globalist strategy in the face of stark evidence of the failures of globalism and 'fears' of a consequential 'backlash against globalisation', puts the discourse of globalism under strain. For example, the quotation above to illustrate the claimed inevitability and irreversibility of 'globalisation' comes from the following paragraph in the official transcript:

> Globalization is an inevitable element of our lives. We cannot stop it anymore than we can stop the waves from crashing on the shore. The arguments in support of trade liberalization and open markets are strong ones – they have been made by many of you and we must not be afraid to engage those with whom we respectfully disagree.

This appears to be an argument, with a claim in the first sentence which seems to be supported by two grounds in the second and third sentences. But it is incoherent because the two grounds are in contradiction – if globalisation is analogous to a natural phenomenon in its inevitability, how can it be open to argument, as the second ground implies? To put the problem in different terms, we have three sentences which are combined in the transcript within a paragraph, which implies coherent relations of meaning between them which are difficult to see. The difficulty lies in the meaning of 'globalisation', a word which is much used in the text but in a way which confuses the 'forces' of globalisation which the US strategy for 'trade liberalisation and open markets' is designed to 'harness', and the (globalist) strategy itself. Here as elsewhere in the speech, an implicit equivalence is constructed between 'globalisation' and 'trade liberalisation and open markets'. In the following paragraph, the implicit equivalence is between 'globalisation' and 'dramatic economic liberalisation':

> In short, the financial crisis has exacerbated fears in developing countries and could fuel a backlash against globalization. Indeed, the optimistic notion only 2 years ago that the world was adopting dramatic economic liberalization as a model for economic and political development is under challenge.

We might counter Eizenstat's argument with the claim that the feared 'backlash' is surely against globalist strategy, not against globalisation as a set of real processes. And for the following extract, with the claim that the 'undeniable risks' surely come from globalist strategy and policies, not from the real processes of globalisation, and that it is by no means 'fruitless' to attempt to stop the former.

> The world must neither resort to protectionist measures in a fruitless attempt to stop globalization nor should we ignore its undeniable risks.

In short, Eisenstat's apologia for globalism in the face of evidence and widespread recognition of its manifest failures is built upon obscuring the difference between globalisation as a set of real processes and tendencies, and one favoured strategy among a number of conceivable and potentially viable alternatives for regulating, controlling and directing a globalising world.

If Eizenstat's speech illustrates the capacity of the strategy and discourse of 'globalism' to accommodate failures and crises without fundamental change, though not without incoherence and contradiction, there is no shortage of alternative and competing strategies and discourses which in some cases, especially since the crises of the late 1990s, constitute a challenge to the hegemony of 'globalism'. The Malaysian government withdrew from the neo-liberal 'global economy' after the Asian crisis and has pursued its own counter-strategy with some considerable success (bin Mohamad 2002). Other Asian governments also have their own strategies for and discourses of globalisation. In the European Union, especially countries with a strong tradition of social democracy (such as Sweden) seek to combine international competitiveness with strong social policies. And some international agencies have pushed for alternatives to globalism (e.g., ECLAC 2002). There are then many non-governmental organisations which produced alternative and competing strategies, including those which reflect the 'limits to growth' perspective such as the Green Party in the UK (Green Party UK 2005). Globalism is still the most influential strategy, but it has had to some extent to come to terms with others, though US policy especially since 11 September 2001 has favoured aggressive unilateralism over accommodation, shifting from what Steger (2005) calls 'soft power' (reliance on persuasion and inducements) to 'hard power' (using economic and military force to compel compliance) in pursuit of a version of globalism which is more nakedly self-interested.

3 Re-scaling

I shall now shift my focus from strategies and discourses of globalisation to the question of how processes of globalisation impact upon specific spatial 'entities' (nation states, cities, regions etc.), how they become globalised. I shall draw upon Jessop's view (2002) of globalisation as the constitution of new scales of social action, interaction and exchange (not only the global scale, but also for instance the 'macro-regional' scale of the European Union or the North American Free Trade Area, and the scale of 'cross-border regions'), and of new relations between different scales. The spatial entity I focus on here is the nation state, taking Romania, one of the 'post-communist' states of Eastern Europe, as an example. The globalisation of a country like Romania can be viewed as a matter of its 're-scaling', its incorporation into new relations of scale.

The strategy of globalism constitutes from this perspective a strategy to constitute a global scale of action, interaction and exchange. As I argued above, the objective is a global scale which is narrowly constrained and one might say reduced in terms of the forms of action, interaction and exchange it entails to, in Eizenstat's words, 'trade liberalisation and open markets', though the political and cultural embedding of economies which I discussed earlier mean that the success of the strategy is conditional upon a more general transformation of social relations, institutions, values, attitudes and identities. Success also requires the dissemination of the strategy and discourse within innumerable spatial entities including nation states like Romania, and their operationalisation and implementation. There are also simultaneously strategies and discourses to constitute macro-regional scales such as the European scale. When we begin to examine these strategies in detail, it becomes clear that although it may be possible to identify overall strategies oriented to both the global and the macro-regional scales, these are 'nodal' strategies around which a multiplicity of more focused strategies are clustered. So in the case of the European Union, a nodal strategy was defined by the Lisbon Council of

2000 (to make the EU 'the most competitive and dynamic knowledge-based economy in the world, capable of sustainable economic growth with more and better jobs and greater social cohesion'), but there are many more focused strategies for constituting a European scale (or 'space' or 'area') of higher education, lifelong learning, competitiveness, social inclusion, and so forth.

These strategies and discourses, as well as many others, are 'recontextualised' (Chouliaraki and Fairclough 1999) in spatial entities at various scales, including nation states like Romania. Recontextualisation is not a simple matter of the spread of strategies and discourses to new contexts. Chouliaraki and Fairclough (1999) argue for seeing recontextualisation as a dialectical process of external 'colonisation' by and internal 'appropriation' of recontextualised elements, which are appropriated within an internal field (or rather complex set of fields) of strategic diversity, contestation and struggle. Romania is said to be a country in 'transition' from a centrally planned economy and one-party state to a market economy and western parliamentary democracy, and it is even after fifteen years of 'transition' a highly complex not to say chaotic and disorganised mixture of old and new. The actual impact on particular nation states of recontextualised strategies and discourses is likely to be variable, unpredictable, and potentially quite different from what strategists may have envisaged. Is for instance 'trade liberalisation and open markets' an accurate way of describing Romania fifteen years after what was effectively a globalist strategy for transition (what came to be known as the 'Washington Consensus') was defined for it as for other post-communist countries? Partly, yes – but Romania is also characterised by a still significant if rapidly diminishing state economic sector, a substantial 'black economy', and the existence of clientelist relations between the state, political parties, public administration and private business which make the word 'open' highly problematic and produce massive corruption and the exorbitant self-enrichment of an elite.

Let me try to make these general observations about re-scaling more concrete by referring to a particular example, the EU's strategy to constitute a European Area of Higher Education (i.e., a European scale in higher education) which would incorporate candidates for EU accession like Romania as well as other countries on borders of the EU as well as EU members, and the recontextualisation of the EU strategy and discourse in Romania. EU strategy is based around the 'Bologna process' which grew out of the Bologna Declaration (2001). Its aim is to achieve 'greater compatibility and comparability of the systems of higher education' in the region in both undergraduate and graduate degrees, in order to 'promote citizens' mobility and employability' and 'the international competitiveness of the European system of higher education'. The latter objective indicates that the process of higher educational reform is actually global, not just European – the Bologna process is a European response to global processes of change, which involve the emergence of a competitive international market in higher education (as part of the moves towards a General Agreement on Trade in Services within the WTO), in the context of the perceived increasing economic importance of higher education in the 'knowledge-based economy' which the EU is committed to, and fears about the EU's lack of competitiveness with the USA and East Asia. The specific targets include standardisation of degree structures in terms of the duration of undergraduate and graduate degrees and the number of credits attaching to each unit, the development of comparable criteria and methodologies for quality assurance, a 'Diploma Supplement' which would make qualifications more easily readable and comparable, and promoting student and staff mobility within European countries.

The discourse associated with the Bologna strategy is internally complex, and we can better refer to it as a nodal discourse which is constituted as a configuration of discourses, including for instance the discourses of 'competitiveness' and 'quality'. Moreover, the Bologna process is an incremental one in which the strategy and discourse have been elaborated over time, at regular biannual meetings of Ministers of Education. For Romania, the selection of this discourse was a selection that made itself, given government policy to achieve accession to the EU, and given the relations of power entailed (for successful accession, involvement is required in the construction of European scales in various domains). One part of measures to secure retention of the discourse, as well as its operationalisation and implementation, has been legislation – a new Law on the Organization of University Studies was passed in 2004, requiring universities to implement the specific targets detailed above. The justification for the new law provided by the government in Parliament was that reorganisation would 'eliminate excessive specialization', contribute to the 'development of professions which are short of specialized and economically and culturally necessary personnel', contribute to 'the development of new qualifications related to current needs and . . . the labour market', and be in line with 'the dynamics of the labour market at national, European and international level'. So the Government's interest was more or less entirely economic, and there were no references to other legitimations which have been prominent in the Bologna documentation such as student mobility or European culture and identity. The new system was put into operation from autumn 2005.

But a promised law on 'quality assurance' has not yet emerged, and it is quality assurance I want to focus on to illustrate the complexities and uncertainties of recontextualisation and re-scaling in Romania. There is a general public cynicism about government discourse and legislation which is constantly expressed in public discourse, including the mass media, in terms of a gap between words and realities. In this case as in others, it is with operationalisation and implementation that the problems begin. To put a complex issue in a simple way, there is considerable scepticism about whether Romanian universities have, or can come to have in the near future, the institutional characteristics which are prerequisites for the Bologna reforms to be actually implemented. Quality assurance is a particularly good illustration of the problems.

The European Association for Quality Assurance in Higher Education (ENQA) has developed 'European standards for internal and external quality assurance, and for external quality assurance agencies' which were approved at the Bergen meeting of Ministers of Education in 2005. The methodology for quality assurance is centred upon 'self-examination' and 'self-evaluation' – the principle that 'providers of higher education have the primary responsibility for the quality of their provision and its assurance' (ENQA 2005). They should establish an inclusive 'culture of quality' (including students, academic staff, administrative staff and other 'stakeholders') which recognises the importance of quality and seeks its continuous enhancement. The role of external quality assurance is to ensure that this process of internal quality assurance is adequate. In internal quality assurance, 'institutions should have formal mechanisms for the approval, periodic review and monitoring of their programmes and awards'; 'students should be assessed using published criteria, regulations and procedures which are applied consistently'; 'institutions should have ways of satisfying themselves that staff involved with the teaching of students are qualified and competent to do so'; that 'the resources available for the support of student learning are adequate and appropriate' and that they 'collect, analyse and use relevant information for the effective management of their programmes of study and other activities'.

The operationalisation of this discourse of quality assurance entails its enactment through the constitution and institutionalisation of new procedures ('mechanisms') which amount to a new set of interconnected genres (on genre 'chains' or 'networks', see Fairclough 2003), such as genres for staff self-evaluation and student evaluation of courses. It also entails, as the idea of a 'culture of quality' suggests, its inculcation in new ways of being, new institutional identities which substantively include new styles. The idea of a 'culture' of quality and an ongoing concern to improve quality through self-monitoring and self-assessment implies changes in 'the way people perceive themselves in relation to their work, to one another and to themselves', changes in 'professional, collegial and personal identity' (Shore and Wright 2000). Thus systems of quality assurance entail profound changes in institutions, their social relationships and practices and the identities of their members, which could fruitfully be researched with CDA as changes in their orders of discourse. They entail social relationships which are open and relatively egalitarian, practices which are transparent and subject to effective institutional regulation, and people who are professionally committed to the institution and well disposed to continuous learning. Consider, for example, staff appraisal. The staff appraisal procedure I am familiar with in one British university is transparently defined as a network of genres: a written self-evaluative report by the appraisee, which is the basis for an interview between appraiser and appraisee so designed as to achieve consensus on an account and evaluation of the appraiser's work in the preceding period, a plan for the next period, and means for fulfilling this plan. The appraisal interview is the basis for a report written by the appraiser and agreed by the appraisee which is confidential to both of them and the Head of Department. For such a procedure to work successfully, the sort of prerequisites I have indicated need to be in place.

The general situation in Romanian universities (there are differences, and exceptions) is that institutional regulation of practices is poor and opaque; social relations are highly hierarchical and predominantly clientelist and the distribution of goods is controlled in often arbitrary and personalised ways by a professorial elite; and people in some cases cynically seek to maximise their own interests, and in most cases are demoralised and alienated by abysmal salaries and conditions and what they perceive as an under-resourced and unjust system. There is already a national council set up for external quality assurance, and internal quality assurance systems are in a more or less advanced stage of preparation in individual universities. Public universities are still subject to a substantial measure of ministerial control, so a quality assurance system and new procedures will emerge. The optimistic view is that systems and procedures will contribute to the profound transformations I have indicated; the pessimistic and perhaps more realistic view is that existing social relations and interests are so entrenched that lip-service will be paid to forms of quality assurance with little substance, and certainly nothing resembling a 'culture of quality'. If the latter happens, there will be new genres and styles – on paper, but probably not in practice.[3]

Quality assurance is just one example of a new technology and discourse of governance which is based upon a principle of 'self-management', 'monitoring' and 'assessment' combined with external 'audit', 'rituals of verification'. 'Where audit is applied to public institutions – medical, legal, educational – the state's overt concern may be less to impose day-to-day direction than to ensure that internal controls, in the form of monitoring techniques, are in place' (Strathern 2000). The technology/discourse is closely associated with the idea of the 'accountability' of public institutions. These developments in governance fall under the general rubric of 'new public management', which is consistent with neo-liberal principles of converting public services into competitive markets (Rose 1999). On the face of it, institutions are 'empowered' to make their own way in the market free of bureaucratic control, but their autonomy is largely illusory, because they are subject to 'audits' which monitor how effective their mechanisms and procedures are for 'assuring' standards of 'quality' which are imposed upon them. The 'open method of coordination' adopted by the EU can be seen as essentially the same technology and discourse of governance. The Bologna strategy thus overlaps with a strategy and discourse to constitute a European scale of governance, and the problems I have indicated for Romania in operationalising the former are compounded as the latter is applied to a variety of institutions.

Let me just add that university reform in Romania as in other countries gives people working in universities a sense of being caught between the devil and the deep blue sea. While few people would wish to defend to existing system, few people are attracted by the subordination of universities to economic demands and interests or the university system turning into just another competitive international market.

4 Media and mediation

Cultural political economy asserts that political economies are subject to cultural conditions, and are culturally embedded. In contemporary societies, mass media are the predominant social field in the creation of these cultural conditions – in the constitution of the public knowledge and information, beliefs, values and attitudes which are necessary for establishing and sustaining economic, social and political systems and orders. Changes in the international political economy of communication have been an important factor for the relative success of globalist strategy and discourse. The emergence of a global communications industry, dominated by powerful transnational corporations such as Rupert Murdoch's News Corporation, is itself a significant part of the emergence of a neo-liberal 'global economy'. The role of these corporations in global political economy is twofold: first, they have provided the infrastructure (hardware and software) that has enabled changes in the pattern of production; second, they are 'the major purveyors of news, information, entertainment and knowledge about the world in general' (Wilkin 2001: 126). They are the main source of views and ideas, of a sense of what is right and what is possible, and the main providers of credibility and legitimacy for the powers that be. They contribute to the dissemination of globalist discourse, claims and assumptions, and of the values, attitudes and identities which are conditions for the successful implementation of globalism, on the basis of an intimate relationship between these corporations and other sectors of business, the public relations industry, governments in the most powerful states, and other agencies. This is not to say that the media as a whole are a mere echo chamber for globalism. Influential independent newspapers and broadcasting still exist in many countries, and they have in many cases played a crucial role in challenging aspects of globalism as well as orchestrating opposition to war (especially in the case of Iraq). But the independent role of the media as a 'fourth estate' fulfilling a public service role, providing accurate and dispassionate information, and, where necessary, exposure and criticism of social ills, is being progressively undermined as the transnational corporations become dominant in the media field internationally.

With respect to news, one can see the partial emergence of a global news agenda whose coverage depends upon a common resource of news agency reports and film, addressed to an increasingly global audience, and producing globalised representations and meanings around particular events. This is particularly clear in the case of news items which top the global agenda, such as natural disasters like the tsunami of December 2004, terrorist attacks like '9/11', wars (most recently the Iraq war), the death of prominent individuals (such as the Pope), or major international political events such as meetings of G8 or the WTO. Meetings of such organisations have become occasions for protest demonstrations by people who are opposed to the way that globalism is actually working with respect to such matters as international debt, terms of trade between rich and poor states, and so forth, and I want to take the coverage of such representations as an example. Such demonstrations have come to be increasingly seen and treated as primarily problems of law and order, and predominant media representations in countries across the world represent them with a focus upon anticipated or actual violence rather than on the major political issues which are at stake, according to what we can call an established narrative schema or template which is applied to new events as they occur. An example of the focus on anticipated violence in the media build-up to such events is a report in the British *Daily Telegraph* on 12 June 2005 about the G8 meeting in Edinburgh in July. The headline was 'Police prepare to make thousands of arrests at G8', and the article began as follows:

The Army is preparing barracks and military bases in Scotland for use as holding camps if, as police expect, thousands of protesters are arrested during the G8 summit of world leaders next month.

The decision to earmark sites where protesters may be held follows warnings from European police forces and intelligence officials that foreign anarchists have already entered Britain and are plotting to disrupt the meeting, to be held at Gleneagles, the luxury hotel and resort in Perthshire, Scotland.

Senior detectives have told *The Sunday Telegraph* that more than 50 dedicated troublemakers with criminal records have slipped into the country, before the imposition of stringent security measures at airports, ferry terminals and on the Eurostar train service in the immediate run-up to the summit.

World leaders including Tony Blair and presidents Putin, Bush and Chirac will attend the three-day meeting and police are straining to protect them and keep protesters at bay. There are fears that anarchists from across Europe will mingle with anti-capitalism campaigners in and around Edinburgh, which is expected to be the focal point of demonstrations against the international financial system.

Their numbers are likely to be swollen by campaigners for African debt relief, who have been urged to descend on the Scottish capital by Bob Geldof.

The political objectives of the planned demonstration are alluded to ('demonstrations against the international financial system', 'campaigners for African debt relief') but parenthetically and in the most general terms. The focus of the story is on preparations for 'disruption' (the term attributed to the police) against the background of evidence that 'dedicated troublemakers' (with, moreover, 'criminal records') and 'anarchists' will be joining the demonstration and are 'plotting' (anarchists are, of course, wont to 'plot') to disrupt them.

Reports of the actual events of and around the G8 meeting were again dominated by violence. What is striking is that very similar reports appeared across the world, from Europe and America to China. On 6 July, CNN, the transnational news channel with the biggest international circulation, used the headline 'G8 protesters clash with police' (notice the implicit agency and responsibility attributed to the protestors in this formulation, in comparison with 'G8 protestors and police clash'). The story began as follows:

EDINBURGH, Scotland – Protesters clashed with police, smashing car windows and throwing rocks, just hours before the world's eight richest nations were set to open their annual meeting in Gleneagles, Scotland.

More than 100 activists, many wearing bandanas and hoods, emerged from a makeshift camp in Stirling early Wednesday morning, The Associated Press reported, one day after clashes sent 100 protesters to court.

A spokesman for Central Scotland Police confirmed to AP that officers had come under attack. Protesters could be seen smashing a police van.

There had been two arrests but no reported injuries, a police spokeswoman told Reuters.

The report did go on to why people were demonstrating, but the focus was on the violence. Needless to say, if the increasingly global character of protest can be countered by an increasingly global message that protestors are violent anarchists or criminals, globalist strategy stands to benefit. Other accounts of such events outside the mainstream media (see, for instance, www.indymedia. co.uk) have accused the latter of focusing upon what were in relative terms minor aspects of the demonstrations, of reporting violence rather than the substantive content of the demonstrations, and of ignoring the ways in which heavy-handed policing was provoking clashes.

5 Globals and locals

Globalised media agendas dominated by a globalised communications industry assume considerable importance, given what Tomlinson (1999) calls the 'deterritorialisation' of local lives whereby 'globalisation lifts cultural life out of its hitherto close connection with physical locality'. People's experience is increasingly a combination of unmediated experience through direct contact with others in their communities, and mediated experience especially through television. Their mediated experience gives them contact with ways of life, information, practices and values (and in discourse analytical terms with discourses, genres and styles) which transcend their unmediated experience. Positively, it vastly increases their access to potential resources, but in so far as agendas, perspectives and values (and discourses, genres and styles) are controlled and limited in the ways I have suggested, it exposes them to the strategies and meanings favoured by the powerful.

Yet the relationship between mediated and unmediated experience is a complex one, and the comments I made in the section on re-scaling about the complexities, uncertainties and unpredictability of recontextualisation apply also here. There can be tensions between them which affect media reception, so that the interpretation of media messages, images and representations may be highly diverse. And while people may add elements of their mediated experience to their resources for living their own lives, these may be hybridised with local resources in diverse and unpredictable ways (Tomlinson 1999). This includes 'interdiscursive hybridity' (Fairclough 1992a), the emergence of new hybrid discourses, genres and styles out of the dynamic relationships and tensions between mediated and unmediated experience. A trap which some academic analysis of globalisation falls into is treating globalisation only in terms of the actions and strategies of agents and 'players' who are dominant on global, macro-regional or national scales, and assuming the local impacts of global processes and tendencies, rather than recognising the need for locality-based analysis to establish these (Burawoy *et al.* 2000).

One issue is the strategies of survival which people develop to deal with the effects of globalisation, such as unemployment. In the following extract (from MacDonald 1994) we have three unemployed people in the North East of England talking on the theme of 'fiddly jobs' – working (illegally) while claiming social security benefits.

Phil: There's enough around. All you have to do is to go into any pub or club, that's where the work is. The person you mentioned he probably just sits around watching the telly. To get a job round here you've got to go around and ask people.

Danny: Most of it is who you know. You've got no chance of getting a job in the Job Centre. . . . You go out to the pub. People who go to the pub go to work.

Stephen: he [the 'hirer and firer'] just shows his face in 'The Rose Tree' or 'The Gate' and people jump and ask him for work. When I was working there I've seen him just drive off in his van around the pubs and he'll come back with another 20 men to work, an hour later. No-one asks any questions.

It's a matter of us being cheaper. It's definitely easier than having a lot of lads taken on permanently. It would cost them more to put them on the books or pay them off. It's just the flexibility. You're just there for when the jobs come up, and he (the 'hirer and firer') will come and get you when you're needed. You need to be on the dole to be able to do that. Otherwise you'd be sitting there for half the year with no work and no money at all.

Jordan (1996) argues that the 'socially excluded' develop their own often effective social capital and social networks to survive – this is evident in this extract, as also is the way such emergent practices are discoursally constructed and sustained through contemporary proverbs – 'People who go to the pub go to work'. Jordan also argues that survival strategies are a perfectly rational response to the conditions people find themselves in, based upon a perception of how the new form of capitalism works which is widely recognised but out-side official public discourse. We can read Stephen here as giving a formula-tion of such a rationale: black labour is part of the 'flexibility' of the new capitalism, but it is so undependable that only people on social security ('the dole') can do it. Notice the word 'flexibility' – Stephen is giving voice to neo-liberal economic discourse, but ironically incorporating it into his rationale for black labour as an alternative to the officially approved course of moving from welfare into poorly paid work.

But the issue goes beyond strategies of survival. 'Global ethnographers' (Burawoy *et al.*, Burawoy and Verdery 1999, 2000) have shown a sort of 'globalization from below' in which people in particular localities develop their own global networks as resources for building and promoting strategies on local issues, drawing upon their mediated experience. Gille (2000) for example has investigated a controversy over the building of a hazardous waste incinerator in a rural area of Hungary which divided the local communities and brought them into alliances with national and international agencies and organisations. Those in favour of the incinerator sought to ally themselves with the global incinerator industry and to justify the project in terms of EU policy on the disposal of hazardous waste, as well as appealing to anti-Romani sentiment by representing the incinerator as a way to 'keep the Gypsies out' of the area. Those opposed to the incinerator sought allies in the Western Green movement, representing the incinerator as part of an EU policy to shift the dis-posal of western hazardous waste to the East. What such examples illustrate is local people actively constructing global links and in so doing developing their own discursive resources, appropriating on both sides discourses, narratives and forms of argumentation from the West. This provides an important cor-rective to the idea of flows of strategies and discourses from West to East which people are passively subjected to.

6 War and terrorism

The US shift from 'soft' to 'hard' power I alluded to above is associated with the rise to power of 'neo-conservatism', particularly when G.W. Bush became President. Neo-conservatism has a continuing commitment to neo-liberalism and globalism, but combined with a willingness to use the USA's economic and military power, unilaterally if necessary, to preserve US global hegemony, which is seen as conditional upon the successful defence and extension of the globalist strategy. The clearest expression of this combination of strategic change and continuity is the US National Security Strategy of 2002 (Chomsky 2003b). I shall discuss an essay (2002, published in Stelzer 2004) on this

Strategy by Condoleezza Rice, National Security Advisor and then Secretary of State in G.W. Bush's administration.

Rice interprets the New York attacks as an 'existential threat' to US 'security' not from other powerful states but from 'terrorists' and 'weak or failed states', a new threat which demands a new strategy. America will 'use its position of unparalleled strength and influence to create a balance of power that favors freedom', and this will include 'military power'.

> We will break up terror networks, hold to account nations that harbour terrorists, and confront aggressive tyrants holding or seeking nuclear, chemical, and biological weapons that might be passed to terrorist allies. These are all different faces of the same evil. . . . the United States must be prepared to take action, when necessary, before threats have fully materialized. Pre-emption is not a new concept. There has never been a moral or legal requirement that a country wait to be attacked before it can address existential threats.

To support this strategy, the US 'will build and maintain . . . military forces that are beyond challenge . . . and seek to dissuade any potential adversary from pursuing a military build-up in the hope of surpassing, or equalling, the power of the United States'. Such a development is more remote than in the past, however, because 'the world's great centers of power are united by common interests, common dangers and . . . common values' and 'share a broad commitment to democracy, the rule of law, a market-based economy, and open trade'. The US 'will fight poverty, disease and oppression because it is the right thing to do – and the smart thing to do. We have seen how poor states can become weak or even failed states, vulnerable to hijacking by terrorist networks'. But 'development assistance . . . will only be available to countries that work to govern justly, invest in the health and education of their people, and encourage economic liberty . . . values must be a vital part of our relationship with other countries.' 'We reject the condescending view . . . that Muslims somehow do not share the desire to be free. The celebrations we saw on the streets of Kabul . . . proved otherwise.' 'We do not seek to impose democracy on others, we seek only to help create conditions in which people can claim a freer future for themselves.' Finally, 'we have the ability to forge a twenty-first century that lives up to our hopes . . . only if we (exercise) our influence in the service of our ideals, and not just ourselves'.

The change in military circumstances which Rice refers to can be seen as the emerging predominance of 'irregular warfare', which is fundamentally about 'weak forces learning how to fight strong', and is a comprehensible response to prolonged domination by the West over the rest (Saul 2005). In reducing this to 'terrorism' and 'tyrants', and adopting an aggressive military strategy, the US government is arguably failing to address basic issues of (in)justice which underlie the proliferation of irregular warfare, and its own responsibility for injustices. 'Terrorism' is, of course, a much contested category – for neo-conservatives it conflates different forms of violence such as 11 September itself, the Palestinian intifada, the Chechyen war, and the resistance to American and British occupation of Iraq, without apparently including the 'state terrorism' practised by US governments themselves in Indo-China or by the Israeli government in Palestine (Honderich 2003) The now routine portrayal of the opposition as 'evil' indicates an important characteristic of neo-conservatism – its links with Christian fundamentalism. The National Strategy includes what Rice misleadingly calls a strategy of 'pre-emption' – to attack nations which are 'seeking' (on what evidence, and in whose view?) nuclear, chemical or biological weapons which 'might' be passed to 'terrorist allies', and 'before threats have fully materialized'. This is not 'pre-emptive' war, which might be justified in international law, but 'preventive' war, which is illegal (Chomsky 2003a). There is a problem of how to legitimise the US claim to permanent hegemony, and the solution is broadly to claim the US is a force for good which operates on the basis of 'values'. It seeks a balance of power which favours 'freedom', a value which few would dissociate themselves from. But the neo-conservative use of the word systematically blurs the distinction between 'free market' and political 'freedom', and treats them as one and them same thing. The desire for 'freedom' is assumed to be universal, shared by Muslims as well as others. And in the words of British Prime Minister Tony Blair, 'values and interests merge': when it come to fighting poverty, disease and oppression, what is 'right' is also 'smart', though aid is conditional upon conformity with values which include the globalist value of 'encouraging economic liberty' (Duffield 2001).

This neo-conservative version of globalist strategy and discourse (which includes the discourse of the 'war on terror' (Jackson 2005)) has been effectively disseminated internationally with the assistance of the global communications industry. In terms of the five positions I distinguished earlier on discourse as a facet of globalisation, what I have said above suggests that the discourse of the 'war on terror' is primarily ideological, effectively legitimising a strategy to preserve and extend US global (and globalist) hegemony for large sections of the global public, including for instance the publics of post-communist countries such as Romania. It has succeeded in marginalising counter-discourses, but without silencing them, and indeed they are gaining strength even in the USA itself and Britain. The discourse is also effective rhetorically in persuading many people to accept restrictions on civil liberties. But it also has constructive effects, including an international restructuring of regimes and apparatuses of security, and the convergence of policies on development with security policies (Duffield 2001).

7 Conclusion

I have adopted a specific, and necessarily highly selective, approach to the very big issue of how language relates to processes of globalisation. Among many omissions there is the questions of languages, and particularly the question of 'global English'. For instance, the recontextualisation of the discourse of globalism and other many discourses which are germane to the re-scaling of Romania also entails the borrowing of a great deal of English vocabulary. To illustrate, readers will recognise the italicised words in the following extract from a statement by the Romanian Minister of Communications and Information Technology at a National Conference on 'Outsourcing' in November 2005, which are either English borrowings or existing Romanian words used in the senses they have in recontextualised discourse:

> *Outsourcingul* este un domeniu de *succes* al *IT&C* – ului romanesc. *Competitia* pe aceasta piata a devenit una foarte stransa, Romania fiind nevoita sa concureze in *satul global* nu doar cu tarile europene, ci si cu cele din Orientul Indepartat sau America Latina. Doar o *strategie* de *marketing* si de *branding* bine structurata si gandita pe termen mediu ne va ajuta sa ne situam pe un loc fruntas in aceasta *competitie globala*.

My approach is based upon the use of CDA in transdisciplinary research on social change which has characterised my recent research and is reflected in the References. In particular, I have used a version of cultural political economy which incorporates a version of CDA. The main point that emerges from this approach is that all the highly complex and diverse contemporary processes of globalisation inherently have a language dimension, because globalisation and indeed social change in general are processes involving dialectical relations between diverse social elements or 'moments', always including discourse. This has been partly recognised as I have indicated in the social scientific literature of globalisation, though little of this research truly does justice to the language dimension, and students of language have a great deal to offer social scientific research in terms of helping it to achieve a more satisfactory treatment of discourse.

Notes

1. It also raises an epistemological problem: what I have referred to as 'actual processes and tendencies of globalisation' are themselves also representations, so we are faced with evaluating different representations in terms of how adequate they are to realities. I shall not address this thorny problem in detail. I shall assume that it is difficult to solve but not unsolvable – that different representations can indeed be evaluated in terms of their relative 'practical adequacy' (Sayer 2000), by reference to social scientific evidence of various sorts on the extent to which what they suggest or imply about social reality actually happens in social reality.

2. I use 'social constructivism' here for the widespread recognition within social science of the socially constructed character of the social world, and not for the particular philosophy of science which goes under that name, which 'in its strong form claims that objects or referents of knowledge are nothing more than social constructions' (Sayer 2000). Like Sayer, I would reject this position, while recognising the socially constructed character of the social world.

3. I don't wish to suggest that the institutional obstacles to effective quality assurance systems I have described are exclusively a problem for Romania or other post-communist countries, they also exist to a greater or lesser degree in at least some Western European countries.

19. Global capitalism, terrorism and war: a discourse-analytical perspective

My general objective in this paper is to consider some aspects of the relationship between discourse and other elements in the social process, and to give a partial presentation of a methodology for addressing this relationship in transdisciplinary research on social change. My more particular objective is to consider, with reference to the American *National Security Strategy* (2002), some aspects of the relationship between discourse and other elements of contemporary processes of 'globalization', especially with regard to their military and security dimensions, including the 'war on terror' and associated 'pre-emptive', 'preventive' or 'aggressive' war – take your choice! – as in Iraq. I want to try to clarify the significance within and effects upon military/security and other dimensions of real processes of globalisation, of the *NSS* document and other broadly similar policy and strategy documents, speeches and so forth; and the particular contribution that discourse analysis can make within transdisciplinary research on these processes.

I am conscious of – and maybe a little uncomfortable about – discussing a document about which a great deal has been said – perhaps even everything there is to say! – in terms of questions about the significance and effects of discourse in the social process about which a great deal has also already been said. I might say in my defence – half-seriously – that there is nothing unusual in this for academics! I cannot promise astounding new insights about either the document or discourse. What I am hoping is that by approaching familiar issues in a particular way I may shed a glimmer of new light on them.

Let me begin with the second paragraph of President Bush's Preface to the *NSS* in which he summarises the strategy in terms of what Condoleeza Rice in a speech on the strategy (*The President's National Security Strategy* 2002) calls its 'three pillars' (which I have italicised):

Today, the United States enjoys a position of unparalleled military strength and great economic and political influence. In keeping with our heritage and principles, we do not use our strength to press for unilateral advantage. We seek instead to create a balance of power that favors human freedom: conditions in which all nations and all societies can choose for themselves the rewards and challenges of political and economic liberty. In a world that is safe, people will be able to make their own lives better. *We will defend the peace by fighting terrorists and tyrants. We will preserve the peace by building good relations among the great powers. We will extend the peace by encouraging free and open societies on every continent.*

Here are a number of comments on this extract which bear upon my broader objectives.

- The national security strategy is not simply a strategy for a *'safer'* world but also for a *'better'* world – it is not simply a military, security, political and diplomatic strategy, it is also a global economic (or more properly political–economic) strategy, in which societies with particular political and economic properties ('free and open') will be 'encouraged' throughout the world.
- The document as a whole is organised around these three 'pillars' apart from the last chapter, which is on 'transforming America's national security institutions'. So there are chapters on 'defeating global terrorism' and 'preventing attacks' and 'preventing our enemies from threatening us with weapons of mass destruction' (first pillar), 'working with others to defuse regional conflicts' and 'cooperative action with other main centres of global power' (second pillar), and 'championing aspirations to human dignity', 'igniting a new era of economic growth through free markets and free trade', and 'expanding the circle of development by opening societies and building the infrastructure of democracy' (third pillar).
- The three pillars are formulated and textured together in a way which integrates them as intended actions with respect to 'the peace'; there is syntactic parallelism between them, and the three means adverbials ('by fighting/building/encouraging' etc.) texture together in a relation of equivalence construals of action which emanate from different discourses – military, diplomatic and political–economic. This is interdiscursive hybridity, and the texturing of a hybrid new security discourse (not strictly new to this document, but new to the strategy which this document gives authority to).
- 'The peace' seems to be used in the sense of *pax* in *pax Romana/ Britannica/Americana* – the state of peace maintained by a dominant

power – and historically an imperial power – and the area in which it obtains (which can thus be 'extended'). America is explicitly identified elsewhere in the document as the 'leading' power – not of course the 'imperial' power – and that is implicit here in the claim to 'unparalleled strength and influence' and the objective of 'creating a balance of power that favors human freedom' (only the dominant power could do that).

So a new entity has been textured – in the sense of textually produced – at this point, and elsewhere in the document: a new hybrid security discourse.

What relationships can this discourse have with reality beyond discourse? – I formulate it in this way to avoid suggesting that discourse stands outside reality.

We might say that the discourse is an *imaginary* for reality, a pre-figuring of a possible and intended reality, which includes an objective ('the peace', 'a balance of power which favors human freedom') and the means to achieve it. Imaginaries produced in discourse are an integral part of strategies, and if strategies are successful and become implemented, associated imaginaries can be 'operationalised', transformed into practice, made real. So one possible relationship is that the discourse can contribute to constructing and reconstructing the wider reality. But the implementation of strategies and operationalisation of imaginaries are subject to certain conditions, including what we might call *practical adequacy* – the world must be such that the imagined reality is possible, the agents imagined as bringing it into being have the power to do so, and so forth – and *conviction* – imaginaries and the strategies they are a part of have to be convincing for the people who need to be convinced. The two are related – people look for practical adequacy in deciding if something is convincing, though they are also likely to consider whether what can be done *should* be done, so there can be tension between the two. This means that there may be motivation for as we might put it 'displacing' a preferred strategy/imaginary deemed practically adequate but unlikely to carry conviction with a different strategy/imaginary deemed more likely to carry conviction. But this displacement cannot be arbitrary: the displacing strategy/imaginary must have reasonable claims to practical adequacy, and moreover sufficiently mirror the displaced and preferred strategy/imaginary for subsequent events and actions to be convincingly construed as operationalisations of it – at least to a certain point.

The point of this is that the strategy as construed here has been widely seen as not quite the strategy that is actually being pursued. Yet before saying more about that, let us listen to what Noam Chomsky (2003a: 4) says about it: the *NSS* is pretty clear and straightforward [. . .] It stated, in effect, that the United States plans to dominate the world permanently, through the use of force if necessary [. . .] And that they are committed to eliminating any potential challenge to their rule that they might detect [. . .] this was unusually brazen and it aroused a lot of concern.

His summary relates particularly to the last chapter, which includes the statements that 'We must build and maintain our defenses beyond challenge [. . .]. Our forces will be strong enough to dissuade potential adversaries from pursuing a military build-up in hopes of surpassing, or equaling, the power of the United States [. . .]. We will be prepared to act apart when our interests and unique responsibilities require'. One can see this as 'in effect' amounting to the way Chomsky summarises it. But even so Chomsky's language is not the language of the document, and though I wouldn't disagree with his summary of what the strategy amounts to, his analysis does not help us with the question of the discourse of the *NSS* and its relationship with reality beyond discourse. The document is not *that* 'clear and straightforward'.

So in what ways is the strategy as construed not quite the strategy as pursued? The intended actions in the three pillars are recognisable in the strategy as pursued – 'fighting terrorists and tyrants', 'building good relations among the great powers' (though also upsetting them at times), 'encouraging free and open societies on every continent' – though the formulations are questionable (only 'encouraging'? 'tyrants'? etc.). It's the formulation of the strategic goal which is most contentious. Has the strategy as pursued really been – not only and most obviously in its actual effects, which inevitably differ from intentions, but also in its intentions – aimed at consolidating and extending 'the peace'? Has it really been aimed at 'building a balance of power that favors human freedom' for 'all nations and societies' rather than 'pressing for unilateral advantage'? And if the answer is 'no', what are we to say about the relationship between this discourse and reality beyond discourse?

Perhaps, returning to the conditions of practical adequacy and conviction, that the discourse has contributed to building a sufficient measure of conviction for a strategy with a somewhat different goal, especially in the USA but also to a degree elsewhere? Though, of course, a great many people both in and outside the USA were never convinced. Perhaps therefore that the discourse is largely or in part *rhetoric*, intended to persuade rather than to truthfully set out intentions? Perhaps, more than this, that the discourse has contributed to consolidating and developing an *ideology*, a generalised belief or assumption that serves to abet American power – the ideology of American exceptionalism, that America here as always acts on principle, on values, for the general good. Maybe so, but let me come back to the point on displacement, and the point that not any displacement will do. Let me put the point this way: it is not plausible to practically pursue one strategy over any length of time – and Bush states in his Preface that 'The war against terrorists of global reach is a global enterprise of uncertain duration' – and explain, interpret and justify what is done in terms of another totally different strategy. The discourse associated with the displacing strategy must provide construals of and imaginaries for actions and events which are practically adequate as well as carrying conviction; and this means actions and events being construed in ways which do correspond in some measure to realities, and actions and events being shaped by these imaginaries as well as other less publicly stated ones. So in opting for 'rhetoric' and/or 'ideology', we are not opting against social construction.

So we might say that a good measure of what is really intended needs to be there in the strategy, discourse and imaginaries which construe it. One reason why Chomsky's summary is acceptable up to a point is that the document, as is characteristic of documents of this sort, is hybrid not only in texturing diverse elements and discourses together into new discourses, but in combining different discourses, sometimes in different parts of the document, that can be in tension with each other or even plain contradictory. And this is partly because the document needs to construe the purported intentions and strategy in a way which make them sufficiently consistent with real intentions and strategies. For a case of contradiction, let us look at the first paragraph of Bush's Preface as well as the second (which is the extract I have been discussing):

> The great struggles of the twentieth century between liberty and totalitarianism ended with a decisive victory for the forces of freedom – and a single sustainable model for national success: freedom, democracy, and free enterprise. In the twenty-first century, only nations that share a commitment to protecting basic human rights and guaranteeing political and economic freedom will be able to unleash the potential of their people and assure their future prosperity. People everywhere want to be able to speak freely; choose who will govern them; worship as they please; educate their children – male and female; own property; and enjoy the benefits of their labor. These values of freedom are right and true for every person, in every society – and the duty of protecting these values against their enemies is the common calling of freedom-loving people across the globe and across the ages.

The first sentence claims that one outcome of the Cold War was 'a single sustainable model for national success: freedom, democracy, and free enterprise'.

What is this 'single sustainable model'? It is 'freedom' and 'democracy', but also 'free enterprise', which is noteworthy in terms of the 'bother to mention' principle – I mean 'freedom' would have 'done'; freedom is 'political and economic freedom', and what 'people want' includes to 'own property' and 'enjoy the benefits of their labor'. Bush here, and the document generally, construes 'economic freedom' in a particular way, not for instance just capitalism, but what is construed in a coded way as 'free enterprise' (coded because although he doesn't precisely say what he means, most readers will know what he means), and more explicitly in the chapter title 'Igniting a new era of economic growth through free markets and free trade', and within that chapter, for instance: 'The concept of "free trade" arose as a moral principle even before it became a pillar of economics. If you can make something that others value, you should be able to sell it to them. If others make something that you value, you should be able to buy it. This is real freedom, the freedom for a person – or a nation – to make a living.' The *NSS* is not a treatise on neo-liberal political economy, but it is pretty clear that the 'single sustainable model' is 'free market' capitalism in the neo-liberal conception. This extract also makes explicit that 'free trade' is basic to the understanding of 'freedom'. The *NSS* is not a treatise on neo-liberal political economy, but it *recontextualises* the discourse of neo-liberal political economy which is more fully elaborated elsewhere, and recontextualising means appropriating within a new context, adapting the discourse to the main purposes at hand, abbreviating and condensing it.

What then of the sentence in the second paragraph: 'We seek instead to create a balance of power that favors human freedom: conditions in which all nations and all societies can choose for themselves the rewards and challenges of political and economic liberty'? 'Freedom' allows 'nations and societies' to 'choose' – to choose 'political and economic liberty'! There is one model, one option – therefore no choice. The sentence is semantically incongruous. Let us assume that a central element of the intended strategy is to extend 'free market' capitalism to as many countries as possible, and that this is seen as the key means to achieving the primary strategic goal, consolidating American global hegemony in a context where it has been seen as endangered. (I'll return to the obvious question: why should we assume this?) This is not fully absent from the document, nor is it fully present in the document. We might see it as present in 'encouraging free and open societies on every continent', but what marks it not being fully present is the verb – 'encourage'. Given the mixture of threats and inducements which have been widely documented for instance with respect to IMF 'structural adjustment' packages, 'encourage' seems to be a detail of the displacement of one strategy, discourse and imaginary by another, which does not so much eliminate the strategic goals, means, etc. of the former as 'translate' them. But back to the semantically incongruous sentence. We might say that the source of its semantic incongruity is that the authors are here seeking to manage a *contradiction* – between the real strategic objective of persuading, cajoling, pushing and of necessary forcing countries to accept the one model, and the objective as it is construed in the document and in indeed in the sentence, 'a balance of power that favors human freedom'.

Let me come back to my assumption about the real strategy as opposed to the strategy as construed, and make two points. The first is that one cannot get far in analysing texts without having to make such assumptions, without taking some position on what is real and what isn't. The second is that just making assumptions makes analysis pretty *ad hoc*. I began by indicating a view of discourse analysis as located within transdisciplinary research. In my recent book on globalisation I worked for instance with a version of 'cultural political economy' (Jessop 2004) which synthesises three elements: a 'Regulation Approach' to economic analysis, a version of Gramscian state theory for political analysis, and 'critical discourse analysis' for analysing discourse (and as a major resource for analysing culture, and ideology). The point here is that rather than assumptions, we need political economic analysis, and for discourse analysis to contribute to social research it needs to be embedded within transdisciplinary frameworks which theorise and develop methodologies for analysing what I see as *dialectical* relations between discourse and other elements. Cultural political economy is just one such framework. And transdisciplinary synthesis means attending to relations and compatibilities between discourse-analytical categories and categories in other disciplines and theories within the synthesis. 'Contradiction' is a political economic category in the version of political economy I work with, and 'semantic incongruity' is a category in analysis of language and discourse; 'strategy' and strategic 'complexity' or 'hybridity' are categories of this version of political economy, and 'interdiscursive hybridity', 'discourse' and 'order of discourse' are categories in discourse analysis. Analysis of texts from this perspective is a matter of identifying specifically discoursal, semiotic and linguistic features of texts, but in ways which allow for textual analysis to be part of a specifically semiotic 'point of entry' into the main concern – analysing *relations between* discourse and other elements of the social processes in focus.

More specifically, I am alluding to particular political economic analyses of globalisation and its military and security dimensions, including that of Steger (2005). It is fruitful to see globalisation as having both structural and strategic dimensions (Jessop 2002) – there are real global structures and structural tendencies, and there are diverse strategies developed by groups of social agents and agencies for 'steering' globalisation and its structural tendencies in particular directions. Strategies as I have indicated inherently include discourses which construe and narrate reality in distinctive ways and produce imaginaries for changed realities which may, contingently, be operationalised – enacted in new ways of acting and interacting, inculcated in new ways of being or identities, materialised in the physical world. The dialectics of discourse, as Harvey (1996) calls it. The political-economic dimension of the strategy of *NSS* has the objective of promoting free-market capitalism, and promoting it across the 'globe'. This combination of neo-liberalism and globalisation emerged after the collapse of the Soviet Union and other European socialist countries at the turn of the 1990s, and is what Steger (2005) calls 'globalism', 'globalist' political-economic strategy. 'Globalism' has been the most influential international strategy for globalisation, for steering it in a particular direction, strongly associated with the doctrine of 'a single sustainable model', not capitalism as such but 'free market' capitalism. Following Steger, I see the *NSS* as globalist, interpreting globalism as a strategy whose continuity has depended upon adaptation. We can see globalism as a 'nodal strategy' around which other strategies and associated discourses cluster, with change in the cluster over time. Steger diagnoses a shift from 'soft power' to 'hard power' in pursuing the strategy of globalism. This is associated with a convergence of globalist political-economic strategy with military and security strategy and the strategy for a 'war on terror', which emerged especially after 11 September 2001 and is evident in *NSS*, though this 'neo-conservatist' militarised globalism was being developed by people who came to hold high office in the Bush Administration (Cheney, Rumsfeld and Wolfowitz) as early as the *Defense Planning Guidance* (1992) and the *Project for a New American Century* (1997). One view is that 11 September provided a manifest justification for the gloves to be taken off, but the roots of official acceptance of the neocon strategy lie in the serious challenges to globalism arising out of growing evidence of its failures in the late 1990s, most notably the East Asian crisis of 1997.

In working with this analysis I am of course making a choice, which I would justify if pressed on grounds of practical adequacy: I think for instance that the sort of things which this analysis suggest are likely to happen have indeed been happening.

Let me now return to the document and look more systematically at its main constituent elements, continuing to identify on the one hand certain semiotic, discoursal and linguistic features and to raise on the other hand questions about the relationship between the discourse and reality beyond discourse – i.e., treating textual analysis as part of a semiotic 'point of entry' into transdisciplinary analysis of relations between discourse and other elements. I am going to focus on Bush's Preface but refer as relevant to other parts of the document.

Both the Preface and the document as a whole have on one obvious level a 'problem–solution' structure, or more exactly they work from narrative of the recent past (basically from the Cold War to the present), to analyses of the present including present problems and dangers, to imaginaries for the future – strategic intentions, objectives and means of realisation. I'll take narrative of the past and analysis of the present together (I've already illustrated part of the narrative of the past), then imaginaries for the future.

The end of the Cold War is 'an historic opportunity' to 'build a world where great powers compete in peace instead of continually prepare for war', and to 'extend the benefits of freedom across the globe' bringing 'the hope of democracy, development, free markets, and free trade to every corner of the world'. It is also a time of new dangers. The task of 'defending our Nation against its enemies [. . .] has changed dramatically'.

> Enemies in the past needed great armies and great industrial capabilities to endanger America. Now, shadowy networks of individuals can bring great chaos and suffering to our shores for less than it costs to purchase a single tank. Terrorists are organized to penetrate open societies and to turn the power of modern technologies against us.

Moreover, 'the gravest danger our Nation faces lies at the crossroads of radicalism and technology'.

> Our enemies have openly declared that they are seeking weapons of mass destruction, and evidence indicates that they are doing so with determination.

In the chapter entitled 'Preventing our enemies from threatening us, our allies and friends with weapons of mass destruction', the 'enemies' are identified as 'rogue states' as well as terrorists: 'new deadly challenges have emerged from rogue states and terrorists'.

> The nature and motivations of these new adversaries, their determination to obtain destructive powers hitherto available only to the world's strongest states, and the greater likelihood that they will use weapons of mass destruction against us, make today's security environment more complex and dangerous.

The document goes on: 'In the 1990s we witnessed the emergence of a small number of rogue states that, while different in important ways, share a number of attributes'. They

> brutalize their own people and squander their national resources for the personal gain of the rulers; display no regard for international law, threaten their neighbors, and callously violate international treaties to which they are party; are determined to acquire weapons of mass destruction, along with other advanced military technology, to be used as threats or offensively to achieve the aggressive designs of these regimes; sponsor terrorism around the globe; and reject basic human values and hate the United States and everything for which it stands.

And finally:

> We must be prepared to stop rogue states and their terrorist clients before they are able to threaten or use weapons of mass destruction against the United States and our allies and friends.

I shall comment on two issues: significant absences, and 'the enemy'.

Texts are selective actualisations of potentials (potential discourses, genres, grammatical constructions, metaphors, vocabularies etc.), and the selection and texturing of actualisations involve agency. Textual analysis seen in these terms needs to attend to what is significantly not 'there' as well as what is 'there' – to significant absences. There is a claim that 'in the 1990s we witnessed the emergence of a small number of rogue states', but there is no explanation or analysis of how or why they 'emerged', why and how states became 'rogue', the motivations for their 'roguery'. The document is slightly more forthcoming on 'terrorism':

> In many regions, legitimate grievances prevent the emergence of a lasting peace. Such grievances deserve to be, and must be, addressed within a political process. But no cause justifies terror.

The implication here is that people may turn to terrorism because of legitimate grievances, though the claim is they are not justified in doing so. But that's all. However, the chapter which deals most with terrorism begins with a quotation from Bush in which he says:

> Our responsibility to history is already clear: to answer these attacks and rid the world of evil.

So we have a national strategy document which provides no analysis or explanation of where the enemy has come from, how it has got to be an enemy, why it is hostile to the USA and its allies. Labelling it as 'evil' implies that no explanation is necessary, or indeed possible. By contrast, the motivation for the US action against these threats is made fully explicit, for instance in the chapter on terrorism:

> In the war against global terrorism, we will never forget that we are ultimately fighting for our democratic values and way of life. Freedom and fear are at war, and there will be no quick or easy end to this conflict. In leading the campaign against terrorism, we are forging new, productive international relationships and redefining existing ones in ways that meet the challenges of the twenty-first century.

And the motives of the USA are repeatedly – sometimes implicitly – represented as unselfish and benign – for instance 'rogue states' 'reject basic human values and hate the United States and everything for which it stands' implies through conjunction that the USA stands for 'basic human values'. This extract also illustrates the value dualisms which proliferate in this discourse – freedom and fear, good and evil, civilisation and barbarism.

The lack of historical depth and of analysis and explanation is a significant absence. We can say it is an absence because there is plenty of analysis of how and why terrorism has developed, why certain states and many people 'hate the United States and everything for which it stands', how past actions on the part of the USA have contributed, and the administration is surely familiar with this. It is in the public sphere, and one might, in fact, say – anticipating something I come to shortly – that failure to enter into dialogue with it is a flaw in the document viewed from the perspective of dialectical argumentation. It is a significant absence because no security strategy can afford to ignore it – for a strategy to be a sound basis for action, it needs to be based upon the serious analysis of the problems or the 'threat'. One can see a rhetorical motivation for this absence: the strategy needs to win conviction, and diagnosing a threat which the USA has failed to avert or diminish though arguably having the power to do so, and indeed contributed to creating, might undermine that. 'Dramatic change' and unexplained 'emergence' are likely to be more convincing. But, again, rhetoric does not preclude socially constructive effects of discourse. We might say that operationising an imaginary which construes the enemy in an ahistorical and irrational way, enacting the imaginary militarily and in other forms of force, has predictably led to perverse effects: the threat is increased rather than diminished, and in a certain sense acting as if the enemy were in reality the flawed construal of it contributes to constructing it as something more closely resembling that construal. Thus acting on the basis of what is arguably the exaggerated threat from international terrorism in this document and elsewhere has – also arguably – contributed to producing a real threat which is closer to the construal. The point is essentially that if you operate on the basis of a discourse that excludes historical analysis of causes and errors, you may well perpetuate the causes and repeat the errors, and aggravate the problems. Here is Chomsky (2003a: 2) again:

> The administration planners [. . .] understand just as well as the intelligence agencies and the intelligence reports they read and the critics that they read [. . .] that the actions that they are undertaking are likely to increase the threat to security of Americans and of the world and a great long-term threat. They don't want that outcome; it just doesn't matter very much. It's a question of priorities. And there are other priorities that are higher, such as the priority of maintaining global hegemony, and maintaining a hold on domestic political power so that they can carry out an extremely radical, reactionary, domestic program.

The actions Chomsky refers to are carried out by actors, including the military, who are imbued with the public discourse represented by this document, in which we might say that the gap left by the absence of analysis is filled by ideology – the ideology of a struggle between good and evil. It was for instance some of these actors who were responsible for the torture and dehumanisation of prisoners in Abu-Ghraib, media images of which would seem to have fed the hatred and resistance and hence the threat. Pinning down the causative effects of discourse in such a case is of course notoriously difficult given the complex character of causality, but it is difficult to believe that the construal of the enemy as dehumanised and irrational has no effect on how the enemy is treated.

A few more comments on 'the enemy'. In some parts of the document the enemy is represented as just 'terrorists' or 'terrorism', for instance in the chapter on terrorism:

> The United States of America is fighting a war against terrorists of global reach. The enemy is not a single political regime or person or religion or ideology. The enemy is terrorism – premeditated, politically motivated violence perpetrated against innocents.

In other parts, there is a dual enemy – 'rogue states and terrorists'. This inconsistency in the document indicates the difficulty of construing a unitary enemy for what is construed and pursued as a single war. How are the two antagonists connected? 'Rogue states' are characterised as 'sponsoring terrorism', they have 'terrorist clients', and both are represented as ready to 'threaten or use weapons of mass destruction against the United States and our allies and friends'. Iraq has of course compromised claims about development and possession of WMD, the threat of them being used particularly against the USA, and the supposed links between 'rogue states' and terrorism.

The construal of the 'enemy' has of course attracted a great deal of critical commentary, and the suggestion that this is a 'made-up' enemy to legitimise military actions whose objectives are not primarily 'defending the peace' but geopolitical and geo-economic – controlling Middle Eastern oil, for example. But terrorist groups are a real enough target; the difficulty is construing the enemy as 'terrorists', or even worse 'terrorism', as such, and operationalising this construal in a way which fails to make crucial discriminations between the perpetrators of the terrorist attacks in New York, London and Madrid and for instance Palestinians who are arguably exercising the right to resistance recognised in UN Resolution 42 (1987), while excluding what is arguably state terror on the part of, say, Israel. 'Rogue states' on the other hand seems like a soundbite in the Reagan tradition which has somehow been taken as a serious category in a vitally important strategy document. Not all of the 'attributes' listed for 'rogue states' are applicable to all the states that have been labelled as 'rogue', and many of them are applicable to 'allies and friends' and even – as has been irrelevantly pointed out – the USA itself. It is, of course, not a category to be taken seriously, though it is serious that it appears to carry so much conviction. Its operational value lies in its arbitrariness and emptiness – it can be added to as and when needed. I shall comment further on 'terrorists' in discussing legitimacy.

Let me move on to imaginaries for the future – the document as I have said is organised in terms of the three 'pillars' of the strategy. I will begin with the third 'pillar', to 'extend the peace by encouraging free and open societies on every continent', but focus on its connections with the first (to 'defend the peace by fighting terrorists and tyrants'), and specifically on the construal of the relationship between development and security. Bush elaborates the third 'pillar' as follows:

> We will actively work to bring the hope of democracy, development, free markets, and free trade to every corner of the world. The events of September 11, 2001, taught us that weak states, like Afghanistan, can pose as great a danger to our national interests as strong states. Poverty does not make poor people into terrorists and murderers. Yet poverty, weak

institutions, and corruption can make weak states vulnerable to terrorist networks and drug cartels within their borders.

It is not only 'rogue states' that pose a threat to the USA, it is also 'weak states' (and 'failed states'). Duffield (2001) argues that there was a convergence from the mid-1990s between the security strategy and development strategy of the USA and its allies which can be summed up in the claim: underdevelopment is dangerous. The point is also formulated in terms of a convergence of values and interests by Rice ('The United States will fight poverty, disease and oppression because it is the right thing to do – and the smart thing to do. We have seen how poor states can become weak or even failed states, vulnerable to hijacking by terrorist networks') and in the Overview chapter of the *NSS* ('The US national security strategy will be based on a distinctly American internationalism that reflects the union of our values and our national interests. The aim of this strategy is to help make the world not just safer but better'.) So an additional motivation for the political-economic strategy and the development strategy attached to it is that it increases international security. Moreover, the linkage of development and security has as Duffield argues led to the use of development aid as a lever for more direct intervention in steering the policies of recipient countries. This is expressed here as the conditionality for aid:

> The United States will deliver greater development assistance through the New Millennium Challenge Account to nations that govern justly, invest in their people, and encourage economic freedom.

And the Preface continues on the theme of the 'responsibilities' of nations:

> In building a balance of power that favors freedom, the United States is guided by the conviction that all nations have important responsibilities. Nations that enjoy freedom must actively fight terror. Nations that depend on international stability must help prevent the spread of weapons of mass destruction. Nations that seek international aid must govern themselves wisely, so that aid is well spent. For freedom to thrive, accountability must be expected and required.

Bush's elaboration of the third 'pillar' of the strategy textures together political-economic, development and security strategies and discourses, and effects their convergence in the national security strategy. This again involves the texturing of relations of equivalence through syntactic parallelism in respect of the 'responsibilities' and 'accountability' of nations, and interdiscursive hybridity. 'Enjoy freedom', 'depend on international stability' and 'seek international aid' are textured as equivalent, as are 'actively fight terror', 'help prevent the spread of weapons of mass destruction', 'govern themselves wisely', articulating together expressions associated with diverse discourses: political-economic, development, and military security. So this is an elaboration of the new hybrid security discourse whose emergence in the text I discussed earlier.

These are the words of the President of the power which is construing itself (not without justification) as the main source and guarantor of the 'goods' which nations are construed as having or wanting ('freedom', 'stability', 'aid'), who would seem to be taking up the position of authoritative source of these demands upon nations, which implies a disciplinary aspect to political-economic and development strategy: the objective not just to include as many countries as possible in the free market economy and the virtuous circle of international aid, purportedly for their own benefit and the general good, but also to use the carrot of inclusion and the stick of exclusion to enforce compliance with the 'war on terror' and the economic and political precepts advocated by the USA as well as other governments and international agencies (World Bank, IMF, WTO etc.). We might say, going back to Chomsky, that this is a point where the document is 'brazen' – it is a pretty transparent *textual* example of the ways in – according to a substantial body of political analysis – the USA to use its power to enforce compliance through inducements and threats.

Let me finally comment on the elaboration of the first 'pillar' ('defending the peace by fighting terrorists and tyrants') with particular respect to the question of *legitimacy*, and relations between discourse and legitimacy. What is at issue here is the legitimacy of a new complex state apparatus for securing not only external security but also internal security, which is partially construed and imagined in the document especially in the final chapter ('Transform America's National Security Institutions to Meet the Challenges and Opportunities of the Twenty-First Century'). This includes transforming military structures designed for the Cold War to meet current 'operational challenges', building new 'bases and stations within and beyond Western Europe and Northeast Asia', developing 'ability to defend the homeland, conduct information operations, ensure US access to distant theaters, and protect critical US infrastructure and assets in outer space', 'transforming our intelligence capabilities and building new ones', ensuring 'the proper fusion of information between intelligence and law enforcement', transforming diplomatic institutions, developing 'a more comprehensive approach to public information that can help people around the world learn about and understand America', recognising that 'our freedom, our cities, our systems of movement, and modern life [. . .] are vulnerable to terrorism', that 'this is a new condition of life' which we must 'adjust to'. The ramifications in terms of internal security, surveillance and curtailment of civil liberties have emerged over the past few years.

Let me go back to what I have called *conviction* as a condition for successful strategies. There are I suggest two relations between discourse and reality beyond discourse associated with conviction: the construction of consent, and the construction of legitimacy. The success of a strategy depends not only on achieving the consent of those whose consent is needed, which can be done through rhetorical means, but also legitimising the applications of power associated with pursuing the strategy. The concept of legitimacy is complex and controversial, but I shall need to short-circuit some of that. Weber linked legitimacy to the willingness to comply with a system of rules or to obey commands. Every 'system of authority', he argued, attempts to establish and to cultivate the belief in its 'legitimacy'. He defined the state in a way which is close to the issues here: 'a human community that (successfully) claims the *monopoly of the legitimate use of physical force* within a given territory' (Weber 1946: 78). Weber's definition has been criticised for conflating belief and legitimacy. Beetham for instance argues (1991) that 'A given power relationship is not legitimate because people believe in its legitimacy, but because it can be justified in terms of their beliefs'. Power can then be said to be legitimate to the extent that: (a) it conforms to established rules, (b) the rules can be justified by reference to shared beliefs, and (c) there is evidence of consent by the subordinate to the particular power relation. A breach of rules leads to *illegitimacy*; a discrepancy between rules and beliefs or the absence of shared beliefs leads to a *legitimacy deficit*, and a withdrawal of consent leads to *delegitimation*. 'Rules' here needs to include a range from legal norms to principles based upon accepted values. Habermas (1976) has pointed to the weakening of cultural systems as sources of legitimacy and a corresponding increase in the significance of ongoing processes of legitimation which cope with threats of delegitimation and if necessary engage in relegitimation. The increasing salience of this dynamic view of legitimation rather than a more static view of legitimacy means that analysis of discourse and of texts emerges as an important resource for research on legitimacy and legitimation – there is a clear case for a semiotic point of entry.

Weber identified three types of legitimate authority: traditional, charismatic, and *rational–legal authority*, and argued that modern states increasingly seek rational–legal authority, which rests 'on a belief in the "legality" of patterns of normative rules and the right of those elevated to authority under such rules to issue commands'. He also identifies a *value–rational* legitimacy, which holds 'by virtue of a rational belief in its absolute value' (Weber 1947: 130). Rational–legal is most relevant in this case, though value–rational authority is also relevant. Notice that both include the word 'rational'. I suggested that consent can be achieved rhetorically, though it can also be achieved dialectically – I am contrasting persuading by any available means, and persuading through the power of argument. Rational–legal and value–rational legitimation on the other hand indicate dialectical means of persuasion. I want to illustrate both forms of legitimation, or attempts at legitimation, in this document.

Note first the sense in which a document of this sort *does* call for textual work of legitimation. What is imagined and intended is the application of state power on a massive scale in the pursuit of security, including externally in wars of what the document calls a 'pre-emptive' nature but others have called 'preventive' at best and 'aggressive' at worst. The unprecedented scale of use of the state's monopoly over the means of violence in what is in a conventional sense a time of peace needs to be legitimated. But so also do unprecedented internal security measures which are indicated here but not detailed, and which have led to a vast increase in surveillance and a curtailment of civil rights, and have as Dillon (2007) puts it produced a terror over security in creating security against terror.

Legitimating such a massive application of state power and violence entails establishing that they are proportionate to the scale of the threat, which entails establishing that the threat itself is unprecedented. There is both rational–legal legitimation here involving claims about danger, and value–rational legitimation involving claims about an attack on 'our values'. Moreover, there is a more positive form of value–rational legitimation involving claims that the security strategy is driven by values, above all 'freedom'. Finally, there is also rational–legal legitimation with the emphasis on 'legal' – the military action envisaged is argued to be 'pre-emptive' and hence defensible in international law. Let me give a few examples, pointing to ways in which they are dialectically flawed – though such flaws have not prevented them from convincing many people and contributing to the legitimation of the strategy.

First, rational–legal legitimation on the basis of claims about danger, using Bush's Preface as an illustration. It contains a sequence of two legitimating arguments of this sort, of which I shall discuss the first:

> Now, shadowy networks of individuals can bring great chaos and suffering to our shores for less than it costs to purchase a single tank. Terrorists are organized to penetrate open societies and to turn the power of modern technologies against us. To defeat this threat we must make use of every tool

in our arsenal–military power, better homeland defenses, law enforcement, intelligence, and vigorous efforts to cut off terrorist financing. The war against terrorists of global reach is a global enterprise of uncertain duration. Our enemies have openly declared that they are seeking weapons of mass destruction, and evidence indicates that they are doing so with determination. The United States will not allow these efforts to succeed. We will build defenses against ballistic missiles and other means of delivery. We will co-operate with other nations to deny, contain, and curtail our enemies' efforts to acquire dangerous technologies. And, as a matter of common sense and self-defense, America will act against such emerging threats before they are fully formed.

The conclusion of the first argument is – to simplify – that we must make war against terrorists of uncertain duration on a global scale. The first two sentences are explicit premises, and there is an implicit premise that making war will defeat the threat. We might criticise the argument with respect to the second explicit threat by questioning whether the threat is not exaggerated, whether it is indeed great enough to justify the *total* character of the proposed response. But more importantly the argument is dialectically flawed with respect to the implicit premise, and in terms of dialogicality: it is highly contentious that war will defeat or even diminish the threat (assuming it is as depicted); it is arguable that it will increase it, and the argument is dialogically (and therefore dialectically) flawed in failing to address these arguments which are widely enunciated in the public sphere (van Eemeren and Houtlosser 2002, Ieţcu 2006). We can say that it comes back to the absence of analysis and explanation – the lack of an analysis of terrorism precludes rational exploration of means to diminish the threats it poses. Terrorism is taken as a given phenomenon, an 'emergence' – there is no room for instance for the argument that the existence of small groups who would happily use WMD against America is not in itself a serious threat, that without large-scale support they would be powerless, and that there are non-military options available for curtailing that support which are more likely to be effective in dealing with the threat than military options.

Value–rational legitimation is not as prominent in this document as it has been in speeches by Bush but also for instance by Tony Blair, who has contributed particularly to developing moral legitimation of war. But here is one example:

In the war against global terrorism, we will never forget that we are ultimately fighting for our democratic values and way of life. Freedom and fear are at war, and there will be no quick or easy end to this conflict.

The argument, condensed and partly implicit, is that a prolonged and difficult war against global terrorism is necessary because we are fighting for our values and way of life, which global terrorism is by implication aiming to destroy, and for freedom and against fear (which, by implication, global terrorism amounts to). It does not necessarily or obviously follow from the fact that there are groups and individuals whose aim is to destroy liberal democracy and consumer society that they are actually in danger, and again the argument is dialectically flawed in not addressing other publicly available arguments which bear upon questions of value in relation to terrorism – for instance that the great majority of those who support terrorist organisations are not driven by objectives of this sort, that the sort of fundamentalism alluded to could be more effectively isolated by means other than all-out war, and so forth.

Finally, let me come to the legal legitimation of intended military action as 'pre-emptive'. There is an elaborate and extended legitimising argument in the chapter on 'rogue states' and their link to terrorism – one point of analytical interest is which claims are argued for and which claims are not, for instance as I said earlier that the claim that 'the only path to peace and security is the path of action' is not argued for, it is simply asserted. The elaboration of the argument in this case would seem to indicate that this is a focus of concerns about legitimacy.

It has taken almost a decade for us to comprehend the true nature of this new threat. Given the goals of rogue states and terrorists, the United States can no longer solely rely on a reactive posture as we have in the past. The inability to deter a potential attacker, the immediacy of today's threats, and the magnitude of potential harm that could be caused by our adversaries' choice of weapons, do not permit that option. We cannot let our enemies strike first.

- In the Cold War, especially following the Cuban missile crisis, we faced a generally status quo, risk-averse adversary. Deterrence was an effective defense. But deterrence based only upon the threat of retaliation is less likely to work against leaders of rogue states more willing to take risks, gambling with the lives of their people, and the wealth of their nations.
- In the Cold War, weapons of mass destruction were considered weapons of last resort whose use risked the destruction of those who used them. Today, our enemies see weapons of mass destruction as weapons of choice. For rogue states these weapons are tools of intimidation and military aggression against their neighbors. These weapons may also allow these states to attempt to blackmail the United States and our allies to prevent us from deterring or repelling the aggressive behavior of rogue states. Such states also see these weapons as their best means of overcoming the conventional superiority of the United States.

- Traditional concepts of deterrence will not work against a terrorist enemy whose avowed tactics are wanton destruction and the targeting of innocents; whose so-called soldiers seek martyrdom in death and whose most potent protection is statelessness. The overlap between states that sponsor terror and those that pursue WMD compels us to action.

For centuries, international law recognized that nations need not suffer an attack before they can lawfully take action to defend themselves against forces that present an imminent danger of attack. Legal scholars and international jurists often conditioned the legitimacy of preemption on the existence of an imminent threat – most often a visible mobilization of armies, navies, and air forces preparing to attack. We must adapt the concept of imminent threat to the capabilities and objectives of today's adversaries. Rogue states and terrorists do not seek to attack us using conventional means. They know such attacks would fail. Instead, they rely on acts of terror and, potentially, the use of weapons of mass destruction – weapons that can be easily concealed, delivered covertly, and used without warning. The targets of these attacks are our military forces and our civilian population, in direct violation of one of the principal norms of the law of warfare. As was demonstrated by the losses on September 11, 2001, mass civilian casualties is the specific objective of terrorists and these losses would be exponentially more severe if terrorists acquired and used weapons of mass destruction. The United States has long maintained the option of preemptive actions to counter a sufficient threat to our national security. The greater the threat, the greater is the risk of inaction – and the more compelling the case for taking anticipatory action to defend ourselves, even if uncertainty remains as to the time and place of the enemy's attack. To forestall or prevent such hostile acts by our adversaries, the United States will, if necessary, act preemptively. The United States will not use force in all cases to preempt emerging threats, nor should nations use preemption as a pretext for aggression. Yet in an age where the enemies of civilization openly and actively seek the world's most destructive technologies, the United States cannot remain idle while dangers gather. [. . .] The purpose of our actions will always be to eliminate a specific threat to the United States or our allies and friends. The reasons for our actions will be clear, the force measured, and the cause just.

'Pre-emptive' action is generally regarded as legitimate self-defence in international law. But 'pre-emption' is conventionally regarded as legitimate only where there is an 'imminent threat', usually clear evidence of preparation and mobilisation for an immediate attack. Part of the argument here is that this concept of 'imminent threat' is out of date and must be 'adapted' to 'the capabilities and objectives of today's adversaries'. The point with respect to 'capabilities' is not new: since the beginning of the nuclear age, the possibility has existed of surprise attack with devastating effect. But it is argued that whereas 'deterrence was an effective defense' during the Cold War, it no longer is, and the reason is not the nature of the weapons but the nature of the enemy – 'rogue states and terrorists', 'the enemies of civilization'. We can concede that there are terrorist groups which do threaten the USA and/or its allies and friends against which deterrence is not an effective defence. But the legitimising argument has a fallacious character which lies in further claims within its premises about the nature of the enemy and the nature of the threat. I have already covered problems in the construal of the 'enemy', and I'll just add a few additional points.

First, there is an assumption that 'rogue states [. . .] seek to attack' the USA, and a claim that they 'rely on acts of terror'. I am not aware of evidence that any of the 'rogue states' has 'sought to attack' the USA, or been responsible for 'acts of terror'. There are claims of support by particular so-called 'rogue states' for terrorist organisations and even complicity in acts of terror. Even if these are true, a generic claim that 'rogue states' *as such* seek to attack the USA and are associated with 'acts of terror' would seem to be totally ungrounded. The same applies to other generic claims about 'rogue states' in this extract (e.g., 'For rogue states, [weapons of mass destruction] are tools of intimidation and aggression against their neighbors').

Second, a threat is implied of use by terrorist groups of WMD ('rogue states and terrorists [. . .] rely on acts of terror and, potentially, the use of weapons of mass destruction'). There no doubt are terrorists who might use WMD if they had access to them and the capability to use them, so we can't dismiss this as a *possibility*. But what is at stake here is *imminent* threat, and no evidence or argument is provided of that. Notice an obfuscation of the boundary between actual and possible, *realis* and *irrealis* claims, which is clearer if we extend the quotation a little:

> Rogue states and terrorists do not seek to attack us using conventional means. [. . .] they rely on acts of terror and, potentially, the use of weapons of mass destruction – weapons that can be easily concealed, delivered covertly, and used without warning. The targets of these attacks are our military forces and our civilian population [. . .]

There is a movement from a realis claim (they rely on acts of terror) to an irrealis claim (they 'potentially' rely on the use of WMD) to realis presuppositions (these attacks happen, these attacks have targets) which works I think rhetorically to make the threat of terrorist attacks with WMD seem more real than it actually is.

The third point is that an answer to the crucial question of how terrorist organisations get access to WMD is only obliquely hinted at:

> Traditional concepts of deterrence will not work against a terrorist enemy whose avowed tactics are wanton destruction and the targeting of innocents; whose so-called soldiers seek martyrdom in death and whose most potent protection is statelessness. The overlap between states that sponsor terror and those that pursue WMD compels us to action.

The last sentence might be regarded as a highly compressed argument for the claim 'we must act (i.e., use force "preemptively")' with implicit premises including the claims that 'states that sponsor terror might develop WMD' and 'if they develop WMD, they might make them available to terrorist groups'), but this makes it seem more transparent than it actually is.

Fourth, despite the claim at the end that 'the purpose of our actions will always be to eliminate a specific threat', the 'threat' is formulated in ways which suggest that it is not in any sense either 'specific' or 'immanent':

> taking anticipatory action to defend ourselves, even if uncertainty remains as to the time and place of the enemy's attack. To forestall or prevent such hostile acts by our adversaries, the United States will, if necessary, act preemptively. The United States will not use force in all cases to preempt emerging threats [. . .].

If there is uncertainty as to time or place, or the threats are 'emerging', they would not seem to be 'immanent' or 'specific'. Notice that the verb 'prevent' is used – indeed this looks more like 'preventive' warfare – which is not legitimate according to international law – than 'pre-emptive' warfare. Arguably this was anyway besides the point in Iraq since there proved to be nothing to prevent let alone 'pre-empt'.

Conclusion

I have been concerned with the texturing of a discourse in this document as part of the development of a strategy, involving the recontextualisation of other texts in some of which the discourse is already textured in similar if not the same ways, and in the light of the extensive and intensive recontextualisation of this document in turn in many other texts of various types. I have selectively analysed the document in such a way as to try to suggest a semiotic 'point of entry' into transdisciplinary analysis of relationships between discourse and other elements of the social process. What I have done is *indicate*, point to, ways of relating features of the discourse to reality beyond discourse, referring to lines of political-economic, political and sociological analysis which could be brought into a synthesis with discourse analysis, without attempting to effect such syntheses, which would be beyond the scope of the paper. Let me first pull together some main aspects and categories of the version of critical discourse analysis I have been working with, but necessarily only illustrated in part, and then sum up the relations I have suggested between discursive features and realities beyond discourse.

One characteristic of textual analysis within this version of CDA is that it is both *interdiscursive* analysis and linguistic analysis in a broad sense (including for instance analysis of argumentation) – in a multimodal text it might have been both linguistic and visual semiotic analysis. Interdiscursive analysis is analysis of hybridity in terms of the categories of *discourses* (ways of representing), *genres* (ways of interacting), and *styles* (ways of being, identities in their discoursal aspect), though in this analysis I have only discussed hybridity of discourses. Interdiscursive analysis mediates between linguistic analysis and social analysis in this version of CDA – thus hybridisation of discourses of the sort we have here is the discoursal or semiotic dimension shifts in boundaries between social fields, in this case convergence between the political-economic, development, diplomatic, and military and security fields; and hybridisation of discourses is realised in the linguistic features of the texts. Another important category I did not use is *order of discourse*, which is a term I use for the semiotic dimension of stabilised networks of social practices, or institutions or social fields. One might for instance talk of the semiotic dimension of the new or at least radically reshaped field (if that's what it is) of *security* as a new order of discourse, interpreting this to mean a particular configuration or articulation not only of different discourses as we have seen, but also of different *genres* and different *styles* – which in plain terms is just to say that a new order of security entails new ways of acting and interacting, and new identities, both of which have a partly semiotic character. A category I briefly used was *recontextualisation*, the movement of a discourse from one context (one network of practices, one institution, one field and so forth) to another, a movement which Chouliaraki and I (Chouliaraki and Fairclough 1999) suggested is a dialectical relationship between colonisation and appropriation. A document of this sort recontextualises discourses from different fields, but then articulates them together according to its own logic and genre. Finally, I have used the category of *operationalisation*, which has a crucial place in discussing relations between discourse and reality beyond discourse, because it subsumes the *enactment* of discourses in ways of acting and interacting, their *inculcation* in ways of being or identities, and their *materialisation* in changes in the physical world.

Let me turn to the relations I have suggested between discursive features and realities beyond discourse. I have discussed the relationship between the discourse of this document and actually existing realities as the *construal* of these realities, a process which condenses these realities, selectively includes and excludes aspects of them. I have also discussed the relationship between the discourse and actions strategically oriented to producing changed realities, and these changed realities themselves. I have argued that the construal of actually existing realities and of actions to change it must have some measure of *practical adequacy*, sufficiently construing things as they actually are and imaging actions which will actually be taken – or constituting a sort of blueprint which is a practically adequate guide to action and which shapes action – for the strategy to be successful, as this one has been to a degree, even if it has also seemed to be failing and unravelling. Thus terrorist organisations which have inflicted and seek to inflict damage on the USA and its allies have really existed, and much of the USA's application of force has indeed been directed at terrorist organisations. I have suggested that *construals* may under certain conditions, which include practical adequacy and achieving conviction, be operationalised, and so come to have *constructive* effects on reality beyond discourse. I suggested for instance that the construal of the enemy as an irrational and evil 'emergent' phenomenon which must be eliminated has had constructive effects on the nature of the military and other action which has been taken against the enemy.

This account has been complicated by what I called 'displacement' – a rhetorically motivated gap between a construal of the strategy for public consumption and a different construal where the intentions and objectives of power are more transparent. I argued the gap cannot be too big – that the public construal also needs a good measure of practical adequacy. Nevertheless, the gap bears upon relations between discourse and reality beyond discourse – in construals which are partly adequate and partly inadequate to reality (e.g., '*encouraging* free and open societies'), and in contradictions which may be textually managed (e.g., the *freedom* to choose, the requirement to choose *freedom*).

In addition to practical adequacy, I have discussed issues of conviction, and the relationship between discourse and beliefs and attitudes. The constructive effects of discourse include the construction of *consent* and the construction of *legitimacy*, both fragile constructs which need to be constructed anew. I suggested that whereas consent can be achieved by rhetorical means, legitimation requires dialectic. The distinction between the two is not a simple one. Rhetoric is persuasion by any available means, dialectic is persuasion through the power of argument. But both are persuasion, and there is a tension between the two, and a tendency which is apparent in this document for the requirements of dialectic to be overridden by rhetoric. My stance on legitimation here has been normative, taking the position that legitimation ought to be dialectically sound, and arguing that it is, in fact, dialectically flawed in legitimising arguments in the document. This normative insistence on the means by which the discursive construction of legitimacy ought to be pursued seems to me to be justified in terms of the standards we should demand of public discourse even if they are rarely satisfied.

In broad terms I have discussed two sorts of constructive effect, mental and material effects, which are, of course, not unconnected. One might say that discourse can have constructive effects on beliefs and attitudes, and so on how people act in and towards the material world, and so on the material world itself. I have also referred to *ideologies*: ideologies might be interpreted in a way that partially brings the mental and material together, as beliefs and values which are naturalised as dispositions to act in and on the material world in certain ways, and as ways of being in the world ('subject positions' adopted as Althusser put it).

Finally, the question of causality. I would say that I have been concerned with the causal powers of discourse, the power of discourse to contribute to change in reality beyond discourse, but on a particular view of the nature of causality. Causality is not the same as regularity. The causal powers of discourse do not necessarily have causal effects in particular instances, because events are standardly subject to diverse causal powers which can block or override each other in contingent ways. This is what has been described as the 'non-Humean' view of causation which separates causality and regularity which has been advanced within 'critical realism' (Sayer 2000), which is a philosophy of social science which can be seen as consistent with the version of CDA I use (Fairclough, Jessop and Sayer 2004).

20. Discourse and 'transition' in Central and Eastern Europe

This chapter is an initial contribution to an area of research I am currently embarking on: the role of discourse in processes of 'transition' (i.e., from socialism to capitalism and Western forms of democratic government) in Central and Eastern Europe (henceforth CEE). My particular focus here is on attempts in CEE, and specifically Romania, to construct a 'knowledge-based economy' (KBE) and 'information society' (IS). I begin with a brief sketch of the version of Critical Discourse Analysis (henceforth CDA), which I am currently working with. I then discuss discourse as an element in processes of 'transition', and the construction of 'objects of research' from research topics such as 'transition', KBE, and IS. The final part of the chapter looks in particular at the recontextualisation of discourses of the KBE and IS, especially the later, in Romania. I shall analyse a specific Romanian government policy text, the 'National Strategy for the promotion of the New Economy and the implementation of the Information Society' (2002).

1 Critical discourse analysis

I have chosen some of the main features of the version of CDA I now work with (Chouliaraki and Fairclough 1999, Fairclough 2003, 2000a, 2000b, Fairclough, Jessop and Sayer 2004), listing them for the sake of brevity:

1. Discourse is an element of all social processes, events and practices, though they are not simply discourse (Fairclough 1992a).
2. The relationship between abstract social structures and concrete social events is mediated by social practices, relatively stabilised forms of social activity (Chouliaraki and Fairclough 1999).

3. Each of these levels has a linguistic/semiotic element: languages (social structures), orders of discourse (social practices), texts broadly understood (social events) (Fairclough, Jessop and Sayer 2004).

4. Social practices and events are constituted as articulations of dialectically related elements including discourse. These are different (and they cannot, for instance, all be reduced to discourse, as some versions of discourse theory claim) but not discrete: discourse internalises and is internalised in other elements (Harvey 1996, Fairclough 2003). For instance, in researching any social organisation, one is faced with its partly discursive character, including its constitution as an operationalisation (putting into practice, 'translating' into its non-discursive as well as discursive facets) of particular discourses. But this does not mean that the organisation is nothing but discourse, or that it can be researched exclusively through discourse analysis – which would be highly reductive.

5. Discourse figures in three main ways in social practices: discourses (ways of representing, e.g., political discourses), genres (ways of [inter] acting, e.g., lecturing, interviewing), styles (ways of being – identities, e.g., styles of management) (Fairclough 2000a, 2000b).

6. Social practices are articulated into networks that constitute social fields, institutions and organisations. Orders of discourse are more exactly the linguistic/semiotic facet of such networks (Chouliaraki and Fairclough 1999).

7. An order of discourse is a social structuring of linguistic/semiotic difference, which is constituted as a relatively stable articulation of discourses, genres and styles (Fairclough 2003). For instance, the political order of discourse, associated with the political field as an articulation of social practices, is constituted in a particular time and place as an articulation of (conservative, liberal, social-democratic etc.) discourses; of genres such as political debate, speech and interview; and of styles, including different styles of political leadership.

8. Social change includes change in social structures, social practices and social events.

9. Change in social practices affects how elements are articulated together in practices; how practices are articulated together in networks; and how discourses, genres and styles are articulated together in orders of discourse (Chouliaraki and Fairclough 1999). Thus the relatively recent development of 'mediatised politics' is a re-articulation of the relationship between the fields of politics and media; their reconstitution as a network, which includes a transformation of the political order of discourse; its genres (e.g., the forms of political interview), discourses (e.g., the

translation of political discourses into popularised, more 'conversational', forms), and styles (political leaders adopt to a degree the 'show business' styles of entertainers).

10. Social change in countries, organisations etc. is often initiated with new discourses. This operates through a dissemination across structural and scalar boundaries which 'recontextualises' new discourses. These may be enacted as new ways of (inter)acting including genres, inculcated as new ways of being including styles, as well as materialised in, for example, new ways of structuring space. Thus liberal and neo-liberal discourses have been recontextualised in 'transitional' countries in CEE, and to varying degrees enacted in new ways of (inter)acting (e.g., in government, including government addressing and interacting with citizens as consumers), inculcated in new ways of being (e.g., people adopting the lifestyles and identities of consumers), and materialised in such new constructions of space as the 'shopping mall'.

11. 'May' is important: there are discursive as well as non-discursive conditions of possibility for discourses having constitutive effects on other elements of the social – the fact that discourses 'construe' the world in particular ways does not necessarily mean that they (re)construct it in those ways (Fairclough, Jessop and Sayer 2004). Social fields, institutions, and organisations are 'intransitive' realities that have properties that make them more or less amenable or resistant to particular directions of change.

12. CDA claims that analysis of social processes and change is productively carried down into detailed textual analysis. More detailed (including linguistic) analysis of texts is connected to broader social analysis by way of interdiscursive analysis of shifting articulations of genres, discourses, styles in texts (Fairclough 2003).

13. As a form of critical social science, CDA analyses social life in its discursive aspects from a normative perspective, i.e., on the basis of a commitment to a set of values of social justice, social equality, democracy – though there are differences in how such values are understood and interpreted.

2 Discourse as an element of processes of 'transition'

The importance of language and discourse in processes of 'transition' in CEE and elsewhere is quite widely recognised in social research (for instance, in Miroiu (1999), and in the conception of influential neo-liberal models of transition as 'discourses' in, e.g., Bourdieu and Wacquant (2001)). But social research has so far produced only a limited understanding of how discourse figures in processes of 'transition'. This is partly a theoretical problem: the theories of discourse which tend to be drawn upon are relatively underdeveloped and do not constitute an adequate basis for providing full and nuanced accounts of how discourse interacts with other non-discursive facets of processes of 'transition'. It is also a problem of data and analytical method: acknowledgement of the importance of discourse in general and abstract statements about discourse in 'transition' or more generally in social change have not generally been translated into detailed analysis texts or talk, so there is little concrete knowledge of how they figure in the unfolding of events or change and continuity of practices in specific types of situation, organisation, locality etc.

Having said that, forms of textual analysis have already been used in Romanian research on 'transition', e.g., on media (e.g., Miroiu 1999, Beciu 2000, Coman 2003a, 2003b), but CDA's particular mix of interdiscursive and linguistic analysis is, I think, a more powerful analytical resource for addressing these issues than those I have seen used (Preoteasa (2002) is one case of CDA being used). I see CDA as a resource for producing richer understanding and analysis of the relationship between discourse and other non-discursive facets of social processes and social change, and of the effects of discourse on wider processes of social change, through a 'transdisciplinary' dialogue with other theories and disciplines. Transdisciplinary research is a form of interdisciplinary research that sees 'Internal' development of a theory or discipline (of their theoretical categories and concepts and methods of research) as emerging out of dialogue with others (Fairclough 2003).

3 Theorising 'transition'

I shall approach the IS and KBE as topics of research by way of recent developments in political economy (Sayer 1995, Pickles and Smith 1998, Stark and Bruszt 1998, Ray and Sayer 1999, Jessop 2002, 2004). In particular, I follow Jessop (2004) in viewing them as strategies for achieving and stabilising a new 'fix' between a regime of capital accumulation and a regime of political regulation in the aftermath of the demise of the 'fix' commonly referred to as 'Fordism'. This formulation derives from 'regulation theory', which has a political-economic rather than a narrowly and purely economic perspective on economic change, arguing that an economic order ('regime of capital accumulation') is dependent upon a political order (a 'mode of regulation') that can produce and sustain the preconditions for its durable operation. The more general claim is that there are non-economic (including, as we shall see, social and cultural as well as political) preconditions for the establishment and reproduction of economies. The dominant international political-economic order since the demise of Fordism has been widely identified as 'post-Fordist', which is indicative of the uncertainty of what follows, or should follow, Fordism.

The significance of the KBE (this is Jessop's focus, though the same could be said for the IS, and for the frequent conjunction of the two which is characteristic of the material I shall look at) is that it seems to be emerging as a strategy for change that can effectively be operationalised in real change. They are strategies but, like any strategy, also discourses, particular ways of representing, or rather imagining (because they are certainly as much predictive as descriptive) a new political-economic order. And they are discourses of a particular kind, what we might call 'nodal' discourses, in the sense that they are discourses which subsume and articulate in a particular way a great many other discourses: technical discourses (e.g., discourses of ICT – information and communications technology), the discourse of 'intellectual property', discourses of governance and government (e.g., 'e-government'), discourses of 'social exclusion' and 'social inclusion', and so forth. As discourses, they constitute selective representations, 'simplifications' (Jessop 2002), 'condensations' (Harvey 1996) of highly complex economic, political, social and cultural realities, which include certain aspects of these realities and exclude others, highlight certain aspects and background others. Not any discourse would work as a strategic nodal discourse for imagining and potentially operationalising, actualising, a new political-economic fix. A discourse can only work in so far as it achieves a high level of adequacy with respect to the realities it selectively represents, simplifies, condenses – in so far as it is capable (as these seem capable) of being used to represent/imagine realities at different levels of abstraction, in different areas of social life (economy, government, education, health, regional and social disparities etc.), on different scales (international, macro-regional [e.g., EU], national, local). It is only if it is a plausible imaginary that it will attract investments of time and money to prepare for the imaginary future it projects, material factors which are crucial to making imaginaries into realities (Cameron and Palan 2004).

In this sense, the KBE and the IS have a partially discursive and partially material character. They are discourses, but not just discourses; they are discourses that are materially grounded and materially promoted. The theoretical framework we need to conceptualise this needs to be not just a political economy (rather than a narrow economics) but also what Jessop calls a 'cultural political economy', a political economy which, among other things, incorporates a theory of discourse and of the dialectics of discourse, of how discursive construals of the world can come to construct and reconstruct the world, without losing sight of the material reality of the world, or the conditions which the material reality of the world sets (as I have briefly indicated) on the discursive (re)construction of the world.

This strategic perspective provides a basis for formulating objects of research for this aspect of 'transition' as a topic of research, and the 'cultural' orientation of the approach to political economy means that objects of research can be formulated to include or highlight questions of semiosis. Objects of research might include the emergence and constitution, hegemony, dissemination and recontextualisation and operationalisation of the strategies of the 'KBE' and the 'IS.' These objects of research might be formulated specifically as objects for CDA research projects in the following ways:

- The emergence of the discourses of the 'KBE' and the 'IS' as nodal discourses in association with the emergence of strategies, their constitution through the articulation of relationships between other discourses, including discourses 'available' within existing or prior nodal discourses.[1]
- Relations of contestation between discourses within the framework of relations of contestation between strategies, and the emerging hegemony of these nodal discourses.[2]
- The dissemination of the discourses of 'KBE' and the 'IS' across structures (e.g., between economic markets, governments, public and social services such as education and health) and scales (between 'global' or international, macro-regional (e.g., EU or NAFTA), national, and local scales of social life), their recontextualisation in new social fields, institutions, organisations, countries, localities.
- The shift of these nodal discourses from 'construals' to 'constructions' (Sayer 2000), from being just representations and imaginaries to having transformative effects on social reality, being operationalised – enacted as new ways of (inter)acting, inculcated in new ways of being (identities), materialised in new instruments and techniques of production or ways of organising space.

These different research objects call for different methods in data selection, collection and analysis. Researching the emergence and constitution of these discourses requires a genealogical approach which locates these discourses within the field of prior discourses and entails collection of historical series of texts and selection of key texts within these series, analysis of the constitution of these discourses through articulation of elements within the field of prior discourses, and specification of the relations of articulation between the diverse discourses which are drawn together within these nodal discourses.

Researching the emergent hegemony of these discourses entails locating these discourses in their relations of contestation with other potentially nodal discourses, which involves, for instance, focusing on dialogical relations between and within texts in key institutions such as the OECD (Godin 2004). Researching dissemination and recontextualisation entails comparing texts in different social fields and at different social scales (e.g., in different societies or localities), and analysing, for instance, how, when these discourses are recontextualised, they are articulated with discourses that already exist within these new contexts. Researching operationalisation calls for ethnographical methods in the collection of data, in that it is only by accessing insider perspectives in particular localities, companies, and so on, that one can assess how discourses are materialised, enacted and inculcated. I shall be discussing only aspects of (the dissemination and) recontextualisation of these nodal discourses.

The predominant form of critique associated with CDA and critical social research more generally has been ideology critique. But we can distinguish three forms of critique that are relevant to CDA: ideological, rhetorical and strategic critique. Whereas ideological critique focuses on the effects of semiosis on social relations of power, and rhetorical critique on persuasion (including 'manipulation') in individual texts or talk, what we might call 'strategic critique' focuses on how semiosis figures within the strategies pursued by groups of social agents to change societies in particular directions. The research objects I have distinguished (emergence, hegemony, recontextualisation and operationalisation) can be seen as objects associated with strategic critique. One might see strategic critique as assuming a certain primacy in periods of major social change and restructuring, such as the one we are going through now. This is not to suggest at all that ideological and rhetoric critique cease to be relevant; it is more a matter of their relative salience within the critical analysis.

The Pickles and Smith (1998) collection on the political economy of 'transition' adopts a regulation approach in combination with theories of governance and elements of cultural theory. One concern is with 're-scaling', which alludes to the category of 'scales', different levels of social process, organisation, structure and strategy: 'global', international, and macro-regional (e.g., the EU and candidate countries), national, micro-regional and local. One aspect of transition is 're-scaling', the emergence of new scales, and the reorganisation of relations between scales (Jessop 2002). The issue of 'globalisation' is significant here, as is what has been referred to as 'glocalisation' (Robertson 1992), a re-scaling which sets up new relations between the local and the global in ways that can to some degree bypass the national.

Ethnographic and other studies of crisis and change in specific localities (Burawoy and Verdery 1999, Burawoy 2000, Anăstăsoaie *et al.* 2003) have shown how 'global' resources are marshalled by local strategists in struggles over, for instance, environmental issues, or attempts to reposition economically depressed cities within global urban networks (Pickles 1998, Gille 2000). These 'global' resources include discourses – for instance, the discourses of internationally organised environmental groups.

On the basis of this literature, one can say the following about 'transition':

1. There is not one form of capitalism but many forms. The market is only one regulatory mechanism within contemporary forms of capitalism, which combines in various ways with others, hierarchies (states), and networks (Sayer 1995, Pickles and Smith 1998, Stark and Bruszt 1998, Jessop 2002).
2. The particular trajectories of 'transition' vary in different countries but also within different countries, depending on legacies, including how the process of extrication from communism took place. The forms of capitalism that develop are consequently also variable (Pickles and Smith 1998, Przeworski 1992, Daianu 2000).
3. Transition entails a mixture of old and new, rather than a simple replacement of the old by the new (Stark and Bruszt 1998, Verdery 2000).
4. Research on transition in a particular country should be sensitive to (a) variation both between and within social fields – economy, government, politics, media etc. – and (b) hybridity (including mixtures of old and new) in particular fields, institutions, practices etc.
5. Transition has semiotic as well as non-semiotic elements. Consequently, variation and hybridity will be in part semiotic variation and hybridity (see, for instance, Miroiu (1999) on variation and hybridity in post-1989 Romanian political discourses) – in the way social life is represented, narrated, imagined (therefore in discourses), in semiotic aspects of forms of action and interaction (therefore in genres), in semiotic aspects of the identities of social actors (therefore in styles).

4   Recontextualisation of the 'knowledge-based economy' and 'information society' in Romanian policy texts

The dissemination and recontextualisation of the strategies and discourses of the KBE and IS in CEE is closely connected to the process of EU enlargement. The Lisbon Council of the EU in 2000 adopted these strategies as part of the 'e-Europe' initiative. The EU's 'strategic goal' is to 'become the most competitive and dynamic knowledge-based economy in the world, capable of sustainable economic growth with more and better jobs and greater social cohesion.' The 'e-Europe 2002 Action Plan' was agreed at Feira in 2000, and the candidate countries for EU membership in CEE were associated with the EU's strategic goal in adopting the 'e-Europe+ Action Plan' in 2001, one reason for which was said to be avoiding a 'digital divide' within the EU. According to the Romanian government's 'National Strategy for the promotion of the New Economy and the implementation of the Information Society' (2002), it was made clear at a conference of ministers of the candidate countries and representatives of the EU in Warsaw (May 2000) that 'the e-Europe initiative will become a basic element of the process of integration'.

The 'e-Europe+ Action Plan' agreed by the candidate countries was explicitly modelled upon the EU's 'e-Europe 2002 Action Plan', and much of the Romanian government's 'National Strategy' document is modelled upon them. The document is partly an 'action plan', but it is also partly a strategy document comparable to an extent with the Lisbon Summit Declaration. The nodal discourse in the Lisbon Declaration is the 'KBE', whereas the nodal discourse in the Romanian document is the 'IS' (the discourse of 'the new economy' could be seen as a secondary nodal discourse). There seems to be no clear and stable relation between the two nodal discourses within the 'eEurope' and 'eEurope+' projects overall; they are articulated together in different ways in different policy documents. In the Romanian position paper on the KBE for the World Bank's 'Knowledge Economy Forum for EU Accession Countries', held in Paris at precisely the same time as the publication of the Romanian 'National Strategy' document (February 2002), the nodal discourse is 'the KBE', even though it refers to virtually the same set of strategies and policies. In the Lisbon Declaration, the 'IS' is one element of one of three 'strategies' for achieving the 'strategic goal' of becoming 'the most competitive and dynamic knowledge-based economy in the world' (see section 5 of the Lisbon Declaration, Text 1, in the Appendix). Although the 'KBE' is not an entity or imaginary or strategic goal in the Romanian 'National Strategy', the 'new economy' is defined partly in recognisably 'KBE' terms as the 'intensification of incorporation of knowledge in new products and services' ('intensificarea înglob rii cunoa terii în noile produse i servicii').

As these comments imply, what is significant with respect to recontextualisation is both the presence or absence of particular discourses in particular texts, and the relations in which diverse discourses are articulated, 'textured', together. One can identify differences between texts in this regard, by analysing the relationship between discourses and features of genre, in the sense that genres can be seen as 'framing' devices for organising relationships between discourses (Chouliaraki and Fairclough 1999). Relevant features of genre include the rhetorical structure and argumentative structure of the text (Fairclough 2003). I shall focus my analytical comments upon these issues. One can see how this selection of focuses for analysis depends upon the particular object of research (recontextualisation), though there are many other analytical issues (such as the presentation of processes and of agency) that are germane to recontextualisation.

In the opening section of the Lisbon Declaration ('A strategic goal for the next decade,' paragraphs 1–7, Text 1, Appendix), predominant features of the rhetorical structure are arguments from problems to solutions and from ends to means. The two paragraphs of the first sub-section ('The new challenge') are both arguments from problem to solution, from what 'is' happening to what 'must' be done in response (from the 'challenge', the changes that are happening, to the necessary responses, what the Union 'must' do, 'needs' to do, what is 'urgent' for it to do, what these changes 'require'). The second section ('The Union's strengths and weaknesses') is also a version of a problem-to-solution argument, arguing for the proposed solution as a response to 'weaknesses' which is timely in the light of 'strengths'. Both paragraphs 5 and 6 in the third section ('The way forward') are arguments from ends ('strategic goals') to means ('strategy'), and paragraph 7 is an argument from ends ('strategy') to means of governance for achieving them.

This rhetorical structure constitutes a frame within which diverse discourses are articulated together in a particular way, within which relations are textured (textually constituted) between these discourses. I am particularly concerned here with the placing of expressions that are associated with different discourses in relations of 'equivalence'[3] through listing and other forms of paratactic connection (Fairclough 2003). One can see this as a process of (re)classifying, texturing relations between expressions as co-members of a class (even if, as is generally the case, the class itself is not named – what van Leeuwen (1996) calls 'association'). In paragraph 5, for instance, the formulation of the 'strategic goal' sets up a relation of equivalence between 'sustainable economic growth', 'more and better jobs', and 'greater social cohesion' (more precisely: there is a comitative structure which sets up a relation of equivalence between the first and the other two phrases, and a coordinate structure which sets up a relation of equivalence between these two), all as attributes of the 'KBE'. Each of these equivalent phrases represents a substantive EU policy area associated with an elaborated discourse (the discourses of growth, (un)employment, social and regional cohesion), and the relations of equivalence among them are linguistic realisations of interdiscursive hybridity (the 'mixing' of discourses).

The formulation of the 'overall strategy', which is the means to achieving the 'strategic goal', again sets up relations of equivalence, among the three listed elements of the strategy ('preparing . . .', 'modernising . . .', 'sustaining . . .'), and within them between 'better policies for the information society and R&D' (and within this, between 'IS' and 'R&D'), 'stepping up the process of structural reform for competitiveness and innovation' (and within this, between 'competitiveness' and 'innovation') and 'completing the internal market'; among 'modernizing the European social model', 'investing in people', and 'combating social exclusion'; and so forth. Again, diverse policy areas and associated discourses (e.g., the 'IS', 'competitiveness', 'social exclusion') are articulated together in particular relations within the nodal discourse of the 'KBE'.

A significant overall feature of the articulation of discourses in the document is that, in the formulation of problems, the strategic goal, and the strategies for achieving it, discourses which represent the economy ('sustainable economic growth' in the strategic goal) are articulated with discourses which represent social problems and policies ('more and better jobs' and 'social cohesion' in the strategic goal).

One notable difference between the Lisbon Declaration and the Romanian 'National Strategy' document is that there is no section in the latter with a comparable rhetorical structure, articulating arguments from problems to solutions with arguments from ends to means. In more general terms, the Romanian document is not based upon arguments from the specific problems facing Romania to strategic goals for dealing with them (and strategies for achieving these). This is on the face of it a surprising absence in a national strategy document, though, as I argue later, not actually at all surprising given Romania's international position. This does not mean that problems are not identified in the document, or that goals and strategies and policies are not specified. They are, but what is significant is the relations that are textured between them. For instance, the relationship between strategic goals and problems is largely reversed: rather than goals and strategies being legitimised in their adequacy and timeliness in responding to a diagnosis of the problems facing the country, the problems are construed as weaknesses and difficulties with respect to achieving the strategic goal, taken as given, of the 'IS'. This is indicated by the wider rhetorical structure of the document: the strategic goal is formulated (as I show below) in Chapters 1 and 2, on the basis of claims about the general benefits (not specific benefits to Romania) of the 'IS' and Romania's international commitments (especially to 'eEurope+'), and specific Romanian problems (of poverty, emigration of skilled labour etc.) are identified only in Chapter 3 within an assessment of the country's current position in respect of the 'IS'.

Arguments for the 'IS' as the strategic goal are largely implicit. The Lisbon Declaration is 'based upon' arguments from problems to solutions in the material sense that the document begins from these arguments. The Romanian document, by contrast, begins with a general chapter about the 'IS' and the 'new economy', which does not directly refer to Romania at all and only indirectly alludes to Romania in the final few paragraphs. In rhetorical structure, the chapter is an extended description of the 'IS', followed by prescriptions about what must be done to construct such a society. The first, descriptive, section construes the 'IS' as actually existing rather than as a strategic goal, representing it in an idealised (and to some degree utopian) way, which construes in universal terms what are commonly claimed to be its potential effects and benefits as if they were actual effects and benefits. Here, for instance, is a translation of the second paragraph:

The information society represents a new stage of human civilisation, a new and qualitatively superior way of life, which implies the intensive use of information in all spheres of human activity and existence, with major economic and social consequences. The information society allows widespread access to information for its members, a new way of working and learning, greater possibilities for economic globalisation, and increasing social cohesion.

It is only in the ninth of its thirteen paragraphs that a strategic perspective on 'constructing the new model of society' ('Construirea noului model de societate . . .') appears. The following paragraphs specify the role of government, business, the academic community, and civil society in this process. By this stage, one can assume that Romania in particular is being alluded to without being explicitly named – this is implicit in the claim that 'national development priorities for the medium-long term' and 'objectives of adhesion to Euro-Atlantic structures' (often formulated in this way in Romanian policy contexts) need to be taken into account. The 'IS' as a strategic goal is covertly established on the basis of idealised claims about the 'IS' as a universal reality.

The second chapter is a review of tendencies and policies internationally and within the EU, including a summary of the 'e-Europe' and 'e-Europe+' initiatives. Romania is a participant in 'e-Europe+'. The 'IS' as a 'development objective' is claimed to be 'an essential condition for participation in the single European market'. It is implied, without being explicitly stated, that this applies to Romania, and that the 'information society' is therefore its 'development objective' (strategic goal). The third chapter is a STEEP (social, technological, economic and political factors) analysis of the current situation with respect to the 'IS' internationally and in Romania, which includes a review of problems and possibilities and policies in Romania – it is here, as I said earlier, that specifically Romanian problems are introduced.

Thus the 'IS' is *implicitly* established as Romania's strategic goal on essentially *extraneous* grounds: the universal benefits it brings as an existing reality, and the commitment to this strategic goal as a part of commitment to the 'e-Europe+' initiative.

It is only in Chapter 4 ('Strategic Directions and Options') that 'strategic choices' for Romania are explicitly addressed. I shall comment on the rhetorical and argumentative structure of the first section (entitled 'Global objectives', see Texts 2 and 3 in the Appendix) and how it frames the articulation of discourses. The rhetorical structure of the section is characterised by arguments from general factual claims about economic changes and their societal consequences in the 'IS', to possibilities, policies and strategies (for, by implication, particular countries). Although these arguments are formulated in general terms without specific reference to Romania (Romania is referred to explicitly only in the last sentence), they can be taken as referring implicitly to Romania – the list of four policies includes what appear to be specifically Romanian policies (especially the fourth, which is very similar to policies advocated explicitly for economic applications of ICT in Romania in the next section of the chapter). The first sentence makes a general factual claim about the consequences of large-scale use of ICTs ('profound implications for socio-economic life, fundamental transformations in the way of producing goods and services and in human behavior'). The second sentence is a conditional formulation of the possibilities opened up: greater use of information technologies 'can ensure the socio-economic progress characteristic of information societies', as long as 'objectives and orientations of a strategic nature are adopted through policies appropriate to the actual societies in which we live'.

Four policies are then listed ('consolidation of democracy and the rule of law', 'development of a market economy and progressive movement towards the new economy', 'improving the quality of life', and, through policies to achieve this, 'integration into Euro-Atlantic structures and the Global Information Society', 'consolidation and development of a national economic framework which ensures the production of goods and services which are competitive on internal and external markets'). The first three elements of this list are structured as arguments from end to means. In the following two paragraphs, there are two sentences making general factual claims about the 'IS', which frame a more specific claim (sentence 3) about the development of knowledge as 'a critical, determining, factor in economic growth and standards of living', which by implication makes it possible (sentence 4) for the 'digital divide' to become, with 'appropriate strategies', the 'digital opportunity'. The pattern of argument from factual economic claim to strategic possibilities is repeated in the following two paragraphs. The final sentence is a recommendation, 'given the example of the countries referred to above and presented in the appendix' (Ireland, Israel, Finland) that Romania 'should make a fundamental choice to develop a branch of the economy which produces the goods and services demanded by the information society, based on ICT'.

The rhetorical structure of the first section of the Lisbon Declaration set up a relationship among diagnosed problems, a strategic goal for solving them, and strategies for achieving it (with means for achieving these strategic ends). Here, by contrast, the strategic goal is taken for granted rather than established on the basis of diagnosis of problems (there is no such diagnosis), and the focus is on possibilities arising from general claims about economic and social change and the strategies for realising them. Thus, at the one point in the document where 'strategic options' specifically for Romania are addressed, there is no attempt to establish strategic goals adapted to Romania's particular problems, and the only strategic choice recommended, in the last sentence (the only one that explicitly refers to Romania), relates specifically and narrowly to economic applications of ICT. The rest of the chapter is taken up with an elaboration of this.

I noted above that, in the Lisbon Declaration, discourses that represent the economy are articulated with discourses that represent social problems and policies. In the Romanian document, there is something resembling this articulation in the list of four policies, but it is significantly different. First, this articulation is only within strategies to achieve the assumed strategic goal of the 'IS', whereas in the Lisbon Declaration the articulation of economic and social discourses is present in the formulation of problems, strategic goal, and strategies for achieving it. Second, and connectedly, it is only social policies that are represented, not social problems. Third, the social policies represented relate to political issues and 'the quality of life', but not, for instance, to standards of living (or the key problem of poverty), employment (or the problem of unemployment), or the major divisions between urban and rural areas and populations.[4] That is, major social problems which one might see as demanding social policies (including those focused upon in the Lisbon Declaration, (un)employment, social and regional cohesion) are not represented.

I shall make a few comments on the articulation of discourses within the listed policies. In the first, a relation of equivalence is textured between 'democracy' and '(the institutions of) the state of right',[5] which one can see as significant in the recontextualisation of the discourse of 'e-government' (as a constituent discourse of both the nodal discourses): the aim of establishing the 'state of right' was one of the key ways in which Romanian society after 1989 differentiated and distanced itself from the Ceausescu era. However, the equivalence relations within the formulation of the means for achieving the policy (between 'the participation of citizens in public life', 'the facilitation of non-discriminatory access to public information', 'improvement of the quality of public services', modernisation of public administration') constitute an articulation of discourses that one might find in the 'e-government' policies of EU members. In the third, the policy of 'improving the quality of life' is represented as a means to 'integration into Euro-Atlantic structures and the Global Information Society'. This is again significant with respect to recontextualisation. 'Integration into Euro-Atlantic structures', subsuming integration into the EU, is often formulated as a Romanian policy objective which has been interpreted as merging in a confused way EU membership and NATO membership (Repere 2004). Policies for improving the quality of life are a *means* to this end in that they are among the conditions Romania must meet (in the *acquis communitaires* and the 'e-Europe' initiative) for joining the EU.

If we look at the arguments and explanations given in the document as a whole for Romania's adoption of the 'IS' as a strategic goal, it may clarify what problems it is covertly construed as a solution to. ICT is 'considered an important engine for boosting the national economy and promoting national interests'. Romania has adhered to the objectives of the 'e-Europe' programme, 'considering them a beneficial framework for the urgent process of integration in the EU'. If Romania is not rapidly integrated into 'Euro-Atlantic structures' (the strategy of the 'IS' is represented as a precondition for this), 'the economic gap between our country and developed countries will grow'. What is noteworthy is that factors to do with the economy, 'national interests', and EU integration are included, but – in contrast with the Lisbon Declaration – social factors (unemployment, poverty, social exclusion, social and regional cohesion) are not.

These are the cases of Romania being specifically and explicitly referred to. There is a much larger number of others, in which arguments for the 'IS' are given in general terms, without reference to particular countries, which can be seen as implicitly applying to Romania. Apart from the first chapter, these are mainly economic arguments (e.g., 'developing countries can obtain certain economic advantages from rapidly capitalising on the opportunities offered by ICT and especially electronic commerce'). In the first chapter, there are a number of general claims about the 'IS' which might be taken as implicit arguments in favour of adopting it as a strategic goal, and these do include solutions to social problems (see the paragraph quoted earlier). But these arguments do not, of course, address Romania's particular and in some ways quite specific social problems (e.g., approximately forty per cent of the workforce is still employed in agriculture).

In Chouliaraki and Fairclough (1999), we argued that recontextualisation is a colonisation–appropriation dialectic. There is both a process of an 'external' discourse colonising the recontextualising practices (country, field, organisation etc.), and a process of the 'external' discourse being appropriated within the recontextualising practices. In principle, one can claim that there is no colonisation without appropriation – recontextualisation is always an active process on the part of 'internal' social agents of inserting an 'external' element into a new context, working it into a new set of relations with its existing elements, and in so doing transforming it. This is often manifested in the interdiscursive hybridity of texts, the mixing of 'external' with 'internal' discursive elements. Moreover, in strategic terms one could argue that strategic relations between 'external' and 'internal' social agents will always be inflected by strategic relations between 'internal' social agents.

However, it is necessary to add two provisos to this theoretical account. First, the degree to which recontextualisation becomes an active process of appropriation entailing potentially substantive transformation of recontextualised elements (which includes the possibilities of them being strategically used by some 'internal' agents in their struggles with others, being contained or marginalised or contested etc.) depends upon the state of the relations between 'external' and 'internal' agents and of relations between 'internal' agents. Recontextualising contexts may manifest degrees of passivity. Second, however active the process of appropriation, one cannot assume that it will be equally active in all practices within the recontextualising context (e.g., a nation state such as Romania).

In general terms, the room for autonomous agency and initiative in contemporary Romania with respect to the main lines of economic and social policy and activity is rather limited. Romania is strongly committed to integration into the European Union and 'Euro-Atlantic structures' and to maintaining good relations with and the support and assistance of the EU, the US, EU states, international agencies (UNO, World Bank, IMF, and so forth), and these come with conditions attached which leave Romania with little room for manoeuvre. I have shown in the analysis of the 'National Strategy' document that, rather than being explicitly legitimised as solutions to Romania's particular problems, strategic goals are implicitly legitimised through idealised claims about the 'IS' construed as a universal reality, and by reference to Romania's international commitments. Any state is faced with the problem of legitimising its goals, strategies, and policies, and these can perhaps be seen as the legitimising strategies adopted by the Romanian government (though such a conclusion would require more extensive analysis of policy documents and other government material). Given its international position, one might argue that Romania does not have the option of formulating goals, strategies and policies on the basis of an analysis of its specific problems and needs. Though Boia (1999), in distinguishing 'defensive' and 'offensive' Romanian responses to integration with 'the West' over the course of modern Romanian history, suggests that it is a characteristic of the 'offensive' (integrationist) responses to proceed with scant regard for the consequences in the already profound social divisions and inequalities in the country.

5 Conclusion

Miroiu (1999) describes the 'mental cramp' she experienced in discussing Romanian problems with Western academics, and her realisation that Romanian realities could not be grasped in their conceptual frameworks. I think this is in part an issue of methodology. Bourdieu's approach to constructing the 'object of research' implies a progressive articulation or rapprochement of topics of research with theories and methods in the course of defining and refining the 'object of research', rather than immediately approaching the topic of research armed with ready-made theories and methods. What is implied is that theories and methods appropriate to the object of research and particular to this object of research should be progressively constructed out of existing resources of theory and method, which can quite legitimately include theories and methods hitherto used only 'elsewhere', be that in different parts of the world, different areas of research, or different disciplines.

We also need to draw distinctions, with respect to theory, among different types of theory. Metatheories (such as 'critical realism' as a philosophy of science) and general theories (such as the theory of discourse I have sketched here, or regulation theory) generally travel better than 'local theories' (e.g., theories focused upon particular social fields in particular sorts of society, such as theories of education, media, or social welfare in social democratic societies). This is not to say that research in particular sorts of society may not lead to specific critiques of metatheories or general theories. There are, for instance, apparently general theories whose covert particularity is revealed by working with them in new contexts – recently influential economic theories are a case in point. And even with general theories, one needs to carefully distinguish what is general about them from particularities that attach to them because of the specific research topics they have been used to address and the specific localities of such research. This is certainly true for CDA: the categories of 'order and discourse', 'discourses', 'genres', 'styles', 'interdiscursivity' are among those which belong to the general theory, whereas categories such as 'marketisation' or 'conversationalisation' which have figured quite prominently in CDA research do not, nor does the use of systemic functional grammar for linguistic analysis of texts. If 'conversationalisation' proved to be a useless category for discourse analytical research in Romania, it would not be a problem for the theory; if 'interdiscursivity' did, it would.

CDA's transdisciplinary way of working makes it difficult sometimes to separate general from particular. For instance, I would say that 'recontextualisation', a category which originated in Bernstein's sociology of pedagogy (Bernstein 1990; Chouliaraki and Fairclough 1999) has become a general category of CDA because it has been fully reinterpreted in discourse-analytical terms and built into the relational structure of the categories of the theory, whereas 'conversationalisation' has not. Moreover the transdisciplinary way of working and the associated methodology I have pointed to entails that, in the course of progressively arriving at one's 'object of research', one is also seeking to find a coherent synthesis between CDA as a general theory and other theories which bear upon one's topic – let us say theories of media and mediation, theories of politics, theories of identity, theories of learning – so that caution is always needed about non-reflexively 'importing' inappropriate or misleading particularities.

Finally, let me note the limited nature of what I have done in this chapter, and point to directions in which this research needs to be developed. Firstly, I have looked at recontextualisation only with respect to policy texts. One would also need material from within particular institutions (e.g., educational), businesses, localities, political parties etc. to arrive at a fuller assessment. Such an extension of the data might also provide evidence of a more active appropriation of these discourses, hybrid relations between these and other discourses, and strategic differences in their recontextualisation, than I have been able to show in this chapter.

Secondly, a commonplace in commentaries on transition is that they are, in the much-used expression of the nineteenth-century Romanian literary critic Maiorescu, 'form without content' – as modernisation and westernisation in Romania have always been, many would add. The language of modernisation is readily 'imitated' from the West, but without much change in social realities. Such claims make it particularly important to go beyond public policy documents in looking at recontextualisation, and especially to research the operationalisation of discourses such as the 'IS' and the 'knowledge economy', not only by looking, for instance, at how imaginaries for 'e-government' are being operationalised in, for instance, the setting up of a government web portal (http:www.guvernare.ro) but also through ethnographic research in localities, companies etc. which can give insights into the relationship among discourses, rhetoric and reality.

APPENDIX

Text 1: Extract from the Lisbon Declaration: ('A strategic goal for the next decade')

The new challenge

1. The European Union is confronted with a quantum shift resulting from globalisation and the challenges of a new knowledge-driven economy. These changes are affecting every aspect of people's lives and require a radical transformation of the European economy. The Union must shape these changes in a manner consistent with its values and concepts of society and also with a view to the forthcoming enlargement.

2. The rapid and accelerating pace of change means it is urgent for the Union to act now to harness the full benefits of the opportunities presented. Hence the need for the Union to set a clear strategic goal and agree a challenging programme for building knowledge infrastructures, enhancing innovation and economic reform, and modernising social welfare and education systems.

The Union's strengths and weaknesses

3. The Union is experiencing its best macro-economic outlook for a generation. As a result of stability-oriented monetary policy supported by sound fiscal policies in a context of wage moderation, inflation and interest rates are low, public sector deficits have been reduced remarkably and the EU's balance of payments is healthy. The euro has been successfully introduced and is delivering the expected benefits for the European economy. The internal market is largely complete and is yielding tangible benefits for consumers and businesses alike. The forthcoming enlargement will create new opportunities for growth and employment. The Union possesses a generally well-educated workforce as well as social protection systems able to provide, beyond their intrinsic value, the stable framework required for managing the structural changes involved in moving towards a knowledge-based society. Growth and job creation have resumed.

4. These strengths should not distract our attention from a number of weaknesses. More than 15 million Europeans are still out of work. The employment rate is too low and is characterised by insufficient participation in the labour market by women and older workers. Long-term structural unemployment and marked regional unemployment imbalances remain endemic in

parts of the Union. The services sector is underdeveloped, particularly in the areas of telecommunications and the Internet. There is a widening skills gap, especially in information technology where increasing numbers of jobs remain unfilled. With the current improved economic situation, the time is right to undertake both economic and social reforms as part of a positive strategy which combines competitiveness and social cohesion.

The way forward

5. The Union has today set itself a *new strategic goal* for the next decade: *to become the most competitive and dynamic knowledge-based economy in the world, capable of sustainable economic growth with more and better jobs and greater social cohesion.* Achieving this goal requires an **overall strategy** aimed at:

- preparing the transition to a knowledge-based economy and society by better policies for the information society and R&D, as well as by stepping up the process of structural reform for competitiveness and innovation and by completing the internal market;
- modernising the European social model, investing in people and combating social exclusion;
- sustaining the healthy economic outlook and favourable growth prospects by applying an appropriate macro-economic policy mix.

6. This strategy is designed to enable the Union to regain the conditions for full employment, and to strengthen regional cohesion in the European Union. The European Council needs to set a goal for full employment in Europe in an emerging new society which is more adapted to the personal choices of women and men. If the measures set out below are implemented against a sound macro-economic background, an average economic growth rate of around 3% should be a realistic prospect for the coming years.

7. Implementing this strategy will be achieved by improving the existing processes, introducing a *new open method of coordination* at all levels, coupled with a stronger guiding and coordinating role for the European Council to ensure more coherent strategic direction and effective monitoring of progress. A meeting of the European Council to be held every Spring will define the relevant mandates and ensure that they are followed up.

Text 2: Chapter 4, section 1, of the Romanian 'Strategia Națională Pentru Promovarea Noii Economii și Implementarea Societații Informaționale'

4.1 Obiective globale

Utilizarea largă a tehnologiilor informaționale și de comunicații (TIC) conduce la implicații profunde în viața social-economică, la transformări fundamentale în modul de a realiza produsele și serviciile și în comportamentul uman. Valorificarea superioară a acestor tehnologii poate asigura progresul economic-social ce caracterizează societatea informațională, cu condiția îndeplinirii unor obiective și orientări de natură strategică prin politici adecvate stării societății în care trăim:

1. **Consolidarea democrației și a instituțiilor statului de drept** prin participarea cetățenilor la viața politică și facilitarea accesului nediscriminatoriu la informația publică, îmbunătățirea calității serviciilor publice și modernizarea administrației publice (e-government, e-administration).
2. **Dezvoltarea economiei de piață și trecerea progresivă la noua economie**, creșterea competitivității agenților economici și crearea de noi locuri de muncă în sectoare de înaltă tehnologie prin dezvoltarea comerțului electronic, tele-lucrului, a unor noi metode de management al afacerilor, de management financiar și al resurselor umane, integrarea capabilităților TIC în noi produse și servicii, dezvoltarea sectorului TIC.
3. **Creșterea calității vieții** prin utilizarea noilor tehnologii în domenii precum: protecția socială, asistența medicală, educație, protecția mediului și monitorizarea dezastrelor, siguranța transporturilor etc. și, pe această cale, *integrarea în structurile euro-atlantice* și în Societatea Informațională Globală.
4. **Consolidarea și dezvoltarea unei ramuri a economiei naționale care să asigure realizarea de produse și servicii competitive pe piața internă și externă**, cerute de evoluția lumii contemporane. O ramură a economiei bazată pe produse și servicii care valorifică TIC pe piața internă și, mai ales, la export, ar permite ocuparea resursei umane în activități caracterizate de eficiență maximă, comparativ cu alte ramuri, prin faptul că produsele și serviciile specifice SI conțin o cotă ridicată a valorii adăugate, asociată cu consumuri minime de resurse materiale și de energie. O asemenea opțiune corespunde previziunilor privind evoluția societății umane în secolul 21, fiind susținută de experiența ultimilor zece ani a unor țări de dimensiuni mici, cum sunt Irlanda, Finlanda sau Israelul. (vezi Anexa nr. 3.)

În ultimii ani au intervenit schimbări importante în evoluția societății, cu un impact major asupra modului în care gândim, muncim, interacționăm, petrecem timpul liber și în mod special, asupra modului în care realizăm produsele și serviciile. Schimbările majore care au produs acest impact și care vor marca evoluția societății în perspectiva noului mileniu sunt legate în principal de globalizarea competiției și a pieței și de progresele obținute în domeniul TIC.

În acest context ce definește Societatea Informațională, asistăm la impunerea cunoașterii ca un factor critic, determinant, al creșterii economice și al standardului de viață. De la o diviziune a lumii în raport cu accesul la cunoaștere și la utilizarea noilor tehnologii din domeniu (*'global digital divide'*) se poate ajunge prin strategii adecvate, elaborate la nivel național și global, la noi oportunități oferite dezvoltării societății la nivel planetar ('global digital opportunity', The Okinawa Summit of the G7/G8', iulie 2000).

Globalizarea și noile TIC impun realizarea produselor și serviciilor la nivelul standardelor existente pe piața externă/globală, în special pe piața internă a UE, în care aceste standarde sunt la nivelul cel mai ridicat.

Realizarea produselor și serviciilor inovative la acest nivel nu se poate asigura decât prin menținerea și dezvoltarea unei capacități de cercetare-dezvoltare-inovare susținută și de un transfer tehnologic activ către producătorii de bunuri și servicii. Conștientizarea acestei stări impune elaborarea unei strategii a dezvoltării economiei naționale și a unor sectoare viabile ale acesteia care să facă față competiției pe piața internă și externă, mai ales a UE.

Având exemplul țărilor amintite mai sus și prezentate în anexe (Irlanda, Israel, Finlanda), România trebuie să facă o opțiune fundamentală pentru dezvoltarea unei ramuri a economiei care să realizeze produse și servicii cerute de societatea informațională, bazată pe tehnologiile informației și comunicațiilor.

Text 3: English translation of Text 2

Overall objectives

The widespread use of ICT produces profound implications for socio-economic life, and fundamental transformations in the way of producing goods and services and in human behaviour. Capitalising more on these technologies can ensure the socio-economic progress characteristic of information societies as long as objectives and orientations of a strategic nature are adopted through policies appropriate to the actual societies in which we live:

1. **Consolidation of democracy and the institutions of the state** through the participation of citizens in political life and the facilitation of

non-discriminatory access to public information, the improvement of the quality of public services and the modernisation of public administration (e-government, e-administration).

2. **Development of a market economy and progressive movement towards the new economy**, growth in the competitiveness of economic agents and the creation of new jobs in the high-technology sector through developing electronic commerce, tele-work, and new methods of business management, financial management and management of human resources, incorporation of ICT capacities in new goods and services and development of the ICT sector.

3. **Improving the quality of life by** using new technologies in areas such as: social welfare, health, education, protection of the environment and monitoring of disasters, transport security etc., and thereby integration **into Euro-Atlantic structures** and the Global Information Society.

4. **Consolidation and development of a national economic framework which ensures the production of goods and services which are competitive on internal and external markets**, as the evolution of the modern world demands. A branch of the economy based on goods and services which capitalise on ICT for the internal market and especially for export would permit a maximally efficient use of human resources, compared with other branches, because specifically information society goods and services contain expanded added value associated with minimal use of material resources and energy. Such an option corresponds to forecasts about the development of human society in the twenty-first century, and is confirmed by the experience of several small countries over the last ten years, such as Ireland, Finland and Israel (see Annex nr 3).

Important changes in the development of society have taken place in recent years, which have had a major impact on the way we think, work, interact, spend our free time and, especially, on the way we produce goods and services. The major changes which have produced these effects and which will shape the development of society in the new millennium are linked especially to the globalisation of competition and the market and progress in the field of ICT.

In this context of the Information Society we are witnessing the implementation of knowledge as a critical, determining, factor in economic growth and the standard of living. From the division of the world on the basis of access to knowledge and use of new technologies in the field ('global digital divide'), we can, with appropriate strategies developed at national and global levels, move towards new opportunities for social development at a planetary level ('global digital opportunity,' The Okinawa Summit of the G7/G8, July 2000).

Globalisation and new ICT mean producing goods and services to the standard of external/global markets, especially the internal market of the EU, where standards are the highest.

The production of innovative goods and services at this level can only be achieved through maintaining and developing a capacity for sustained research-development-innovation and for active technology transfer between producers of goods and services. Making people aware of this entails developing a strategy for development of the national economy and for viable sectors within it, which can compete on internal and external markets, especially the EU.

Given the example of the countries referred to above and presented in the appendix (Ireland, Israel, Finland), Romania should make a fundamental choice to develop a branch of the economy which produces the goods and services demanded by the information society, based on ICT.

Notes

1. Godin (2004) lists some 75 terms for societal transformation between 1950 and 1984 alone, including 'post-industrial society', 'neocapitalism', and 'management society'.

2. The stance of key states (notably the US, European states, Japan) and international institutions and agencies (the World Bank, the IMF etc.) towards strategies and discourses is one important factor in the outcome of struggles for hegemony. Godin (2004) traces the displacement of 'national systems of innovation' (NSIs) by 'knowledge-based economy' as the favoured strategy of the OECD in the 1990s.

3. In Fairclough 2003, I suggest analysis of the texturing of relations of 'equivalence' and 'difference' as the operationalisation in textual analysis of the view of the political (which one can extend more generally to social action) in Laclau and Mouffe (1985) as constituted through the simultaneous operation of the 'logics' of 'equivalence' and 'difference'. I see this as a case of textual analysis being enriched through transdisciplinary dialogue.

4. The discourse of 'social exclusion', which is widely used in the EU, is not widely used in Romania. The discourse of 'poverty', which was, for instance, displaced by the discourse of 'social exclusion' in the UK in the language of New Labour (Fairclough 2000b), is, by contrast, widely used, though it appears only once in this document – the issue of poverty is not otherwise referred to.

5. I use the term 'state of right' as equivalent to the German term 'Rechtsstaat'.

Section G

Language and education

Introduction

The two papers in this final section of the book represent an educational application of CDA developed with Lancaster colleagues specialising in various aspects of educational linguistics, especially Romy Clark, Roz Ivanič and Marilyn Martin-Jones. A joint paper was presented at the 1987 annual meeting of the British Association for Applied Linguistics, and subsequently published as Clark, Fairclough *et al.* (1990, 1991), and later developments were brought together in a collection of papers (Fairclough 1992b). This work was a response to the enthusiasm during the 1980s for 'language awareness' in schools (Hawkins 1984, NCLE 1985). Our concern was that language awareness programmes should be informed by critical views of language and discourse, as well as a conception of language learning which integrated the development of language awareness with the learner's own prior experience and with the development of capacities for practice, including creative and innovative forms of practice.

'Critical language awareness and self-identity in education' locates education within the general social problematic of language and power in contemporary society. Not only is education itself a key domain of linguistically mediated power, it also mediates other key domains for learners, including the adult world of work. But it is additionally at its best a site of reflection upon and analysis of the sociolinguistic order and the order of discourse, and in so far as educational institutions equip learners with a critical language awareness, they equip them with a resource for intervention in and reshaping of discursive practices and the power relations that ground them, both in other domains and within education itself. The paper contrasts the assumptions and objectives of critical and non-critical approaches to language awareness. It then turns to a particular application of critical language awareness work in the reflexive analysis of relations of power which are implicit in the conventions and practices of academic discourse, and in struggles on the part of learners to contest and transform such practices. I use this example for some reflections on the difficulties facing those dealing with issues of language and power in the complex sociocultural circumstances of contemporary societies, and argue that critical language awareness must not go beyond providing a resource for people to use in making their own decisions – it must scrupulously avoid setting out blueprints for emancipatory practice.

Paper 22 ('Global capitalism and critical awareness of language') was published in 1999, a decade after the early papers on critical language awareness. They were based upon the conviction that because of changes affecting the role of language in social life, a critical awareness of language was 'a prerequisite for effective democratic citizenship, and should therefore be seen as an entitlement for citizens, especially children developing towards citizenship in the educational system' (Fairclough 1992b: 2–3). We argued that CLA should be a basic concern in language education. Has the case for this weakened or strengthened in the intervening years? I argue in this paper that as the shape of the new global social order has become clearer, so too has the need for a critical awareness of language as part of people's resources for living in new ways in new circumstances. Our educational practices have some way to go before they begin to match up to our educational needs. At the same time, it has also become clearer that what is at issue is a critical awareness of discourse which includes other forms of semiosis as well as language: visual images in particular are an increasingly important feature of contemporary discourse (Kress and van Leeuwen 1996).

I discuss several key features of recent society which help make the case for critical awareness of discourse: the relationship between discourse, knowledge and social change in the 'information' or 'knowledge-based' society; what Smith (1990) has called the 'textually-mediated' nature of contemporary social life; the relationship between discourse and social difference; the commodification of discourse; discourse and democracy. I then draw these together by tying the case for CLA to the nature of the new global capitalism.

21. Critical language awareness and self-identity in education[1]

The issue of language and power in education is just a part of the more general social problematic of language and power, and ought not in my view to be isolated from it. At least in developed capitalist countries, we live in an age in which power is predominantly exercised through the generation of consent rather than through coercion, through ideology rather than through physical force, through the inculcation of self-disciplining practices rather than through the breaking of skulls. (Though there is still unfortunately no shortage of the latter, and indeed there has been a reversion to it on the grand scale in certain parts of the world (e.g., the former socialist countries) in the past few years.) It is an age in which the production and reproduction of the social order depend increasingly upon practices and processes of a broadly cultural nature. Part of this development is an enhanced role for language in the exercise of power: it is mainly in discourse that consent is achieved, ideologies are transmitted, and practices, meanings, values and identities are taught and learnt. This is clear from the generally acknowledged role of the mass media as probably the single most important social institution in bringing off these processes in contemporary societies. And it is recognised in the salience given to language and discourse (the 'linguistic turn') in the work of theorists of modern and contemporary society including Heidegger, Foucault, Derrida, Bourdieu and Habermas.

We also live in an age of great change and instability in which the forms of power and domination are being radically reshaped, in which changing cultural practices are a major constituent of social change, which in many cases means to a significant degree changing discursive practices, changing practices of language use. I have discussed, for example, how the marketisation of discursive practices is constitutive of more general processes of institutional marketisation, and discursive facets of sociocultural processes of detradition-alisation and informalisation (Paper 4) and the technologisation of discourse as a peculiarly contemporary form of intervention in discursive practices to shape sociocultural change (Paper 5).

Educational institutions are heavily involved in these general developments affecting language in its relation to power. First, educational practices themselves constitute a core domain of linguistic and discursive power and of the engineering of discursive practices. Much training in education is orientated to a significant degree towards the use and inculcation of particular discursive practices in educational organisations, more or less explicitly interpreted as an important facet of the inculcation of particular cultural meanings and values, social relationships and identities, and pedagogies. Second, many other domains are mediated and transmitted by educational institutions. For example, one general consequence of processes of societal post-traditionalisation and informalisation for various domains of work (in the context of the emergence of the supposedly dehierarchised, 'flat', organisation) is a great increase in expectations of and demands upon the dialogical capacities of workers, which educational institutions are widely expected to meet through a new emphasis on spoken language 'skills'. Third, educational institutions are to a greater or lesser extent involved in educating people about the sociolinguistic order they live in. In some cases they are aiming to equip them with what has in my view become, because of the enhanced social and cultural role of language and because of the technologisation of discourse, an essential prerequisite for effective democratic citizenship, the capacity for critique of language. No doubt the critique of language is in the best cases already carried out reflexively, i.e., is directed at the practices of the educational institution itself (and even at the practices of the critical classroom) and towards issues of language and power in education.

Anticipated changes in the linguistic and discoursal needs of work are a major factor in shaping language education in schools. The established shift towards the service sector at the expense of manufacturing is one element, entailing a focus on interaction with publics, customers or clients. Another is the shift from a Fordist, Taylorist mode or organisation within manufacturing to a post-Fordist organisation, alluded to above. There is an emphasis on the future worker as 'multiskilled', on work as exploiting talents it has not hitherto exploited, including a range of what have hitherto been seen as 'life skills' rather than occupational skills, including conversational forms of talk. Hence in part the new official interest in spoken language education. Barnes (1988) has pointed to the often uncomfortable coexistence of Old Right and New Right priorities in official educational policy: on the one hand maintenance of traditional language practices and values around standard English with 'back to basics' appeals on spelling and grammar; on the other hand the new emphasis on oracy and spoken language education. The Kingman and Cox reports on the teaching of English in schools (DES 1988, DES 1989) contain elements of both (Fairclough 1990b).

I believe that the problematic of language and power is fundamentally a question of democracy. Those affected need to take it on board as a political issue, as feminists have around the issue of language and gender. If problems of language and power are to be seriously tackled, they will be tackled by the people who are directly involved, especially the people who are subject to linguistic forms of domination and manipulation. This is as true in educational organisations as it is elsewhere. Struggle and resistance are in any case a constant reflex of domination and manipulation: the will to impose discursive practices or engineer shifts in discursive practices from above is one thing, but in actuality the conditions in which such a will to power must take its chance may include a diversity of practices, a resistance to change, and even contrary wills to transform practices in different directions. Of course, struggle against domination has varying degrees of success, and one factor in success is the theoretical and analytical resources an opposition has access to. Critical linguists and discourse analysts have an important auxiliary role to play here in providing analyses and, importantly, in providing critical educators with resources for programmes of what I and my colleagues have called 'critical language awareness' (Clark, Fairclough et al. 1990, 1991, Fairclough 1992a) – programmes to develop the capacities of people for language critique, including their capacities for reflexive analysis of the educational process itself.

I have described in other papers an approach to the general societal problematic of language and power, and I want to indicate here its particular applicability to the forms which that problematic takes within educational organisations. The first element in this approach is the development of a critical tradition within language studies and discourse analysis, which has been extensively discussed elsewhere in this book. The second element, which is described in the next section, is the application of this critical theory and method in the development of critical language awareness work within schools and other educational organisations. In the final part of the paper I shall discuss an example, based upon analyses carried out by colleagues at Lancaster University, of how critical language awareness work can lead to reflexive analysis of practices of domination implicit in the transmission and learning of academic discourse, and the engagement of learners in the struggle to contest and change such practices. I shall finally use this example for some reflections on the difficulties facing those dealing with issues of language and power, in education and elsewhere, in the complex and often confusing socio-cultural circumstances of contemporary societies; and the opportunities and dangers faced by CDA as its focus shifts from critique of existing practices to exploration and even advocacy of possible alternatives.

1 Language awareness: critical and non-critical approaches

In recent years, language awareness, knowledge about language, has been widely advocated as an important part of language education in Britain, by those associated with the 'language awareness' movement (Hawkins 1984, NCLE 1985), independently and in some cases earlier (Doughty *et al.* 1971), and in reports on the teaching of English in schools within the national curriculum (DES 1988, DES 1989). While welcoming this development, I think language awareness work has been insufficiently critical: it has not given sufficient focus to language-related issues of power which ought to be highlighted in language education, given the nature of the contemporary socio-linguistic order. What is needed is an approach based upon a critical view of language and language study such as the one described in this book. In this section I shall contrast such a critical language awareness (henceforth CLA) with the non-critical conception just referred to (henceforth LA – I shall refer mainly to Hawkins (1984)), in terms of: rationale for language awareness work; conceptions of language awareness work; the relationship envisaged between language awareness and other elements of language education.

A rationale for critical language awareness work emerges from the general contemporary problematic of language and power described at the beginning of the paper: given that power relations work increasingly at an implicit level through language, and given that language practices are increasingly targets for intervention and control, a critical awareness of language is a prerequisite for effective citizenship, and a democratic entitlement. There is some similar-ity between this rationale for CLA and part of the rationale for LA, in that the latter attempts like the former to use language education as a resource for tack-ling social problems which centre around language. But the arguments are cast in very different terms. In Hawkins (1984), this dimension of the rationale for LA refers to social aspects of educational failure (which I discuss below), a lack of understanding of language which impedes parents in supporting the language development of their children, and an endemic 'linguistic parochialism and prejudice' affecting minority languages and non-standard varieties. These are indeed problems which language awareness can help to address, but from a CLA perspective they are just particular points of salience within the much broader contemporary problematisation of language I have indicated. A fundamental difference between LA and CLA is their assumptions about what language awareness can do for such problems. Within LA, schools seem to be credited with a substantial capacity for contributing to social harmony and integration, and smoothing the workings of the social and sociolinguistic orders. Language awareness work is portrayed as making up for and helping to overcome social problems (e.g., making up for a lack of 'verbal learning tools' in the home, extending access to standard English to children whose homes do not give it to them). In the case of CLA, the argument is that schools dedicated to a critical pedagogy (Giroux 1983, Freire 1985) ought to provide learners with understanding of problems which cannot be resolved just in the schools, and with the resources for engaging, if they so wish in the long-term, multifaceted struggles in various social domains (including education) which are necessary to resolve them. I shall suggest below, in discussing the treatment of standard English, that the LA position can in fact have unforeseen detrimental social consequences.

There are a number of other elements in the rationale for LA. I referred above to social aspects of educational failure, and Hawkins refers in this connection to evidence that schools have had the effect of 'widening the gap' between children who get 'verbal learning tools' at home and those who don't (1984: 1). Language awareness work can help all children 'sharpen the tools of verbal learning' (1984: 98). LA is particularly sensitive to the need to improve study skills in the 'difficult transition from primary to secondary school language work, especially the start of foreign language studies and the explosion of concepts and language introduced by the specialist secondary school subjects' (Hawkins 1984: 4). The poor record of British schools in foreign language learning is part of the rationale; there is an emphasis upon developing 'insight into pattern' and 'learning to listen' as conditions for success in foreign language learning. A related educational problem which LA seeks to address is the absence of a coherent approach to language from the child's perspective, including a lack of coordination between different parts of the language curriculum. There is also (NCLE 1985: 23) reference to the particular linguistic demands arising from rapid social change, where 'many more events require interpretation', especially interpretation of linguistic signals.

Although CLA highlights critical awareness of non-transparent aspects of the social functioning of language, that does not imply a lack of concern with issues such as linguistic dimensions of educational failure or inadequacies in foreign language learning. Nor, turning to a comparison of conceptions of language awareness work, does it imply a lack of concern with formal aspects of language, which take up a large proportion of LA materials. I would see the position of CLA rather as claiming that these important issues and dimensions of language awareness ought to be framed within a critical view of language; for example, we must develop the capacity for sensitive attention to formal linguistic features of texts, and the capacity to frame such textual analysis within a critical discourse analysis. Having made these points, I shall focus my comparison of conceptions of language awareness work upon views of linguistic variation, and especially the treatment of standard English.

LA, like the Kingman and Cox Report (DES 1988, DES 1989), takes the position that it is vital for schools to teach pupils standard English, while treating the diversity of languages in the classroom as 'a potential resource of great richness', and recognising that all languages and varieties of languages 'have their rightful and proper place' in children's repertoires and 'each serves good purposes' (Hawkins 1984: 171–5). Standard English and other varieties and languages are presented as differing in conditions of appropriateness. Vigorous arguments are advanced for the 'entitlement' of children to education in standard English, especially standard written English, as part of the 'apprenticeship in autonomy' which schools should provide (Hawkins 1984: 65). Stigmatisation of particular varieties or accents is attributed to parochialism or prejudice.

There is no doubt whatsoever that learning standard English does give some learners life chances they would not otherwise have. On the other hand, this view of standard English and language variation misses important issues and can I think have detrimental effects. Firstly there is an assumption that schools can help iron out the effects of social class and equalise the 'cultural capital' (Bourdieu 1984) of access to prestigious varieties of English. I think this assumption needs cautious handling, because it is easy to exaggerate the capacity of schools for social engineering; the class system is reproduced in many domains, not just education. Secondly, there is no sense in LA work that in passing on prestigious practices and values such as those of standard English *without* developing a critical awareness of them, one is implicitly legitimising them *and* the asymmetrical distribution of cultural capital I have just referred to. Thirdly, portraying standard English and other languages and varieties as differing in conditions of appropriateness is dressing up inequality as diversity: standard English is 'appropriate' in situations which carry social clout, while other varieties are 'appropriate' at the margins. Fourthly, attributing the stigmatisation of varieties to individual prejudice papers over the systematic, socially legitimised stigmatisation of varieties. Elevating the standard means demoting other varieties. Again, there is likely to be a mismatch between the liberalism and pluralism of the schools, and the children's experience. It is these mismatches, based upon well-meaning white lies about language variation, that carry the risk of detrimental effects; either they will create delusions, or they will create cynicism and a loss of credibility, or most probably a sequence of the former followed by the latter. I think a CLA position on the treatment of standard English is that one should teach written standard English for pragmatic reasons, but one should also expose learners to views about standard English, including the critical views I have alluded to here. And one should raise with the learners the question of whether and why and how dominant rules of 'appropriateness' might be flouted and challenged (see further below).

At the root of the different conceptions of language awareness work are different conceptions of language, and of sociolinguistic variation. LA is based in a tradition which sees a sociolinguistic order as a given and common-sense reality, effectively a natural domain rather than a naturalised domain, which is 'there' to be described. The question of *why* it is there scarcely arises, and there is certainly not the focus upon sociolinguistic orders being shaped and transformed by relations of power and power struggle, which characterises the critical approach to language study.

Let me come finally to the relationship envisaged between language awareness and other elements of language education. There is agreement between LA and CLA that, as Hawkins puts it (1984: 73–4), 'awareness' affects 'competence' – or as I would prefer to put it, awareness affects language capabilities. LA does not, however, set out to build into language education explicit connections between developing awareness and developing capabilities: language awareness work is isolated from other parts of language education as a separate element in the curriculum. By contrast, a central theme in a critical approach is that language awareness should be fully integrated with the development of practice and capabilities.

The diagram below (from Clark *et al.* 1991) gives one representation of this integration. This model incorporates the important principle that critical

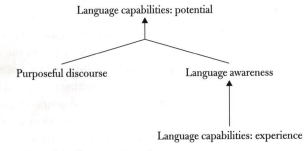

Figure 21.1 A model of language learning

language awareness should be built from the existing language capabilities and experience of the learner. The experience of the learner can, with the help of the teacher, be made explicit and systematic as a body of knowledge which can be used for discussion and reflection, so that social causes for experiences (e.g., of constraint) can be explored. At the same time, links should constantly be made between work on the development of language awareness and the language practice of the learner. This practice must be 'purposeful': that is, it must be tied in to the learner's real wishes and needs to communicate with specific real people, because this is the only way for the learner to experience authentically the risks and potential benefits of particular decisions. When critical awareness is linked to such decisions, it broadens their scope to include decisions about whether to flout sociolinguistic conventions or to follow them, whether to conform or not conform (in the use of standard English, for instance, as mentioned above). It also allows such decisions to be seen as in certain circumstances collective rather than individual ones, associated with the political strategies of groups.

2 Critical language awareness in practice: identity in academic writing

Critical language study and critical language awareness work can, as I indicated earlier, be reflexively applied within educational organisations to the practices of such organisations. They constitute a resource for investigating, and intervening in, issues of language and power in education. I have been suggesting that there is an intimate relationship between the development of people's critical awareness of language and the development of their own language capabilities and practices. Accordingly, such reflexive work could involve learners and teachers in analysis of and possibly change in their own practices, as speakers and listeners (and viewers), writers and readers. In this section I want briefly to describe one sort of reflexive application of CLA in work by colleagues at Lancaster (Clark 1992, Ivanic and Simpson 1992), and to use this example for some closing reflections on the difficulty of tackling issues of language and power in complex and often opaque contemporary societies.

The focus of this research is on what I earlier referred to as the identity function of discourse, and specifically the sort of self-identities that are constituted by/for writers in the process of academic writing. Traditional forms of academic discourse, especially in science and social science, demand an impersonal style, and part of the 'apprenticeship' of a student in an academic discipline is the effacing of prior identities in academic writing in order to join the new 'discourse community' (Clark 1992). This can be an uncomfortable and alienating process, perhaps especially for older students with extensive experience or established professional backgrounds. The pressure on students to conform is illustrated in an example given by Clark. An academic made the following comment on an essay written by one of Clark's students: 'Your arguments are undermined by the use of the personal pronoun (meaning the first person pronoun *I*). [Name of student] is not an established authority . . . or not yet, anyway. Avoid the use of personal pronouns and expressions like "in my view" in all academic work'.

Both the Clark paper and the Ivanic and Simpson paper describe experiences of working with a CLA framework with students who are resistant to the constraints of conventional academic writing. In both cases, there are attempts to develop styles of writing which allow students to project self-identities which they feel more comfortable with. Clark's paper reports her work on a study skills course for postgraduates taking Diploma or MA degrees in a department of politics (see also Clark, Constantinou *et al.* 1990). The focus of the course is the written assignments which students have to produce for their politics courses (their practice on the course is thus 'purposeful' in the sense of the last section). The course begins with an exercise designed to raise students' consciousness about the writing process (more fully described in Clark and Ivanič 1992), and the ongoing discussion of the writing process then informs and is fed by collaborative writing workshops and tutorials in which students work on assignments set for their politics courses. Discussion of the writing process leads to work on the development of critical awareness of linguistic resources and conventions, which in turn feeds back into the students' writing. The class used a past student essay to focus a debate on issues of objectivity and impersonalness in academic writing, and these issues are then dealt with in more concrete terms by looking at specific decisions academic writers need to take – whether to use the first person singular pronoun or not, whether to use modality and tense forms which express strong commitment to propositions, or modal forms and hedges which tone down commitment, and so forth. The objective of the study skills course is to 'empower' students by giving them a critical awareness of academic conventions, their social origins and effects. The course provides students with the means for 'emancipation' through the flouting of conventions and the development of non-conventional forms of academic writing, though it is up to students themselves whether they do so (not all do). A major theme of the paper is that students are faced with the dilemma, which they must resolve for themselves, of whether to conform or not conform, whether to lean in the direction of fulfilling obligations or of claiming rights. (On emancipation as a concept in CLA, see also Janks and Ivanič (1992).)

The Ivanič and Simpson paper reports on co-research between an academic (Ivanič) and a mature student (Simpson) who had recently entered higher education, into the latter's development as an academic writer (see also Ivanic and Roach 1990). This paper also focuses upon problems of identity: given the overwhelming prestige of 'impersonal', 'objective' academic style, how can a student – this student – project his own identity in his writing, 'find the "I"', show himself as the sort of person he wants to be? 'Finding the "I"' is a matter of responsibility to oneself and to one's readership: it is a way towards truthfulness and clarity. The authors suggest that writers may be better able to tackle their dilemmas over identity if they become conscious of the 'casts' or 'populations' of identities in the texts they read as well as in their own writing (Talbot 1990). This is a matter of raising their critical awareness of the standard conventions of academic writing, and their effects upon identities. The paper includes an analysis in these terms of three assignments written by Simpson. The 'population' consists of tutors who set the assignments, the people who wrote what he read, the writer himself, the people he writes about, and the people who read what he writes. What emerges is a tense relationship between the pressures upon him to conform to the norms of traditional academic style and his own often cautious and nervous attempts to project his own identity and evolve his own academic style. One noteworthy feature of the paper is that as well as writing about Simpson's attempts to tackle the problem of identity, the authors are explicitly trying to tackle it together in the way in which they write the paper.

The two papers provide useful practical techniques for using CLA in educational organisations to work on one problematic aspect of the interface of language and power in such organisations: the constraints which organisations, and powerholders within them, place upon the discursively constituted self-identities of learners. Evidently, there is a microscopic emphasis in both papers, upon how individual students cope with the tension between a will to resist the impositions of conventional academic writing and requirements to conform, and how critical language awareness programmes can help clarify (if not resolve) such dilemmas. The outcomes of this tension in students' work can be described using the framework for critical discourse analysis discussed elsewhere in this book. One feature of the student work discussed in the two papers is that its 'discourse practice' tends to be complex, involving the mixing of genres and discourses (traditional academic ones and, often, ones drawn from the private domain), and this is realised linguistically in texts which tend to be heterogeneous in style, meanings and forms. I want, however, to explore a little how this microscopic focus relates to a more macroscopic view of the state of hegemonic relations and hegemonic struggle in the orders of discourse of educational organisations, in order to raise some issues which have a more general relevance to the problematisation of language and power in education.

In my view, a microscopic focus upon individual calculations of risk and benefit should always be complemented with and contextualised within a macroscopic view. Student resistance to academic conventions is widespread in contemporary higher education, but the situation is not unified academic institutions stolidly defending traditional practices against reluctant students. Traditional practices have already been extensively undermined from within. For instance, as Ivanic and Simpson point out, academic writing is 'becoming less segregated from informal speech'. There has already been a hegemonic shift which constitutes a favourable environment for the sort of reflexive CLA work that Clark, Ivanic and Simpson are engaged in: practices of academic writing which achieve a hybridisation of traditional academic styles and colloquial, informal, spoken styles are now well positioned within the order of discourse. Personalised writing, space to project identities which academic writers feel comfortable with, are part of this evolution. This shift is often construed in terms of a suspect contrast between one's 'real self' and the artificial identities taken on in academic writing. What is I think actually at issue is pressure for specialised academic identities to give way to private domain or 'lifeworld' identities. It would be a mistake to overstate the hegemonic shift or underestimate the continuing power of traditional forms within certain types of institution and particular disciplines. Nevertheless, the shift is clear.

But this shift in educational discursive practices and orders of discourse needs to be explained, i.e., it needs to be situated within wider sociocultural changes which it is a part of. I would like at this point to strike a cautionary note: it is often difficult to assess the full social and cultural import of a change in discursive practices, and therefore its effect upon power relations and power struggle in the institution concerned. This underlines for me the importance of avoiding directive, top-down interventions designed (perhaps by well-intentioned theorists like myself) to shift practices in a particular emancipatory direction: such decisions must be left to the people directly involved, 'on the ground', who are generally better able to weigh up the complex odds and interpret the sometimes ambivalent, complex, and contradictory values, risks and benefits.

Consider for instance the case in point, in the light of my comments in Paper 6 on the ambivalence of the 'conversationalisation' of public discourse. The impetus in educational organisations to break down barriers between academic discourse and the more informal and personal practices of the private sphere is not isolated: it is part of a general rejection in contemporary societies of elite, professional, bureaucratic, etc., practices, and a valorisation of ordinariness, naturalness, 'being oneself' and so forth, in discourse and more generally. It is part of the conversationalisation of public discourse, and it ties in with the informalisation of contemporary society and its post-traditional properties. Seen in these terms, it can be interpreted positively as a democratising development.

But the push for democracy is not the only source of attacks on tradition, and not the only impetus for the breaking down of barriers. Education like other institutions has been and is being marketised, incorporated into the consumer society and culture. This entails a standardisation of practices across institutions on the model of the market. One obvious and indeed notorious surface example of this standardisation is the generalisation of the persona and vocabulary of the 'consumer' (or 'customer') across institutions, including the reconstruction of students as consumers. The difficulty is that it is not always easy to distinguish between attacks upon and attempts to reconstruct traditional academic practices which are democratically rooted and those which are rooted in marketisation. How for instance might one decide whether a student who is resisting the impersonalness of academic writing is operating from a democratic rejection of elitism, or as someone who wishes to assert his or her authority as consumer? (On the 'authority of the consumer', see Keat, Whiteley and Abercrombie (1994) and Fairclough (1994).) One way of reading the difficulty in this case is in terms of appropriation: one could see the impetus towards marketisation of education as having appropriated some of the themes and values, and discursive practices, of the historically earlier impetus towards anti-elitism – the 1960s being appropriated by the 1980s, so to speak.

The point is not in any way to retreat from reflexive critical language awareness work, still less to defend traditional practices. It is to highlight the difficulty in contemporary society in being entirely confident about the target, in the sense of what needs changing, and what it needs changing to. People on the ground must make up their minds about these complex issues, as they will whether critical language work is in progress or not. We need CLA work of a sensitive, non-dogmatic and non-directive sort. We also need, in support of it, critical discourse analysis research into the complex and ambivalent interdependencies between discursive practices and sociocultural systems and transformations in education.

This example raises a more general issue. There have recently been proposals that CDA should partly shift its emphasis from critique of existing discursive practices to exploration of alternatives.[2] This is broadly welcome:

the founding motivation for critical analysis is emancipation and the building of emancipated forms of social life, not critique *per se*. Such work must, however, proceed with caution. Critical analysis can be 'turned' and appropriated by dominant social forces, and critical interventions to build new practices can look uncomfortably similar to what I have called technologisation of discourse. A more productive orientation on the part of CDA must, I believe, be framed within a profound commitment to democracy. CDA can contribute to the social imaginary, to the stock of feasible Utopias which can inform choices which people make individually and collectively, but the choices must be made by the people concerned and affected on their own behalf.

Notes

1. The first and third sections of this paper appeared in a modified form as part of a paper with the same title in a book edited by D. Corson, *Language and Power in Education*. The second section ('Language awareness: critical and non-critical approaches') draws upon collective work with colleagues in Lancaster, reflected in Clark, Fairclough, Ivanič and Martin-Jones (1991).
2. Voiced for instance by Gunther Kress at a conference on Discourse and Ideology in Vienna, December 1993.

22. Global capitalism and critical awareness of language

[handwritten marginalia: "textually" mediated' nature of contemporary society' "social life"]

As the shape of the new global social order becomes clearer, so too does the need for a critical awareness of language as part of language education. I discuss, with a focus on discourse, several key features of late modern society which help make the case for critical awareness of discourse: the relationship between discourse, knowledge and social change in our 'information' or 'knowledge-based' society; what Smith (1990) has called the 'textually-mediated' nature of contemporary social life; the relationship between discourse and social difference; the commodification of discourse; discourse and democracy. I then draw these together by tying the case for CLA to the nature of the new global capitalism, and conclude the paper with discussions of how CLA is anchored in 'critical discourse analysis' (and, through that, in critical social science generally), and of how the question of CLA is framed within the wider question of the nature and purposes of education.

It is over 10 years since an initial paper on critical language awareness (CLA) was given at the British Association for Applied Linguistics annual conference (later published in Clark *et al.* 1990, 1991, see also Ivanič 1990, Fairclough 1992b). The work on CLA was based upon the conviction that because of contemporary changes affecting the role of language in social life, a critical awareness of language is 'a prerequisite for effective democratic citizenship, and should therefore be seen as an entitlement for citizens, especially children developing towards citizenship in the educational system' (Fairclough 1992b: 2–3). We argued that CLA should be a basic concern in language education. Has the case for this weakened or strengthened in the intervening years? I want to argue that as the shape of the new global social order becomes clearer, so too does the need for a critical awareness of language as part of people's resources for living in new ways in new circumstances. Our educational practices have some way to go before they begin to match up to our educational needs. At the same time, although I continue using the expression 'critical language awareness' because it is relatively well known, it has also become clearer that what is at issue is a critical awareness of discourse which includes other forms of semiosis as well as language: visual images in particular are an increasingly important feature of contemporary discourse (Kress and van Leeuwen 1996).

1   An example: the discourse of 'flexibility'

I shall begin with an example which points to a number of features of social life in contemporary ('late modern') society which demand a critical awareness of discourse. Most accounts of change in contemporary social life give a more or less central place to change in the economic system: the change from 'Fordism' to 'flexible accumulation', as Harvey (1990) puts it. Fordism is the 'mass production' form of capitalism (named after the car magnate Henry Ford) which dominated the earlier part of this century. Flexible accumulation is a more complex concept but it basically means greater flexibility at various levels – in production (the production process can be quickly shifted to produce small batches of different products), in the workforce (part-time and short-term working, extensive reskilling of workers), in the circulation of finance, and so forth. Harvey points out that some academic analysts see 'flexibility' as no more than a new discourse which is ideologically motivated – if working people can be persuaded that 'flexibility' is an unavoidable feature of contemporary economies, they are more likely to be 'flexible' about their jobs disappearing, the need to retrain, deteriorating pay and conditions of work, and so forth. Harvey disagrees. Flexibility is a real feature of contemporary economies for which there is ample scientific evidence – though that does not mean that 'flexible accumulation' has totally displaced 'Fordism'; the reality is rather a mix of old and new regimes. Nor does it mean that the discourse of flexibility is irrelevant to the reality of flexible accumulation. Far from it: *the discourse is an irreducible part of the reality*. The change from Fordism to flexible accumulation is inconceivable without the change in economic discourse. Why? Because the emerging global economy is the site of a struggle between the old and the new, and the discourse of flexibility is a vital symbolic weapon in that struggle. It is as Bourdieu (1998a) has put it a 'strong discourse', that is a discourse which is backed by the strength of all the economic and social forces (the banks, the multinational companies, politicians, and so on) who are trying to make flexibility – the new global capitalism – even more of a reality than it already is. Neo-liberal discourse contributes its own particular, symbolic, form of strength to the strength of these social forces.

Let me briefly clarify my example. My focus is on the metaphor of 'flexibility' which is at the centre of the economic discourse of 'flexible accumulation' for which Harvey (1990: 47–97) gives an analytical account – including, for example, its construction of the labour market in terms of 'core' and 'periphery' employees. Elements of this discourse, and especially the metaphor of flexibility itself, are widely distributed within many types of non-economic discourse (examples shortly). The discourse of flexible accumulation enters complex and shifting configurations with other discourses within a field I am calling 'neo-liberal discourse' – for instance, with a management discourse which centres on the 'mission statement' which Swales and Rogers (1995) have described. This is a complex and unstable area which needs detailed research.

One accessible place to find the discourse of flexibility used within this struggle over global economy is in the books written by management 'gurus' which seem to dominate airport and railway station bookshops (for example, Peters 1994). But it is a discourse that turns up in many other contexts. One of them is politics – New Labour's 'Third Way', for instance, can be summed up as follows: economic flexibility (on the model of the World Bank and the IMF) is inevitable, but government must strive to include those it socially excludes. Here is Blair in his first major speech after becoming Prime Minister:

> We must never forget that a strong, competitive, flexible economy is the prerequisite for creating jobs and opportunities. But equally we must never forget that it is not enough. The economy can grow while leaving behind a workless class whose members become so detached that they are no longer full citizens. (Blair 1997)

But the discourse of flexibility also penetrates into everyday language. Here for instance is an extract from an ethnographic interview with 'Stephen' from Cleveland in north-east England who does 'fiddly jobs', i.e., works illegally in the black economy while claiming social benefits. He is talking about the work he does:

> It's a matter of us being cheaper. It's definitely easier than having a lot of lads taken on permanently. It would cost them more to put them on the books or pay them off. It's just the flexibility. You're just there for when the jobs come up, and he [the 'hirer and firer'] will come and get you when you're needed. You need to be on the dole to be able to do that. Otherwise you'd be sitting

there for half the year with no work and no money at all. (Quoted in MacDonald 1994: 515)

We might pessimistically think of everyday language as colonised by this discourse of the powerful, and that is no doubt partly true, but here is 'Stephen' appropriating the discourse in constructing his own perfectly coherent rationale for his (illegal) way of living. One aspect of economic flexibility from his perspective is that companies need the flexibility of workers doing fiddly jobs.

Like other prominent discourses, the discourse of flexibility draws some comment and critique – a critical awareness of language is not wholly something which has to be brought to people from outside, it arises within the normal ways people reflect on their lives as part of their lives. But this ordinary form of critique has its limits. People need to know about discourses like this – for instance, what insights it gives us into the way economies work or could work, and what other insights it cuts us off from; whose discourse it is, and what they gain from its use; what other discourses there are around, and how this one has become so dominant. People practically need to know such things, because not knowing them makes it harder for them to manage in various parts of their lives: as trade unionists – whether resisting shifts to part-time and short-time work is fighting the inevitable; as managers – what strengths and limitations the metaphor of flexibility has for their organisations; as citizens – whether there is a 'Third Way'; as parents – what sort of world to prepare their children for. But such knowledge about discourse has to come from outside, from theory and research, via education.

I want to proceed by discussing, with a focus on discourse, several key features of late modern society which this example touches on, and which I think help make the case for critical awareness of discourse. Actually the earlier ones arise more easily from the example of the discourse of flexibility than the later ones. I discuss these features of late modernity under the following headings: the relationship between discourse, knowledge and social change in our 'information' or 'knowledge-based' society; what Smith (1990) has called the 'textually-mediated' nature of contemporary social life; the relationship between discourse and social difference; the commodification of discourse; discourse and democracy. I shall then draw these together by tying the case for CLA to the nature of the new global capitalism, and conclude the paper with discussions of how CLA is anchored in 'critical discourse analysis' (and, through that, in critical social science generally), critical discourse awareness and critical pedagogy.

2 Discourse, knowledge and social change

The example points to a relationship between change in economic discourse, new economic knowledge, and change in economic practices. As I stated earlier, it is a matter of discourse, not just language – knowledges are increasingly constituted in multi-semiotic ways in contemporary society (Kress and van Leeuwen 1996, New London Group 1996). Information- or knowledge-based late modern societies are characterised, as Giddens has put it, by enhanced reflexivity – we are constantly reshaping our social practices on the basis of knowledge about those practices. This is true in the domain of work but also, for instance, in how people conduct their personal relationships – the media are full of expert advice. On one level, reflexivity is an inherent property of all social practices – any social practice includes the constructions of that practice produced by its practitioners as part of the practice. What is different about late modernity is the ways in which 'expert systems' (such as the sciences and social sciences) are systematically integrated into reflexive processes (Giddens 1991).

These expert systems can be thought of as evaluating existing knowledges in the practical domain in focus (for example, the economy) and producing new knowledges. Since knowledges are constituted as discourses, particular ways of using language, this means that they are in the business of evaluating and changing discourses. Evaluating discourses means setting them against shifting understandings of what material possibilities there are in the practical domain concerned (for example, the economy), which are, in turn, instantiated within new discourses. In such practical contexts, discourses are evaluated not in terms of some impossible 'absolute truth', but in terms of 'epistemic gain' – whether they yield knowledges which allow people to improve the way in which they manage their lives.

The business of evaluating and changing knowledges and discourses is something which an increasing number of people are involved in as part of the work they do. It is a major concern of educational institutions to teach them how to do this, and part of the current preoccupation with 'learning to learn', and other thematisations of 'learning' in contemporary education and business – 'the learning society', businesses as 'learning organisations', 'lifelong learning' – see, for example, the Dearing Report on universities *Higher Education in the Learning Society* (National Committee of Inquiry into Higher Education 1997). What I want to argue is that the resources for learning and for working in a knowledge-based economy include a critical awareness of discourse – an awareness of how discourse figures within social practices, an awareness that any knowledge of a domain of social life is constituted as one discourse from among a number of coexisting or conceivable discourses, that different discourses are associated with different perspectives on the domain concerned and different interests, an awareness of how discourses can work ideologically in social relations of power, and so forth. It is on the basis of such understandings of how discourse works within social practices that people can come to question and look beyond existing discourses, or existing relations of dominance and marginalisation between discourses, and so advance knowledge. If on the other hand language and other semiotic modalities are viewed as simply transparent media for reflecting what is, the development of knowledge is likely to be impeded.

3 Textually mediated social life

The presence of the discourse of flexibility in Stephen's talk is an illustration of the textual mediation of social life: in contemporary societies, the discourses/knowledges generated by expert systems enter our everyday lives and shape the way we live them. Contemporary societies are knowledge-based not only in their economies but even, for instance, in the ways in which people conduct their personal relationships. Expert knowledges/discourses come to us via texts of various sorts which mediate our social lives – books, magazines, radio and television programmes, and so forth. These processes of textual mediation bind together people who are scattered across societies into social systems – one of Smith's examples is how textually mediated constructions of femininity lock women scattered across social space into the economic system of commodity production and consumption, in that femininity is constructed in terms of the purchase and use of commodities such as clothes (Smith 1990). Moreover, the distances in space and time across which these processes of textual mediation operate are increasing. Modernity can be seen as a process of 'time/space compression', the overcoming of spatial and temporal distance, and late modernity is marked by a twist in that process which is widely referred to as 'globalisation' (Harvey 1990, Giddens 1991). The vehicles for this spatio-temporally extended textual mediation are the new media – radio, television and information technology.

As everyday lives become more pervasively textually mediated, people's lives are increasingly shaped by representations which are produced elsewhere. Representations of the world they live in, the activities they are involved in, their relationships with each other, and even who they are and how they (should) see themselves. The politics of representation becomes increasingly important – whose representations are these, who gains what from them, what social relations do they draw people into, what are their ideological effects, and what alternative representations are there? The example of Stephen's talk is a case in point. His representation of his own life in the black economy draws upon the discourse of flexibility. We might question whether his construction of his own life and identity has been ideologically invested, drawn into the social relations between the powerful groups who control economies and back neo-liberalism and the rest of us. However, the picture is more complex and more hopeful. As I suggested earlier, his talk does not simply reproduce the discourse of flexibility, it works it in a particular – and ironic – way into a rationale for his own way of living based on a perfectly coherent, if non-standard, view of the new capitalism – part of the flexibility that companies need is the flexibility of illegal black labour. The example shows that people are not simply colonised by such discourses, they also appropriate them and work them in particular ways. Textually mediated social life cuts both ways – it opens up unprecedented resources for people to shape their lives in new ways drawing upon knowledges, perspectives and discourses which are generated all over the world. But in so doing it opens up new areas of their lives to the play of power. There is a colonisation–appropriation dialectic at work. Whether on balance people gain or lose depends on where they are positioned in social life – the fact that new possibilities are opened up does not mean people are unconditionally free to take them. But my main point is this: if people are to live in this complex world rather than just be carried along by it, they need resources to examine their placing within this dialectic between the global and the local – and those resources include a critical awareness of language and discourse which can only come through language education.

4 Discourse, social difference and social identity

Discourses are partial and positioned, and social difference is manifest in the diversity of discourses within particular social practices. Neo-liberal economic discourse, for instance, is only one of many economic discourses and, as I have indicated earlier, it corresponds to a specific perspective and set of interests. Critical awareness in this case is a matter of seeing the diversity of discourses and their positioned nature.

But there are other aspects of social difference. Late modern societies are increasingly socially diverse societies, not only in that migration has led to greater ethnic and cultural diversity, but also because various lines of difference which were until recently relatively covered over have become more salient – differences of gender and sexual orientation, for example. Differences are partly semiotic in nature – different languages, different social dialects, different communicative styles, different voices, different discourses. The

of the universe of discourse' (Marcuse 1964) – the predominance of a single economic–political discourse across the political spectrum.

We might see the narrowing of political discourse as a symptom of the political system becoming cut off from the sources of political diversity and change in social life. This has been widely debated in recent years as a crisis of the 'public sphere' (Habermas 1989, Calhoun 1992), troubles to do with the apparent absence of effective spaces and practices where people as citizens can deliberate over issues of common social and political concern, and their deliberations can shape the policy decisions that are made. The broadcast media are full of dialogue on such issues, but it is a dialogue that is deeply flawed in terms of its public sphere credentials – in terms of who has access to it, in terms of what gets onto its agendas, in terms of who controls its flow, and in terms of it being designed to maximise audience and entertain. The task of reconstructing the public sphere is at the heart of the defence and enhancement of democracy. It is already being undertaken within social movements which are active outside the official political system. But it is also a task for educational institutions including schools and universities, whose standing as public spheres has been undermined by recent institutional changes (Giroux 1997). One way forward here is suggested by Billig (1991): that we conceive of teaching people to think as teaching people to argue, and put our energies into making educational institutions as open as possible as spaces for argument. Negotiating across difference is again a central concern for the contemporary public sphere – political dialogue in socioculturally diverse societies has to be oriented to alliances around particular sets of issues. In this case, a critical awareness of discourse is essential for the work of experimentation and design which is necessary to find effective forms of dialogue which facilitate open argumentation and forms of action in common and which do not suppress difference (Fairclough 1998).

7 Critical awareness of discourse and the new global capitalism

I began from the example of neo-liberal economic discourse. The choice of example was not incidental, because it is the new global capitalism which this discourse simultaneously represents and constitutes that makes critical awareness of discourse an increasingly necessary resource for people. The new global capitalism opens up new possibilities for people yet at the same time creates new problems. A critical awareness of discourse is necessary for both – on the one hand, for opening up new knowledges in the knowledge-based economy, and for exploring new possibilities for social relationships and identities in socially diverse communities; on the other hand, for resisting the incursions of the interests and rationalities of economic, governmental and other organisational systems into everyday life – such as the commodification of the language of everyday life, the colonising incursions of textually mediated representations and the threat of global capitalism to democracy, for example, in the ways it manipulates national governments. Late modernity is characterised by increasing reflexivity including language reflexivity, and people need to be equipped both for the increasing knowledge-based design of discursive practices within economic and governmental systems, and for critique and redesign of these designed and often globalised practices as workers, consumers, citizens, members of social and lifestyle groups (for example, as women, Blacks, trade unionists, environmental activists, and so forth).

8 Critique: social science, discourse analysis, discourse awareness

The need for critical awareness of discourse in contemporary society should make it a central part of language education in schools, colleges and universities. I come to some educational issues later. Such a critical discourse awareness programme would rest upon and recontextualise (Bernstein 1990) critical research on discourse, which in turn is based in critical traditions in social science. While these are obviously not the focus of this paper, readers may find useful a brief sketch of one view of critical discourse analysis and critical social science, starting with the latter.

Social life can be seen as constituted by networks of social practices, each of which consists of various elements including discourse (as well as material activities, institutional rituals, social relations, beliefs and values) articulated together in a dialectical relationship, such that each element internalises all others without being reducible to them – each element has its own distinctive logic and generative power (Collier 1994, Harvey 1996, Chouliaraki and Fairclough 1999). A critical social science explicates both structural relations between and within social practices within such networks, and the dialectical tension between structure and event which makes structures both preconditions for events and (transformed) outcomes of them (Bourdieu and Wacquant 1992, Chouliaraki and Fairclough 1999). One view of critique is the concept of 'explanatory critique' associated with 'critical realism' (Bhaskar 1986, Collier 1994): critique involves four stages – identification of a problem, identification of what it is in the network of social practices that gives rise to the problem, consideration of whether and how the problem is functional in sustaining the system (for example, whether it works ideologically), and identification of real possibilities within the domain of social life in question for overcoming the problem. What constitutes a problem can only be established through dialogue between those involved – often not an easy process, or one that yields clear answers.

Critical research on discourse has been carried out under the names of 'critical discourse analysis' and 'critical linguistics' (Fairclough and Wodak 1997). Critical discourse analysis aims to provide a framework for systematically linking properties of discoursal interactions and texts with features of their social and cultural circumstances. The network of social practices is described from a specifically discoursal perspective as an 'order of discourse' consisting of discourses and genres in particular relationships with each other, but with an orientation to shifts in boundaries within and between orders of discourse as part of social and cultural change. Particular discursive events and longer-term series of events tied to specific social conjunctures are described in terms of the potentially innovative ways in which they draw upon the orders of discourse which condition them – it is that relationship to orders of discourse that mediates the connection between detailed semiotic/linguistic features of texts and interactions, and social and cultural structures and processes. Problems of two sorts are in focus: needs-based problems – discursive practices which in some way go against people's needs (for example, forms of doctor–patient communication which do not allow patients to recount what they see as all the relevant aspects of their health problems); and problems with representations (for example, constructions of social groups such as women or cultural minorities which have detrimental social consequences for them).

Critical discourse awareness programmes will be concerned to recontextualise this body of research in ways which transform it, perhaps quite radically, into a practically useful form for educational purposes, including a metalanguage.

8.1 Critical discourse awareness and education[1]

Recent educational reforms have sharply raised the question of what education is for, and for whom. The dominant view of education – evident, for instance, in the recent Dearing Report *Higher Education in the Learning Society* (National Committee of Inquiry into Higher Education 1997) – sees it as a vocationally oriented transmission of given knowledge and skills. What is perhaps most distinctive about this view of education is its focus upon the teaching and learning of 'key skills' which are seen as transferable from one sphere of life to another, and as the basis for future success including successful 'lifelong learning'. Given that one of these key skills is 'communication' (the others identified in the Dearing report are numeracy, information technology and learning to learn), this view of education rests upon a view of discourse – discourse as 'communication skills'.

What is wrong with seeing discourse as communication skills? Let me focus on three problems. First, it is assumed that a communication skill, once learnt, can be freely transferred from one context to another. I think there is an interesting connection between this assumption and the tendencies I have identified as textually mediated social life and the technologisation of discourse – discursive practices are indeed transferred across contexts in late modern social life. But what this first assumption misses is what I have referred to as the colonisation–appropriation dialectic (which is also a global–local dialectic) – even where such transfers take place, it does not mean that we find the same discursive practice in all contexts, for even the most globally dispersed discursive practice is always locally recontextualised, transformed and appropriated. It is inviting disaster to assume that if you have learnt to interview candidates for admission to university, you know how to interview personalities on a television chat show.

Second, it is assumed that there is a simple relationship between what is actually said (or more generally done) in the course of some social practice, and skills, internalised models of how to say/do it – that discourse is a mere instantiation of such models (Fairclough 1988). On the contrary, discourse is a complex matching of models with immediate needs in which what emerges may be radically different from any model, ambivalent between models, or a baffling mixture of models, and where flair and creativity may have more impact than skill. Thirdly, and most seriously, it is assumed that there is a given and accepted way of using language to do certain things, as if discourse was a simple matter of technique, whereas any way of using language which gets to be given and accepted does so through applications of power which violently exclude other ways, and any way of using language within any social practice is socially contestable and likely to be contested. From this point of view, any reduction of discourse to skills is complicit with efforts on the part of those who have power to impose social practices they favour by getting people to see them as mere techniques.

In critiquing the view of discourse as communication skills, I am also critiquing the view of education as a transmission of knowledge and skills. For viewing discourse as skills is just one aspect of viewing knowledge and skills in general as determinate, uncontested, and given externally to the learner; and it is only on such assumptions about what is to be taught and learnt that the process can be viewed as 'transmission'. We can broaden out the argument against discourse as skills into a different view of knowledge and skills in education:

they are always provisional and indeterminate, contested and, moreover, at issue in social relationships, within which all teachers and learners are positioned. In a critical view of education, knowledge and 'skills' are indeed taught and learnt, but they are also questioned – a central concern is what counts as knowledge or skill (and therefore what does not), for whom, why, and with what beneficial or problematic consequences. In the Dearing Report, higher education promotes knowledge, skills and understanding; my comments here take understanding to mean a questioning of knowledge and skills, and problematise the foregrounding of 'key skills' in the Report.

Perhaps it has always been the case that education has been relatively critical for some, though usually for a small elite. In the new work order (Gee *et al.* 1996), there is a need for a small elite of symbolic–analytic workers for whom the new system may demand a critical education (including a critical awareness of discourse). The danger is a new form of educational stratification which separates them from those likely to become other categories of workers (routine production workers, and workers in service industries) or to join the 'socially excluded' (including unemployed). That would be in line with the contemporary tendency of the purposes of education to narrow down towards serving the needs of the economy. The alternative is some vision of education for life within which a critical awareness of discourse is necessary for all.

Note

1. Although pedagogy is not my major concern here, I envisage the sort of four-part pedagogy set out by the New London Group (1996). Its elements are: development of the ability to engage successfully in a range of practices through immersion in authentic Situated Practice; an awareness and understanding of these practices through Overt Instruction; a capacity to critique those practices as socially particular and partial actualities from within a wider range of possibilities through Critical Framing; and Transformed Practice, experimentation with new practices reflexively informed by Overt Instruction and especially Critical Framing. What is envisaged, then, is a link between awareness and practice, awareness opening up new possibilities for practice.

Bibliography and references

Abercrombie, N., Hill, S. and Turner, B. (1980) *The Dominant Ideology Thesis.* London: Routledge.

Ackroyd, S. (2000) Connecting organisations and societies: A realist analysis of structures. In S. Ackroyd and S. Fleetwood (eds), 87–108.

Ackroyd, S. and S. Fleetwood (eds) (2000) *Realist Perspectives on Management and Organisations.* London: Routledge.

Adorno, T.W. (1951/1974) *Minima Moralia: Reflections from Damaged Life.* (E.F.N. Jephcott, trans.) NLB: London.

Adorno, T.W. (1966/1973) *Negative Dialectics.* (E.B. Ashton, trans.). London: Routledge & Kegan Paul.

Adorno, T.W. (1994) *Hegel: Three Studies.* (S.W. Nicholson, trans.). Cambridge, Mass: MIT Press.

Althusser, L. (1971) Ideology and ideological state apparatuses, *Lenin and Philosophy and Other Essays.* London: New Left Books.

Althusser, L. and Balibar, E. (1970) *Reading Capital.* London: New Left Books.

Anăstăsoaie, V. *et al.* (2003) *Breaking the Wall: Representing Anthropology and Anthropological Representations in Post-Communist Eastern Europe.* Cluj-Napoca: EFES.

Ansel, C.K. (2001) Legitimacy: political. *International Encyclopedia of Social and Behavioural Sciences.* Elsevier, Amsterdam, 8704–6.

Archer, M. (1982) Morphogenesis versus structuration: on combining structure and action. *British Journal of Sociology,* 33(4): 455–83.

Archer, M. (1995) *Realist Social Theory: The Morphogenetic Approach.* Cambridge: Cambridge University Press.

Archer, M. (2000) *Being Human.* Cambridge: Cambridge University Press.

Arendt, H. (1958) *The Human Condition.* Chicago: University of Chicago Press.

Argyle, M. (1978) *The Psychology of Interpersonal Behaviour* (Third edn). Harmondsworth: Penguin.

Aristotle (1991) *The Art of Rhetoric*. H.C. Lawson-Tancred (Trans.). London: Penguin Classics.

Aristotle (1998) *The Metaphysics*. H.C. Lawson-Tancred (Trans.). London: Penguin Classics.

Atkinson, J. and Drew, P. (1979) *Order in Court*. London: Macmillan.

Austin, J. (1962) *How to Do Things with Words*. London: Oxford University Press.

Bakhtin, M. (1981) *The Dialogical Imagination*. Austin: University of Texas Press.

Bakhtin, M. (1986) *Speech Genres and Other Late Essays*. Austin: Texas University Press.

Barat, E. (1998) Women's identities: A tension between discourses and experience. Paper delivered at conference on Critical Discourse Analysis, Brasilia, May.

Barbu, D. (1999) *Republica absenta*. Bucharest: Editura Nemira.

Barnes, D. (1988) The politics of oracy. In M. Maclure *et al.* (eds) *Oracy Matters*. Milton Keynes: Open University Press.

Barnett, A. (1998) All power to the citizens, *Marxism Today*, special edition on New Labour, 44–47.

Barratt Brown, M. and Coates, K. (1996) *The Blair Relevation* Spokesman Books.

Barthes, R. (1977) Introduction to the structural analysis of narratives, *Image, Music, Text*. London: Fontana.

Bauman, Z. (1998a) On glocalization: Or globalization for some, localization for others. *Thesis Eleven*, 54: 37–49.

Bauman, Z. (1998b) *Globalization*. Cambridge: Polity Press.

Beciu, C. (2000) *Politica discursiv: practici politice într-o campanie electoral*. Bucharest: Polirom.

Beck, U. (1992) *The Risk Society: Towards a Different Modernity*. London: Sage.

Beetham, D. (1991) *The Legitimation of Power*. Atlantic Highlands NJ: International Humanities Press.

Bell, A. (1991) *The Language of News Media*. Oxford: Blackwell.

Bell, A., Coupland, N., Jaworski, A. and YlaÈnne-McEwen, V. (1997) Editorial. *Journal of Sociolinguistics*, 1: 1–5.

Bell, D. (1976) *The Cultural Contradictions of Capitalism*. London: Heinemann.

Benhabib, S. (1992) *Situating the Self*. Cambridge: Polity Press.

Benhabib, S. (ed.) (1996) *Democracy and Difference*. Princeton University Press.

Benson, D. and Hughes, J.A. (1983) *The Perspective of Ethnomethodology*. London: Longman.

Benton, T. (1981) Realism in Social Science. *Radical Philosophy*, 27: 13–21.

Bergmann, G. (1951) Ideology. *Ethics* 61(3): 205–218.

Bernstein, B. (1975) *Class, Codes and Control 3: Towards a Theory of Educational Transmissions*. London: Routledge.

Bernstein, B. (1982) Class, modalities and cultural reproduction: a model. In M. Apple (ed.) *Cultural and Economic Reproduction in Education*. London: Routledge.

Bernstein, B. (1990) *The Structuring of Pedagogical Discourse*. London: Routledge.

Bernstein, B. (1996) *Pedagogy, Symbolic Control and Identity*. London: Taylor & Francis.

Berti, E. (1978) Ancient Greek dialectic as expression of freedom of thought and speech. *Journal of the History of Ideas*, 39(3): 347–370.

Bhaskar, R. (1979) *The Possibility of Naturalism*. Hassocks: Harvester.

Bhaskar, R. (1986) *Scientific Realism and Human Emancipation*. London: Verso.

Bhaskar, R. (1989) *Reclaiming Reality*. London: Verso.

Billig, M., Condor, S. *et al.* (1988) *Ideological Dilemmas*. London: Sage.

Billig, M. (1991) *Ideology and Opinion*. London: Sage.

Billig, M. (1995) *Banal Nationalism*. London: Sage.

bin Mohamad, M. (2002) Extracts from speech at the East Asia Economic Summit Executive Intelligence Review Online, 18 October 2002.

Birch, D. and O'Toole, M. (1988) *Functions of Style*. London: Frances Pinter.

Blair, T. (1997) Speech at the Aylesbury Housing Estate, Southwark, 2 June.

Blair, T. (1998a) *The Third Way: New Politics for the New Century*, Fabian Society pamphlet.

Blair, T. (1998b) 'Publication of annual report', speech 30 July.

Blair, T. (1998c) Speech at the Confederation of British Industry Annual Dinner, 27 May.

Bloom, S.F. (1943) Man of his century: A reconsideration of the historical significance of Karl Marx. *The Journal of Political Economy*, 51(6): 494–505.

Boden, D. (1994) *The Business of Talk: Organisations in Action*. Cambridge: Polity Press.

Boden, D. and Zimmerman, D. (1991) *Talk and Social Structure*. Cambridge: Polity Press.

Boia, L. (1999) *History and Myth in Romanian Consciousness*. Budapest: Central European University Press.

Boltanski, L. and Chiapello, E. (1999) *Le nouvel esprit du capitalisme*. Paris: Gallimard.

Boltanski, L. and Thévenot, L. (1991) *De la justification*. Paris: Gallimard.

Bora, A. and Hausendorf, H. (2000) Annex 1 of the final PARADYS research submission to the EU. IWT, Bielefeld University, PO Box 10 01 31, D-33501 Germany.

Bora, A. and Hausendorf, H. (2001) Communicating citizenship in decision making procedures. Towards an interdisciplinary and cross-cultural perspective. *Outline of an international and interdisciplinary workshop at the Centre for Interdisciplinary Research* (ZiF). Bielefeld, June 2001. IWT, Bielefeld University, PO Box 10 01 31, D-33501 Germany.

Bora, A., Furchner, I., Hausendorf, H. and Münte, P. (2001) State of the art report: Currents of thought on the main issues of the PARADYS project. IWT, Bielefeld University, PO Box 10 01 31, D-33501 Germany.

Borzeix, A. (2003) Language and agency in organizations, in A. Müller and A. Kieser (eds) *Communication in Organizations*. Frankfurt-am-Main: Peter Lang, 65–79.

Bourdieu, P. (1977) *Outline of a Theory of Practice*. (R. Nice, trans.), Cambridge: Cambridge University Press.

Bourdieu, P. (1984) *Distinction: A Social Critique of the Judgement of Taste*. (R. Nice, trans.), London: Routledge and Kegan Paul.

Bourdieu, P. (1988) *Homo Academicus*. Cambridge: Polity Press.

Bourdieu, P. (1990) *The Logic of Practice* (R. Nice, trans.) Stanford, CA: Stanford University Press.

Bourdieu, P. (1991) *Language and Symbolic Power*. London: Polity.

Bourdieu, P. (1998a) A reasoned utopia and economic fatalism. *New Left Review*, 227: 125–130.

Bourdieu, P. (1998b) L'essence du neo-liberalisme. *Le Monde Diplomatique*, March: 65–7.

Bourdieu, P. (1998c) *Practical Reason: On the Theory of Practice*. London: Polity.

Bourdieu, P. (2000) *Pascalian Meditations*. London: Verso.

Bourdieu, P. and Wacquant, L. (1992) *An Invitation to Reflexive Sociology*. Cambridge: Polity Press.

Bourdieu, P. and Wacquant, L. (2001) New Liberal Speak: Notes on the New Planetary Vulgate. *Radical Philosophy*, 105: 2–5.

Brown, B.M. and Coates, K. (1996) *The Blair Revelation: Deliverance for Whom*. Nottingham: Spokesman.

Brown, G. (1994) *Fair is Efficient*, Fabian Society pamphlet.

Brown, G. and Yule, G. (1983) *Discourse Analysis*. Cambridge: Cambridge University Press.

Brown, P. and Levinson, S. (1978) Universals of language usage: politeness phenomena. In E. Goody (ed.) 1978, 56–324.

Brunsdon, C. (1990) Television: aesthetics and audiences. In P. Melancamp (ed.) *Logics of Television*. Bloomington, IN: Indiana University Press.

Buci-Glucksmann, C. (1980) *Gramsci and the State*. London: Lawrence & Wishart.

Burawoy, M. *et al.* (2000) *Global Ethnography*. Berkeley, CA: University of California Press.

Burawoy, M. and Verdery, K. (1999) *Uncertain Transition: Ethnographies of Change in the Postsocialist World*. New York: Rowan and Littlefield.

Burks, R.V. (1949) A conception of ideology for historians. *Journal of the History of Ideas*, 10(2): 183–198.

Butler, J. (2000) Dynamic Conclusions, in J. Butler, E. Laclau, and S. Zizek, *Contingency, Hegemony, Universality: Contemporary Dialogues on the Left*. London: Verso, 263–280.

Calhoun, C. (1992) *Habermas and the Public Sphere*. MIT Press.

Callinicos, A. (1987) *Making History*. Cambridge: Polity Press.

Cameron, A. and Palan, R. (2004) *The Imagined Economies of Globalization*. London: Sage.

Cameron, D. (1985) *Feminism and Linguistic Theory*. London: Macmillan.

Cameron, D. (1995) *Verbal Hygiene*. London: Routledge.

Campbell, D.T. (1969) Variation and selective retention in socio-cultural evolution. *General Systems*, 14: 69–86.

Candlin, C. and Lucas, J. (1986) Interpretation and explanation in discourse modes of 'advising' in family planning. In Ensink, T. (ed.) *Discourse Analysis and Public Life*. Foris Publications.

Cardiff, D. (1980) The serious and popular: aspects of the evolution of style in radio talk 1928–1939. *Media Culture & Society*, 2.1.

Carpignano, P., Anderson, R., Aronowitz, S. and Difazio, W. (1990) Chatter in the age of electronic reproduction: talk television and the 'public mind'. *Social Text*, 25/26: 33–55.

Carver, T. (1998) *The Postmodern Marx*. Manchester University Press.

Castells, M. (1996) *The Rise of the Network Society*. Cambridge: Blackwell.

Chia, R. (1995) From modern to postmodern organizational analysis. *Organization Studies*, 16/4: 580–605.

Chiapello, E. and Fairclough, N. (2002) Understanding the new management ideology: A transdisciplinary contribution from critical discourse analysis and new sociology of capitalism. *Discourse and Society*, 13/2: 185–208.

Chilton, P. (2004) *Analysing Political Discourse*. London: Routledge.

Chilton, P. (2005) Missing links in mainstream CDA: modules, blends and the critical instinct, in R. Wodak and P. Chilton (eds) *A New Agenda in (Critical) Discourse Analysis*. Amsterdam: John Benjamins.

Chomsky, N. (2003a) Where's the Security in Bush's National Security Strategy?, Lecture at the University of Florida, October 21, 2003.

Chomsky, N. (2003b) *Hegemony or Survival: America's Quest for Global Dominance*. New York: Metropolitan Books.

Chouliaraki, L. (1998) Regulation in 'progressivist' discourse. Individualized teacher–pupil talk. *Discourse and Society*, 9: 5–32.

Chouliaraki, L. (1999) Media discourse and nationality: Death and myth in a news broadcast. In R. Wodak and C. Ludwig (eds), *Challenges in a Changing World: Issues in Critical Discourse Analysis*. Passagen Verlag.

Chouliaraki, L. and Fairclough, N. (1999) *Discourse in Late Modernity*. Edinburgh: Edinburgh University Press.

Chouliaraki, L. and Fairclough, N. (2000) Language and power in Bourdieu: on Hasan's 'The Disempowerment Game'. *Linguistics and Education*, 10(4): 399–409.

Cicourel, A.V. (1976) *The Social Organisation of Juvenile Justice*. London: Heinemann.

Clark, R. (1992) Principles and practice of CLA in the classroom. In Fairclough, N. (ed.) *Critical Language Awareness*. London: Longman.

Clark, R., Constantinou, C., Cottey, A. and Yeoh, O.C. (1990) Rights and obligations in student writing. In Clark, T. *et al.* (eds) *Language and Power: Proceedings of the BAAL Annual Meeting, Lancaster 1989*. London: CILT.

Clark, R., Fairclough, N., Ivanic, R. and Martin-Jones, M. (1990) Critical language awareness Part 1: A critical review of three current approaches. *Language and Education*, 4(4): 249–60.

Clark, R., Fairclough, N., Ivanic, R. and Martin-Jones, M. (1991) Critical language awareness Part 2: Towards critical alternatives. *Language and Education*, 5(1): 41–54.

Clark, R. and Ivanic, R. (1992) Consciousness-raising about the writing process. In Garrett, P. and James, C. (eds) *Language Awareness*. London: Longman.

Clark, R. and Ivanič, R. (1997) *The Politics of Writing*. London: Routledge.

Clarke, J. and Newman, J. (1997) *The Managerial State*. London: Sage.

Clarke, J. and Newman, J. (1998) *A modern British people? New Labour and the reconstruction of social welfare*. Department of Intercultural Communication and Management, Copenhagen Business School. Occasional Paper.

Cole, P. and Morgan, J. (eds) (1975) *Syntax and Semantics 3: Speech Acts*. New York: Academic Press.

Colletti, L. (1975) Introduction. In Marx, K. (1975). *Early Writings*. (Livingstone, R. and Benton, G. trans.), (pp. 7–56). London: Penguin.

Collier, A. (1994) *Critical Realism*. London: Verso.

Coman, M. (2003a) *Mass Media in România Post-comunista*. Bucharest: Polirom.

Coman, M. (2003b) *Mass Media, Mit i Ritual*. Bucharest: Polirom.

Conein, B. *et al.* (1981) *Materialités discursives*. Lille: Presses Universitaires de Lille.

Connerton, P. (ed.) (1976) *Critical Sociology: Selected Readings*. Harmondsworth: Penguin.

Connolly, W. (1991) *Identity/Difference*. Ithaca: Cornell University Press.

Cook, D.J. (1982) Marx's critique of philosophical language. *Philosophy and Phenomenological Research*, 42(4): 530–554.

Coulthard, M. and Montgomery, M. (eds) (1981) *Studies in Discourse Analysis*. London: Routledge & Kegan Paul.

Coupland, N. (1998) What is sociolinguistic theory? *Journal of Sociolinguistics*, 2: 110–117.

Courtine, J.-J. and Marandin, J.-M. (1981) Quel object pour l'analyse de discourse? In Conein (1981).

Coward, R. and Ellis, J. (1977) *Language and Materialism: Developments in Semiology and the Theory of the Subject*. London: Routledge & Kegan Paul.

Crowley, T. (1989) *The Politics of Language*. London: Macmillan.

Daianu, D. (2000) *încotro se îndreapt rile postcommuniste?* Bucharest: Polirom.

Davis, K. (1988) *Power under the Microscope: Toward a Grounded Theory of Gender Relations in Medical Encounters*. Dordrecht: Foris.

D'Entreves, M. (1994) *The Political Philosophy of Hannah Arendt*. London: Routledge.

Department for Education and Employment (1998) *The Learning Age*. London: The Stationery Office.

Department of Education and Science (DES) (1988) Report of the Committee of Enquiry into the Teaching of English Language. London: HMSO. (Kingman Report.)

Department of Education and Science (DES) (1989) English for Ages 5 to 16. London: HMSO. (Cox Report.)

Department of Social Security (1998) *New Ambitions for Our Country: A New Contract for Welfare* (Green Paper on Welfare Reform). London: The Stationery Office.

Department of Trade and Industry (1998) *Our Competitive Future: Building the Knowledge-Driven Economy*, London: HMSO. http://www.dti.gov.uk/comp/competitive.wh_int1.htm.

Derrida, J. (1978) Structure, sign and play in the discourse of the human sciences. In *Writing and Difference*. Chicago: University of Chicago Press, 278–293.

Derrida, J. (1994) *Specters of Marx*. London: Routledge.

Dews, P. (1988) *Logics of Disintegration*. London: Verso.

Dillon, M. (2007) Governing terror: the state of emergency of biopolitical emergence, in: *International Political Sociology*, 1: 7–28.

Doughty, P., Pearce, J. and Thornton, G. (1971) *Language in Use*. London: Edward Arnold.

Drew, P. and Heritage, J. (1992) *Talk at Work*. Cambridge: Cambridge University Press.

Dreyfus, H. and Rabinow, P. (1982) *Michel Foucault: Beyond Structuralism and Hermeneutics*. Brighton: Harvester Press.

Driver, S. and Martell, L. (1998) *New Labour: Politics after Thatcherism*. Cambridge: Polity Press.

Dubiel, H. (1985) *Theory and Politics: Studies in the Development of Critical Theory*. Cambridge, Mass: MIT Press.

Duffield, M. (2001) *Global Governance and the New Wars: the Merging of Development and Security*. London: Zed Books.

Eagleton, T. (1991) *Ideology*. Verso.

Eagleton, T. (2000) *The Idea of Culture*. Oxford: Blackwell.

ECLAC (2002) UN Economic Commission for Latin America and the Caribbean report 'Globalization and Development', (http://www.eclac.cl).

Edmondson, W. (1981) *Spoken Discourse: A Model for Analysis*. London: Longman.

Eizenstat, S. (1999) On the threat to a more open global system, speech to the Democratic Council (http://canberra.usembassy.gov/hyper/WF990120/publog3.htm).

Ellis, J. and Ure, J. (eds) (1982) Register Range and Change. *International Journal of the Sociology of Language*, 35.

Engels, F. (1976) (1877–78) *Anti-Dühring*. Peking: Foreign Languages Press.

ENQA (European Network for Quality Assurance in Higher Education) (2005) Follow-up to the Bologna declaration: a European quality assurance system, a position paper submitted to Bergen meeting of Ministers of Education (http://www.enqa.net.bologna.lasso).

Fairclough, N. (1982) Review of Bolinger, Language – the Loaded Weapon. *Language in Society*, 11: 110–120.

Fairclough, N. (1985) Critical and descriptive goals in discourse analysis. *Journal of Pragmatics*, 9: 739–63.

Fairclough, N. (1988a) Register, power and sociosemantic change. In D. Birch and M. O'Toole (eds) *The Functions of Style*. London: Pinter Publications.

Fairclough, N. (1988b) Discourse representation in media discourse. *Sociolinguistics*, 17: 125–39.

Fairclough, N. (1989a) *Language and Power*. London: Longman.

Fairclough, N. (1989b) Michel Foucault and the analysis of discourse. *Centre for Language in Social Life Research Paper 10*. Lancaster University.

Fairclough, N. (1989c) Language and ideology. *English Language Research Journal*, 3: 9–27.

Fairclough, N. (1990a) What might we mean by 'enterprise discourse'? In R. Keat and N. Abercrombie (eds), *Enterprise Culture* (pp. 38–57). Routledge.

Fairclough, N. (1990b) Critical linguistics, 'New Times' and language education. In R. Clark *et al.* (eds) *Language and Power: Proceedings of the BAAL Annual Meeting, Lancaster 1989*. London: CILT.

Fairclough, N. (1992a) *Discourse and Social Change*. Cambridge: Polity Press.

Fairclough, N. (ed.) (1992b) *Critical Language Awareness*. London: Longman.

Fairclough, N. (1992c) Review of B. Torode (ed.) Text and Talk as Social Practice. *Sociolinguistics*, 18: 144–50.

Fairclough, N. (1992d) The appropriacy of 'appropriateness', in Fairclough 1992b.

Fairclough, N. (1992e) Discourse and text: linguistic and intertextual analysis within discourse analysis, *Discourse & Society*, 3.2: 193–217.

Fairclough, N. (1993) Critical discourse analysis and the marketization of public discourse: the universities, *Discourse and Society*, 4/2: 133–168.

Fairclough, N. (1994) Conversationalisation of public discourse and the authority of the consumer. In R. Keat, N. Whiteley and N. Abercrombie (eds) *The Authority of the Consumer*. London: Routledge, 253–68.

Fairclough, N. (1995a) *Critical Discourse Analysis*, first edn. London: Longman.

Fairclough, N. (1995b) *Media Discourse*. London: Edward Arnold.

Fairclough, N. (1996) Technologisation of discourse. In C. Caldas-Coulthard and M. Coulthard (eds) *Texts and Practices: Readings in Critical Discourse Analysis*. London: Routledge.

Fairclough, N. (1997) Discourse across disciplines. Discourse analysis in researching social change. *AILA Review*, 12: 3–17.

Fairclough, N. (1998) Public space as discourse: Monarchy – the Nation Decides. *Quaderni di studi linguistici*, 4/5.

Fairclough, N. (1999) Democracy and the public sphere in critical research on discourse. In R. Wodak and C. Ludwig (eds) *Challenges in a Changing World: Issues in Critical Discourse Analysis*. Vienna: Passagen Verlag.

Fairclough, N. (2000a) Discourse, social theory and social research: the discourse of welfare reform: *Journal of Sociolinguistics*, 4.2, 2000: 163–195.

Fairclough, N. (2000b) *New Labour, New Language?* London: Routledge.

Fairclough, N. (2000c) Represenciones del cambio en discurso neoliberal. *Cuadernos de Relaciones Laborales*, 16, 2000: 13–36.

Fairclough, N. (2001a) The discourse of New Labour: Critical discourse analysis. In M. Wetherell, S. Taylor and S. Yates (eds) *Discourse as Data: a Guide for Analysis*. London: Sage/Open University, 229–266.

Fairclough, N. (2001b) Review of A Giddens the Third Way and its Critics. *The Spokesman*, 70: 77–81.

Fairclough, N. (2001c) The dialectics of discourse. *Textus*, 14, 231–242.

Fairclough, N. (2003) *Analysing Discourse: Textual Analysis for Social Research*. London: Routledge.

Fairclough, N. (2005a) Critical discourse analysis, organizational discourse, and organizational change. *Organization Studies*, 26: 915–939.

Fairclough, N. (2005b) Critical discourse analysis, *Marges Linguistiques*, 9: 76–94.

Fairclough, N. (2005c) 'Transition' in Central and Eastern Europe, British *and American Studies* (University of Timisoara), 11: 9–34.

Fairclough, N. (2005d) Critical discourse analysis in transdisciplinary research. In R. Wodak and P. Chilton (eds) *A New Agenda in (Critical) Discourse Analysis*. Amsterdam: John Benjamins (2005), 53–70.

Fairclough, N. (2006) *Language and Globalization*. Routledge, London.

Fairclough, N. (2009) Language, reality and power. In J. Culpeper, F. Katamba, P. Kerswill and R. Wodak (eds) *English Language and Linguistics*. London: Palgrave Macmillan.

Fairclough, N. *et al.* (2000) *Language in new capitalism*. [Online collection] Available from the World Wide Web: http://www.uoc.es/humfil/nlc/LNC-ENG/lnc-eng.html.

Fairclough, N., Graham, P., Lemke, J. and Wodak, R. (2001) Introduction. *Critical Discourse Studies*, 1(1).

Fairclough, N., Graham, P., Lemke, J. and Wodak, R. (2004) 'Editorial'. *Critical Discourse Studies*, 1: 1–7.

Fairclough, N., Jessop, B. and Sayer, A. (2004) Critical Realism and Semiosis. In J. Joseph and J. Roberts (eds) *Realism, Discourse and Deconstruction*, 23–42. London: Routledge.

Fairclough, N. and Ivanic, R. (1989) Language education or language training? A critique of the Kingman model of the English language. In J. Bourne (ed.) *The Kingman Report*, Committee on Language in Education.

Fairclough, N. and Thomas, P. (2004) The globalization of discourse and the discourse of globalization. In D. Grant *et al.* (eds) *Handbook of Organizational Discourse*. London: Sage, 379–396.

Fairclough, N. and Wodak, R. (1997) Critical discourse analysis. In T. van Dijk (ed.) *Discourse as Social Interaction*, 258–84. London: Sage.

Featherstone, M. (1991) *Consumer Culture and Postmodernism*. London: Sage.

Fenves, P. (1986) Marx's doctoral thesis on two Greek atomists and the post-Kantian interpretations. *Journal of the History of Ideas*, 40(3): 353–368.

Firth, J.R. (1957) *Papers in Linguistics 1934–1951*. London: Oxford University Press.

Fishman, J.A. (1972) The relationship between micro- and macro-sociolinguistics in the study of who speaks what language to whom and when. In J. Pride and J. Holmes (eds) *Sociolinguistics*. Harmondsworth: Penguin, 15–34.

Forgacs, D. (1988) *A Gramsci Reader*. London: Lawrence & Wishart.

Foucault, M. (1971) *L'ordre du discours*. Paris: Gallimard.

Foucault, M. (1972) *Archaeology of Knowledge*. London: Tavistock Publications.

Foucault, M. (1979) *Discipline and Punlish: The Birth of the Prison*. Harmondsworth: Penguin.

Foucault, M. (1981) *History of Sexuality* vol. 1. Harmondsworth: Penguin.

Foucault, M. (1984) The order of discourse. In M. Shapiro (ed.) *Language and Politics*. Oxford: Blackwell, 108–138.

Fowler, R. (1991) *Language in the News*. London: Routledge.

Fowler, R., Hodge, R., Kress, G. and Trew, T. (1979) *Language and Control*. London: Routledge.

Fowler, R. and Kress, G. (1979) Rules and regulations. In Fowler *et al.* 1979.

Franklin, B. (1998) *Tough on Soundbites, Tough on the Causes of Soundbites: New Labour and News Management*. Catalyst Pamphlet 3. London: The Catalyst Trust.

Fraser, L. (1986) Where? What? And How? Awkward questions in the theory of ideology. *Language and Politics Working Paper*, 1986. Lancaster University.

Fraser, N. (1989) *Unruly Practices*. Cambridge: Polity Press.

Fraser, N. (1995) From redistribution to recognition? Dilemmas of justice in a 'post-socialist' age. *New Left Review*, 212: 68–93.

Freire, P. (1985) *The Politics of Education*. London: Macmillan.

Frow, J. (1985) Discourse and power. *Economy and Society*, 14.

Furusten, S. (1999) *Popular Management Books*. London: Routledge.

Galbraith, J.K. (1955) *The Great Crash 1929*. London: Hamish Hamilton.

Garnham, N. (2001) *The Information Society: Myth or Reality?* Bugs, Globalism and Pluralism Conference, Montreal, Quebec.

Gee, J., Hull, G. and Lankshear, C. (1996) *The New Work Order: Behind the Language of the New Capitalism*. London: Allen & Unwin.

Giddens, A. (1976) *New Rules of the Sociological Method: A Positive Critique of Interpretative Sociologies*. London: Hutchinson.

Giddens, A. (1981) Agency, institution and time–space analysis. In K. Knorr-Cetina and A.V. Cicourel (eds) *Advances in Social Theory and Methodology: Towards an Integration of Micro- and Macro-Sociologies*. London: Routledge & Kegan Paul.

Giddens, A. (1984) *The Constitution of Society*. Cambridge: Polity Press.

Giddens, A. (1991) *Modernity and Self-Identity*. Cambridge: Polity Press.

Giddens, A. (1994) *Beyond Left and Right*. Cambridge: Polity Press.

Giddens, A. (1998) *The Third Way*. Cambridge: Polity Press.

Gille, Z. (2000) Cognitive cartography in a European wasteland: multinational capital and Greens vie for village allegiance. In Burawoy (ed.) (2000) 240–267.

Girin, J. (2001) La théorie des organisations et la question du langage. In A. Borzeix and B. Fraenkel (eds) *Langage et Travail*. CNRS Editions, 167–185.

Giroux, H. (1983) *Theory and Resistance in Education: A Pedagogy for the Opposition*. New York: Heinemann.

Giroux, H. (1997) *Pedagogy and the Politics of Hope*. Boulder, CO: Westview Press.

Givón, T. (1979) *On Understanding Grammar*. New York: Academic Press.

Godin, B. (2004) *The Knowledge-based Economy: Conceptual Framework or Buzzword?* Project on the History and Sociology of S. & T. Statistics, Working Paper, 24.

Goody, E. (ed.) (1978) *Questions and Politeness*. London: Cambridge University Press.

Gould, P. (1998) *The Unfinished Revolution: How the Modernisers Saved the Labour Party*. London: Little, Brown & Co.

Graham, P. (1999) Critical systems theory: A political economy of language, thought, and technology. *Communication Research*, 26(4): 482–507.

Graham, P. (2000) Hypercapitalism: A political economy of informational idealism. *New Media and Society*, 2(2): 131–156.

Graham, P. (2001) Space: irrealis objects in technology policy and their role in a new political economy. *Discourse & Society*, 12(6): 761–788.

Graham, P. (2002) Hypercapitalism: New media, language, and social perceptions of value. *Discourse & Society*, 13(2) [special issue on Language in the New Capitalism. N. Fairclough, issue editor]: 227–249.

Graham, P. (forthcoming) Critical discourse analysis and political economy of communication.

Gramsci, A. (1971) *Selections from the Prison Notebooks*. London: Lawrence & Wishart.

Grant, D. and C. Hardy (2004) Introduction: Struggles with organizational discourse. *Organization Studies*, 25/1: 5–13.

Grant, D., Harvey, C., Oswick, C. and Putnam, L. (2004) 'Introduction: Organizational discourse, exploring the field' in *Handbook of Organizational Discourse*. London: Sage, 1–35.

Grant, D., Keenoy, C. and Oswick, C. (2001) Organizational discourse: key contributions and challenges. *International Studies of Management and Organization*, 31: 5–24.

Gray, J. (1993) *Beyond the New Right: Markets, Government and the Common Environment*. London: Routledge.

Green Party UK (2005) *Manifesto* (http://manifesto.greeparty.org.uk/).

Gregory, M. and Carroll, S. (1978) *Language and Situation: Language Varieties and Their social Contexts*. London: Routledge.

Grice, H.P. (1975) Logic and conversation. In P. Cole and J. Morgan (eds) 1975: 1–58.

Grote, G. (1872) *Aristotle* (Vol. 1). London: John Murray.

Haberland, H. and Mey, J. (1977) Editorial: Linguistics and pragmatics. *Journal of Pragmatics*, 1: 1–12.

Habermas, J. (1976) *Legitimation Crisis*. London: Heinemann.

Habermas, J. (1977) Hannah Arendt's communications concept of power. *Social Research*, 44: 44–65.

Habermas, J. (1984) *The Theory of Communicative Action*, vol. 1. London: Heinemann.

Habermas, J. (1987) *The Philosophical Discourse of Modernity: Twelve Lectures*. Cambridge: Polity.

Habermas, J. (1989) (1962) *Structural Transformation of the Public Sphere*. Cambridge: Polity Press.

Habermas, J. (1996) *Between Facts and Norms*. Cambridge: Polity Press.

Hall, S. (1982) The rediscovery of 'ideology': return of the repressed in media studies. In M. Gurevitch, T. Bennet, J. Curran and J. Woollacott (eds) *Culture, Society and the Media*. London, Methuen, 56–90.

Hall, S. (1988) The toad in the garden: Thatcherism among the theorists. In C. Nelson and L. Grossberg (eds) *Marxism and the Interpretation of Culture*. London: Macmillan.

Hall, S. (1994) Some 'politically incorrect' pathways through PC. In S. Dunant (ed.) *The War of the Words: The Political Correctness Debate*. London: Virago Press, 164–184.

Hall, S. (1998) The great moving nowhere show, *Marxism Today* special issue on New Labour, 9–14.

Hall, S., Critcher, C., Jefferson, T., Clarke, J. and Roberts, B. (1978) *Policing the Crisis*. London: Macmillan.

Halliday, M.A.K. (1978) *Language as Social Semiotic*. London: Edward Arnold.

Halliday, M.A.K. (1993) New ways of meaning: a challenge to applied linguistics. In *Language in a Changing World*. Applied Linguistics Association of Australia, 1–32.

Halliday, M.A.K. (1994a) 'So you say pass . . . thank you three muchly': How conversation means – contexts and functions. In A. Grimshaw (ed.) *What's Going on Here? Contemporary Studies of Professional Talk*. Norwood, NJ: Ablex, 175–229.

Halliday, M.A.K. (1994b) *An Introduction to Functional Grammar*, second edn, London: Edward Arnold.

Halliday, M.A.K. and Hasan, R. (1976) *Cohesion in English*. London: Longman.

Halliday, M.A.K. and Hasan, R. (1985) *Language, Context and Text*. Geelong: Deakin University Press.

Hansen, A.H. (1921) The technological interpretation of history. *Quarterly Journal of Economics*, 36(1): 72–83.

Haroche, C., Henry, P. and Pêcheux, M. (1971) La sémantique et la coupure saussurienne: langue, langage, discours. *Languages*, 24.

Hart, K. (1999) *The Memory Bank: Money in an Unequal World*. London: Profile.

Harvey, D. (1990) *The Condition of Postmodernity*. Oxford: Blackwell.

Harvey, D. (1996) *Justice, Nature and the Geography of Difference*. Oxford: Blackwell.

Harvey, D. (2003) *The New Imperialism*. Oxford: Oxford University Press.

Hasan, R. (2000) The disempowerment game: a critique of Bourdieu's view of language. *Linguistics and Education*, 10.

Hawkins, W. (1984) *Awareness of Language: An Introduction*. Cambridge: Cambridge University Press.

Hay, C. (2007) *Why We Hate Politics*. Cambridge: Polity.

Hay, C. and Marsh, D. (2000) Introduction: demystifying globalization. In C. Hay and D. Marsh (eds) *Demystifying Globalization*. London: Palgrave, 1–17.

Hay, C. and Rosamond, B. (2002) Globalization, European integration and the discursive construction of economic imperatives. *Journal of European Public Policy*, 9.2.

Hegel, G.W.F. (1807/1966) *The Phenomenology of Mind*. J.B. Baillie (trans.). London: George Allen & Unwin.

Hegel, G.W.F. (1830/1998) Philosophy of subjective spirit. In S. Houlgate (ed.) *The Hegel Reader*. London: Blackwell, 293–318.

Hegel, G.W.F. (1833/1995) *Lectures on the History of Philosophy (Vol. 1): Greek philosophy to Plato*. E.S. Haldane (trans.). London: Nebraska University Press.

Hegel, G.W.F. (1910) *The Phenomenology of Mind* vol. 2, translated J.B. Baillie. London: Sonnenschein.

Held, D., McGrew, A., Goldblatt, D. and Perraton, J. (1999) *Global Transformations: Politics, Economics and Culture*. Cambridge: Polity Press.

Heller, A. (1999) *A Theory of Modernity*. Oxford: Blackwell.

Henriques, J. *et al.* (1984) *Changing the Subject*. London: Methuen.

Hennessy, R. (1993) *Materialist Feminism and the Politics of Discourse*. London: Sage.

Hermann, E. and Chomsky, N. (1988) *Manufacturing Consent: The Political Economy of the Mass Media*. Pantheon Books.

Hobsbawm, E. (1977) Gramsci and political theory. *Marxism Today*, July 1977.

Hochschild, A.R. (1983) *The Managed Heart*. Berkeley: University of California Press.

Hodge, R. and Kress, G. (1988) *Social Semiotics*. Cambridge: Polity Press.

Hoey, M. (2001) *Textual Interaction*. London: Routledge.

Honderich, T. (2003) *After the Terror* (revised edition). Edinburgh: Edinburgh University Press.

Hook, S. (1928a) The philosophy of dialectical materialism I. *The Journal of Philosophy*, 25(5): 113-124.

Hook, S. (1928b) The philosophy of dialectical materialism II. *The Journal of Philosophy*, 25(6): 141-155.

Horkheimer, M. and Adorno, T. (1947/1998) *Dialectic of Enlightenment*. London: Verso.

Huczynski, A. (1993) *Management Gurus: What Makes Them and How to Become One*. London: Routledge.

Huxley, J. (1950) New bottles for new wine: Ideology and scientific knowledge. *Journal of the Royal Anthropological Institute of Great Britain and Ireland*, 80(1/2): 7-23.

Hymes, D. (1972) On communicative competence. In Pride, J. and Holmes, J. *Sociolinguistics*. Harmondsworth: Penguin.

Iedema, R. (1998) Institutional responsibility and hidden meanings. *Discourse & Society*, 9(4): 481-500.

Iedema, R. (1999) Formalizing organizational meaning. *Discourse & Society*, 10(1): 49-66.

Iedema, R. (2003) *Discourses of Post-bureaucratic Organization*. Amsterdam: John Benjamins Publishing.

Iedema, R., Degeling, P., Braithwaite, J. and White, L. (2004) 'It's an interesting conversation I'm hearing': the doctor as manager. *Organization Studies*, 25/1: 15-33.

Ieţcu, I. (2006) *Discourse Analysis and Argumentation Theory: Analytical Framework and Applications*. Bucharest: Editura Universităţii Bucureşti.

Ivanič, R. (1990) Critical language awareness in action. In R. Carter (ed.) *Knowledge about Language - The LINC Reader*. London: Hodder & Stoughton.

Ivanič, R. (1997) *Writing and Identity: The Discoursal Construction of Identity in Academic Writing*. Amsterdam: Benjamins.

Ivanič, R. and Roach, S. (1990) Academic writing, power and disguise. In Clark, N., Fairclough, N. *et al.* (eds) (1990).

Ivanič, R. and Simpson, J. (1992) Who's who in academic writing? In Fairclough, N. (ed.) (1992b).

Jackson, B. (2001) *Management Gurus and Management Fashions*. London: Routledge.

Jackson, R. (2005) *Writing the War on Terrorism*. Manchester: Manchester University Press.

Jakobson, R. (1990) *On Language*. Cambridge: Cambridge University Press.

Jameson, F. (1984) Postmodernism, or the cultural logic of capitalism. *New Left Review*, 146.

Janks, H. and Ivanic, R. (1992) Critical language awareness and emancipator discourse. In Fairclough, N. (ed.) (1992b).

Jessop, R. (2000) The crisis of the national spatio-temporal fix and the ecological dominance of globalizing capitalism. *International Journal of Urban and Regional Studies*, 24(2): 273-310.

Jessop, B. (2001) Institutional (re)turns and the strategic-relational approach. *Environment and Planning A*, 33(7): 1213–37.

Jessop, B. (2002) *The Future of the Capitalist State*. Cambridge: Polity Press.

Jessop, B. (2004) Critical semiotic analysis and cultural political economy. *Critical Discourse Studies*, 1(2), 2004: 159–74.

Jessop, B. (2008) The cultural political economy of the knowledge-based economy and its implications for higher education. In Norman Fairclough, Bob Jessop and Ruth Wodak (eds) *Education and the Knowledge-Based Economy in Europe*. Amsterdam: Sense Publishers.

Jessop, B. and Sum, N.-L. (2001) Pre-disciplinary and post-disciplinary perspectives in political economy. *New Political Economy*, 6: 89–101.

Jessop, B. and Sum, N.-L. (2006) *Beyond the Regulation Approach*. London: Edward Elgar.

Jones, N. (1999) *Sultans of Spin: The Media and the New Labour Government*. London: Victor Gollancz.

Jordan, B. (1996) *A Theory of Poverty and Social Exclusion*. Cambridge: Polity Press.

Jordanidou, A. (1990) Read Me the Old News: A Study of Discourse Practice. Lancaster University PhD Thesis.

Kanter, R.M. (2001) *Evolve!* Boston: Harvard University Press.

Keane, J. (1984) *Public Life in Late Capitalism*. Cambridge: Cambridge University Press.

Keat, R. and Abercrombie, N. (1990) *Enterprise Culture*. London: Routledge.

Keat, R., Whiteley, N. and Abercrombie, N. (1994) *The Authority of the Consumer*. London: Routledge.

Keenoy, T. and Oswick, C. (2004) Organizing textscapes. *Organization Studies*, 25/1: 135–142.

Kennedy, E. (1979) 'Ideology' from Destutt de Tracy to Marx. *Journal of the History of Ideas*, 40(3): 353–368.

Kennedy, P. (1998) Coming to terms with contemporary capitalism: beyond the idealism of globalisation and capitalist ascendancy arguments. *Sociological research online*, 3(2). [Online journal]. Retrieved 7 October 1998 from the World Wide Web: http://www.socioresonline.org.uk/socioresonline/3/2/6.html.

Kieser, A. and Müller, A. (2003) Foreword. In A. Müller and A. Kieser (eds) *Communication in Organizations*. Frankfurt-am-Main: Peter Lang, 7–17.

Kress, G. (1988) *Linguistic Processes in Sociocultural Practice*. Oxford: Oxford University Press.

Kress, G. (1993) Cultural considerations in linguistic description. In D. Graddol *et al.* (eds) *Language and Culture*. London: Multilingual Matters.

Kress, G. and Hodge, B. (1979) *Language as Ideology*. London: Routledge & Kegan Paul.

Kress, G. and van Leeuwen, T. (1996) *Reading Images: The Grammar of Visual Design*. London: Routledge.

Kress, G. and van Leeuwen, T. (2000) *Multimodal Discourse*. London: Arnold.

Kristeva, J. (1980) Word, dialogue and novel. In Kristeva, J. (ed.) *Desire in Language*. Oxford: Blackwell.

Labov, W. and Fanshel, D. (1977) *Therapeutic Discourse*. New York: Academic Press.

Labov, W. and Waletzky, J. (1967) Narrative analysis: oral versions of personal experience. In J. Helms (ed.) *Essays on the Verbal and Visual Arts*. University of Washington Press.

Laclau, E. (1979) *Politics and Ideology in Marxist Theory*. London: Verso.

Laclau, E. (1996) Why do empty signifiers matter in politics? In *Emancipations*. London: Verso, 36–46.

Laclau, E. and Mouffe, C. (1985) *Hegemony and Socialist Strategy*. London: Verso.

Langholm, O. (1998) *The Legacy of Scholasticism in Economic Thought: Antecedents of Choice and Power*. Cambridge, Mass: Cambridge University Press.

Larrain, J. (1979) *The Concept of Ideology*. London: Hutchinson.

Larrain, J. (1989) *The Concept of Ideology*. London: Hutchinson.

Lash, S. (1990) *The Sociology of Postmodernism*. London: Routledge.

Latour, B. (2004) *Politics of Nature: How to Bring the Sciences into Democracy*. Catherine Porter (Trans.) Cambridge, MA: Harvard University Press.

Lave, J. (1998) *Cognition in Practice*, Cambridge: Cambridge University Press.

Law, J. (1994) *Organizing Modernity*. Oxford: Blackwell.

Lawson-Tancred, H.C. (1998) Introduction. In Aristotle, A. (1998) *The Metaphysics* (pp. xi–lviii). (Lawson-Tancred, H.C. trans.). London: Penguin Classics.

Leech, G.N. (1974) *Semantics*. Harmondsworth: Penguin.

Leech, G.N. (1983) *Principles of Pragmatics*. London: Longman.

Lemke, J. (1988) Text structure and text semantics. In R. Veltman and E. Steiner (eds) *Pragmatics, Discourse and Text: Systemic Approaches*. London: Pinter.

Lemke, J. (1995) *Textual Politics*. London: Taylor & Francis.

Lemke, J. (1998) Resources for attitudinal meaning. Evaluative orientations in text semantics, *Functions of Language*, 5, 1: 33–56.

Lepschy, G. (1985) Linguistics. In Z. Baranski and G. Short (eds) *Developing Contemporary Marxism*. London: The Macmillan Press, 199–228.

Levinson, S. (1979) Activity types and language. *Linguistics*, 17: 365–99.

Levinson, S. (1983) *Pragmatics*. Cambridge: Cambridge University Press.

Levitas, R. (1998) *The Inclusive Society? Social Exclusion and New Labour*. London: Macmillan.

Lipset, S.M. (1966) Some further comments on 'The End of Ideology'. *The American Political Science Review*, 60(1): 17–18.

Livingstone, S. and Lunt, P. (1994) *Talk on Television*. London: Routledge.

Lyotard, J.-F. (1984) *The Postmodern Condition*. Manchester: Manchester University Press.

Lyotard, J.-F. (1986/7) Rules and paradoxes and the svelte appendix. *Cultural Critique*, 5: 209–19.

Lyotard, J.-F. (1988) *The Differend: Phrases in Dispute*. Manchester: Manchester University Press.

MacDonald, R. (1994) Fiddly jobs, undeclared working and the something for nothing society. *Work, Employment and Society*, 8(4): 507–30.

MacIntyre, A. (1985) *After Virtue: A Study in Moral Theory*. Second edition. London: Duckworth.

Maguire, S. (2004) The co-evolution of technology and discourse: A study of substitution processes for the insecticide DDT. *Organization Studies*, 25(1): 113–134.

Maingueneau, D. (1987) *Nouvelles tendances en analyse du discours*. Paris: Hachette.

Makdisi, G. (1974) The scholastic method in mediaeval education: An inquiry into its origins, law, and theology. *Speculum*, 49(4): 640–661.

Maldidier, S. (1984) Michel Pêcheux: une tension passionnée entre la langue et l'histoire. In *Histoire et linguistique*. Paris: Editions de la Maison des Sciences de L'homme.

Malinowski, B. (1923) The problem of meaning in primitive languages. Supplement 1. In C. Ogden and I.A. Richards (eds) *The Meaning of Meaning*. New York: Harcourt Brace.

Mandel, E. (1978) *Late Capitalism*. London: New Left Books.

Marcuse, H. (1964) *One-Dimensional Man*. London: Abacus.

Margerison, C. (1987) *Conversation Control Skills for Managers*. London: Mercury Books.

Marquand, D. (1998) The Blair paradox, *Prospect*, May, 19–22.

Marsden, R. (1999) *The Nature of Capital: Marx after Foucault*. London: Routledge.

Martin, J. (1989) *Factual Writing*. Oxford: Oxford University Press.

Martin, J. (1992) *English Text*. Amsterdam: John Benjamins.

Marx, K. (1843/1975) *Critique of Hegel's Doctrine of the State*. In Marx, K. (1975) *Early Writings*. R. Livingstone and G. Benton (Trans.). London: Penguin, 157–198.

Marx, K. (1844/1975a) *Economic and Philosophical Manuscripts*. In Marx, K. (1975) *Early Writings*. R. Livingstone and G. Benton (Trans.). London: Penguin, 279–400.

Marx, K. (1844/1975b) *Excerpts from James Mill's 'Elements of Political Economy'*. In Marx, K. (1975) *Early Writings*. R. Livingstone and G. Benton (Trans.). London: Penguin, 259–278.

Marx, K. (1844/1977) *Economic and Philosophic Manuscripts of 1844*. London: Lawrence & Wishart.

Marx, K. (1851-2/1973) The Eighteenth Brumaire of Louis Bonaparte. In *Surveys from Exile*. Harmondsworth: Penguin, 38–64.

Marx, K. (1857/1973) *Grundrisse: Foundations of the Critique of Political Economy* (M. Nicolaus, Trans.). London: Penguin.

Marx, K. (1875/1972) *Critique of the Gotha program*. In R.C. Tucker (ed.), *The Marx-Engels Reader*. New York: W.W. Norton, 382–405.

Marx, K. (1970) *A Contribution to the Critique of Political Economy* (S.W. Ryazlanskaya, Trans.). Moscow: Progress.

Marx, K. (1974) Capital. *A Critique of Political Economy* (Vol. 1), (S. Moore and B. Aveling Trans). London: Lawrence & Wishart.

Marx, K. (1976) *Capital: A Critique of Political Economy* (Vol. 1), (B. Fowkes, Trans.). London: Penguin.

Marx, K. (1978) *Capital: A Critique of Political Economy* (Vol. 2), (D. Fernbach, Trans.). London: Penguin.

Marx, K. (1981) *Capital: A Critique of Political Economy* (Vol. 3), (D. Fernbach, Trans.). London: Penguin.

Marx, K. and Engels, G. (1846/1972) *The German Ideology*. In R.C. Tucker (ed.), *The Marx–Engels Reader*. New York: W.W. Norton, 110–166.

Marxism Today. Special Issue on Blairism. October 1998.

McKeon, R. (1928) Thomas Aquinas' doctrine of knowledge and its historical setting. *Speculum*, 3 (4): 425–444.

McTaggart, J.E. (1893) Time and the Hegelian dialectic. *Mind* [New Series], 2(8): 490–504.

Melucci, A. (1996) *Challenging Codes: Collective Action in the Information Age*. Cambridge: CUP.

Meehan, J. (1995) *Feminists Read Habermas*. London: Routledge.

Mey, J. (1985) *Whose Language? A study in Linguistic Pragmatics*. Amsterdam: John Benjamins.

Michel, V. (1927) Why scholastic philosophy lives. *The Philosophical Review*, 36(2): 166–173.

Miroiu, M. (1999) *Societatea Retro*. Bucharest: Editura Trei.

Mischler, E. (1984) *The Discourse of Medicine. Dialectics of Medical Interviews*. Norwood NJ: Ablex.

Montgomery, M. (1999) Speaking sincerely: public reactions to the death of Diana. *Language and Literature*, 7: 5–33.

Morley, D. (1980) *The 'Nationwide' Audience*. London: BFI.

Morley, D. (1983) Cultural transformations: the politics of resistance. In H. Davis and P. Walton (eds) *Language, Image, Media*. Oxford: Blackwell.

Mouffe, C. (2005) *On the Political*. London: Routledge.

Mouzelis, N. (1990) *Post-Marxist Alternatives*. London: Macmillan.

Mumby, D. and Clair, R. (1997) Organizational discourse. In T.A. van Dijk (ed.) *Discourse as Structure and Process: Discourse Studies Volume 2*. London: Sage.

Mumby, D.K. and Stohl, C. (1991) Power and discourse in organizational studies: Absence and the dialectic of control. *Discourse and Society*, 2: 313–332.

Mumby, D.K. and Stohl, C. (1996) Disciplining organizational communication studies. *Management Communication Quarterly*, 10/1: 50–73.

Muntigl, P. (2002) Politicization and depoliticization: Employment policy in the European Union. In P. Chilton and C. Schäffner (eds) *Politics as Text and Talk*. Amsterdam: John Benjamins, 45–79.

Myers, G. (1998) Displaying opinions: topics and disagreements in focus groups. *Language in Society*, 27: 85–111.

National Committee of Inquiry into Higher Education (1997) *Higher Education in the Learning Society (The Dearing Report)*. London: HMSO.

National Congress on Language in Education (NCLE) (1985) *Language Awareness*. London: CILT.

Neill, T.P. (1949) The physiocrats' concept of economics. *Quarterly Journal of Economics*, 63(4): 532–553.

Nellhaus, T. (1998) Signs, Social Ontology, and Critical Realism. *Journal for the Theory of Social Behaviour*, 28(1): 1–24.

New London Group (1996) A pedagogy of multiliteracies: Designing social futures. *Harvard Educational Review*, 66(1): 60–92.

Nietzsche, F. (1990/1886) *Beyond Good and Evil*. Harmondsworth: Penguin.

Norris, C. (1992) *Uncritical Theory*. London: Lawrence & Wishart.

O'Barr, W. (1982) *Linguistic Evidence: Language, Power and Strategy in the Courtroom*. New York: Academic Press.

Ollman, B. (1993) *Dialectical Investigations*. London/New York: Routledge.

O'Neill, J. (2001) Markets and the environment: The solution is the problem. *Economic and Political Weekly*, 36(21): 1865–1873.

Palonen, K. (1993) Introduction: From policy and polity to politicking and politicization. In K. Paolonen and T. Parvikko (eds) *Reading the Political: Exploring the Margins of Politics*. Helsinki: FPSA, 6–16.

Parker, I. (1992) *Discourse Dynamics*. London: Routledge.

Pêcheux, M. (1982) *Language, Semantics and Ideology*. London: Macmillan.

Pêcheux, M. (1988) Discourse: structure or event? In Nelson, C. and Grossberg, L. *Marxism and the Interpretation of Culture*. London: Macmillan.

Perri 6 (1997) *Holistic Government*. London: Demos.

Perri 6 (1998) Problem-solving government. In Ian Hargreaves and Ian Christie (eds) *Tomorrow's Politics*. London: Demos, 50–63.

Peters, T. (1994) *The Tom Peters Seminar*. London: Vintage Books.

Pickles, J. (1998) Restructuring State Enterprises: Industrial Geography and Eastern European Transitions. In J. Pickles and A. Smith (eds) *Theorising Transition: The Political Economy of Post-Communist Transformations*. London: Routledge, 172–96.

Pickles, J. and Smith, A. (1998) *The Political Economy of Transition*. London: Routledge.

Pieterse, J. (2004) *Globalization or Empire?* London: Routledge.

Pilger, J. (1992) *Distant Voices*. London: Vintage.

Platt, S. (1998) *Government by Task Force*. Catalyst Paper 2. London: Catalyst.

Polanyi, K. (1944) *The Great Transformation*. Boston: Beacon Press.

Poster, M. (ed.) (1988) *Jean Baudrillard: Selected Writings*. Cambridge: Polity Press.

Potter, J. and Wetherell, M. (1987) *Discourse and Social Psychology*. London: Sage.

Poznanaski, K. (2000) The morals of transition: decline of public interest and runaway reforms in eastern Europe. In S. Antohi and V. Tismaneanu (eds)

Between Past and Future: The Revolutions of 1989 and their Aftermath. Budapest: CEU Press.

Pratt, N.L. (1981) The ideology of speech act theory. *Centrum* (new series), 1: 5–18.

Preoteasa, I. (2002) Intellectuals and the public sphere in post-communist Romania: a discourse analytical perspective. *Discourse and Society*, 13: 269–92.

Przeworski, A. (1992) The neoliberal fallacy. *Journal of Democracy*, 3 (3): 67–84.

Putnam, L. and Fairhurst, G. (2001) Discourse analysis in organizations: Issues and concerns. In F.M. Jablin and L. Putnam (eds) *The New Handbook of Organizational Communication: Advances in Theory, Research and Methods.* Newbury Park, CA: Sage, 235–268.

Rancière, J. (1995) *On the Shores of Politics.* London: Verso.

Rancière, J. (2006) *Hatred of Democracy.* London: Verso.

Randall (Jr), J.H. (1940) The development of scientific method in the school of Padua. *Journal of the History of Ideas*, 1(2): 177–206.

Ranney, A. (1976) 'The divine science': Political engineering in American culture. *The American Political Science Review*, 70(1): 140–148.

Ray, L. and Sayer, A. (1999) *Culture and Economy after the Cultural Turn.* London: Sage.

Rawles, K. (1998) Philosophy and the environmental movement. In D. Cooper and J. Palmer (eds) *Spirit of the Environment: Religion, Value and Environmental Concern.* London: Routledge, 131–45.

Reed, M. (2000) In praise of duality and dualism: Rethinking agency and structure in organizational analysis. In S. Ackroyd and S. Fleetwood (eds) (2000), 45–65.

Reed, M. (2004) Getting real about organisational discourse. In D. Grant *et al.* (eds) *Handbook of Organizational Discourse.* London: Sage, 413–420.

Rentoul, J. (1997) *Tony Blair* (revised edition). London: Warner Books.

Repere 2.1 (2004) *România în lumea contemporan* (Colloquium at New Europe College).

Ricoeur, P. (1997) *L'idéologie et l'utopie.* Paris: Seuil.

Ringer, Fritz K. (2000) *Max Weber's Methodology: The Unification of the Cultural and Social Sciences.* Cambridge, MA: Harvard University Press.

Robertson, R. (1992) *Globalization.* London: Sage.

Rose, N. (1999) *The Powers of Freedom: Reframing Political Thought.* Cambridge: Cambridge University Press.

Rose, N. and Miller, R. (1989) Rethinking the state: governing economic, social and personal life. (Working Paper.)

Roucek, J.S. (1944) A history of the concept of ideology. *Journal of the History of Ideas*, 5(4): 479–88.

Sacks, H. Schegloff, E. and Jefferson, G. (1978) A simplest systematic for the organization of turn-taking in conversation. In J. Schenkein (ed.) (1978): 7–55.

Salskov-Iversen, D., Hansen, H. and Bislev, S. (2000) Governmentality, globalization and local practice: transformations of a hegemonic discourse. *Alternatives*, 25: 183–222.

Sartori, G. (1969) Politics, ideology, and belief systems. *The American Political Science Review*, 63(2): 398–411.

Saul, J.R. (1992) *Voltaire's Bastards: The Dictatorship of Reason in the West.* Maryborough, Australia: Penguin.

Saul, J.R. (1997) *The Unconscious Civilization.* Maryborough, Australia: Penguin.

Saul, J.R. (2005) *The Collapse of Globalism and the Reinvention of the World.* London: Atlantic Books.

Saussure, F. de (1966/1916) *Course in General Linguistics.* London: McGraw Hill. (Wade Baskin, Trans.)

Sayer, A. (1995) *Radical Political Economy.* Oxford: Blackwell.

Sayer, A. (2000) *Realism and Social Science.* London: Sage.

Sayer, A. (2005) *The Moral Significance of Class.* Cambridge: Cambridge University Press.

Scannell, P. (1991) *Broadcast Talk.* London: Sage.

Scannell, P. (1992) Public service broadcasting and modern public life. In P. Scannell *et al.* (eds) *Culture and Power.* London: Sage.

Schank, R. and Abelson, H. (1977) *Scripts, Plans, Goals and Understanding.* New York: Lawrence Erlbaum.

Schegloff, E. (1992) On talk and its institutional occasions. In P. Drew and J. Heritage (eds) (1992): 101–34.

Schenkein, J. (ed.) (1978) *Studies in the Organization of Conversational Interaction.* New York: Academic Press.

Secretary of State for Social Security and Minister for Welfare Reform (1998) *New Ambitions for Our Country: A New Contract for Welfare.* London: The Stationery Office.

Selden, R. (1990) The rhetoric of enterprise. In R. Keat and N. Abercrombie (eds) (1990).

Shore and Wright (2000) Coercive accountability: the rise of audit culture in higher education. In Strathern (ed.) (2000).

Silverstone, R. (1999) *Why Study the Media?* London: Sage.

Sinclair, J. and Coulthard, R.M. (1975) *Towards an Analysis of Discourse: The English Used by Teachers and Pupils.* London: Oxford University Press.

Skogstad, G. (2003) Legitimacy and/or policy effectiveness?: Network governance and GMO regulation in the European Union. *Journal of European Public Policy*, 10(3): 321–338.

Smith, A. (1776/1997) *The Wealth of Nations* (Books I–III). London: Penguin.

Smith, A. (1776/1999) *The Wealth of Nations* (Books IV–V). London: Penguin.

Smith, D. (1990) *Texts, Facts and Femininity.* London: Routledge.

Sondermann, K. (1997) Reading politically: national anthems as textual icons. In T. Carver and M. Hyvärinen (eds) *Interpreting the Political: New Methodologies.* London: Routledge, 128–42.

Spencer, J. and Gregory, M.J. (1964) An approach to the study of style. In N. Enkvist *et al.* (eds) *Linguistics and Style.* Oxford: Oxford University Press.

Sraffa, P. (1960) *Production of Commodities by Means of Commodities: Prelude to a Critique of Economic Theory*. Cambridge: Cambridge University Press.

Stark, D. and Bruszt, L. (1998) *Postsocialist Pathways: Transforming Politics and Property in East Central Europe*. Cambridge: Cambridge University Press.

Steger, M. (2005) *Globalism: Market Ideology meets Terrorism*. Lanham: Rowman & Littlefield.

Stelzer, I. (ed.) (2004) *Neo-Conservatism*. London: Atlantic Books.

Strathern, M. (ed.) (2000) *Audit Cultures: Anthropological Studies in Accountability, Ethics and the Academy*. London: Routledge.

Stubbs, M. (1983) *Discourse Analysis: The Sociolinguistic Analysis of Natural Language*. Oxford: Basil Blackwell.

Swales, J. and Rogers, P. (1995) Discourse and the projection of corporate culture: the mission statement. *Discourse and Society*, 6(2): 223–42.

Talbot, M. (1990) Language, Intertextuality and Subjectivity: Voices and the Construction of Consumer Femininity. PhD Thesis Lancaster University.

Tannen, D. (1986) *That's Not What I Meant! How Conversational Style Makes or Breaks Your Relationship with Others*. New York: William Morrow.

Tannen, D. (1991) *You Just Don't Understand: Women and Men in Conversation*. London: Virago.

Tannen, D. and Wallat, C. (1986) Medical professionals and parents: a linguistic analysis of communication across contexts. *Language in Society*, 15: 295–312.

Taylor, C. (1986) Foucault on discourse and truth. In D.C. Hoy (ed.) *Foucault: A Critical Reader*. Oxford: Blackwell.

ten Have, P. (1989) The consultation as a genre. In B. Torode (ed.) *Talk and Text as Social Practice*. Foris.

Therborn, G. (1980) *The Ideology of Power and the Power of Ideology*. London: Verso.

Thibault, P. (1991) *Social Semiotics as Praxis*. University of Minnesota Press.

Thibault, P. (1997) *Re-reading Saussure*. London: Routledge.

Thompson, J.B. (1984) *Studies in the Theory of Ideology*. Cambridge: Polity Press.

Thompson, J.B. (1990) *Ideology and Modern Culture*. Cambridge: Polity Press.

Thorne, N., Kramarae, C. and Henley, N. (1983) *Language, Gender and Society*. London: Newbury House.

Threadgold, T. (1989) Talking about genre: ideologies and incompatible discourses. *Cultural Studies*, 3(3): 101–27.

Tolson, A. (1991) Televized chat and the synthetic personality. In P. Scannell (ed.) (1991).

Tomlinson, J. (1999) *Globalization and Culture*. Cambridge: Polity Press.

Touraine, A. (1997) *What is Democracy?* Westview Press.

Tsoukas, H. and Chia, R. (2002) On organizational becoming: Rethinking organizational change. *Organization Science*, 13/5: 567–585.

Tucker, R.C. (1972) Introduction. In R.C. Tucker (ed.), *The Marx-Engels Reader*. New York: W.W. Norton xv–xxxiv.

Turner, W. (1904) Recent literature on scholastic philosophy. *The Journal of Philosophy, Psychology and Scientific Methods*, 1(8): 200–207.

Ure, J. (1982) Introduction: approaches to the study of register range. In J. Ellis and J. Ure (eds) (1982).

van Dijk, T. (1987) *Handbook of Discourse Analysis*. 4 vols. New York: Academic Press.

van Dijk, T. (1988) *News as Discourse*. Erlbaum.

van Dijk, T. (1998) *Ideology: An Interdisciplinary Approach*. London: Sage.

Van Eemeren, F. and Houtlosser, P. (eds) (2002) *Dialectic and Rhetoric: The Warp and the Woof of Argumentation Analysis*. Dordrecht: Kluwer.

van Leeuwen, T. (1987) Generic strategies in press journalism. *Australian Review of Applied Linguistics*, 10(2): 199–220.

van Leeuwen, T. (1993) Genre and field in critical discourse analysis. *Discourse & Society*, 4(2): 193–223.

van Leeuwen, T. (1995) Representing social action. *Discourse and Society*, 6(1): 81–106.

van Leeuwen T. (1996) The Representation of Social Actors. In C.R. Caldas-Coulthard and M. Coulthard (eds) *Texts and Practices*. London: Routledge.

Van Leeuwen, T. (2007) Legitimation in discourse and communication. *Discourse & Communication*, 1: 91–112.

Van Leeuwen, T. and Wodak, R. (1999) Legitimizing immigration control: a discourse-historical analysis. *Discourse Studies*, 1.1: 83–118.

Veblen, T. (1907) The socialist economics of Karl Marx and his followers. *Quarterly Journal of Economics*, 21(2): 299–322.

Verdery, K. (2000) Privatisation as Transforming Persons. In S. Antohi and V. Tismaneanu (eds) *Between Past and Future: The Revolutions of 1989 and Their Aftermath*, 87–104. Budapest: Central European University Press.

Volosinov, V.I. (1973) *Marxism and the Philosophy of Language*. New York: Seminar Press.

Warminski, A. (1995) Hegel/Marx: Consciousness and life. *Yale French Studies* (88). [Depositions: Althusser, Balibar, Macherey, and the Labor of Reading], 118–141.

Weber, M. (1946) Politics as a vocation. In H. Gerth and C.W. Mills (eds) *From Max Weber: Essays in Sociology*. Oxford: Oxford University Press, 224–46.

Weber, M. (1947) *The Theory of Social and Economic Organization*. New York: Free Press.

Weick, K. (1979) *The Social Psychology of Organizing*. 2nd edn. Boston, MA: Addison-Wesley.

Weinberg, J. (1968) Abstraction in the formation of concepts. In P.P. Werner (ed.) *Dictionary of the History of Ideas: Studies of Selected Pivotal Ideas*: Vol. I. New York: Charles Scribner and Sons, 1–9.

Wenger, E. (1998) *Communities of Practice: Learning, Meaning and Identity*. Cambridge: Cambridge University Press.

Wernick, A. (1991) *Promotional Culture*. London: Sage.

West, C. and Zimmerman, D.E. (1983) Small insults: a study of interruptions in cross-sex conversations between unacquainted persons. In N. Thorne *et al.* (eds) (1983).

Wilkin, P. (2001) *The Political Economy of Global Communication: An Introduction*. London: Pluto Press.

Williams, G. (1999) *French Discourse Analysis*. London: Routledge.

Williams, R. (1976) *Keywords*. London: Fontana.

Williams, R. (1981) *Culture*. London: Fontana.

Winograd, T. (1982) *Language as a Cognitive Process v.1*. London: Addison-Wesley.

Wodak, R. *et al.* (1990) '*Wir Sind Alle Unschuldige Täter*'. *Diskurshistorische Studien zum Nachkriegsantisemitismus*. Frankfurt-am-Main: Suhrkamp.

Wodak, R. and Meyer, M. (2001) *Methods in Critical Discourse Analysis*. London: Sage.

Woolgar, S. (1988) *Science: The Very Idea*. Chichester: Ellis Horwood.

Woolgar, S. (2002) Interpreting public concerns about GMOs: Questions of meaning. In C. Deane-Drummond and B. Szerszynski (with R. Grove-White) (eds) Re-*Ordering Nature: Theology, Society and the New Genetics*. Edinburgh: T&T Clark, 221–248.

Wouters, C. (1986) Formalization and informalization: changing tension balances in civilizing processes. *Theory, Culture & Society*, 3(2): 1–18.

Zima, P. (1981) Les mécanismes discursifs de l'idéologie. *Revue de l'institut de sociologie (Solvay)*, 4.

Index